✦ CURRICULUM ✦

✦ CURRICULUM ✦
Perspective, Paradigm, and Possibility

WILLIAM H. SCHUBERT
The University of Illinois at Chicago

MACMILLAN PUBLISHING COMPANY / **COLLIER MACMILLAN PUBLISHERS**
New York London

Macmillan Publishing Company
866 Third Avenue, New York, New York 10022

Collier Macmillan Canada, Inc.

Library of Congress Cataloging in Publication Data

Schubert, William Henry.
    Curriculum: perspective, paradigm, and possibility.
    Bibliography: p.
    Includes index.
    1. Curriculum planning.   I. Title.
LB1570.S3476   1986   375   85-302
ISBN 0-02-407760-7

Printing: 1 2 3 4 5 6 7 8   Year: 6 7 8 9 0 1 2 3 4 5

ISBN 0-02-407760-7

For SP

✦ Preface ✦

Why should you want to read a curriculum book? Surely, this is a reasonable question to ask, whether you are a practicing educator (teacher, supervisor, administrator), an aspiring scholar in education, or an established scholar in education or a related area. Maybe, too, you are a parent or a group leader and see yourself as an informal educator. It is a reasonable question, too, if you simply picked up the book at a library or bookstore, or if someone required or recommended that you read it. The primary reason for reading a book, or for doing anything in life, should be because it will do some good. How, then, can this book do you some good?

Perhaps, I can respond best to this question by being a bit autobiographical. What led me to an interest in curriculum studies? I come from a family of educators; my mother, father, grandmother, and two great aunts were teachers. My father was also a school administrator, and his father educated through the ministry, while my mother's father educated informally in the political sphere. For some time I thought that I wanted to go into any number of other professions, both because my interests were broad (athletics, biology, journalism, architecture, psychology, religion, philosophy, theater, poetry, and history) and because of the adolescent rebelliousness of wanting to be different. Although several of my relatives were teachers—and they were very good teachers—the most profound educative impact on my outlook came from four kinds of experiences that they provided for my life: (1) the multitude of fictional activities, stories, sports, and fantasy games that we experienced together; (2) the annual travels that we planned together; (3) the deep sense of compassion that they exhibited; and (4) the consistent and growing set of values that they exemplified.

Without consciously realizing the profound and lasting impact of these forces on my outlook while growing up on a farm in a small Indiana town called Butler, I turned for meaning and direction to a few close friends and to the prevailing fundamentalist religion of the area. School seemed to be about things—information detached from the meaning of life.

In a small liberal arts college, Manchester, I was introduced to the world of ideas and great books. There, my early love for imaginative stories was re-awakened by literature and the arts; the study of history and social and natural science broadened my basis of compassion for humanity and its ecological context; and philosophy, theology, and psychology opened doors of value complexities unknown in fundamentalist religion. These were the formative influences of my parents and family, expanded by the vast heritage of human culture. The whole experience was a journey that I pondered and planned much as I had done for our family vacations each summer.

Toward the end of the four years at Manchester, I began to conclude that what I had just done for myself—creating the course of my study, a curriculum—was so rewarding to my own sense of meaning and direction that I wanted to help others do it, too. This, I thought, would be my calling; pondering how to do it was the essence of my growing interest in philosophy, and I discovered it was the reason I turned to literary classics as well. So I took my growing collection of books to Indiana University, where I studied history and philosophy of education for more than a year.

Feeling ready to help others develop a journey of learning, a curriculum, that might give greater meaning and purpose to their lives, I embarked on a seven-year public school teaching career in the Chicago area. This experience involved me in self-contained classrooms, open-space and team-teaching arrangements, and departmentalized organizations. One indelible observation that teaching gave me was that at its heart should lie a central question of philosophy: What does it mean to live a good and fulfilling life? The basic curriculum problem follows quite automatically: What kind and quality of knowledge and experience enable a person to live a good and fulfilling life?

This struck me, not merely as an interesting or important question, but as *the* most important question. Educators, I thought, who do not ask this question and do not make their work a continuous effort to respond to it, fail to realize fully the worth and magnitude of their calling.

Thus, it seemed to me that I should study more thoroughly what has been written about this question. This I did under the able guidance of J. Harlan Shores at the University of Illinois at Urbana-Champaign, where I received a Ph.D. in 1975.

My work for the past ten years has been as a faculty member of the College of Education at the University of Illinois at Chicago. If there is one purpose I have had as a teacher of undergraduate preservice teacher education majors, as coordinator of a masters degree program in Instructional Leadership, as a professor of doctoral students, and as a consultant to many schools and other educational institutions, it is to help professional educators perceive the profound contribution that they can make. By reflecting deeply on the influence that they can have, by inquiring broadly into the spheres of literature that speak to curriculum issues, and by carefully developing a curriculum philosophy that is always growing, educators in many walks of life can help others to embark on journeys of meaning that lead them to lives more fulfilling to themselves and to those with whom they interact.

My own experiences with my parents, my children, other relatives, teachers, friends, students, authors, and most assuredly my wife, Ann, have taught and continually teach me of the worth of such a journey. I feel fortunate indeed to experience such a journey, to be engaged in work that is a serious–playful continuation of it, and to be able to share the journey with Ann, who always enriches my commitment and insight.

This book is an attempt to share some of the considerations that my studies reveal are important for those who want to enable others to develop the curriculum of their own educational lives.

W.H.S.

✦ Acknowledgments ✦

I am more grateful than I can express for the loving, insightful, and encouraging contributions of my wife, Ann, to this book and to all my endeavors. I appreciate greatly her careful reading and commenting on the manuscript.

I thank Heidi Ann for understanding that Daddy had to "color" on those yellow notebook pads for over three-fourths of the first eighteen months of her life. I thank Elaine, Karen, and Heidi, who have taught me much about curriculum without realizing it, as one's children invariably do. I greatly appreciate the interest and support extended by Madeline Schubert, my mother. Pearl Kanaley, Helen Lopez, Frank Lopez, and Doris Devine were all helpful in their thoughtful questions about how the book was progressing at frequent junctures.

Early influences on my educational thought by J. Harlan Shores, J. Myron Atkin, Bernard Spodek, Frederick Raubinger, Harry S. Broudy, Hugh Chandler, Peter Shoresman, L. Thomas Hopkins, Charles Elmlinger, Stanley Ballinger, A. Stafford Clayton, Malcolm Skilbeck, Paul Keller, Russell Bollinger, Esther Mae Ashley, and Charles Hampel are certainly part of me and thus contributed to this book. So are conversations with friends and fellow teachers during earlier episodes of my life.

Encouragement and feedback from a number of educational researchers have been beneficial: Michael Apple, Daniel Tanner, Laurel Tanner, Nelson Haggerson, Max van Manen, Virginia Macagnoni, Elliot Eisner, Craig Kridel, Paul Klohr, William Pinar, Noreen Garman, Philip L. Smith, Ted Aoki, William F. Connell, Louis Rubin, Herbert Kliebard, Edmund Short, Barry J. Fraser, Ralph W. Tyler, Antoinette Oberg, Edward and Geneva Haertel, Sheldon Rosenstock, and Gerald Jorgenson.

I am grateful for the support of colleagues at the University of Illinois at Chicago: Gary Griffin, Ernest Pascarella, David Wilson, Larry Nucci, Susanna Pflaum, Tanis Bryan, Eugene Cramer, Patricia Charlier, Marilyn Fiduccia, Aimee Strawn, Vicky Hare, Isaac Balbus, Bruce McPherson, and Julius Menacker.

I especially appreciate the many organizational efforts of Merry Mastny, head of the word processing center in the College of Education, and the others in that unit (particularly Mike Korenchan, Sam Karnick, Ellen Patterson, Debbie Allen, Lynn Casey, Kirt Menon, Alma Jakimavicius, Renee Okonek, Tina Ku); and secretaries Sharon Coleman, Marilyn Geron, Mamie Gray, Patricia Tyrrell, and Linda Camacho have been exceedingly helpful. I also thank students in Education 330, 474, and 431, who responded to early drafts, content, and pedagogical approaches in the book. Among these graduate students, I especially note Nancy Crowley, David Laske, Benjamin Lowe, Jenny Wojcik, and Georgiana Zissis. I cannot omit seven years of elementary school students in Downers Grove, Illinois, who helped shape my curricular perspectives, and the influences of many teachers and administrators who have been students in my courses and workshops during the past ten years.

For permission to quote sizable passages, I acknowledge the following: Thomas Barone, Elliot Eisner, and Macmillan for sections by Barone from *The Educational Imagination* (Macmillan, New York, first edition, 1979, pp. 240–245); The National Society for the Study of Education and Kenneth J. Rehage, Editor for the Society, for "List of Fundamental Questions on Curriculum-Making" in *The Foundations of Curriculum-Making* (Harold Rugg, editor), The Twenty-Sixth Yearbook of The NSSE (Part II), Public School Publishing Company, Bloomington, Ill., 1927, pp. 9–10; and Francine Holt Hultgren for permission to build upon a chart developed in F. H. Hultgren, "Reflecting on the Meaning of Curriculum Through a Hermeneutic Interpretation of Student-Teaching Experiences in Home Economics," unpublished Ph.D. dissertation, The Pennsylvania State University, 1982, p. 121.

I greatly appreciate the administrative expertise, professional understanding, and personal regard of Lloyd C. Chilton, Jr., Executive Editor of the College Division for Macmillan, Pat Cabeza, Production Supervisor, and the other editors who helped to prepare the manuscript for publication. Finally, now that I know their identity, I want to thank Arthur Costa, Nathalie Gehrke, Ronald E. Comfort, Edmund C. Short, and George Willis for their candid, perceptive, and helpful reviews of the manuscript for this book.

Quite apart from all of the above, as well as the influences of many authors whom I have read and acknowledge but have not known personally, I alone accept responsibility for what is said here.

W.H.S.

✦ Contents ✦

3

Precedent: Historical Antecedents 54

4

Panorama: Relevant Contexts 93

5

Philosophy: The Realms of Assumptions 116

6

Policy: Curriculum Creation   140

PART II

Paradigm

7

Paradigms in Curriculum   169

8

Paradigm of Perennial Analytic
Categories: Purpose   188

9

Paradigm of Perennial Analytic Categories: Content or Learning Experiences   212

10

Paradigm of Perennial Analytic Categories: Organization   233

11

Paradigm of Perennial Analytic Categories: Evaluation   261

12

Paradigm of Practical Inquiry   287

13

Paradigm of Critical Praxis   313

PART III

Possibility

14

Problems Facing Curriculum   341

15

Professional Development and Curriculum Improvement   371

16

Promising Directions in Curriculum: A Personal Hope   410

1

✦ Preparation: Introducing This Book ✦

It is through good education that all the good in the world arises.
IMMANUEL KANT *Education* (1803)

True education . . . is at once a fulfillment and a spur; always at the goal and never stopping to rest, it is a journey in the infinite, a participation in the movement of the universe, a living in timelessness. Its purpose is not to enhance particular abilities; rather, it helps us to give meaning to our lives, to interpret the past, to be fearless and open toward the future.
HERMANN HESSE *Reflections* (1974)

SETTING THE STAGE

What knowledge is most worthwhile? Why is it worthwhile? How is it acquired or created?

These are three of the most basic curriculum questions. They are the "bottom line" of all activities commonly associated with educational theory and practice. All of the educational research, all of the debate by school district committees, all of the financial planning, all of the inservice and preservice teacher education, all of the school board agenda items, all of the public relations, all of the collective bargaining, all of the textbook adoptions, all of selection of instructional hardware and software, all of the teacher preparation, all of the politically charged interest group lobbying, and all of the activities engaged in by students are for naught if they are not infused with these fundamental questions. Without direct consideration of *what* is worthwhile to know and its correlates of *why* and *how*, the foregoing activities are devoid of defensible meaning, purpose, and direction. When fundamental curriculum questions are not addressed by educators, economic or political caprice leads the way and educational practice is governed by default.

In this book, I assume that educators (be they teachers, administrators, teacher educators, policymakers, researchers, or parents) want to make decisions that best facilitate the growth of children, youth, and learners of all ages. To do this, educators must be committed to a process of discovering what knowledge is valuable, why it is valuable, and how it can be acquired. Notice that I say *a process of discovering*, not *having discovered*. Final answers depend on specific situations. They are never fully made, but always in the process of being created and reconstructed to fit needs of changing circumstances.

Given this orientation, how can a book such as this one help you, as an educator, to address curriculum questions with greater effectiveness?

PURPOSES OF THIS BOOK

If fundamental curriculum questions, like all other truly significant problems, do not have precise, easy-to-follow answers, how can a book on curriculum be helpful to those who must deal with day-to-day curriculum problems? In an overall sense, it can enhance the curriculum knowledge at your disposal. This, then, is the first of five purposes that we will consider.

To Provide a Background of Curriculum Knowledge

By *curriculum knowledge*, I refer to perspectives, paradigms, and possibilities, the three main parts into which the book is divided. *Perspectives* form the context or background that nourishes the development of a set of beliefs or assumptions. These are central pillars of one's philosophy of curriculum. The building of perspective provides a fuller and richer image of what the state of affairs is in the curriculum world. It also provides vision of what ought to be. *Paradigms* are the conceptual lenses through which curriculum problems are perceived. It is well known that one's frame of mind often dictates what one sees. The conceptual frameworks that we use to deliberate about curriculum problems shape their character and impel us to acceptance of some forms of evidence and rejection of others. In similar light, paradigms that guide our work as educators govern the kinds of questions we ask and the ways in which we view the consequences of our efforts. *Possibilities* provide a range of responses for meeting needs and addressing problems.

When faced with problematic situations, increased knowledge of perspectives, paradigms, and possibilities enables us to be better decision makers. A confusing and baffling dilemma becomes a well-articulated problem as it is given shape through our paradigms of inquiry. A proposal is more adequately critiqued because our perspective gives criticism a more defensible basis. Consequences of probable courses of action emerge in bold relief as our repertoire of possibilities is augmented. Similarly, heightened awareness of possible consequences of actions taken gives greater insight and sensitivity to the much neglected domain of unintended outcomes. I will say more about the value of perspectives, paradigms, and possibilities as I sketch an overview of the book in subsequent sections of this chapter.

This book is, thus, intended to provide a background of curriculum knowledge for both scholars and practitioners. Already familiar with the information, literature, and research reviewed here, curriculum scholars may be interested in the configurations that I use to portray curriculum studies. This is directly related to the matter of interpretation. Every book is an interpretation, and curriculum books are no exception. As authors study a topic or phenomenon, they interact with it; their writing about it portrays both themselves and the phenomenon under study. The completely objective account is a myth. This, however, is not to say that any one account is as good as another. A book can still be judged on such criteria as fairness to alternative perspectives, informed and defensible arguments, and imaginative but realistic proposals. Thus, curriculum scholars who educate teachers, administrators, policymakers, and future scholars should be interested in the way in which the book interprets the curriculum field.

My primary purpose, however, is to convey the character of curriculum knowledge to those who will need to use it. Clearly, it is addressed to those who plan to be curriculum leaders in schools as well as to scholars. Similarly, because curriculum questions are fundamental to all domains of educational deliberation, I intend to provide perspective for those who plan to go into any realm of educational research. Those who seek administrative positions in schools or other educative agencies will invariably be faced with curriculum problems. They will develop, criticize, and revise policies; they will motivate, inform, monitor, and evaluate educational practice.

The book is offered, as well, to a too-often-forgotten class of curricularists, teachers. Unfortunately, teachers are frequently considered mere recipients of already packaged curriculum; they are viewed as implementors of prescriptions, not creators. I want to acknowledge the key role that teachers have in developing curriculum. Their daily decision and action provides a vast proportion of the experience that students have in school. This is equally true for human service professionals, those who teach in nonschool educative institutions (e.g., churches, scouting, youth clubs, sports groups, occupational training, counseling services, and the burgeoning host of educators in the mass media). These educators plan programs to influence the knowledge, skills, attitudes, and values of others; therefore, they are curriculum developers. They are able to do this work more effectively if they are familiar with the research and theory that can inform the curriculum development process. Finally, there is another nonschool educator—perhaps the most important and unsung of all—the parent. Parents fashion curricula for their children on a daily, almost momentary, basis, as do teachers. Curriculum issues are highly complex. When educators in any sphere do not make use of existing curriculum perspectives, they are at a disadvantage. Greater knowledge enables a higher level of conscious attention to and reflection upon curriculum matters.

To Enable Socialization to Roles Within the Curriculum Field

To become socialized to roles within a field of inquiry is not dissimilar to becoming socialized to a society. One learns to adopt the forms of perception and conceptualization, the language and values, and the habits, mores and folkways of the social group. The curriculum field is not only a body of knowledge but a loosely coupled social organization. To come to understand it requires more than reading; it also necessitates involvement or immersion in the experience of the group. A book can only take one part way, but practical experience in the absence of literature is also limited exposure to a professional field.

To know a field of inquiry, one must both become involved in it and become acquainted with its literature. Here, again, the overarching topics of *perspective, paradigm,* and *possibility* arise. Discussions of each provided in the chapters of this book should take you a sizable distance into the field of curriculum. You will learn about the language of curriculum discourse; dominant and alternative modes of perceiving, examining, and experiencing curricular phenomena; and historical treatments of curriculum problems. Through the bibliographical essays that conclude each chapter, the citations within each chapter's text, and the reference list at the end of the book, you will have ample exposure to curriculum literature to enable a great deal of further study. This, of course, requires that you be an active rather than a passive reader.

An active reader is one who reflects carefully while reading and afterward as well. Alfred North Whitehead said it well when discussing the purpose of a university: "The justification for a university is that it preserves . . . the imaginative consideration of learning" (1929, p. 93). This, I argue, is also a purpose of a book of this kind. Although in some ways more difficult to accomplish in a book than in a seminar, lecture hall, or tutorial, I still hope that we can engage in a kind of conversation as you read. In view of this hope, I try to provide writing of a conversational tone. The real meaning of the book comes from a joining of the experience and imagination of both author and reader. This in itself is a significant kind of socialization.

To Convey the Importance of Curriculum Study

Why is it the case that curriculum problems lie at the heart of the education process? There should be no more defensible reason for bringing people together in an educational setting than to provide educational experiences for them. Yes, we occasionally hear of the custodial rationale that schools keep children off the streets while parents work and provide a place for youth until the economic system has room for them. While there is admittedly some truth in these assertions, they are hardly *educational* justifications for schools.

Educational justification for schools must reside in the character of the educative experience that schools provide. When educative institutions and agencies are established, the justification for their existence is usually that they enable certain kinds and qualities of learning to occur that would not occur (or would occur less effectively or efficiently) outside of the educative setting provided by the institution in question.

In a very broad sense, *curriculum studies* refers to an area of inquiry in higher education that focuses on what is learned and should be learned in educative institutions and to a lesser (but not less important) extent to what is and should be learned in noninstitutionalized educational situations. As noted earlier, the questions of *why* and *how* flow readily from this central concern. We should also round out the list with questions about *where, when,* and *for whom* the learning is appropriate. A major question, which will be raised time and again throughout this book, is: To what extent can answers to these questions be answered generically and to what extent must answers be situationally specific? If one assumes that curriculum problems can be answered by general pronouncements, one also assumes that the needs of human beings and their circumstances are essentially alike. In contrast, if one assumes that problems in different situations require unique solutions, then human individuality is affirmed.

To grapple with such questions requires that we travel back to the dawn of civilization. The first parents who reflectively considered how they should prepare a child to live in the world were, in effect, addressing fundamental curriculum questions. By consciously addressing the question of what knowledge is most worthwhile, one moves beyond the state of merely taking for granted what social circumstance dictates as proper answers to the great curricular questions. Thus, the unrecorded history of human striving, of parents wondering what is good for their children, of individual human beings at any age thinking about what will make them more fully human, and of social groups' quests to understand better themselves and their world are all prime examples of curriculum inquiry as a formative human enterprise.

The great treatises on philosophy and social thought from antiquity to present indelibly address ideas that relate directly to issues about the most worthwhile kinds of knowledge. Readers of classics, from Plato's *Republic* to Dewey's *Democracy and Education* (1916), become acutely aware that penetrating consideration of questions about worthwhile knowledge invokes the concomitant question: Worthwhile for what? To pursue this question leads into the depths of philosophy, natural science, history, psychology, the arts, social science, and literature. It pushes one to discover more about human nature and the most desirable characteristics to nurture in human beings and compels one to think about the kind of society that exists, to dream what might be, what should be, and how to move toward such ideals.

While such issues have been discussed throughout human history, the universal schooling movement of the early twentieth century brought increased attention to fundamental curriculum questions. It became a political necessity to ask them. In the United States, for example, at the onset of the twentieth century, only 5 to 10 percent of the secondary school age group attended school, and by the early 1930s the number rose to more than 50 percent. With rapid increases in the population of students who attended school came heightened consciousness of the need to ask what is important to know. As schools became more complex in an effort to serve the larger public that attended them, certain administrators were given specific curriculum responsibilities. An era of rapidly growing specializations in many fields was quick to label them curriculum specialists. Meanwhile, colleges of education emerged on a broader scale within universities, and the preparation of curriculum specialists became one of their hallmarks. To support such study, curriculum scholars began to amass a body of literature that accumulated to more than eleven hundred books published in English alone during the first eighty years of the twentieth century (Schubert, 1980a).

A central purpose found throughout curriculum literature is to convey the importance of curriculum studies. "Nothing matters more than curriculum matters," is the way the point was made by Elliot Eisner of Stanford University and Philip Jackson of the University of Chicago, as Eisner turned over the leadership of the three thousand–plus member Curriculum Studies Division of the American Educational Research Association (AERA) to Jackson at the 1983 Annual Meeting in Montreal. The point can be made quite simply and directly: What can be more serious or more important than the experiences through which we choose to induct the young into the human race? The future of the individual, society, and civilization is at stake when we ask: What is worthwhile to know? If we shirk the responsibility to address this question, then convention, mindless action, and taken-for-granted patterns of behavior will provide answers. Differentiated from other forms of life largely by their consciousness, human beings must engage in conscious reflection and deliberation about the growth of their progeny.

Far indeed from the tedium of lesson plans, textbook adoptions, bulletin boards, motivational tricks, curriculum guides, course syllabi, and other mundane facets of schooling too often equated with curriculum, curriculum must be seen as central to the maturing process of the human race. While the mundanities of schooling may be necessary, they are far from sufficient. Separated from the ideal that connects curriculum to the growth of the human beings and their culture, they are meager tinkerings indeed. The etymological roots of curriculum can be interpreted to reveal this ideal. The term *curriculum* derives from Latin roots to mean "the course of a chariot race." Yet a race course need not be thought of as a preestablished track to follow; instead, it can be seen as a metaphor for a journey of learning and growth that is consciously developed. However, such curriculum development is ahistorical and ill conceived if it is not grounded in knowledge of accumulated curriculum literature.

To Encourage Educators to Ask Basic Curriculum Questions

A fourth purpose of this book is to note that educators at all levels need to address fundamental curriculum questions. It is too often assumed that curriculum is only created by experts who have appropriate titles to legitimate such activity: curriculum director, curriculum developer, curriculum consultant, supervisor of instruction, associate superintendent for curriculum, and so forth. Surely persons in such positions perform a valuable curriculum development service, but they are certainly not the only ones who do so. Furthermore, they may not be the most important ones. Building principals can create an atmosphere that fosters the development of curriculum and instruction in specific schools, as do assistant principals. Sometimes they set a tone that counteracts productive attention to curriculum matters.

Teachers have greater direct impact on students than any other educator in a school system. The interpretation that teachers give to subject matter and the classroom atmosphere constitutes the curriculum that students actually experience. Parents, too, are the first educators and exercise their teaching by design and example during the immensely impressionable early years as well as later.

Finally, and most overlooked among educators, are the learners themselves, be they children, adults, or entire communities. While parents, teachers, administrators, supervisors, consultants, and scholars must all ask what is worthwhile to know for others, every individual in the final analysis must direct his or her own learning. Thus, every person, regardless of his or her age, is in charge of his or her own self-education. We are all recipients of our own advice more than that of others. No one can know an individual more fully than the individual can know himself or herself.

The individual who infuses his or her life with the quest to discover what is most worthwhile may be well on the road to self-education or self-realization. I often wonder how educational experience would be different if this spirit of asking basic curriculum questions became the curriculum rather than the answers generated by credentialed experts who are commissioned to ask such questions.

Whatever the level of your experience as an educator or whatever you hope to become (whether a teacher, parent, principal, central office administrator, a curriculum scholar, consultant, educational researcher in a subfield other than curriculum, or a better educated human being), the basic curriculum questions are your responsibility.

To Convey the Problematic Character of Curriculum Knowledge

I want to establish in this book that there are no pat answers, no recipes for solving fundamental curriculum questions. You should not expect to come away from this book with a set of plug-in techniques that will solve school attendance problems, raise scores on college entrance examinations, or convince students to learn more about math, history, grammar, and the like. To expect generic answers to such questions is to expect magic. Yet there are many purveyors of one or another kind of magic. Beware of them; many even wear the badges of science and technology, which makes them even more dangerous given the ready acceptance we give to such labels today.

Instead of receiving panaceas from this book, you should come away with a broader and deeper perspective on curriculum problems, and their historical, ideological, and social contexts. You should also become more aware of possible courses of action that have provided and might provide answers to basic curriculum questions in specific settings. You should become more aware of intents and criticisms for such possibilities. Moreover, I hope to convey that we all view the world and our own functioning in it through a paradigm or conceptual framework that accepts certain assumptions about such matters as the nature of inquiry, reality, and values. To view educational phenomena through different paradigms is analogous to viewing a society through the language and values of different cultures. Perhaps we need to be multi-intellectual in much the same way that values of multiculturalism have arisen in recent years to counteract ethnocentrism. In intellectual matters, we can suffer from a kind of centrism of inquiry.

Recent growth in the area of curriculum theory has moved productively in the direction of recognizing the possibility of conducting educational inquiry through different paradigms. There is considerable time lag between the writing and reading of scholarly books. The awakening of the curriculum field to the idea of alternative inquiry paradigms, for example, began in the early 1970s; nevertheless, few curriculum texts published in the early 1980s devote substantial space to this fundamental issue.

To prevent the tendency for books to be obsolete before they come off the press, one must realize that many educational trends reflect only the surface structure of curriculum. As powerful as they are in stirring public and professional concern, they are often fleeting and ephemeral. They ride on a bandwagon pulled by economic and political expedience. Because of their power, however, they must be addressed. But the way in which we address them is a key. John Dewey's position (1938a) on this nearly fifty years ago rings true today as it did when he stated it:

> *It is the business of an intelligent theory of education to ascertain the causes for the conflicts that exist and then, instead of taking one side or the other, to indicate a plan of operations proceeding from a level deeper and more inclusive than is represented by the practices and ideas of the contending parties. [p. 5]*

In this book, we will examine samples of past and present bandwagon trends; however, we will not let them guide our inquiry. We will probe underlying assumptions, contextual influences, and alternative possibilities. All the while, we must remember the magnitude of fundamental curriculum questions. We are not merely dealing with choices among textbooks or learning packages, although that is encompassed by a broad conception of curriculum inquiry. What we are addressing is as profound and serious an issue as humankind can address: the fate of our children and youth and what it means to turn their lives toward greater growth, goodness, and enlightenment.

Embarking on such inquiry means putting aside simplistic hopes for certainty and all-encompassing solutions. Again Dewey, in his *The Quest for Certainty* (1929a), admonished students of every field not to be taken in by the enticing grasp of the myth of certain knowledge. Decker Walker (1980) argued that we need to appreciate the worth of the vehement debates that characterize curriculum literature. He labeled this a *rich confusion*. I somewhat prefer the label *productive uncertainty*, but the meaning is essentially the same.

Why should this state of acceptance of the uncertainty of curriculum knowledge persist? Why should a rich confusion be prized? Dwayne Huebner (1975a) insightfully states the case:

> *Think of it—there standing before the educator is a being partially hidden in the cloud of unknowing. For centuries the poet has sung of his near infinitudes; the theologian has preached of his depravity and hinted at his participation in the divine; the philosopher has struggled to encompass him in his systems, only to have him repeatedly escape; the novelist and dramatist have captured his fleeting moments in never-to-be-forgotten esthetic forms; and the man [sic] engaged in curriculum has the temerity to reduce this being to a single term—"learner." [p. 219]*

Indeed, how can we be more certain about curriculum problems than we are about the great philosophical questions that have always plagued humankind, especially when we realize that the former are contingent upon the latter?

Let us now turn to an overview of this book, chapter by chapter, and notice how the foregoing purposes are interwoven.

PERSPECTIVE: PART 1

Part I consists of five chapters, each of which treats a different aspect of the intellectual and practical environment that surrounds curriculum and gives it meaning. Together, these chapters treat curriculum as a domain of both inquiry and practice.

Portrayal: The Curriculum Field (Chapter Two)

Chapter Two provides perspective on curriculum by portraying it as a professional field of inquiry and activity. It begins with a discussion of alternative characterizations of *curriculum* and their relative strengths and weaknesses. Through a wide-angle lens, curriculum is portrayed as part of an interdependent network of subdivisions of educational inquiry, for example, administration, supervision, teaching, and research methodology. The theme of variety within unity is emphasized by identifying domains of specialization within curriculum inquiry. Acknowledging that one book cannot possibly provide a complete overview of curriculum for the reader, resources are discussed to guide further study: professional associations, journals and newsletters, and books of various types.

Precedent: Historical Antecedents (Chapter Three)

Many fields today are criticized for being ahistorical, overly unaware of their past. The curriculum field is no exception. There is a tendency for curriculum developers to respond uncritically to the pressures of the day. Innovations heatedly promoted by school districts via workshops and inservice education one year are frequently dropped for a new agenda the next year. Compounding this problem, and decreasing the credibility of educational innovation, is the fact that what is promoted as novel are often old ideas with new labels.

Educational innovators need to be able to use the successes and failures of the past to renew their own contributions. Thus, Chapter Three begins by presenting roots of theory and practice that extend from antiquity to the late nineteenth century. It builds upon this background by presenting a sample of critical episodes in curriculum drawn from the late 1800s to present. The purpose of this background grows from the assumption that curriculum development in the present is more defensible if it proceeds from an awareness of precedent. Different orientations to the conduct of historical curriculum inquiry are presented.

Panorama: Relevant Contexts (Chapter Four)

The curricular present, as well as the past, exists within a panorama of contexts. Curriculum cannot be created in a vacuum. Instead, much of what curriculum becomes is forged by political, economic, and value contexts that surround and interpenetrate it. As with all forms of existence, curriculum achieves its character from an ecological embeddedness. The use of the term *ecological* here implies that these contexts of the larger society interact with teachers, learners, other curriculum developers, and the culture of classroom life all at once—each interacting with and influencing the others.

Chapter Four provides perspective on three general categories of forces that affect the curriculum that emerges for students at any level. The first category includes the political, economic, and value contexts that affect education from the outside. The second is the culture that occurs within the school environment, and includes both planned and unplanned factors that shape the experiences, thus the learnings, of students, such as organizational and physical structures of the school, peer culture, hidden curricula, and extracurricular activities. The third category applies the idea of curriculum to nonschool experiences of students (e.g., the media, families, jobs, hobbies) and asserts that they constitute a kind of natural curriculum that must be taken into account by any who purport to educate other human beings.

Philosophy: The Realm of Assumptions (Chapter Five)

All of our everyday decisions and most of our actions are based upon assumptions. Activities in all fields of inquiry are based upon assumptions. Many of our assumptions are dimly recognized and seldom articulated. To gain insight into the taken-for-granted assumptions that guide our lives is to gain meaning and direction. An educator's curricular life is a subset of his or her life generally; thus, assumptions about everyday life apply with equal force to our work as educators. Perhaps they apply with even greater power because those who create curriculum are, by definition, directly striving to influence the lives of other human beings.

Philosophy was once considered the overarching discipline that offered perspective to all other areas of knowledge and action, and should continue to be so utilized. In portraying this value of philosophy for curriculum, Chapter Five begins with a model that links curricular action and common sense with policy and finally with philosophical assumptions. Perennial domains of philosophical inquiry and schools of philosophy are analyzed for their relevance to curriculum theory and practice. Further, the chapter explores the nature and function of curriculum theory as it relates to practice as well as philosophy.

Policy: Curriculum Creation (Chapter Six)

Chapter Six is the final chapter in the Perspective part of the book and is a fitting culmination because the relatively new field of policy studies is an integrative and interdisciplinary enterprise. Curriculum is depicted as a form of policy. Its relevance to public or social policy is explored. The nature of curriculum policy is examined through four different frameworks represented in the literature. Since policy itself is inseparable from policymakers, a discussion is presented of categories of persons who influence curricular policy.

PARADIGM: PART II

Part II of the book develops the idea of paradigm by relating the dominant paradigm or conceptual framework used to discuss, research, and work with curricular phenomena. It also sets forth alternative paradigms that fall under the labels *practical inquiry* and *critical praxis*. While categories of the dominant paradigm are most frequently applied as a basis for understanding and doing curriculum work, it is imperative that curricularists study alternative criticisms and proposals carefully.

Paradigms in the Curriculum Field (Chapter Seven)

The purpose of this chapter is to provide an introduction to Chapters Eight through Thirteen by elaborating the idea of paradigms of inquiry and by applying them to curriculum inquiry. The dominant paradigm, developed by Ralph Tyler (1949), includes the analysis of puposes, content or learning experiences, organization, and evaluation. Each of these perennial categories and more recent elaborations within them are treated in Chapters Eight through Eleven. A second curriculum paradigm is based on critique of educational research developed by Joseph Schwab (1969, 1971, 1973), who illuminated the distinction between theoretic inquiry that seeks generalized knowledge for its own sake and practical inquiry that seeks situational knowledge for understanding, decision, and action. Schwab's advocacy of the latter leads to a conception of curriculum characterized by the interaction of teachers, learners, subject matter, and milieu. A third paradigm focuses on the critique of social and psychological barriers to more enlightened action, and supports efforts to develop personal and political freedom as a basis for curriculum. Practical and critical paradigms are presented in Chapters Twelve and Thirteen. Four chapters, Eight through Eleven, are devoted to the perennial paradigm because of its extensive impact on curriculum theory and practice.

Paradigm of Perennial Analytic Categories: Purpose (Chapter Eight)

Since the beginning of curriculum as a field of inquiry, purposes, aims, goals, and objectives have been a primary consideration. Ways in which curriculum literature and practice deal with purposes are the focus of Chapter Eight. The stance taken on the nature and use of purposes has profound reverberations throughout the entire curriculum system. Criteria are presented for analyzing the substance and form of objectives, and examples of different kinds of purposes are examined and criticized.

Paradigm of Perennial Analytic Categories: Content or Learning Experiences (Chapter Nine)

In its traditional sense, the curriculum is academic content; more recently, it has also been considered as activities and/or learning experiences. Chapter Nine considers the relative advantages and disadvantages of different conceptions of content and criteria for its selection. Different images of content in subject matter areas such as social studies, language arts, science, mathematics, the arts, and vocational training are aired and critiqued.

Paradigm of Perennial Analytic Categories: Organization (Chapter Ten)

Chapter Ten presents a range of topics that each play an important part in giving patterns of organization to curriculum. Ways of responding to the need for breadth and depth of learning are presented and criticized under the topic of curricular scope. Issues concerned with a defensible basis for sequence or order in curriculum are investigated. Different kinds of learning environments are presented and criticized. Finally, the controversial relationship between curriculum and instruction is addressed by treating instruction as a means of organizing curriculum for learners. The debate about the scientific versus artistic character of teaching is discussed, models of teaching are presented, and a broad array of instructional arrangements and approaches are compared and contrasted.

Paradigm of Perennial Analytic Categories: Evaluation (Chapter Eleven)

Evaluation, the fourth of the perennial curriculum categories identified by Tyler (1949), is portrayed as it emerged throughout the twentieth century: from evaluation as judging and grading students, through the measurement movement, the broadening of evaluation in the Eight Year Study, to evaluation for divese purposes such as program improvement, national and international comparisons, accountability, personal growth, and human liberation. Contemporary orientations to curriculum evaluation are presented and criticized.

Paradigm of Practical Curriculum Inquiry (Chapter Twelve)

Assumptions of practical inquiry are compared with the usual theoretic interpretations of the perennial paradigm. Curriculum derived from practical inquiry is examined in light of four commonplaces: teachers, learners, subject matter, and milieu or environment. Arts of eclectic inquiry are shown to support practical curriculum deliberation that speaks to particular needs of teachers and students. This is expanded by illustrations of ways in which teachers, learners, subject matter, and milieu interact with one another in an ecological web of mutual influences that is the curriculum experienced by students.

Paradigm of Critical Praxis (Chapter Thirteen)

A third paradigm, one that focuses on the ideological ramifications of curriculum, is presented here. *Ideology* is a general term that encompasses the political, economic, psychological, and cultural character of curriculum. Curricularists in this paradigm critically analyze, interpret, and evaluate the kind and quality of knowledge reproduced by schools. They are particularly concerned with the impact of ideology on social justice as evidenced in inequities attributed to race, gender, and socioeconomic class. Moreover, they seek to contribute to social justice by critical praxis (a union of critical theory and action) that reduces such inequities through curricular interventions.

This chapter looks at precedents for critical theory in the history of reconstructionist and reconceptionalist writings on curriculum. The chapter concludes with a discussion of critical questions and their relevance to teaching and learning in schools.

POSSIBILITY: PART III

One of the great purposes of education is to project possibilities imaginatively. When confronted with a dilemma, an educator must be able to formulate imaginatively needs and problems that conceptualize the disrupted state of affairs. When faced with a problem, an educator should not be content with one ready-made solution. Instead, he or she should be adept in the art of generating an array of possible solutions or courses of action. This is not a ponderous and technical process; rather, it is often spontaneous. Teachers and administrators know well, and researchers are beginning to admit, that educators' work involves a continuous flow of decisions in action. To imagine and project possibilities involves the ability to imagine possible consequences of decision and action. To see the ideal in the ordinary and the ordinary in the ideal, to make the strange familiar and the familiar strange, to see the taken-for-granted as it might be otherwise—this is the realm of possibility. Its value is to bring greater meaning, direction, and "wide awakeness" (Greene, 1978) to learning in the lived world.

Problems and Proposals Facing Curriculum (Chapter Fourteen)

Two levels of problems affect the professional educator as he or she engages in curriculum inquiry. The first I label *instructional and institutional problems*. These reside within the education profession and include apathy, discipline, high-tech education, basics, life skills, drug education, test score decline, multicultural and bilingual education, education for the handicapped, and global education, among others. I label the second level of curriculum problems as *societal and ideological*. These are broad cultural, often global problems such as poverty, autocracy, indoctrination, dissolution of the family, prejudice, alienation, war, and greed, among others. The category scheme is drawn from Goodlad and Richter (1966). Each of the problems at both levels is discussed through the perspective of three quite different orientations to curriculum theory and practice. Curriculum implications are discussed from each perspective, as are proposals for the resolution of the problems discussed.

Professional Development and Curriculum Improvement (Chapter Fifteen)

A great deal of attention has been devoted, over the years, to curriculum on paper (policy statements, curriculum guides, lesson plans, textbooks, instructional systems). Meanwhile, evidence accumulates to suggest that the same curriculum documents in the hands of teachers in comparable settings yield quite different, sometimes vastly different, results. Policy, support services, physical learning facilities, and materials receive much attention as curriculum changes and improvements are planned and implemented. To be sure, these are all important; however, the human element too often has been omitted from the plans. It follows that professional development is essential to effective curriculum improvement. This includes preservice teacher education, inservice teacher education, and supervision. Alternative approaches in each of these three areas of educator development are presented along with criticism and commentary about their contribution to curriculum improvement.

Promising Directions in Curriculum: A Personal Hope (Chapter Sixteen)

In the concluding chapter, I sketch the directions that my studies and value system lead me to suggest as most promising. First, I attempt to glean a central message that I tried to convey in each chapter. This is not a summary of the chapter, but an effort to point toward promising developments that seem to be emergent in curriculum theory and practice today.

In the second part of the chapter, I unleash some of my own curricular fantasies. I grant myself ten wishes or hopes for curriculum theory and practice in the future and encourage you to respond to them and develop your own list of hopes.

THREE CURRICULUM ORIENTATIONS

In my classes and workshops during the past ten years I have developed a technique that I refer to as the "guest speaker" approach. I use this approach to illustrate the problematic state of curriculum knowledge. Using the approach, I role play as three respondents or critics to topics I teach. The three speakers are labeled *intellectual traditionalist*, *social behaviorist*, and *experientialist*. Although I have used these labels for schools of curriculum thought in past writings (Schubert 1980a, 1982a, 1982b), I do not argue here that they represent distinct schools of thought. Let us merely say that they are three orientations to curriculum theory, research, and practice. Each of the three positions is rather wide ranging, and there is undoubtedly some overlap among them.

The advocates will "speak" to you at various junctures throughout this book. They will speak in a somewhat intellectualized, but conversational, tone, and they will often draw upon literature to support their positions. Just because one of these "guest speakers" cites a given author, you should not classify that author under the commentator's label. It is the very rare author in the curriculum field who is purely a social behaviorist, intellectual traditionalist, or experientialist. As you read, you may wonder which of the speakers I am, as author of this book. The fact is that I could not act as each of them in my classes, nor could I write in character with their position, without having some of each inside of me. Nevertheless, my own position is closest to the experientialist, with heavy doses of intellectual traditionalist. As an experientialist of Deweyan persuasion, I share John Dewey's conviction that steadfast pursuit of one's interests and needs leads one to realize the value of intellectual classics and disciplines of knowledge for practical affairs. Pursuit of one's deepest needs and interests also leads to a continuous quest for personal growth and to the commitment to reduce ideological oppression that prevents opportunity for such growth. The experientialist and intellectual traditionalist positions have been neglected as the social behaviorist orientation has dominated curriculum work. While social behaviorists offer much to technical curriculum problems, their preoccupation with technique and procedure has greatly limited the perspective and sense of the possible that curriculum inquiry and practice desperately need. Despite my own position, which I believe should be explicated to you at the beginning of this book, I will make every attempt to present each orientation as fairly and accurately as possible.

Instead of merely telling *about* each commentator, I will let each tell you about himself or herself. I have "asked" our three presenters to provide a concise statement that introduces their position, using the framework of What? Why? How? Who? Where? and When? to clarify their curriculum orientation.

Intellectual Traditionalist

(Standing at podium in nearly formal attire; obviously steeped in the classics.) I am pleased to be here and I hope that I can shed some light on a greatly misunderstood curriculum position that has been with us now for approximately twenty-five hundred years. Let me say at the outset that I am convinced that great ideas have emerged in every era. They are embodied in the best poetry, paintings, essays, plays, sculpture, music, dance, novels, stories, myths, philosophy, mathematics, history, and social thought. They speak to us of good and evil, human nature, the nature of the cosmos, beauty, logic, politics, religious belief, and the nature of knowledge itself. Now, science is a contributor to this wisdom, but it should not be overemphasized; today, it is almost deified as the sole avenue to truth. In proper perspective science is one route to truth that developed in the five hundred years known as modern times. However, the accumulated wisdom of all ages, from all parts of the world, is the curriculum. Through this curriculum, we can introduce human beings to that which is excellent in the blotted history of human civilization on earth.

What?   The curriculum should consist of the liberal arts tradition. By this I mean that learners should be exposed to the great books. The Britannica Great Books of the Western World, The Harvard Classics, and so on convey the idea; yet the reading need not be confined to these sets. A prerequisite to all this is, of course, facility in the technique and art of reading, writing, and computing.

Why?   The benefits are twofold: to develop the mind and to become acquainted with life's great ideas and questions. To develop the mind is to develop powers of reason, logic, imagination, and the like. As for the great ideas and questions, Mortimer J. Adler speaks of six great ideas: truth, beauty, goodness, liberty, equality, and justice (Adler, 1981). The perennial questions pertain to those themes that recur timelessly in great literature, art, philosophy, and elsewhere. Robert Ulich refers to these as the "great events and mysteries of life: birth, death, love, tradition, society and the crowd, success and failure, salvation, and anxiety" (Ulich, 1955, p. 255).

How?   Acquaintance with the great books develops the mind and introduces the great mysteries and events of life. This derives from serious reading, contemplation, and discussion. It can be motivated by excellent lectures and Socratic questioning. It can be refined by rigorous writing.

Who?   Ideally, everyone should have this type of education. Even young children can be exposed to great myths, fables, poetry, songs, paintings, and stories. I suspect that more of the so-called "basics" can be learned in conjunction with such substantive examples as these. Students are probably bored with the drudgery of learning basics in isolation. In short, anyone who will willingly study and learn should have this sort of curriculum. "Who" also refers to the teacher. The teacher must be a person who is becoming liberally educated himself or herself. I say "becoming" because we never can be completely educated. As Gilbert Highet (1950) says, teaching is an art that requires teachers who know and like both their subject and their students.

Where?   Ideally, one should always pursue one's education. Formal education, however, should take place in schools or in tutorials.

When?   Education should proceed throughout life. It should especially be available to the young, say ages five through twenty-five or thirty. I think our age groupings are about right—kindergarten through graduate school. What we do with this important time period is what is so questionable and so lamentable.

Some people respond that what I propose is "old hat." I say it has never been tried on a broad scale in public education, except in the most superficial way.

Social Behaviorist

(Exudes efficiency; appears as typical physical scientist of forty to fifty years ago; paces about the front of the room while speaking.) I have no difficulty being succinct. It is my business to be parsimonious. To be economical and to rule out inert ideas, the fat of armchair philosophizing, is one of my major goals. Suffice it to say that science and its practical offspring, technology, have transformed society in the twentieth century. In the past eighty years, many diseases have become extinct and others are moving in this direction, the comfort level of all socioeconomic classes has markedly improved, communication and transportation have made strides that earlier generations only could refer to as magic. But it is not magic that brought these benefits; it is science and technology. Science and technology are insufficiently applied to educational planning and curriculum development today. Similarly, they must become the mainstay of the curriculum itself.

What?   The curriculum should consist of operationally designed skills and knowledge. Such knowledge, insofar as possible, should be warranted by scientific studies as useful to society in the modern age. Such knowledge consists of modern correlates of traditional subjects, often called basics, such as mathematics, social sciences (not the meager "social studies" of the past), natural sciences, and the humanities and arts. The latter have been overemphasized for the social benefits that accrue from them. Much more emphasis should be placed on science, technology, and mathematics, and on preparation for the world of work. Finally, I must add that these basics cannot be pursued without solid grounding in basic skills of reading, writing, arithmetic, and, I would add, computer and media literacy.

Why?   We moved beyond the agricultural revolution in the first part of the twentieth century and built the Industrial Revolution. Science and technology have now brought us into a postindustrial society where communication is the mechanism by which economies flourish. Students must be prepared to enter this kind of existence. We are making headway, but many educational systems remain at the industrial and agricultural levels.

How?   First, we need to apply the knowledge that scientific educational research has placed at our disposal for the design of curriculum and instruction. Second, we need more and better educational research on how learning takes place, how different categories of learners can best be taught, and on technologies of instructional engineering.

Who?   This question pertains to several categories of professional educators. First, we need more and better educational researchers who help us to understand how learning takes place. This is basic research. Second, we need applied researchers who develop technologies for using the fruits of basic research in experimental schools. Third, we need educators (administrators and teachers) in real-world schools who are able and willing to design curricular packages and instructional procedures based on this research. To the question of who should be educated, I respond that it should be everyone; everyone according to their capacity, that is. We are continuously refining our ability to assess students and place them in appropriate educational settings.

Where?   Appropriate curricula can be most efficiently delivered by schools and technical institutions. Within these institutions there should be planned variation of learning environments to accommodate the particular skills needed by categories of carefully evaluated student needs.

When? Formal education should begin earlier and, in our continually changing society, should also be available to retrain people who need new skills and technical abilities throughout adult life. This is the case whether they be involved in the operation of innovative high-tech equipment or performance in unsophisticated service technologies or in human relations. *When* also has a specific meaning with regard to the sequence of instruction. I will address this later; suffice it to say at this point that discovery of the correct ordering of instruction is one of the primary tasks for educational researchers to analyze.

Experientialist

(A relaxed, easygoing speaker who seems open to many individual preferences; at the same time, intense about social inequality and injustice.) I hope that the three of us will be able to enter into dialogue later on, because I am quite disappointed with the position set forth by the two previous speakers. No doubt, they will be disenchanted with my position as well.

I've already mentioned dialogue. It is central to my view of curriculum. Curriculum itself must be an interchange of experiences and ideas, not just among experts or from experts to recipients, but among everyone engaged in the educative process. That means all of us, especially students. Students must be given opportunity to reconstruct their experience, study its possible meanings, and interpret its significance for their own sense of meaning and direction.

Yet my position does not begin and end with the individual. It is centered as well in community and in the right of all publics to grow as both individuals and groups. Thus, I am oriented to a notion of democracy that realizes with Dewey (1916) that democracy and education must grow symbiotically, each nourishing and replenishing the other. Yet neither democracy nor education can flourish in a state where autocratic leaders or wealthy social classes repress others. The broadest interpretation of the curriculum question (What is most worthwhile to know, be, and do?) must be asked and acted upon by all members of a society in relation to the consequences that their action has on others.

Why? The experiential approach to curriculum acknowledges the essential goodness of each individual. It holds that as individuals reflect on their own experience, they are drawn together in sharing with others who are embarked on similar journeys. This makes all persons, not just experts, agents of their own learning. When each person's learning grows from his or her own experience, when its direction or purpose is conceived by the individual or group in question, only then can it truly be *for* that learner or learning community. This is both root and flower of democracy as captured in Abraham Lincoln's phrase "a government of, by, and for the people." Unfortunately, most schools are the antithesis of this position, although some thrust forth its rhetoric with great profusion.

How? As Dewey argued (1916), we must begin with the *psychological* and move to the *logical*. This means that we begin with learners' genuine interests that are embedded in their experience and enable them to pursue those interests gradually by becoming acquainted with the disciplines of knowledge. Here *interests* are not momentary whims; rather, they lie deep within the human spirit. One of the most fundamental human interests is personal and collective liberty that seeks equality and justice. In today's world most human beings are subjugated; they need to learn by pedagogy that emancipates them from the oppression that prohibits their pursuit of education and democratic action and leads to the good life. Paulo Freire (1970) has written eloquently of this in *Pedagogy of the Oppressed.*

Who? The separations of teachers from students and school from community are artificial and debilitating. Experientialist curriculum must involve teachers, students, community members, and curriculum leaders in a shared community of growth. All of them must acknowledge that they can both teach and learn from the others in honest and worthwhile ways.

Where? Everywhere people exist, perhaps more outside of formal educative institutions than within them. This is because the autocracy and oppressive control exerted by institutionalized education, as it presently exists, mitigates against self-direction and democracy. This is not to say that institutions are unable to support experientialist curricula. Allow me to modify my initial statement in response to the *where* question: anywhere that human beings can genuinely reflect on their experience and act on the fruits of that reflection to reconstruct their personal perspectives and political institutions.

When? Continuously throughout life.

SUGGESTED READING

Each chapter in this book will conclude with a brief essay in which I recommend further reading that augments the ideas, information, and issues developed in the chapter. I have selected the bibliographical essay because it has advantages over both a bibliographical list and an annotated bibliography. A list does not inform beyond the title, author, place of publication, publisher, and date. An annotated bibliography provides more information but usually presents it in alphabetical rather than logical order. Each of the bibliographical essays will be selective in order not to provide an unwieldy number of sources. For the most part, references discussed in the bibliographical essay will be of overarching relevance to the entire chapter. Supplementary reading for specific topics is represented by parenthetical notation of author and date in the textual discussion. Full citations for such references in the text as well as those in the bibliographical essays may be found in the reference list at the end of the book.

This chapter began with a most basic curriculum question: What knowledge is most worthwhile? Herbert Spencer is often credited with raising this question for the consideration of modern educators. In his 1861 book, *Education: Intellectual, Moral, and Physical*, he devoted a chapter and much attention to a slightly different phrasing of the question: "What knowledge is of most worth?" In one way or another, this question has been a mainstay of curriculum inquiry throughout history. Witness the array of selections of Western and Eastern thought compiled by Robert Ulich in *Three Thousand Years of Educational Wisdom* (1954). Ulich provides selections on education from more than fifty classics of philosophical, religious, and social thought, from Lao-Tse and Plato to Jefferson, Froebel, and Dewey. For all of them, the question of worthwhile knowledge is at the center of the discussion. In the twentieth century, when curriculum study became a specialized endeavor, we can see the influence of many philosophers and social thinkers who pursued the question that Spencer summarized. Sometimes twentieth-century educators addressed the question directly, as we shall see when we consider various national commission reports, and sometimes the question was ignored as curricularists became preoccupied with the technical delivery of information and skill regardless of its defensibility. A 1967 publication entitled *The Knowledge Most Worth Having,* edited by Wayne C. Booth, provides an excellent collection of papers from a University of Chicago conference on the topic in question. Authors include Wayne C. Booth, F. Champion Ward, Northrop Frye, John Cockcroft, J. A. Simpson, John R. Platt, Anne Firor Scott, James M. Redfield, Richard McKeon, and Edward H. Levi.

Although I do not intend to comment here on books related to individual chapters mentioned in the overview, I will note that the book you are reading falls within a long tradition of synoptic curriculum books. These are books that represent attempts to provide state-of-the-art presentations of curriculum knowledge. In addition, the best of them have offered novel conceptualizations of the curriculum field and have developed key ideas for it. More will be said about synoptic curriculum books in chapters that follow. Among the most widely used synoptic texts in the past are Caswell and Campbell (1935), Gwynn (1943), Smith, Stanley, and Shores (1950 and 1957), Taba (1962), Saylor and Alexander (1954, 1966, 1974, 1981 with Lewis), Doll (1964, 1970, 1974, 1978, 1982), and Tanner and Tanner (1975 and 1980). Any of these might be consulted for overviews of the state of curriculum thought and practice at earlier junctures. (Only the most recent editions of each are cited in the bibliography at the end of the book.)

Numerous sources will be given by each of the guest speakers throughout this book. As noted previously, it is difficult to find pure forms of each; however, I will provide the following sources of orientation. A book that best represents the intellectual traditionalist position is not a curriculum book at all; it is not even a book on education. Instead, it is a compendium of elaborate and well-referenced quotations on great ideas edited by Mortimer J. Adler and Charles Van Doren (1977). Entitled *Great Treasury of Western Thought,* its 1771 pages provide more than an introduction to sources that the intellectual traditionalist would consider the essence of what curriculum ought to include. I have often thought that were I limited to only one book to ponder for the remainder of my life, I would do well to select this one. A much shorter book, this one written directly for education and also by Adler (1982), is the well-publicized *Paideia Proposal: An Educational Manifesto* representing an intellectual traditionalist outlook, along with its sequels, *Paideia Problems and Possibilities* (Adler, 1983) and *The Paideia Program* (Adler, 1984).

The social behaviorist is imbued with the scientific tradition in education from Thorndike's *Educational Psychology* (1903) and Bobbitt's *The Curriculum* (1918) to such "bibles" of research methodology as Campbell and Stanley (1966) and Kerlinger (1973) and is exemplified by works in curriculum and instruction by Gagné (1977), Beauchamp (1981), and Gage (1978).

The experientialist position is well represented by Dewey's *Democracy and Education* (1916), probably his most thorough treatise on education, and the more contemporary and revolutionary *Pedagogy of the Oppressed* by Paulo Freire (1970).

RECOMMENDATIONS FOR REFLECTION

Each chapter will conclude with recommendations that readers are encouraged to use to reflect on the content of the chapter, to relate that content to their personal and professional lives, to pave the way for subsequent chapters, and to use the essence of what is said here for increased meaning and self-direction. Most of the questions/activities are designed to be most beneficial if they are considered individually, followed by dialogue with others.

1. How do you respond to the basic curriculum question: What knowledge is most worthwhile? When you respond, attempt to divorce yourself from knowledge of what schools usually teach. Why do you consider certain knowledge to be of worth? Is there anything in life that you think is more worthwhile than what you just selected? Perhaps you did not include it because you do not classify it as knowledge. Why don't you classify it as knowledge? Should schools include it among the experiences that they provide, anyway?

2. If you were suddenly endowed with magical powers and could bestow five characteristics on every human being in the world, what five characteristics would you select? Why? Try to communicate your definition of each characteristic to someone else. Share characteristics with others who have made similar lists. Compare, debate, and build ideas together. Add to your list and refine it.

3. How do your lists for activities 1 and 2 compare? At what points can they be contrasted? Is the choice of characteristics to give others (activity 2) fundamentally different from a decision about what knowledge is most worthwhile for people to have (activity 1)? If so, what is different about it? If not, why are the two similar?

4. Select one of your responses to activities 1 or 2 that you have particularly strong feelings about, and translate it into curriculum. Is it susceptible to transformation into curriculum? If you decide that it is not, why is it not? If it is important for people, can it not be learned? If it is susceptible to being translated into curriculum, what would a curriculum be like that is designed around the characteristic or aspect of knowledge that you selected as its organizing center? Describe it and share your translation with others who have thought about similar translations.

5. If you are in a situation in which you are able to share with others, think about the politics of your interactions. What is the nature and intensity of your deliberations? How are they similar to or different from a situation in which you might be determining curricula for an actual school?

6. When have you asked what is most worthwhile to know for your own life? Can you recall particular times in which it was very important for you to ask this question (i.e., when you made major contributions to your own development)? What were the conditions that prompted this fundamental questioning? Did your questioning occur under the auspices of an educational institution or elsewhere? Is such questioning a rare or ordinary occurrence for you? Do you think it should be rare or ordinary? What are its consequences for you?

7. What are the sources of your own conception of what is worthwhile to know? List at least five. Compare your sources with those of others. Are your sources essentially similar to or different from those of others? What are some possible explanations for the similarities or differences? To what extent did the sources come from formal education experiences?

8. From your first impression of the three "guest commentators," what do you think are three major strengths and weaknesses of each: intellectual traditionalist, social behaviorist, and experientialist?

9. Also from your initial impression, with which of the three orientations to curriculum theory and practice are you most aligned? What reasons support this alignment? Keep your choice in mind and see if the "commentators" are effective in convincing you to alter your position as you continue to read this book.

10. Restate in your own words the central purposes of this book, and interpret their meaning for the value of curriculum studies. In relation to this, what is the worth of curriculum amid the larger enterprise of educational practice?

PART I

✦ Perspective ✦

2

✦ Portrayal: The Curriculum Field ✦

Every man takes the limits of his own field of vision for the limits of the world.

ARTHUR SCHOPENHAUER "Further Psychological Observations"
Parerga and Paralipomena (1851)

He who lets the world, or his own portion of it, choose his plan of life, has no need of any other faculty than the ape-like one of imitation. He who chooses his plan for himself, employs all his faculties. He must use observation to see, reasoning and judgment to foresee, activity to gather materials for decisions, discrimination to decide, and when he has decided, firmness and self-control to hold his deliberate decision.

JOHN STUART MILL *On Liberty* (1859)

SETTING THE STAGE

The purpose of this chapter is to sketch with broad strokes the academic area that, during the past century, has come to be known as the curriculum field. While some who technically differentiate terms such as *field*, *discipline*, and *area of study* debate whether curriculum really is a field (see Westbury and Steimer, 1971; Jackson, 1980), use of the term *curriculum field* is widespread. This usage generally denotes the range of theorists, practitioners, and researchers who devote most of their professional time and energy to proposing, developing, studying, defending, and/or criticizing the content and experiences taught and learned in schools and other educative situations.

What kinds of images of curriculum exist in the curriculum field? How is curriculum related to other subfields of education? What subfields of specialized concern exist within the curriculum field? What resources are available to enable one to find one's way around the curriculum field? These are the main questions that this chapter is designed to address.

IMAGES OF CURRICULUM

A quick survey of a dozen curriculum books would be likely to reveal a dozen different images or characterizations of *curriculum*. It might even reveal more, because the same author may use the term in different ways. Authors may intentionally provide different images of curriculum to portray what others have said or to represent different conceptualizations of curriculum; or they may do so without realization and thus provide inconsistency or contradiction. I use the terms *image* and *characterization* rather than *definition* because they denote a broader conceptualization than the label for a thing. To make curriculum an object reduces its richness and rules out presentation of certain key conceptualizations that are essential to an understanding of the field.

To analyze and discuss all of the images that have been advanced would be a massive undertaking, since more than eleven hundred curriculum books have been written in the present century (Schubert, 1980a, p. 11). Moreover, the scholarly worth of such an endeavor would be dubious. What can be done more economically is to categorize major conceptions of curriculum, with examples, intents, and criticisms of each.*

Curriculum as Content or Subject Matter

The most traditional image of curriculum stems back to antiquity and the seven liberal arts, usually divided into the *trivium* (grammar, rhetoric, and dialectic) and the *quadrivium* (arithmetic, geometry, astronomy, and music). Curriculum is equated with the subjects to be taught.

Examples. Today, if one asks administrators of secondary or elementary schools to describe their curriculum, they usually expound a litany of subjects taught and times that they are offered. In my years as an elementary school teacher, "curriculum night" was an evening early in the school year in which teachers explained the curriculum to parents. Most parents actually expected a rendition of the daily schedule and an explanation of how this routine made sense as an overall program of subject matter.

Intent. Educators who use this image intend to explicate clearly the network of subjects taught, interpretations given to those subjects, prerequisite knowledge for studying certain subjects, and a rationale for the ways in which all subjects at a particular level of school fit together and provide what is needed at that level. Needs may be defined by programmatic labels such as college preparatory, commercial curriculum, general studies, advanced placement, remedial, honors, and so on.

Criticism. The exclusive focus on subjects does not account for other planned or unplanned activities that are a major part of students' experiences in schools. In fact, it only accounts for topics to be covered and neglects such important dimensions as

---

*Throughout this book, alternative ideas and positions are presented and supported by a statement of *intent* or *advocacy*. *Criticism* sections are written from a counteradvocacy vantage point. The technique is used to convey controversial issues and differences of opinion, interpretation, and argument.

cognitive development, creative expression, and personal growth. There is much more involved in planning than the subject to be taught. Instructional strategies, sequencing procedures, the scope of the subject, motivational devices, evaluation instruments, and interpretations of content are but a sample of planned attributes that make an immense difference in the character of a subject. Unplanned aspects such as the student's prior knowledge, student attitude about the subject and learning, teacher attitude and mode of interaction with students, students' interactions with each other, and messages about learning conveyed by the social, organizational, and physical features of the learning environment are powerful forces in what is learned. Likewise, the many informal social interactions among students in corridors, on playgrounds, and during lunch and free periods, as well as the formal organizations and events that make up extracurricular features of education, are major factors in what is learned. Thus, an image that equates curriculum with subject matter or formal content is easy to use but it simplifies and limits the problem too much. Schools provide learnings for students that go far beyond the confines of subject matter. Such learnings, as well as those unintended and embedded in the culture of schooling, must be included to give us a comprehensive view of curriculum.

Curriculum as a Program of Planned Activities

By focusing on a comprehensive view of all activities planned for delivery to students, this image of curriculum incorporates scope and sequence, interpretation and balance of subject matter, motivational devices, teaching techniques, and anything else that can be planned in advance. This view of curriculum as a plan is embraced by Saylor, Alexander, and Lewis (1981). The nature of a plan can be quite wide ranging. One way to view the extensiveness of this concept is from two extremes, one viewing curriculum as a written document (Beauchamp, 1981) and the other accepting plans that are in the minds of educators but remain unwritten. P. H. Taylor (1970), for example, has carefully observed teacher planning of courses and has emphasized that while it may involve written notes, much teaching is based on a curriculum of unwritten plans.

Examples. Written documents range from daily lesson plans to curriculum guides. Anyone who has passed through a teacher education program knows what a lesson plan is and can quickly recall its familiar categories: general purpose, specific goals, materials needed, procedures, evaluation, and so on. Curriculum guides are usually constructed locally by school administrators and/or districtwide committees of teachers, administrators, and sometimes outside consultants and community representatives. Some guides are rather brief and give the "bare-bones" structure of what is to be covered in each subject at given grade levels. Others are exceedingly elaborate and provide background information for teachers, and suggest teaching strategies, arrangements for learning environments, supplementary materials, outside resources, and modes of evaluation. Larger school districts often have sizable central office staffs and produce many curriculum guides for different subject matter areas. University libraries compile collections of these guides to supplement teacher education programs. Projects are now available that provide curriculum guides on microfiche.

Teachers' manuals for published textbooks and other instructional materials serve as another version of curriculum guides. Although they usually do not unify curriculum areas into an overall programmatic thrust, as do locally designed guides, they provide a great deal of extra material for teachers to use as they organize their classroom and think about the specifics of teaching a lesson or unit. Some school systems legislate specific requirements that teachers must cover a certain number of activities from the guide or be at a certain page or chapter in the textbooks by specified dates. Others recognize curriculum guides and textbooks as helpful resources rather than mandates to follow to the letter.

Those who have taught for several years know that planning is a great deal more than that which is written down. I recall, for example, team teaching situations in which teachers would discuss possible courses of action and arrive at a plan. The plan would be implemented, each teacher doing his or her part, and nothing would be written down. Teachers will sometimes get bright ideas on the spur of the moment or will have to change plans in midstream because of altered circumstances (an unannounced assembly, student lack of responsiveness, unavailable equipment). Teachers may do a great deal of planning while driving to and from work or when pondering the next day just before falling asleep at night. These and similar activities are all plans, yet they may never be written.

Intent.   The common thread in all of these notions of planning, written or unwritten, is that they are planned activities. As in the case with elaborate curriculum guides, there is more provided than activities; however, the end of planning is to see that certain desired activities are delivered to students. Granted, all these plans have purposes for which the activities are the vehicle. Yet it is the activity—what students do—that is the curriculum.

Criticism.   To characterize curriculum as planned activities is to place major emphasis on outward appearance rather than inner development. It values outcomes and neglects the learning process. Emphasis on activities implies that more careful attention should be given to ends than means. For example, many teachers and school districts are so intent on seeing that certain activities are implemented that the activities become ends in themselves. There is a tendency to lose sight of purposes that the activities serve, such as their impact on the learning process or personal meaning. Attention to prespecified activities obscures consequences that cannot be readily anticipated. For example, twenty children who engage in the same creative writing activity have twenty quite different responses. Thus, it may be more sensible to focus on what each student experiences than on the planned activity itself.

Curriculum as Intended Learning Outcomes

Some authors (Johnson, 1977a; Posner, 1982) contend that curriculum should not be the activities but should focus directly on the intended learning outcomes. This shifts emphasis from means to ends. Intended learning outcomes are a convenient way to specify purposes. Purposes no longer remain stated in such global rhetoric as, "an appreciation for our cultural heritage." Instead, a structured series or sequence of learning outcomes is set forth; all activities, teaching, environmental design, and the like serve the acquisition of specified ends. Intended learning outcomes are not precisely equated with curriculum; rather curriculum is the realm of intentionality that fosters the intended learning outcomes.

Examples.   An intended learning outcome in a high school social studies class may be to identify the arguments for and against the buildup of nuclear armaments. The curriculum design would detail all the materials, plans, and arrangements that would enable students to do this. The process of determining, designing, and realizing intents would, of course, involve a great deal of analysis of contextual and philosophical factors.

Intent.   The purpose is to be explicit and defensible regarding what is offered to students.

Criticisms.   Focus on intended learning outcomes as the prime factor in curriculum draws attention away from the unintended outcomes, which many claim are an exceedingly powerful force in what students learn in schools. These are outcomes of the culture of schooling or hidden curriculum. While all the students in a class may demonstrate that they have acquired the intended learning outcome, the consequences of its acquisition may be quite different from one student to another. Knowledge that helps one student when it combines with the rest of his or her cognitive and affective repertoire may be enlightening, while the same intended learning outcome may indeed be harmful to another student. Less harmful, but still quite powerful, is the impact that differing organizational environments and instructional strategies can have on an outcome. The same intended outcome may become quite different when taught by an inquiry, simulation, and lecture method. The central point here is that intended results may be very different from actual ones, even within a group of students who seem to have acquired the intended outcomes.

Curriculum as Cultural Reproduction

Some hold that curriculum in any society or culture is and should be a reflection of that culture. The job of schooling is to reproduce salient knowledge and values for the succeeding generation. The community, state, or nation takes the lead in identifying the skills, knowledge, and appreciations to be taught. It is the job of professional educators to see that they are transformed into a curriculum that can be delivered to children and youth.

Examples.   The patriotic events of national history; the dominant economic system whether communistic, capitalistic, or another; the cultural conventions, mores, and folkways; the religious values in parochial schools or in public schools where no separation of church and state exists.

Intent.   In advanced industrial societies, it is impossible for parents who have specialized jobs themselves to teach adequately all the complicated capabilities that their children need. Moreover, in earning a living, they scarcely have the time to do so, even if they do have the knowledge, inclination, and ability. Thus, they need special institutions to reproduce the culture for their children.

Criticisms.   To hold that curriculum *should* be uncritical cultural reproduction assumes that the status quo is good enough (i.e., that cultural and social improvements are not needed). As argued by Apple (1979), Anyon (1980), Giroux (1983), and others, the problem runs much deeper than simply asserting that the status quo is perpetuated; they identify massive inequities associated with prolonging unjust social hierarchies. The wealthy and powerful remain in control of middle and working classes; they, along with the poor and destitute, remain unable to grow and develop as human beings who can govern their own lives. It is, of course, a mistake to view impositions of cultural reproduction as uncontested (Apple and Weis, 1983). Oppressed persons find ways to resist. Yet, when educators tacitly assume that schools are powerless to influence social or cultural change, they perpetuate existing injustices. The question is not whether schools alone can change a society, but whether they, as one of many institutions in a society, can exert forces for greater freedom, equality, and justice. To claim that institutions within a society are less powerful than the society itself misses the point that a society is a composite of institutions and individuals who all contribute to the character and dynamic of the whole.

Curriculum as Experience

The idea that curriculum should be a set of activities or predetermined ends was resisted by John Dewey, who advocated a means-ends continuum. This position holds that educational means and ends are inseparable parts of a single process: experience. To attend to one's experience reflectively and to strive continuously to anticipate and monitor the consequences of one's thought and action relative to the good that they bring is a continuously evolving curriculum. The teacher is a facilitator of personal growth, and the curriculum is the process of experiencing the sense of meaning and direction that ensues from teacher and student dialogue.

Examples.   Learners are seen as vast reservoirs of potential. In his or her own way, each learner is deemed unique and worthwhile. Teachers and learners discuss the importance of determining worthwhile activities; however, the notion of activity is not as central to this definition of *curriculum* as is the concept of experience. Ralph Tyler (1949) contrasted course content and activities with learning experience. Learning experience is the curriculum that students actually come to know or realize. It is a function of purposes; content or activity; organizational patterns of persons; instructional materials; instructional practices; evaluation modes; and hopes, desires, and philosophies of educators. Yet learning experience is to be equated with none of these, for it is fashioned finally when it meets the experiential repertoire of the learner. The same plans will often have quite different consequences when actualized as experience amid the knowledge, skills, attitudes, and values of different learners.

Intent.   Curriculum as actual learning experiences is an attempt to grasp what is learned rather than to take for granted that the planned intents are in fact learned. Experiences are created as learners reflect on the processes in which they engage. Curriculum is meaning experienced by students, not facts to be memorized or behaviors to be demonstrated. While ideals are indeed indispensable in giving direction to action, they are fashioned as teachers and learners interact amid a milieu and with subject matter that gives substance to learning. Four commonplaces of curricular experience are set forth by Schwab (1973): teacher, learner, subject matter, and milieu. Whenever a change occurs in any one or a combination of these common-places, and such alterations are always occurring, the curricular consequences change that meet the learner and his or her storehouse of experience. Thus, ends and means are united in constant interaction. The perceptive educator, as collaborator with the learner, must artistically facilitate the learner's search for experiences that contribute to personal growth.

Criticism.   While curriculum as personal experience and growth sounds wonderful in principle, it is impossible in practice. Given the realities of the teaching situation, how can one high school teacher who meets 150 or more students per day enter into dialogue with each one and work out a curriculum for personal growth? Although a bit more feasible, how can an elementary school teacher do this with 30 students? Even when considering a small enough group, say, less than 10 students, one might be able to plan a personalized curriculum with each, but it is impossible to get inside of each student's being well enough to know the consequences of teacher, other learners, subject matter, and milieu on his or her personality, character, outlook, beliefs, behavior, and so on. For the same reasons, this conception of curriculum is so broad that it defies research. How could one ever study the short- and long-term consequences of the totality of school experience on the whole of the prior experience of the learner?

Curriculum as Discrete Tasks and Concepts

The curriculum is seen as a set of tasks to be mastered, and they are assumed to lead to a prespecified end. Usually, that end has specific behavioral interpretation such as learning a new task or performing an old one better. This approach derives from training programs in business, industry, and the military.

Examples.   Acquisition of rules of grammar, mathematical algorithms, penmanship style, or phonics rules at the elementary school level and in occupational training, learning a new system of filing for an office, a new maneuver with a military vehicle, the operation of a new machine for folding envelopes in a stationery factory, or running a program with a microcomputer are carefully specified at a defined level of performance. Potential learners are pretested to assess the level of knowledge of the desired skill that they possess and perhaps their aptitude for acquiring it as well. Minutely detailed sequences of learning tasks are identified that build the larger skill; these are implemented and, eventually, posttests are conducted.

Intent.   Just as a skill may be defined in terms of its constituent behaviors, knowledge and appreciation can be analyzed in terms of the affective, cognitive, psychomotor, and social concepts that characterize it.

Criticism.   While task analysis may be highly appropriate for learning certain mechanical activities, it is very limited. The whole of most tasks, even mechanical ones, is greater than the sum of its parts. Therefore, a simple additive set of procedures may produce the appearance of a skill well learned, but it will not provide for variation that is so essential in our changing world. This requires a knowledge of principles, not isolated skills or even concepts. Even more difficulty is found in the assertion that more sophisticated knowledge and appreciation can be derived from training. The ancient Greeks called this procedural knowledge *techné*, and they contrasted it to *aréte* which refers to the quest for excellence, virtue, and goodness. Although concept analyses are available on the appreciation of, say, impressionist painting, and they may convey certain rules or criteria to observe, they could never provide an adequate substitute for the educated imagination that comes from careful study and considerable experience with that which is to be discussed or appraised.

Curriculum as an Agenda for Social Reconstruction

Dare the School Build a New Social Order?   This is the title of a book by George S. Counts (1932b), one of the fathers of the social reconstructionist position in education. Championed by Theodore Brameld in the 1940s and 1950s, and inspired by many of Dewey's works, this view of curriculum holds that schools should provide an agenda of knowledge and values that guides students to improve society and the cultural institutions, beliefs, and activities that support it.

Examples.   Application may begin within the school itself. Students are given a major role in planning and implementing life in the school. They address what the purpose of schools should be, and they develop and defend a design to implement that purpose. Another variation involves students in the identification and study of major national and international issues, the result of which would be activist participation. Still another interpretation is that educators and students would determine utopian plans for a better world. In any of these alternatives, the purpose of schooling is to improve the social order (e.g., to prepare students who enter the world with a fervor to provide greater racial equity or more empathic understanding among wealthy, middle, working, and poor classes of people).

Intent.   Based on the assumptions that no culture or society is perfect and that the purpose of education is to improve it, the cultural reconstructionist sets out to build a better society. The orientation may involve considerable input from students, or it may be dominated by educator decisions about how students should be taught to reconstruct society. The methodology may range from teaching students desirable changes that should be made to equipping them with critical thinking abilities and a desire to ask and act on the question: What should be changed, how, and why? In either case, the curriculum is an agenda for cultural reconstruction.

Criticism.   It is doubtful that schools, large but not particularly influential institutions, are politically powerful enough to exert major social changes. If they would become powerful enough to do so, the desire of educators to foist their political beliefs on children and youth is tantamount to indoctrination of a very serious kind. It sparks the memory of youth in totalitarian nations who are brainwashed to support a revolution or to spy on their own families and report infractions of rules. Even in less severe cases, the question arises as to the right of educators to play deity in the dictating of social change.

Curriculum as "Currere"

One of the most recent positions to emerge on the curriculum horizon is to empha-size the verb form of *curriculum*, namely, *currere*. Instead of taking its interpretation from the race course etymology of *curriculum, currere* refers to the running of the race and emphasizes the individual's own capacity to reconceptualize his or her autobiography. Illustrated by Pinar and Grumet (1976), the individual seeks meaning amid the swirl of present events, moves historically into his or her own past to recover and reconstitute origins, and imagines and creates possible directions of his or her own future. Based on the sharing of autobiographical accounts with others who strive for similar understanding, the curriculum becomes a reconceiving of one's perspective on life (Grumet, 1980). It also becomes a social process whereby individ-uals come to greater understanding of themselves, others, and the world through mutual reconceptualization. The mutuality involves not only those who are in im-mediate proximity but occurs through the acquisition of extant knowledge and ac-quaintance with literary and artistic expression. The central focus, however, is auto-biographical. The curriculum is the interpretation of lived experiences.

Examples.   Students write autobiographical accounts that focus on striving to know who, how, and why they have developed as they have. Teachers and/or other stu-dents respond through written or oral comment on the writing. Dialogue ensues and creates reconceived visions of self, others, and the world. Relevant literature is introduced, and the curriculum becomes the process of reconceptualization.

Intent.   The purpose of reconceptualization is individual emancipation from the constraints of unwarranted convention, ideology, and psychological unidimensional-ity. It is to explore other provinces of meaning, to envision possibilities, and to fashion new directions for oneself, others, and the world, through mutual reconcep-tualization.

Criticism.   This striving for self-knowledge cannot be done in schools by teachers and students. It requires the intense expertise of a psychiatrist, psychoanalyst, or other professional therapist. Even if it could be done in schools, it should not be, for it goes far beyond the purpose of schools to transmit knowledge, skills, and values of a culture. Children and youth need objective knowledge. Self-understanding is a pa-rental and personal responsibility, not that of the government or other agencies that sponsor schools.

Continuing the Images Debate

Each of the images of curriculum just presented ends with a critical assessment. You should not be swayed unduly by the argument advanced, and you certainly should not conclude that because of the existing disagreement none of the positions have merit. The statements of intent and the examples make clear some of the positive features of each image. The reader is challenged to imagine a continued debate. How would a proponent of each of the images respond to the criticisms raised?

How might the conflicting positions be productively analyzed? One way is to identify the metaphors that they utilize. In a brief but powerful article, Herbert

Kliebard (1972) emphasizes that we think in metaphors. He characterizes three root metaphors found in curriculum literature and practice: production, growth, and journey. Production provides an industrial model that envisions the student as raw material to be transformed by a skilled technician who uses rigorously planned specifications, avoids waste, and carefully sees to it that the raw materials are used for the purposes that best fit them. The growth metaphor perceives the teacher as an insightful gardener, who carefully gets to know the unique character of the plants (students) and nurtures their own special kind of flowering. In the travel metaphor, the teacher is a tour guide who leads students through a terrain rich in knowledge, skills, ideas, appreciations, and attitudes. The tour guide knows that each traveler will respond differently to the trip because of his or her unique configuration of background, ability, interests, aptitudes, and purposes.

The etymological origins of curriculum as the course of a chariot race might lead one to believe that a travel metaphor is closest to the original. The original, however, is not sacred, and we must be willing to alter meanings as knowledge and ideas improve. This notwithstanding, I encourage you to return to each of the characterizations and ask whether it is best represented by the production, growth, travel metaphor, or perhaps a different metaphor that you invent. Perhaps, too, each is a combination of several metaphors. It might be the case that the original journey metaphor is sufficiently comprehensive to incorporate each of Kliebard's metaphors. While it is obvious, for example, that travel is a journey from place to place, growth is a journey in which the self expands, differentiates, and becomes more complexly integrated (Hopkins, 1954). Production is a journey from raw material to sophisticated product.

Just as we have emphasized that curriculum knowledge as a whole is problematic, is it also contributory to conceptual richness to have several extant images of curriculum? Might this invigorate debate? Or, as some suggest (Johnson, 1977b), is it stupid to posit the existence of a field of study when its members cannot agree on the definition of what is studied? Might a reasonable compromise be to argue that different images are needed for different purposes? As you look back at the characterizations provided, can you state a practical situation in which each of the images would be useful? In other words, might each image be appropriate to some aspects of the curriculum realm but not to others?

Here, the parable of the blind men and the elephant seems fitting. Each of several blind men touched a different part of the elephant; one grasped the leg and concluded that an elephant was like a tree, another examined the trunk and described the elephant as a large snake, another touched an ear and thought of a huge fan, still another felt the tusks and likened the elephant to a sharp spear. Could it be that staunch advocates of one image of curriculum are only examining one of many facets of the entire realm? Should we continue to cultivate a variety of images in an effort to move closer to an understanding of the whole picture of curriculum? Or do some images contradict and rule out the use of others?

CURRICULUM AND RELATED SUBDIVISIONS OF EDUCATION

To portray curriculum as a field of inquiry and practice, it must be viewed in its interdependence with other subdivisions of education. This invokes an ecological perspective in which the meaning of anything must be seen as continuously created by its interdependence with the forces in which it is embedded. Thus, the character of curriculum shapes and is shaped by its external relationships with knowledge, perspectives, and practices in other educational domains: administration, supervision, foundations, policy studies, evaluation, research methodology, subject areas, educational levels, teaching or instruction, special education, educational psychology, and so on. Some of these areas have more direct relevance to curriculum than others; therefore, they will be treated in greater depth elsewhere in this book.

Administration

School administrators set the tone for curriculum development. They orchestrate the system through which curriculum is developed and implemented. Administrators generally fall into two broad categories: line and staff. Line administrators begin with the superintendent, who develops overarching policy with the school board and sees that it is delivered and refined by assistant superintendents (district superintendents in very large school systems), building principals and their assistant principals, department heads, and teachers. This is the line of command, to use a military or business analogy. Staff administrators serve in a consulting capacity and provide advice to teachers and principals. They may be specialists in subject matter areas, classroom management, testing, teaching methods, and so on.

The *modus operandi* of administrators is often categorized as autocratic, *laissez-faire*, or democratic. It is obvious that each of these orientations has quite different influences on the character of curriculum. For example, one might look again at each of the images of curriculum and consider how different it would be if applied within an autocratic, *laissez-faire*, or democratic administrative climate. One might also try to align images of curriculum with administrative orientations that would be most likely to facilitate them. This is to say that the administrator is a curricular leader by virtue of the stage he or she sets for teaching, directly or indirectly. Administrators may set a system in motion with the direct intent of mandating certain prespecified curriculum practices, or they might enable most curriculum practices to evolve at the classroom level. Line administrators may, on the contrary, see their responsibility as the removal of obstacles to curriculum development, assuming that curriculum can be determined more appropriately by teachers and staff administrators.

One matter is certain; curriculum is a prime reason for the exercise of administration. Administrative decision and action bypasses its purpose if it is not designed directly or indirectly to enable the maintenance and improvement of curriculum. In other words, the end of administrative endeavors should be to facilitate what is taught and learned. A growing curriculum depends on good administration, and curriculum gives final meaning to school administration.

Supervision

Teachers who are actively employed are generally supervised by principals at the elementary school level and assistant principals or department heads in the secondary school. This act of overseeing teachers with the intent of enabling them continuously to improve learning experiences for students has both formal and informal dimensions. Both relate to administration, for it is staff and line administrators who supervise. Formal supervision may take the form of carefully planned classroom observation and feedback that includes reflection on problem solving and possibilities for improvement. Informal supervision occurs in the form of everyday interaction among teachers and administrators but also includes subtle suggestion, encouragement, reduction of impediments to creative teaching, and modeling of both better interaction with students and more appropriate teaching methods. Supervision, in other words, embraces the whole domain of staff development, and the latter is inextricably entwined with curriculum development.

Educational Foundations

Foundational courses in education usually include history and philosophy of education, and sometimes sociological, political, economic, anthropological, and even literary perspectives. Some foundational courses provide an integrated treatment of most of these. It is hoped that such courses will provide educators with an intellectual context from which to judge and defend decision and action. According to the American Educational Studies Association, the principal professional group for professors in this area, the purpose of foundational studies is to provide interpretive, normative, and critical perspectives and analyses (Task Force on Academic Standards, 1978).

Foundational studies enable curriculum scholars and practitioners to analyze more carefully and defend the programs that they propose and implement. Historical studies help to prevent the needless rediscovery that characterizes too much of educational practice. Sociological, political, and economic perspectives help to situate curriculum and curricular discourse within a vast network of forces that pull, push, and persuade educators in many directions simultaneously. Philosophical inquiry probes deeply into the assumptions that are too often taken for granted in curricular proposals, procedures, and practices. Moreover, philosophy facilitates the clarification of values and language, both of which are central to curriculum research and practice. In short, foundational studies provide perspectives essential to understanding and working in the curriculum field.

Educational Policy Studies

This relatively new area on the educational scene is an outgrowth of departments of educational foundations in universities. Policy studies or policy analysis evolved as an effort to make educational foundations more responsive to problems and issues faced by educational institutions. Some also argue that it emerged in the 1960s to get for professors of educational foundations a share of the pie baked by creators of the Great Society funding programs.

Curriculum may be conceived as policy. The development or formulation of curriculum, its implementation, evaluation, and revision, is a multifaceted policy issue that involves fundamental questions: How do (and how should) educational institutions generate and deliver the goods and services (in this case knowledge, skills, and attitudes or values) deemed most worthwhile to students? What forces within educative institutions and society at large support and resist the creation and utilization of curriculum knowledge?

Evaluation

Evaluation is a key ingredient in the perennial curriculum paradigm as the fourth question in the Tyler Rationale (Tyler, 1949), which includes considerations of purposes, learning experiences, organization, and evaluation. Evaluation is separated from curriculum at this point, however, because it has in the past twenty-five years emerged as a specialized domain of inquiry. Embracing several academic areas, evaluation is both a professional and research field, sometimes referred to as *program evaluation* rather than curriculum evaluation.

The call for accountability in all professional spheres of society today has given rise to massive emphasis on research and teaching about evaluation in political science, economics, business and management, and medical sciences, as well as education, other professional areas, and applied sciences. With funding has come intense pressure to insure that money is well utilized. Increased public awareness of policies that meet their direct goals but neglect attention to side effects (e.g., ecological problems that resulted from headlong attention to dollar signs in quarterly reports by executives in business and industry) intensifies the need for careful evaluation of unintended as well as intended consequences in programs of many kinds. In the curriculum field, the emphasis on unanticipated consequences signaled the emergence of *hidden curriculum* as an evaluation concern. It also called for direct attention to evaluation that substantiated or refuted the realization of goals through the gathering of empirical evidence.

Research Methodology

During the past twenty-five to thirty years, the sophistication of research methods in education experienced a great upsurge. During the late 1950s and throughout the 1960s, this was represented by a borrowing and adapting of behavioral research design and quantitative methodology from the social sciences, which earlier borrowed and adapted from the natural sciences. Throughout the 1970s and thus far in the 1980s, social science research has continued to develop and naturalistic, ethnographic, and a variety of case study approaches have been applied to education. Drawing from the arts, humanities, and traditions in social thought from continental Europe (e.g., phenomenology, existentialism, Marxism, and psychoanalysis), educational research has broadened to include a whole range of inquiry types (Feinberg, 1983; Bredo and Feinberg, 1982). In the curriculum area, this increased variety of inquiry might be considered inconsistent with the canons of science and contributory to confusion in a field already fraught with controversy. It might, on the contrary, be seen as promising because it opens up new ways to investigate curricular phenomena; different situations can be illuminated by different methods of inquiry, and most situations can be disclosed by examining them through the lenses of multiple forms of research. During the past fifteen years, much scholarly attention has been given to the nature and function of curriculum inquiry. It is inappropriate to present the curriculum field without devoting substantial attention to the kind and quality of inquiry that creates it.

Subject Areas

Many colleges of education have designed majors in curriculum and instruction for specific subject areas taught in schools. Mathematics, science, social studies, reading, language arts, art, and music are prominent examples. Similarly, books on curriculum often focus on one subject area or another instead of attempting to cover curriculum more generically. Many professional journals and associations likewise are geared to specific subject areas.

There exists, then, an interplay between those whose concerns lie primarily with teaching of subject areas and those whose interests reside more generally in curriculum. The subject matter specialist draws heavily upon the cognate disciplines that pertain to the subject area of interest and to research and methods of teaching that focus directly on that subject. The general curriculum specialist is more concerned with processes of curriculum development and design that can be applied to any subject areas. Concomitantly, the generalist is interested in overarching theory, research, history, and change in the curriculum field as a whole, whereas the specialist is interested in these topics primarily as they pertain to specific subject areas.

No small debate has occurred in the curriculum field about the nature of interdependence desirable between curriculum generalists and subject specialists. A sample of positions on this topic is available in the January 1983 *ASCD Update*. Historically, many have seen attention to subject matter as a major culprit in the alienation of school from life. As Dewey (1931) argued, the confused state of education and its lack of perceived relevance to students is due to the unnatural lines of demarcation that separate one subject from another. Others argue more positively that in our age of specialization, we need a continuous exchange of knowledge between generalists and specialists. Only then can both generalist and specialist be invigorated, updated, and provide a sense of wholeness.

Levels of Schooling

Departments and areas of specialization in universities as well as journals, books, and professional organizations specialize in the following: early childhood or preschool education; elementary education; junior high school, secondary or high school, and higher education. Recently, additional specializations have emerged: education in the professions as a form of higher education; primary (grades 1 through 3) and intermediate (grades 4 through 6) as variations within elementary education; community colleges or junior colleges as a form of higher education; the middle school as a transition that includes various combinations of grades formerly at the end of elementary schooling with those of the junior high; and adult education as an ongoing extension of education or training that is postsecondary and often postcollegiate.

Some curriculum writers argue that each of these areas is unique, so that the principles of curriculum development that pertain to it do not adequately serve the other areas. Thus, they produce separate curriculum books and articles on each level of schooling. Others argue that students at any level are human beings and that people don't learn in significantly different ways simply because they are at different age levels; instead, it is held that regardless of age, individual variation must be considered when developing curricula.

Education for Equity

Legal mandates and increased awareness of certain disadvantaged groups in society have brought the emergence of special education, bilingual and multicultural education, and compensatory education. A wide range of provisions have been made through programs for the mentally, physically, emotionally, behaviorally, and socially handicapped; for those whose language and cultural values differ from those that dominate a society; for those whose economic, racial, ethnic, and/or sexual characteristics and circumstances provide unequal access to goods and services that meet physical, psychological, and social needs; and for those who are beset by learning disabilities of different kinds.

Evidence for the growth of equity programs in education resides in the fact that bilingual education and special education are now major departments in many colleges of education, the fact that funding sources in these areas have made a major impact on school programs, and the plethora of professional literature and related organizations that have emerged. Such areas cannot be treated as just another dimension of subject matter or levels of schooling, for they transcend both. Education for equity needs to be treated as a major area of education in its own right.

During the past quarter of a century, curriculum scholars and practitioners have become more attuned to these special problems. Literature and pressure groups increasingly call for an end to the unfortunate neglect of such groups that has blotted the history of education and society. The means to providing equity are indeed complex. It is a topic with which curricularists are beginning to grapple and for which much work needs to be done.

Educational Psychology

Educational psychology is a wide-ranging domain with nearly as many subspecialties as psychology itself. Measurement and psychometrics have had major impacts on educational research and practice through the steady growth of the testing industry. Nearly all schools use standardized tests of achievement and cognitive ability. A large proportion of educational research studies uses results of such tests as measuring sticks, often unquestioningly equating test results with the construct to be measured. Witness the use of standardized tests as a measure of ability in college entrance requirements. Behavioristic psychology also has a sizable following in education through operant conditioning and behavior modification. This emphasis is highly evident in special education programs. Developmental psychology has grown markedly in the past two or three decades; its applications focus on the analysis of the developmental appropriateness of curricular and instructional programs.

Developmental, clinical, and personality psychology have continued to exert great influence on conceptions of human development and learning, which in turn affect all areas of the curriculum, teaching methodology, and counseling. Perhaps the greatest growth in educational psychology in recent years is in the area of cognitive psychology, which focuses on the intricacies of long- and short-term memory, draws upon the neurosciences, and relates cognitive structures and functions to the learning process. Through the influence of cognitive psychology, those who design and implement curriculum and instruction are more inclined to monitor student responses to learning situations. They know that students bring a storehouse of knowledge to the learning situation and thereby mediate or influence the learning that is intended.

Instruction

A major debate exists in the curriculum field over the relationship between curriculum and instruction. In this book, instruction is treated as a subdimension of curriculum. There are, however, a sizable number of curriculum writers who consider the two as related but separate entities (e.g., Beauchamp, 1981; Johnson, 1977a). They want curriculum study to be about the *what* of education and instruction to treat the *how*. Advocacy of this kind relegates those concerned with instruction to a more technical status. They deal with the delivery process. They are given the package to deliver, and it is their job to determine how to reach its destination in the learner. Those concerned with technical delivery are often labeled instructional designers or technologists. In the past, many of them focused on programmed learning and teaching machines; today, some of this group have turned to computer-assisted instruction. Instructional design advocates often see curricularists as specialists in the particular areas of knowledge, skills, values, appreciations, and the like that should be taught. Foshay and Foshay (1980) discuss differences and similarities between curriculum generalists and instructional designers, noting that the former are more concerned with the problem of worthwhile knowledge and the latter with technical delivery.

Many others in the curriculum field hold that the separation between curriculum and instruction is artificial and contrived (e.g., Dewey, 1916; Macdonald and Zaret, 1975). They argue that curriculum generalists must be concerned with the whole process because instruction is not merely delivery. They think that creation and modification of instructional practices sends reverberations throughout the entire system, from the determination of purposes through the selection and organization of learning experiences, to evaluation, revision and meaning that accrues in the personal lives of learners.

Regardless of one's position on the relation between curriculum and instruction, one point is clear: they are both central ingredients in teaching. Recent research on teacher effectiveness, for example, has implications for the whole curriculum process. Similarly, critical perspectives on curriculum, arguing that it reproduces knowledge and values that support ruling classes while subjugating middle, working, and lower classes, are as applicable to instruction as they are to curriculum.

DOMAINS WITHIN CURRICULUM STUDIES

Now that curriculum has been situated amid related areas of educational studies, I shall identify prominent subdivisions of curriculum study itself. Some scholars specialize in one or another of these areas while others attempt to deal with the whole. Practice can be influenced by all of the subdivisions.

Curriculum Theory

Curriculum theory has many forms that may be derived from overarching philosophies (e.g., pragmatism, idealism, realism, existentialism, phenomenology, scholasticism, and critical theory). Curriculum theory is often characterized as either prescriptive or descriptive. Prescriptive theory asks, What is worthwhile to know, how do we know it is worthwhile, and how can its worth be justified? Prescription deals with the realm of *ought*. Descriptive theory deals with the realm of *is*; taking their cue from empirical science, descriptive theorists ask: How can reality be modeled so that we know its salient features, thus enabling us to explain, predict, and control curricular activity and behavior? One might also ask: What do I, as an educator, believe should be taught, how do I defend its worth, conceptually explicate it, validate and refine it? Here we invoke a kind of personal theory that includes an image of both what *is* and *ought* to be in curriculum. Curriculum theory can also be interpreted as the act of clarifying meanings and the uses of language. Still another notion of curriculum theory refers to the act of theorizing and reflecting. Finally, *metatheory* is the comparative study of different conceptions of theory and the categories used by theorists.

Curriculum History

Curriculum history deals with processes of describing, analyzing, and interpreting past curriculum thought and practice. By studying our past we better understand our present because we develop a better sense of origins. By studying the past we can profit from insights and approaches to problems that relate to similar circumstances today. Study of the forces that have inhibited or supported curricular innovation, decision, and action in the past places educators in a better position to analyze present conditions and chart future courses of action.

Curriculum Development

One of the most widely used labels in the field, sometimes taken to be synonymous with curriculum study itself, *curriculum development*, refers to the process of deciding what to teach and learn, along with all the considerations needed to make such decisions. Brought into full bloom in 1935 by Caswell and Campbell through their book entitled *Curriculum Development*, the term has been used in the titles of several of the most prominent curriculum texts: Stratemeyer et al. (1957); Smith, Stanley, and Shores (1957); Taba (1962); and Tanner and Tanner (1980). Each of these books symbolizes the vast array of considerations (historical, philosophical, cultural, political, psychological, and economic) that need to be taken into account in curriculum development. Moreover, each shows that all individuals in the process must be given careful attention, as well as the usual issues of purposes, content or learning experiences, organization, instruction, evaluation, and change.

Curriculum Design

Sometimes equated with curriculum development, curriculum design is usually more specific. The planning of curriculum guides, the analysis of instructional materials, the development of instructional units, the preparation of computer software, and the creation of instructional games and programmed learning materials all require attention to key elements of curriculum design: intent or objectives, content or activities, organization, and evaluation. The curricularist concerned with design analyzes the consistency and congruence within and among each of these areas. This is done on a large scale for an entire program, for a grade level, or for a subject area. It is also done for individual units of study, textbooks, instructional packages, and even lesson plans.

In addition to the analysis function in design, there is also much attention given to the creation of curriculum. This is traditionally done by proceeding from assumptions, to purposes and objectives, and to the selection of content or activities that facilitate acquisition of objectives. The latter is followed by careful organization of materials and environment in which the content and activities can be delivered and finally includes evaluation for purposes of revision. Design or redesign may also begin through intervention at any one of the stages noted and proceeds to others affected.

Curriculum Implementation

Traditionally seen as the delivery process, implementation can be considered a system of engineering that takes design specifications through various channels to the teacher and classroom. Other conceptions of implementation directly focus on the teaching or instructional process. Thus, the study of how faithfully teachers carry out instruction in a school district could be considered curriculum implementation research (see Brandt, 1980; Fullan and Pomfret, 1975).

Another quite different conception holds that the purpose of curriculum is not to "teacherproof" the instructional process. Instead of being so carefully specified as to prevent teacher innovation, teachers are seen as curriculum creators and adapters. In this case, implementation is not the following of orders but the development of learning experiences based upon knowledge derived from a continuous flow of interactions with learners.

Curriculum Evaluation

Evaluation is the attempt to assess or judge the worth of students and educational practices, materials, or programs. It can serve as a starting point, an end, or a means of continuous monitoring and renewal of curriculum. Its purposes can be as narrow as grading and assessing students or as broad as program improvement. Methods of evaluation may be the traditional experimental or quasi-experimental study or more recently developed qualitative or ethnographic portrayals. The more traditional applications of evaluation in curriculum involve the attempt to see if prespecified goals are reached by using prespecified means.

Curriculum Change

Falling also under the labels *revision*, *renewal*, *improvement*, and *innovation*, change literature in curriculum was originally patterned after change literature in agriculture. The careful planning of change, the involvement of all concerned, the analysis of resisting and supporting forces, and the development of both organizations and individuals, all geared toward the end of improving the curriculum, are still mainstays of this literature.

Curriculum Inquiry

It is indefensible to study curriculum without investigating the nature of curriculum inquiry. Although the terms *research* and *inquiry* can be used synonymously, research is often given narrower meaning than inquiry. While the former generally applies to the logical positivist and objectivist orientations, the latter includes these plus a wide range of philosophical, historical, interpretive, normative, and critical forms of investigation. There is a sense in which curriculum inquiry penetrates every aspect of the curriculum field, for no dimension of curriculum could proceed apart from inquiry that precedes, accompanies, and reflects upon action.

RESOURCES FOR CURRICULAR KNOWLEDGE

In one book, even one of this length, it is impossible to provide a comprehensive overview of the curriculum field. Therefore, I provide the following section intended to alert readers to sources of further information and ideas. These include professional associations, periodicals, and books.

Professional Associations

Information, ideas, and collegial exchange are the benefits of professional associations. They are a seedbed for the maintenance and growth of a field of inquiry. In the curriculum field there are associations for theorists and researchers, others for practitioners, and still others that attempt to bridge the gap between the two. Some of these associations are established for general audiences of educators, while others are designed primarily for those in curriculum. Notable are the National Education Association (NEA) and the American Federation of Teachers (AFT) as prime examples of organizations designed for general audiences. They cater mainly to practitioners, although both also serve scholars in universities. The collective bargaining, the journals published (*Today's Education* of the NEA and *American Educator* of the AFT), the workshops and instructional materials produced and the other benefits that accrue from membership all have direct or indirect impact on curriculum.

The American Educational Research Association (AERA), the National Society for the Study of Education (NSSE), and the American Educational Studies Association (AESA) are of primary interest to curriculum scholars. AERA is by far the largest of these three organizations, having a membership of more than twelve thousand. AERA is organized into nine divisions and over seventy special interest groups (SIGs) that correspond to areas of research interest. The Curriculum Studies Division has more than three thousand members, and the SIG on Creation and Utilization of Curriculum Knowledge has approximately one hundred members. This association has an annual meeting that attracts several thousand researchers and publishes seven journals. Among them, *Educational Researcher* provides general perspectives on research and information about the association, *Review of Educa-*

tional Research specializes in integrative interpretations of research studies on a single topic, *Educational Evaluation and Policy Analysis* deals with two topics of great interest in curriculum, and *Contemporary Education Review* provides a host of reviews of a wide range of books on education. AESA, a much smaller organization of scholars concerned with foundation and policy areas, produces one journal, *Educational Studies*, primarily a book review journal, that discusses books of direct and indirect interest to curricularists. AESA meets annually, publishes a newsletter, and works toward the purpose of providing greater integration among educational foundations areas (philosophy, history, psychology, sociology, policy studies, economics, and cross-national systems) as they bear on educational issues. The NSSE publishes a two-volume yearbook annually. Each volume addresses a major educational topic from the perspective of several noted scholars in the field. At the end of each yearbook is a complete listing of previous yearbook titles dating back to 1902, when the Society was founded, as successor to the National Herbart Society. The yearbook titles alone produce a kind of history of contemporary issues in education in the twentieth century, and many relate directly to curriculum. In recent years, the NSSE has produced a "Contemporary Series" of books on additional topics of interest. Similarly, AERA provides occasional monographs and an annual volume, *Review of Research in Education*.

Several associations reach both scholars and school-based curriculum administrators. Principal among them is ASCD (the Association for Supervision and Curriculum Development). Its journal—*Educational Leadership*, the *ASCD Yearbook*, special publications, an annual convention, training institutes, and state affiliates have provided a mainstay in the diet of curriculum leaders for over forty years. Professors of Curriculum, a group of curriculum scholars that holds an annual meeting just prior to that of ASCD, has a membership by invitation policy and is limited to one hundred members. Its purpose, since its founding in 1959, is to establish a forum whereby major contributors to curriculum thought and practice can address fundamental curriculum problems together. Another major associate group of ASCD is the World Council for Curriculum and Instruction, established to generate global dialogue on problems of curriculum and instruction in many cultures. They, too, meet in conjunction with the annual ASCD conferences and, in addition, hold regular international conferences at different locations throughout the world.

Other smaller groups remain independent of large organizations (in much the same way that Professors of Curriculum is not officially part of ASCD), but hold meetings in conjunction with them in order to economize on travel and the costs of meeting and to remain in close contact with curriculum leaders in schools. The Society for the Study of Curriculum History, founded in 1977, meets just prior to the Annual Meeting of AERA. Its purpose is to further interest and scholarship in the history of curriculum thought and practice through the development of a network of scholars, presentation of papers at meetings, and publication of proceedings. Another group is not a formal organization with membership but is a loosely knit group of persons concerned with curriculum theorizing, most of whom are subscribers to the *Journal of Curriculum Theorizing*. They have held annual conferences since 1973 and have gradually engaged practitioners as well as scholars who wish to extend the boundaries of curriculum reflection beyond its traditional limits to embrace new philosophical, ideological, literary, psychological, artistic, and interpretive perspectives. The John Dewey Society (founded in 1935) discusses, interprets, and extends the spirit of Dewey's philosophy relative to contemporary and historical issues involving education and culture. It holds annual meetings with such groups as AESA and ASCD, publishes books that expand its annual invited lecture by a distinguished scholar, and publishes members' ideas in *Insights* and monographs on contemporary issues.

Finally, two educational honor societies should be noted: Phi Delta Kappa and Kappa Delta Pi, which publish *Kappan* and *Educational Forum*, respectively, two of the best known journals for educational scholars and practitioners alike. These two societies publish numerous books, occasional papers, and monographs and engage in special projects. For example, PDK is well known for its "Fastbacks," small books on contemporary issues, and KDP is engaged in a sizable research project designed to identify good schools.

Professional Periodicals

While many periodicals are affiliated with professional associations, a number of first-rate curriculum journals are independently operated. *Curriculum Inquiry,* formerly initiated as *Curriculum Theory Network* in 1968, began in 1976 at the Ontario Institute for Studies in Education in Toronto. The *Journal of Curriculum Studies,* a British journal, started publication in 1969, and now has Australian, U.S., Canadian, European, and British editors. In the United States, *The Journal of Curriculum Theorizing* was born in 1979, and in 1980 *Curriculum Perspectives* emerged in Australia. These dates are indicative of the youth of the curriculum field. All four journals have an international readership, and they publish articles using a variety of inquiry modes to extend scholarship on curriculum theory, research, and practice.

In addition to journals, newsletters of several associations help to keep curriculum scholars and practitioners abreast of current research and other perspectives. Examples include *The Newsletter of the AERA SIG on Creation and Utilization of Curriculum Knowledge, The Newsletter of the Society for the Study of Curriculum History, ASCD Update, Practical Applications of Research* by Phi Delta Kappa, the *Newsletter of the World Council on Curriculum and Instruction, Curriculum: Newsletter of the Canadian Association for Curriculum Studies,* the newsletter of the Australian Curriculum Studies Association (formerly the Curriculum Interest Group), and a newsletter of the Curriculum Studies Division (Division B) of AERA, begun in 1985.

Educational Leadership of ASCD has the greatest circulation of any curriculum journal. It appeals to both scholars and practitioners, with curriculum leaders in schools comprising the largest proportion of its readership. Its articles tend to be short, informative, and conversational in style, and they cover an eclectic range of contemporary educational issues. In 1985, however, ASCD sponsored a new journal, *Journal of Curriculum and Supervision,* in an effort to speak to the more scholarly needs and interests of the profession. Other periodicals of interest to curriculum administrators are *Curriculum Review* (a U.S. publication that reviews textbooks, instructional materials, and children's literature as well as provides articles on related topics) and *Curriculum,* an issues-oriented journal of the British Association for the Study of Curriculum. Educational Products Information Exchange (EPIE) specializes in nonpartisan consumer reports on instructional materials and textbooks and also provides workshops and study guides on the process of selecting curricular and instructional materials.

In addition to periodicals designed exclusively for curriculum writing, articles on curriculum theory, research, and practice may be found in a variety of other journals such as the following: theoretical treatments in *Teachers College Record, Harvard Educational Review, American Journal of Education* (formerly *School Review*), *The Journal of Education, Educational Theory, Phenomenology and Pedagogy, Theory into Practice;* research presentations in *Review of Educational Research, British Journal of Education Studies,* the *High School Journal,* the *Elementary School Journal;* ideas and research for practitioners in *The Elementary Principal, The Reading Teacher, Language Arts, Science and Children, The Arithmetic Teacher, Social Education, Learning, Teacher,* and *Instructor.* These are but samples; numerous other journals of merit exist.

Beyond this, I encourage you to scour the library; use the *Education Index* and the *Cumulative Index to Journals in Education* (CIJE) to locate topics of interest in many different journals; check topics in *Dissertation Abstracts;* look for book reviews by using *Book Review Digest* and *Book Review Index;* learn to use the Educational Resources Information Center (ERIC) system to find documents relevant to your interests; learn to use the ERIC computer search facilities and similar data bases in most university libraries for generating citations and abstracts. Locate other professional organizations, for example, those that specialize in a subject area or other educational topic that interests you.

Books on Curriculum

A field of inquiry is known by the books it produces. Major journal articles eventually make their way into books of readings. Prominent examples include collections by Hass (1983), Giroux et al. (1981), Bellack and Kliebard (1977), Van Til (1972, 1974), Pinar (1974, 1975), and Short and Marconnit (1968). Texts that summarize major contributions to curriculum thought and practice, and thereby present an overview or state-of-the-field portrayal such as this book, are referred to as *synoptic texts* (Schubert, 1980a, pp. 76–77). Some synoptic texts go beyond summarization to add new dimensions to the literature portrayed; for example, Alberty and Alberty (1962) interpret an innovative core curriculum; Stratemeyer et al. (1957) relate the curriculum to persistent situations in student lives; Smith, Stanley, and Shores (1957) integrate dimensions of scientific curriculum making with social reconstruction; Taba (1962) adds careful diagnosis and unit construction to the conventional categories of curriculum planning; Firth and Kimpston (1973) present a continuum of perspectives that includes precedents, parameters, programs, and potential; and Tanner and Tanner (1980) provide elaborate historical perspectives.

In addition to synoptic texts and collections of readings, there are many curriculum books that specialize in a particular subject area, level of schooling, or specific aspects of curriculum development such as organization, purposes, learning environments, selection of content, and evaluation. Studies of practice are also highly recommended, such as Goodlad (1984), Reid and Walker (1975), Smith and Geoffrey (1968), and Willis (1978), as well as inquiries into the nature of theory and practice such as Schwab (1978), Pinar (1975), McCutcheon (1982a), Eisner (1982), Apple (1979), and Giroux (1983).

Reference books on education are also a valuable resource. The fifth edition of the *Encyclopedia of Educational Research* sponsored by the American Educational Research Association (Mitzel, 1982) has several curriculum articles in its four volumes and many related others. Similarly, *The International Encyclopedia of Education* (Husen and Postlethwaite, 1985) is a much larger reference work that treats all aspects of education, providing many articles on different aspects of curriculum in broad, intercultural context.

COMMENTARIES

Each of the guest commentators is asked to comment on the foregoing sections of this chapter: images of curriculum, subdivisions within educational curriculum studies, and resources for broadening one's horizons about curriculum. Each is also asked to characterize his or her interpretation of major contributions to curriculum theory, research, and practice.

Intellectual Traditionalist

On my image of curriculum I simply ask, Where can we turn to find defensible knowledge and great ideas? The answer, of course, is to the disciplines. I cannot see how curriculum could be conceived seriously as anything but content or subject matter. Certainly planning is necessary, but it must be done in moderation. One cannot merely dive into the disciplines at random; however, it must be remembered that the disciplines have a structure of their own. So does the individual who studies them. Thus, the interaction between individuals and the disciplines often yields unpredictable outcomes, expressions, and ideas. This is healthy and requires artistry of teaching of the kind implied in the famous comment attributed to President Garfield that he would rather have his son sit on the opposite end of a log from the great teacher, Mark Hopkins, than have him attend preparatory schools of highest rating. This is why too much planning or predetermination of outcomes is a mistake. The true educator fashions a lasting relationship between the student and the great ideas. This is what makes teaching an immortal profession (Highet, 1976). Surely, personal growth, cultural reproduction, cultural reconstruction, and reconceptualization may be outcomes of this high-quality liberal education, but to strive directly for such benefits is, as the adage goes, the surest way to miss them.

As for the context of curriculum within the other subdivisions of education, I believe the point is overblown. First, education is not a discipline; at best, it is an area of inquiry. It does not have a body of subject matter, a structure, and methods of inquiry that are unique. Thus, it is unlike chemistry, mathematics, sociology, architecture, history, the study of languages, and the like. Instead, educational scholars draw upon many areas of knowledge in an eclectic fashion. Since education is not a discipline itself, it is contradictory to think of curriculum, administration, educational psychology, foundations, and so on as subdisciplines.

It seems more appropriate to think of the subdivisions as inextricably united with the whole. This is especially the case if we move away from the dilapidated notion that equates the study of education with the study of schooling. What we must do, instead, is emphasize a conception of education that is akin to the German notion of *bildungsroman* (Schubert and Schubert, 1982; Swales, 1978), which holds that education is the self striving to become fully developed and directed toward the good, the virtuous, and excellent life as best exemplified in the Wilhelm Meister novels by Goethe. If we accept this broader idea of education as self-conscious life development, it makes more sense to view curriculum as the whole substance (or journey) of this development.

Therefore, it becomes necessary for curriculum scholars to tap the resources of all knowledge, not merely that which falls within education. This is especially the case since curriculum and education are an inseparable union. Hence, it is much more sensible to set curriculum studies within the context of all of the disciplines: natural sciences, social sciences, the arts, the humanities, and even some of the better established professions such as law and medicine. Given this orientation, it makes little sense to subdivide curriculum into theory, development, implementation, and the like, except for the most banal analytic purposes.

Curriculum theory, research, and practice must be seen holistically, as inquiry into human nature, knowledge, values, society, reason, and pedagogy. Historically, Plato and Aristotle are still the great exemplars. Plato shows the inseparable connection of education and all fundamental human concerns. Aristotle developed the disciplines of knowledge and demonstrated the necessity of coupling education and the pursuit of wisdom within them. It is to the tradition of great philosophers who emulated Plato and Aristotle that we should turn for curricular insights. See, for example, the collection of excerpts on curriculum and education provided by Ulich (1954).

Today, places called Colleges of Education would be labeled more appropriately "Colleges of Schooling." They focus on an institution, not on the process whereby human beings are educated. In actuality, the latter occurs throughout many spheres of life, not schooling alone. So-called educational researchers who spend their energies analyzing schooling and their work, with few exceptions, speak inadequately to the broad educational process by which people become more human. The ideas of Hutchins (1936), Adler (1982), Broudy (1961), King and Brownell (1966), Phenix (1964), and Whitehead (1929) speak to the value of the disciplines in a liberal education.

The overall point is that we lose perspective when we view twentieth-century curriculum literature as the last word. Most of this literature pertains to the technology of schooling and not to fundamental ideas about the nature of human education. For the most part, we are better off to turn to the philosophical and literary classics for insight about curriculum. There, curriculum problems are addressed in an alive, humanistic context, not in the dry and lifeless vacuum of service delivery, social engineering, and institutionalized systems.

Social Behaviorist

I see why the intellectual traditionalist is labeled *intellectual*. There is no reasonable way to produce the ideals so glowingly set forth. The eloquence of the intellectual traditionalist's rhetoric, however, is offset by the fact that it is unproductive in the real world.

In the real world of postindustrial society, schooling has become the means for education. We have a highly refined and specialized society that brings us countless goods and services, most of which we take for granted. Admittedly, schooling is far behind the medical, legal, mass media, or engineering professions in terms of sophisticated service delivery. We can use these more advanced professions as models to emulate. While I too acknowledge that education is broader than schooling, we must accept the fact that each person's private life is his or her own. We do not have the right to say that everyone needs a pervasive liberal education. What we can defensibly say is that the common needs of persons in all industrialized societies (and those striving in that direction) are basic skills of communication and computation, foundational knowledge of the world and how it works, and to some extent a sense of the values appreciated by the culture in which they live.

These needs can be provided by combining careful analysis of the subject matter with diagnosis of student capabilities for acquiring it. As this is done, curriculum becomes a structured series of intended learning outcomes, a carefully planned course of study. See Posner and Rudnitsky (1982) for a detailed analysis of the contingencies to be considered in designing course plans of this kind. I would favor a definition of curriculum that focuses on results, intended outcomes that can be observed and measured. Otherwise, how do we know where we are or what we have produced? It is best to have these outcomes and their rationale carefully described in the form of a written document or policy that serves as a treatment specification for curriculum implementation. Without careful definition and prespecification of products intended for delivery to students, it is absurd to proceed because there is nothing to verify or evaluate. Without verification and evaluation, it is impossible to know whether a curriculum works or is worthwhile.

Regarding the situating of curriculum within the other subdisciplines of education, I am convinced that it is important to delineate carefully the boundaries among them and the responsibilities of each. Only then can we achieve a level of rigor and sophistication that is worthy to be called a discipline. Only when the function of each component of the whole system is explicitly related to the others can progress be made. Thus, administrators, instructional technologists, psychologists, philosophers of education, and so on must all know the scope and limits of their work and their interdependence with one another. Curriculum developers must see themselves as one very important cog in the overall machine of schooling.

This concept of interdependent systems applies to many levels; thus, within the curriculum domain, it must be made clear exactly what functions are to be carried out by curriculum theorists, historians, developers, designers, implementors, evaluators, change agents or organization development experts, and researchers. This, of course, implies that each person (be they principal, supervisor, consultant, teacher, or scholar) involved in curriculum should know the aspects of each of the tasks involved in his or her role.

As for contributions to research, theory, and practice, most of them have been made in this century. I would go further to say that the majority of important contributions have been made in the past twenty-five years. Prior to this century and for a good part of it, educators were long on armchair philosophy and short on scientific evidence. The science of education began with E. L. Thorndike, Charles H. Judd, John Dewey, and in curriculum Franklin Bobbitt and W. W. Charters, all prior to the 1930s. However, the methods of science and the value of rigorous specialization were not fully realized in education until social scientists and behavioral psychologists began to study educational problems in the post-*Sputnik* curriculum reform movement and during the Great Society education programs that required accountable demonstration of uses of funding.

A great deal more systematic empirical research has been done in instruction than in curriculum. Evaluation methodology has also made great strides. The close link between curriculum and instruction would cause me to give high recommendation to the three fine *Handbooks of Research on Teaching* (Gage, 1963; Travers, 1973; Wittrock, 1985). Together they portray the growth of a wide range of research on teaching, including recent research on teacher effectiveness, mastery learning, time on task, and so on. If curriculum research is to aid practice as well as has research on teaching, curricularists would do well to follow the scientific guideposts set forth in the curriculum theory of Mauritz Johnson (1977a) or George Beauchamp (1981).

Experientialist

The curriculum should be defined as growth experiences that lead to a continuous reconceptualization of culture, individuals, and groups. The social behaviorist concentrates so much on management that efficiency is given precedence over worth, and in practice research takes precedence over education. Meanwhile, the intellectual traditionalist blatantly assumes that subject matter that looks worthwhile in theory will in fact be worthwhile when it enters the growing repertoire of each student's experience. This assumption is unwarranted; if a learner is not capable of interpreting a body of subject matter or deriving meaning from a fine literary classic, the effects may be deleterious. Similar harm can result from the social behaviorist propensity to focus on goals for the sake of evaluation and research rather than to focus on experience and reflect on its impact on learner outlook. It is, in other words, indefensible to subject students to content or activity without accepting responsibility for its consequences.

Since the consequences of learning are holistic, and since real-world problems are not arranged to fit subject boundaries, it is not particularly useful to divide educational or curricular labor into rigid job specifications. For example, a good teacher must do all of the following: administer a classroom; be his or her own best supervisor; build perspective from educational foundations; have expertise in matters of policy, evaluation, research, subject areas, and instruction; possess strong expertise in educational psychology; and be able to deal with a host of problems of educational equity. This is equally true for the principal, consultant, central office administrator, and any other curriculum decision maker. Similarly, when the curriculum design, implementation, and evaluation are done by different groups, a great disservice is done to communication and articulation. To segment responsibility in this way dashes the best of plans on the rocks of misinterpretation. Furthermore, one whose work is limited to design may not feel a vested interest in implementation. It is better that every educator be considered a curriculum theorist, developer, designer, implementor, evaluator, researcher, change agent, and the like. It is much too easy to be seduced into the tendency to specialize inquiry. Few remain who can see the whole, as was brilliantly pointed out by Kelley and Rasey (1952) over thirty years ago, and by many before them from Plato to Dewey.

The major contributions to curriculum theory and research have not been made by persons whose jobs were defined as theorists or researchers, but by educators who have exemplified sensitive, thoughtful interaction with others. Such a conception of theory and research may be found in the emphasis on reflective thinking in many works by John Dewey, especially *The Child and the Curriculum* (1902), *Democracy and Education* (1916), and *Experience and Education* (1938a). Popular renditions of teaching experiences (e.g., Ashton-Warner, 1963; Dennison, 1969; Freire, 1970; Holt, 1964; Kohl, 1968; Kozol, 1967; Neill, 1960) are perhaps the best recent examples of an integration of theory, research, and practice conceived as reflective, educative interaction. Justificatory argument for this integration can be found in Hopkins (1954), Pinar (1975), and Schwab (1978). I would only add that this broadening and unifying of the notion of curriculum inquiry should infuse every aspect of life, not merely schooling. We must begin to see the natural curricula that educate us quite profoundly through families, peer groups, vocations, avocations, media, nonschool organizations, and informal relationships. For it is the journey of learning in all such areas, including schooling, that shapes the outlook or personal theory of all persons. To neglect consideration of the whole is to miseducate.

SUGGESTED READING

Most of the readings that enhance perspective on the curriculum field were mentioned in the "Resources for Curricular Knowledge" section of this chapter. However, I will mention a few overviews of the field here. (Full citations for all works mentioned are in the bibliography at the end of the book.)

Rather brief summaries of five aspects of curriculum may be found in the fifth edition of the *Encyclopedia of Educational Research* (Mitzel, 1982): "Curriculum and Instruction in Higher Education" by Paul L. Dressel, "Curriculum Development and Organization" by Edmund C. Short, "Curriculum History" by Daniel Tanner, "Curriculum Research" by William H. Schubert, and "Qualitative Curriculum Evaluation" by Gail McCutcheon.

Relevant articles include Lawrence Cremin's (1971) widely cited piece, "Curriculum-making in the United States"; Decker Walker's (1976) "Toward Comprehension of Curricular Realities"; William Pinar's (1978) "Notes on the Curriculum Field"; John D. McNeil's (1978) "Curriculum—A Field Shaped by Different Faces"; and William H. Schubert's (1982a) "The Return of Curriculum Inquiry from Schooling to Education." An excellent bibliographical essay on journal articles on curriculum is written by Linda McNeil (1977).

Among recent synoptic texts, two stand out for their portrayals of the curriculum as a field of study (Zais, 1976; Tanner and Tanner, 1980). In addition, collections edited by Short and Marconnit (1968); Eisner and Vallance (1974); Van Til (1972, 1974); Bellack and Kliebard (1977); Orlosky and Smith (1978); Gress and Purpel (1978); Giroux, Penna, and Pinar (1981); and Hass (1983) provide samples of widely cited articles from curriculum literature.

Few books have been devoted exclusively to a perspective on the curriculum field as a whole. Schubert's (1980a) *Curriculum Books: The First Eighty Years* provides an elaborate bibliography with commentary on the development of the field 1900–1979, and Seguel (1966) offers an overview of contributions by major figures in the formative years of the field. A series of six books published in 1976 under the editorship of David Jenkins also provides a fine panorama of the curriculum field with a broadly balanced flavor of ideas throughout the English-speaking world. The six small books are *Curriculum: An Introduction* by Jenkins and Shipman (1976), *Designing the Curriculum* by Sockett (1976), *Changing the Curriculum* by MacDonald and Walker (1976), *Curriculum Evaluation* by Hamilton (1976); *Knowledge and Schooling* by Pring (1976), and *Culture and the Classroom* by Reynolds and Skilbeck (1976). Finally, Rosales and Short (1985) provide an interesting view of the field through their analysis of results of a survey of curriculum professors' knowledge and use of 36 major references in curriculum literature.

RECOMMENDATIONS FOR REFLECTION

1. What is your own image of curriculum? What justification or rationale do you give for its usefulness or worth? Discuss your image and rationale with others. Provide criticism and make suggestions for mutual improvement.

2. With which of the images of curriculum presented in the first part of this chapter do you agree most? Which do you feel is the most widespread among educators? Among noneducators? Which one differs most from your own image?

3. Are some of the images compatible with others? Which ones? Are some incompatible? Which ones? What makes some compatible and others contradictory or inconsistent?

4. In which of the subfields of education do you have most experience, either direct or vicarious? To what extent are curriculum issues and problems dealt with in that area? To what extent should they be addressed there?

5. Reflect on each of the subareas of education (administration, supervision, evaluation, foundations, and the like). How do educators who specialize in each area facilitate the process of curriculum development and implementation? How might they hinder it?

6. How do the several subdivisions of curriculum inquiry relate to one another? Try to draw a model that depicts their interdependence. Is one of the subdivisions the center of focus or are they all of equal balance?

7. Go to your college or university library and do a survey of the resources available for curriculum study. Which of the resources mentioned in this chapter help to give you an overview of the curriculum field? Which resources seem most useful to your particular needs and interests in curriculum? Recall the characteristic that you selected for activity 4 at the end of Chapter One. What resources would be most helpful to you as you think about developing it as a curricular area?

8. With which of the guest commentaries do you agree most: intellectual traditionalist, social behaviorist, or experientialist? Can you rank them and give reasons for your ranking?

9. Select a curriculum issue that is popular today. Develop a response from each orientation: social behaviorist, intellectual traditionalist, and experientialist. How would each be likely to criticize the stance taken by the other two?

10. Identify a part of the argument of each guest commentator that provoked your thinking. Was it a positive or a negative provocation? Why do you think the argument or idea affected you as it did? How did it influence your outlook on curriculum? On education generally?

11. Select any one of the three commentators. Imagine that you are each of the other two. What counterarguments could you build to the position advanced by the one selected?

12. Relative to the several images of curriculum presented in this chapter, select one or two and continue the argument as a debate. In other words, respond to the criticism in character with the statement of intent and respond again as the critic might. Continue for two or three episodes.

3

✦ Precedent: Historical Antecedents ✦

Those who cannot remember the past are condemned to repeat it.
> GEORGE SANTAYANA *The Life of Reason* (1905–1906)

Human history becomes more and more a race between education and catastrophe.
> H. G. WELLS *The Outline of History* (1920, 1921)

History is the essence of innumerable biographies.
> THOMAS CARLYLE "On History" (1830)

We can chart our future clearly and wisely only when we know the path which has led to the present.
> ADLAI STEVENSON Speech, Richmond, Virginia (September 20, 1952)

SETTING THE STAGE

To be ahistorical, devoid of perspective on one's past, is indefensible. If people have thought and worked in one's area of concern, one must take responsibility to learn about what has gone on before.

The curriculum field is new as a formal area of academic inquiry, but as a basic human interest, its concerns are perennial. Parents and other members of society throughout history have wondered how best to help their young grow and mature. Their response to this problem constitutes an unwritten history of informal curriculum thought and action. As societies became more formal and as institutions developed within them to meet specialized needs, schools evolved to help students grow more efficiently, to introduce them to the ways of their society, and to help them acquire understanding of their cultural heritage.

The assumption that society must be responsible for the development of its young has been addressed with great seriousness by perceptive members of humanity. Philosophers, social theorists, political leaders, religious leaders, and an unknown array of good parents and teachers have asked questions about what should be taught and learned. Some dared to question the taken-for-granted answers. This questioning and the answers that emerged are the historical roots of curriculum studies.

First, we shall look at those roots by turning our attention back to highlight theory and practice that evolved prior to the twentieth century. Second, we shall focus on the development of curriculum theory and practice as curriculum studies emerged during the twentieth century. Following this, the guest commentators respond to the study of curriculum history, noting what they consider to be the most significant developments.

PRE–TWENTIETH-CENTURY CURRICULUM HISTORY

To understand contemporary curriculum problems and proposals, it is necessary to be acquainted with the history of curriculum thought and practice that stretches back to antiquity. Much of what follows is geared to the Western traditions. It would be desirable to have more perspective drawn from the Eastern, African, Latin American, Islandic, and other non-Western educational history, but this goal awaits further historical research in education.

The Ancient World

In *Before Philosophy* (1946), Frankfort and others interpret the intellectual adventure of ancient man in the Near East; it is possible to see in their historical essay a central thread of education that pervaded ancient life in Egypt and Mesopotamia. What we know about the early half of Egypt's six-thousand-year history indicates a primary emphasis on practical as opposed to abstract thought; however, conceptions of good, evil, and justice were dealt with through religious institutions and family life. It was in the latter that education took place, with greatest emphasis on sons being taught by their fathers. The curriculum was largely vocational, with apprenticeship systems that followed training in the home. The most able were apprenticed as scribes in court schools or in government. Heavy emphasis was placed on writing through the learning of hieroglyphic symbols, due to the central role of documents that governed Egyptian life through leadership of a powerful class of conservative priests in whose hands rested higher education. Traditionally, it was assumed that the emphasis on practical mathematics, astronomy, medicine, engineering, and geography contributed to the architectural wonders of ancient Egypt, although some accounts attribute this to psychic and even extraterrestrial powers. However, many scholars believe that the decline of Egyptian civilization is related to lack of imaginative literature, philosophical thought, and scientific inquiry that sought abstract or generalizable knowledge.

In ancient China, we find a rather different situation. Two dominant educational orientations emerged, one attributed to Lao-Tse (sixth century B.C.) and the other to Confucius (fifth century B.C.). Lao-Tse saw education as the fruit of contemplation. The spiritual life brought a state of mind that was necessary if other achievements were to have meaning and importance. Confucius was more oriented to society than to the individual and saw education as a process for preserving society and its institutions. While Confucius held that curriculum should reproduce society's traditional habits, customs, and laws to make good citizens, Lao-Tse believed that good citizens can only come from persons who have attained great spiritual insight.

In ancient India, the curriculum was the sacred text (e.g., the *Upanishads*, *Vedas*, and *Gitas*). Religious life and education were inseparably entwined with the goal of life itself, which was to move along the path toward Nirvana in which the human soul finds union in the World Spirit.

Curriculum in Ancient Greece and Rome

The primary origins of curriculum today can be traced to ancient Greece. For education to develop fruitfully for both individuals and the state, the Greeks, particularly the Athenians, realized that leisure time is essential. Leisure was not regarded as frivolity, but as the opportunity to contemplate the significance, worth, meaning, and aesthetic value of one's life and contributions. The goal was achievement of a well-rounded development of mind and body based on principles of moderation and balance. Even the Olympic games involved contests in music, poetry, art, and drama as well as athletics. One must, however, balance the great achievements by noting that the contemplative middle class was supported by slaves at a ratio of six slaves to one citizen and that women were not considered citizens.

A multitude of philosophers in ancient Greece contributed to educational thought. Aristippus (435–355 B.C.) advocated hedonism or pleasure as the goal of life and education. Epicurus (341–270 B.C.), on the contrary, advocated simplicity, abstinence, and moderation, while Zeno of Citium (340–265 B.C.) pushed this position further, by emphasizing the stoic life of self-denial of material possessions. These, their contemporaries, and the pre-Socratics developed philosophical perspectives that contributed greatly to educational thought in the Western world; nevertheless, the three greatest contributors were Socrates (470?–399 B.C.), Plato (428–348 B.C.), and Aristotle (384–322 B.C.).

Little is known about Socrates apart from his characterization in the renowned *Dialogues* of Plato, his student. His method of questioning, his use of discussion to spur inquiry, and his dedicated quest for virtue are well known and revered today. Socrates abhorred the Sophists who thought they had certain knowledge, emphasized vocational education, institutionalized education, and taught for payment. These criticisms speak too powerfully to be taken seriously by many of today's educators who are more Sophistic than Socratic. Plato's *Dialogues* are replete with curricular implications, especially *Crito*, *Protagoras*, *Meno*, *Phaedro*, and *The Apology*. However, in *The Republic* Plato most explicitly set forth his curricular recommendations for the ideal state. He saw education as essential to the development of a republic, both because citizens must be enlightened in order to provide maximum contributions to their particular station and because he considered education a process by which the virtue and wisdom of preceding generations could be passed along to suceeding generations.

Curriculum in Plato's *Republic* was a lengthy process that began at age six and extended to age eighteen for both boys and girls. Music, mathematics, and gymnastics were the main areas of study, although they were to be interpreted more broadly than they are today. Music included literature and history and was believed to foster noble emotions. Mathematics involved the organization of knowledge; by connecting reason with the processes of the natural world, one could control one's environment. Gymnastics included the study of dance, rhythm, athletics, and military arts and emphasized the interdependence of physical and mental growth. Following the first twelve years were two years of military training, which terminated with an examination that dictated the students' futures. Those who failed became soldiers and laborers, while those who passed studied abstract subjects such as epistemology, politics, ethics, psychology, and law, for the next ten years. Further examinations placed some students in bureaucratic government jobs, while the most elite became philosopher-kings who governed the republic.

One can easily see roots of many contemporary curricular practices in Plato's proposal. In his *Laws*, written later in life, Plato took a more conservative stance, arguing that more control was necessary and that knowledge did not automatically produce the political and moral capacity to govern soundly. If one wants to read Plato's most profound educational insights, however, Robert Ulich (1950, pp. 8–9) recommends the *Symposium*:

> One who wishes to understand the deepest of what Plato had to say about education should immerse himself in the poetic symbolism of the *Symposium*. *He ought to pay special attention to the narrative of Socrates about his conversation with the noble woman Diotima of Mantinea, who told him that Eros, or Love, the son of Plenty and Poverty, creates in man the instinct of immortality and the desire for the good and beautiful. Eros inspires man also with the ever-lasting harmony of the universe of which we are a part. . . . [p. 9] The harmony and the proportions we discover in the growth of plants, in music, and in the movements of the stars, man's feeling of an embracing love for all that resembles divine creativeness, beauty, and perfection—all these powers flow into nature and us through the mysterious channels which connect individual life with the soul of the whole. [p. 8]*

Although we can turn to Plato for the roots of a liberal education, it is his student Aristotle who should be studied for the full-blown idea. In Books VII and VIII of *The Politics*, Aristotle argued that a liberal education leads to personal improvement, which in turn brings dedication to the state. The end of philosophy, politics, and education, for Aristotle, is happiness, which brings human good. Thus, the curriculum must be broad, but not directed to vocations. It should include gymnastics, or education of the body, and health, which yields growth of mind; refinement of passions, desires, and appetites through music, aesthetics, and ethics; and the education of reason through philosophy and the sciences. As the great systematizer of knowledge, Aristotle invented the disciplines that have been passed on to the contemporary generations. Yet knowledge alone is not enough to bring virtuous living. Both experience and habit are required. One should choose to practice the moral habits that lend to the development of good character, which brings happiness. Thus, for both Plato and Aristotle, education was more than discovering the truth about what is; it also involved the quest for what should be.

Education in ancient Rome built heavily on Greek influences, as did the entire Roman culture. Like the Egyptians who preceded them, Romans were excellent engineers. Their systems of law and the Latin language have had great influence on education to the present day. Several major periods of Roman civilization brought different forms of education. Education was first conducted in the home (700–275

B.C.), mainly by the parents, who were highly respected and whose social standing determined their children's vocations. During the second period (275–130 B.C.), curriculum was based on a Greek model of philosophy, literature, and rhetoric. As this was assimilated into the Roman life-style, it became more Latin oriented, eventually creating the Latin grammar school, which was the model for Western education. Private Latin grammar schools emphasized the training of orators, who were at this time the symbols of success. Revolutions changed this, and, as the Roman republic gave way to the empire, success routes changed. Public support of arts and sciences brought public schools, which led to government control of teaching. Eventually (300–500 A.D.), the curriculum became effectually separated from life. Memorization of literary matters and strict control of students was the mainstay. Only technical education remained connected to real-world activities. Censorship of ideas and the separation of scholar from statesman is thought by some as contributory to Rome's fall (Maxwell et al., 1963).

Among the major educators in Rome's history were Cicero, Plutarch, and Quintillian. Cicero (106–43 B.C.) was the paragon of orators and deemed rhetoric the central study. Conceived broadly, rhetoric included the liberal arts and humanities based on life experience and detailed study of the character of great orations that moved masses in earlier days. Plutarch (46–120 A.D.) was a Greek among Romans; he was eclectic, collected perspectives from numerous sources, and established the image of the broadly educated gentleman that emerged in the Renaissance. Quintillian (35–95 A.D.) set forth educational principles in his *Institutes of Oratory* that remind one of progressive education in the twentieth century. For example, he argued that an inspiring teacher could make unnecessary the strict discipline usually imposed on students and that students learn better when the curriculum is varied. But, alas, Quintillian's call for orators as liberally educated, practical philosophers fell largely on deaf ears. Roman emperors wanted administrative functionaries who would implement their policies, not intelligent critics and creative thinkers. It remained for the humanist revival of the Renaissance for the curricular insights of Quintillian to make their mark on history. At its best, however, Roman curriculum was designed to develop a practical philosophy of living more than the philosophy of detached contemplation exemplified by the Athenians. Cicero, Quintillian, and Marcus Aurelius exemplified this more practical philosophy that guided action in the affairs of state.

In concluding their historical study of exemplars of teaching method, Broudy and Palmer (1965) observe that

> *If we have learned anything from our brief survey of teaching methods, it is that the success routes of an era dictate the dominant patterns of schooling and styles of teaching. [p. 159]*

Thus, there is an important sense in which the mode of education of any time period caters to the paths that bring success in that era. As we have seen, the Romans valued prowess in practical activities, and this is what their educational system fostered. Even those who promote a broader idea of education that reaches to greater breadth and depth than others of their time cling to society's success routes. For example, Cicero and Marcus Aurelius supported liberal education, but its purpose was still persuasion through oratory and political leadership. Before this, in Athens, we find the Sophists, who led the citizen of leisure toward greater wealth or power. Even Socrates, Plato, and Aristotle, who eschewed wealth and power, perpetuated the citizen of leisure, which linked education with elitism. In Egypt, China, and India, one can also find obvious connections between educational systems, success routes, and the great thinkers of the day.

I do not argue that it is inappropriate for curriculum to be tied to success routes of the time period. The point is to be aware of it, look for it, reflect on curriculum in light of historical context, and focus on the relation of curricular experiences to social and historical contexts.

Curriculum in the Christian World

The educational curriculum of the Middle Ages was indisputably Christianity. It was the lens through which people focused their life and meaning; thus, it became the leading force in the Western world both in and out of school.

To gain perspective on curriculum thought and practice in the Middle Ages, one must begin with the origins of Christianity. During a time when the Roman Empire (27–476 A.D.) expanded by conquering and assimilating small states, assimilated peoples needed a greater source of meaning and stability. The teachings of Jesus met this need for many. These teachings embodied a curriculum that held the knowledge most worth knowing to be that the human soul is immortal, immutable, and more important than the material world. Appealing to those not wedded to stock in the material world, Jesus spoke to the impoverished and uneducated as well as to many of the scholarly and well-to-do. Jesus reached their emotional, moral, and spiritual needs and compelled them to acknowledge the principles of love of fellow human beings brought by a common love of God. He took away the ritual of Hebrew church law and dogma as well as the Greek and Roman deification of reason and worldly knowledge and granted each person the right to a life sustained by personal communication with God. To submit oneself to God's will meant to grant Him the kingdom, power, and glory in one's own life, thus overcoming a life of striving for vain and perishable rewards.

Fitting with the success routes of the times, which respected the teacher or rabbi, Jesus took on a form of that role to convey his message. In so doing, he used a conversational method and illustrative parables. It was through his personality more than specific concepts that he reached the emotions of listeners and convinced them to change their lives. This change focused on doing good to others who are inseparably united with oneself and anticipating the experience of a life of unity with God after death that extricates one from suffering on earth.

Recorded in the gospels of the *New Testament*, memories of the teachings of Jesus were preserved in both written and oral traditions. Opposed vehemently for nearly three centuries, Christian beliefs were gradually assimilated into Roman culture, and by 300 A.D., Constantine secured Christianity as the official religion of the Empire. The propensity of Romans to value legalized forms of policy statements transformed spiritual community into doctrine and bureaucratic hierarchy. Similarly, philosophers of the day wrestled with Christian ideology and its relation to pagan religion and secular philosophy.

The attempts to reconcile the Christian, pagan, and secular with one another and with tendencies toward legalization and bureaucratization brought the problem of interpretation in bold relief. What occurs in the translation of once liberating ideas as they pass from generation to generation of disciples is well characterized by Isaiah Berlin (1980), the political theorist:

> *The history of thought and culture is, as Hegel showed with great brilliance, a changing pattern of great liberating ideas which inevitably turn into suffocating straitjackets and so stimulate their own destruction. [p. 159]*

The spiritual community of humanity and love in the teachings of Jesus were strait-jacketed by institutionalized rules and regulations in the name of Christianity. Similarly, Socrates' belief in a life of questioning and his abjuration of certainty were straitjacketed by followers who accepted Plato's reflections on what a republic might be as if they were mandates. For example, by the second century A.D., Plotinus (205–270 A.D.) fashioned an entire scale of goodness supposedly based on Plato's philosophy. There is great need to look carefully at the ways in which self-appointed disciples put straitjackets on liberating ideas throughout the history of curriculum thought.

Let us now consider a few examples of transformation in curriculum influenced by various interpretations of Christianity throughout the Middle Ages. In the second century A.D., Tatian looked at the corruption perpetuated by those who espoused the Greek and Roman intellectual heritage and denounced it in favor of Christianity. St. Augustine (354–430 A.D.), however, moved in a more reconciliatory direction by attempting to join the teachings of Plato with those of the Church. In his *Confessions*, he concludes that truth is not found in sensory impressions of the material world but in connection with absolutes in the world of ideas. The Plato of Plotinus most influenced Augustine, and Church doctrine was his source of interpretation for the hierarchy of truth and goodness. Thus, the ends of the Church were given precedence over the value of knowledge for its own sake. Knowledge became valuable because it was instrumental in the propagation of Christianity. Although Augustine held love and commitment to be at least as necessary as intellect, he was also convinced that children needed to be told what was valuable to learn and that they should be severely punished if they did not follow adult direction. When one looks at the rampant corruption of Roman life at the time, one might gather justification for Augustine's insistence on the development of curricula that led to a strict moral code.

The leaders of the Church, particularly the monastic orders, were responsible for the perpetuation of education in the West during the remainder of the Middle Ages. Prior to the overt sacking of Rome in 476, St. Basil (330–379) developed a communal form of monasticism in Greek-speaking areas. Believing that the Church should practice brotherhood (as well as merely preach it and engage in self-degradation as did many monastic orders), he instituted orphanages in monasteries and advocated a curriculum that drew the most noble characters and lessons from pagan literature in an effort to provide a broader base of knowledge to educate the young in Christian principles. Following the fall of Rome, St. Benedict (480–546) continued this broader emphasis on human growth, reviving the Greek emphasis on moderation. Benedictine monasteries spread throughout Europe and largely replaced orders that practiced torturous self-sacrifice. These self-sufficient monasteries were bastions of preservation for the arts, scholarship, agriculture, and even trade, as well as religion. Among the religious beliefs taught to the young by the Benedictines were humility and obedience in light of Church authority.

The seat of Western culture during the Middle Ages was Constantinople, the capital of the Eastern Roman Empire from 330 to 1453. Many of the most valuable documents were housed there during Rome's decline under the leadership of Constantine the Great (287?–337) and thus preserved after its fall. Those at Constantinople looked with envious eye, however, at their counterparts in the Islamic world with which they fought the Crusades. The Islamic levels of learning and luxury in the Moorish cities of Toledo and Granada in Spain, in the Turkish Bagdad in Mesopotamia, and Cairo in North Africa were in many respects superior to that of the West. From these centers the Western idea of universities emerged and a more cosmopolitan connection with the Far East developed. As might be expected, great educators emerged in these cultures although we know too little of them. Al-Ghazali (1058–1111) stands out as one who "realized the incapacity of human reason if confronted with the great mysteries of God, immortality, and eternity and tried to overcome the menace of skepticism by mysticism and an ascetic life" (Ulich, 1954, p. 193), as revealed in Al-Ghazali's essay entitled "My Child." Three hundred years later, Ibn Khaldoun (1332–1406), who some historians consider the greatest intellect of the century, attempted in his *Historical Prolegomena* to interpret the evolution of civilization in light of intellectual, climatic, and social conditions. In this work he discussed instructional methods and procedures (see Ulich, 1954, pp. 199–201).

It was not only to the Islamic and Byzantine empires, however, that one could turn for scholarly achievement. At the end of the Dark Ages, Charlemagne, leader of the Franks, established a palace school, attempted to bring the monks and clergy to a higher level of education, and issued a proclamation in favor of general learning in 782. Most important, he invited Alcuin (735–804) to head his palace school in Frankland. Alcuin was a noted poet and was widely regarded as the greatest scholar of the day. In teaching method he enlivened learning with the use of riddles and other courtly puzzles and games. He reinstituted the liberal arts as a major curricular emphasis and did much to promote the serious study of languages as a means to religious enlightenment. His students eventually headed most of the Western European educational centers of the period.

In the thirteenth century, several orders of friars emerged. St. Thomas Aquinas (1225–1274), an Italian Dominican friar known for his excellence as a teacher, administrator, scholar, and writer, succeeded in building a philosophical basis for Catholicism by unifying Aristotelian philosophy with Church doctrine and belief. He moved toward perfecting the scholastic method of argument, which began by selecting a topic such as the interpretation of a doctrine. Articles or subtopics were enumerated, and then a systematic process of support or rejection was provided on each point. This method was used a century earlier by Peter Abelard (1079–1142) of France as a teaching strategy that involved lecture, repetition, and disputation or debate. Abelard was so skilled at the latter that young scholars traveled long distances to observe his cogent use of dialectic as he outargued opponents at Notre Dame in Paris. It is reported that twenty of his pupils eventually rose to the position of cardinal, while another fifty became bishops (Broudy and Palmer, 1965, p. 60).

Throughout most of the history of Christian education, educators thought curriculum was good for students, but they lamented the fact that students did not realize its benefits. Therefore, most believed that it had to be forced upon them through a process of strict discipline. It awaited the efforts of John Gerson (1363–1429), chancellor of the University of Paris, near the end of the Middle Ages, actually to apply Christian principles of love and goodness to children and youth. He advocated leading students to Christianity through gentleness instead of using coercion and punishment. In a pamphlet entitled "*On Leading the Young Towards Christ*," Gerson says,

> *But where there is no love, what good is instruction, as one neither likes to listen to it nor properly believes in the words heard nor follows the commandments! Therefore it is best to forgo all false dignity and to become a child among children. Yet all sins have to be avoided and all signs of impure love have to be held at bay . . . . Our nature prefers guidance to force. . . . He will not be able to convince them unless he smiles kindly at the laughing ones, encourages those who play, praises their progress in learning, and when remonstrating, avoids all that is bitter or insulting. [Gerson in Ulich, 1950, p. 101]*

Curriculum in the Renaissance, Reformation, and Enlightenment

Beginning in the mid- to late 1400s, a new attitude toward scholarship began to emerge. Scholars in Western Europe and England turned again to the humanistic literatures of ancient Greece and Rome. While they revived substantive learning available in classical literatures, they even more importantly revived the spirit of inquiry. In education, this involved a critical, Socratic questioning and a practical and humanistic pedagogy derived from Quintillian. To study classical literature, it was necessary to achieve a high degree of literacy in Latin, Greek, and classical culture. The great educators of the period were also the great scholars: Vittorino da Feltre of Italy (1378–1446), Aenea Sylvio of Italy (1405–1464), Desiderius Erasmus of Holland (1466–1536), Thomas Elyot of England (1490–1546), and Michel de Montaigne of France (1533–1592). Da Feltre's school at Mantua prepared children of the wealthy to be cultured gentlemen through a curriculum of the seven liberal arts (dialectic, rhetoric, grammar, astronomy, arithmetic, geometry, and music), Greek and Latin languages, history, and fine arts. Whereas da Feltre's school had to rely on lecture and memorization, Sylvio and others who followed benefited from the printing press. Sylvio's book *On the Education of Boys* explained his teaching methods and his advocacy of Greek literature with its emphasis on reason, beauty, and virtue. Erasmus was the first since Quintillian to place great stress on teaching methodology, arguing in several books for the need to base instruction upon both an understanding of the learner and the psychology of learning. He also held that play could be integral to learning and that audiovisual aids were helpful teaching devices. It was Montaigne, however, whose theories of curriculum were the most progressive. The importance of observation, direct experience, interaction with the world, integration of mind and body, and emphasis on student needs and interests have their roots in Montaigne's *Essays*. Elyot also drew upon Quintillian, advocated classic languages and the seven liberal arts, and added dance and physical education.

The title of Elyot's book, *Governor*, symbolizes the fact that the education advocated by Renaissance educators was intended for the aristocracy, to prepare them for leadership or positions of nobility. This is one condition that spurred the Reformation, which was not only a religious movement but a popular movement as well. The invention of the printing press by Gutenberg was a mainstay in the development of the Reformation, as it aided in the communication of protests that were primarily directed at the Church. The Church was viewed as corrupt in placing great wealth in the hands of a few and by attempting to control lives of private individuals. The rise of cities, the beginning of secular government, the rise of a distinction between civic and canon law, and an increase of nationalism all contributed to educational strategies that attended to the needs of the masses and the value of the individual.

Martin Luther of Germany (1483–1546) and John Calvin of France (1509–1546) were major contributors to curricular changes brought by the Reformation. Luther's emphasis on education was steadfast because he believed that the people had to be educated if the Church were to be reformed. He called for compulsory education of boys, girls, rich, and poor. Such education should be controlled by the state, and religious education should be in vernacular languages. He added music and physical education to the curriculum, and favored classical languages in academic subjects. Both Calvin and Luther emphasized the importance of homes in education and saw parents as foundation builders of sound discipline. Calvin went as far as to develop home supervision to ensure that parents taught the catechism correctly and that they provided no educational activities that were contrary to proper religious principles. While Luther saw the state as responsible for education, Calvin thought state and church alike should be directed toward religious purposes. Luther, however, held that state schools should be carefully monitored and started a system of school surveys and supervision to ensure accountability to standards.

In response to the Reformation, the Roman Catholics attempted to regain credibility and stature. The principal figure in this movement was Ignatius Loyola of Spain (1491–1556), founder of the Jesuit Order, whose *Ratio Studorum* expounded Jesuit educational beliefs about teaching methods, school administration, teacher supervision, and curriculum. All courses related to a common theme of theology in secondary and higher education. Such subjects were classical languages and the seven liberal arts. Courses were taught one at a time, instead of several simultaneously. Teachers were given detailed instructions, the first curriculum guides, and were even expected to use a common or uniform instructional method. The latter consisted of two phases: prelection (lecture) and repetition (clarifying questions and memorization). The Jesuits also instituted teacher education programs and student teaching.

Also during the sixteenth century, there emerged a number of realist educators who were precursors of the Age of Reason scholars who argued that there was more to know than one could find in ancient classics. While they respected the classics, they sought historical and scientific insight from careful observation and analysis of their own design. Juan Luis Vives, also Spanish, (1492–1540) promoted a student-oriented curriculum for both sexes that was taught in the student's language, humanistic in character, and based upon the empirical scientific study of psychology. Vives wanted education for all, especially the poor, and stressed the arts, nature, and morals as important subjects of study. In France, Francis Rabelais (1483–1553) argued that the aim of learning should be to enjoy study; therefore, students should learn from experience in observation, interpretation, and evaluation of life, not merely from textbooks. Many of his educational reforms were presented through the keen use of satire. Thus, the realists were more life centered than their humanist predecessors, and they shared the reformation's call for universal education.

This spirit was realized in full bloom in the Age of Reason of the seventeenth and eighteenth centuries. Set off by scientific discoveries by Copernicus (1473–1543), Galileo (1564–1642), and Newton (1642–1727), philosophers, social theorists, and educators turned with increased confidence to scientific inquiry. Francis Bacon of England (1561–1626), sometimes called the father of scientific method, dared to question the pronouncements of Aristotle that had guided intellectual work for a thousand years. According to Bacon, knowledge, except that which clearly fell under the province of the Church, should be subjected to critical analysis and empirical verification. Thus, induction began to replace, or at least attain equal status with, the deductive logic of Aristotle as promulgated by the scholastic method of medieval theologians. It is, Bacon asserted, through the empirical method of testing ideas against experience that we can break away from the idols of prejudice couched in the limits of human nature, social class, communication, and authority.

Philosophers Thomas Hobbes of England (1588–1679) and René Descartes of France (1596–1650) continued to develop reason and empiricism in ways that had major implications for curriculum. Hobbes is often credited with the birth of modern psychology because of his theories that sense impressions produce images in the brain that trigger imagination, memory, and the like. Just as influential was Hobbes's political theory that declared the primacy of the state over the individual and argued that human survival meant joining together to form social units that overcame anarchy and destruction spawned by the evil of human nature and the laws of nature itself. As Hobbes's state evolved, it achieved complete power over the individual— morally, religiously, and educationally. Descartes sought to reconcile the vast differences among religion, science, and philosophy that emerged with the Renaissance and Reformation. Starting from a position of complete doubt, he wanted to learn whether valid knowledge was achievable through the senses and whether it was possible to know more than the senses provide. He concluded by developing a proof of God that was his basis for arguing that truth can be reached through the intellect, not only by empiricism and imagination but through intuition.

Descartes's doctrine of the dualism of mind and body had a major impact on Western philosophical and educational thought into the twentieth century. In fact, the belief in two irreducible elements, mind and matter, is clearly with us today. We see the widespread separation of cognitive and noncognitive aspects of schooling, for example, and in religious education, the separation of faith and reason. The American Founding Fathers were influenced by Descartes's perspective in their decision to separate church and state. Such separation is quite different from the Eastern view of the oneness of all things (Watts, 1961), and the West awaited the work of Froebel and Dewey in education to deal with problems in dualistic thought. In the same century that Descartes wrote of dualism, however, Dutch philosopher Baruch Spinoza (1632– 1677) argued for a pantheistic position that holds that God is manifested in all material and nonmaterial aspects of the universe. This unifying force dissolved the dualistic separation of mind and body. A free thinker himself, Spinoza advocated a state that sponsors freedom of thought, schools, and the right of educators to raise fundamental questions. He believed that educators should stimulate both the senses and the mind, and thus called for experience and reason to be united in the curriculum. The central purpose of the curriculum, according to Spinoza, was to help students reach their potential, for only in such pursuit could they function happily in society. Spinoza, however, rejected the use of recipes for teaching method and called for teachers to exercise their freedom of thought and experience to determine the best methodology for the situation. Too liberal for his time period, Spinoza had greater effect on philosophers and educators of subsequent centuries.

Two of the most influential educators of the seventeenth century were John Amos Comenius of Moravia (1592–1670) and William Petty of England (1623–1687). Comenius devoted concerted attention to developing a philosophy of education that joined teachings of the Church with the scientific method. He opposed both social class and national distinctions and called for an equal education for all persons, who should be educated with uniform curriculum and methods. Comenius made a major contribution to method by advocating that it be linked to child development and that methodology should involve discovery through sensory experience. Set forth in *The Great Didactic*, these methods were to begin at birth, when mothers should be expected to begin to prepare children for a local school to be attended between ages seven and thirteen. Both the mother and local school teachers should conscientiously relate curricular content to learner needs and individual rates of learning. At these levels, instruction would be provided in the child's own language, although the ideal for Comenius was to develop *pansophia*, a universal language. Ages thirteen to eighteen would be spent attending a Latin School, and university study and travel concluded the process of formal education up to age twenty-four. Throughout these levels Comenius maintained his emphasis on the senses, or empirical learning. This is most evident in his schoolbook, *Orbis Pictus*, and his renewal of methods for teaching Latin. The influence of Comenius had profound impact on nearly all educational thinkers who followed, and he is often thought of as the father of modern education.

Like Comenius, Petty was a reformer who called for universal education. His curriculum stressed what we now call "the basics" or "three R's," reading, writing, and arithmetic. Like many today, he saw this as a prerequisite for obtaining a job and thus contributing to society. Keeping with his practical thrust, Petty thought that all (including the wealthy) should know about the trades, and he preferred scientific and technical content to languages and the liberal arts. He envisioned schools that included museums and galleries within them.

English philosopher, John Locke (1632–1704) exerted great influence on educational thought by arguing that experience is the source of learning. The mind, he asserted, is a *tabula rasa*, or blank slate, upon which sense impressions "write" the learning that transpires for an individual. This assertion set Locke apart from the main line of philosophers from Plato through Descartes, who held that innate ideas govern the development of the human mind. Moreover, Locke's historical studies, which revealed no universal or innate ideas, also led him to discredit the universal idea of original sin accepted by Church doctrine that holds adult human beings to be depraved and children to be merely adults in miniature. To Locke, education was not primarily intellectual growth but moral habit and self-control, which are the basis for intellectual as well as other development. Born with equal capacity, children develop differently because of their environment. Teachers can motivate them when they adequately determine what they are ready to learn at a given time. The best stance from which to make such determination, according to Locke, was the tutorial relationship. Since only the wealthy could afford private tutors, Locke's writing pertained more to the education of the upper than the lower classes, although he was concerned about the latter, too. Often credited with the advocacy of a useful curriculum, Locke's notion of usefulness rested on a desire to develop the virtuous citizen. Thus, the curriculum was that of a practical, liberal arts education—in short, the education of a gentleman. It also included continental languages for communicative utility, physical education for a healthy body conducive to a sound mind, mathematics for its transferability to reason, and travel to develop cosmopolitan attitudes.

Curriculum from the Enlightenment to Twentieth Century

Influenced by Locke, Benjamin Franklin (1706–1790) continued opposition to classical education in America, preferring instead to emphasize education directly related to professional affairs of life. In this interest he founded the Academy, a practical form of secondary education that used English rather than classical languages and came to dominate the scene in the United States from 1830 for the next forty years. The curriculum, said Franklin, should be meaningful to the expansive middle class of business-oriented citizens who needed to deal with contemporary problems.

French philosopher, Jean Jacques Rousseau (1712–1778) laid groundwork for progressive philosophies of education that were to follow Franklin's Academy in the United States and the enlightened pedagogy of Basedow, Pestalozzi, and Froebel in Europe. Taking an opposite tack from Hobbes, who asserted the primacy of the state, Rousseau charged that the state is the seat of corruption of the individual, who is pure in nature. To purge the evil of society, Rousseau argued in his *Social Contract*, adults must become reeducated by the purity of children who are educated apart from the contamination of perverted values in adult society. Children who are educated apart from adult society, as Rousseau portrayed in *Emile*, are able to create a renewed society, a new "social contract." The curriculum should allow for free play in natural settings during the first five years of life. During the next seven years children should engage in sensory experience with concrete rather that abstract learning being the focus. Concepts, ideas, and reason are developed between ages twelve and fifteen, at which point the youth enters society with an understanding of nature that provides a basis for judgment about good and just ways of living together. Child-centered curriculum, with its emphasis on individual needs and interests, owes a great debt to Rousseau.

Both influences, Rousseau and Locke, can be seen in German curricular reform of Johann Basedow from Germany (1723–1790) who added such practical subjects as nature study, natural history, anatomy, and physical education. An advocate of learning by direct experience, Basedow initiated field trips or brief excursions to learn about practical topics from firsthand exposure to them. He also contributed to the improvement of textbooks, school facilities, and milder forms of discipline.

Basedow's experimental school, the Philanthropinum, influenced Swiss educational reformer Johann Heinrich Pestalozzi (1746–1827), whose work clearly builds upon Rousseau's ideals. His most popular books (*Leonard and Gertrude*, 1782, and *How Gertrude Teaches Her Children*, 1826) has widespread influence and contributed much to the early growth of elementary schools. He called for the natural, balanced, and harmonious development of all capacities of the child and spoke of the need for balanced growth of head, heart, and hand. A staunch proponent of educating the poor to gain dignity, Pestalozzi wanted discipline to be based on love and respect for students as individual human beings. Such was the basis for improving society. For twenty years Pestalozzi actively practiced his doctrines in an experimental school at Yverdun, Switzerland. There he introduced *object lessons* that were devoted to the study of actual objects or pictures; he placed prime importance on individual differences, and he taught only those subjects that involved sense perception and could be actively experienced. The latter excluded most of historical and literary studies. Pestalozzi prepared children for educative experiences and sequenced instruction from the known to the unknown. He carefully studied child development and developed some of the first scientific principles of teaching. By using such principles along with slates and pencils, Pestalozzi was able to teach larger classes of impoverished and handicapped children, yet it was principally through his devoted personality that he was able to accomplish so much. As Ulich (1950) observes,

> *In the studies of Old Swiss and German schoolmasters one could often find a reproduction of a painting of Pestalozzi, in which we see him, with a profound expression of love on his ugly and wrinkled face, embracing the children of peasants who, clad in rags, enter the simple schoolroom. . . . Pestalozzi's example of "Let the little children come unto me" probably had a greater effect on modern education than all that philosophers ever said or wrote about the tasks and character of education. [p. 264]*

In another source Ulich (1954, p. 480) points to the far-reaching idealism in Pestalozzi's little known *Evening Hour of a Hermit*, which says "deeper things about the character of values, about liberal and vocational education, and about the relation between 'individual' and 'general' truth than are contained in many voluminous reports of our time."

The eloquent oratory of Johann Gottlieb Fichte in 1807 convinced the Prussian people to build a modern Germany on the shoulders of a Pestalozzian curricular orientation following their losses to Napoleon. This led to free public education in Germany, a realization of Pestalozzi's desire to see social improvement emerge from education as an instrument of the state rather than the Church. The ideals of Pestalozzi by the 1860s had sizable impact in the United States through the efforts of William T. Harris, who was an eminent idealist philosopher as well as United States commissioner of education.

The idealism of Harris and other educators of the eighteenth and nineteenth centuries was rooted in the philosophy of Immanuel Kant (1724–1804) and Georg Wilhelm Hegel (1770–1831), both of Germany. Kant saw education as critical to the improvement of human life. Developing Rousseau's emphasis on the individual, Kant called for curriculum adapted to student needs and abilities and maintained that students should be free to pursue their interests as long as they did not impinge upon those of others. Hegel saw education as a process that continued throughout life, enabling the individual to achieve increased sophistication in reason that dialectically synthesized apparent opposites. This he thought could be achieved through a liberal arts education that revived the study of Greek, Latin, literature, philosophy, and history. Hegel's emphasis on the state's responsibility to provide such an education influenced Horace Mann and Henry Barnard as well as Harris. He added that the interactive experience of teacher and student constitutes a kind of synthesis as well.

Influenced by both Kant and Hegel as well as Pestalozzi was the German educator and philosopher, Johann Freidrich Herbart (1776–1841), known as the father of both the science of education and of modern psychology. Despite these influences, much was original with Herbart and he went on to influence many educators into the early years of the twentieth century (DeGarmo, 1895; Dunkel, 1970; Connell, 1980, pp. 53–70). For example, Herbart's disciples developed five steps of method and propagated their use throughout the continent and United States: (1) *preparation* or developing connections between what is known and what is about to be learned; (2) *presentation* or setting forth material to be learned in a manner that is psychologically sound for the learner; (3) *association* or developing analogies with prior learning; (4) *generalization* or moving from concrete instances to abstract principles; and (5) *application* or using the newly acquired knowledge as a basis from which to pursue more knowledge.

Teachers and curriculum developers were often so preoccupied with following the sequence in their lesson plans that they became straitjacketed (recall the quotation by Berlin earlier in this chapter), unable to see the larger purposes envisioned by Herbart. Herbart's main educational intent was the development of a cultured human being who strove to find and be guided by the highest ethical values. In the final analysis, then, education was a moral enterprise for Herbart, intended to evoke the goodness that he considered innate in each individual. Grounded thusly in philosophy, Herbart also operated from a strong psychological base. The child was believed to grow in the pattern of the evolution of human culture (i.e., from primitive to civilized), and it was the teacher's job to intervene by directing and stimulating child development toward greater civilization. A curriculum that ranged from mythology and ancient history through modern literature and history would facilitate this process. Throughout this sequence, the teacher attempted to enlarge and enrich the child's perspective, or *apperceptive mass*, by bringing him or her into contact with knowledge that related to previous experience and enhanced moral growth. According to Herbart, "The worth of a man is measured by his will, not by his intellect" (Herbart, translated by Lange, 1901, p. 40); "Instruction will form the circle of thought, and education the character. The last is nothing without the first. Herein is contained the whole sum of my pedagogy" (Herbart, 1901, p. 44). At this point Herbart's emphasis on pedagogy went beyond Locke and Rousseau, who relied more on the child's own capacity for natural, educative experience.

While English educators such as Joseph Lancaster (1778–1838) and Andrew Bell (1753–1832) experimented with a monitorial system in which more students could be taught for less expense by having younger children taught by older ones, Robert Owen developed a kind of utopian school to improve the morals and religious toleration of children of workers at his textile mill in Scotland.

Building upon the example and ideas of Pestalozzi, Friedrich Froebel of Germany (1782–1852) developed the first kindergarten in 1837 and paved the way for the emergence of progressive education in the next century. From his own experience with children and from Friedrich Schelling's philosophy of identity between mind and nature, Froebel created a doctrine of unity. He held that everything, including the child, has a unity of its own and is also a part of a larger unity; the concept expands eventually to include the unity of all existence. As education helps individuals to become more mature, it contributes to the larger unity of human evolution. Similarly, childhood does not merely transfer to youth and adulthood, but each is part of the unity of a human life. Each unity, for example, childhood play or games, has a worth and meaning of its own. It does this unity a disservice merely to treat it as a means to something more important in later life.

Froebel's curriculum was truly child centered and provided for individual differences. All subjects involved religious mysticism because Froebel contended religious mysticism enables humans to better understand their own nature and become more mature, open minded, and free thinking. Activities in art, manual training, natural science, language, music, and mathematics were provided within an atmosphere of cooperation and play. Play to Froebel was educative, not frivolous and yields self-development because it unites the physical, spiritual, emotional, and intellectual. Like Rousseau, Froebel assumed that the child is basically good; therefore, the child's play is a free expression of human goodness. Froebel's curriculum occurred within a gardenlike environment. In the midst of nature, children could actively explore themselves and the unities that surround them.

The middle of the nineteenth century brought conditions that fostered a general call for universal schooling in the United States. The rise of nationalism is often accompanied by universal education as a means to sustain patriotism. Social welfare concerns brought an attitude of greater regard for the common person and a heightened desire for equality. The time was right for a fuller realization of Thomas Jefferson's 1779 *Bill for the More General Diffusion of Knowledge*, and Horace Mann (1796–1859) steadfastly worked for a school that would be common to all children of all races, religious beliefs, and socioeconomic classes in the United States. He thought that such schools would uplift society morally by integrating persons from different backgrounds. Supported by taxes from the general public, the common school would provide a democratic dissemination of culture that was formerly reserved for the wealthy elite. Such education was not to be merely distributed to the masses; rather, it was to be controlled and created at the community level. Thus, Mann contributed substantially to the Jeffersonian ideal of excellence and equality; as Ulich (1954) observed, the former without the latter is privilege and the latter without the former yields mediocrity.

Ralph Waldo Emerson (1803–1882) captured the essence of American individualism in his idealist philosophy derived from Plato, Kant, Pestalozzi, and Froebel. To him, the aim of education should be moral and spiritual self-reliance. The great books can help if presented at appropriate times, but experience and imagination are the keys to education that need not occur in school. Students will become better educated if they are encouraged to wonder about life's great mysteries and if allowed to imagine and accomplish something that they deem worthwhile. This, of course, rests upon an assumption that humans are basically moral. A good teacher's enthusiasm will help students to enjoy drill and work toward self-discipline to meet high standards. This should move the student toward the ideal of good citizenship in the deepest and broadest sense.

The emergent spirit of science was given great impetus by Herbert Spencer (1820–1903) of England in his *Education: Intellectual, Moral, and Physical* (1861). He rated scientific studies (sociology and politics as well as physics and biology) as more important than cultural and humanistic education because they contributed more to self-preservation. This position was doubtless related to Spencer's high regard for the work of Charles Darwin. Spencer's renowned question, "What knowledge is of most worth?" (Spencer, 1861), is a mainstay of curricular thought, and his answers to it, which involve health, vocation, citizenship, home, and leisure, were reflected in statements of purpose for the next hundred years.

In the same year as the appearance of Spencer's *Education* (1861) and in considerable contrast to it, the great novelist Leo Tolstoy (1828–1910) returned to his Russian homeland from travels throughout Europe during which he became acquainted with the educational methods used by followers of Pestalozzi, Herbart, and Froebel. He disliked the now routinized object lesson that once had been alive in the personality of Pestalozzi and similarly eschewed imposed discipline and recitation of barren facts. Instead, he established an elementary school where students could come and go freely, where children could play with ideas, and where children learned by discussion with teachers and others in real-life situations outside of school. Far ahead of his day, Tolstoy's brief experiment anticipated the most liberal aspects of progressive education and saw curriculum as primarily embodied in the teacher. As Curtis and Boultwood (1965) describe it,

> *Believing as he did that a teacher should be one who knows his subject and "communicates it in a spirit of love," he gave an important place to teaching by "infection" not only in intellectual matters but also in emotional and moral education. [p. 500]*

Curricular orientations of considerable variety entered the stage as the nineteenth century progressed. Edward Austin Sheldon (1823–1897) headed the Oswego Primary Teachers' Training School, the first city training college for teachers in the United States. There he established the main center for Pestalozzian methods in America. William Torrey Harris (1835–1909), noted earlier, was a major force in post–Civil War educational history in the United States and advocate of building psychological foundations to educational practice. An idealist with strong Hegelian roots, he attempted to apply Hegel's thought to education as well as all other disciplines. He established the first public kindergarten in the United States as superintendent of the St. Louis schools and later became United States commissioner of education.

Often entering into colorful debate with Harris was Colonel Francis Wayland Parker (1837–1902) who began as a follower of Sheldon's version of Pestalozzi and later traveled to Europe, visiting Herbartian, Pestalozzian, and Froebelian schools. He returned to the United States and disseminated his ideas through normal schools in Chicago between 1883 and 1902. His emphasis on child-centered interests and experiences and his criticism of traditional education laid groundwork for progressive education and had considerable influence on John Dewey (Fraley, 1981).

CURRICULUM IN THE TWENTIETH CENTURY

The study of the emergence of the curriculum field in the twentieth-century most properly begins in the 1890s. A great many forces were interacting during this period, which Kliebard (1982a) aptly calls "a crucible for curriculum change." Here we find origins of the three orientations represented by "guest commentators" who conclude each chapter. A period of great revolution was occurring in science: Darwin's theories of evolution, Einstein's theory of relativity, Max Planck's quantum theory, and innumerable applications of science in technology and medicine. Would-be psychologists and educators from America streamed to Europe to study with Herbartians, Froebelians, and Pestalozzians. They also sought the tutelage of Spencer, proponents of psychological measurement such as Francis Galton in England and Alfred Binet in France, and especially Wilhelm Wundt (1832–1920) who founded the first psychological laboratory in Leipzig, Germany, in 1879. A sizable proportion of the founders of the curriculum field can be traced to Wundt (Schubert and Posner, 1980).

Pressed by the rising tide of universal public schooling in the United States, educators set about to discover the best methods for delivering the service of schooling. I use the term *method* because prior to the twentieth-century *curriculum* was sparsely used. The Herbartians emphasized *method* and broadened it to the extent that it was nearly comparable to *curriculum*. Americans who studied with Herbartians include Charles DeGarmo, Frank McMurry, and Charles McMurry. G. Stanley Hall (1844–1924) was a psychologist who drew deeply upon Herbart's theory of cultural epochs and extended the idea that the growing child recapitulates the evolution of the human race to the point of suggesting that children also reflect the mental processes of the past. Known for his emphasis on careful study of children and adolescents as a prerequisite for teaching them, Hall advocated child study by Steachers to determine methods that were developmentally appropriate. Hall's emphasis on experimental study derived from his study with Wundt and his subsequent creation of the first experimental psychological laboratory in the United States. While a faculty member at Johns Hopkins University, Hall influenced the thought of a young doctoral student named John Dewey.

Dewey (1859–1952), whose main interest was philosophy, had impressed William Torrey Harris sufficiently to have him accept his writing for publication in the Hegelian-oriented *Journal of Speculative Philosophy* while Dewey was still a high school teacher in Oil City, Pennsylvania. While at Johns Hopkins, Dewey also was taught by Charles Sanders Peirce (1839–1914), who, with William James (1842–1910) of Harvard laid the basis for pragmatic philosophy, which would be carried further in education by Dewey than anyone else. James, a psychologist as well as a philosopher, argued against the associationist theory of the Herbartians and asserted that learning proceeded through the acquisition of habits. Implications of his *Principles of Psychology* (1890) for education are sketched in his *Talks to Teachers* (1899). Among other things, James asserted the need to study the nervous system, which reveals that good habits are internalized by acting on resolutions, not by merely verbalizing about them.

In James was a biological basis for learning by doing that greatly influenced Dewey. Moreover, Dewey was born in 1859, the year that Darwin's *Origin of the Species* was published and Horace Mann died. The democratic spirit of Mann, with its Jeffersonian link between democracy and education (see Dewey's *Democracy and Education*, 1916) and Darwin's illumination of the connectedness of experience and biology (see Dewey's *Experience and Nature*, 1925) had a marked influence on many of Dewey's published works throughout his ninety-three-year life, which extended from before the Civil War to the end of the Korean War.

Viewing education as experimentalist philosophy, Dewey established the Laboratory School at the University of Chicago, where educational practice served as both an experiment with theoretical principles and as a seedbed for further ideas. Out of this experience, Dewey produced two small books that were the foundation stones of the Progressive Education Movement: *The School and Society* (1900) and *The Child and the Curriculum* (1902). In these books Dewey argued that the experience of the child must be the basis for education. The educator must realize that children are active learners who are already involved in meaningful social life. It is up to the teacher and curriculum developer to start with the psychological (sources of meaning and interests in child life) and move to the logical (the accumulated knowledge of the human race) by demonstrating that personal interests can become more meaningful and fulfilling as one grows in acquaintance with relevant knowledge. Thus, the connection between school and society should be inseparable. The purposes of school should be to resolve social problems and to build a better society. To do this, educators must focus on each child as a unique and whole being, the growth of whom contributes to society's growth. For Dewey, there was no dualistic separation between mind and body, individual and society, work and play, nature and culture; rather, these apparent opposites had a reciprocal benefit for one another. In the testing ground of action, such intellectualized separations blend, as Dewey exemplified in a host of activist causes in which he illustrated his philosophical position that truth and goodness must be viewed relative to the consequences of a proposal or action being judged.

In 1904, Dewey moved from Chicago to Columbia University in New York City. There he continued his work in philosophy, maintaining its inseparable link with education. In 1916, he published his major work on education, *Democracy and Education*. In this book he made clear the importance of democratic living and problem solving to ensure personal and public growth in present action. He saw the school as a simplified society, the goal of which was mutual cooperation that brings growth in all involved as they actively engage in learning, in contrast to the passive recipients that Dewey saw students become in most traditional schools. Instead of obedience and conformity, students were expected to develop initiative, originality, social awareness, and responsibility for consequences of their actions. Thus, Dewey viewed education as life itself, not primarily preparation for future life, although he considered a high quality of meaning and sense of direction in present living the best preparation for living that followed.

A contemporary of Dewey and also a professor at Columbia University was Edward L. Thorndike (1874–1949). Although he studied with William James and admired the scientific studies of Darwin, Thorndike differed greatly with Dewey. Thorndike was heavily influenced by experimental psychology through the teaching of his mentor James McKeen Cattell who studied with Wundt. Thorndike's hope to build a scientific discipline of education is evident in his influential *Educational Psychology* (1913), in which he laid the foundations of behaviorist stimulus-response theory. This led to education based on reward and to a regard for individual differences that maintained that learning involves specific associations.

Another student of Wilhelm Wundt, Charles Hubbard Judd (1873–1946), became dean of the School of Education at the University of Chicago after Dewey left for Columbia. Although he shared Thorndike's hope for a science of education and together they were a powerful force in the educational measurement movement, they differed on one crucial account. While Thorndike saw learning as occurring by specific associations, Judd held that learning involved the realization and application of principles that provide general, not merely specific, knowledge.

Dewey, who also hoped for a science of education (Dewey, 1929b), differed with both Judd and Thorndike, arguing that science should be conceived as the process of inquiry in ordinary human experience (Dewey, 1938b). This difference pitted the formal science controlled by experts characteristic of social behaviorists such as Thorndike and Judd against progressivists or experientialists who saw science as the continuous improvement of everyday problem solving by individuals and groups.

Debate such as this was far from new to the embryonic curriculum field. In the 1890s debates raged on the question of worthwhile knowledge. Experiments by William James in the 1890s demonstrated that classical subjects did not train faculties of the mind better than other subjects and later Thorndike corroborated and augmented the findings. This reduced the power of advocates of classical liberal arts curricula such as W. T. Harris, who justified the worth of such study on the grounds that it trained the faculties of mind.

In 1893 an influential report was produced by the Committee of Ten on Secondary School Studies of the National Education Association. The committee, commissioned to study the problem of college entrance requirements, was chaired by Charles W. Eliot, president of Harvard, who was also a humanist and advocate of liberal education. His intimate acquaintance with Harvard's long tradition of elective subjects led him to conclude that any subjects taught well trained the mind. When the committee determined that all disciplines would qualify students for college, it was a boon for Herbartians, advocates of new sciences, and pragmatists who all (for differing reasons) wanted to move beyond the limits of a classic curriculum. At the same time the door was opened to a plethora of subjects, making the curriculum suffocate from overcrowdedness.

In response, Francis Parker called for another committee to study *curriculum correlation*. In doing so he used this term much differently from the interpretation of the Committee of Fifteen that was called together to study the problem under the chairmanship of William T. Harris. Harris essentially led this committee in 1895 to defend the inviolability of his five windows on the soul or basic divisions of knowledge: (1) mathematics; (2) biology; (3) art and literature; (4) grammar, which included psychology and logic at a higher level of sophistication; and (5) history, which involved sociopolitical theory.

G. Stanley Hall led an attack on the Committee of Ten, asserting indefensibility in their assumption that all students should be taught in the same way, all subjects were of equal value, and that readiness for college required the same background as readiness for life. Hall decried the tendency of such committees to put great stock in quantitative accumulation and to disregard the connection between curricular content and human development. If the response to the Committee of Ten report was heated, that to the Committee of Fifteen and especially to Harris was a blazing fire. As Kliebard (1982a, p. 19) reports, the newly organized Herbartians (including Dewey) "at an 1895 meeting of NEA in Cleveland . . . felt ready for a direct confrontation with the person they saw as the embodiment of conservatism and reaction" (viz., Harris). When, for example, Harris used the term *correlation*, it was pointed out that he referred to correlating the pupil with the spiritual and natural environment instead of using *correlation* as Herbartians intended (i.e., in relating content to and concentrating it on the cultural epoch theory of development). Parker, who had proposed the committee, was disappointed with the results, claiming that the whole debate left out the main character, namely, the child. Parker, precursor to Dewey, wanted others to see the child as the experientialist organizing center for curriculum correlation. Frank McMurry (1927) lamented not perceiving this in his recollections some thirty years later:

> *As I look back on it now, he (Parker) was searching for the problem or project of work, where you find your starting point for both curriculum and method within the child rather*

than within some branch of knowledge. In that tendency he was a long way in advance of the rest of us. [p. 331]

Another critic of Harris and traditional educational practice in the 1890s was Joseph Mayer Rice, a pediatrician who studied with Herbartians in Europe and in 1892 surveyed American schools in thirty-six U.S. cities. In a series of articles in *Forum*, later published in a book (Rice, 1893), he attacked the public schools for incompetence, inadequate pedagogic knowledge, and lack of quality in teaching. Despite intense criticism by school people, Rice continued his studies, trying to discover why some schools were better than others. These comparative studies exemplified a new kind of scientific reasearch in education, and Rice's dim view of the teaching and leadership, he found, caused him to conclude that educational practitioners need scientific management, strict supervision, carefully defined goals and standards, and valid measurement of results (Rice, 1913). Rice was indeed a harbinger of those social behaviorists who called for social efficiency in education and often aligned with the tests and measurement movement, and with the behaviorist psychologists who followed Wundt and Thorndike.

Kliebard (1982a) identifies another influential line of thought in the late nineteenth century, one that emerged with Dewey's. The social and historical work of Lester Frank Ward, a botanist, attacked the social Darwinism propagated by Herbert Spencer (Ward, 1883, 1893). Spencer argued that social life among humans also followed the survival of the fittest, a principle that explained the unequal distribution of personal, national, and corporate wealth. This seemed to many to be consistent with Spencer's (1861) insistence that self-preservation was more worthwhile than the classical studies. It also seemed consistent with a free-market capitalism and rugged individualism often assumed to be characteristically American. Ward disputed Spencer by arguing that intelligence and a sense of justice made it unnecessary for humans to submit mindlessly to the laws of nature. In fact, Ward claimed that it was actually the legacy of maldistribution, not innate differences, that caused some individuals or groups to appear unequal to others. Ward saw the schools as a major force in social improvement and looked toward a day when partisan interest groups would be replaced in government by *"meliorism,* the science of improvement or amelioration of the human or social state" (Ward, 1893, p. 290).

Out of this crucible of change evolved the specialized field of curriculum studies. Much that transpired in America was paralleled in other parts of the world as well. The child study of G. Stanley Hall, Francis W. Parker's child-centeredness, and main-line Herbartianists such as Charles DeGarmo and Frank and Charles McMurry combined with the social meliorism of Ward and the pragmatic psychology of James to give rise to progressive education in the work of John Dewey and his experientialist followers. From the social Darwinism of Herbert Spencer; the propensity for psychological experimentation in Wundt, Galton, and Binet (and their followers, Thorndike and Judd); and from the empirical surveys and emphasis on efficiency by Rice, we can see the social behaviorist tendencies of curricularists Franklin Bobbitt and W. W. Charters. From the long tradition of classical education recently epitomized in Harris and from its modifications with electives as advocated by Charles W. Eliot, we find continued emphasis on intellectual traditionalist curricula advocated by Robert Maynard Hutchins, Alexander Meiklejohn, Gilbert Highet, and Mortimer J. Adler.

The first two decades of the twentieth century brought the work of Dewey (1900, 1902, 1910, 1916) into prominence. The Progressive Education Association was founded in 1919 to promote the theory and practice of Dewey as succinctly summarized in "My Pedagogic Creed" (Dewey, 1897). But even as the work of Dewey was held in high esteem in America, three major progressive educators made exceptional contributions in Europe. In Italy, Maria Montessori (1870–1952) encouraged the spontaneous development of mental, physical, and spiritual personality through educational activities that emphasize sensory stimulation and can be fostered during sensitive periods of growth by appropriate use of didactic apparatus. She used her methods successfully with retarded and poor children and transferred the techniques to a variety of ability levels and socioeconomic backgrounds. The Montessori method was adapted to needs and interests of children who were allowed to develop at their own rate with only intrinsic rewards. A primary goal of her individualized instruction was to help children to care for themselves. Her methods were spread throughout the world by six-month training sessions.

The two other major European figures in progressive education were Georg Kerschensteiner (1854–1932) of Germany and Ovide Decroly (1871–1932) of Belgium. Decroly established the most widely noted activity school in Europe at the L'Ecole de l'Ermitage, maintained for twenty-five years beginning in 1907. He organized the curriculum around centers of childhood interest. "Decroly was dedicated to the task of humanizing and enlivening the education of children. He had the common sense of a scientifically trained person, and the democratic feeling of a devoted social worker. He was a modest, unassuming man, who could enter empathically into the concerns of children and find ingenious and satisfying ways of catering to their needs and interests. Decroly is the representative man of progressive education" (Connell, 1980, p. 144). Kerschensteiner was a school administrator, reformer of elementary education, and supporter of activity schools. He managed to establish the successful practice of progressive education on a large scale in a public school system for a considerable time period as Director of Education in Munich from 1894–1919. In so doing, he influenced other administrators in such places as Hamburg, Vienna, and Russia in the 1920s (Connell, 1980, p. 143).

In America, the year 1918 marks a time of certainty that the curriculum field was likely to be quite permanent on the educational horizon. Three major contributions occurred in that year. William Heard Kilpatrick published an article entitled "The Project Method" in *Teachers College Record* that was read around the world as a concrete embodiment of Deweyan curricular philosophy. According to Kilpatrick, the teacher and student arrive at a common purpose centered on a typical life situation, and the project takes place in a social situation, as something to be produced or consumed, a problem to be resolved, or a drill to be mastered.

The second event of 1918 was the publication of *The Curriculum* by Franklin Bobbitt, who was the father of the social efficiency movement in curriculum. The curriculum should be formulated, he advocated, by scientifically analyzing activities of adult life and translating them into behavioral objectives. The process was known as *activity analysis*, and was detailed more fully in his *How to Make a Curriculum* (1924).

The third event that represents at least as great a curriculum landmark as that brought by Bobbitt (1918) and Kilpatrick (1918) was NEA's Commission on the Reorganization of Secondary Education (1918) report entitled *Cardinal Principles of*

Secondary Education. It will be recalled that the NEA also sponsored the Committees of Ten and Fifteen reports. Those reports (though criticized as conservative by developmentalists such as Hall and by proponents of child-centered curriculum such as Parker, and as mere speculation by behavioristic measurement types as well), continued the development of an expanded version of classical curriculum tailored to the needs of life. Seguel (1966) reports that in the period prior to 1890, learned societies appeared at a rapid rate. New areas of study and prestigious academies arose in an expression of faith in the usefulness of knowledge, especially *new scientific* knowledge. Thus, there is little wonder that the Committee of Ten, under the leadership of Charles W. Eliot, advocated four alternative curricula: classical, modern languages, English, and scientific. The Cardinal Principles report of 1918 continued this trend from the classic to the practical and was reminiscent of Spencer's (1861) claim that knowledge was worthwhile in proportion to its preservation of life. It called for seven cardinal principles or aims of secondary education: (1) health, (2) command of fundamental processes, (3) worthy home membership, (4) vocational preparation, (5) citizenship, (6) worthy use of leisure time, and (7) development of ethical character. This breadth of advocacy pointed to the value of unified studies, responsiveness to realities of life, a break with subservience to colleges and universities for curricular guidance, and a realization that comprehensive high schools were needed to meet needs of a growing population of students. Lawrence Cremin went so far as to say about the Cardinal Principles report, "Most of the important and influential movements in the field since 1918 have simply been footnotes to the classic itself" (Cremin, 1955, p. 307).

The 1920s began with a flurry of work in "scientific curriculum making," which stemmed from the work of Bobbitt and indirectly from Judd and Thorndike. The trend of this work was twofold: (1) toward increased specification and precision and (2) toward responsiveness to current social needs, rather than carrying on traditional, classic subjects for the sake of custom. Frederick Bonser (1920) used principles of job analysis to determine common knowledge, skills, attitudes, and appreciations to all walks of life in America, as a basis for determining the curriculum for elementary education. David Snedden (1921) argued that curricular objectives should be developed by empirical analysis of the needs of adult life, in physical, civic, cultural, and vocational areas. W. W. Charters (1923) provided a theoretical base for Bobbitt's activity analysis. He said that the first step was to identify *ideals* of socially efficient persons in the society. These ideals and common activities were then analyzed into objectives and were arranged in order of importance for children and youth to acquire, so that they might efficiently fit society's needs. In a widely used book (1924) Bobbitt concretely explained how to develop curricula in a concise manner that served as precedent for other writers who wanted to provide a kind of recipe for curriculum developers to follow. Henry Harap's *The Techniques of Curriculum Making* (1928) exemplifies a popular how-to manual of this type. Although Harap and others who followed retained the prescriptive recipe orientation, they moved away from the rigid acitvity analysis procedures of Bobbitt and Charters.

In opposition to these social behaviorists in the 1920s, we also find a strong force of adherents to Dewey. W. H. Kilpatrick continued to attract great numbers of students to Teachers College of Columbia University, where much ferment in curriculum thought was taking place. George D. Strayer emerged as a leader in conducting school surveys that remind one of the penetrating work of Rice a quarter of a century before. Strayer, however, surveyed schools in over fifty cities for the purpose of providing constructive feedback and helping them improve their curriculum. This and the general trend of scientific curriculum study led to statewide, as well as local, curriculum revision projects. According to Tanner (1982, p. 415), this brought about the Curriculum Bureau at Teachers College, which served as a clearing house to distribute information on curriculum development. Strayer had been influenced by Herbartians and Dewey, as well as by Thorndike, and wanted to decentralize authority for curriculum development more than did the social efficiency advocates. Harold Rugg, in Deweyan democratic spirit, called for curriculum committees at the local level and an attitude of research by all involved in the curriculum. As he revealed in *The Child-Centered School* (Rugg and Shumaker, 1928), and as Kilpatrick (1926, 1936) reiterated, the student's role in this process must be central. Curriculum inquiry became conceived as a process of teachers and students entering into dialogue to determine together what is worthwhile to learn and how to pursue it. This was a process that L. Thomas Hopkins began to develop in the late 1920s (see Hopkins, 1929) and would continue to develop for the next five decades.

In the debate between social behaviorists (with their adherence to measurement, precision, efficiency, and mechanical technique) and experientialists (with their child-centered, progressive, democratic, problem-solving orientation), we find a monumental difference in perspective that plagues the curriculum field to this day and centers on two opposing notions of science. The social behaviorist seeks inquiry that controls others through highly generalized knowledge derived by credentialed experts, and the experientialist searches with others for insights about the consequences of daily courses of action on growth for all involved. Boyd Bode (1927) grasped this dichotomy by the horns and, using insightful wit, wrestled with its inconsistencies, criticized zealots in both camps, and emerged with faith in democracy strengthened by philosophic and scientific inquiry.

In the late 1920s several European influences began to penetrate American educational thought. British philosopher-mathematician Alfred North Whitehead's essays on education were put together in a volume called *The Aims of Education* (1929) three years after he took a post at Harvard University. His admonitions to maintain the wholeness of knowledge, to root out inert ideas, to engage in imaginative dialogue, and to attend to the rhythms of the learning process are well known. Such rhythms, patterns, or stages of development were treated nowhere more intensely than in the work of Swiss psychologist Jean Piaget (1926, 1928, 1929). The *gestaltist* psychology of Max Wertheimer and the psychoanalytic writings of Freud, Jung, and others also began to enter American educational thought.

The differences between intellectual traditionalist proponents of liberal arts and their opponents who opposed each other, the social behaviorists and experientialists, were creating great dissension within the emergent curriculum field that was little more than a decade old. Another way to state the problem (rather than in terms of method of inquiry) is to focus on the value attributed to each of three sources of curriculum emphasis: (1) the learner, (2) society, and (3) subject matter. In 1902, Dewey argued that these three factors must be treated as interdependent (see Tanner, 1982). Yet his advice was not to be heeded. Intellectual traditionalists turned to subject matter, while social behaviorists focused on society and experientialists attended to the learner.

So great was the fragmentation that Harold Rugg invited major figures from each camp to participate in deliberations, beginning in 1924 and lasting for over two years, in an effort to achieve a consensus on central curriculum issues and questions. The participants included William C. Bagley, Franklin Bobbitt, Frederick G. Bonser, W. W. Charters, George S. Counts, Stuart A. Courtis, Ernest Horn, Charles H. Judd, Frederick J. Kelly, William H. Kilpatrick, George A. Works, and Rugg, who chaired the group. Their first task was to devise questions that needed to be answered. If a common set of questions could be agreed upon, it was thought that the curriculum field would have a chance of staying alive, and if some consensus could be achieved on the answers, there was even greater chance that the field would progress. The committee (Rugg, 1927b) produced a set of eighteen fundamental questions about curriculum making:

1. *What period of life does schooling primarily comtemplate as its end?*
2. *How can the curriculum prepare for effective participation in adult life?*
3. *Are the curriculum-makers of the schools obliged to formulate a point of view concerning the merits or deficiencies of American civilization?*
4. *Should the school be regarded as a conscious agency for social improvement?*
   a. *Should the school be planned on the assumption that it is to fit children to "live in" the current social order or to rise above and lift it after them? Are children merely to be "adjusted" to the institutions of current society or are they to be so educated that they will be impelled to modify it? Are they to accept it or to question it?*
5. *How shall the content of the curriculum be conceived and stated?*
6. *What is the place and function of subject matter in the education process?*
   a. *Subject matter is primarily matter-set-out-to-be-learned. It is the conscious and specific end of school activity (educative process), and the learning activity is exactly and precisely means to this end.*
   b. *Subject matter and learnings are properly both subsequent and subordinate to some normal life activity or experience (the educative process) already under way from other considerations. Subject matter is called for when, and because, this life activity has been balked for lack of a certain way of behaving. This needed way of behaving, as it is sought, found and acquired, is what we properly call subject matter. Its function is to enable the balked activity to proceed.*
7. *What portion of education should be classified as "general" and what portions as "specialized" or "vocational" or purely "optional"? To what extent is general education to run parallel with vocational education and to what extent is the latter to follow on the completion of the former?*
8. *Is the curriculum to be made in advance?*
9. *To what extent is the "organization" of subject matter a matter of pupil-thinking and construction of, or planning by, the professional curriculum-maker as a result of experimentation?*
10. *From the point of view of the educator, when has "learning" taken place?*
11. *To what extent should traits be learned in their "natural" setting (i.e., in a "life-situation")?*
12. *To what degree should the curriculum provide for individual differences?*
13. *To what degree is the concept of "minimal essentials" to be used in curriculum-construction?*
14. *What should be the form of organization of the curriculum? Shall it be one of the following or will you adopt others?*
    a. *A flexibly graded series of suggestive activities with reference to subject matter which may be used in connection with the activities? Or,*

      b. *A rigidly graded series of activities with subject matter included with each respective activity? Or,*

      c. *A graded sequence of subject matter with suggestion for activities to which the subject matter is related? Or,*

      d. *A statement of achievements expected for each grade, a list of suggestive activities, and an outline of related subject matter, through the use of which the grade object may be achieved? Or,*

      e. *A statement of grade objectivities in terms of subject matter and textual and reference materials which will provide this subject matter without any specific reference to activities?*

15. *What, if any, use shall be made of the spontaneous interests of children?*

16. *For the determination of what types of material (activities, reading, discussion problems and topics, group projects, etc.) should the curriculum-maker analyze the activities in which adults actually engage?*

      a. *For skills and factual material?*

      b. *For group activities?*

      c. *For problems and issues of contemporary life?*

17. *How far shall methods of learning be standardized? For example, is it probable that current principles of learning will favor the use of "practice" devices? For individuals? For groups? How is drill to be provided?*

      a. *By assignment, under penalty, of specially chosen drill material?*

      b. *By such personal practice as the felt connections call for?*

18. *Administrative questions of curriculum-making.*

      a. *For what time units shall the curriculum be organized?*

      b. *For what geographic units shall the curriculum be made?*

        i. *In the United States*

        ii. *Individual states*

        iii. *A county*

        iv. *An individual school*

      c. *Shall a curriculum be made especially for rural schools?*

      d. *What is the optimal form in which to publish the course of study? [pp. 9–10]*

These questions were followed by a seventeen-page consensus statement signed by the participants. Its central thrust was quite experientialist in tone, although much compromise was evident. It recognized the great contributions of the concepts, principles, and ideas that constitute the organized disciplines of knowledge, and at the same time, the authors acknowledged the need to develop curriculum that fits the needs and interests of learners. The curriculum, they said, was to help learners solve problems relevant to their own lives. Thus, curricular content should be drawn in interdisciplinary fashion, instead of maintaining separate subject status. In fairness to the participants, it should be added that each was given opportunity to respond (provide a minority report) to the composite statement with supplementary comments, and these comments occupied 133 pages. Combined with pages of quotations from Dewey and several Herbartians, the proceedings of these deliberations were published as Part II of the Twenty-sixth Yearbook of the NSSE (Rugg, 1927b).

    This second volume was accompanied by a first volume also edited by Rugg (1927a). This was a much longer volume that reconstructed a history of curriculum development in the United States and provided significant reports on innovative practices and programs of that period. Troubled by the trend away from child-centered curriculum, Rugg gave special attention to writings by Dewey, Parker, and the Herbartians and called for curriculum development that carefully returned the child to the process.

In the 1930s the debate continued. Dewey returned to the scene with new publications on education. In 1931 he argued that the way out of educational confusion was to cease being controlled by a separate subject curriculum. He called for a curriculum that was integrated by attention to learner interest and need. In 1932b George S. Counts asked if schools should build a new order, emphasizing the social aspect of curriculum making and initiating a social reconstructionist orientation to curriculum that held that schools should change society rather than perpetuate the status quo. Bode (1938) reiterated Dewey's (1902) call for balanced attention to the learner, society, and subject matter. In a project published in 1937, L. Thomas Hopkins brought together scholars from diverse desciplines to address the problem of curricular balance; they determined that it could be achieved by integrating the curriculum around the learner. If this were done, Hopkins reasoned, the society's needs would be met by growing human beings who tap the disciplines for insights.

Schools that moved in this direction, Dewey reflected, gave more attention to individual needs, expressive activities, and cooperation between teachers and students and among students themselves (Dewey, 1940, pp. 280–281). Nevertheless, the practice of progressive education turned increasingly to the individual. Dewey (1938a, p. 84) protested vehemently against catering to student caprice: "Some teachers seem to be afraid even to make suggestions to the members of a group. . . . I have heard of cases in which children are surrounded with objects and materials and then left entirely to themselves, the teacher being loath to suggest even what might be done with the materials lest freedom be impinged upon. Why, then, supply materials?" At another point Dewey (1938a, p. 32) says of the teacher: "There is no point in his [sic] being more mature if, instead of using his greater insight to help organize the conditions of experience of the immature, he throws away his insight." Here Dewey is saying that all members of a situation must cooperate if growth is to accrue in democratic fashion, and he reminds us that "the school cannot be a preparation for social life excepting as it reproduces, within itself, the typical conditions of social life" (Dewey, 1938a, p. 34). Moreover, to continue consistently with his call for balance among society, learner, and subject matter, Dewey summarizes the task of curriculum in action: "Utilizing of interest and habit to make of it something fuller, wider, something more refined and under better control, might be defined as the teacher's whole duty" (1938a, p. 126).

Bode, too, was incensed with mindless preoccupation with childhood whims, warning that, "If progressive education can succeed in translating its spirit into terms of democratic philosophy and procedure, the future of education in this country will be in its hands. . . . If it persists in one-sided absorption in the individual pupil, it will be . . . left behind" (Bode, 1938, pp. 43–44). The conflict that beset progressive educators was epitomized by a 1938 rift in the Progressive Education Association between those who favored child study and those who advocated social reconstruction. When reflecting on the situation, Paul Hanna said that this difference never healed and did much to bring dissolution of the movement (Hanna, 1984).

Social behaviorists were steadily on the rise, too, in the 1930s. They questioned the glowing platitudes of progressive theorists, and they criticized reports of success by progressive teachers who had nothing but enthusiastic self-reports to substantiate their claims. They asked for scientific evidence, and little was available. In the early

1930s the Progressive Education Association (P.E.A.) became bothered by this problem, too. In the 1927 NSSE Yearbook, Part One, Rugg and Counts had called for more scientifically controlled studies of innovative practices. There is a sense in which this seemed like a contradiction to many experientialists who adhered to a notion of science centered in everyday problem solving and reflective thinking. Nevertheless, most members of the P.E.A. wanted increased credibility generated for what their experience told them was obvious, namely, that progressive education was superior to traditional education. Later, Dewey (1938a) would cogently summarize fundamental differences between traditional and progressive practices:

> *To imposition from above is opposed expression and cultivation of individuality; to external discipline is opposed free activity; to learning from texts and teachers, learning through experience; to acquisition of isolated skills and techniques by drill, is opposed acquisition of them by means of attaining ends which make direct vital appeal; to preparation for a more or less remote future is opposed making the most of opportunities of the present life; to static aims and materials is opposed acquaintance with a changing world. [pp. 5–6]*

Some members of the P.E.A. lamented the fact that they, as teachers and curriculum makers, could not be inventive because of rigid college entrance requirements. Many realized that the Great Depression brought a massive increase of the student-age population into the secondary schools. Finally, the group enlisted the cooperation of several hundred colleges and universities and developed a study in which thirty school systems participated as experimental schools. These schools agreed to experiment with the curriculum, and the colleges agreed to drop the usual entrance requirements for students from them. The study followed students from the freshman year of high school through college; hence, it was named "The Eight Year Study." Students were compared in pairs (one from a traditional school and one from an experimental progressive school) and matched for similar background characteristics. On a multitude of measures, ranging from academic to personal and social adjustment and accomplishment, students from the experimental schools equaled or excelled students from the control group of traditional high school students, except in the foreign language area. It should be kept in mind that experimental schools often did not have courses in areas emphasized by most of the colleges but traditional high schools had such courses. Thus, one might think that students from traditional high schools would be better prepared for college, since colleges usually offered a traditional curriculum. Such was not the case, however.

One is forced to conclude that students from the progressive schools learned something more important, for example, how to direct their own learning, a greater love for learning, problem solving, a sense of meaning and direction in their own lives, personal responsibility, resourcefulness. Perhaps students from traditional schools learned more docility, compliance, and how to follow directions. Since no uniform treatment was given to progressive schools in the study, some critics assumed that schools that had experimented least (those who had "learned to love their chains") were essentially comparable to traditional schools. To this criticism the study compared only students from the six schools that departed most from tradition with their traditional counterparts and found that those who experienced the most experimental curricula far excelled the traditional students (Chamberlin et al., 1942). These highly experimental schools often involved students in self-designed learning projects and elective courses with few or no required courses. The study is reported in five volumes and is summarized in the first volume by Aikin (1942). It should be added that when a follow-up study was done twenty years later by Margaret Willis (1961) on the graduates of one of the most experimental schools (The Ohio State University Laboratory School), they were found to be considerably self-satisfied, involved in stable family situations, and making high levels of leadership contributions in relation to the general population.

One of the most important contributions to curriculum literature in the 1930s was made by Hollis Caswell and Doak Campbell. Their text, *Curriculum Development* (1935), marked the first in a continuing series of synoptic curriculum texts. The *synoptic text* (Schubert, 1980a) is a book that attempts to summarize the state of the art of curriculum studies for the professional educator who intends to devote full-time effort to curriculum development and/or scholarship. By the mid-1930s, when the student population suddenly doubled as a result of the Depression, when curriculum thought was moving in several different directions, when many different kinds of curriculum books were becoming available, it was becoming impossible to expect aspiring curriculum developers to master over two hundred books available on different aspects of curriculum studies. Thus, Caswell and Campbell (1935) tried to provide a book that brought a balanced awareness of the comtemporary curriculum scene. They wanted to provide curriculum developers with a guide for reflection on issues, problems, ideas, and procedures that they should be aware of in order to do curriculum development. In 1937, they published a supplementary collection, *Readings in Curriculum Development*. As subsequent decades brought a greater proliferation of curriculum books, articles, and technical reports, synoptic texts and collections of readings were developed to bring curriculum knowledge together. As interpretations, synoptic texts always leaned in one direction or another. This fact led to another contribution that the authors made—to provide a new way of viewing the curriculum field. Caswell and Campbell (1935) leaned toward Dewey and progressive thought, as is evident in their attention devoted to purposes that pupils themselves have.

The 1940s continued the trend in synoptic texts. Some reached in the direction of the student, some emphasized the society, and others focused on disciplines of knowledge. All these texts formed a means of socialization for budding curricularists. A few such texts were appealing enough to appear in revised editions. *The Child and His Curriculum* (1940, 1950, 1960) by Lee and Lee is one such example that leaned in the direction of the child. Gwynn (1943, 1950, 1960, 1969) emphasized the society. Alberty (1947, 1953, 1962) centered discussion on the high school and focused on the core curriculum that did much to blend emphasis on students, society, and disciplines of knowledge. Stratemeyer (1947, 1957) emphasized students with her idea of "persistent life situations" or perennial areas of interest.

Finally, the conclusion of the 1940s brought Ralph W. Tyler's (1949) *Basic Principles of Curriculum and Instruction*. This small book drew conceptually upon Dewey, Charters, Rugg, Bode, the Eight Year Study (Giles, 1942), and other sources to formulate four fundamental topics that frame curriculum study: (1) purposes, (2) learning experiences, (3) organization, and (4) evaluation. Moreover, Tyler echoed Dewey's call for balance among subject matter, students, and society as bases of curriculum development. Here emerged the perennial paradigm of curriculum studies that dominates the field to this day.

The work of special commissions was influential enough that by the 1940s an Education Policies Commission of the NEA came into its own. Established in 1935 with a grant of $250,000 from the General Education Board, the EPC offered a number of policy statements during the next thirty-three years (see Ortenzio, 1983, pp. 31–34), which affected state and local curriculum policy in no small measure.

Throughout the 1940s, the trend begun in the 1930s toward different plans for grouping students continued. Special attention was devoted to provisions for the gifted and talented, and enabling more students to attend college. Yet a great deal more time, energy, and money was devoted to developing the school building and the business of running it than to what it was supposed to provide for learners, namely, the curriculum. However, "attention was being given to audiovisual instruction, guidance programs, functional reading, and increasing community involvement in school affairs" (Doll, 1982, p. 14).

In the 1950s, one of the major classics among synoptic curriculum texts appeared: *Fundamentals of Curriculum Development* by Smith, Stanley, and Shores (1950, rev. 1957). This text brought the balance of attention more toward the society, although it melded this with focus on student interest through the core curriculum, which enabled students to study contemporary problems of interest to them by drawing upon different disciplines.

The 1950s also brought a conservative, back to the "nuts and bolts" reaction, spearheaded by Arthur Bestor (1955) and others who called for serious attention to basics in an effort to counter life-adjustment education that was popular in the late 1940s. Just as William C. Bagley led a back-to-basics movement during the post–World War I era, so too Bestor and others led a similar venture in the 1950s following World War II and the Korean conflict. The sentiment seems to be one of getting down to serious intent that will prepare future generations better for troubles that might lie ahead.

From an American viewpoint, however, trouble did emerge too soon. The major catalyst to curriculum activity in the 1950s was the successful orbit of a Soviet satellite named *Sputnik*. U.S. education was seen by many as the culprit who let the Russians get ahead. Experts from the disciplines were called upon to improve the educational system in the United States. Already developed ideas, such as a new approach to the teaching of mathematics, later known as "new math" or "modern math" (developed in the early 1950s by Max Beberman), were capitalized on and billed as an answer to the U.S. lag in the space race. In 1960, Jerome Bruner published *The Process of Education*, which outlined an image of what education might be if it were adequately responsive to disciplinary, social, and individual needs. Despite Bruner's attention to individual needs and interests of learners, post-*Sputnik* curriculum reform clearly pushed the curriculum balance toward the disciplines of knowledge in the interest of social and political ends.

Not only was scientific content promoted but the study of curriculum and teaching took on the character of scientific research. Gage (1963) provided a summation of accomplishments of research on teaching and advocated that more be pursued. The 1956 *Taxonomy of Educational Objectives: Cognitive Domain*, by Benjamin Bloom, was revived as a basis for some of the research and as a means for more systematic curriculum planning. By 1964, an "affective domain" of the taxonomy had been developed by Krathwohl.

The 1960s also brought the idea of a comprehensive high school into popular as well as professional vision. The efforts of James Bryant Conant (1959) to see that high school could meet the needs of all youth in a society had begun to be realized through the assistance of the Carnegie Foundation that enabled extensive dissemination of *American High School Today* (Conant, 1959). Such a high school would have provisions for college preparatory, vocational, and general education. It would enable a broad basis for all in English, foreign language, science, mathematics, social sciences, and the humanities.

While the proponents of the post-*Sputnik* reform projects in sciences and other areas (see Goodlad, Von Stoephasius, and Klein, 1966, and Eisner, 1971, for summaries and criticisms of this movement) tried to "teacher proof" the curriculum, other authors advocated a more active role by teachers (e.g., Burton, 1951; Sharp, 1951; Spears, 1951; Corey, 1953; Hopkins, 1954; Pritzkau, 1959).

The year 1968 marked the end of the Educational Policies Commission, which in no small measure was brought about by the influx of foundations (Ford, Carnegie, Rockefeller, etc.) that, in effect, governed educational policy by regulating funding. With the large-scale entry of the federal government, first through the National Defense Education Act in 1958, the National Science Foundation, and subsequently by the Elementary and Secondary Education Act of 1965, government linked with private funding sources to forge a new prime mover in curriculum policy. By carrying the purse, these forces effectually overpowered humanistic education (see ASCD, 1962) and open education movements (see Barth, 1972; Spodek and Walberg, 1975). Such movements were strongly related to A. S. Neill's (1960) classic, *Summerhill*, Charles Silberman's (1970) *Crisis in the Classroom*, and Carl Rogers's (1969, 1983) *Freedom to Learn*. Both these and the popular education writings of Herb Kohl, John Holt, Jonathan Kozol, George Dennison, and others beginning in the 1960s attracted much attention but by comparison to foundation and government-supported projects were infrequently applied on a large scale.

As funding agencies demanded accountability for their expenditures in the 1960s and 1970s, greater specification of treatment (such as behavioral objectives) and evaluation of results became commonplace. The changing winds of fundable topics, political and legal responses to pressure groups, and the ever-capricious bandwagon of curricular novelties brought greater attention to curriculum as a political phenomenon (Schaffarzick and Sykes, 1979).

Much greater attention was given to nurturing cultural diversity and to equity for the handicapped in the 1960s and 1970s. This has continued into the 1980s accompanied by increased problems of poverty, especially in urban education, with ramifications for equality of educational opportunity for different socioeconomic, racial, ethnic, and sexual groups. The 1980s brought new qualitative research methodologies for probing the complexities of such problems in an effort to study educational outcomes as more subtle than products turned off an assembly line. The 1980s also brought a public conservatism that called for a return to fundamentals. Paradoxically, at the same time, the public called for education that speaks to a moral an ethical bankruptcy that contributes to social violence and disharmony. The preoccupation with technological advance with which the twentieth century began became more accentuated in the 1980s with the computer revolution. The depressed economy made job acquisition a further demand on curriculum. Moreover, reports by a large number of "blue ribbon" commissions between 1982 and 1985 demanded that schools upgrade curricula to meet the needs of a rapidly changing, diverse society.

SUMMARY

The foregoing may seem extensive to one who is becoming acquainted with curriculum as a field of study; however, it is essential that anyone interested in curriculum realize that it has a history that parallels the whole of human history. Actually, what is presented here is a brief encounter with curriculum history. The most recent decades of the twentieth century were presented with even greater brevity because they are drawn upon elaborately in the other chapters of this book. The overriding point of this chapter is that it is imperative for those who engage in curriculum work to reflect carefully on the past. Precedent must be a constant guide to present decision and action. Without knowledge that enables historical reflection, curricularists will always be tyrannized by the present.

COMMENTARIES

Due to the length of this chapter, the guest commentators are asked to be as succinct as possible. Rather than respond to each movement and major figure, they will emphasize overall responses.

Experientialist

Although I think of myself as one who is well aware of history, I must admit that I want to reread some of the writers of the past. Many of them remind me of Dewey and the twentieth-century progressive educators. I recall that even Dewey commented in his intellectual autobiography that Plato was the philosopher he most liked to read (Dewey, 1930). It must be in the encounters between Socrates and others that Dewey found the essence of educative dialogue. I want to return to these and look at them for pedagogic insight. I suspect that such insight is conveyed more by the medium than the intended message of Plato's philosophy.

I was struck by the relevance of Quintilian, John Gerson, Montaigne, Comenius, and especially Rousseau. Their messages of concern for the well-being of children, what we can learn from their experiences, and what they can teach us by the way they are if we will only listen are likely to be exceedingly important. Herbart, Emerson, Pestalozzi, Froebel, Tolstoy, and Francis Parker are of course paragons of progressive education before it was known by that label. In addition, I had not fully realized that the progressive education movement was of worldwide origin. Therefore, I want to learn more about the writings and/or schools of Claperede, Montessori, Kerschensteiner, and DeCroly in Europe. I now have an overview about these great contributors, and I want to experience primary sources, what they and their contemporaries said.

I do, of course, want to study again twentieth-century advocates of child study and social reconstruction (i.e., followers of Dewey such as Kilpatrick, Bode, Counts, Rugg, and Hopkins). I am increasingly convinced that they have much in common with the popular, radical writers of today (Holt, Kohl, Illich, Freire) as well as some of the scholars of curriculum who are labeled among the reconceptualists (Pinar, Grumet, Huebner, Macdonald, Giroux, Apple). Such possible connections need to be studied for similarities and differences. We need to know where we've been before; if we can experience it vicariously, we need not rediscover it.

As for methods of historical research, it is very important to acknowledge openly that any way of doing history is value laden. There is no purely factual form of curriculum history, just as there is no purely objective kind of educational research. Therefore, I think that we need more revisionist history because the value base of the researcher is admitted from the start. Among curriculum writers, Macdonald (1977a) made this clear nearly a decade ago. This is a prerequisite to surveys of curriculum thought and practice, analyses of movements, and biography. We need more detailed biographies of people involved in many spheres of curriculum, not only curriculum scholars, but curriculum developers, administrators, teachers, and students. To know more about the biography of those with whom one works and lives enables better working together. Likewise, to know more of one's autobiography yields self-education. These laudable goals, self-education and living well together, are a good deal more important to pursue than limiting oneself to the biography of well-known educators.

Social Behaviorist

I found it only mildly interesting to traverse the history of curriculum presented in this chapter. After all, the curriculum field began in the early twentieth century. I don't see why we have to spend so much space on pre–twentieth-century matters. This is not to say that nothing important happened before 1900. Clearly, forerunners of contemporary curriculum and methods are to be found in earlier times and places. Yet most of what went on before is bound to different cultural and social eras. Besides, curriculum has become a science since the early work of Bobbitt and Charters. "Inert ideas," to use Whitehead's words (1929), are ruled out by the methods of science. Were I the author of this book, I would devote a great deal more attention to what we now know through the process of scientific verification. The fine synthesis of research on teaching provided by Wittrock (1985) in *The Third Handbook of Research on Teaching* and by Hosford and others (1984) in the 1984 ASCD Yearbook entitled *Using What We Know About Teaching* are exemplary, the first for the scholar and the second for the practitioner.

This is not to say that it is not useful to know the early origins of educational thought. These led to the current state of scientific achievement and productivity that we have reached today. It is indeed interesting to know that the task and job analysis began in rudimentary ways in Ancient Egypt, that Confucius had the sense to preserve the rules and conventions of society through education, and that the inkling that the world is intelligible through sense experience evolved among Pre-Socratic philosophers. Scientists today are in a remote sort of way indebted to Aristotle for his logic and classifications of knowledge, and more directly indebted to Renaissance empiricists such as Copernicus, Bacon, Galileo, Descartes, and especially Hobbes and Locke. Hobbes, after all, gave us a faith in the possibility of scientific explanations of human nature and society on which psychology, the parent discipline of education, rests today. In the past century, the works of Spencer, Wundt, and Rice were monumental in bringing experimental research to education. Thorndike and Judd continued this job in the first decades of this century. More should have been said in this chapter about the many other great early contributors to educational science such as Alfred Binet, E. Meumann, Wilhelm Lay, and F. Galton, among others. For historical perspective on ways in which researchers have changed American schools (1840–1983) I cite Travers (1983).

These forerunners of educational science are the intellectual ancestors of the curriculum field. This chapter might well have begun with them. It is the essence of their methodology that should be applied to historical reasearch in curriculum. By this I mean that data should be examined systematically to test hypotheses. Data should be presented quantitatively whenever possible, and every effort should be used to maintain objectivity, reliability, validity, parsimony, replicability, power of explanation, and accuracy of prediction. In this way historical findings can provide a scientific basis for policy.

Intellectual Traditionalist

It is absolutely essential to provide curriculum developers and scholars with a strong historical basis. It is especially important that they attend to the happenings and ideas that evolved in other cultures, times, and places. This gives a kind of distance from which educators can reflect on their own culture; doing this enables one to discard the taken-for-granted and to realize that curricular patterns fit cultural patterns. In fact, I would go so far as to say that persons preparing to be curriculum scholars and developers should study the original works of the educational theorists noted here. If they did this, they would have the added advantage of not succumbing to today's appeal of science as the only defensible way of knowing. Too many programs that prepare students for doctoral and master's degrees in curriculum neglect historical perspective. Some of those that do provide it offer history that pertains only to the country in which the study takes place. This defeats the central purpose of historical studies.

Historical studies should be embedded in both intellectual and political history. They should, therefore, deal with curriculum thought, practices, and movements. Biographies of great educators should be central to such study. These have the added advantage of providing exemplars for current theorists and practitioners of curriculum. It is, after all, through the humanistic study of education as part of the liberal arts tradition that one can best prepare to be an educator of the first rank. I do wish that this chapter devoted more time to recent advocates of liberal education such as Herman Harrell Horne, Jacques Maritain, Robert M. Hutchins, Alexander Meiklejohn, Jacques Barzun, and Mortimer J. Adler. Horne's idealism, Maritain's return to the classics, Hutchins's application of a liberal education at the University of Chicago as a basis for democracy, Meiklejohn's Experimental College at the University of Wisconsin prior to the Great Depression, Barzun's *Teacher in America*, and Adler's Paideia Proposal are all important to read and ponder.

One of the most important statements on general education is the Harvard Committee Report on General Education published in 1945 under the title *General Education in a Free Society*. Unlike many advocacy statements on liberal education that smack of elitism, authors of the Harvard Report wanted to gain insight into the relationship between liberal education and universal schooling that fosters democratic living. As a matter of fact, there is evidence (Kridel, 1984) that ample student participation contributed to the Harvard Report. They posed a telling question, the answer to which is what a democracy should be about; I leave this question with you:

How can general education be so adapted to different ages and, above all, differing abilities and outlooks, that it can appeal deeply to each, yet remain in goal and essential teaching the same for all? [Harvard Committee, 1945, p. 93]

SUGGESTED READING

For an excellent sampling of excerpts from primary sources from Confucius to Dewey, I suggest Ulich (1954). I also suggest his companion piece to that volume for a fine, scholarly interpretation of major thinkers of the same time span (Ulich, 1950).

An overview of educational thought and practice in historical context is also important, and for this I recommend any of four sources: Good (1969), Boyd (1965), Curtis and Boultwood (1965), and Butts (1973). Many insights into curriculum history may be gleaned from such surveys.

Historical treatments that relate exclusively to the curriculum field are few indeed. Kliebard's (1986) history of American curriculum, 1890–1958, is particularly noteworthy. I suggest Seguel (1966) who portrays the thought and contributions of the McMurry brothers, Dewey, Bobbitt, Charters, Rugg, and Caswell. Fraley (1981) provides an historical look at innovation and schooling. Schubert (1980a) attempts a portrayal of the field from 1900 to 1979 through more than eleven hundred books that have served as the mainstay of the field during its first eighty years. Although Tanner and Tanner (1980) is not exclusively a book on curriculum history, it has several sections that deal carefully with curriculum history, and I recommend them. I also recommend Zais (1976) and Firth and Kimpston (1973) as rare synoptic texts with well-developed historical sections. The proceedings of the Society for the Study of Curriculum History are also suggested: Tanner (1981); Nelson (1983); Jorgenson and Schubert (1985).

Finally, I recommend two histories of education in the twentieth century: Lawrence Cremin's *Transformation of the School* (1961) and William Connell's *A History of Education in the Twentieth Century World* (1980). Both are histories of education, not specifically of curriculum, but they have much relevance to curriculum. Connell provides a broad-ranging history that extends throughout many parts of the world. Cremin paints the history of progressive education in twentieth-century America with special attention to societal context.

While the sources just cited focus on the substance of curriculum history, it is also important to realize the variety of methods or approaches used in doing curriculum history.

Orientations to Curriculum History

Curriculum history is studied in a number of different ways, including the following: surveys of thought, surveys of practice, analyses of movements, case studies, revisionist critiques, and biography. Rarely, however, do we find histories that focus exclusively on curriculum. Instead, we must turn to general histories of education in an effort to ferret out curriculum history. In commenting on the state of curriculum studies in the early 1970s, a number of scholars pointed out a need for more serious work in curriculum history (e.g., Cremin, 1971; Bellack, 1969; Kliebard, 1970; Ponder, 1974). Toward this end, The Society for the Study of Curriculum History emerged under the leadership of Laurel Tanner in 1977 and has since published three sets of proceedings (Tanner, 1981; Nelson, 1983; Jorgensen and Schubert, 1985). Thus, curriculum history has become a more visible area of study since 1980. That it is such is attested to by Tanner's (1982) article on the topic in the *Encyclopedia of Educational Research* (one of only five major articles on curriculum), an article by Kliebard and Franklin (1983) in the *Historical Inquiry in Education* published by AERA, and several articles in the *International Encyclopedia of Education* (Husen and Postlethwaite, 1985).

Surveys exist that focus primarily on curricular practice. After John Dewey and his daughter Evelyn surveyed the United States in an effort to locate exemplary progressive schools, they published their findings in *Schools for Tomorrow* (1915). Another sample is Part (Volume) I of the Twenty-sixth NSSE Yearbook (Rugg, 1927a), which consists of an elaborate survey of innovative schools.

Beginning in Boise, Idaho, in 1910, the school survey movement in the United States provides a different type of survey that grew out of the early twentieth-century tendencies in many nations to assess social conditions as a basis for allocating welfare, a growing interest in social relationships in schools, and a desire for more efficient management of institutions (Connell, 1980). The school survey consisted of a process of bringing experts into large-city school systems to assess them and make recommendations for future policy developments. The assessments increased in sophistication, as did the measurement instruments employed, as the practice of utilizing surveys increased in popularity well into the 1920s and 1930s. The 25-volume report on the Cleveland Survey 1915–1916 is a classic example (Ayers, 1917), and in it one can clearly identify a seedbed for the measurement and evaluation movement discussed in Chapter Eleven.

On the other side of the educational fence from the measurement movement was progressive education. *The Transformation of the School* by Lawrence Cremin (1961) is a splendid example of the intellectual history of a movement in education. He interprets the origins, emergence, and fading of progressive education in American culture. While Cremin's book treats the interplay of educational thought and practice and thus exemplifies one kind of history of a movement, George Herbert Mead's *Movement of Thought in the Nineteenth Century* (1936) is a rendition of movements that transports the reader from Kant, through romanticism, utilitarianism, and socialism, to twentieth-century industrialization, scientific research, pragmatism, behaviorism, individuality, and the self. Thus, Mead's work is an excellent prerequisite to that of Cremin (1961), Connell (1980), or Kneller (1984).

Some histories focus on a particular country, such as *A History of Education in the American Culture*, a widely read survey by Butts and Cremin (1953), and the portrayal of critical choices in American education by David Tyack (1967) in *Turning Points in American Educational History*.

Case studies are yet another method of doing history, and educational history that focuses directly on curriculum is represented by Caswell and Associates (1950), who provided a caselike rendition of curriculum improvement projects in school systems throughout the United States. More in-depth, politically oriented case studies began to appear twenty-five years later, as exemplified by Reid and Walker (1975). To focus on one particular setting in depth is a quite different form of history than the broad survey, although it seems to be a descendent of early reports of practice (e.g., Dewey and Dewey, 1915; Rugg, 1927b) already mentioned.

Some historical studies in education, like that of Seguel (1966), focus on the biographical. An excellent earlier example is *The Social Ideas of American Educators*, by Merle Curti (1935), a sociology of ideas centering on major contributors to American education from the early 1600s to the midtwentieth century. Surely, too, in the biographical realm one can turn to works on a single educator, such as Dykhuizen's (1973) intellectual biography of Dewey and Monaghan's (1982) biographical work on the contributions of Noah Webster. Autobiography has been a window on the educational life in its broadest sense from St. Augustine's *Confessions* to the *Confessions* of Jean Jacques Rousseau and the *Autobiography of Benjamin Franklin*. One recent effort consists of William Van Til (1983), a well-known contributor to educational and curricular thought, taking account of the insights derived from his own experience. Some authors make historical contributions in the biographical vein by interpreting educational and curricular implications of contemporary philosophers (such as Kierkegaard, Nietzsche, Marx, Buber, and Mannheim) whose work is not explicitly directed to education (Hill, 1973), while others provide critiques of the contributions of educational theorists (such as J. B. Conant, Theodore Brameld, Jacques Barzun, B. F. Skinner, and Paul Goodman) as set forth by James E. McClellan (1968). Oral history of educational scholars and practitioners also contributes to insight into the curricular past, as evidenced in the extensive collections of oral history tapes developed by O. L. Davis, who, with two colleagues, provided a guide to oral history techniques and benefits for teachers (Sitton, Mehaffy, and Davis, 1983).

Slices of educational history that bear heavily on curriculum appear on many topics. Alexander Meiklejohn (1932) portrayed his experience in establishing a thoroughgoing liberal arts, core curriculum in the Experimental College at the University of Wisconsin, 1927–1932. Ruth Miller Elson's (1964) history of U.S. schoolbooks in the nineteenth century is a well-researched exposure of the values about nature, God and man, nationality, the individual, economics, society, and politics revealed in them. Ida DePencier's (1967) history of the University of Chicago Laboratory School (1896–1965) is another type of history, one in this case written by a woman who was involved for thirty-three years as a teacher in the school about which she wrote. Broudy and Palmer (1965) present a history of teaching method through characterizations of exemplars from Socrates to Kilpatrick. Raymond Callahan's (1962) critique of the efficiency movement, David Tyack's (1974) critical history of urban education in America, and Edward A. Krug's (1964) history of the American high school are additional examples of educational history that offer considerable insight into curriculum. The wide-ranging character of historical studies that bear on curriculum is further illustrated by Julia Wrigley's (1982) analysis of social class politics and public schools in Chicago from 1900 to 1950 focused on that one city, while Atkin and House (1981) surveyed federal government involvement in curriculum development over a thirty-year span, 1950–1980, in the United States.

In the early 1970s, a number of books offered a challenge to standard histories of education, the early paragon of which is Cubberley's *Public Education in the United States* (1934) and *The History of Education* (1920). These new historians came to be known as *revisionists*, and they argued that it is a myth that schools will integrate the poor, oppressed, and racially and ethnically diverse. They point out that far from building the traditional "American dream" of democratic participation, schools effectuate social control in the service of a corporate state. Against this powerful force, they argue that educational change has been illusory (e.g., Greer, 1972; Spring, 1972; Katz, 1971; Bowles and Gintis, 1976).

RECOMMENDATIONS FOR REFLECTION

1. Make a list of the major curricular events that you can remember as a teacher and a student. Read some historical commentaries about them. How does reading about what you have experienced differ from reading about earlier events?

2. What do you consider to be the five most difficult problems facing curriculum today? Can you identify precedent for them earlier in history? Bear in mind the admonition of Broudy and Palmer (1965) to judge educational events relative to the success routes of the day.

3. If you could select from five to ten figures in the history of curriculum to study in greater detail, who would they be and why would you select them?

4. Remember Isaiah Berlin's (1980) observation that disciples of those who create great liberating ideas tend to "straitjacket" them into recipes? Has this been done by any of the followers of those whom you selected for activity 3? Is it necessarily negative that this recipe making be done? Is it always straitjacketing, or does it have liberating results as well?

5. As you think back on the ideals that you identified in Chapters One and Two, which of the curriculum thinkers of the past deal with similar ideals?

6. Which historical time period interests you the most? Why? What relevance does this period have to today's curriculum problems?

7. Read samples of different types of curriculum history: history of ideas, history of practices, biography, history of movements, case studies, revisionist histories. Which do you think is the most useful approach? Can you identify strengths and weaknesses of each approach?

8. Which of the three bases for curriculum development identified by Dewey and others who followed him is most important: the learner, the society, or knowledge? How should the choice be made, and what balance among the three is most appropriate?

9. Where do you now stand with respect to each of the guest commentators? Which do you now agree with most? Which do you disagree with most?

10. How would you answer the eighteen questions posed by the authors of the Twenty-sixth Yearbook of the NSSE? How do you think most schools today (and/or

your school in particular) answer those questions? Are the questions relevant today? What questions should be added? What questions should be deleted?

11. Write a brief sketch of how you think history will portray the current era of curriculum thought and practice. Share it with those written by others.

12. If you could interview any of the great educators of the past about their curricular ideas, what would you ask them? Select three, pose three questions to each, and explain why you selected the questions. How do you imagine each would respond to your questions?

4

✦ Panorama: Relevant Contexts ✦

What a man is depends on his character; but what he does, and
what we think of what he does, depends on his circumstances.
> GEORGE BERNARD SHAW Preface, *Major Barbara* (1905)

I am myself plus my circumstance and if I do not save it, I cannot
save myself.
> JOSÉ ORTEGA Y GASSET "To the Reader" *Meditations on
> Quixote* (1914)

The friend of humanity cannot recognize a distinction between
what is political and what is not. There is nothing that is not
political.
> THOMAS MANN *The Magic Mountain* (1924)

SETTING THE STAGE

When we look in depth at any period in history, or indeed when we magnify any
current educational situation, it is clear that curriculum does not occur in isolation.
Curriculum thoughts, decisions, and practices are socially, politically, and culturally
constructed. They are powerfully governed by the economic and legal contexts in
which they exist. Moreover, the values of the day exert profound influence on
curriculum. The character of interpersonal and bureaucratic transactions of a given
time and place play an important role in curriculum planning and action.

All this is not to suggest a highly deterministic portrayal of curriculum as forged by
impersonal forces over which curriculum workers have no control and to which they
can only react. At a meeting of the John Dewey Society in Chicago in 1974, a
discussion took place that reveals the point I wish to make here. The setting was a
discussion session following presentations that painted a rather bleak picture of the
role of educators in a technocratic society. Positions ranged from the then novel

revisionist assertion that schools merely reflect the inequities harbored in dominant social class value structures to outright accusations that school people are so ineffectual that they functioned as mere automatons. The discussion became increasingly dispirited, at which point the clarion voice of progressively oriented William O. Stanley (in his midseventies) rang clear. He movingly acknowledged that contextual forces influence educational theory and practice *and* at the same time that educators themselves are active forces with some weight to throw around. Stanley, whose *Education and Social Integration* (1953) was one of the last major contributions to literature of the Deweyan social reconstructionist genre, added balance to a discussion that had become weighted toward the position that the school is merely a pawn carrying out society's will.

The curriculum literature, however, is decidedly weighted in the opposite direction. One ordinarily finds among synoptic curriculum texts a chapter on social forces or influences. Such chapters indicate that curriculum workers should realize that such influences exist and should note that they will need to deal with them from time to time. This is altogether too naive an orientation. What curriculum workers need to realize is that their lives and work are embedded in a history and context that both creates what they are and do and is created by what they are and do. Thus, this chapter deals with the impact of outside-of-school contexts (political, value, and economic), inside-of-school contexts, and nonschool curricula in student lives.

OUTSIDE-OF-SCHOOL CONTEXTS

Beyond the daily struggles, activities, and satisfactions that constitute the school day lie the politics, economics, and values that do much to create the school climate. Out of this climate school programs come into being. Yet their existence in turn affects the climate. The interplay of this mutual creation is a continuous process in the reality of school life. Let us look more closely at the politics, economics, and value contexts of curriculum and several subcategories of each.

Political Contexts

When in ordinary life activities, be it everyday conversation or in exposure to mass media, we hear the term *politics*, we think of the government. Perhaps we invoke memories of a government or political science class in high school or college. Or perhaps we think of only the pejorative connotation of *political* and focus only on matters of clout, intrigue, and subterfuge by which some elected and appointed officials try to secure the expedient.

It is unfortunate that such limited concepts of *the political* dominate the conventional wisdom. *Politics,* as noted in Chapter Five, pertains to the way in which people join together to accomplish what they could not accomplish alone. The study of politics then becomes the generation of knowledge about how persons engage in such endeavors, criticisms of the latter, and recommendations about how this might be accomplished more adequately.

When we think of the complexities of political interactions that contribute to school conflict and decision making, it is possible to identify levels of analysis such as the local community, the state, the courts, and the federal government that Wirt and

Kirst (1982) have set forth from a systems analysis perspective. It is also possible to move progressively outward to expanding horizons of influence as we will do here, beginning with administrative design and moving to school board decision, interest group lobbies, legislative mandates, court rulings, and global interactions. The purpose of the following discussion is to illustrate the general impact of several levels of politics on curriculum. The central point is to show that curriculum making is situated within a context of political forces, as amply demonstrated by Kirst and Walker (1971) and by Short (1983).

Administrative Design.   How does the school curriculum actually become designed? This is a question that Decker Walker (1971) set out to research by carefully following curriculum committees as they conducted their work. His naturalistic research revealed that their work is quite different from the ideas set forth in the Tyler Rationale (Tyler, 1949). Curriculum committees, he found, do not attend meticulously and thoughtfully to the study of society, learners, and disciplines of knowledge. They spend little time developing a philosophy and studying the psychology of learning. Furthermore, while they may pay lip service to Tylerian categories of purposes, learning experiences, organization, and evaluation of curriculum, they rarely engage in systematic development of them. Walker observed that the process instead is much more political and much less rational than the Tyler Rationale says it should be.

Walker concluded that a naturalistic model of curriculum has three major dimensions. The first he calls *platform,* using the image of a political platform metaphorically. This refers to the vast array of beliefs, attitudes, backgrounds, hidden agendas, abilities, biases, pet ideas, ideals, and hopes of the committee members. When a person comes to the curriculum committee meeting, this baggage is not left at home. It enters the discussion or *deliberation,* which is the second dimension of Walker's naturalistic model of curriculum development. This is the act of transaction among participants, a dialogue that often has more of a political than rational character. Finally, like it or not, the real world of schooling is under severe time constraints, and the third dimension, *design,* occurs when decisions must be put into practice. This means that administrative curriculum design is often only partially complete. A general, maybe even confusing, and motley configuration of guidelines is provided. If the guidelines are to become practicable, the transformation must be accomplished by the creative work of teachers and students.

School Board Decision.   School boards represent a somewhat more removed political entity in curriculum decision. Traditionally, they represent the public interest, and through personnel and policy decisions they delimit the parameters of curriculum deliberations conducted by administrators and teachers who serve on curriculum committees. Some hold that school boards have the responsibility to select purposes that they, in turn, commission professional educators to deliver. This service delivery interpretation reduces the professional educator's responsibility to a status of technician who deals primarily with matters of how rather than matters of what and why. Others suggest that the school board's decision to hire certain personnel over other candidates is akin to electing representatives to whom one extends confidence that they will make good decisions. In this case the professional educators are hired with the understanding that they will study the community, develop an educational philosophy commensurate with it, clarify its educational needs, and develop curricula that meet those needs. Their work would, of course, be monitored by school board members. Nevertheless, this stance involves professional educators much more fully in matters of what and why as well as how. A compromise position between these two extremes sees professional educators and board members as engaged in continuous dialogue over curriculum matters. In this process educators are able to ask a host of questions to encourage board members to clarify their philosophical assumptions, perceive more alternative courses of action, and anticipate the probable consequences of action.

While the latter position might seem like a worthy ideal, many educators and board members alike question its practicality. They see it as overly idealistic to propose that school boards spend much time on curriculum because they have so many problems to deal with that relate to finances, management, buildings, institutional arrangements, compliance with legislative and judicial mandate, and assuagement of interest group demands. Critics of this position, however, argue that it is senseless to spend all of one's energies developing a delivery system if little time is spent on what should be delivered. That which should be delivered to learners is the bottom line, they say; in other words, it is curriculum that matters most. Meanwhile, these laudable ideals pale as we realize that board members, like curriculum committee members in Walker's (1971) naturalistic model, all have their platforms and the public and private constituencies that they represent. This adds to the contention that school boards, too, are more political than rational.

Interest Group Lobbies.   The number, range, type, and variety of political interest groups are legion. Essentially, the label refers to any kind of group of any size that directs pressure or persuasion upon educational policymakers. Teachers' unions such as the American Federation of Teachers, professional associations such as the National Education Association, and parent associations such as the National Congress of Parents and Teachers (PTA) are large and powerful lobbyists at the federal, state, and local levels. These groups lobby on a host of issues ranging from student exposure to drugs and mass media to racial and economic inequities and classroom learning conditions. Many of their efforts have great influence on curriculum in an indirect if not direct manner. Other interest groups deal with educational matters as one among many concerns, for example, the NAACP's quest for racial equity, NOW's pressure for women's equity, the Center for Science in the Public Interest's work for fair and accurate research on science and technology in everyday life, and the ACLU's advocacy of justice in all segments of society. There are many narrowly defined interest groups that address a single cause. Some of these groups are organized on a permanent basis; others emerge informally to meet a given issue, such as religious fundamentalists who lobby to remove certain books, promote classroom prayer, or oppose teaching evolution. Many neighborhood groups exert a powerful, direct influence on the local school but have little or no impact on the city, state, or nation. At the local level a small group of parents concerned about textbooks or other curriculum materials may have profound effects on a school and its personnel. Such concern has been known to mushroom to state and national proportions as in the work of groups of textbook critics in Texas. A professional educational consumer group such as EPIE (Educational Products Information Exchange) provides a service that guards against false advertising by those who promote instructional materials.

Corporate interests, too, are one of the largest lobbyists for their own welfare. Not only do they station permanent lobbyists in Washington to support their interest, but they lobby continuously through advertisements in the mass media. The latter saturates the "curriculum" of our daily lives. Moreover, corporate interests directly influence school curriculum through the variety of instructional material that they produce for classroom use. See, for example, the disclosure of such activities by the Center for the Study of Responsive Law in *Hucksters in the Classroom* (Harty, 1979).

It should, of course, be added that interest groups can be productively educative. They can provide a forum of accessibility between the beliefs and values of citizens and professional educators who serve them. Thus, interest groups can help education to become more truly public. Time and again, interest groups have drawn the attention of educators and other citizens to educational inequities that resulted in better treatment of racial and ethnic minorities and the handicapped. Broad and varied groups such as Afro-Americans have a heritage of educational thought and practice that has been much neglected and suppressed. Curriculum policy could be enriched, as Gordon (1983) argues, by careful attention to this valuable resource.

At the same time, interest groups can be self-interested to the point that they are myopic to needs, interests, and life-styles other than their own. Their provincialism and inability to project the adverse consequences of their causes can be damaging to educational progress.

Legislative Mandate.   Lawmakers at the national, state, and local levels often have important influence on curriculum. The legal principles that provide for separation of church and state and relegate education to the states and localities are perhaps the most overarching of influences that legislators have had on curriculum, because these principles infuse debate on countless other legal and judicial matters that pertain to curriculum.

For other more specific examples of the influence of legislative mandate in the United States on curriculum, we might turn to the 1852 Massachusetts Law on Compulsory Schooling. It had great curricular impact by setting a precedent followed by other states to see that a vastly increased number of youngsters attended school. To meet needs of this expanded population, curriculum that spoke to practical as well as intellectual needs was developed. The Committees of Ten and Fifteen in the 1890s were developed precisely to respond to these needs. While the Land Grant College Act of 1862 had direct and obvious effect on college curriculum, it also "made the federal government a partner in the development of higher education throughout the states" (Krug, 1966, p. 83). Both the practical or occupationally oriented curriculum and the link between federal and state powers were felt in the secondary and elementary school. Ground was broken for federal involvement in the state education of its publics, and practical or occupational subjects were given greater impetus. The latter were furthered considerably by the Smith-Hughes Act of 1917, which encouraged vocational education.

This illustrates the point that almost as important as a piece of legislation itself is the precedent it sets for future legislation. When, for example, the College Entrance Examination Board was established in 1900 it would have been difficult to predict the mushrooming of legislation that enabled the massive test industry of today. Such testing, used continuously as the prime measure of student worth and school accountability, profoundly affects curricular decision. We live in an era when curriculum is molded to fit demands of evaluation mechanisms that are already in place. Thus, too often educational philosophy and curricular purpose are developed to comply with the standards of evaluation rather than calling for evaluation that facilitates philosophy and purpose.

In the past thirty years, we have notably experienced effects of the 1958 National Defense Education Act (with Amendments of 1964), the Economic Opportunity Act of 1964, the Civil Rights Act of 1964, the Elementary and Secondary Education Act of 1965 with its numerous *titles* (more recently *chapters*), and the Education for All Handicapped Children Act (P.L. 94-142) of 1975. All of these have had massive influence throughout the schools of America.

Through such legislation, children and youths who had heretofore received much less than their fair share of educational advantage began to be treated more equitably. Curricular materials and approaches were provided to help equalize what was more widely recognized as an unjust distribution of goods and services. Congress appropriated over a billion dollars for the Head Start program to improve educational opportunity for culturally disadvantaged children in 1965. This was followed by projects Follow Through, Upward Bound, and others that continued the effort. In the 1980s, in the wake of commission reports and research studies that denounced U.S. education for lagging behind in science and technology, the National Science Foundation appropriated increased funding in an attempt to upgrade scientific and technological education in a manner reminiscent of the post-*Sputnik* era. Not only is funding available through legislative political action, but it spurs a race among researchers and curriculum developers to meet the criteria for acquiring it. In meeting the criteria, curriculum is altered. Thus, legislation not only affects curriculum by what it mandates but by what it makes available and the paths it designates toward that availability.

Court Rulings.   The countenance of American curriculum has been continually altered by a flow of significant court cases. For example, the Fourteenth Amendment to the U.S. Constitution was furthered by interpretations of *Brown* v. *Board of Education* in 1954 and 1955 and by *Swann* v. *Charlotte-Meklenberg* in 1971 that ordered busing to end segregation. This led to classrooms of a new racial mix and, thus, to a curriculum of classroom cultural relations that was impossible before. The teachings of classroom life itself were also affected by the *Goss* v. *Lopez* decision of 1975, which established due process for student discipline. More students, therefore, learned by experience that they had a right to live under a system governed by uniform procedures rather than by the autocratic caprice that too often rules the young in schools. This, too, is a part of the hidden curriculum that can powerfully influence students' images of governance and justice. More clearly related to the overt curriculum is the *Lau* v. *Nichols* decision of 1974, which determined that schools must provide special language instruction for students who need it or be held in violation of the Civil Rights Act of 1964. These are but a few of the many court cases that have implicitly or explicitly altered the curriculum.

Global Interactions.   We live in an interdependent world; thus, the political context of curriculum does not stop at national boundaries. Curricular initiatives seem to be guided or misguided (depending on one's political outlook) by the perceived need to compete with, outperform, and/or overpower other nations. The smallness of our planet, our spaceship Earth, is well depicted by McLuhan and Fiore (1968), and the need for a politics of international cooperation is persuasively advocated by Berman and Miel (1983) as leaders in the World Council for Curriculum and Instruction. That there is much to be learned from international perspectives on education is evident in the comparative work of Taylor and Johnson (1974), Connell (1980), and Ignas and Corsini (1981). Conceptions of the nature of curriculum research itself can also be enriched by cross-cultural studies such as Popkewitz's (1984) inquiry into the role of ideological vision and contradiction in Soviet pedagogical science and van Manen's translations of the work of the eminent Dutch pedagogue and theorist, Martinus Jan Langeveld (1983), whose work reveals deep insights into the phenomenological life worlds of children.

Spheres of Power: An Overarching Note. No discussion of politics would be complete without addressing the issue of power. Power resides in the formal political hierarchy, to be sure, that is, in the legislative, judicial, and executive branches of government, in corporate leadership ladders, in school boards, and in the administrative line and staff of school districts. Nevertheless, informal power also carries great weight, sometimes dwarfing that of the formal hierarchies by comparison. Every social group from the classroom and social club to corporate giants and national governments is governed informally by power wielders who exert subtle influence on those who hold formal positions. This is revealed in few places more fully than in community power studies (see Kimbrough, 1964) in which the barons of power rarely hold political office, yet they frequently do hold strings that control office holders. Even at the school or classroom level, one can identify small groups and individual students whose attitudes carry considerable weight. Just as it profits a teacher to receive the support of such groups, it behooves superintendents to conduct informal power studies of their communities—to discover who serves on the most boards of directors and advisory councils. At all levels, power wielders (the "power elite" according to C. Wright Mills, 1956) form interlocking directorates. They move easily from power positions in one domain to another. The shifts of top-level educators from government, to foundations, to business, to universities and prestigious schools are legion. Educators of all levels should be aware of the intricacies of power.

Value Contexts

Values are inextricably entwined with curriculum. Curriculum deals with the issue of what should be taught. Decisions about should or ought are value decisions. In this case they are value decisions about knowledge and experiences that are considered worthwhile in that they enable learners to move toward better lives. At least four dominant spheres have great bearing on the values held in a society: mores and folkways, social class, mass media, and personal beliefs.

Mores and Folkways. A society's glue can be found in its *mores*, those deep-seated ideas about what is proper. To run naked in the streets, to have several wives and families in different locales, to engage in incest or cannibalism are examples of taboo mores in most advanced industrial countries today. *Folkways* is a term that usually refers to customs and conventions that do not run so deeply into the heart of a culture's value structure. William Graham Sumner's (1906) classic work, *Folkways,*

however, deals with a comparative study of mores and folkways, and many anthropologists use the terms interchangeably. The point for the curriculum worker is
to remember that choices in any culture about what should be taught reflect the
mores, folkways, and other conventions that give members of that society a sense of
cohesiveness, commonality, and stability.

Social Class.   To a large extent, different social classes live in different worlds.
Members of the upper socioeconomic classes live by different rules and conventions,
sometimes even different mores and often different folkways than do middle-class,
proletarian (working-class), and lower-class members of the same society. Fussell
(1983) insightfully and wittily depicts some of the prime differences among outward
appearances of values in American culture today. He further characterizes an X class,
the members of which consciously attempt to determine their own values and rules
rather than mindlessly taking for granted those ascribed by income, birth, and association. Havighurst (1981) also noted the increment of an *underclass*, particularly in
major cities, which refers to those who have no income, connections, or even social
identity. They are "down-and-outers" who are almost always there to stay.

Some curriculum writers (Apple, 1979, 1982a, b; Apple and Weis, 1983; Giroux,
1981, 1983) argue that curriculum decisions reflect values that maintain social class
hierarchies as they presently exist. This hegemonic process effectually prevents social mobility, democratic action, and the exercise of personal growth. In other words,
each class is taught the values that keep it in place, thus ensuring the continued
power of the upper classes. Populated by faculty who are middle or working class,
most public and parochial schools promote middle-class values. Thus, they are quite
familiar places to middle-class students, somewhat familiar to working-class students,
but quite foreign to the few upper-class and many lower-class students who attend
them. While some educational research points to the power of schools to transform
students' lives (Good, Biddle, and Brophy, 1975), work by other empirical and
critical sociologists alike (Coleman et al., 1966; Jencks et al., 1972; Connell et al.,
1982; Willis, 1977; Wexler, 1977, 1983) suggests that the socioeconomic background
of students provides profound impact on the kind and quality of education they
experience (i.e., that home and social class are more influential than school in a
person's outlook, education, and accomplishment).

Mass Media.   A third value context derives from the influence of mass media and
includes the impact of television, film, video, radio, and computer games as well as
print in magazines, books, newspapers, and other sources. Some of these influences
are overt and obvious, such as the vast array of information at our disposal through
the alleged value-neutral presentation of news media and through the direct admonishment to buy products from advertisers. Other influences are much more subtle,
such as the "medium is the message" presentation by McLuhan and Fiore (1967) in
their inventory of effects of electronic technology on values as they reshape patterns
of human interdependence. Since the time of McLuhan's writing, scholars have been
intrigued with subliminal as well as overt influences of the media on human values.
The entire issue of the Fall 1982 *Daedalus*, journal of the American Academy of Arts
and Sciences, addressed the interplay and impact of print and video culture. In
Inside Prime Time Todd Gitlin (1983) argues that television has replaced government

as the preeminent authority figure in our culture, but even more dangerous, he suggests, is the discontinuity it produces in the human psyche—segments of life and the world quickly move on and probably offset the human capacity to give sustained attention to problems and possibilities in everyday experience. Bagdikian's (1983) research demonstrates that a mere fifty corporations monopolize what America hears, reads, and views; the power of the media in shaping human values may be greater than we think. Yet Graber (1984) says that the media are unable to get people to attend to information that they find uninteresting, irrelevant, or contradictory to their existing understandings and beliefs. In any event, those who create curriculum and those who learn from it are both conditioned by mass media in ways unexperienced by those of two generations past.

Personal Beliefs.   The personal beliefs of all engaged in the educative process invariably affect the experiences that bring learning in schools. Beliefs of administrators who determine what resources shall be appropriate or what funding strived for are key factors in decisions. Beliefs of teachers who interpret curriculum to students often make a profound difference in the image that curriculum takes in student lives. For example, the elementary school teacher who dislikes science and teaches it with reluctance will communicate a lack of enthusiasm to his or her students. Similarly, a teacher who receives curriculum guidelines for a unit involving controversial social issues and is instructed to present several positions on those issues in a nonpartisan manner will convey, if successful, an attitude of neutrality to students. Thus, writers of the curriculum may contradict the purpose of interesting students in social issues because their belief in neutrality may foster neutrality itself or a blasé attitude toward those issues. Studies reported by Klein, Lacefield, and Griffin at the 1984 Annual Meeting of AERA point to the integral part played by beliefs in all levels of curriculum decision making.

There is also ample evidence that beliefs of students affect the ways in which they receive curriculum and instruction. Posner (1982) illustrates this with examples drawn from cognitive psychology. From critical theory, Apple and Weis (1983) point to the contestation and resistance that students exert on curriculum as their perspectives meet differing value systems embedded in the curriculum. In a broad sense, the realm of beliefs involves that of personal psychology, the understanding of which might be derived from personality theories of such writers as Freud, Jung, Gordon Allport, Alfred Adler, Abraham Maslow, George Kelly, Walter Mischell, and a range of developmental psychologists such as Piaget and Kohlberg.

Economic Contexts

In seeking to understand curriculum, one should remember the song from the musical, *Cabaret*, that says, "Money makes the world go around" or the advice of "Deep Throat" in *All the President's Men* that the road to key culprits behind the Watergate break-in is to "follow the money." One of the most underrated forces in curriculum literature is economics. Do economic factors of a given historical period dictate a tendency toward conservative or liberal curricular practices? Do the purse strings, in other words, control the character of thought that propels educational innovation? Let us continue to raise questions such as these in greater specificity.

Schools as Paths to Success.   The conventional wisdom holds that schooling yields socialization, social mobility, and self-realization. These are three major functions that Ralph Tyler (1981) observes should be performed by schools; nevertheless, there is often a great hiatus between that which is and that which should be. What does it mean to become socialized? Does it mean to learn to take for granted the values, norms, and rules of one's group? Does it mean to adhere to the values of one's social class, and if it does, is this not a hindrance to social mobility? Does socialization in schools lead to more than students learning to adhere to peer-developed codes of behavior? To what extent does mobility up the economic ladder support or retard self-realization?

Occupational Promotion.   Increasingly greater attention is given to job preparation through school. Work-study programs are a common occurrence. Politicians running for office rarely disagree on one matter in the 1980s, namely, the need for more jobs and the desirability to get all citizens of working age and in good health involved in the work force. Is the assumption of this need a warranted one? In advanced technological societies, do we need to maintain the ideal of everyone working? Or would it be better to encourage all students to think seriously about what it means to lead a worthwhile life? Behind the cries for jobs, we hear about the need for "high-tech" jobs. Simultaneously, we hear of the need for greater equity, social justice, and nononsense liberal education courses as opposed to life-adjustment education. Responding to the acknowledged and mandated need to integrate racial, ethnic, and socioeconomic groups, many large urban school systems created magnet schools. Often, these magnet schools augmented their attractiveness by designating a specialty (e.g., classics, arts, sciences, foreign languages). In Houston, for example, as of 1983 magnet schools totaled thirty-three elementary school programs, thirteen middle school programs, and fifteen high school programs (Borman and Spring, 1984). Borman and Spring also identify the tendency for magnet schools to move away from their original purposes, to promote liberal arts and to integrate diverse groups in society, toward occupational preparation. In effect, this tracks students in occupations that solidify their retention in the economic class of their home. Witness magnet schools that prepare secretaries, police, performing artists, and so on. One might legitimately argue that such schooling prepares students for the world of work, but it does not prepare them for social mobility in the world. How powerful is our governance by corporations that want people's labor so forcefully that it prevents their growth? To what extent does schooling for jobs prevent education for self-realization and for building a better world? Or is sound occupational preparation the way to build a better world?

Publisher Sales.   Educational Products Information Exchange (EPIE, 1979) contends that 85 to 90 percent of classroom time is based on commercially published curricular materials—textbooks, workbooks, skills management systems, worksheets, learning packages, computer software, and so on. If their estimates are correct, the authors of such materials must be considered principal curriculum developers for schools. What are their purposes? Like any capitalistic business enterprise, the bottom line for publishers is profit. Profit usually accrues from systematic study of the laws of supply and demand. What will be most marketable, that which sells best, is that which is sold. Can that which sells best be equated with that which *is* best? To what extent do authors of commercially prepared curriculum materials genuinely determine purposes and content based upon the serious study of educational philosophy, psychology of learning, consultation with subject specialists, study of society, and study of learners? How can their materials be tailored to unique needs and interests of particular communities, racial and ethnic populations, socioeconomic classes, and individuals? When one finds textual variation (say, the absence of integrated photographs in regions known for racial bias or the removal of information on evolution in fundamentalist Christian areas), one can assume that the market has prevailed over concern for educational quality.

Sources of Funding. The rush toward the latest funding priority established by major foundations and government agencies is a well-known phenomenon in universities. Newsletters and special bulletins carry messages of the most fundable research initiatives, and representatives are sent to Washington to acquire the latest "scoop" on next developments in funding. Faculty members are often evaluated on the basis of the number of research dollars they are able to bring into the university.

This state of affairs is nearly as heated in large school districts where state, federal, and private monies are available to those who can make the best case for need. This might mean that priority is given to those who can identify large quantities of minority populations, mentally or physically handicapped students, pockets of poverty, or who can creatively justify programs that seek to overcome the latest deficiencies of schools such as those identified by the high-tech needs of industry and given special attention by the mass media.

If educational institutions do not enter into the competition for funds, do they not soon lose status and fail to acquire their most laudable educational goals? If they do enter the competition for funding have they, however, not exchanged bandwagonism for the pursuit of excellence—the desired for the desirable? Yet, if they have an image of excellence but not the wherewithal to move toward it, what good does the image do? But can the image of excellence survive for those who hold onto the bandwagon of funding fads as the prime motivator? Or, do the authors of funding guidelines actually have a solid image of what is genuinely needed?

Multinational Corporations. In his last book, *GRUNCH of Giants* (1983), twentieth-century Renaissance man R. Buckminster Fuller warned vehemently of the torrid rise of multinational corporations from the military-industrial complex that began to evolve following World War II. He argues that since these economic titans have outgrown the capacity of contemporary political units to govern them, they threaten to reap world bankruptcy. If Fuller's predictions are true, is it not all the more necessary that education not follow and support but lead, rebuild, and invent new forms of governance that can overcome GRUNCH, which Fuller explains as a quasi-acronym for Gross Universal Cash Heist? But is it possible to lead when education is so meek? Or might the meek be able to lead one day?

We have dealt with macrocontexts thus far. While politics, values, and economics play a major role in what curriculum becomes, their impact is certainly not the whole picture. Let us now turn to what occurs within the school environment itself.

INSIDE-OF-SCHOOL CONTEXTS

The politics, values, and economics of a society are indeed powerful in providing boundaries and prerequisites for what is done in schools. To be sure, they set the tone for curriculum that might and might not be developed and experienced. Nevertheless, *might* is a key term here; these forces indicate what is probable, but they do not determine what is possible. Those who live, work, and act in the school environment itself are not mere automatons. They build upon, contest, and exclude, as well as accept values, politics, and economics of the larger society. In other words, those who live in schools have considerable weight to throw around in determining what those schools are like and what kind of curriculum is offered by them. Let us now identify seven interrelated dimensions of within-school contexts that create curriculum.

Overt Curriculum

The intended or explicit curriculum is what the schools formally admit to teaching. It usually consists of skills, concepts, principles, appreciations, and values that school officials overtly provide for students. Statements of policy, purpose, and mission that appear in curriculum guides usually delineate overt curricula, although some of it is merely understood. For example, all of the topics in textbooks used by a school are not explicated in curriculum guides and other policy statements; neither is the range of content tested on achievement tests that are used as a measuring stick of student performance and school accountability. In sum, the overt curriculum is what schools admit they teach or at least offer to learners.

Frame Factors

Two Swedish educational researchers, Urban Dahllöf (1971) and Ulf Lundgren (1972), have identified and sought to understand better organizational features of school that contribute to student achievement. Thus, they developed the concept of *frame factors* to define elements in the context of schooling that affect achievement. Frame factors that lie beyond the control of teachers and local building administrators are school location, general ability of students, and large-scale scheduling policies such as the duration of the school year, length of school day, and vacation dates. Frame factors that are within the command of teachers are the level of objectives that they teach, intraclass grouping practices, and the quantity and quality of time on task. The frame of time has had much exposure in the literature, and often is applied to the ways in which teachers use time to maintain attention to the tasks to be accomplished. Harnischfeger and Wiley (1976), however, observe that we need more work on actual pupil pursuits in relation to time. Bloom (1984) and his colleagues and students have done considerable work on the relation of time to quality and type of instruction, and he points to the value of tutorial relationships as a model for time use in mastery learning.

Physical Plant

The structural design of the school building itself shapes curriculum in numerous ways. The traditional egg-crate design of school buildings can instill the conception of learning as something that occurs passively after one enters a designated room with a teacher who has specialized in a certain age level or subject matter area. Here students of the same age, and often similar background, are given the same treatment or subject matter and learning activities. An implicit assumption holds that like parts are fashioned as uniform products; the factory metaphor depicts taken-for-granted practices of this kind.

Occasionally, a new form of school construction reaches a sizable degree of popularity; in the late 1960s and early 1970s, this was the open space school. American architects caught the fancy taken by some American educators toward the British primary school and also noticed interest in the counterculture free schools often located in storefronts and other makeshift environments. They observed, as well, the popularity of humanistic psychology (e.g., Rogers, 1969, 1983; ASCD, 1962) and deduced that they could convince school administrators that schools with large open spaces instead of conventional rooms would lead to greater openness among human beings. As administrators from school systems with good reputations built open-space schools, others followed suit. With the new architecture came curricular modification, sometimes by careful planning and at other times by trial and error.

The middle school movement (Kindred and Wolotkiewicz, 1976) in the late 1970s and early 1980s is another example. A new style of school plant was built ostensibly to overcome certain difficulties found in working with junior high school students. In fact, the slight alteration in grade level (taking the sixth grade out of the elementary school) was done for economic rather than educational reasons in many places.

While it is clear that both the examples of open space schools and middle schools sometimes are guided by well-planned educational ideologies, it is also the case that many practices in the name of such innovations go unguided by carefully developed rationales, reflection, and study. Lacking the latter, they are illustrations of educational bandwagonism at its worst and demonstrate how a desire for new styles in physical school buildings can preempt, obfuscate, and even guide curriculum. Moreover, the lack or possession of physical facilities (from desks, to libraries, to computers) can provide similar effects as the structure of the building itself. Many are the instances in recent years of school districts purchasing large-scale skills management packages or computer hardware without having a curricular rationale that guides their use. Such purchases are too often done without attention to congruence with the rest of the program or the feasibility of implementation of using current personnel, facilities, and finances.

Hidden Curriculum

The hidden curriculum of schooling is that which is taught implicitly, rather than explicitly, by the school experience. Since the late 1960s, school has been acknowledged as a subculture with rules, mores, folkways, and emergent values of its own. Thus, ways of life derived from school experience convey learnings. Though often unintended or unnoticed (hence, *hidden*), these constitute a curriculum that frequently carries profound learnings. For example, Jackson's study of elementary school students, *Life in Classrooms* (1968), shows the great impact of school socialization on learning that takes place in schools; students learn from a curriculum of living in a crowd of agemates, living under conditions of power, and incurring frequent evaluation. Dreeben's sociological study of schooling, *On What Is Learned in School*

(1968), demonstrates that the societal contexts of the factory, the military, and the church make their way into school organizations in subtle but pronounced ways. In the ASCD, attention to the "unstudied" curriculum under the leadership of Norman Overly (1970), and in the same year Snyder's (1970) illustration of hidden curricula in the lives of college students promoted greater consciousness about implicit curricula in student lives. These sources point out that students learn well "the ropes" of classroom success. Students learn to look attentive, express admiration for the teacher's insights, nod appropriately in the midst of lectures, and efficiently sort out the real requirements from the total array of suggested readings and assignments. In short, students learn much from the social context of classroom and corridor life. It shapes their thoughts and feelings about themselves and others and is a guiding force in their lives.

Another form of hidden curriculum accrues from messages that are subtly intended. When teachers model behavior, when they reinforce some students' behavior with positive comments, they do not explicitly say, "do such and such," but they implicitly convey that meaning. The teacher dresses neatly, says "pardon me" when he or she yawns, or places a paper in the waste basket without loudly crumpling it into a ball. He or she calls for a response from the student who quietly raises a hand but ignores the one who speaks out without permission and praises the row of students who sit quietly with tidy desks at the end of the day and allows them to exit first. These are examples of a kind of intended hidden curriculum.

Finally, it is obvious in the examples of teacher modeling that teachers don't model universal values; rather, they usually exhibit values and life-styles of the middle class. If schools perpetuate values of the middle class, how does this influence students from lower, working, and upper classes? Curriculum writers such as Apple (1979, 1982a, 1982b) and Giroux (1983) argue that schools essentially reproduce class hierarchies and inequities by failing to attend critically to the knowledge they provide as curriculum. For example, the textbook that predominates in most classrooms can be seen as symbolizing knowledge as a commodity received from experts as contrasted with knowledge as something produced by ordinary experience. One might argue that children who learn to see knowledge as a received commodity begin to view themselves primarily as clients, patients, and spectators, as well as students. Anyon (1980) and others provide evidence that children of different social classes are treated differentially by the hidden curriculum of schooling. Children from higher social classes are treated as being capable of generating knowledge while those of lower classes are taught to be docile recipients of it. The message that upper classes control production of values and knowledge as well as material commodities is transmitted by schools, while they also depict lower classes as consumers of the same. Knowledge and values, to put it blatantly, are treated similarly to soaps, deodorants, soft drinks, beer, and automobiles on television ads.

Extracurricular Activities

Noncourse experiences such as athletics, clubs, musical organizations, dramatics, and student government are far from hidden. Some argue that students, parents, and even educators themselves take extracurricular activities more seriously than school subjects. This is not to say that extracurricular activities do not have hidden dimensions. It may be the intent of interschool athletic teams to foster sportsmanship, loyalty, and determination, whereas, they may subtly teach overzealous competition and a win-at-all-costs attitude.

Otto (1982) points out that "extracurricular activities are extra not because they exist outside of the formal learning process and curriculum, but because they provide an additional learning experience" (p. 226). He reviews research that could serve as a basis for policy. Some argue vehemently for the worth of extracurricular activities on the basis that they teach useful content and social skills, enhance peer status, and help one make important contacts. Yet research neither confirms nor rejects such assertions in any overall sense. Otto (1982) raises questions that are in need of investigation:

> *Are the benefits more pronounced if participation occurs early or late in high school years? Do benefits occur primarily in individual or team activities? Same-sex or coeducational activities? High or low supervision programs? Do activities that closely parallel the structure of the curriculum have stronger effects than less compatible programs? Does group size make a difference? [p. 225]*

It may well be that these questions cannot be answered in highly generalizable ways. Nevertheless, they are important for school teachers and administrators to address in light of their own particular situations.

Null Curriculum

"Null curriculum," a term coined by Eisner (1979, pp. 83–92), refers quite simply to the curriculum not taught. It may seem strange to think of the curriculum that is not taught, but we often teach by our silence on many matters. When art, for example, is taught only once a week (and then as a construction paper, glue, and scissors project), much of the appreciation of art's role in culture and perception is missed by the students. If social studies is all history and geography and not anthropology, economics, sociology, and political science, the latter are part of the null curriculum. Advocates of values education, death education, drug education, family life education, and technological education are lobbying for the inclusion of topics that have been part of the null curriculum. The prevalence of autocratic classrooms often means that democracy (as a way of life as distinguished from precepts about it) is often part of the null curriculum. Folk singer Biff Rose once said, "Be prepared to meet those persons who, in their silence, will convert you." We need to realize that students in our schools continuously meet curricula that provide an absence that converts them in many ways. We need to ask ourselves: What worthwhile knowledge and experiences do we leave out as we make curricular decisions?

NONSCHOOL CURRICULA

When we consider the fact that every human being learns from experience, and when we reflect on the sizable amounts of time students spend outside of school, it is obvious that a great deal of learning transpires in nonschool organizations, mass media, peer groups, homes and families, vocations, and avocations.

To purport to teach students without knowing the knowledge that they have acquired from nonschool experience is akin to sitting in the physician's waiting room and receiving a prescription from page 47 of the *Physician's Desk Reference* along with others whose symptoms and needs may be very different. Yet it is the case in schools, as ludicrous as it may seem, that students whose knowledge and experiences we scarcely know are given treatments anyway.

Granted, the use of the term *curriculum* for the structure of knowledge acquisition in nonschool settings may seem strange. One can, of course, find a process that appears curricular in the succession of activities needed for one to achieve higher ranks in scouting and related formal organizations for children and youth. Yet there is nothing like an overt plan or curriculum guide in homes, peer groups, and hobbies or avocations. Likewise, although mass media such as television programming and vocations or jobs are carefully planned, it is difficult to think of either as learning experiences. What is needed since children and youth (all of us) learn from each of these areas is a broadened conceptualization of curriculum. If we learn from an experience, there must be within it implicit purposes, content, organization, and evaluation. Thus, as I have argued elsewhere (Schubert, 1981), these and other curricular categories may be used as means to analyze descriptively nonschool experiences for curricular implications.

While it is possible to gain knowledge of nonschool domains of learning from psychological and sociological literatures, it is even more important that educators develop a knowledge base about nonschool learning in the lives of students. Such knowledge could surely derive from formal research studies that produce general knowledge. Of greatest concrete benefit to particular schools and classrooms, however, would be knowledge that administrators and teachers gather through interaction with their own students. While some teachers and administrators do this informally, how can it be accomplished on a broader scale?

First, teachers and curriculum leaders must acknowledge that the ecology of classroom life does not stop at the schoolhouse walls. It extends far and wide into the community and culture (Schubert and Schubert, 1982). Second, they must realize that the outlooks of their students are wrought by impacts from a number of nonschool sources in their lives: homes and families, peers, media, nonschool organizations, vocations, and avocations or hobbies.

While teachers and curriculum leaders might read and benefit from sociological and psychological literature on each of these areas, they need more specific insights into the lives of their students. They need to know about the experiences that fashion the outlooks embodied in the learners who sit before them. To advocate what a given student needs to enhance his or her growth toward greater maturity by this or that mode of teaching would seem to be impossible without a fairly accurate picture of the current status of that student's outlook. To be honest, however, this goes on in widespread fashion in schools today. Curricular prescriptions are made with little or no knowledge of the outlooks of students, the lives outside school that forged those outlooks, and the world to which students must return with the changed outlooks that are designed to enhance their lives. It may be that we do more harm than good when we accomplish what we set out to do. A paucity of writing exists on how knowledge of nonschool curricula can be obtained in practical situations by teachers and curriculum leaders. Let us consider some of the questions that teachers might ask about students in their classrooms to gain information about their nonschool curriculum in the following areas: homes and families, peer relationships, mass media, formal organizations, vocations and avocations.

Homes and Families

What messages do students get about the value of schooling? What do they see it as good for? Can discussion broaden this conception? Do students come into contact with persons who are actively attempting to become educated in their homes and families? Is such education of a formal or informal variety? Do family members take an interest in and discuss ideas or projects dealt with in school? What does the family environment teach? Is it worthwhile to know and experience? How can teachers take an interest in students' family life without being nosy or prying?

Peer Relationships

What do informal peer associations teach students that is worthwhile to know and experience? To what extent does this support or hinder purposes of school curriculum? What needs that students experience in their peer groups should be addressed in the school curriculum? How can teachers relate peer group concerns to the subject matter they are expected to teach?

Mass Media

What television, movies, music, and written materials do students experience? Why is their interest focused in these areas? What needs do the content of television programs, movies, music, and written material (magazines, books, newspapers, etc.) meet for the students? What needs are met by the form of these media? For example, students can choose what to view or read in the outside world. They can listen, read, or watch for their own purposes. Are these needs revealed and met in student experience with media that school curriculum could respond to more adequately? Can teachers and curriculum makers learn about content or method from the media that attract their students outside of school? How can content of media that captures student interest be used as a springboard for developing concepts, skills, and ideas that curriculum developers deem worthwhile to teach?

Formal Organizations

The range of such organizations is vast: from Scouting and 4-H to church groups, street gangs, musical groups, sport leagues, and service clubs. What do these organizations teach? Which students belong to which organizations? What seems to make a student join one or another? How can school teachers relate these outside activities to purposes of the school experience? How can the teachers acknowledge interest in their students' out-of-school pursuits? Many of these organizations have a curriculum that teaches a great deal (both overtly and covertly). How do the purposes, learning experiences, instruction, environment, and evaluation in these organizations compare with that provided by schools? Can curriculum developers in schools learn from the ways curriculum in nonschool organizations enhance interests and meet needs?

Vocations

Students of high school age often have part-time jobs. What do they learn from these jobs? What are their thoughts and feelings about their lives as workers? How does this compare with their thoughts and feeling about school work? Students who do not have jobs are still surrounded by a world of vocations. Family members have jobs, are striving to find jobs, suffer from joblessness, or are independently wealthy. In any case, what images of vocation do they have? How realistic is their conception of requirements for certain jobs? What are the students' aspirations vocationally, if they have any? Does school curriculum speak to these aspirations? How might it do so better?

Avocations

What hobbies or outside interests do students have? What do they know a great deal about? How might their expertise be tapped in school? How can school learning be enhanced by making productive analogies between students' school work and that which they know well outside of school?

Toward Curricular Ecology

These are but a few of the kinds of questions that teachers might reflect on as they consider the ecology of curricula that exists in their culture. It is interesting to note that in analyzing each of these out-of-school curricular areas, one could use categories that are usually reserved for school curricula. Using Tyler's Rationale (1949), one could inquire into purposes, learning experiences, organization, and evaluation. Although these are rarely explicated except in some of the formal organizations, they are there implicitly and learning of some kind is taking place. Alternatively, one could analyze these domains in terms of the Schwab's (1973) interaction of teachers, learners, subject matter, and milieu. In so doing, these terms become metaphors for those who teach, those who are taught, that which is taught, and the context of teaching.

The main point is that varieties of curricula, often bearing contradictory messages, infuse student lives daily. Educators at all levels must strive to understand these curricula better, especially their interrelationships. Such understanding could serve at least five central purposes: (1) to provide greater background for teachers and curriculum leaders to create curriculum that responds to particular needs and interests of students, and thereby enables more personalized teaching; (2) to learn more about the ingredients that often make students more responsive to nonschool curriculum than to that of school, and thereby use insights of nonschool educators to enhance education that takes place in school; (3) to enable professional educators in schools to share their knowledge about curriculum development and teaching with nonschool educators, and thereby enable the latter to realize their purposes more effectively; (4) to create greater knowledge of the spectrum of life experience that educates, and thereby contribute to research on how human beings arrive at perspectives or outlooks that guide their lives; and (5) to establish greater communication among all who educate children and youth, and thereby create the possibility of an ecological response to developing curricula that meet their overall needs more fully.

CONCLUSION

We have now seen that numerous contexts set the stage for curriculum. Outside-of-school contexts of political, economic, and value character provide a very broad and penetrating milieu. At the same time, forces within the school provide inner context: overt curriculum, frame factors, the school plant, hidden curricula, extracurricular activities, and the null curriculum. Finally, nonschool curricula are seen to have a profound influence on student lives.

COMMENTARIES

Experientialist

I want to go further than the author of this chapter. He claims that contexts (political, value, and economic) are not *mere influences* and asserts that they are much more profound factors in the creation of curriculum. He is on the right track but stops short of realizing that the total configuration of contexts in fact, *is* the curriculum, that is, the lived experience that is wrought by one's situation.

At the broadest level, this lived experience is an interaction among, or integration of, political, economic, and cultural values. They are inseparable in action. As defined by the author, I would say that values and economics are most important. This is because political dimensions often refer to formal hierarchies. The real decisions in any society, the most important political exchanges, are more subtle. They occur behind the scenes.

The basis of any society's value context lies, of course, in the composite of individual belief systems. For this reason, I assert that community is the most important sector in an individual's life. The nonschool curricula are salient features of the curriculum of community life; yet I am surprised that the author did not develop the idea of community further as the configuration of nonschool curricula. This is done well by John Bremer (1979), founder of the Parkway School Without Walls in Philadelphia, a secondary school that actually used the community as its classroom. The city itself can be seen as a living curriculum as developed by Mayberry (1980) with special reference to urban education.

When dealing with urban education, we find that economic and social class hierarchies come through more blatantly than anywhere else. The contrasts of rich and poor, and those of majority and minority racial, ethnic, and ideological groups, stretch before our eyes in a single continuum in today's major cities. The quality of community life afforded those who live in different sectors of the city is immensely diverse; thus, curriculum as a function of social life differs greatly from place to place within our large urban environments. These are, however, microcosms of whole societies and of the world itself. We must come to grips with the unequal distribution of knowledge that parallels the unequal distribution of goods and services throughout our world as well as within individual societies.

These broad and penetrating factors make the curriculum of schools what it is. The overt curriculum is analogous to overt political systems; both are largely ineffectual in the provision of the deepest human needs and interests. The real messages of curriculum in schools are communicated by the hidden and null curricula, just as real political messages derive from economic and interpersonal transactions behind the political facade. The social life of the school, as that of everyday experience, teaches the most important knowledge, skills, and values. This is why it is so important to recognize the importance of Dewey's (1916) call for the integration of democracy and education that recognizes the social construction of knowledge and has been heeded all too seldom. If democratic participation rather than autocratic coercion were the lived experience and spirit of our schools, a new vision of life would be possible. Through it we could reconstruct a more just and equitable society.

Intellectual Traditionalist

The value of having a common curriculum for all regardless of social or economic stature, or of racial or ethnic origins, is that it provides for equal opportunity. As a matter of fact, it provides for more opportunity than does the experientialist, who caters to individual interests, and more than the social behaviorist, who devises strategies that supposedly fit needs and learning habitudes. I say this at the beginning of my comments on context because I am often unfairly accused of being elitist. The elitism that I proffer, if any, is one that holds that all persons are elite in the sense that they are worthy to receive excellence in their education.

Thus, my position transcends many of the forces brought by context. While the values propagated by media, mores, folkways, social class, and personal beliefs play a role, they are tempered by being tested against the wisdom of the ages. The transitory nature of pronouncements of political pundits comes up against the challenge of political thought of the greatest theorists of all time. Furthermore, the best test of the study of ideas for its own sake lies in students and teachers alike who realize that the benefits of such study supersede the banality of the marketplace that offers the temptation of jobs, funding, false images of success, and the ebb and flow of corporate wiles as substitutes for truth, beauty, and goodness.

If the sights of educators are set high enough that they keep the classics in the fore, the overt curriculum will so infuse the life of the school that there will be no time left for the likes of hidden curriculum. Null curriculum will be anticipated and will be granted null status only because it is less important, and extracurricular activities will play an insignificant (if not a nonexistent) role because students will be interested in matters of greater consequence for their lives. Finally, on the matter of nonschool curriculum, who would deny that media, peers, families, jobs, hobbies, and nonschool organizations shape ideas? But that is beside the point. The point is that classics are classics because they speak to all walks of life. Knowing individual backgrounds of students is of little importance to educators whose subject matter speaks to all when taught with commitment, understanding, and enthusiasm.

Social Behaviorist

The context consists of a huge number of factors that influence curricular decision making. Sometimes the influence is great, and at other times it is small. What is important is to delineate as many specific influences as possible and to plan research that reveals the magnitude and nature of each influence. We also need research that demonstrates successful ways to deal with political, cultural, and economic forces. Armed with verifiable strategies, curriculum administrators should be able to deal more productively with such forces than when they are forced by lack of knowledge to make policy by sheer guesswork. More research needs to be brought together as a basis for curriculum policy and productivity as Walberg presents for educational policymakers in *Improving Educational Standards and Productivity* (1982).

The key, however, to dealing with context is to so thoroughly coordinate the design of curriculum around the conditions germane to learning (see Gagné and Briggs, 1979, and many issues of *The Journal of Instructional Development*) that the impact of contextual variables is controlled, lessened, and, if possible, extinguished. While the scientific basis for dealing with contextual variables is in its infancy, that of designing instructional technology to implement curriculum design is at a rather mature level. Hence, it is possible to design learning that virtually eliminates undesirable values and political and economic influences and controls for SES (socioeconomic status), racial, and ethnic orientation. Moreover, carefully designed treatment specifications that are systematically verified during implementation take into the plan variations in school plant and frame factors. Likewise, sound design builds extracurricular activities into the program. It all but eliminates the hidden curriculum, for sound planning leaves no stone unturned. Research also provides a basis for deciding among competing responses to the question of what should be taught. Thus, the null curriculum is no surprise; it is null by choice if based on thorough research and planning.

Nonschool learning is an important new area for research, but it should not be labeled *curriculum*. Curriculum is carefully and systematically planned by professionals who use research findings as a basis for their work. Nonschool areas rarely do this. However, it is important to tap the social science research literature on effects of mass media, family, peer group, formal organizations, and work on children, youth, and adults whom we purport to educate. These findings can serve as important generalizations from which research specifically related to school curriculum can evolve.

SUGGESTED READING

I argue that the best book on the relation of social context to curriculum and the educative process is still Dewey's *Democracy and Education* (1916). Readers who wish to know what significant past theorists have said about the relation of curriculum to society should consult Curti (1935), Rugg (1947), or Stanley (1953), three classics in the field of social foundations of education.

Contemporary overviews include a fine collection on value conflicts and their connection with curriculum issues, edited by Schaffarzick and Sykes (1979); a collection of articles that appeared during the revolutionary period of the 1960s in *Educational Leadership*, by Robert Leeper (1971); an NEA publication edited by Edinger, Houts, and Meyer (1981); and an article on bureaucracy and curriculum theory by Kliebard (1971).

Two general books on the politics of education are cited even though curricular aspects need to be extrapolated; both are by Frederick Wirt and Michael Kirst (1975, 1982).

Works by Michael Apple are recommended for the influence of economics of social class on educational practice (Apple, 1979, 1982b, 1983 with Weis).

An excellent collection of articles and excerpts from books that deal with the hidden curriculum is provided by Giroux and Purpel (1982). Also suggested is Jackson's *Life in Classrooms*, (1968), which did much to air the hidden curriculum issue. Chapter Five of Elliot Eisner's *The Educational Imagination* (1985) is the best source for contrasting the explicit, implicit, and null curricula.

On the issue of nonschool curriculum, I suggest my own article in *Educational Forum* (Schubert, 1981) and the recent NSSE Yearbook (Part 1) on nonschool learning edited by Mario Fantini and Robert Sinclair (1985) under the title, *Education in School and Nonschool Settings*.

For a careful methodology for developing a language of the schooling process in social context, I suggest *Dilemmas of Schooling* by Ann and Harold Berlak (1981). Reynolds and Skilbeck (1976) provide a cultural perspective on the classroom and curricular issues that interpenetrate it.

Finally, I would be remiss if I did not acknowledge the contribution of synoptic texts to the social foundations of curriculum. It is interesting to compare the treatment of contextual forces in synoptic texts of different eras, for example, Smith, Stanley, and Shores (1957), Taba (1962), Zais (1976), and Tanner and Tanner (1980).

RECOMMENDATIONS FOR REFLECTION

1. Reflect on your image of what a good learning situation is. If you are currently teaching, for example, think of your current situation. Now, list five to ten of the contextual factors that prevent your ideal image from being realized.

2. Try to recall a situation, out of school, in which you grew a great deal. (Broadly speaking, growth involves learning.) Identify five of the salient features of this context that spurred you on to greater growth.

3. How could the contextual features listed in activity 2 be applied to the situation in which you teach?

4. Characterize the political, value, and economic situation that surrounds your educational situation. In what ways do these forces inhibit the best education? How do the prevailing contextual forces facilitate good teaching?

5. Look again at each of the specific influences under the categories of politics, values, and economics. Rank these influences from strong to weak in your situation. Do strong and weak parallel direct and indirect, or is it possible to have some very strong but quite indirect forces?

6. Teachers and administrators are more familiar with in-school influences. Identify how frame factors, physical plant, publisher sales, funding sources, hidden curriculum, extracurricular activities, and null curricula influence the overt curriculum in your situation.

7. Can you identify ways in which the overt curriculum actually fashions or contributes to the impact of hidden curriculum, extracurricular activities, and null curriculum?

8. Pretend that you are a visitor from a distant galaxy (a kind of intergalactic educational anthropologist) observing your own educational situation. What do you see differently about the several aspects of your school curriculum?

9. What are some of the significant nonschool curricula in your own life; that is, what forces have contributed to the ways in which you see the world and the perspectives you have on life?

10. What do you know about the nonschool curricula in your students' lives? Use a list of your students' names and see how much you can say about the influence of the following on them: home, family, peers, mass media, nonschool organizations, jobs, hobbies. How can you discover more about these aspects of your students' lives? Try to do so.

11. What might curriculum or learning experiences be like if you were able to use findings from activity 10 as organizing centers for curriculum development? Discuss one or two scenarios of this type.

5

✦ Philosophy: The Realms of Assumptions ✦

You can't do without philosophy, since everything has its hidden
meaning which we must know.
>   MAXIM GORKY *The Zykovos* (1914)

It might be a hard thing to expect educators to be philosophers,
but can they be anything else?
>   MAX BLACK *Harvard Educational Review* (1956)

It is better to emit a scream in the shape of a theory than to be
entirely insensible to the jars and incongruities of life and take
everything as it comes in forlorn stupidity.
>   ROBERT LOUIS STEVENSON "Crabbed Age and Youth"
>   *Virginibus and Puerisque* (1881)

Philosophy begins in wonder. And, at the end, when philosophical
thought has done its best, the wonder remains.
>   ALFRED NORTH WHITEHEAD *Modes of Thought* (1938)

SETTING THE STAGE

Philosophy lies at the heart of educational endeavor. This is perhaps more evident in
the curriculum domain than in any other, for curriculum is a response to the question
of how to live a good life. The latter is presupposed when we ask what is worthwhile
to know or experience. What is the reason for knowing or experiencing something, if
it is not to live a better life? John Dewey (1916) supported this emphasis when he
suggested that education is the testing ground of philosophy itself. This idea implies
that the worth of philosophical inquiry is determined by the human growth or education that accrues from it.

These observations reflect the problem of the relationship between theory and practice that has beset curriculum inquiry since humans began to ponder the ways in which others should be inducted into the human race. Of what use are these ponderings, the reflections, the theory, the philosophy? How do they affect practice? How does practice influence theory? What good can theory and practice do for one another?

One way to respond to such questions is to realize that theory or philosophical assumptions are ever present, whether we consciously reflect on them or not. Even if we refuse to think about the assumptions that underlie our practical work as educators, some set of assumptions always rules. If we go to an instructional materials display and select materials primarily because they will keep students busy, or because they are easy to store, or because they contain pretty illustrations, we have already accepted certain assumptions. In the case of these examples, priority is given to expedience, custodial care, and entertainment as contrasted to defensible notions of genuine learning, and cosmetic appearance is granted precedence over educational desirability.

Any time that we alter our mode of educating others, we indirectly influence the character of some of our other assumptions about education. If a workshop on classroom management convinces us that a new mode of discipline should be used in our classroom, implementing this change will subtly or profoundly affect the assumptions upon which we operate. It may conflict with assumptions that guide other aspects of our curriculum. If the accepted model is behavioristic and most of our curriculum is humanistic, there is conflict. The new mode will have reverberations throughout the entire curriculum system. It will affect all aspects of classroom life and culture.

The assumptions that we report possessing may not be the ones that actually guide us. The old adage applies: our actions may speak so loudly that it is impossible to hear what we say. We may espouse humanistic and democratic principles, but our autocratic propensity to control others may betray them.

In similar light, we sometimes take special effort consciously to reflect on our philosophy of education and attempt to explain our beliefs or assumptions. This is indeed admirable, and it is what we should strive to do. Nevertheless, to articulate a philosophy of education does not necessarily mean that we practice it successfully. We must realize that it is necessary to look continuously at our own thought and action and to discover more about its character and consistency.

To clarify some of the dimensions of curricular assumptions, I will begin with the discussion of a model that conceptually links action and assumption, practice and theory. Then the value of perennial realms of philosophical assumptions for curriculum deliberation will be considered, followed by a look at implications of different schools of philosophy for curriculum. Finally, three orientations to curriculum theory are discussed, and the guest commentators conclude the chapter with observations and debate.

A MODEL OF THEORY AND PRACTICE

The model in Figure 5-1 may be read from action to assumption, assumption to action, or one may begin at any point between the two and work to the extremes. I say this at the onset of discussion because it is so prevalent to think of only one kind of

Action	Common Sense	Policy	Philosophical Assumptions
Practical Problem-solving	Perception	Excellences to Foster	Metaphysics
Reflection	Daily Goals	Virtues and Dispositions to Foster	Epistemology
Situational Adaptation	Habits		
Practical Ambiguity	Interests	Procedural Rules	Axiology
Spontaneous Decision	Needs	Results of Empirical Research	Ethics
Volitions and Reactions	Routines	Models and Constructs	Politics
Intuitive Leaps	Daily Plans	Political Pressure	Aesthetics
		Scholarly Inquiry	Logic

FIGURE 5-1. *Model of Theory and Practice*

direction (i.e., theory into practice). Theory, philosophy, scientific basis, and assumptions are too often thought of as authoritative and controlling agents. Practice is too frequently viewed by scholars and administrators as the passive reception and implementation of wisdom from high places. Wisdom, compassion, and prudent judgment in the course of action by those who are intimately familiar with the situation are considered here to be of equal importance with theory that emanates from outside sources.

As you read the description of the model, I suggest that you reflect upon your own professional work as an educator. For example, you are engaged in some form of daily professional *action*. The action that you take is certainly not arbitrary or random. You encounter dilemmas within a succession of practical ambiguities. You must attempt to make sense of them; therefore, you rely a good proportion of the time on the second pillar of the assumption-action scheme, namely, *common sense*, which includes habits, daily plans, sense perceptions, routines, and impressions of needs and interests. You cannot make decisions about every circumstance in your daily activity; thus, it is most useful to draw upon these pillars of experience. For example, you notice that a student reminds you of another student in your class five years ago, and you think that some variation on the theme that motivated him will motivate her. You establish schedules for classroom cleanup and other menial tasks and have daily rituals for homework, recitation, classroom deportment, and the like. It would be impossible to make decisions anew about matters such as these as they arise in every different circumstance.

We do, however, encounter a sizable number of situations that are inadequately met by habit, common sense, daily plans, and our usual modes of perception, conceptions of needs, and interests. This requires us to use habits and daily plans as remote guides or precedent for problem solving. We often find, however, that these guides only take us part way. They are too idiosyncratic and do not provide principles upon which to make decisions. Thus, we must move to another pillar that includes scientific knowledge and statements about desirable excellences, which may be called the level of *policy*. Some view it as the realm of theories, constructs, and models. It includes broad goal statements of conviction that usually have logical and institutional support and set forth descriptions of knowledge, skill, appreciation, and values that are considered desirable. These are coupled with policy statements about how this knowledge might be acquired and what its essential nature is; such statements are usually supported by research and are, therefore, considered by some to be more warranted than idealistic statements of virtues or excellences to be taught.

Policy, however, is not considered the final arbiter. Generalization based on science and prescriptive theory rests on certain arguments, and convictions about excellences to be fostered are justified in a higher court. Here we probe into philosophy, the realm of assumptions about the nature of truth, wisdom, goodness, beauty, reason, justice, and so on. This is the level of basic or *fundamental assumptions*. Whenever we act, we implicitly assume something about these matters, whether we can explicitly state it or not. To realize connections between our actions and assumptions is to be in a better position to control and liberate our lives. Knowledge of this connection enables more defensible and justifiable action, which in turn brings educational growth. Thus, we see truth in the adage attributed to Aristotle and others that nothing is so practical as a good theory.

PERENNIAL REALMS OF ASSUMPTIONS

Throughout much of the history of human thought, philosophy was considered to be a kind of discipline of the disciplines. It evolved out of the everyday wonder of persons who wanted to know more about their origins, beliefs, and sense of meaning and purpose. The difficult task of judging the defensibility of claims about knowledge and values became philosophy. Those who engaged in it extensively became philosophers. It was philosophy to which scholars turned for integrated wisdom gleaned from the several disciplines. Philosophers took as their job the imaginative consideration of knowledge; they were challenged by speculation about the frontiers of knowledge, by the problems of truth, beauty, goodness, justice, value, reason, and so on. Such were the concerns of philosophers from Plato and Aristotle to Augustine, Aquinas, and Abelard; from Bacon, Spinoza, and Descartes to Voltaire, Kant, and Hegel; from Schopenhauer, Nietzsche, Marx, Mill, Locke, and Rousseau to Bergson, James, Russell, Wittgenstein, Dewey, and Whitehead. As one reads philosophers, one finds that the many dimensions of life and education are an integral part of their thought. They provide extensive ideas on matters of perennial concern to all persons.

In the twentieth century, however, much of philosophy became a technical enterprise. Dewey, Bergson, and Whitehead, Sartre, and others are notable exceptions. Academic philosophy and philosophy of education became for some time preoccupied with language analysis. While language analysis is certainly important, the tendency became so great that an eminent educational philosopher commented to me in the early 1970s that the tables have turned so substantially that one who wants to study human nature and other traditional philosophic concerns should go to the language departments and read great literature, whereas one who desires to learn about language should enroll in the philosophy department. During the past decade, a shift back toward the more overarching role of philosophy has been prompted by such philosophers as Jürgen Habermas, Jacques Derrida, Richard Rorty, Richard Bernstein, Michael Foucault, and others who recognize the importance of tracing intellectual roots back to critical theorists such as Marx, Adorno, and Marcuse; to existentialists such as Sartre and Camus; to phenomenologists such as Husserl, Heidegger, and Merleau-Ponty; to pragmatists such as Peirce, James, and Dewey; or to psychoanalysts such as Freud, Jung, and Fromm.

This return to the breadth of concern that characterized much of the history of philosophy has emerged in education and curriculum discourse during the past ten years. While recent reconceptualizations in philosophy and education are qualitatively different from the ancient traditions, the two possess the common purpose of seeking wisdom, understanding, and insight that transcends the specialized disciplines, the techniques of science and logical analysis, and everyday custom and convention.

Philosophy can be discussed in terms of its perennial categories: metaphysics, epistemology, axiology, ethics, aesthetics, politics, and logic. To look briefly at each helps to point out dimensions of assumptions that lie at the heart of all educational policy and action. Each category will be characterized, elaborated by typical questions that it addresses, and illustrated by showing its relevance to contemporary curriculum practice. The categories are offered because those who make educational decisions need a strategy for probing their assumptions.

Metaphysics

Metaphysics is the division of philosophy that is concerned with the nature of reality. The term *meta* means beyond and *physics* refers to nature. Thus, *metaphysics* is the study of that which lies beyond or is the basis of natural phenomena.

The term *metaphysics* is sometimes used synonymously with *ontology*, which is derived from the terms *onto* (to be) and *ology* (study of). Thus, ontology is the study of being, or what it means to be or exist. Some philosophers see this question as a subset of metaphysics; others view it as quite separate.

These issues may, at first glance, seem quite thoroughly removed from concerns of the educator. However, one has only to reflect on the basic curriculum question (What knowledge or experience is most worthwhile?), and the relevance of metaphysics and ontology becomes more obvious. A major feature of our curriculum, as unexplicated and taken-for-granted as it might be, is that we make reality better known to students. We want students to acquire the reality of the natural world through science, the reality of the social world through social studies, and the reality of communication through reading and language arts. Yet how often do we seriously reflect on the nature of reality that we attempt to convey or offer? Do we treat the ontological problem of existence as problematic, or do we act as if the answers are obvious? Does reality or the true nature of existence lie behind or within appearance? Do we teach the superficial conventional wisdom, or do we probe more deeply?

Within the problem of the nature of reality lies the enigma of human nature. Have human beings been created, or did they evolve along with the rest of reality? Are the students we teach essentially mind, body, or spirit? While it is easy to respond that they are all three, even a casual glance at school practice reveals that we treat them largely as minds. When introducing students to the human race and its accomplishments, do we give as fair a treatment to physical, emotional, and spiritual aspects of human nature as we give to the mental or cognitive?

Free will and determinism have brought forth no small amount of metaphysical controversy. Are human beings free to determine their own destiny? Can we make choices, or does it only seem that way in a deterministic world? Is the world governed by the laws of probability as is assumed by most research in the natural and social sciences, or do we live under the rule of coincidence a great deal of the time, as Arthur Koestler (1972) brilliantly argues?

Time itself is a major concern in metaphysics. Is time merely a human contrivance, the belief in which alters our relation to reality? When we insist that students learn about and adhere to usual conventions of time, what are we teaching them? Are we teaching them to depart from their "childish" fantasies and to accept adult contrivance as reality? We all know that an hour of conventional time can be very brief if we are having a conversation with someone we respect and admire; on the other hand, it can be very long if we are waiting for the dentist to finish drilling our tooth. Thus, personally experienced time—which Bergson (1889) termed *duration*— is prominent in early childhood, but replaced with clocks and calendars in the lives of students by those who prepare them for adulthood. Is such emphasis warranted?

Cosmology, another branch of metaphysics, deals with the nature of the universe, how it came to exist, and the problems of causality, space, and time. Modern physics and astronomy, with the search for quarks, black holes, pulsars, and quasars, the discovery of four universal forces (gravity, electromagnetism, strong force, and weak force), and the emphasis on interdependence augment our notions of reality (Toben et al., 1976), and thereby have numerous implications for education. Insights about reality require that we help students to understand it in new ways. Moreover, these insights have implications for learners, teachers, and the nature of knowledge and learning.

Theology and religion may seem far removed from education where schools are considered an arm of the state, legally separated from the church. Numerous forms of education, however, are not separated from religion. Moreover, questions about the nature or existence of God play a central part in the life and thought of many persons. When such persons enter school buildings, they do not leave their religious beliefs behind. In fact, such beliefs serve as prominent lenses through which they interpret knowledge to be acquired. Further, some have argued (e.g., Macdonald, 1980) that education itself, when entered into with serious intent toward growth, is a personally religious endeavor. It reaches into the depths of one's spirit and invokes the quest for goodness. The religious in a nondoctrinaire sense is a genuinely spiritual endeavor, whether spiritual is interpreted mystically or humanistically.

Epistemology

Epistemology is probably the branch of philosophy that most directly speaks to education. It deals with the nature of knowledge and the knowing process. More specifically, epistemology deals with such questions as, Does knowledge have a structure? Do different kinds of knowledge have different structures? Is it adequate to categorize knowledge in its several disciplinary domains (e.g., chemistry, psychology, and history)? Is there a deep character of knowledge that lies behind its superficial appearance and gives us a sense of origins? By what methods can knowledge be acquired and validated? What are the limits of knowledge? To what extent is knowledge generalizable, and to what extent does it depend on particular circumstances?

Positions or general responses to these and related questions have evolved in philosophical literature over the centuries. The acceptance or rejection of such responses has profound implications for curriculum. Let us now turn to the implications of several different ways of knowing.

1. Authority is one of the oldest ways of gaining knowledge. Think of the authority of the tribal leader in prehistory, the authority of the sage, the poet, the priest, the ruler in ancient times, and our pervasive tendency to report in informal conversations, "Well, you know what *they* say . . . ." In school, the textbook, the encyclopedia, the teacher, and the administrator are custodians of authoritative knowledge. Even in our scientific age, authority plays a much greater role than we are prone to admit.

2. Early in human history revelation was considered a major source of knowledge. The sun god, ancestor worship, the forces of nature, the colorful and multifarious gods of the ancient Greeks, Germanic and Norse tribes, Hindu ascetics, African and islandic tribes were said to reveal prescriptions for human behavior as do major religions of today. Who, it is asserted, has the right to challenge the deity, the ultimate authority revealed in sacred scriptures, interpretation of prophets, and direct contacts? Think of the massive influence of religion on education throughout history. Couple this with the fact that in any period, the most powerful "religious" faiths are accepted as truth rather than belief. Some assert that science is one of today's most profound sources of knowledge; they assert that science reveals and technology ministers.

3. If there is a source of knowledge older than authority and revelation, it is empiricism. Contrary to its usual association with formalistic sciences and research, the term *empirical* simply means the use of sense perceptions as our means to truth. Through the senses we experience; how many times have we heard the adage that "experience is the best teacher"? Our daily decision and action surely are based on informally gathered empirical data. In schools we take for granted that students have approximately equal access to knowledge that can be acquired through seeing, hearing, touching, and so on. If students are demonstrably different, they are placed in special classes or are classified with generic special labels. Knowledge gained from experience and observation is called *a posteriori knowledge,* in contrast to *a priori knowledge,* which comes from theory, revelation, intuition, and other sources of first principles.

4. Reason is yet another way of knowing. Whatever survives the test of rational or logical analysis is granted special credibility. In schools we can find logical reasoning in mathematics. We sometimes see emphasis placed on the identification of assumptions, the differentiation of fact from opinion, the construction of a defensible line of argument, the recognition of propaganda techniques, the drawing of inferences from data, and so on. These are aspects of reason and have been accorded a central role in the acquisition of knowledge since ancient times.

5. The scientific method, a hybrid of reason and empiricism, evolved since the Renaissance and emerged in full force in the twentieth century. Its steps (summarized by Dewey, 1938b) include (a) sensing a dilemma, (b) stating the problem clearly, (c) gathering data or precedent, (d) formulating hypotheses or possible courses of action and anticipating their consequences, (e) testing the hypotheses, (f) selecting and applying a course of action to solve the problem, and (g) assessing the resolution in view of its consequences. Pursued by specialists in natural and social sciences, this way of knowing is rigorous and rather formal. Done by anyone in everyday activities, the scientific method can be interpreted as a practical means of problem solving.

6. Intuition is yet another widely used form of knowing, although it is given minimal credibility in academic institutions. Intuition refers to a variety of means of immediate apprehension of knowledge. One thinks of immediate grasp of affinity with certain aspects of nature or the social world, which brings to mind such topics as love at first sight and psychic phenomena as well as an intuitive or poetic grasp of a great principle (Newton's insight into laws of motion or Einstein's presage of relativity). Although discounted in scholarly circles, it is ironic how substantial a part is played by intuition in the decision and action of everyday life. Teachers often admit to a kind of intuitive development of curriculum and methods as they teach. Yet they seldom give credence to student use of intuition. It seems that those in control of others admit to the use of intuition but do not deem it worthwhile for use by their subordinates. Teacher educators pride themselves in intuitively knowing how to relate to would-be teachers, but they attempt to instill in their students mechanistic, recipelike strategies of teaching and curriculum planning.

Those who study educational psychology and learning theory, and, of course, those who advocate application of instructional strategies or ways of managing learning environments, set forth positions that are deeply rooted in epistemological assumptions. Those who develop curriculum and/or teach constantly act on such assumptions. The serious teacher, policymaker, and curriculum leader realizes that if such assumptions are not probed and studied, critical inconsistencies may accrue and an unruly array of assumptions will rule by default.

Axiology and Ethics

The terms *axiology* and *ethics* are sometimes used interchangeably. Axiology addresses the question: What is valuable? Ethics refers to: What is good and evil? This general domain of philosophic inquiry is too often underestimated by educators. At first glance, it would seem that epistemology is more thoroughly related to curriculum than is axiology or ethics. However, when one reflects on the fact that most educational policies, and certainly all curricula prescribe what ought to be done, the centrality of ethics and axiology becomes indelible. When we provide a curricular offering, we implicitly (if not explicitly) assume that it is for personal or public good that we do so. To say that curricular offering x should be provided for a range of students y is to say that it is good for them unless, of course, our intent is evil or that of blatant self-interest. If we assume that x is good for y, we assume that it enhances the good life. The nature of the good life, a basic philosophical question, thus lies at the heart of all curricular decision and action. If it is not, it is clear that it should be.

For what other purpose can schools be said defensibly to exist except for that of contributing to the quality of life? Now, this opens another, much more complex problem: What, in fact, does enhance the quality of life and what do we mean by "quality of life"? Education cannot be carried on meaningfully without addressing this question.

A principal question of axiology is: which is more worthwhile, the desired or the desirable? Some theories hold that they are the same (i.e., that following self-interest is the key to sound values). They might argue for curriculum that enables students to acquire expediently knowledge that fits their own interests. Others hold that decision and action must be valued with respect to consequences for other persons, places, and things, not merely to the self. Here a curriculum would need to place emphasis on personal and public responsibility and on the ability to perceive consequences. Still others see values as having existence that is independent of human beings instead of being created by them. To them, values are to be discovered and taught; those who develop curriculum must see that these true values are learned. There are those who hold that values depend on the situation; these relativists are engaged in perennial debate with absolutists who advocate a universal set of values.

The literature of aims and purposes of the curriculum is saturated with values and conceptions of goodness. Such questions bear on the aims, purposes, and directions of society in which educational systems are embedded. Can curricula do anything except reflect the values that dominate the society? Or can curriculum be developed to redirect societal values?

Aesthetics

Assumptions about the nature of beauty are the province of aesthetic studies. At first glance, one might think that this area has more limited applicability to curriculum, that it pertains only to teaching in art, music, dance, theater, and other performing, visual, and fine arts. If, however, one looks more deeply, as does Harry Broudy (1977), and asks, "How basic is aesthetic education?" one learns that art orders feeling by giving it expressive form perceptible to the senses. Through aesthetic perception human beings develop what Broudy calls an "imagic store," a context of ideas and concepts that gives meaning to reading, any other symbolic learning, and to life experience itself. Thus, Broudy (1979) asserts that the arts are necessary, not merely nice. Elsewhere, he argues that arts are basic to higher levels of thinking (associative, applicative, and interpretive) that schools so often neglect in favor of replicative thought, which merely reproduces what has been presented and is soon forgotten (Broudy, 1982a). Kenneth Boulding, the eminent economist, wrote a book entitled *The Image* (1956) in which he demonstrated with great facility that life itself is a process of building an image by which we interpret the events of our life. Indeed, Eisner (1982) recently argued for an aesthetic view of cognition that markedly broadens the usual parameters of curriculum by showing the value of imaginative perception for any curricular area.

Perception of patterns is a basic means by which human beings orient themselves to life. We perceive patterns in the personality of others and configurations of environmental conditions. Our decision, action, and consciousness itself are forged by imaginative, perceptive interactions among past and present experiences and future expectations. In referring to John Dewey, who well realized the power and pervasiveness of aesthetic awareness in life and education, Maxine Greene (1981) pointed to the freedom that comes from aesthetic imagination by providing the capacity to see things as they could be otherwise.

There is a sense in which aesthetics has a close relation to axiology and ethics. When referring to judgment about art objects, the problem of the desirable versus the desired is invoked. Friedrich Schiller (1965) went much farther with the value of aesthetic education to claim that only aesthetics holds the key to relationship with the harmony and rhythm of the universe. From this necessary basis human beings are better able to know what is worthwhile to do. It provides a grounding that enables one to create a life of meaning and value to oneself and others. As Sir Herbert Read succinctly argued, education in art evokes within the child "that *instinct of relationship* which, even before the advent of reason, enables it to distinguish the beautiful from the ugly, the good from the evil, the right pattern of behavior from the wrong pattern, the noble person from the ignoble" (Read, 1943, p. 70).

Logic

Logic is the branch of philosophy that deals with the nature of reason, and the study of it is an attempt to set forth standards or rules by which reason should proceed. It provides a basis for making inferences based upon data. There are at least three formal orientations to logic: deduction, induction, and dialectics. Variations on the theme of each can be seen in everyday experience.

Deductive reasoning refers to the syllogism that consists of two or more premises and a conclusion. The most widely used example, stemming from ancient origins, is

Major premise:	All men are mortal.
Minor premise:	Socrates is a man.
Conclusion:	Therefore, Socrates is mortal.

The premises, however, must be regarded as true, usually by acknowledging their epistemological basis in *a priori* or *a posteriori* knowledge. The major premise identifies a class of topics and a characteristic of that class, while the minor premise situates a specific instance within the general class. Validity of deduced truth relies on the truth of the premises. Traditional adherents to the rules of deductive logic hold that one cannot deduce value-oriented conclusions from solely factual premises. Thus, it is faulty reasoning to conclude that one ought to drink orange juice from the major premise that vitamin C fights infection and the minor premise that orange juice contains high levels of vitamin C. It is of course logical to conclude that orange juice helps to fight infection. To deduce that one ought to drink orange juice, it is necessary to introduce a premise that says one ought to fight infection or that one ought to pursue a healthy life and fighting infection is one way to do this. Without such a premise it is considered the *naturalistic fallacy* (by logical analyst G. E. Moore and his followers) to derive conclusions of *ought* from *is* premises.

This has profound bearing on curriculum because curriculum workers are continuously in the process of advocating what ought to be taught and learned. Where do they derive their basis for such advocacy? Prevalent sources of justification include cultural assumptions and the authority of experts. One frequently hears: *"They say it is what should be taught."* Who is this omniscient *they* and how do they acquire their omniscience? In some cases it is the accumulation of social conventions. In other cases it is "scientific" educational researchers. The mission of scientific educational research is, however, to provide greater insight into what is or what works. What is and what works constitute premises of the *is* variety. By themselves, they do not provide adequate warrant for deducing conclusions of *ought*. Philosophers would say that they may be necessary but are not sufficient to justify conclusions that assert *ought*. Curriculum, by its very nature, is a matter of asserting *ought*. Thus, it is necessary to have premises of ought. One of the great lessons provided for curriculum decision makers by deductive logic in our era marked by reverence for science is that scientific knowledge insufficiently provides a basis for curriculum advocacy. The need for ought premises makes it necessary to give equal emphasis to philosophical development of excellences or virtues that provide a sense of direction from which curricular aims and purposes can be derived.

Induction is the second form of logic that we shall examine. Here the move is from particular to general rather than from general to particular as in deduction. It begins by gathering a set of particular instances that characterize or explain a defined range of phenomena. This process is a basis for scientific method that moves toward truth by converting the confusion of a dilemma into a clarified problem, by observing and/or experimenting with key variables, by forming an hypothesis or hypothetical solution or explanation, and by testing the solution in controlled circumstances. By use of sampling techniques, one can increase the external validity or probability that the conclusion may be generalized more widely. If hypotheses are supported, they are then accepted as a form of scientific truth. The logic of induction, however, does not provide absolute certainty. It deals in probabilities. It remains possible, though perhaps improbable, that a counterexample of an assumed truth will be discovered. Hypotheses heretofore supported always remain subject to falsification (Popper, 1972). While induction provides a basis for premises used in deduction, it warrants the *is* more than the *ought*. *Oughts* must be derived from experience, judgment, prudence, and the like. Inductive knowledge certainly can be used as guidance for ought premises, but it cannot provide full justification for them.

One must use caution, therefore, when relying on scientific educational research as the basis for curriculum. It may well provide helpful knowledge of what is likely to occur under certain circumstances, the methods that would be likely to work, and a whole range of technical procedures. But the large question of what should be taught and why remains the purview of philosophical and practical judgment.

The final category of logic that we shall discuss is dialectical reasoning. The most common form is to move from thesis, to antithesis, to synthesis. This can be interpreted as starting with a position (thesis) about a problem and to argue its soundness, to then argue the opposite position as cogently as possible, and finally to arrive at a synthesis or position that contains the best dimensions of both thesis and antithesis. To stop here is misleading, however. The synthesis becomes a new thesis and the process proceeds by continuously renewing itself. Such a process is exemplified in the Socratic dialogues of Plato, in the writings of Hegel on philosophy of history, and in the class struggle theory of Marx. Recently, dialectics is associated with hermeneutic inquiry in phenomenology. Originally, *hermeneutics* referred to the interpretation of religious texts and took the form of writing new interpretations beside older ones; thus, over a considerable period of time, the new interpretations gave deeper meaning to the text. The recent use of hermeneutics is metaphoric and refers to discourse itself. Human communication can be conceived as a form of dialectical or hermeneutic logic that contributes to the evolution of society.

The importance of logic for curriculum is at least twofold. First, it establishes forms for acceptable deliberation and discourse about curriculum problems. It justifies the way in which we link assumptions and consequences of reasoning. Second, a sizable proportion of education in any field of the curriculum involves the teaching of reasoning. What is reasonable or what constitutes sound reasoning is problematic, not obvious. If we intend to teach learners to reason, we must address the complex philosophical domain of logic. Otherwise, we operate on hearsay and taken-for-grantedness.

Politics

Political or social philosophy deals with questions of how humans should live together. Assumptions about the relation of individual and group needs, wants, and interests are paramount among problems addressed by political philosophers. The group involved may be as large as international bodies and national and state governments, or it may refer to individual communities or institutions such as businesses or schools.

During the past fifteen to twenty years, the influence of politics on education generally and curriculum in particular has become more widely acknowledged. Curriculum is not a purely rational enterprise in its conception or practical application. It is laden with political and ideological values (see Apple, 1979; Giroux, 1983; Young, 1971). Curriculum is, in fact, shaped by a highly complex network of public and private political forces as revealed in Chapters Four and Six.

SCHOOLS OF PHILOSOPHICAL THOUGHT

Books on philosophy and philosophy of education often are organized around schools of philosophical thought, or *isms*. Some of the most prominent "isms" are idealism, realism, scholasticism, pragmatism, naturalism, and existentialism. A brief characterization of each shows that the categories of philosophical inquiry (metaphysics, epistemology, and the like) are answered differently for each school of thought. As a matter of fact, it is possible to develop a matrix to compare and contrast the positions.

Such a matrix (Figure 5-2), however, is only provided for heuristic purposes. That is, it is intended to stimulate you to think about, study, compare, and contrast schools of philosophic thought. Rather than fill in the matrix with answers and substitute the appearance of certainty for elaborate discourse and argument, I leave it open ended and encourage you to ponder each cell and to think about the richness of possible inclusions derived from your own study.

Those who create and implement curriculum operate on positions represented by these schools of thought, whether or not they are conscious of them, although such positions are not necessarily distinct and consistent with formal schools of thought, nor should they be necessarily. To the extent that curricularists are able to articulate their own philosophical assumptions and relate them to existing schools of thought, however, the better they are able to know themselves and the sense of direction that they are striving to help others realize. In short, such awareness enables realization

	Idealism	Realism	Neo-Thomism	Naturalism	Pragmatism	Phenomenology	Existentialism
Metaphysics							
Epistemology							
Axiology							
Ethics							
Aesthetics							
Logic							
Politics							

FIGURE 5-2. *Comparing Assumptions of Philosophical Orientations: A Heuristic Device*

of the converse of the Socratic maxim that the unexamined life is not worth living; to wit, the examined life *is* worth living. The curricular correlates would be that the unexamined curriculum is not worth offering and the examined curriculum *is* worth offering. With this in mind, let us consider very briefly some of the curriculum assumptions brought to light by major schools of curriculum thought.

Idealism

When one sees educational practice in which the learner is viewed as a mind to be molded by the teacher, when classics of subject matter are deemed the best answer to ideas that have stood the test of time, when rigorous discipline of the mind is considered the means to these ideas, and when emulation of the teacher is considered a prime inducement to learning, one would do well to explore roots in idealism. Such roots trace to Plato, who saw a universe of ideas that was more real than sensed events. The spirit of idealism was integrated with Christianity in the Middle Ages and perpetuated in the eighteenth and nineteenth centuries by Immanuel Kant (who advocated the existence of "things-in-themselves" beyond ordinary experience), George Wilhelm Hegel (who posited the existence of absolute mind), and their followers in the twentieth century.

Realism

Those educators who emphasize the validity of the senses to interpret the physical world, who promote the acquisition of skills necessary to acquire and master factual knowledge, and who strive to adjust learners to realities of the physical world and behavior sanctioned by adult culture should turn their attention to the heritage of realism. Such educators promote heavy doses of science and mathematics, systematized packages and procedures for teaching and learning, scientific educational research, and highly technical modes of evaluation and testing that are believed to possess objectivity. Although the history of realism is complex and variegated, it is clear that its origins trace back to Aristotle, and it was revived and perpetuated during the Enlightenment by John Locke, who argued that all knowledge is provided by experience. Bertrand Russell was an exemplary realist in the twentieth century. Everyday activity in the twentieth-century world is heavily weighted in realist assumptions, although few probe such origins sufficiently to be consciously articulate of them.

Neo-Thomism

Those who advocate a religious, Catholic education, who join reason and faith to train what they often call the faculties of the mind through the study of formal disciplines of knowledge, have their roots in the work of Thomas Aquinas who, in the eleventh century, created a blend of Aristotelian realism and basic Christian beliefs. Jacques Maritain is a twentieth-century proponent of this orientation. There is also a strong secular voice among neo-Thomists represented by Robert Hutchins and Mortimer Adler, who emphasize reason as an absolute object of study. The advocacy of studying the Britannica Great Books of the Western World and related classics is characteristic of the latter group. Both secular and religious factions are sometimes referred to as essentialists or traditionalists.

Naturalism

Those who advocate education that is focused on individual development, do not interfere with what the child wants to learn and experience, do not impose social conformity, and encourage close contact with nature should realize that their orientation is perhaps oldest of all. It traces back to pre-Socratic philosophers such as Thales, Empedocles, Democritus, and Epicurus. In modern times the philosopher Jean Jacques Rousseau's *Emile* is perhaps the best example of naturalism. The great educators from Comenius to Pestalozzi, Herbart, and Froebel all have naturalist leanings, acknowledging the emotional, spiritual, and psychological aspects of education. Although not as romantic as was Rousseau, Herbert Spencer was a naturalist in that he believed nature to be basic reality. His 1861 book *Education: Intellectual, Moral and Physical* had much influence on broader conceptions of education and curriculum that were to emerge in the twentieth century. A. S. Neill's *Summerhill* (1960) is surely a contemporary classic of naturalistic educational thought and practice.

Pragmatism

Some educators call for careful attention to the experiences of students. They want to begin with the psychological (student interests) and demonstrate to students that they can resolve meaningful problems by moving toward the logical (knowledge, organized by human culture). They believe and teach that reality is in a state of continuous flux, that the truth of ideas or propositions depends upon their consequences in the broadest sense of the public and personal good they bring, and that human beings create knowledge through the reconstruction of experience. Pioneers of pragmatism are primarily of the nineteenth and twentieth century: Charles Sanders Peirce, William James, and most notably John Dewey, whose *Democracy and Education* (1916) is the key educational work in pragmatic theory. The Progressive

Education movement, promoted by such scholar-practitioners as Boyd Bode, William Kilpatrick, and L. Thomas Hopkins, led to curricula of problem solving through personal scientific inquiry and emphasis on individual differences, the need to educate the whole child, and the desirability of building curricula on experiences of learners. In practice these emphases took the form of child-centered schools, the project method, learning by doing, and integrating learning with personal experience. Although a number of these phrases are looked at as clichés today, a careful look at the literature of the era reveals the original depth and intent of their meaning.

Existentialism and Phenomenology

Those who see the world as essentially absurd and alienating, and who thus conclude that the only way to deal with the predicament of existence is to take responsibility to create one's life, can be identified as among existentialists. One's own experiences are considered the only viable basis for self-realization. Teachers should encourage students to look deeply within themselves to develop greater self-knowledge and thereby be in a better position to initiate choice and action. Only by addressing directly the great mysteries and events of life such as the meaning of existence and death can students be enabled to build more authentic lives for themselves. Roots of existentialism trace to Sören Kierkegaard in the nineteenth century and to Martin Heidegger, who was influenced by Kierkegaard, and is more often associated with phenomenology. While phenomenology also began to be articulated in the nineteenth century under the leadership of Edmund Husserl, there was a kind of blending of existentialism and phenomenological writing by midtwentieth century.

Educational philosophers and curriculum theorists of this vein usually tap sources in both phenomenology and existentialism. The close connection can be seen in Husserl's definition of phenomenology as the descriptive analysis of subjective thought processes. Heidegger continued this thrust by seeking to analyze the historical and temporal character of phenomena in human existence. For example, his studies of dread as a human phenomenon yielded insight that concern (Sorge) is a fundamental principle of all beings. Today the work of such noted existentialists as Jean-Paul Sartre, Albert Camus, and Karl Jaspers (and to an extent Christian existentialists such as Paul Tillich and Reinhold Niebuhr) often are referred to in the same literature as phenomenologists such as Maurice Merleau-Ponty, Alfred Schutz, and Hans-Georg Gadamer. These are combined frequently, as well, with the neo-Marxist tradition found in members of the Frankfurt School such as T. W. Adorno, Herbert Marcuse, and Jurgen Habermas. Other continental European philosophers such as M. Foucault, R. Barthes, J. Derrida, and G. Lukas are drawn upon. Together these and related authors form a network of literature that provides integrated perspectives from existentialism, phenomenology, critical theory, radical psychoanalysis, and literary criticism. To get a sense for this emphasis in curriculum literature, one has only to read works by Maxine Greene (1973, 1978), William Pinar (1974, 1975, and 1976 with Madeleine Grumet), Michael Apple (1979, 1982a,b), and Henry Giroux (1981, 1983), van Manen (1982, 1984a), and survey issues of *The Journal of Curriculum Theorizing* and *Phenomenology and Pedagogy*.

There are those in the curriculum field (e.g., C. A. Bowers, 1983) who argue that there are better ways to introduce educators to philosophy than through the *isms*. Bowers asserts that educators should study philosophy of culture because curriculum is derived from the repertoire of a culture. He argues that they should study philosophy of language because teaching itself is language and this is the medium for communicating curriculum. Finally he suggests that since we are interested in ends or outcomes, we should study the patterns of thought, for it is in acquired perspectives, not behavior alone, that the depth of curricular influences can be discovered. Thus, Bowers would directly focus philosophical inquiry in education on that which is central to curriculum, instruction, and evalution.

CURRICULUM THEORY

Curriculum theory is treated here as a subset of philosophy, the parent discipline that treats fundamental questions and assumptions undergirding all disciplines and areas of study: natural sciences, social sciences, humanities, the arts, professional studies, technical training, vocational education, and everyday life. Cutting across several of these, we find curriculum studies. Thus, curriculum theory is a strange amalgam, and one finds a number of different orientations to it.

Some (e.g., Beauchamp, 1981) argue that curriculum theory is a relatively new domain, younger than the general field of curriculum studies that is often said to have begun at the onset of the twentieth century. Beauchamp acknowledges the contributions of theoretical debate that went into deliberations on questions that formed a consensus statement for the Twenty-Sixth Yearbook of the National Society for the Study of Education (Rugg, 1927b), as noted in Chapter Four. But a 1947 curriculum theory conference at the University of Chicago, he asserts, was the birthplace of curriculum theory. The proceedings, edited in 1950 by Virgil Herrick and Ralph Tyler, included papers by noted curricularists of the day who addressed the question of what curriculum theory should entail. One important reason that Beauchamp and others see this as a milestone publication in curriculum theory is doubtless that it was a major call for scientific theory building in the positivistic vein that Beauchamp's own work went on to develop.

Those who do not adhere to this tradition of positive science might go so far as to say that all serious, philosophical writing about the aims and nature of education is curriculum theory. This would include a range from the pre-Socratics to present. If one confines oneself to the twentieth century alone, surely it should be admitted that John Dewey is among the finest of curriculum theorists.

The purpose of this section, however, is not to paint a history of curriculum theory. Rather, it is to sketch some of the different kinds of work regarded as curriculum theory. First, we shall look at a category scheme that includes descriptive, prescriptive, critical, and personal conceptions of curriculum theory. Second, we shall examine a brief sample of the other ways in which to categorize curriculum theory.

As an overall position, Kliebard (in Lavatelli et al., 1972) stated well the general purpose of curriculum theory and its relation to curriculum studies:

> *The field of curriculum is devoted to the study and examination of the decisions that go into the selection of what is taught. Implied in such a study is the notion that a curriculum may be planned with basic principles in mind. These principles, when they are reasonably consistent and coherent, constitute the essence of curriculum theory. [p. 85]*

Descriptive Curriculum Theory

Examples. Theorists who conduct research to model certain aspects of educational or curricular reality believe that they pattern their work after theorists in the natural sciences who have created models of the atom, the cell, food chains, and the like. they want to describe generalizable tendencies, and they see their mission as explaining and predicting behavior for the applied purpose of controlling it.

Intent. The purpose or aim of descriptive, behavioral theory is set forth by Kerlinger (in Beauchamp, 1968) as follows:

> *A theory is a set of interrelated constructs (concepts), definitions, and propositions that presents a systematic view of phenomena by specifying relations among variables with the purpose of explaining and predicting the phenomena.* [p. 13]

Thus, descriptive theorists analyze that which is. They gather empirical data and from it attempt to construct explanatory propositions that provide insight into definitions, axioms, relationships, and the like. The function of such theory is to define, describe, predict, and direct (Beauchamp, 1982, pp. 23–27).

Criticism. Because descriptive theory is patterned after theory in the natural sciences, it is deemed free of ideological values. If it is value free, the users of it commit the naturalistic fallacy of deriving *ought* from *is* when they use models or descriptions to control or direct behavior. Moreover, a wide line of theorists from a diverse range of philosophical orientations (pragmatism, existentialism, phenomenology, critical theory) argue convincingly that all theory (including scientific or descriptive) is value laden, not value free. They argue that many forms of descriptive or positivistic theory constrict or enslave their users. The latter are unable to see beyond the fetters of a narrow epistemological, metaphysical, axiological, and political base.

Prescriptive Curriculum Theory

Examples. Prescriptive theory is based on the assumption that curriculum is a form of recommendation. Curriculum documents of all kinds (teachers' guides, textbooks and teachers' editions of them, instructional material packages, school board directives) as well as that which teachers decide to do for students in their unique classroom setting constitutes a form of prescription. They all advocate, and advocacy rests on principles. Prescriptive curriculum theory seeks to clarify and defend principles upon which advocacy rests.

Intent. The aim of prescriptive theory is to establish norms for action and is ably characterized by Paul Hirst (in Tibble, 1966):

> *It is the theory in which principles, stating what ought to be done in a range of practical activities, are formulated and justified.* [p. 55]

Criticism. The purpose of theory is not to advocate; moreover, values (the base of advocacy) have no place in theory. Policymakers advocate, but researchers and theorists have the job of discovering true knowledge. Uncritical advocacy merely perpetuates the society and its value systems; it restricts growth and inhibits renewal.

Critical Theory

Critical theory derives from the work of post-Marxist theorists often characterized as the Frankfurt School. Principal figures in the movement include Adorno, Marcuse, Horkheimer, and Habermas. Critical theory deals with careful reflection on the taking for granted of socioeconomic class structure and the ways in which curricularists unwittingly perpetuate such structures. Such perpetuation, it is argued, effectually enslaves subjugated classes. In his widely acclaimed work with Brazilian peasants, Paulo Freire (1970) demonstrates how a *problem-posing pedagogy* can replace the prevalent *banking* pedagogy to help emancipate oppressed persons. The further point is that subjugated classes predominate every culture and require a liberating pedagogy.

Intent.   The purpose of critical theory according to Henry Giroux (1983), who has interpreted its pedagogical character, is to

> *Assess the newly emerging forms of capitalism along with the changing forms of domination that accompanied them . . . to rethink and radically reconstruct the meaning of human emancipation [p. 7] . . . and (to engage in) self-conscious critique and . . . to develop a discourse of social transformation and emancipation that does not cling dogmatically to its own doctrinal assumptions. [p. 8]*

Thus, critical theorists intend to penetrate and expose social relationships that take on the status of things or objects. For instance, by examining notions such as money, consumption, distribution, and production, it becomes clear that none of these represents an objective thing or fact, but rather all are "historically contingent contexts mediated by relationships of domination and subordination" (Giroux, 1983, p. 8). In pointing out contradictions in culture, it becomes possible to distinguish what should be from what is and to strive compassionately for the former as the conditions of suffering are recognized and articulated (Giroux, 1983, pp. 8–9).

Criticism.   Despite its worldwide currency in intellectual circles, critical theory is attacked by political conservatives and reactionaries because it stems from Marxist origins. It is also criticized by moderates who view theory as scientific, hold that there is no place in scientific work for ideology, and assume that it is possible for inquiry to be free from ideology and values. Opposition also centers on critical theorists' advocacy of radical change and concomitant destabilization of society.

Personal Theorizing

Examples.   The term *theorizing* has taken on a particular meaning in curriculum thought since the mid-1970s. It is associated with the work of writers who seek to reconceptualize the field of curriculum. Such writers are categorized as *reconceptualists* in works by William Pinar (Pinar, 1974, 1975; Pinar and Grumet, 1976; Giroux, Penna, and Pinar, 1981). Pinar intentionally uses a verb form to express curriculum concerns, namely, *theorizing rather than theory* (1975). With Madeleine Grumet (1976), Pinar probes the etymological root of curriculum and emphasizes the verb form again, *currere*, which "refers to my existential experience of external structures" (Pinar and Grumet, 1976, p. vii). In this work, the authors illustrate a "regressive-progressive-analytic-synthetic" mode of theorizing characterized thusly:

> *The first step of the method of* currere *is regressive, the free associative remembrance of the past. We work to excavate the present by focusing on the past, work to get underneath my everyday interpretation of what I experience and enter experience more deeply. The next step, the progressive, asks me to ponder meditatively the future, in order to uncover my aspiration, in order to ascertain where I am moving. Third, I analyze what I uncover in the first two sections, an analysis devoted to intuitive comprehension as well as cognitive codification. I work to get a handle on what I've been and what I imagine myself to be, so I can wield this information, rather than it wielding me. The beginning of agency. Now the antithesis, the synthetical stage. More deeply, now, in the present, I choose what of it to honor, what of it to let go. I choose again who it is I aspire to be, how I wish my life history to read. I determine my social commitments; I devise my strategies: whom to work with, for what, how. [p. ix]*

Intent.   The work of Pinar and Grumet sketched here constitutes only a portion of the conceptualizations and theorists that Pinar (1975) includes as reconceptualists. (More is said about this in Chapter Thirteen.) Looking broadly at the curriculum field, Pinar (1975) criticizes *traditionalists* who are concerned with the uncritical guiding of curriculum development in schools and *conceptual empiricists* who use methods of behavioral science to identify variables and their relationship and use these to explain and predict behavior. Contrasting these efforts with reconceptualists, he asserts

> *Reconceptualists tend to concern themselves with the internal and existential experiences of the public world. They tend to study not "change in behavior" or "decision making in the classroom," but matters of temporality, transcendence, consciousness, and politics. In brief, the reconceptualist attempts to understand the nature of the educational experience. [pp. xii–xiii]*

Criticism.   There are many, those who Pinar classifies as traditionalists and conceptual empiricists, who argue that what is advocated by theorizing is not theory and it is not curriculum. It is dismissed by some as merely subjective, personal reflection, and is not deemed worthy of the *theory* label, meaning an extant theory of the descriptive or prescriptive variety. Others discount the reconceptualist position because it has nothing to do with the curriculum of schools; they assert that it does not offer something that can be used by schools.

More to Come

The preceding discussion is merely a whetting of the appetite for curriculum theory. Part II of this book is a more elaborate discussion of curriculum theory because it treats different paradigms of curriculum thought that directly embrace several dimensions of curriculum theory.

The four-part categorization of curriculum theory developed here is one of many found in the literature. Each of the following categorizations offers a different configuration and, thus, adds to the richness of the topic. We have, for example, just become acquainted with Pinar's division of curriculum theorists into three camps: traditionalists, conceptual empiricists, and reconceptualists. Elliot Eisner has developed five orientations to or conceptions of curriculum theory: (1) the development of cognitive processes, (2) academic rationalism, (3) personal relevance or consumatory experience, (4) social reconstruction and adaptation, and (5) curriculum as technology (Eisner, 1985; Eisner and Vallance, 1974). Orlosky and Smith (1978) offer four-part classification of styles of curriculum theory: (1) humanistic, (2) disciplines of knowledge, (3) technological or analytic, and (4) futuristic. Mauritz Johnson (1977a) develops an elaborate blend of descriptive and prescriptive approaches, but rejects as inappropriate personal theorizing and critical theory. Dorothy Huenecke (1982) differentiates among three types of theorizing: (1) structural, (2) generic, and (3) substantive. Structural theory refers to analyses of components of curriculum policy or practice and/or examinations of decision making and planning. Generic theorizing is an attempt to understand the curricular impact of society and culture as mediated by schooling on social groups and individual persons. It is concerned with the broader environment of schooling and with education as a cultural phenomenon. Substantive theorizing deals with the question of what is most worth knowing or learning. It also relates to the development of arguments for the inclusion or exclusion of certain subject matter in the curriculum.

COMMENTARIES

The commentators represent an additional categorization for curriculum theory. Intellectual traditionalists, social behaviorists, and experientialists each speak to particular stances on what theory is, how it should be developed, and what its uses are.

Intellectual Traditionalist

It does my heart (should I say mind?) good to see a curriculum book emphasize philosophy. One chapter, however, is not nearly extensive enough to develop the relevance of curriculum and philosophy to each other. I would, in fact, like to see many (or most) of the education courses in universities replaced by good, sound philosophy courses. If some students are interested in education, then let them draw implications for curriculum from the study of philosophy.

The model of theory and practice is useful. It makes those who work in applied fields, such as curriculum, think about the role of assumptions in their lives. I particularly like the use of the traditional areas of philosophical inquiry (metaphysics, epistemology, axiology and ethics, aesthetics, logic, and politics). If curricularists immerse themselves in these concerns, they will realize how massively complex the problem of curriculum is.

On the issue of schools of philosophy, I certainly set my allegiances with the idealist. I did think the author's treatment of idealism to be a bit biased. It was so brief. Clearly, we must read and reread Plato. All the major philosophic questions are dealt with by Plato, as are most of the educational and curricular issues of our day. The reason for this is, of course, the fact that sociocultural change is merely transparent; real change occurs behind the scenes in the more fundamental ideas embedded in the universe. These ideas are universal, absolute, and immutable. They are reflected in the great works of literature and the arts. Most of our students, and adults for that matter, see only the shadows of reality (referring to Plato's allegory of the cave). We need teachers who emerge from the cave and glimpse the source of illumination. It is they who must return to the cave to help others see the reality of the realm of ideas. By contrast, realism is such a banal acknowledgment of the obvious. Neo-Thomism has many good qualities, especially in its more secular dimension as exemplified by Hutchins and Adler. The rest are mere modern aberrations; by comparison, they make even realism look inviting.

As for curriculum theory, the only type worthy of being discussed is prescriptive theory. We know that the great books offer the best education; it remains only to advocate them in a way that will be widely accepted. It is silly to describe and explain, as descriptive theorists want to do, when what is focused on is so blatantly superficial. Unfortunately, we are faced with the descriptive theorist's deification of science. The other two modernists I would call hopelessly naive. Both critical theorists and personal theorists want to remake the world. They ignore the dark side of human nature that the great books reveal along with the virtuous side.

Social Behaviorist

True to my propensity for parsimony, I plan to be economical in what I say. Yes, I agree that we need a philosophy to do research well and to offer viable prescriptions for practitioners. But we don't need to beat a dead horse, as the saying goes. Armchair philosophers are a dime a dozen today, even with inflation. We can't spend the day pondering when there is work to do. Anyone who has looked at schools, unlike the intellectual traditionalist and experientialist, knows that there is plenty of work to do. We need to clarify and define our philosophy of education and then get to work putting it into practice.

As for my philosophy, I am certainly a realist; I rely on my senses and my analysis of overt behavior. We can never know what's hidden in the black box of consciousness (or preconsciousness), and I can't say that it matters much. Productive performance is what is important. I used to think this value made me a pragmatist, at least until I read the author's account of pragmatism. I believe in what works! Maybe I'm eclectic; I draw from whatever philosophy works for the problem that needs resolution.

My curriculum theory orientation is clearly descriptive. We need more good research studies to reveal what works. Then we can exert the kind of control necessary to acquisition of specified treatment. To know what exists, what works, is the only solid ground I know of for deciding what should be. Thus, sound descriptive studies are the basis of defensible prescriptions. They allow us to predict and control behavior. The other two curriculum theories aren't theories at all; they are ideological radicalism and softminded subjectivism. I don't know why they are even included in this book.

Experientialist

The worth of this chapter depends on how it is used. I guess that makes me a pragmatist. I believe that the theory-practice model should be used by each reader to clarify and develop his or her perspective on curriculum. The great categories of philosophical questioning should not primarily be used to find out what the masters say and internalize it (as the intellectual traditionalist would advocate), nor is it to discover some absolute answer to each question. The purpose is to continue the questioning and always to grow. The categories provide the best set of dimensions that I know for building a well-integrated holistic philosophy of curriculum.

I am not so keen on the use of *isms;* summary treatments do an injustice to the richness that can be gained from reading philosophers to understand the experiential style in which they create ideas. If forced to respond to the schools of philosophic thought, I would claim to be eclectic. I see some good in each and can imagine situations in which each might give the quality of perspective that I need. I do have a heavy leaning toward pragmatism as interpreted through Dewey in contrast to the social behaviorist, who defines consequences as "what works" and who doubtlessly views what works as what promotes self-interest. We need more attention to consequences for others; thus, the critical theorist's attention to those who suffer and the need for compassion speak strongly to me. It seems, too, that careful observation of the interdependency or ecology of nature can give us clues about living together in more empathic understanding. There is no better avenue toward this end than to realize, as the existentialist does, the need to take responsibility for creating one's world. Similarly, I can think of no better way to do this than through conscientious, personal theorizing. As more people embark on such theorizing and consciously create their better worlds for themselves, I can't help but think that the world at large will become better too.

I guess that I have talked about schools of philosophy and orientations to curriculum theory at the same time. Rather than criticize the positions that I did not mention, I wish to end on a positive note (at least this time). It is in the continuous doing of philosophy, in the questioning of the taken-for-granted, in the admission that each of us can always grow, expand, and mature that the world can become a better place.

SUGGESTED READING

Quite a number of sources have been mentioned throughout the chapter. I will present, therefore, mostly additional sources for those who wish to read more.

On both the basic philosophical questions and schools of thought, I recommend appropriate sections of the eight-volume *The Encyclopedia of Philosophy* (Edwards, 1967) published by Collier-Macmillan. Similarly, I recommend the five-volume *Dictionary of the History of Ideas* (Weiner, 1974) published by Charles Scribner's Sons. There are a great many histories of philosophy: *The Story of Philosophy* (1961) by Will Durant and Bertrand Russell's *Wisdom of the West* (1959) are two of the best known. Emile Brehier's *The History of Philosophy* in seven volumes (published during the late 1960s by the University of Chicago Press) is recommended for the more ambitious. In addition, there are numerous anthologies of excerpts from philosophical classics.

With particular reference to philosophy of education, I suggest *Philosophies of Education* by Philip Phenix (1961a) for an excellent collection and *Building a Philosophy of Education* by Harry S. Broudy (1961) for those who want to entertain the great questions systematically. Two yearbooks of the National Society for the Study of Education: The Forty-first (Part I, Henry, 1942) entitled *Philosophies of Education* and the Eightieth (Part I, Soltis, 1981a) entitled *Philosophy and Education* portray the development of the area quite well. I would add to this pair *Philosophy of Education Since Mid-Century* edited by Jonas Soltis (1981b). For a concise summation of orientations to educational philosophy in recent years, I recommend Kneller (1984).

Concerning curriculum theory, such work as Beauchamp (1981 and previous editions), Eisner (1985), Eisner and Vallance (1974), Giroux (1983), Herrick and Tyler (1950), Pinar (1975), Molnar and Zahorik (1977), Levit (1971), and others have already been mentioned. Other texts such as Tanner and Tanner (1980), Schiro (1978), and Zais (1976) contain informative treatments of curriculum philosophy and theory. In addition, I want to note a special issue of *Theory into Practice* (Winter 1982, *21*(1)) edited by Gail McCutcheon. The volume contains articles by a wide range of curriculum theorists (Herbert Kliebard, George Beauchamp, Jean Anyon, Max van Manen, Elizabeth Vallance, William Pinar, Madeleine Grumet, James B. Macdonald, Decker Walker, Tom Barone, Gail McCutcheon, and Cleo Cherryholmes).

RECOMMENDATIONS FOR REFLECTION

1. What are three to five principles that you, as an educator, use to guide your educational situation? How do these principles or guidelines relate to curriculum?

2. Think of a problematic situation that you faced recently. Explain how you drew upon each of the above principles or guidelines as you dealt with the situation. To what extent were your actions in harmony with your principles? To what extent might your actions have been adapted to be more compatible with the principles? To what extent do your actions reveal that your principles themselves should be reconstructed to represent your actions more fully?

3. Think of the action on which you reflected in activity 2. (Or select another situation that you remember well.) Think backward to deeper levels that show origins of your decision and action. Use the "Model of Theory and Practice" (Figure 5-1). Begin at the level of action and characterize your situation relative to the terms within pillar I. Then move to pillar II and ask: How was my situational decision and action derived from various contributors to common sense? Do the same for the policy level, pillar III. Then proceed to pillar IV and ask: What basic assumptions are represented by my decision and action case?

4. Reflect on pillar IV of the "Model of Theory and Practice." Can you sketch some of your basic assumptions in each of the dimensions of philosophical inquiry? Review the characterization of each in the chapter.

5. Compare your response to the last question in activity 3 with the characterization of your position on the major philosophical questions in activity 4. Is there any discrepancy? There usually is, so don't be alarmed. Realize that everyone's philosophy should be a growing process. Sometimes one's action leads the way and later becomes part of one's philosophy. At other times one has difficulty realizing the ideals that one sets for oneself.

6. Can you identify basic assumptions that you currently have that were different last year at this time? Five years ago? Ten years ago? Would you characterize your philosophy as continuously growing or relatively fixed? What accounts for its growth or fixity?

7. How does your practical experience influence your curriculum philosophy? How do policy mandates in your professional situation affect your philosophy and your practical action? How does your philosophy guide your daily decision and action? What influences that which we usually call common sense? In short, consider the dynamic interplay among action, common sense, policy, and philosophy in your life.

8. How does your philosophy of curriculum compare with that of the institution for which you work (or have worked in the past if not currently working)? What are the major similarities and differences? At the institutional level? At the building level? At the department level? At the interpersonal level?

9. Try to fill in the open-ended cells of Figure 5-2 to portray assumptions of philosophic schools. If you were to characterize your own philosophy of education as closest to one of the schools of philosophy, which would it be most consonant with? Can you rank the others in order of their affinity to your own position?

10. Which school of philosophy would you like to learn more about? Which orientation to curriculum theory? Why did you select the one that you selected? How might you go about learning more about it?

11. What school of philosophy and what orientation to curriculum theory best characterizes your school or place of work, or former places where you have worked in an educational capacity? Which best characterizes institutions of higher education that you have attended? What about the program you are now taking?

12. What do you consider to be three strengths and three weaknesses of each of the four orientations to curriculum theory presented in this chapter? Which orientation do you think is most helpful to the future of the curriculum field? Why?

6

✦ Policy: Curriculum Creation ✦

It is evident that the state is a creation of nature, and that man is by nature a political animal.
> ARISTOTLE *Politics* (Fourth Century B.C.)

Policy sits above conscience.
> WILLIAM SHAKESPEARE *Timon of Athens* (1607–1608)

I could not be leading a religious life unless I identified myself with the whole of mankind, and that I could not do unless I took part in politics.
> MOHANDAS K. GANDHI *Non-Violence in Peace and War* (1948)

SETTING THE STAGE

The history of policy perspectives on curriculum is short; nevertheless, such perspectives are of sufficient interest to merit special attention in this book. Until the mid-1960s, most colleges of education had departments of history and philosophy of education, variously referred to as foundations of education. In 1965, Stanley E. Ballinger called for a refocus of history, philosophy, and social foundations of education on matters of public policy in education. Over a decade earlier Daniel Lerner and Harold Lasswell (1951) made a similar point with reference to all disciplines and areas of study. They argued that *policy sciences* should make problematic and worthy of study any realm of knowledge that potentially or actually has impact in the public sphere. The essence of Lasswell's call was for attention to the impacts of knowledge. This was what Ballinger wanted for knowledge about education in particular. Both wanted greater attention given to the political consequences of inquiry.

Persons not associated with academic or governmental work, if faced with the term *policy*, still would be likely to think of insurance policies. Nevertheless, the use of the term is more widespread than it was twenty years ago. Indeed, one finds it rather frequently in the popular news media: television, radio, magazines, and newspapers. Similarly, *policy* has increasingly found its way into educational discourse to the extent that today we have departments of educational policy where we once had educational foundations and history and philosophy of education. Thus, a concerted effort is being made to analyze and influence the principles and plans that guide educative endeavors.

Although policy studies in the general field of education have come to the fore, this is not yet the case in curriculum. Nevertheless, if we reflect on the subject matter of the other chapters in Part I of this book, it becomes quite obvious that policy is the logical concluding chapter. Why should there be a curriculum field, as depicted in Chapter Two, if it is not to influence the realm of professional action? Why should we review historical antecedents, Chapter Three, if not to derive precedent for present and future policy? Why should we study contexts of curriculum, Chapter Four, if not to enable us to situate curricular principles and practices within a social, economic, and value setting? Finally, why should one deal with the realm of philosophical assumptions, Chapter Five, if it is not to clarify meaning and direction that informs action?

These questions point to the need to treat curriculum as a policy problem. The results of many phases of educational inquiry eventually deal with curricular concerns. In the next part of this chapter, we look at curriculum policy as a subset of educational policy, as a subset of public policy, and as the end of inquiry in both of these domains. Then we address three conflicting conceptions of curriculum policy. This is followed by a consideration of a number of different actors who contribute to curriculum policy.

CURRICULUM AS POLICY

The study of educational policy (sometimes referred to as "educational policy analysis" or "educational policy studies") is often conducted by a hybrid of scholars in educational foundations and educational administration. The policy analysis function is done primarily by those whose background is in history, philosophy, and social foundations of education. These scholars seek to bring analytic, interpretive, normative, and critical perspectives to bear on educational policies and proposals. They study such dimensions of policy as assumptions, consistency of argument, political context, and historical precedent. Toward this end, the American Educational Studies Association issued a statement of standards to guide academic and professional instruction in foundations of education, educational studies, and educational policy studies (Warren, DeVitis, et al., 1978). Graduate study in school administration is primarily designed to prepare policymakers and implementors for administrative positions in school systems. Of course, major universities also prepare scholars and researchers of educational administration, but this occurs in very small numbers compared with the process of educating educational administrators whose job is to make and implement policy decisions. Thus, two large spheres of educational policy studies might be termed policy analysis and policy development.

A Subset of Educational Policy

Curriculum policy is a subset of educational policy. Some educational policy pertains to the machinations of budgetary planning, to personnel matters, to maintenance of buildings and grounds, to legal issues, to staff development, and to community relations. But one must ask: What is the purpose of concern for community relations, staff development, legal issues, buildings and grounds, personnel, budget, and the like? It would seem that policy orchestrations that facilitate such areas should be done for a better reason than the mere self-preservation of educational bureaucracy. Instead, it would seem reasonable to assume that the final purpose of all educational policy is to arrive at better educational experiences for children and youth. This means better curriculum.

There is, therefore, a very real sense in which curriculum itself is a form of educational policy. When it is written, it is the policy of intended learning experiences or content (together with its purpose, organization, and evaluation) that a school system decides to provide for its students. Even when it is unwritten, and it is often a combination of document and practical action, curriculum is a school system's policy about the knowledge and experiences that students should have. To say, for example, that science classes will be taught by the inquiry approach, that homogeneous ability grouping will be used in middle school reading instruction, or that children's expressed interests will be the starting point of curriculum development is to assert a portion of an overall curricular policy.

A Subset of Public Policy

Public policy is the larger sphere of rules, regulations, and modes of operation within which educational policy falls. It can be distinguished from private policy by its primary relationship to government as differentiated from private enterprise. Nevertheless, this distinction fades with the increasing merger of public and private spheres. That which is private enterprise, for example, television advertising, has a distinct and intended public effect on public images, and thereby qualifies for inclusion in a broad definition of public policy.

In large part, public policy represents attempts to maintain or change certain attitudes, outlooks, and behaviors. Broadly speaking, those who make public policy educate. One can, of course, argue with the substance or viewpoint taught, but hardly with the fact that learning takes place. Learning certainly need not be equated with education if by *education* we include a value direction. In other words, if to educate means to draw out or to inspire knowledge that yields goodness, then education cannot be equated with an immoral or amoral notion of learning. The latter notion of learning could include the evils implicit in Nazi brainwashing, but education would not. Put another way, public policy is usually regarded as that system of rules, regulations, principles, and procedures that guides decision and action in any public domain. This could include policy as the means to achieve the narrow object of self-interest; it could also include carefully deliberated strategies to attain freedom, cooperation, and social justice. Or policy could fall on a continuum between these two extremes.

In any case the development and practice of public policy involves a voyage of learning. This journey metaphor is deeply curricular and demonstrates that learning requires a sequence of events or situations, a curriculum. A curriculum brings learning. Learning, even of the most rudimentary type such as compliance or obedience, cannot occur without substantive experiences that foster it. Therefore, if policy is to be actualized, learning must take place, and for learning to occur, curriculum must exist.

This argument, however, leaves open the most crucial question: When is learning educative; when does it edify? In other words: What kind of public policy is instructive toward morally desirable ends? My distinction here is between learning as a more inclusive category (amoral acquisition of knowledge and experience that changes one conceptually, behaviorally, and/or attitudinally) and education, which is learning directed toward the development of good and just living. This, of course, invokes the philosophical question of what is good and just living. One response is to provide an overarching definition. Another response is that it is impossible to answer this question in general; instead, it must be answered in terms of specific situations. Still another response is that such questions are never answered fully, even in situations; rather, only a continuous reflection on the question of goodness in the course of daily experience brings us closest to the good, the wise, and the just.

What these kinds of fundamental questions evoke more than anything else is the profoundly moral character of policy studies, taken seriously. Thomas Green depicted it well when he said:

> After all, though policy problems *may be technical, the participants in policy debates are moral persons. . . . There is thus a profound and tenuous balance that must be secured in our institutions. They must be malleable enough so that good and skillful persons who dream of what is not yet, but might be so, can be free to decide and act. But our institutions must also be sufficiently resistant to change so that those whose conscience is merely technical and limited to skills of managing the political apparatus, but who are rootless in their souls, may not do irreparable harm. Rootedness and vision ultimately is what provides both the only salvation there is of those institutions and the only fixed point for the guidance of persons engaged in public policy. [pp. 27–28]*

An End of Educational and Public Policy

Is a given course of action good? That is, Does it bring desirable qualities to those involved? What are desirable qualities, and who should determine them? Is a proposed or existing course of action just? Does it distribute consequences fairly? Have its side effects been perceived as carefully as its intended consequences? The continuous asking of such questions in daily activity of policymakers and the general public lies at the heart of both public policy analysis and public policymaking. In fact, one might argue that it is only when the public at large asks such questions that "public policy analysis" actually becomes public.

To ask these questions on a broad public scale is analogous to proposing that the basic curriculum question identified throughout this book should be asked by all students and teachers: What knowledge and experiences are most worthwhile? To take this line of reasoning full cycle is to argue that curriculum questions are the *sine qua non* of both educational and public policy. The reason for the existence of noncurricular educational policy problems is ultimately to provide better educational experiences (curriculum) for students; moreover, students as the future of society are evidence that an educative curriculum in the broad sense is the *raison d'être* of public policy itself.

ALTERNATIVE CONCEPTIONS OF CURRICULUM POLICY

As is the case with the definition of *curriculum* and other key terms used in this book, there are several different interpretations of the term *policy*. What does it mean? What alternative uses abound in policy literature and how do they redound on curriculum? As applied here, four conceptions of *policy* are now sketched. First, policy as guidelines for practice; second, policy as carefully specified treatment that must be verified; third, policy as simply and broadly that which occurs; and, finally, policy as an evolving sense of direction and responsibility. Each speaks to a different orientation to curriculum policy or at least a different aspect of how it might be conceived. The presentation of each position is characterized briefly by explanation and example, advocated by an intents statement, and then criticized.

Curriculum Policy as Guidelines for Practice

Curriculum policy can be conceived of as required and/or recommended courses of action to be taken in a range of circumstances, conditions, and situations. This is a very prevalent form of curriculum policy, which may or may not be provided in written form.

Examples.   School systems, universities, and other educational institutions have legal and extralegal statements of their mission, purposes, and governance procedures. Such documents speak to curriculum and academic programs in both direct and indirect ways. A school system's line hierarchy may or may not include the director of curriculum, for example. If this office is held by an assistant or associate superintendent who has line authority over principals of individual schools, his or her role can be quite different from that of an advisory staff member who consults but does not issue directives. There are, of course, advantages and disadvantages associated with each of these positions, but the point is that they represent differences in governance policy that indirectly influence curriculum. Thus, they illustrate a form of curriculum policy.

Other guidelines for practice relate quite directly to curriculum. In universities, the graduate and undergraduate catalogues or bulletins are official policy on curricular matters. Each college or department has written and unwritten elaboration that provides further curricular guidance for faculty, staff, and students. School districts are usually less formal than this, except for particularly large or affluent ones. However, they do produce curriculum guides for subject matter areas, grade levels, and special topics. They often make available resource units, teaching units, consumable materials (e.g., worksheets, workbooks, sample lesson plans), and nonconsumable materials (e.g., textbooks, audiovisual materials, computer software). These constitute both guidelines for practice and actual curriculum materials used in the teaching process. Examinations, those made within a school district and those purchased from outside sources, often guide practice. Since standardized tests are used as measures of productivity and success, it is a temptation to develop curriculum and to teach for performance on the tests. Thus, there is a tendency for the content of tests to be used as guidelines for practice.

At a level more removed from guidelines determined within the schooling institution are national mandates for change that generally come from commissions of the "blue ribbon" variety. These are often appointed by government, foundations, or professional associations. For example, the National Educational Association, you recall from Chapter Three, established the influential Committee of Ten and Committee of Fifteen in the 1890s and in 1913 appointed the Commission on the Reorganization of Secondary Education, which produced the renowned seven cardinal principles of education reported in 1918. By 1936 the NEA established the exceedingly active Educational Policies Commission, which "produced 98 major policy statements from 1936 to 1968, with a total distribution of over two and one-half million copies" (Ortenzio, 1983, p. 34). Among its most powerful statements are *The Purposes of Education in American Democracy* (1938), *A War Policy for American Schools* (1942), *Education and the People's Peace* (1943), *Education for All American Youth* (1944), and *Education and National Security* (1951).

The regard granted to the EPC declined during the post-*Sputnik* curriculum reform of the late 1950s and early 1960s. During that period, a new force gave behind-the-scenes impetus to school improvement policy, namely, the U.S. government and private foundations such as Carnegie, Ford, and Rockefeller. By 1968, the EPC was phased out, and curriculum reform was sponsored by the U.S. government under auspices of the National Defense Education Act of 1958, the Elementary and Secondary Education Act of 1965, and other funding sources, as well as major charitable foundations established by multinational corporations. While both these sources of funding diminished as the 1970s advanced, the 1980s brought renewed government and corporate attention to education. The National Task Force on Excellence in Education produced a report in 1983, *Nation at Risk*, that was given extensive media coverage and generated immense public interest. Other foundations and government agencies were simultaneously making reports during the 1982–1984 period (see Figure 6-1). Finally, in 1984 a scholarly society, the American Educational Studies Association mustered the strength to respond to calls for school improvement by issuing its own report on the state of American schools and called for schools that provide excellence for *all* the people (Raywid, Tesconi, and Warren, 1984).

Public and professional response was great indeed. Paul Peterson (1983) reported in the *Brookings Review* that more than 260 "blue ribbon" commissions were created by late 1983 to study the state of education in the United States generally and in the several states and localities. While major reform statements in the two decades that followed *Sputnik*, such as Conant's *American High School Today* (1959) and Silberman's *Crisis in the Classroom* (1970), pointed toward a liberalizing trend in which more variety of knowledge and freedom of choice were offered students, the reform reports of the early 1980s represent a pulling back on the reins. They called for more basics or fundamentals expected of all learners and focused directly on standards and testing as well as curriculum and teaching. This emphasis on uniformity is a far cry from the thrust toward diversity and pluralism in education that exudes from the reports of the 1970s such as *The Reform of Secondary Education* conducted by the Kettering Commission (Brown et al., 1973), the National Panel on High Schools and

Title	Sponsor and/or Author(s)	Source
Academic Preparation for College (1983)	Educational Equality Project of The College Board, 46 pp. (Free)	888 Seventh Avenue New York, NY 10106
Action for Excellence (1983)	Education Commission of The States Task Force on Education for Economic Growth, 53 pp. ($5.00)	Suite 300 1860 Lincoln Street Denver, CO 80295
America's Competitive Challenge: The Need for a National Response (1983)	The Business-Higher Education Forum, 51 pp. ($17.50)	Suite 800 One Dupont Circle, NW Washington, DC 20036
Educating Americans for the 21st Century (1983)	National Science Board (Free)	National Science Foundation 1800 G Street, NW Washington DC 20550
High School: A Report on Secondary Education in America (1983)	Ernest L. Boyer for the Carnegie Foundation for the Advancement of Teaching, 363 pp. ($15.00)	Harper & Row 10 East 53rd Street New York, NY 10022
Horace's Compromise: The Dilemma of the American High School (1984)	Theodore R. Sizer for the National Association of Secondary School Principals and the National Association of Independent Schools (1984) (Note: Two additional volumes are planned by Robert L. Hampel and Arthur G. Powell.) ($16.95)	Houghton Mifflin 2 Park Avenue Boston, MA 02107
Making the Grade (1983)	Twentieth Century Fund ($6.00)	41 East 70th Street New York, NY 10021
A Nation at Risk (1983)	National Commission on Excellence in Education, 65 pp. ($4.50)	Superintendent of Documents U.S. Government Printing Office Washington, DC 20402
The Paideia Proposal (1982) *Paideia Problems and Possibilities* (1983) *The Paideia Program* (1984)	Mortimer J. Adler and the Paideia Group ($2 to $5 price range)	Macmillan Publishing 866 Third Avenue New York, NY 10022
A Place Called School (1984)	John I. Goodlad as the major report on his "Study of Schooling", 416 pp. ($18.95)	McGraw Hill Book Princeton Road Highstown, NJ 08520
Pride and Promise: Schools of Excellence for All the People (1984)	Mary Anne Raywid, Charles A. Tesconi, and Donald R. Warren for The American Educational Studies Association	Pride and Promise, AESA P.O. Box 598 Westbury, NY 11590

FIGURE 6-1. Major Commission Reports to Influence Curriculum Policy: 1982–1984.

Adolescent Education (Martin et al., 1976), and *High School* by Gross and Osterman (1971). The pendulum again swung in the direction of a conservative, control-oriented educational policy.

Advocacy.   It is obvious from the examples just provided that there is great range among policy guidelines for practice. Curriculum guides and instructional materials created by local school districts are highly specific, whereas national commission reports are quite general. Authors of the latter realize that specific interpretations must be made in the light of local needs and circumstances. Thus, the purpose of a guidelines conception of curriculum policy is to provide (1) authoritative guidance for practitioners and (2) a modicum of uniformity in practice. The former recognizes the importance of external and internal sources of expertise that give institutional stability, and the latter provides a more standardized educational product. Without guidelines for practice, practitioners would flounder in a sea of idiosyncracy. Duplication and inconsistency would reign supreme. Furthermore, it is not the case that professional autonomy would be abrogated; on the contrary, guidelines help educators to function more effectively through an interdependence with other professionals.

Criticism.   Despite the assertions of those who advocate a guidelines conception of curricular policy, guidelines have a way of becoming requirements, and they somehow mushroom into increasingly rigid mandates. National guidelines almost invariably have political motives and economic self-interest behind them. Approximately a year after *A Nation at Risk* was published, and just as the 1984 election campaign was getting under way, President Reagan announced that studies and reports indicated that the nation's educational problems had now been turned around. According to Passow (1984, p. 676), "Many educators fear that the new 'get tough' approach to excellence will jeopardize the drive for educational equity." The call to a pull-yourself-up-by-the-bootstraps policy does little good and shows an absence of empathy when directed to those who have no boots and have not heard of them. Continuing this metaphor, as did Carolyn Trice of the American Federation of Teachers (1984), we need to teach students what boots are and how to wear them. While this may be the case, it is necessary to remember Theodore Sizer's (1984b) admonition not to confuse standards with standardization. To have uniform schedules, texts, minutes per subject area, and the like is merely to have standardization, not standards.

Standardization of the curriculum that derives from national pronouncements creeps (sometimes races) into local guidelines as well. Guidelines issued by central office administrators no longer become helpful guidance and possibilities, but mandates to be followed. Teachers are, in effect, removed from their role as professionals and are relegated to the level of automatons who merely follow directives. For example, this is especially the case when teachers are expected to follow instructional sequences by which they must be on a particular page on a specified date. Thus, policy as guidelines for practice is criticized on the grounds that it opens a "Pandora's box" of requirements that makes the teacher less professional by relying more on authoritative expertise than professional responsibility.

Policy as Treatment Specification

In the 1970s, when the golden age for educational funding began to wane, political power wielders demanded evidence for results of appropriations made. When many looked back to the lack of success of the post-*Sputnik* curriculum reform, they demanded more accountability for programs such as Head Start and its several follow-up projects. The primary response to such demands was made by social scientists and behavioral psychologists who entered education during the discipline-centered reform movement of the 1960s. Using sophisticated technical modes of quantitative research, these researchers and evaluators advocated rigorous specification of treatments, careful verification of the extent to which treatments were implemented, and detailed measurement of results. Practice of these intents, however, often fell short.

Examples.   The treatment specification and verification model of curriculum policy can be seen as a research-oriented approach to the guidelines position. It begins with an operational definition of the treatment that a carefully defined population would receive. This includes goals, stated in behavioral terms whenever possible, and a detailed action plan that explains the interventions designed to affect the treatment population in a particular way. Summative evaluation is designed to assess the degree to which the results of the study match prespecified goals. Formative evaluation is designed to determine the extent to which the action plan actually delivers the intended program.

Reflection on the post-*Sputnik* curriculum reform projects often reveals that the lack of prespecified outcomes actually stemmed from failure to implement the treatment. For example, when Goodlad, Klein, and Associates (1970) went behind the classroom door to look at implementation of the reform projects, they discovered that the rhetoric of reform but not its substance prevailed. Clearly, when no implementation existed, it meant that no experiment had been conducted; therefore, results were untenable. Hence, formative evaluation was seen to be a necessary accompaniment to summative evaluation (Scriven, 1967; Bloom et al., 1971). Formative evaluation provides unobtrusive interventions in a project to verify the extent to which original specifications are being implemented. If not implemented according to specification, it can be readjusted and put back on track. When this was done, evaluation researchers could be more certain that summative evaluation really examined a policy that had been implemented in the prespecified manner.

Advocacy.   The purpose of a treatment specification-verification approach to curriculum policy is to link closely policy formulation, implementation, and evaluation. Often these three functions in the creation of policy are carried out by different groups of persons or even by different institutions, increasing the possibility that there will be little communication among them. Implementors may not know what formulators had in mind, and the intents of both may be lost to the evaluators. At the local school district level, the committee that formulates a new approach in the reading curriculum may have something quite different in mind from that which is mediated through district consultants and building principals to teachers. Similarly, teachers at the building level who develop a new social studies unit conceive of and implement it much differently from teachers who receive it a few years later and were not participants in its formulation.

All this is to illustrate the need for careful communication that assures a match or fit among formulation, implementation, and evaluation. Only when the formulation of policy is explicitly specified can it be implemented with accuracy and reliability. Only when careful specifications exist can formative evaluation accurately verify the consistency between goals and implementation. And only when both specification and verification are consistent can one have a strong basis for making evaluative inferences about a policy's formulation and implementation. Evaluation of this type provides a defensible basis for revision and change.

Criticism.   To put too much faith in prespecified goals and action plans can bring disaster to curriculum policy. When a policymaker prespecifies an entire course of action, he or she assumes a very thorough knowledge of the implementation conditions. In reality, the participants in the implementation situations know their needs better than the distant policymaker. One can, of course, argue that the policymaker can study the needs of those in the implementation situation before making prespecifications. This is the essence of a needs assessment. The problem is that the only truly worthwhile needs assessment occurs continuously and its results are fed back into the system for improvement on an ongoing basis. In the treatment specification-verification model, feedback and revision only occur at the end of the project.

When formative evaluation is used only to get a project back on its prespecified track, it abrogates the responsibility to say that this track itself may be ill conceived. The fact is that it is impossible for an outside expert in a brief encounter to understand the needs of a situation as fully as those do who live in it. Moreover, situations change between needs analysis and project implementation. Needs discovered during analysis and prespecification phases are not necessarily the same as those discovered during implementation. Project implementors may also develop deeper and broader insights into the situation through their interaction than were possible by formulators of prespecifications. Thus, formative evaluation must be reconceived to allow for revision of mistaken prespecifications. This is especially the case when it is obvious to implementors that continuation of a prespecified course of action will result in more harm than good. Researchers intent on producing published results too often prevent themselves from accepting the fact that their prespecifications need to be revised for the benefit of those affected by the treatment. They do not want their research to be endangered by altering the treatment specifications. It is indeed a sad state of affairs, however, when educators give precedence to research about treatments over the effects of those treatments on people.

Policy as That Which Occurs

Some scholars assert that policy is neither planned guidelines nor treatment specifications. They argue that it is a much less systematic and more thoroughly political activity. In other words, prespecified policy statements bear little relation to what actually occurs. What occurs, the activity of public transaction, is what needs to be studied. The situation is much the same as the comparison of a politician's campaign promises with his or her actual performance during a term in the office. One may bear little relation to the other. Thus, the argument continues, those who want to study educational policy should study practice, not primarily proposals.

Examples.   The perennial paradigm or conceptual framework for curriculum for the past twenty-five years has been the Tyler Rationale (Tyler, 1949). Tyler's four central topics for curricular analysis—purposes, learning experiences, organization, and evaluation—could serve as a basis for descriptive and interpretive analyses of extant curricular practices. However, this has not been their primary use. The categories have been used by followers of Tyler as recipelike guidelines for developing curricular policies and practices.

Many statements of curricular "oughts," policies developed by schools and other educative institutions, are not congruent with the practices of those institutions. Decker Walker's (1971) naturalistic model of curriculum development (discussed in Chapter Four) is descriptive rather than prescriptive and affirms the fact that curriculum design in practice often accumulates unsystematically. The important point here is that curriculum policymakers are not suddenly transformed from human beings, with all the foibles that accompany that station, into rational and just decision makers simply because they engage in curriculum policymaking. Practitioners have not the luxury to deliberate as long as academics; thus, curriculum design (rudimentary as it is) emerges when students appear who are to be influenced by the curriculum in question. The ongoing presence of students necessitates that deliberation with all its incompleteness and inconsistency becomes design as it meets a situation with teachers, learners, and subject matter. Instead of trying to understand a curriculum policy by asking how its creators determined purposes, learning experiences, organization, and evaluation and by describing principles from which practices were rationally determined in advance, Walker (1974) suggests that the following questions be asked in an attempt to comprehend curriculum policy in any situation:

1. *What are the significant features of a given curriculum?*
2. *What are the personal and social consequences of a given curriculum feature?*
3. *What accounts for stability and change in curriculum features?*
4. *What accounts for people's judgments of the merit or worth of various curriculum features?*
5. *What sorts of curriculum features ought to be included in a curriculum intended for a given purpose in a given situation? [pp. 217–218]*

Studies of curriculum policymaking during the past ten years illustrate another trend in which practice differed from proposal. Although it had been taken for granted that authority and governance in curricular matters rested primarily at the local level with guidance from the state, a review by Short (1983) of curriculum policy research reveals that the trend is toward multidimensional governance of curriculum in the United States. State, local, and federal levels and legislative, executive, and judicial branches of government all share in the creation of curricular policy. Thus, again we see how the study of practice reveals policy that counters that which is espoused.

Advocacy. We all know the saying, "What you are speaks so loudly that we can't hear what you say." This is precisely what this approach to policy studies attempts to capture on the institutional scale. Everyone knows that huge discrepancies exist between what school officials say they do with their public relations hat on and what they actually do. Maybe it should be this way, but if we are concerned with the reality that affects the lives of students and teachers, we should not be preoccupied with the rhetoric of policy and pronouncements. Thus, the proper study of policy should be an attempt to glean the central principles upon which practice is based. These are best discovered by careful observation of practice. Such principles, when discovered, in any situation should be analyzed for contradictions and inconsistencies. Principles that guide practice in a given situation should then be compared with those that guide related situations. This is the way to generate a defensible theory of curriculum policy formulation and implementation.

Criticism.   To assume that curriculum policy is what occurs is to sever a major portion of the function of policy, namely, the *ought*. To relegate the study of policy wholeheartedly to the realm of *is* is to tread in the direction of the naturalistic fallacy, discussed in Chapter Five. If we could generate a verifiable set of principles that guide policy formulation and implementation (is), this would still not tell us what we should do (ought). Policymaking is essentially a value-laden process of determining worthwhile directions in which to move in a range of situations. Even policy analysis cannot defensibly be only analysis of policies that exist; it also must be the considera-tion of what should be. Granted, those who determine what should be in curriculum can profit immensely from having a strong background in what is. But to neglect the *ought* dimension of policy analysis is to leave the Prince of Denmark out of *Hamlet*. It is to analyze without a defensible basis for critique.

Policy as Disposition

So long as policymakers or policy analysts stand apart from the situation in which the policy is to be applied, they take on the role of expert authorities. An alternative emerges, however, when those in authority realize that the best they can do is establish a sense of direction in dialogue with those who live in the situation where the policy is to be applied. Those in the situation must take responsibility to help the sense of direction evolve. In this case, policy formulation becomes the clarification of a disposition or sense of direction, not rigid guidelines or invariant prespecifications. Policy implementation becomes a process of evolution, or continuous, conscious refinement by those who live under the policy (see Wildavsky, 1979; Pressman and Wildavsky, 1979). This orientation radically alters the character of formative evalua-tion as interpreted in the treatment specification–verification model. Formative evaluation becomes not a readjustment of practice to comply with prespecified treat-ment, but a continuous process of revision, tailoring, and adapting of initial disposi-tions to meet the needs of an increasingly better understood situation.

Examples.   Wildavsky (1979) argues that "It is more important to create organiza-tions that want to learn than to tell them what they ought to learn" (p. 39). This is exemplified by Ronald Swartz (1983), who distinguished the curricular policy of Mortimer J. Adler from that of A. S. Neill. Swartz sees Adler as a modern advocate of policy by expert authority who assumes with Plato and Aristotle that there should be a special category of persons, deemed more reliable than others, who make authoritative educational decisions for the rest. In the *Paideia Proposal*, Adler (1982) tells readers that, "The best education for the best is the best education for all" (p. 7). This is curriculum policy of expert authority. Those who learn receive the policy and are influenced by it. They have little or no hand in its making.

Swartz (1983) argues that a liberal critique of this position has arisen against policy of expert authority and is exemplified in philosophy by Socrates and Bertrand Rus-sell. They argued that the essence of an education is to be found in the grappling with fundamental curriculum questions. Unfortunately, proponents of policy by expert authority set aside that realm for themselves and thereby exclude the heart of the educative process from learners. Swartz (1983) contends that A. S. Neill offers an alternative, the "policy of personal responsibility" (pp. 9–11). In his renowned school, Summerhill (Neill, 1960), Neill engages students in the process of asking what is important to know and be. They determine worthwhile experiences, sources of meaning, and a sense of direction. In doing this for their own lives, they engage in policy of personal responsibility.

Advocacy. To have a broad, open-ended conception of policy allows for participation in its creation by those who are affected by that policy. This gives those who are influenced by the policy a primary role in its development and evolution. The disposition or sense of direction may be very much open to interpretation as illustrated by the Golden Rule, the Socratic admonition to seek virtue, or the Buddhist teaching to eschew greed. The situational interpretation of any of these dispositions or excellences is the personal responsibility of participants. The curriculum of learning to achieve such ends is always problematic and never given, since full realization of these ideals cannot be achieved and since the situations in which the dispositions need to be achieved are always changing.

Criticism. Most people are incapable of engaging in dialogue about fundamental educational questions. It would be nice if they were, but they need experts who specialize in such matters to tell them what is worthwhile. Throughout history, people have clamored for experts to give them such answers. They have turned to priests, magicians, political leaders, sages, barons of industry, and scientists. It is the responsibility of policymakers and policy analysts to do more than merely set the stage for deliberation. They must take the responsibility to decide. Policymakers and analysts are given time and resources by the society in which they work. Thus, they should be expected to produce substantive conclusions, not merely pass along the work to the general citizenry. This is also essentially the case with the relationship between teachers and their students who are even more immature than the citizenry at large.

CURRICULUM POLICYMAKERS

Who makes curriculum policy? As research by Short (1983) reveals, curriculum policy is made by a broad network of persons and institutions at many different levels. In the sections that follow, we consider briefly a number of such policymakers. The list is not inclusive; rather, it is illustrative. We also consider the extent to which each example should influence curriculum policy.

Curriculum Administrators

If any one person is looked to as the principal instigator of curriculum policy within a school district, it is the curriculum administrator. The title given to this person is usually associate or assistant superintendent for curriculum and instruction or curriculum director. These persons are usually in charge of establishing committees that determine curriculum policy. Policy often accumulates indirectly through decisions about selections of textbooks and other instructional materials and through decisions about what to include in curriculum guides for various grade levels and subject areas. In addition, central office curriculum administrators are usually in charge of faculty and staff development, informing building principals of new policies, maintaining curriculum materials collections and professional libraries, and overseeing the entire academic program from inception through evaluation.

These duties are, of course, impossible for one person or even a team of curriculum administrators. Many of the tasks must be carried out through productive decentralization by principals and teachers whose professional judgment develops responses in light of particular situations. On the other end of the power structure, the curriculum administrator must comply with legislative and judicial rulings. He or she is responsible to the superintendent, school board, and state education officials and to federal agencies for federally funded programs. It is difficult for the curriculum administrator to move beyond the dictates of community values, the kinds of materials provided by commercial publishers, and the trends of the educational bandwagon devised by researchers, teacher educators, and professional associations. Thus, the curriculum administrator's hands are both free and tied. He or she works within a network of other policymakers.

Building Principals

Traditionally, building principals are thought of as instructional leaders of schools. Research is mixed on this matter; some studies such as the effective schools literature (Squires et al., 1983, and theme issues of *Educational Leadership:* "Leadership Up Close," February 1984, and "Toward More Effective Schools," December 1982) reveal that good schools have principals who are instructional leaders. In contrast, Morris et al. (1984) derive from their study of urban principals a conclusion that most principals do not exercise direct leadership in curriculum and instruction. A sizable proportion of principals may lead insofar as they set the stage for teachers to make key decisions about curriculum and instruction, but most do not engage in curriculum decision making much of the time as Donmoyer (1984) and Hannay and White (1984) contend from their research on effective principals.

This debate may be moot because while schools generally may not find principals to be leaders of curriculum and instruction, the most effective schools may indeed have principals who both directly and indirectly exercise curriculum leadership. Thus, the issue may again be one of confusion between *is* and *ought*. The prescriptive literature on principals has agreed over the years that they *should be* curricular and instructional leaders. This literature did not assert that most principals are curricular leaders. If some studies of principals reveal that they do not take curriculum leadership, it should be seen as verification of what was believed to be the case, not as a recommendation that principals should not be curricular leaders. Moreover, the finding of strong curricular and instructional leadership in effective schools points to the desirability of principals as curriculum leaders.

Principals, like central office curriculum administrators, experience numerous encumbrances as curriculum leaders. They are seen as the arm of the central office policy at the building level and, thus, are subject to all of the community, state, and national policies that shape central office curriculum policy. In addition, principals are the closest administrators to the teachers, students, and families at the local level. They must be artists of policy adaptation who can fit it to situational needs and interests without contradicting official mandate. In their attempts to balance needs and interests of many contending parties, principals do much to set the tone for functioning within the school building. This tone has immense influence, direct and indirect, on the curriculum. It becomes an important, indirect form of curriculum policy.

Superintendents

Just as principals establish the tone for individual school buildings, superintendents set the tone for entire school districts. Their personalities, modes of public relations, pet ideas, methods of negotiation, and establishment of priorities all establish an atmosphere for the kind and quality of knowledge and learning experiences students have in that school system. The superintendent must play the dual role of the professional educators' representative on the school board and school board's representative among the teachers, supervisors, and administrators within the school system. Together with professional educators within the district, the superintendent formulates policy that is subject to review and approval by the school board. Together with the school board, the superintendent develops policy that must be implemented and evaluated by professional educators.

As the highest-ranking professional educator in the school system, it is up to the superintendent to provide up-to-date information on state-of-the-art theory, research, and practice. Similarly, it is the superintendent's job to make certain that the school district is aware of all legal, financial, political, and professional matters that affect the school system's functioning. It is the superintendent's job to make decisions on these and related matters that at first glance seem far removed from basic curricular concerns. Nevertheless, in the final analysis, all of the superintendent's decisions affect curriculum decisions, indirectly if not directly. Despite the fact that policy decisions dealing with selection of textbooks, other curriculum materials, and the content of curriculum guides are usually delegated to curriculum administrators, the superintendent's decisions about finance, physical facilities, legal matters, public relations, and political negotiations are not ends in themselves. They shape the scene for the kind and quality of learning experiences that teachers may provide and students may realize.

School Boards

School boards are the official educational policymaking bodies for school systems in the United States. Whether elected or appointed, board members are, in principle, representatives of the community. There are those who assert that school board members represent only the interests of the dominant social and economic classes. Others claim that they quite accurately represent the needs and concerns of different interest groups. Increasingly, over the past fifty years, school boards have moved from a position of the dominant force in curricular policy formulation to one among many forces. Legislative, judicial, and executive branches of state and federal government (Short, 1983), as well as a host of private, corporate, personal, and global powers have emerged to allay the once supreme power of the local board of education. Indeed this raises the question: On our planet made small by communication and transportation can we ever again completely rely on local policymakers alone?

Can we assume that students who are prepared for entry into the life of a local community are ready for life in the world outside that community? A further, and perhaps more complex, question emerges: Do the national, global, community, and private interest groups that naturally emerge with perspectives on what curriculum should be like adequately represent interests that ought to determine curriculum? Is it legitimate, in other words, to assume a free market conception of influences on curriculum? Do charlatans not emerge to dominant positions as they often do in the world of corporate advertising? In other words, what kinds of checks and balances apply and should apply to policymaking by local boards of education?

Communities

The foregoing questions progress from school board to community quite logically. Who best knows the community interest? How can all groups with legitimate concerns be represented? Is it the case that fair representation within the community (if it could be possible) results in curricular policy that adequately prepares students for life in a mobile and interdependent world? Or is the local community a microcosm (a miniature version) of the world itself? Therefore, would those prepared well for life in any community automatically be prepared to live in any other community or region of the world? These are significant public policy questions that bear directly on curriculum.

On another plane, how should community and professional educator responsibility be divided? A popular view in the 1940s and 1950s held that communities should articulate general purposes and that professional educators should determine their specific meaning and how to deliver them to the children and youth of that community. This, of course, raises the question of the community's capacity to know what is best for itself educationally. Are professional educators with their advanced study of education in a better position to determine what is of worth for the community in which they work? To what extent should professional educators and community representatives enter into dialogue to determine fundamental curriculum policy?

All of the foregoing questions are contingent upon the level of community discourse that can be generated on curriculum issues. The progressive ideal is that families and small groups within communities would engage in serious discourse about experiences and knowledge most worthwhile to pursue. Moreover, this sense of small community would merge into larger units with the ultimate ideal of conjoining humankind in dialogue about its curricular ends. This is surely an ideal, yet its image must be preserved. Harry Broudy has called the generation of public seriousness about education the master question (Broudy, 1972), and such seriousness is implicit in this ideal.

Lawmakers

Those who deliberate on bills and create laws in state and national legislatures and those who interpret the laws relative to specific situations have a powerful influence on curriculum. In Chapter Four we reviewed some of the legislation and court cases that have exerted strong effects on curriculum. At the local level, too, deliberations at city hall frequently affect curriculum. At the national, state, or local level this is illustrated by monetary appropriations for one or another dimension of education.

Similarly, school discipline, library materials, and other topics needing conflict resolution in curriculum-related domains make their way into the courts. While courts and legislatures make important decisions that bear on curriculum, it is important for professional educators to handle as many curriculum problems as they can within their own realm, reserving only the unusual and excessively complicated ones for official lawmakers.

Educational Researchers

When educational researchers publish results, they often stir the interest of policymakers. In recent years, we have heard much about the value of time on task, teacher effectiveness, effective schools, mastery learning, and learning styles. Considerable research has been done in each of these areas, not to mention a certain amount of media "hype" that brought attention to research in these areas. Past research on such topics as behavior modification, positive reinforcement, and self-fulfilling prophecy has become so much a part of educational discourse that it seems that they are second nature. Such terms as *cognitive* and *affective* development were seldom used prior to the work of Benjamin Bloom (1956) and David Krathwohl (1964) on taxonomies of educational objectives. In this overarching sense, educational researchers have a powerful impact on policy. Policy statements are filled with terms that represent ideas developed through years of research.

Similarly, the educational philosophy of John Dewey has resulted in widespread use of such rhetoric as *the whole child, problem solving, experiential learning, begin where the child is*. Such terms and phrases seem commonplace, even trite, but they were introduced by Dewey and the Progressives with great meaning and fervor attached to them. Few also realize when they read the so-called steps or stages in the scientific method that the formulation was Dewey's (1910, 1938b), although the conceptions trace to Bacon and Descartes.

One often sees the topics *purposes* (goals, aims, objectives), *learning experiences* (content, activities, subject matter), *organization* (environment, procedures, scope and sequence, instructional strategies), and *evaluation* in curriculum guides, methods books, lesson plan forms, instructional units, teachers' manuals, and the like. However, one rarely reflects on the fact that they were given formulation by Ralph Tyler (1949), probably the most widely cited curriculum researcher of our day. Thus, while researchers should not be deemed demigods, their contributions to policy should be acknowledged. They are frequently called upon to testify before state and national legislators on issues that pertain to their areas of expertise.

Teacher Educators

Curriculum policy is affected in subtle ways by teacher educators, at least by virtue of the ideas, methods, and conventional wisdom that they purvey to prospective teachers. Teacher educators teach prospective teachers, for example, to write lesson plans that include (1) general purposes, (2) specific purposes, (3) materials needed, (4) procedures to be followed, and (5) means of evaluation. Along with instructional and resource units, these become part of the curricular psyche of graduates who embark on teaching careers and are merely illustrations of a considerable repertoire that teachers receive from preservice and inservice teacher education experiences.

Insofar as teachers mediate and/or create curriculum policy, it is obvious that teacher education plays a key role in it. Teachers not only teach the way they were taught; they teach, in part at least, the way they were taught to teach.

Teachers

Perhaps the least acknowledged curriculum policymakers among professional educators are teachers. How should they be involved in curriculum development? Many school systems place teachers on curriculum planning committees at district and/or building levels. But the issue runs much deeper than this. Despite what the curriculum guides and central office mandates say, teachers go into classrooms daily, close the door, and teach as they see fit. This may be viewed positively or negatively. Some teachers do harm to students by letting their self-interest overpower their desire to help them. It is hoped that such teachers as these are few. Research does not reveal their numbers.

On the positive side, teachers who are more professional carefully assess the needs of their students to experience curriculum that differs from the policy bestowed by external authority. They often create alternatives carefully tailored to the needs and interests of their students. Teachers frequently discover that general needs responded to by overarching guidelines set forth by school systems or publishers inappropriately meet needs of individuals in their classrooms. Thus, they feel professionally compelled to modify such policy, and sometimes they teach in opposition to it. Against this issue of the teacher's professional autonomy vis-à-vis received policy, the question of teacher involvement on school system curriculum policy committees pales despite the fact that this, too, is important.

Should teachers be curriculum policymakers in their own bailiwick, and if so, how does this relate to curriculum policy developed at higher levels and bestowed upon teachers? The vast amounts of time that students spend with teachers alone enlivens the meaning of the adage: "Teachers are the curriculum." The daily decision and action of teachers forges a kind of unwritten policy that greatly influences the lives of students whether it is formally recognized as policy or not.

Publishers

Those who design commercially available materials for curriculum and instruction (textbooks, learning packages, worksheets, workbooks, computer software, skills management systems, etc.) must also be regarded as curriculum policymakers. The amounts of school time spent using some form of purchased curricular material is immense. In fact, only a tiny proportion of the day in most classrooms is not based on some form of commercially prepared instructional material. This means that publishers create policy, not in the form of policy documents, but in the texts and other materials that a school system chooses to use. An adopted text in reading or social studies becomes the policy of content covered in a school that uses it. As with teachers, consequences may range from positive to negative. If published materials are carefully developed and if they are selected and adapted to fit local needs and circumstances, they can be a very useful form of policy. On the contrary, they may be developed solely for market value without regard to educational worth and selected on the basis of hucksterlike advertising. In either case, or in the range of cases between these extremes, it is clear that publishers are another prominent contributor to curriculum policy.

Accrediting Agencies and State Departments of Education

National and regional accrediting agencies and state departments of education play important roles in curriculum policy. Their periodic visitations, review processes, and establishment of standards create limits on what may be done at the local level. Requirements of courses to be taken, time allotted to different subject areas, and statements of purposes to be served by education overtly and covertly determine what is worthwhile. They determine parameters within which schools and universities may innovate.

To the extent that decision making by such agencies is wise and well informed, they may prevent practice that is harmful to students. Their review processes may also enable those in schools or colleges to reflect more adequately on what they do and the reasons for doing it. Nevertheless, these agencies often react to political and economic winds without a defensible basis; thus, they can do a disservice to local situations by pushing standards that do not fit situations. Such pressure can make it more difficult for professional educators to exercise their judgment at the local level and their genuine commitment to curriculum issues. "Recent surveys of state policy makers suggest that curriculum development has been receiving less attention than other basic state policy domains during the last few years" according to a review by Mitchell and Encarnation (1984, p. 9). Much depends on the quality and dedication of particular individuals who work for accrediting agencies and state offices of education.

Parents

We have discussed communities as creators of curricular policy, but parents deserve separate consideration. By virtue of their impact on the outlook of their own children, they contribute to curriculum policy in several ways. Parents help their children form educational outlooks or attitudes; from the parental relationship can spring a level of curiosity, a willingness to learn, a sense of discovery, a process for dealing with problems, and a facility with ideas. These and related characteristics are built by example as well as by direct teaching. Thus, by the educational outlook that parents help to shape in their children, they set limits on the kinds of curriculum policy that schools can implement. Certain ideals are practical in the policy realm only if students are capable of realizing them. It is what parents have helped their children to become that has great effect on curricular policy.

Surely, too, parents are among the most actively concerned community members on matters of school curriculum. Because of their vested interest, they seek direct involvement through formal organizations such as the PTA and through informal communication with a variety of school personnel. Grumet (1981) has suggested that some parents may become involved in school policy as a sort of last-chance grappling to have at least some say in their children's lives, feeling so little control of their own. Some critics see parental passion as too subjective to do policymakers much good. Parents, they claim, are naturally too partial to their own children to be able to focus on the general well-being of all students. Others claim that intense, loving concern of parents is what is most needed for sound educational policy.

A major question on parental participation, as with community participation, is how to involve parents in curriculum policy in meaningful ways. How should the line be drawn between input best suited to parental background and aspects of policy better reserved for professional educators? The issue becomes compounded when one considers the immense variety of parental backgrounds. Parents who are psychologists, educators, financial analysts, scientists, attorneys, laborers, physicians, and so on, all have different areas of expertise. Not only should parents be involved, but they should be involved differentially according to their expertise. Finally, a very practical question: How can parents who are otherwise immensely busy with jobs and family life devote the time and energy necessary to engage meaningfully in curriculum policy deliberations?

Nonschool Educators

School personnel are not the only makers of curriculum policy. Those whose work is to rehabilitate the ill, infirm, and aged create curriculum policy, as do those who design activities and programs for such organizations as scouting groups, little league sports, and other clubs for young people. They ask questions about what experiences or activities are worthwhile to the growth and development of participants. Even if they don't ask such questions directly, they answer them implicitly as they make policy. This means that by selecting activities or experiences, they act on certain assumptions, whether consciously articulated or even realized. If the Boy Scout leaders take the troop to the local wrestling match, auto race, or rifle range, certain assumptions are implicit in what they deem worthwhile. Similarly, television program policymakers create a form of curriculum policy as they decide what the public will view, and the same is true of the advertising agencies that devise the commercials with which the public is bombarded. Families, too, in the course of their daily routines and special outings act on principles that are often unarticulated or unrealized. Nevertheless, decisions that families make involve implicit assumptions about how children learn, what is worthwhile experience, who should decide on the nature of learning experiences, what kinds of learning experiences are relevant, how learning situations should be organized, how children should be taught, and how they should be evaluated. Hope Jensen Leichter (1974, 1979) has done a great deal to study the family as educator by bringing noted scholars from different disciplines together to focus on issues related to that topic.

A central point, then, is that it is possible to study nonschool environments from educational or curricular perspectives. In reassessing the Tyler (1949) Rationale, Ralph Tyler (1977) noted that he would place greater emphasis on nonschool learning. In the past ten years educators have studied the implicit curriculum in media, youth clubs, athletic organizations, medical facilities, museums, and families. I have argued elsewhere (Schubert, 1981) that it is essential for those who design school curriculum to know more about the effects of out-of-school agencies, relationships, and institutions on the outlooks of children and youth. Otherwise, efforts at curriculum policymaking in schools are conducted with little knowledge of the perspectives and outlooks of students. Surely it is important to ask: How can we defensibly advocate knowledge and experience as worthwhile for students whose current knowledge and experience we scarcely know?

Mario Fantini has consistently argued that we need to make curriculum policy within a context of educational systems rather than school systems (Fantini and Sinclair, 1985). By this, he means that school systems are only one of the important educative institutions in a society, and educational policymakers must consider the total configuration of institutions that influence the knowledge and experience of children, youth, and adults. The objection to such work is that it is too complex and insurmountable (i.e., it is a nice idea but impossible to coordinate). To this kind of criticism Nobel laureate Peter Medawar speaks cogently when he reminds us in *The Hope of Progress* (1973) that the hope comes only from proceeding steadfastly in directions to which we are committed.

Students

By far the most underestimated group of curriculum policymakers is students. Many would recoil at the very mention of their possible role in curriculum policy. It conjures up the image of six- and eight-year-olds sitting on curriculum committees. Or one thinks of the misguided classroom practice of having whole classes, in the name of progressive education, vote on the next chapter to study. More genuine involvement of students occurs when teachers get to know them well and engage with them in dialogue about what is worthwhile to know and how coming to know it relates to their lives both in and out of school. This is the essence of democratic curriculum as envisioned by Dewey and many of the progressives. Intrinsic to this idea is a conception that curriculum policy is primarily a creation of teacher-student dialogue and reflection.

A more subtle way that students affect curriculum policy, progressive or any other, is simply by mediating it. Curriculum is altered as it enters the minds and lives of students. Students' repertoires of experience interact with classroom activities to transform curriculum in many different ways. Research is neither sophisticated nor subtle enough to tell us much about the individual's response to curriculum. However, cognitive psychologists offer considerable perspective to curricularists (e.g., Resnick, 1985; Posner, 1982) that bears out the observation that different students conceptualize the same aspects of curriculum in quite different ways due to the unique character of their cognitive storehouses of experience. Any experienced teacher will admit that the same teaching strategy, unit, or aspect of content affects students with different backgrounds, aptitudes, and attitudes with widely differing results. Without realizing it, a single comment that a teacher utters can elicit glee in one student, pensiveness in another, depression in another; it can bore others, stimulate some, and bypass a few who have no experiential hooks with which to grab hold of it. Thus, it is by their response, the way in which they *realize* curriculum (as Walker, 1977, phrased it), that students exert a strong influence on curriculum policy.

COMMENTARIES

Each of the commentators will now respond selectively to topics from this chapter, taking care not to duplicate statements of advocacy and criticism offered throughout.

Experientialist

Curriculum policy is the way in which we actually influence children and youths in classrooms and other learning situations. As such, it is the end or most important realm of educational policy and public policy. There is no more important dimension of public policy than that of preparing children to become more fully functioning members of the public. Policy cannot be regarded as that which is proposed or even mandated on paper. Instead, true policy is that which occurs. However, that which occurs should not occur without forethought and reflection; thus, I support the notion that policy begins as a sense of direction derived from group dialogue and then evolves as a group tries to put disposition into action. I might add that I heartily support the notion of policy as personal responsibility in contrast to policy as expert authority (referring to the earlier discussion of Swartz, 1983). This means that I decry the treatment specification model of policy as well as that of rigid guidelines for practice. Little in the field of education has done as much to diminish the professional decision-making power of teachers as have rigid guidelines and treatment specification models of policy. The former undermines teacher judgment by trying to "teacherproof" the curriculum, whereas the latter makes research more important than people. Neither of these approaches to policy adequately realizes the variability of human beings and their situations. Both positions naively assume that general guidelines and uniform treatments meet needs of changing situations, persons, and groups.

The centrality of the situation in which policy becomes action, and the need to recognize the creative insight of those intimately involved in situations in the development of policy that affects their lives leads me to propose that teachers, students, and community (including parents) should be the major developers of curriculum policy. They know their situation, and it is imperative that we recognize the capacity of persons of all ages to know what is best for them or to figure out how to use resources to help them do so. It is the proper role of all curriculum policymakers who are removed from the local situation (from administrators and lawmakers to researchers and publishers) to see their role as facilitators of local efforts. The opposite has been the state of affairs that has evolved—outside experts have achieved increasingly greater control over local groups and individuals. Those who experience educational life the most in a particular situation should be allowed and encouraged to take responsibility for curriculum policy in their domain. Dewey (1927) put it well:

> No government by experts in which the masses do not have the chance to inform experts as to their needs can be anything but an oligarchy managed in the interests of the few. And the enlightenment must proceed in ways which force the administrative specialists to take account of the needs. The world has suffered more from leaders and administrators than from the masses. [p. 208]

Intellectual Traditionalist

If the public assiduously pursued the quest to understand the great mysteries and events of life, there would be little need for public policy, with the exception of regulatory conveniences such as traffic flows. The problem is that some persons haven't the will to pursue such a quest and many others are so engrossed in mundane work for basic survival that they haven't the time or energy. This is a sad state of affairs in a world with so much potential to relieve the public from mundane work through automation and computerization.

I know that this emphasis may sound a bit strange coming from me, but the point is that modern society has its priorities upside down. It sees education as the means to technology that it values for its own sake and for acquisition of mundane jobs. Instead, it should see technology and jobs not as ends but means to achieve time to study classics and consider problems of truth, beauty, justice, and the good life. This is what will make our world better, and for the first time in history, technology makes a life of study a possibility for all, not just for the affluent. This, of course, would require a redistribution of budget priorities so that more people would be in a position to engage in meaningful pursuits. If public policymakers and analysts want to be useful, they should figure out a way to provide for this kind of a life. Education should be the end of public policymaking. By this I do not mean schooling, but education that is a lifelong participation in the great conversation that each of us can have with the greatest thinkers of all time through the great books and other great works of art and science.

Given the fact that some haven't the will and many more haven't the background, time, or energy to pursue a first-rate education, curriculum policymakers must provide guidelines that translate superficial interests into will. They need to create guidelines that enrich backgrounds, increase time, and inspire energy to enable all students to value education and engage in the pursuit of higher learning.

As for the issue of who the principal policymaker should be in the curriculum realm, I say it should be the teacher. I refer to the great teacher; only he or she who is well on the way to a liberal education can make curriculum policy. Similarly, any of the policymakers who are more removed from the classroom environs should be in thorough pursuit of a liberal education. (I say "in pursuit" and "on the way" because no one fully reaches a liberal education; there is always the potential for enrichment.)

The job of local administrators, national and state officials, scholars, teacher educators, and so on should be to clear the way for great teachers to do the work that they can do so well, namely, to engage in the art of teaching great ideas and images. Hospital administrators provide a good analogy; they pave the way for physicians to engage in their art and science. They do not boss the physicians around. Can you imagine the debased character of a "physicianproof" hospital? The fundamental task faced by those policymakers who hope to improve curriculum is to locate and attract great teachers who are as fully qualified as the best physicians.

Social Behaviorist

I am rapidly tiring of the vague platitudes of the experientialist and intellectual traditionalist. Nothing short of magic would make their rhetoric become reality. We have a definite shortage of magic. Soothsayers and medicine men were discarded in more primitive times.

Fortunately, we now have science and technology, which, if utilized pragmatically, will help us a great deal. First, policymakers must turn to research and to their own situation. They must conduct a needs assessment by drawing upon representatives of all constituencies to be affected by the policy to be made (English and Kaufman, 1975). Simultaneously, they must consult the research on needs assessments in situations similar to their own. How did those who faced like dilemmas identify needs? What research is available on methods of meeting those needs?

Based on sound research, they do the following: (1) define a policy as a treatment specification, (2) devise an operationalized (stepwise, detailed action plan) strategy for putting the policy into practice, (3) develop methods for monitoring the implementation to verify its adherence to the prespecified treatment, (4) set forth a final evaluation of the extent to which the policy and its implementation resolves the problem it was built to deal with, and (5) revise the policy to meet the needs of similar problems more fully. I should add that it would be wise to conduct a limited pilot study of the policy using an experimental or quasi-experimental design before applying it on a full-scale version. This process is merely the application of scientific method to a curriculum problem. After all, a policy, as I see it, is a guiding hypothesis.

A network or unified system of such hypotheses would form a generalized set of guidelines for curriculum implementors to follow. This would constitute a rather rigorous curriculum policy framework that would spell out responsibilities of curriculum administrators, principals, supervisors, and teachers in the orchestration of a coherent set of purposes, learning activities, organizational plans, and evaluations. Any plan must be devised with full realization of the relevance of the law, community values, research, accrediting regulations, state requirements, board policy, parental attitudes, and student needs to the policy context in question. All relevant parties should be represented. Publishers, however, should be interviewed to determine the capacity of their product to fulfill policy; texts and instructional materials should not be chosen first and allowed to dictate policy. Thus, it is through the rigorous efforts of well-structured committees that curriculum policy should be formulated. Such formulations should define certain decisions as open to principals, teachers, and others in the hierarchy. Decided by well-represented committees, professional educators throughout the system should understand how and why policy is made and that careful adherence to it brings consistency of program throughout an educational institution. This process ushers in accountability as a part of the policy procedure itself.

SUGGESTED READING

To gain perspective on policy generally it is important to read a noneducational text on the matter. I can think of none better than Aaron Wildavsky's *Speaking Truth to Power: The Art and Craft of Policy Analysis* (1979). It is a modern classic in this new field. Though not regarded as a book in the new field of public policy, John Dewey's *The Public and Its Problems* (1927) remains one of the best statements on the matter before public policy studies was a recognized area of study.

Moving into the educational policy realm, I suggest *Political and Social Foundations of Education* (1975) by Wirt and Kirst, the *Handbook of Teaching and Policy* (1983) by Shulman and Sykes, and *Policy Making in Education* (1982) by Lieberman and McLaughlin.

Specific book length treatment of curriculum policy is provided by William Reid

(1978) who argues for a practical and humanistic orientation to policy matters when thinking about curriculum problems. Schaffarzick and Sykes (1979) have prepared a fine collection of policy studies and essays on the relation of value conflicts to curriculum issues. I also suggest Daniel Mulcahy's *Curriculum and Policy in Irish Post-Primary Education* (1981) for both its comparative value and its general relevance to discourse on aims, general education, pedagogy, and reform. The Spring 1984 issue of *National Forum* is devoted entirely to the theme "Public Policy and Education."

RECOMMENDATIONS FOR REFLECTION

1. Think of your own educational situation. List five policies that are bestowed upon you, that you are expected to implement. Are they written or informally communicated expectations? Or are they some of each? Why might they be written, unwritten, or some of each? How were they formulated? How is implementation monitored? How are the policies evaluated? Do you play a decision-making role in the formulation, implementation procedures, or evaluation of these policies?

2. How do the foregoing policies fit with the principles that guide your professional activities—principles that your experience has shaped over the years? Make a list of five or more of these principles. What if there are contradictions between the policies that you are asked to implement and the principles that guide your professional life? How do you deal with this?

3. How might educational systems develop greater harmony between policies and principles of professional educators?

4. Some have argued that policy comes from bad dreams. In other words, administrators mistrust teachers and, therefore, create rigid guidelines for them to follow; teachers mistrust administrators and saddle them with union contracts. Both teachers and administrators mistrust students and impose tough standards and examination requirements on them. Is there anything to this notion that people won't do what they should do unless somehow forced? What if we granted unconditional positive regard to all levels of persons in the educational system (even students)—a sort of innocent until proven irresponsible position in contrast to a position that holds persons guilty of irresponsibility until proven responsible? Is it possible to prove one's responsibility while following orders, or does this merely indicate obedience?

5. Which of the four alternative conceptions of curriculum policy presented in this chapter do you agree with most: (a) guidelines for practice, (b) treatment specification, (c) that which occurs, or (d) disposition and evolving sense of direction? What reasons do you have for your choice? Do you feel that some of the alternatives actually complement each other and could work together without contradiction? How?

6. Which curriculum policymakers do you think currently have the greatest influence? The least? Should it be this way? What would be a better (your ideal) balance of influence?

7. Where do you now stand with respect to the guest commentators?

8. Do you agree or disagree with the position that curriculum policy is a legitimate end for public policy and educational policy? Is it really that important? Reasons?

9. Look again at statements of advocacy and criticism provided in the section on "Alternative Conceptions of Curriculum Policy." Continue the argument as an advocate and then as a critic of each position. Work with a partner and then switch roles.

10. Relate an experience that you have had in creating curriculum-related policy. Share it with other educators and compare your experiences. What did you learn from the exchange?

PART II

✦ Paradigm ✦

7

✦ Paradigms in Curriculum ✦

**It is not enough to take steps which may some day lead to a goal;
each step must be itself a goal and a step likewise.**

JOHANN WOLFGANG VON GOETHE quoted in Johann Peter
Eckermann's *Conversations with Goethe* (September 18, 1823)

**The past is the *terra firma* of methods, of the roads which we
believe we have under our feet.**

JOSÉ ORTEGA Y GASSET "In Search of Goethe from Within,
Letter to a German" *Partisan Review* (December, 1949)

**A philosophy is characterized more by the formation of its
problems than by the solution of them.**

SUSANNE K. LANGER *Philosophy in a New Key* (1942)

SETTING THE STAGE

This chapter is an introduction to the next six chapters of the book. These chapters
present a range of orientations to how work in the curriculum field should be conducted and what it entails.

Part I of this book provided perspective for addressing these questions by interpreting curriculum as a field of study, and by situating the work of curriculum studies
within historical, philosophical, socioeconomic, and policy contexts. Part II asks:
Within these contexts, how do we proceed? How do we address questions about the
nature of worthwhile knowledge and experiences? I am reminded of the old "Think
and Do" books that were used for years in the elementary school. Part II essentially
deals with the "think and do" of curriculum itself. *What* do we think about, what
considerations are most relevant when we do curriculum? *How* do we think about
these matters?

Such questions as these invoke the consideration of paradigms. For more than twenty years, philosophers of science have been concerned about paradigms of inquiry. Much of this interest was generated by Thomas Kuhn's *The Structure of Scientific Revolutions* (1962). Kuhn drew upon data from philosophy, history, and psychology as well as from the natural sciences to argue that the doing of science in any era proceeds from a conceptual framework. This framework or paradigm is a loosely connected set of ideas, values, and rules that governs the conduct of inquiry, the ways in which data are interpreted, and the way the world may be viewed. While there is a fairly wide latitude within such inquiry, it does have rather definite boundaries. The territory within these boundaries, the paradigm or conceptual framework thus defined, is called "normal science" by Kuhn. As scientists of any era proceed using inquiry defined by the assumptions of normal science, they may begin to discover *anomalies* or occurrences that they cannot explain. Over a period of time, after a number of such anomalies have accumulated, it becomes apparent that normal science is inadequate to deal with certain categories of problems. As these problems are deemed significant enough, a state of crisis emerges, and it is necessary to alter the world view (the value structures and rules) that guides inquiry. In the physical sciences, for example, the interactions of matter and energy within the atom could not be explained sufficiently by Newtonian physics. Similarly, problems regarding the speed of light and the nature of time and space in the universe of astrophysics necessitated new forms of inquiry. Thus, we find a shift of scientific paradigms from Newton's clockwork universe to the relativity theories of Einstein and the quantum theory of Max Planck after the turn of the twentieth century. Similarly, one can refer to other revolutions in science: the move from a geocentric to a heliocentric conception of the solar system sponsored by discoveries of Galileo, Copernicus, and others; the move to a microbe theory of disease promoted by Pasteur, Lister, and others; the transition from Euclidian to non-Euclidian geometry in mathematics; and even the gradual acceptance of a round earth instead of a flat one.

Although the intervening years have brought criticism of Kuhn's analysis (e.g., Lakatos and Musgrave, 1970), a positive outgrowth has been the raising of conscious attention in many scholarly areas to focus on paradigms that guide inquiry. The social sciences have done much in this regard in recent years. So, too, has education.

Curriculum theory, perhaps as much as any other area of educational studies, has given serious attention to the question of paradigms. There are two major ways, returning to our what/how distinction, that we will look at paradigms in the curriculum field. The first pertains to *what* questions are asked and the second to *how* curriculum inquiry is conducted. At first, this distinction will hold clearly enough; however, as we move into Chapters Twelve and Thirteen, it begins to fade. We will eventually see that while the what and how can be productively separated for analytic purposes, they become integrated in actuality.

But let us maintain the distinction for the present. Tanner and Tanner (1980) and Schubert (1982a) argue that Ralph W. Tyler's (1949) *Basic Principles of Curriculum and Instruction* synthesizes the paradigmatic questions of the curriculum field. This is one answer to the *what* question. We shall see that an ample supply of others have challenged the paradigm represented by Tyler; nevertheless, it has persisted and certainly should be recognized for the widespread influence it exerts. The *what* question does not directly refer to the *what* that should be taught; instead, it centers on what considerations should be made when analyzing or developing curriculum.

The *how* question refers to how research or, more broadly, inquiry should be conducted. Here we see that attention is placed on epistemology. How can we know about curriculum? What is valuable curriculum knowledge? Relative to this problem, we will consider Joseph Schwab's critique (1969, 1971) of *theoretic* or *empirical/ analytic* orientations to curriculum inquiry and his proposal for *practical* inquiry, which leads to a paradigm of curriculum (Schwab, 1973) that can be seen as an alternative to the Tyler Rationale. The practical paradigm links the what and the how, providing perspective that relates to a loosely connected array of curriculum theorists who argue that curriculum should be interpretive and/or emancipatory. We will consider this in more detail by comparing three paradigms of curriculum inquiry: (1) the perennial or empirical/analytic, (2) the practical or interpretive, and (3) the critical or emancipatory. Each of these is examined briefly in this chapter and then is given expanded treatment in the next six chapters. Because of its significant influence, the perennial or analytic paradigm is discussed in Chapters Eight through Eleven, one chapter for each of its key topics: purposes, learning experiences or content, organization, and evaluation. Chapter Twelve elaborates the practical or interpretive paradigm, while Chapter Thirteen reveals a paradigm of critical praxis.

One further point is necessary to the setting of the stage for both this chapter and the others that comprise Part II. My intent is not to provide *the answers*, but to illustrate the structure of the paradigms presented and to engage the reader in a consideration of questions and sample answers that each paradigm evokes. The presentation of a curriculum cookbook would be an insult to practitioners who are fully capable of engaging in meaningful curriculum inquiry, especially if given access to the kinds of questions that scholars address.

THE DOMINANT CURRICULUM PARADIGM:
RALPH W. TYLER'S CATEGORIES

Tyler's (1949) paradigm was first written as course syllabus for Education 360, which he taught at the University of Chicago. It found its way into book form when the clamor for copies from other universities became loud enough. The book has continued to be used widely, has had many reprintings, and has been translated into at least ten languages. It is doubtless the most widely cited curriculum book, and in a study conducted by Harold Shane (1980), Tyler's book was rated along with John Dewey's *Democracy and Education* as one of the two most influential books on curriculum thought and practice.

Tyler (1949) identified four questions that should provide the parameters for curriculum study and uses the questions as his chapter titles as follows:

1. *What Educational Purposes Should the School Seek to Attain?*
2. *How Can Learning Experiences Be Selected Which Are Likely to Be Useful in Attaining These Objectives?*
3. *How Can Learning Experiences Be Organized for Effective Instruction?*
4. *How Can the Effectiveness of Learning Experiences Be Evaluated?*

Admittedly, the widespread use of this book is due in part to the educational reputation that Tyler had already developed as director of evaluation for the Eight Year

Study, dean of the Division of Social Sciences at the University of Chicago, evaluation director of the U.S. Armed Forces Institute, educational advisor to several U.S. presidents, and numerous positions with other governmental agencies and private foundations in education that he has actively continued to fulfill well into the 1980s. In a 1980 interview with Tyler (1980b) he openly acknowledged that his 1949 rationale was an attempt to summarize and synthesize what had been said earlier by other curriculum writers such as Franklin Bobbitt, W. W. Charters, John Dewey, Boyd Bode, Harold Rugg, and Henry Harap. In fact, Cremin (1971) identifies the curriculum field's indebtedness to William T. Harris who, in the late nineteenth century, set forth concerns that one can relate to those of Tyler. Yet the manner in which Tyler handled the questions, by pointing out criteria and principles for decision, makes his work unique.

Curriculum research grew rapidly since the 1950s (Schubert 1980a), and much of it can be categorized within each of the key terms of Tyler's four questions (Schubert, 1982a): purposes, learning experiences, organization, and evaluation. Chapters Eight, Nine, Ten, and Eleven, respectively, are devoted to a presentation of the numerous subcategories that have emerged in each of these perennial categories of curriculum, giving special attention to interests and criticisms of this knowledge for educational practice.

The simplicity and parsimony of Tyler's "Rationale" accounts in no small measure for its appeal. Four central questions, from a practitioner's view, were much less unwieldy than were the eighteen produced in 1927 by Harold Rugg and others for the Twenty-sixth Yearbook of the National Society for the Study of Education or the more subtle and complicated questionings of philosophers of education of the Progressive era such as John Dewey (1916, 1938a), L. Thomas Hopkins (1929), and Boyd H. Bode (1927).

In the years that followed Tyler's (1949) book, aspiring curriculum and instruction writers, enticed by technology, translated the intent of Tyler's Rationale into a how-to manual. More will be said about this in the next four chapters. Others (Kliebard, 1975) criticized Tyler for not attending to political dimensions of curriculum and for lack of precision in language. We now turn to the mode of inquiry that merged with the Tyler Rationale in the decades following its publication.

In the late 1950s and throughout the 1960s, behavioral science research methods became the dominant form of educational research. These are epitomized by Campbell and Stanley (1966) and Kerlinger (1973, 1979). There are many reasons why this occurred, too many to discuss fully here, but a few are worth mentioning. There was already a long line of powerful researchers in curriculum that stretched back to E. L. Thorndike at Teachers College, Columbia University, and Charles H. Judd at the University of Chicago, who both trace a line of mentorship to Wilhelm Wundt and his first experimental psychological laboratory in Leipzig, Germany. There was the increasing reverence for science in the culture at large, which steadily crept into the social sciences and especially the professions (such as education) that sought greater academic respect. A powerful manifestation of this phenomenon was in the post-*Sputnik* curriculum reform movement. Specialists from the subject matter areas were called upon to develop curriculum commensurate with the structure of their discipline, and psychologists were asked to provide systems of learning that conveyed the disciplinary knowledge. As time passed, curriculum projects or packages were implemented, and it became clear that they needed to be evaluated. Psychologists and educators whose training was in empirical, analytic, behavioral, and objectivist research methodology, were called upon to assess outcomes.

The press for accountability was even greater with the educationally oriented Great Society programs of the late 1960s and early 1970s, such as Head Start, Follow Through, and Upward Bound. Quantitatively expressed data were seen as the prime source of truth and the only avenue to credible reports of accomplishments (Broudy, 1982b), and statistical virtuosity became more politically persuasive than did careful argument and interpretation of experience as a basis for funding. Governmental officials and citizens alike were caught in the difficult dilemma of trying to determine the meaning of true and credible reports of alleged successes of educational programs.

The empirical-analytic mode of research became ubiquitous, not only in evaluation but in the host of studies that compared one curriculum or instructional method with another. In short, it became the paradigm, the governing rules, for the conduct of educational research and remains prominent today, as is obvious from a cursory glance at educational research journals. Even educational philosophy and other foundational studies adopted a rather technical application of concept analysis in the 1960s, derived from analytic philosophy. Together, the behavioristic psychologists and the concept analysts brought a technical rationality to educational scholarship. In the curriculum field, this technical rationality merged with the Tyler Rationale to make the perennial paradigm more mechanistic and positivistic than it had been as it evolved from Tyler's extensive interaction with and responsiveness to schools in the Eight Year Study and elsewhere. Tyler's original emphasis on a broad notion of behavior (including how learners think and feel), his attention to their experiences in and out of school, and his advocacy of the need for active involvement of students in their own learning experiences became overshadowed by cookbook approaches that translated the Tyler Rationale into a theoretic recipe for curriculum development. This reinterpretation of the perennial paradigm became the object of criticism by those who advocated practical and critical orientations.

A PRACTICAL PARADIGM FOR CURRICULUM INQUIRY

In "The Practical: A Language for Curriculum," Joseph Schwab (1969) argued that curriculum was moribund due to its preoccupation with the technical, behavioristic research paradigm, which he labeled *theoretic*. Schwab's use of this term refers not to its everyday usage, but harkens back to Aristotle's distinction between theoretic and practical knowledge. Drawing from his Aristotelian roots, Schwab constructed a case against the domination of a theoretic language (paradigm) in educational research. Not only did he build a compelling critique, unlike many writers who stop with criticism, he also provided an image of what should be, namely, a practical paradigm.

Schwab's critique is not about *what* the curriculum should be like; rather, it concerns *how* curriculum inquiry should proceed. His use of the term *language* is analogous to paradigm. He identified signs of crisis evident in the "flight" of educational researchers away from the phenomena that they purport to study: actual educational situations. There is the flight to experts in other fields to solve curriculum problems; witness the turn to psychologists and subject matter specialists in the post-*Sputnik* curriculum reform movement. There is the flight to discourse about the field instead of action that resolves problems within the field, a flight to the sidelines to comment on the field but not become involved in its problems, and a tendency to repeat the old knowledge under new labels as evidenced by well-known cycles of the educational bandwagon of trends and pseudosolutions (Schwab, 1970, an expanded version of the 1969 article).

These and other signs set forth a crisis of principle that required a paradigm shift from the theoretic to the practical, quasi-practical, and eclectic. The salient elements of the theoretic and practical paradigms can be contrasted relative to Aristotle's four well-known categories of causation: formal, material, efficient, and final (see Figure 7-1).

The *formal cause* or problem source of the theoretic exists as a mere state of mind, whereas that of the practical is in an actual state of affairs. In other words the theoretic researcher perceives bits and pieces of problems and asks a broad question such as: What characteristics do good high school science teachers have? For example, the theoretic researcher might ask: What traits can be discovered that high school science teachers whose students score above a certain level on achievement tests have in common? The practical researcher, in contrast, would want to focus on a particular setting, for example, a particular high school and a problem actually experienced there: How can attendance be improved at high school A? The practical inquirer, however, would not be content to solve the problem by dealing with symptoms alone. Instead, he or she would seek root causes. Such research might reveal that activities in high school A had little to do with sources of meaning, sense of direction, or personal growth in student lives. A behavioral solution of providing T-shirts or other extrinsic motivation to increase attendance would be viewed as antithetical to the search for excellence or virtue that should be the driving force behind curriculum.

The *material cause* asks: What is the subject matter under inquiry? What is the nature of the knowledge being sought by inquiry? The theoretic researcher, taking physical science as a model, seeks generalizations that are broadly applicable, reminiscent of the laws of motion or gravity. The practical researcher sees this as a false hope when dealing with a field that is composed of persons in changing contexts, not things. Therefore, the advocate of practical research recommends that the search be for insights into situationally specific problems. It is enough to discover why students in high school C respond negatively to the use of formal lectures by science teacher B. It is viewed as unproductive to inquire further, as the theoretic researcher would, to seek to discover and verify a lawlike principle that students achieve less or more when taught by formal lecture methods.

The third cause, the *efficient*, deals with the kind or method of inquiry to be used. This is probably the point at which there is to be the greatest hiatus between the theoretic and practical. The theoretic researcher reveres induction that separates the inquirer from the situation studied for the sake of objectivity. Induction, in this sense, is thought to result in propositions that can serve as premises in deduction. The practical researcher sees immersion in the problematic arena itself as necessary. Thus, interaction is the practical counterpart of induction. One who has lived for years in a public housing project in the inner city knows life there better than a sociologist does who surveys the residents over a four-day period. Teachers who live in classrooms are in a better position to understand them than are the theoretic

	Theoretic	Practical
Problem Source of Inquiry (formal cause)	state of mind or abstract conceptualization of researcher	state of affairs or dilemma experienced
Method of Inquiry (efficient cause)	induction on phenomena by detached researcher and hypothetical deduction relative to findings	interaction with state of affairs; embeddedness and encounter as lived experience
Subject of Inquiry (material cause)	generalizations lawlike statements generic knowledge or information data	situationally specific insights increased meaning and sense of direction
End of Inquiry (final cause)	knowledge *qua* knowledge knowledge (data) *qua* publication	decision meaning sense of direction action

FIGURE 7-1. *Comparison of Theoretic and Practical Paradigms*

researchers who have amassed generic knowledge about classrooms by spending an hour or two gathering data in each. What can be generalized broadly about classroom life is quite limited. There remains the host of ways in which each classroom is different, subtly or profoundly, from others. If this rich uniqueness is left out of the picture, generalized renditions provide a distorted, impoverished, and lifeless portrayal.

The end of inquiry, or final cause, in the theoretic paradigm is knowledge for the sake of knowledge, which treats persons and situations as broad categories instead of acknowledging their unique needs and interests. The distinction is not merely that between basic and applied research, both of which are part of the theoretic orientation. The practical researcher is interested in sense of meaning and direction and in improved decision and action, and argues that inquiry in fields such as curriculum must focus on issues of quality of life and worthwhile experience in actual dilemmas. Moreover, the practical researcher criticizes the theoretical researcher on the grounds that his or her real goal is not to acquire knowledge but publications.

Some readers of Schwab's first article on practical inquiry (1969, 1970) criticized him for not believing in the worth of theories. They could hardly have been farther off target. Others argued that Schwab may not understand the technical character of behavioristic research; therefore, he opted for what Lindblom (1959) has called the "science of muddling through." These critics, too, were far from the truth. Schwab, a theoretical and statistical geneticist, surely had a strong background in quantitative measurement. He is a philosopher as well, one who advocates and exemplifies the value of a strong background in theories from many disciplines. This value was spelled out in a second article, "The Practical: Arts of Eclectic" (Schwab, 1971), in which he emphasized the need for practical researchers to have a broad, liberal background in as many bodies of theoretical literature as possible. If one has little background, one has little capacity to be eclectic. If one does have a background of theories, it is necessary to learn how to use them in the resolution of practical problems. This leads to three eclectic arts. The first is the ability to match theoretic perspectives with problems. The limitation of this art is that often the two don't make a good match. Thus, the second eclectic art is to tailor, adapt, and combine theoretical perspectives to fit situations. Bodies of theory, however, do not exist that offer relevant guidance to many situational problems. Therefore, the third eclectic art is to invent new solutions that fit situations. Thus, we see that Schwab's castigation of the theoretic paradigm was a specialized use of the term *theoretic* and that he staunchly advocates knowledge of theory as a basis for practical inquiry.

After the first two articles, some questioned why Schwab claimed to be writing about curriculum. Responding, he provided a third: "The Practical 3: Translation into Curriculum" (Schwab, 1973). There he identified four classroom commonplaces that he considered to be the essence of curriculum: teachers, learners, subject matter, and milieu. The derivation of these commonplaces is integrally connected with the principles of the practical paradigm. If one wants to *decide and act* with greater understanding in a *particular curriculum situation*, one should develop insight by *interacting* with that situation, which consists of teachers, learners, subject matter, and milieu. Milieu refers to the environment, including its physical, social, economic, and psychological aspects.

There is a further point about interaction—one of great importance. The teachers, learners, subject, and milieu interact and continuously influence one another. In Figure 7-2, for example, one could ask: How does the teacher affect other teachers? Or, how does he or she affect himself or herself? How does the teacher influence the learners? The process can be continued for every cell in the matrix. Yet such questions cannot be answered once and for all. They must be asked continuously. How can a researcher be present in every classroom to ask such questions? The only practical answer is that there is a teacher in every classroom, and there are also twenty to forty students. It is to them that we must turn for practical inquiry and for deliberation about the continuously changing dynamics of the commonplaces.

Schwab has not fully explicated this last point at the classroom level, although he moved in that direction in "The Practical 4: Something for Curriculum Professors to Do" (Schwab, 1983) by suggesting that teams of school personnel and outside resource persons be formed to deliberate (interact and discuss) about curriculum problems at the school building level. In Chapter Twelve, we will extrapolate further implications of the practical position.

A PARADIGM OF CRITICAL PRAXIS FOR CURRICULUM INQUIRY

Derived from existentialism, phenomenology, critical theory, and personal theorizing, this paradigm became visible in the mid-1970s through collections edited by William Pinar (1974, 1975). A history of the development of this loosely connected paradigm is provided by Mazza (1982), and a sampling of articles by Giroux, Penna, and Pinar (1981) appear under the label *reconceptualists*. The latter are set in juxtaposition with traditional and conceptual empiricist selections, largely because of their emphasis on a blending of action and inquiry (praxis) by reflection on what it

	Teachers	Learners	Subject Matter	Milieu
Teachers	T/T	L/T	SM/T	M/T
Learners	T/L	L/L	SM/L	M/L
Subject Matter	T/SM	L/SM	SM/SM	M/SM
Milieu	T/M	L/M	SM/M	M/M

FIGURE 7-2. *Interaction Among Practical Classroom Commonplaces*

Focus on a specific commonplace and read: How does _____ (category at top) affect _____ (category at left)? For example, How do teachers affect other teachers? How do teachers affect learners? Continue this process throughout the sixteen cells.

means to engage in worthwhile experience and how the latter can be pursued in the face of constraints on social justice.

Among the principal, current curriculum authors who emphasize different forms of critical praxis or emancipatory theorizing are Michael Apple, William Pinar, Henry Giroux, Madeleine Grumet, and their former students, and in turn their former students, as well as earlier curriculum writers and educational philosophers who inspired them, such as James B. Macdonald, Dwayne Heubner, Maxine Greene, John S. Mann, Ross Mooney, Paul Klohr, Ted Aoki, and Paulo Freire.

A strong theme in the work of these writers is their drawing to consciousness the taken-for-grantedness of one dominant epistemological paradigm (the theoretic, to use Schwab's language; the conceptual empiricist, to use Pinar's designation; the social behaviorist, to use Schubert's characterization; and the neopositivist, to use conventional philosophic discourse). Moreover, critical praxis seeks liberation from ideological constraints as well. It is argued that special attention needs to be given to the impact of race, socioeconomic class, and gender on education, quality of life, outlook on life, and capacity to grow and become more fully liberated.

Others, too, produce work that is influenced by, related to, or influences more mainstream emancipatory theorizing. Robert Donmoyer (1981), Thomas Barone (1983), Gail McCutcheon (1981), and Elizabeth Vallance (1982) build upon a model of educational criticism related to an artistic rather than scientific approach to qualitative research as explicated by their mentor, Elliot Eisner (1981). The phenomenological work presented by George Willis (1978) is also a major contribution in this domain. So, too, is Max van Manen's phenomenological theorizing based on the writings of philosopher Martin Heidegger, images of student life worlds by Martinus Jan Langeveld of the Netherlands, and others. Swedish curriculum theorists Ulf Lundgren and Daniel Kallos are also recognized for their contributions to research that pertains to critical praxis.

While contributors to critical praxis are varied and wide ranging, central tendencies were captured by Paul Klohr (1980) who noted nine commonalities within this highly divergent paradigm of reconceptualized curriculum thought. Klohr, mentor of William Pinar and numerous other scholars who maintain a connectedness with reconceptualist thought, identified salient tendencies that will serve as topical guides to the portrayal of emancipatory theorizing, which is discussed in Chapter Thirteen. Sketched briefly now, these characteristics should be viewed as tendencies, not as operational definitions or criteria for membership in a reconceptualist club. No such club exists; however, certain intellectual interests provide informal linkages among many of the scholars noted.

1. Organic View of Nature.   Nature is viewed as an interdependent, holistic, dynamic, ecological unit. Human beings are integrally embedded in nature. They are not mere outside observers.

2. Individuals as Creators of Knowledge and Culture.   Individual human beings are not simply viewed as receivers of knowledge through the educative process or of culture via socialization or enculturation. Rather, human beings interact with their environment, derive knowledge from it, and use that knowledge to contribute to the cultural milieu. Not only do power wielders, government officials, barons of business, famous writers, artists, and musicians, media personalities, wealthy socialites, scientists, and scholars create knowledge; every person does. The history of ordinary lives has made extraordinary contributions to human life and culture, although it goes largely unacknowledged.

3. Experiential Base of Method.   Method is a means of inquiry, of finding ways of coming to know oneself as organically embedded in culture and history and needing to rely more on experience. Heretofore, reliance has rested on authority, revelation, science and other sources of knowledge outside the individual who is striving to learn, grow, and become emancipated. Thus, the experience of one's autobiography, in the restitution and reconstitution of one's educational experiences, as Madeleine Grumet (1980) writes, is the seedbed of epistemological and pedagogical method.

4. Preconscious Experience.   Dominant educational and curricular literatures focus on behavior and consciousness, and mostly the former. Behavior is the prime concern, the main source of evidence, for theoretic (Schwab's term) researchers, conceptual empiricists (Pinar's term), and social behaviorists (Schubert's term). Others argue that it is the thought that counts (Posner, 1980, 1982), that the conscious interaction of new learning within the repertoire of long- and short-term memory should be the focus of attention. While the latter represents a major advance of cognitive over behaviorist psychology applied to curriculum, it does not address the preconscious to any sizable degree. The preconscious may pertain to Freudian and post-Freudian notions of subconscious and unconscious factors in personality or to more social and biological dimensions in Jung's collective unconscious, that is, archetypes derived from historical and mythological dimensions of the human psyche. It may also pertain to the array of contemporary literature on body-mind interaction or to spiritual dimensions of the individual and social self.

5. New Sources of Literature for Curriculum. Literatures of existentialism, phenomenology, radical psychoanalysis, critical theory, and to some degree Eastern thought are studied by those in the paradigm that deals with emancipatory theorizing. So, too, we find considerably more emphasis on poetry, theater, short stories, novels, films, and a variety of social and artistic criticism. One explanation for this broadening of literature is the fact that curriculum studies are seen as a pervasive human phenomenon, not relegated to and constricted by schooling alone and by the service delivery image of knowledge and skills implied by it (Schubert, 1982b).

6. Liberty and Higher Levels of Consciousness. Liberty or emancipation is not merely a label associated with political rhetoric. Rather, it is viewed as a central dimension of the growing person. To perceive through different lenses enriches and liberates cognition (Eisner, 1982). Similarly, Maxine Greene speaks of "wide awakeness," of seeing through multiple perspectives, of being more "perspectival," of learning to make the familiar strange and the strange familiar. This is a quality of development that is never fully made; it is always in the state of being created. It proceeds to increasingly higher levels of consciousness, not preidentified stages through which learners are expected to progress, but new levels created by persons who wish to grow and to liberate themselves from constraints of previous levels. The central assumption here is that higher levels of consciousness yield personal emancipation.

7. Means and Ends That Include Diversity and Pluralism. As Dewey argued on numerous occasions, means and ends are not opposite poles; neither are they equivalent to cause and effect. They are an integral part of the same process. Means, as Dewey reminds us, are ends-in-view. Thus, emancipatory pedagogy grows from involvement in diversity and pluralism. At the same time, it promotes diversity and pluralism, through engagement in varieties of educational situations and methods and by providing access to many different kinds of knowledge, skills, ideas, and interpretations.

8. Political and Social Reconceptualization. Personal and public growth is assumed to be impossible or least greatly impeded if social and economic conditions so thoroughly constrain the individual that he or she is unable to move toward higher levels of consciousness. The need for food, shelter, clothing, and other life-preserving requirements also may be so great that an individual cannot attend to anything but meeting those needs. Those who have work, often a full-time preoccupation with the mundane, are usually too tired to strive for personal growth and liberation. A vast majority of human beings do not experience the quality of life that enables meaningful, liberating endeavors without having to work at a mundane job. Those who are fortunate enough to organize their lives around the search for worthwhile experience are characterized by Paul Fussell (1983) as X class persons who have managed to move beyond taken-for-granted class characteristics and have reflectively created their own ways of living. The point is that the likelihood of attaining wide-awakeness, of having a chance to become emancipated through higher levels of consciousness, is today contingent upon socioeconomic class. If the vast majority of persons is to engage in emancipatory pedagogy, it must be liberated from constraints that perpetuate forces of oppression. This calls for a paradigm of critical praxis, which requires political and social reconceptualization and reconstruction. Curriculum and pedagogy derived from such a paradigm enable oppressed persons to realize that they are oppressed and that there are other levels of consciousness to be explored. Concomitantly, it necessitates the realization by oppressors that they do, in fact, oppress and that their acts of repression (unconscious though they may be) return in the form of repression to themselves as well as to the subjugated (Freire, 1970). The point that advocates of critical praxis try to make is that those who are concerned with curriculum cannot defensibly ignore the inequality of access to emancipatory knowledge that socioeconomic class demarcates.

9. New Language Forms. The language that one uses has great influence on both communication and on the way in which one views the world. As was noted in our discussion of Schwab's proposal for a language of the practical, the reference is to a mode of inquiry that invokes world view or outlook. The dominant curriculum language (that of the theoretic, conceptual empiricist, or social behaviorist) reveals a world of persons as potential products who are forged on the assembly lines of schools and are judged by methods of quality control that utilize technical, quantitative jargon. If students do not conform to the factory model of growth, they are reshaped by the military model of control and obedience to authority. If certain socioeconomic groups do not learn well enough, they are expected to exercise a puritanical will-power and "pull themselves up by their bootstraps."

These illustrations of models that pervade our educational thought and practice, it is argued, work contrary to emancipation. They control and dominate. Languages of moral compassion and sensitive aesthetic imagination are needed, as argued by Dwayne Huebner (1975a). New languages of discourse can enable us to think and act with greater perspective and to join together in the creation of pedagogy that emancipates. Such a unity of thought and action is the mainstay of critical praxis.

A COMPARATIVE MODEL OF PARADIGMS

Jurgen Habermas is one of the most widely cited contemporary philosophers who deals with the theory of knowledge and its cultural implications. In *Knowledge and Human Interests* (1971) and other sources (1973, 1975, 1979, 1984), he outlines a comparative analysis of three paradigms of inquiry, which he calls *sciences.* His use of the term *science* is interpreted broadly as study or inquiry. In contrast, the usual use of science in educational literature today is confined to the canons of replicability, validity, parsimony, and reliability and is usually associated with analyses of quantitative data derived from experimental and quasi-experimental research (patterned after such writers as Glass and Stanley, 1970; Kerlinger 1973; Cook and Campbell, 1979; Campbell and Stanley 1966). This rather specific interpretation of science is often referred to as empirical-analytic, positivist, or neopositivist. It dominates educational research literature today.

The conceptual-analytic mode also dominates public policy research with its linear emphasis on policy formulation, implementation, and evaluation, or what we referred to (in Chapter Six) as the treatment specification model. However, we also discussed other perspectives, drawing from Bernstein's *The Restructuring of Social and Political Theory* (1976), especially alternatives from phenomenology and critical theory. Similarly, the emergent acceptance of alternative paradigms for educational research is portrayed in an excellent collection by Eric Bredo and Walter Feinberg (1982). First, they present articles that illustrate the positivistic approach to social and educational research (such authors as B. F. Skinner, George C. Homans, James S. Coleman); then they proceed to set forth an interpretive orientation (e.g., Nelson Goodman, Peter Winch, Nell Keddie); and finally they adopt a critical approach (Paul Willis, Pierre Bourdieu, Jurgen Habermas).

This portrayal of alternatives parallels Habermas's analysis of three types of science already noted. His analysis is depicted in the modified version of a chart developed by Francine Hultgren (1982) in Figure 7-3. Drawing upon the work of Giroux (1980) as well as Habermas, Hultgren explicates three types of science (empirical-analytic, interpretive, and critical) relative to three characteristics they embody: the interests they serve, the kinds of social organization that they represent, and the mode of rationality they exhibit.

Empirical-Analytic Science Paradigm.   Empirical-analytic science serves technical interests. It does not admit to a value or ideological orientation of its own; yet its values are implied by the positivist or theoretic assumptions it represents. Its social organization is that of work. Work implies a hierarchical structure in which certain individuals are granted control over others by virtue of their position in bureaucracies. An instructional technologist, for example, might agree to design delivery systems for conveying information to others, or an evaluator would accept the task of data generation as a means to judgment. They would do so without questioning the ideological ramifications of their work. They are there to do a job.

The mode of rationality holds a faith in the certainty of knowledge generated by

TYPE OF SCIENCE OR INQUIRY	Empirical/Analytical	Hermeneutic	Critical
INTEREST SERVED	Technical	Practical	Emancipatory
SOCIAL ORGANIZATION	Work	Interaction	Power
	MODE OF RATIONALITY		
	Posits principles of control and certainty Operates in the interests of law-like propositions that are empirically testable Assumes knowledge to be value free Assumes knowledge to be objectified Values efficiency or parsimony Accepts unquestioningly, social reality as it is	Emphasizes understanding and communicative interaction Sees human beings as active creators of knowledge Looks for assumptions and meanings beneath texture of everyday life Views reality as intersubjectively constituted and shared within a historical, political, and social context Focuses sensitively to meaning through language use	Assumes the necessity of ideological critique and action Seeks to expose that which is oppressive and dominating Requires sensitivity to false consciousness Makes distorted conceptions and unjust values problematic Examines and explicates value system and concepts of justice upon which inquiry is based

**FIGURE 7-3.   *Habermas's Comprehensive Theory of Knowledge*
[derived from Hultgren (1982) and based on Habermas (1971),
*Bernstein (1976), and Giroux (1980)]***

empirical-analytic rules. Researchers who operate in this mode see themselves as searchers for lawlike propositions and seekers of verification of such propositions. Most of what they do is based on the value that the universe is explainable by probabilities; yet they hold that knowledge is value free and may be objectified, that is, made into a commodity to be delivered to others. Social reality, as it exists in overt behavior, is taken-for-granted as the basis for truth. To provide knowledge is to reflect the overt behavior or appearance of nature, not primarily the deeper or unseen mysteries that lie behind the surface. The most efficient avenue to this notion of truth is the best one.

Hermeneutic Science Paradigm.   Hermeneutic science involves practical interests; recall Schwab's practical paradigm. Its social organization is interaction among persons and the cultural and historical circumstances in which they are embedded. The mode of rationality looks for meaning that enhances interaction with others and events. Education or pedagogy is not pursued by service delivery systems; rather, human beings communicate thoughtful attempts to reveal that which lies deep within them and speaks through them, connecting their being to that of existence itself. Reality is not merely the way things appear; rather, it is created by communication among persons, a process known as intersubjectively constituted meaning. This process both depends on and contributes to historical, political, and social context. Of particular interest to hermeneutic sciences are hidden meanings that participants who are sensitive to language can evoke as a basis for continuous growth.

Critical Sciences Paradigm.   Proponents of critical praxis purport to go beyond the hermeneutic by emphasizing more emancipatory political interests. They claim that the search for meaning and virtue is impossible if not accompanied by a social organization that empowers human beings to transcend constraints imposed by socioeconomic class and its controlling ideologies. Meaning and virtue desired by practical interests can only be pursued if pedagogy goes beyond interaction to provide for socioeconomic equity and justice. Thus, critical praxis combines inquiry and action in an attempt to realize and expose that which is oppressive and dominating. Forces of oppression and domination prevent insight into one's own circumstances by contributing to a "false consciousness" or a perspective that maintains the control of dominant groups. Critical praxis combines sensitivity to false consciousness with conscious attempts to perceive and expose unjust values. To identify certain values as unjust, it is imperative that those who engage in critical science explicate the values that they hold. It is their position, furthermore, that empirical-analytic sciences are value laden without realizing it and that hermeneutic sciences do not sufficiently incorporate political action.

SUMMARY

We have discussed the notion of paradigm as a conceptual framework of values and rules that guide inquiry. In curriculum we identified two uses of paradigm. One pertained to the *what* or kinds of substantive topics addressed; the other pertained to the *how* or methods of inquiry used. We noted that Tyler's purposes, learning experiences, organization, and evaluation summarize four topics that have dominated the curriculum field since its inception at the turn of the twentieth century. We also noted that an empirical-analytic mode of inquiry evolved along with these perennial curriculum topics to create the dominant curriculum paradigm that we shall refer to as the "paradigm of perennial analytic categories." Each of the four substantive topics of this paradigm is presented separately in Chapters Eight through Eleven. Two alternative paradigms that have emerged in recent curriculum literature were introduced: the "paradigm of practical inquiry" and the "paradigm of critical praxis." These are elaborated in Chapters Twelve and Thirteen, respectively.

Finally, paradigms of inquiry were discussed relative to Habermas's theory of knowledge. His three categories (empirical-analytic, hermeneutic, and critical) can be related to the foregoing discussion of paradigms in curriculum literature. The empirical-analytic relates quite directly to the theoretic paradigm that Schwab criticizes and to that which the Tyler Rationale has become as it was merged with positivistic science. Schwab's practical paradigm is largely in harmony with the hermeneutic, except that Schwab is more of a pragmatist in the Deweyan sense than a phenomenologist as is usually associated with hermeneutics. One would do well to turn to the work of Max van Manen (1979, 1982, 1984a,b) for a more thorough phenomenological perspective. The critical perspective is a basis for emancipatory theorizing (e.g., Apple, 1979; Apple and Weis, 1983; Giroux, 1983).

COMMENTARIES

The guest commentators have been asked to keep their remarks on this chapter brief because the next eight chapters relate to specific dimensions of this one. Thus, they will confine their comments to matters of overview.

Intellectual Traditionalist

As long as we are discussing new terminology, I want to add an important point about the label bestowed upon me by the author. I am worried that it might be confused with the ordinary use of the term *traditionalist*, which is more commensurate with traditionalist used by Pinar (1975). Both have been clarified in this book, but I want to reemphasize the point because to equate intellectual traditionalist and traditionalist would be a *most serious error*. We are poles apart. I am in favor of a liberal education for all. The *traditionalist* of everyday educational discourse simply refers to strictly disciplined, subject-oriented schooling of the recent past. Pinar's *traditionalist* who includes such educators also takes society and its values for granted as they remain unreflectively instrumental in dealing with curriculum problems. Such traditionalists are both technical and concerned with liberal arts in name only, if at all. Traditionalism is a banal and hollow form of curriculum if it is not intellectual. In contrast, I draw upon the great intellectual traditions, the best literatures and ideas humanity has produced.

As for the topics of this chapter, I find the Habermas theory of knowledge compelling and interesting. It strikes me as a sad commentary that it is so seldom realized that interpretive and critical studies are much older and more venerable than are the empirical-analytic. Yet advocates of the latter (most education researchers, I gather) decry scholars who write from hermeneutic or critical perspectives as uninitiated newcomers. How ahistorical! The conceptual empiricists or social behaviorists fail to realize that they actually are the newcomers. Moreover, they are researchers, not scholars. There is an obvious difference.

Let me make short order of the rest. *Paradigm* is an overworked term; it's one of those bandwagon terms like *interface* and *infrastructure* and *entropy*. Nevertheless, the idea needs to be dealt with, so I will tolerate the term's use in this book.

Tyler's four topics seem to be common knowledge. What excellent teacher would have to be taught to think of purposes, learning experiences, organization, and evaluation? It should come as second nature. As for Schwab, Aristotle did the job of distinguishing theoretical from practical. In addition, Aristotle made explicit the connection of *aréte* or the search for excellence to practical inquiry. Schwab doubtless realizes its centrality but does not make it explicit enough. Without the search for excellence, the practical is merely trial and error, with no basis for critique or sense of direction. Schwab demonstrates that he realizes this by his advocacy of the arts of eclectic and the need to ground inquiry in a strong liberal education. Of course, I agree that we need to attend to Schwab's four commonplaces, especially subject matter, the commonplace that must be the hub of all learning.

I am not so favorable toward this emancipatory paradigm, however. It is not that it isn't a wonderful ideal, but idealist though I am, I cannot sustain hope in the dissolution of societal extremes of rich and poor, controllers and oppressed. There is too much naive Marxism in it for my taste. If literature teaches us anything about this topic, it is that the dark side of human nature will always bring socioeconomic oppression. The only way to liberate is within the life of the mind.

Social Behaviorist

It is amusing how long it takes for the intellectual traditionalist to be brief.

I guess I must admit to being one of those dastardly empirical-analytic neopositivists. There is nothing more practical than a good theory, an empirically verified one. I think Schwab gives a false picture of research under his label of *theoretic*. We need pure research that discovers knowledge unencumbered by having to justify its application. We also need applied research. Both can have practical value, the first in the long term and the second immediately. But both *must* adhere to the canons of science: replicability, objectivity, validity, reliability, parsimony, and the like. We already have excellent bodies of research of this kind on Tyler's four topics and on Schwab's commonplaces. The emergence of sophisticated empirical and analytic research techniques is the most valuable contribution to educational and curriculum inquiry yet. I don't see that there is so much to lament as I hear being lamented!

Finally and of greatest import, it is necessary to avoid connecting research with values and ideology. When these enter, researchers turn from their responsibility to be dispassionate. Advocates have no place in research. Research is a powerful tool. The new brand of scholars who sponsor ideology need to be reminded by Lord Acton and many others of similar insight that power tends to corrupt and that absolute power corrupts absolutely. I have as little use for their ideological and revolutionary rhetoric as I have for their subjectivity. It is an ingenious ploy to argue that reality lies behind the sensed world. Then one can make reality anything one wishes. Thus, their manufactured mysteries at the heart of the universe can be used as a basis for peddling ideology. They should get out of the academic business and join movements. To call their work *science* is to debase the term.

Experientialist

It is important to acknowledge a plurality of paradigms. It is good that Schwab's commonplaces and Tyler's questions draw our attention to different aspects of reality. We need different conceptual lenses, a variety of substantive categories through which to gain a more comprehensive image of our changing reality. The major problem is when one dominates. There are other categories, too. Frymier (1967) draws attention to artifacts, actors, and events; Walker (1971) to platform, deliberation, and design; Lundgren (1972) to a variety of frame factors. It is not important to explain each of these here (some are elaborated elsewhere in the book); instead, they are illustrative of the variety of lenses through which we might look at curriculum.

The paradigms of inquiry are similar but to an extent only. I do believe that there are certain problems that can be dealt with by empirical-analytic or theoretic means; others can best be treated by practical, interpretive, or critical inquiry. The point is that very few problems can be treated effectively by the technical approach of the empirical-analytic mode alone, and it is the dominant mode. A massive turnabout is needed. I subscribe to the hermeneutic mode of inquiry, thus to Schwab's practical, but I believe that it must be augmented and strengthened by critical praxis. I believe that my roots in progressive education support this. Dewey was a practical (almost hermeneutic) scientist. The recipe-oriented, theoretic researcher so prevalent today would have been a curse to him. Dewey, as one who wanted to reconstruct society, embodied a sizable spark of emancipatory theorizer. It is difficult to imagine that one so desirous of connecting democracy and education would not support emancipatory pedagogy. He supported similar ideas and movements in his day, so I suspect he would do so today as well.

SUGGESTED READING

There are many sources listed in the text of the chapter. Some are noted here along with others for those who wish to study the chapter topics in greater depth.

On the idea of paradigms I suggest Kuhn's (1962) classic and commentary on it by Lakatos and Musgrave (1970). One should also see Drengson's (1983) work on shifting paradigms.

Ralph Tyler (1949) is the best source on Tyler, as is a 1977 reassessment by Tyler in an ASCD publication edited by Molnar and Zahorik (1977). Kliebard's (1970) critique of the Tyler rationale is worth reading as well. The work of Ralph Tyler is being catalogued by the Ralph W. Tyler Project at the National Foundation for the Improvement of Education in Washington, D.C., under the leadership of Helen Kolodziey.

Schwab's work is collected in an edited volume by Westbury and Wilkof (Schwab, 1978). All three essays on practical inquiry are there; also particularly relevant to his notion of inquiry are "Eros and Education" and "What Do Scientists Do?" Schwab's more recent statement on the practical appeared in the Fall 1983 *Curriculum In-*

quiry under the title: "The Practical 4: Something for Curriculum Professors to Do." There, he conveys his image of how to organize schools for practical curriculum deliberation.

Emancipatory theorizing is represented by Apple (1979, 1982a), Apple and Weis (1983), Greene (1973, 1978), Giroux (1981, 1983), Freire (1973), Pinar (1974, 1975), Pinar and Grumet (1976) and Young (1971). Giroux (1983) is a most readable and thorough development of a resistance pedagogy that opposes domination. Paul Willis (1977) presents an incisive account of the relationship of education to social class in *Learning to Labor*. Paul Fussell (1983) provides a vivid, witty, and well-written interpretation of social class characteristics in the United States.

Paradigmatic contrasts developed by Habermas are elaborated in his *Knowledge and Human Interests* (1971). Bernstein (1976) interprets similar paradigms for social and political thought, as is done by Feinberg (1983) for educational research. Bredo and Feinberg (1982) amplify the characteristic differences among positivistic, interpretive, and critical inquiry in a fine set of readings with selections on each orientation or paradigm. Overview classifications of several different orientations to educational inquiry are provided with incisive clarity by Kneller (1984) and Soltis (1984). Implications for curriculum inquiry are readily identifiable from their analyses.

RECOMMENDATIONS FOR REFLECTION

1. Where do you now stand with respect to the commentators? Have your views changed or remained essentially the same?

2. Do you believe that Tyler's four categories are in conflict with Schwab's commonplaces? Do they complement one another in some ways and conflict in others? Please elaborate.

3. Can you find research studies that illustrate the theoretic and practical modes discussed by Schwab?

4. Analyze your own educational situation in terms of the matrix (Figure 7-2) based on Schwab's commonplaces.

5. Analyze your own educational situation in terms of Tyler's four topics: purposes, learning experiences, organization, evaluation.

6. Compare and contrast the insights revealed by activities 4 and 5. Which is most revealing? Why? Is there a sense in which the approaches enrich each other? Do they lead to any conflicting interpretations?

7. What theoretical knowledge (bodies of theory) serves as a basis for your own eclectic decision making? What disciplines or theories would enable your decision making to improve?

8. Which of the three types of science identified by Habermas (Figure 7-3) is in greatest harmony with your own outlook? Which is most dissonant with your outlook? What reasons can you give to defend your choices?

9. Why does the paradigm of critical praxis bring so much resistance from educators? Try to think of possible explanations.

10. What are the advantages of practical and theoretic inquiry as developed by Schwab? Which do you think best meets the needs of contemporary curriculum problems?

11. Why isn't there one best form of curriculum inquiry? Should the achievement of one best form be a goal for curriculum scholars?

8

✦ Paradigm of Perennial Analytic Categories: Purpose ✦

Many persons have a wrong idea of what constitutes true happiness. It is not attained through self-gratification but through fidelity to a worthy purpose.
HELEN KELLER *Helen Keller's Journal* (1938)

The great and glorious masterpiece of man is to know how to live in purpose.
MICHEL EYQUEM DE MONTAIGNE "Of Experience" *Essays* (1580–1588)

The secret of success is constancy to purpose.
BENJAMIN DISRAELI *Speech* (June 24, 1870)

SETTING THE STAGE

As might be suspected from Chapter Seven, the topic of purposes is not without controversy. First, a variety of terms are used in connection with the topic—purposes, aims, goals, objectives, ends—and the list could go on and on. Some curriculum writers treat these terms as essentially synonymous. Others see them as levels in a hierarchy from general to specific. Within this group, differences exist as to which terms are more specific. Some hold aims as most general, purposes as more specific, followed by particular goals and highly specialized instructional objectives. The point is that one should be wary of those who dogmatically assert this or that as the accepted hierarchy, because no definitional scheme for these terms is widely accepted in curriculum literature.

The next major point is that many insist that the four basic questions of the 1949 Tyler Rationale constitute a stepwise curriculum recipe. Many of the major, synoptic curriculum texts over the past thirty years use curriculum development or design diagrams, supposedly based on the Tyler Rationale, that solidify it into a mechanistic formula for designing curriculum. In some of these books, a plethora of curriculum guides, and many teachers' manuals for school books or instructional packages, we see evidence of the influence of Tyler's four questions. Too often we see vast distortion by those who have not remembered the last page of Tyler's book (1949), wherein he cautioned:

> *Another question arising in the attempt at curriculum revision by a school or part of a school is whether the sequence of steps to be followed should be the same as the order of presentation in this syllabus. The answer is clearly "No." [p. 128]*

In discussions with Tyler on this matter, he emphasized to me that his categories of purposes, learning experiences, organization, and evaluation are intended to be analytic topics, not necessarily prescriptive directives. This perspective should be kept in mind as you read Chapters Eight through Eleven, each of which is built on one of Tyler's four categories.

In this chapter we begin with a look at four different orientations to the form that purposes should take. Midway in the chapter we discuss substantive and procedural criteria that may be used as a basis for selecting purposes, which is followed by an explanation of four general categories of substance with which purposes are likely to deal. Throughout the discussion of purpose, the reader should realize that form and substance exist in dynamic interplay; their separation is only for purposes of analysis.

It would be useful, here, to differentiate between usual uses of *curriculum development* and *curriculum design*. Curriculum development is the broader of the two terms and incorporates curriculum design within it. It is exemplified by such classic curriculum works as *Curriculum Development* by Caswell and Campbell (1935), *Developing a Curriculum for Modern Living* by Stratemeyer et al. (1947, 1957), *Fundamentals of Curriculum Development* by Smith, Stanley, and Shores (1950, 1957), *Curriculum Development: Theory and Practice* by Taba (1962), and *Curriculum Development: Theory into Practice* by Tanner and Tanner (1975, 1980). Curriculum development involves the broad consideration of curriculum vis-à-vis social issues, foundations of education, organization for change and revision, program administration, the nature of subjects or disciplines, human relations, organization development, theory, practice, supervision, research, and personnel issues as well as design.

Curriculum design usually focuses more exclusively on some variation of the Tylerian (1949) questions. This may be broadly conceived as by Pratt (1980), who includes foundational considerations and instructional design. Or it may be more specifically focused on the design of courses, as exemplified by Posner and Rudnitsky (1982). In short, design magnifies the technique of dealing with purpose, content or experience, organization, and evaluation, whereas development includes design plus its context and treats ways and means of formulating, implementing, evaluating, and changing curriculum. Some would say that design deals with devising the plan and characteristics of the plan itself and that development treats the whole orchestration necessary to actualize the planning and the plan. One need only look at such sources as Saylor, Alexander, and Lewis (1981), English (1983), Doll (1982), Wiles and Bondi (1984), and Hass (1983) to learn that development and design have much overlap in the literature. But one thing is certain: all treatments give high priority to the nature and function of purposes.

There is one further caveat, a reminder that book-length treatments exist on the nature and function of purposes in curriculum and philosophy of education (e.g., Morris, 1972; Taylor, 1966; Nisbet, 1968; Goodlad, 1979). In one chapter one cannot hope to cover all bases. I do, however, hope to give you enough of a springboard to ask important questions. This is done, in part, by a strategy of efficiently listing examples, intents or advocacy statements, and criticisms of each position set forth. The examples, intents, and criticisms are not comprehensive, only illustrative, and they are written in the spirit of advocacy and counterargument.

ORIENTATIONS TO PURPOSE

In this section I identify four different orientations to the form that curricular purposes should take: global, behavioral, evolving, and expressive. By *form* I mean the ways in which purposes are stated and used, in contrast to substance, or that which is actually advocated. Each form represents a special philosophical outlook. (That is the case for substance of purpose too, which is treated later in the chapter.) Some contend that purpose is, in fact, the embodiment of the whole educational process that guides and efficiently manages curriculum development or design. Many curricularists at least view purpose as the hub or directive force from which the remainder of design and/or development processes emanate.

Global Purposes

Broadly based or global statements of the purposes of curriculum date back to antiquity. Plato saw the virtuous life as the ultimate goal; Aristotle's vision was one of happiness. The specifics that they advocated for educational practice were directed to these ends. Even in the more practical realm of ancient Rome, the specifics of Quintillian's curriculum were designed to produce the great orator, a symbol of excellence signifying learning and the educated man. Throughout the history of educational thought, the guiding power of some global conception of the good life exists in almost every proposal for curriculum and teaching.

Examples.   In recent years universal education has caused curricularists to broaden their outlook from the "cultured man" to conceptions of education that best serve the public at large. In 1861, Herbert Spencer identified five comprehensive purposes of education that lead to a full life: (1) direct self-preservation, (2) necessities of life, (3) rearing of offspring, (4) proper social and political relations, and (5) gratification of tastes and feelings. Here he set curriculum concerns in a broader perspective of moral and physical as well as intellectual development. Bearing close kinship with Spencer's notions of purpose is the 1918 statement of the *Cardinal Principles of Secondary Education* developed by the Commission on the Reorganization of Secondary Education appointed by the National Education Association. Under the leadership of Clarence Kingsley, the commission stated seven global purposes of education: (1) health, (2) command of fundamental processes, (3) worthy home membership, (4) vocation, (5) citizenship, (6) worthy use of leisure time, and (7) ethical character. As Edward Krug (1966, p. 117) described it: [this] "32-page pamphlet, drab in appearance but not in content . . . established for at least three decades the major dimensions of discussion about secondary schools." The discussion of issues raised by this document was considerably longer than thirty years and extended well into the grammar school and collegiate debate as well. The thirty-two pages discussed and interpreted the seven cardinal principles but did not specify their precise meaning, intentionally leaving them broad and inclusive.

Advocacy.   Global purposes are designed to provide educators general, prescriptive guidelines. This keeps the door open for interpretation that needs to be made during educational practice. Building-level administrators and teachers play important roles in interpreting the meaning of global purposes. Thus, implementation of the same purposes by different professional educators should look quite different, depending upon unique, situational needs, conditions, and circumstances. Although neither Spencer's purposes nor the Seven Cardinal Principles are overtly used today, they are subtly present in statements of purposes published by many school districts and state departments of education. In addition to purposeful guidelines for promoting basic skills and knowledge of the disciplines, which are often stated globally, Goodlad's (1983) massive study of schooling found: "state goals include a highly idealistic array pertaining to democratic processes, enculturation, truth and values, moral integrity, effective use of leisure time, personal flexibility, creativity and aesthetic expression, self-confidence, and the setting of life goals, particularly pertaining to continued learning" (p. 10). More often than not, we find school district goal statements that refer to the development of critical thinking, well-rounded growth, lifelong learning, and fully functioning personalities. These goals are intended as open-ended principles supporting the idea that professional educators should not be given recipes, but rather should be expected to interpret global goals creatively to fit situational needs.

Criticism.   No sane person could deny the value of health, worthy home membership, command of fundamental processes, and the like. Who would be in favor of illness, deranged home life, and the inability to deal with fundamental processes? The problem comes with what these general terms mean. "Worthy use of leisure" for ten different educators may hold ten vastly different interpretations. Global objectives are simply not explicit enough. A second problem is that each global purpose, if taken seriously, involves more than can be accomplished reasonably (Goodlad, 1978). In fact, the several national reports of the 1980s on the state of education in the United States (e.g., National Commission on Excellence in Education, 1983; Boyer, 1983; Goodlad, 1984; Sizer, 1984a) can be seen as reassessments of the broad mission of schooling as promoted by global purposes. These reports explicitly or implicitly blame the Cardinal Principles and similar statements for expecting schools to respond to too many social needs. To accomplish, or even approximate, the Seven Cardinal Principles would require that schools shoulder the burden of solving all social ills. This is impossible for one institution. We need to decide specifically what it is that schools should do, what kind of contribution they should make to society. Then they can set out to accomplish it more realistically. Otherwise, we wind up with a watered-down version of each. Moreover, global objectives are a political trick in that they are sufficiently vague that the crafty administrator can adapt or twist them to be expedient to any problem that might arise.

Behavioral Objectives

Historically, behavioral objectives were probably part of apprenticeship systems; though they were rarely stated in writing, apprenctices were expected to master certain tasks. Franklin Bobbitt (1918, 1924) first made the process explicit in the curriculum field. After making detailed observations of successful adult activities, he translated them into specific, itemized lists of objectives for student learning activities. W. W. Charters (1923) refined this activity analysis process by basing it on objectives built on societal ideals. In the 1960s and 1970s, we saw this spirit rekindled in the widespread behavioral objectives movement led by Mager (1962), Popham (e.g., Baker and Popham 1973), and others. Behavioral objectives were seen as very specific statements of purpose for which an end result, or terminal behavior, is stated in observable terms.

Examples.   To say, "The student will learn correct uses of the comma" is not a behavioral objective because there is no prespecified, observable, terminal behavior. The objective should read something like this: "The student will demonstrate knowledge of five comma rules (specify which ones) by stating them and correctly inserting commas in sentences where commas are omitted." Usually a proportion of items answered accurately and conditions under which answers are to be provided within a certain time frame is added to the specification.

Advocacy.   Behavioral objectives are intended to overcome the vagueness provided by global objectives. If teachers state the behavioral objectives for all of the lessons that they teach, they will be clearer and more explicit about what they are doing. Moreover, they can communicate accurately to parents, supervisors, and students exactly what they intend to teach. By stating objectives behaviorally, it is much easier to evaluate because it becomes obvious what is to be recognized as evidence of attainment of the objectives. Thus, behavioral objectives contribute greatly to acountability.

Due to the work of Benjamin Bloom (1956), David Krathwohl (1964), and others, behavioral objectives writers are able to specify levels of cognitive and affective functioning. Bloom developed a taxonomy of behavioral objectives in the cognitive domain that moves through six phases from lesser to greater complexity: recall or memory, comprehension, application, analysis, synthesis, and evaluation. Similarly, Krathwohl and others developed an affective or emotional hierarchy beginning with receiving, and moving through responding, valuing, organization (which perceives interrelationships among values), to a value complex (which is akin to world view or philosophy of life). Anita Harrow (1972) developed a psychomotor taxonomy that moves through observing, imitating, practicing, and adapting. Elaborate work in the late 1960s and 1970s was done to write behavioral objectives at higher levels within each taxonomical area, thereby attempting to provide greater breadth and depth to curricula that too often focus on the lower levels of recall, receiving, and observing.

Criticism.   Travers (1980) argued that the taxonomies improperly model biological sciences and do not justify their label adequately. Others object to the taxonomies because they inappropriately separate integrated aspects of human functioning. In other words, they cause teachers and curriculum developers to perceive students themselves as having separate affective or cognitive or psychomotor sides. A teacher may believe that a lesson is cognitive and ignore its affective consequences and implications, for example. These, of course, were not the intent of Bloom, Krathwohl, and others who originally developed the taxonomies as an analytic tool to help researchers and practitioners look more broadly at the relationships between educational objectives and the complex processes of cognitive and affective functioning.

A more widespread criticism of behavioral objectives goes beyond taxonomies to their style and assumptions. Staunch advocates of behavioral objectives assume that learning can be atomized into discrete components, that it is not holistic, and that these minute entities can be manageably dealt with. John Goodlad argues that there is no logical or epistemological justification for doing this (1978). If, in fact, it were possible to catalogue all behaviors involved in the learning process, the single act of orally reading a sentence would involve a vast array of behaviors. This makes the task of accurately listing the behaviors of a lesson or a day insurmountable, let alone those for all students in a school for a year.

Another problem has to do with time and prespecification. We often do not know, and cannot anticipate, how new knowledge or experience will fit with a learner's accumulated repertoire of knowledge. Some learning, perhaps a great deal, is not fully realized until much later than the classroom setting, perhaps years later.

Finally, how can the acquisition of values, understandings, attitudes, and appreciations be explicated in terms of observable behavior? They are matters of consciousness, not mere behaviors. Even if some values and attitudes can be incorporated into the overt curriculum, more are taught and learned through the hidden curriculum and, therefore, cannot be prespecified.

Close cousins of behavioral objectives are competency-based programs, performance objectives, task analyses, and results-oriented instruction. These are soundly criticized by Atkin, Stake, Stenhouse, Eisner, and others in Hamilton et al. (1977). Such techniques also assume that tasks, competencies, results, and performances can be prespecified in advance as atoms of learning to be delivered to learners. This assumes that needs do not change during implementation, that learners have no expertise about their own needs, that discrete elements of the learning process can be extracted without affecting the whole, and that observable behavior is more important than consciousness. There is no scientific basis to support these claims.

Evolving Purposes

John Dewey argued (1902, 1916, 1938a) that objectives are not the prespecifications of educative experience, but the outcomes of such experience. Experience is educative if it provides increased capacity for growth. Growth can be fostered in many ways, but one is through dialogue between teachers and learners who together create and pursue a sense of direction.

Examples. Students as human beings want to engage in experience that satisfies their needs (Hopkins, 1954). They have what Dewey referred to as ends-in-view. Teachers engage in discussion with them about the probable consequences of these student-centered purposes. Together they work out a process of problem solving that enriches the students' experience by enabling them to reconstruct and reflect on their situation with greater perspective. For teachers and students, purposes are not directives, documents, or curriculum guides; rather, they are a sense of direction that values growth.

Advocacy.   Growth may seem to be a vague sense of direction, but it is intentionally maintained in this state. To define growth operationally would defeat the purpose of evolving purposes. Neither curriculum developer nor teacher can impinge on students' self-determination by deciding what is best for them. No curriculum without representation might be the maxim of democratic education equivalent to no taxation without representation. Students are engaged in asking what is worthwhile to learn and what would be the personal and social consequences of doing so. As they pursue learning of this kind, they become acquainted with existing bodies of knowledge when they are relevant to them; thus, they are assimilated more permanently in this way. As problems are solved or interests are pursued, students generate new problems, perceptions of worth, and projections of consequences. This cycle continues throughout life; thus, a curriculum based on evolving purposes promotes lifelong learning.

Criticism.   Evolving purposes sound good in principle, but they are too idealistic. First, the use of evolving purposes requires teachers who are able to engage in meaningful dialogue with students. Most have not been trained to do this. Second, even if there were a large number of teachers trained to engage in dialogue, some would not want to use this interactive method because of the extra effort and planning required. Teaching, for many teachers, is a job—not a life mission. But suppose that a large number did accept the mission; they could not engage in dialogue with each of 30 elementary school students (or 150 to 200 students for secondary school teachers). Third, students do not know what is good for them; they want to be told what to do. Finally, the process is too open ended. Students would never get around to seeing the relevance of certain essential subjects such as grammar, algebra, physics, and the like.

Expressive Objectives

This form of objectives, advocated by Elliot Eisner (1969), assumes that it is sometimes desirable to provide activities for students without prespecification or even a clear idea of what the outcomes will be.

Examples.   A teacher may read excerpts from *Huckleberry Finn* or another work of great literature to students for twenty minutes a day for several weeks. Time might be set aside to discuss the book, but no prespecified outcomes are given. A teacher may play a Mozart symphony and ask students to dance or draw expressing their response to the music.

Advocacy.   Students would not be constrained by predetermined goals. Teachers and students would be able to discover what the experience had in store for them. Eisner observes that few, if any, persons set forth objectives before attending a play or movie (Eisner, 1985). Nevertheless, we can learn and grow a great deal by attending such an activity.

Criticism. Expressive objectives are too vague. Schools should deal with intended or prespecified learning outcomes (see Johnson, 1977a). When the teacher sets out the paints and paper, she has many intended learning outcomes: that the students will learn to use paints, that they will begin to appreciate the kind of expression that paints can produce, that they will gain skill or technique by watching one another and the teacher, that they will, in fact, express a feeling or idea that might later be discussed, that their expression might open doors to interests that could be studied. Even when we choose to attend a movie or play or concert, we have usually heard something about it from a friend, have read a review, or have simply gathered from a newspaper ad that it would speak to an interest. In this sense, it is not merely amorphous expression but a rudimentary sense of personal, intended learning outcome that impels us to act in the interest of our own growth. Furthermore, as with evolving purposes, there is no guarantee with expressive purposes that desirable material would be covered. Only a little bit here and there is what students get from ordinary, unguided life experience. School, institutionalized education, should be a structured series of intended learning outcomes (Johnson, 1977a; Posner and Rudnitsky, 1982).

SUBSTANTIVE CRITERIA FOR SELECTING PURPOSES

In *Fundamentals of Curriculum Development*, Smith, Stanley, and Shores developed principles or criteria for validating curricular objectives. This was a further refinement of a similar procedure included in the 1950 first edition of their widely cited text. Of their five criteria, three are substantive and two are procedural (Smith, Stanley, and Shores, 1957, pp. 108–123). Their substantive criteria for selecting purposes are basic human needs, social adequacy, and democratic ideals, while procedural criteria include consistency, noncontradiction, and behavioral interpretation. Tyler (1949) similarly identified sources of purposes: study of learners, study of contemporary life outside the school, and suggestions from subject matter specialists. He further asserts that philosophy and psychology of learning are "screens" or criteria through which purposes are mediated.

These two books, Tyler (1949) and Smith, Stanley, and Shores (1950, 1957) were two of the most influential texts in twentieth century curriculum literature, and both acknowledged the importance of supporting assertions of curricular purpose with a rationale. They encouraged curriculum developers and designers to recognize that purposes are derived from assumption about learners, society, and knowledge. They argued that none of the three can be left out of the curricular decision-making equation. It is important to rank and balance these three key elements that trace back to Dewey as they relate to different situations and circumstances. To do justice to the magnitude of the problem of developing defensible purposes, however, recall Huebner's (1975a) admonition (quoted in Chapter One) that questions about the nature of knowledge, society, and learners are among the most profound that human beings can address. If there are no easy answers to these questions, there are no easy answers to the problem of what purposes the curriculum should promote. It requires that curriculum developers address head on the issue of what it means to lead a good life and what knowledge, social system, and kind of learning contributes to it.

This emphasis by Tyler (1949) and Smith, Stanley, and Shores (1950, 1957) on the search for a rationale as a basis for curriculum development derived from study of learners, society, and knowledge has been continued in many subsequent curriculum texts. See, for example, the widely used synoptic texts by Oliva (1982, p. 160); Saylor, Alexander, and Lewis (1981, p. 165); McNeil (1981, pp. 93–95); Tanner and Tanner (1980, pp. 83–90); and Wiles and Bondi (1979, p. 223).

Daniel Tanner (1982) reminds us that this tripartite procedure for developing purposes has been present in curriculum literature since the field began. For example, Dewey (1902) emphasized three fundamental factors in the educative process: learner, subject matter, and society. In discussing the deliberations of the renowned Twenty-sixth Yearbook Committee of the National Society for the Study of Education (Rugg, 1927b), Chairperson Harold Rugg observed that committee members agreed that learner, subject matter, and society were "fundamentally interdependent factors in curriculum development" (Neil, 1983, pp. 9–10). Similarly, curriculum consultants from the Eight Year Study developed a model based on three factors: adolescent needs, specialized subject matter, and social demands (Giles, McCutchen, and Zechiel, 1942, pp. 22–48). Hilda Taba, protégé of Tyler, perpetuated the study of learners, knowledge, and society or culture as a foundational prerequisite to the process of curriculum planning (Taba, 1962, pp. 16–192). One can even find rudiments of these three domains in the early work of William Torrey Harris prior to the twentieth century (see Cremin, 1971).

Let us now look at learner needs, social needs, and disciplines of knowledge as criteria for selecting purposes, considering examples, advocacy, and criticisms of them. It is important to realize that these three sources of purpose are not distinct alternatives; rather, they are to be weighed for their relevance to situational needs.

Basic Human Needs of Learners

Examples. We often hear of basic human needs of food, shelter, clothing, water, and oxygen, and social-cultural-biological needs of affection, love, recognition, and so on. These are examples of essentials that foster individual growth.

Advocacy. It is essential that curriculum developers carefully study research on learner needs and on the conditions that should exist for learning to occur. This involves the study of both human nature and the psychology of learning. One should realize what is known in these areas if one hopes to build a curriculum. The search for knowledge of human nature and the learning process relates to general knowledge, but the criterion of basic human needs of learners pertains to idiosyncratic knowledge of individuals as well. Thus educators at all levels (especially school district, building, and individual) must continuously augment their knowledge of the particular learners whom they teach.

Criticism. There is the risk of exclusive focus on the learner that leads to an imbalance of consideration given to society and knowledge. Dewey's emphasis on the learner led some of his would-be disciples in the progressive education era to base teaching on superficial whims of their students rather than to demonstrate to students that their learning could be enriched by investigating its social context and consequences and by realizing the disciplines of knowledge have much to offer any

inquiry that begins in personal interest. A second criticism is somewhat more penetrating. It challenges the certainty on which curricularists act after a cursory study of
human nature and the learning process. If the greatest philosophers, poets, theologians, dramatists, novelists, artists, and scientists have only scratched the surface of
human nature, it is ironic for curriculum developers to assume hastily that they know
learners well enough to say conclusively what they must learn.

Social Needs

Examples.   A classic example is found in the methods of curriculum formulation
developed and perpetuated between 1915 and 1935 by Franklin Bobbitt, W. W.
Charters, and other social behaviorists who drew purposes from the study of existing
society, and accepted its values and modes of operation as worth perpetuating.
Referred to as activity analysis, the process involves observation of what effective
adults do, assuming that they should be the models for the young, and converting
these activities and the ideals they represent into behavioral objectives and learning
activities.

John Dewey, George S. Counts, and others analyzed society with quite different
results from Bobbitt and Charters. Dewey advocated democracy as a perpetual
means whereby society can renew itself. Counts, Brameld, and others envisioned a
better society and sought to bring it into being through reconstructing school curriculum.

Today, it is quite evident that the values of society are perpetuated through
schooling. When a thrust toward patriotism of one sort or another is made, schools
are given a large share of the burden. Children of poverty are found hungry and
schools provide meals for them. Drugs, alcohol, and teenage pregnancy are found to
be social evils among youth, and school programs are instituted to combat these
problems. Resolutions for overcoming racial and ethnic separatism are needed, and
school busing is mobilized and magnet schools are developed. Nations find themselves inferior in technological or military prowess, and schools are expected to
upgrade future scientists, engineers, and technicians. Schools have always been used
as instruments of nationalism, patriotism, and the perpetuation of whatever economic system prevails in a society.

Advocacy.   Curriculum should perpetuate or improve the existing social order. To
perpetuate it means that schools pass along social values, rules, conventions, and the
like that are deemed desirable. To improve implies that curriculum promotes a
better form of society or sets in motion a process that can bring about improvement,
such as deliberation or democracy. Usually, some combination of these interpretations prevails rather than a pure form of one of them.

Criticism.   Exclusive focus on social needs creates an imbalance among society,
learners, and subject matter in which attention is denied learners and subject matter
as a basis for determining purposes. Thus, in the extreme, the learner becomes an
automaton of the state or merely an agent of social change. Inattention to knowledge
could result in conveyance of only that knowledge that the government, economic
system, power wielders, or particular interest groups want the society to acquire.

While this is the extreme, there are those who argue (e.g., Apple, 1979, 1982a,b) that in many subtle ways schools reflect and perpetuate socioeconomic class hierarchies and inequities that exist in any society. In a telling study, Anyon (1980) demonstrates that children of working-class, middle-class, and upper-class backgrounds are taught quite differently. The curriculum of the former teaches more docility, while that of the latter more independence and self-directiveness. Thus, critics argue that we need curricula and teaching that help to reconstruct the social order, to make it better, not merely to follow suit (Counts, 1932b; Brameld, 1956; Giroux, 1983). While such writers argue against curriculum that uncritically reproduces the social order, they sometimes bring an imbalance among the criteria by focusing so fully on social critique and reform that they neglect individual growth of learners and give too little attention to the disciplines of knowledge.

Disciplines of Knowledge

Examples.   Scholars are called upon to oversee and advise the construction of textbooks in their areas of expertise, because they are assumed to have the best grasp of subject matter. In the 1960s post-*Sputnik* curriculum reform movement Jerome Bruner (1960) and others (Ford and Pugno, 1964; Elam, 1964) called attention to the structure of the disciplines. Each discipline was asserted to have a basic structure that, if understood, would enable all other aspects of information in that area to fall conceptually into place.

Advocacy.   The curriculum, after all, is the dissemination of knowledge that is not easily accessible through ordinary experience. Furthermore, the disciplines are the most important conceptual pillars of knowledge that should be learned, and subject matter specialists can best tell us what the structure of each discipline is. While structure is obvious in disciplines such as mathematics, physics, and chemistry, it is less overt in areas of study such as the arts, French literature, Russian history, anthropology, and education. Nevertheless, each of these areas has an integrity that gives it internal cohesion.

Criticism.   Subject matter specialists may know their discipline well, but on what basis can they judge its relevance to learners without knowledge of specific groups of learners and society? If they have little background in psychology of learning, how can they determine the extent to which students are capable of learning a given discipline? What gives specialists the capacity to judge the worth of one discipline compared with another in a world that has far more areas of knowledge than it is possible to offer even in the most "comprehensive" schools?

PROCEDURAL CRITERIA FOR SELECTING PURPOSES

Procedural criteria deal with the process of deciding what the substantive purposes shall be. Thus, procedural criteria provide means of employing substantive criteria as one seeks to create and discover the actual substantive purposes that guide the curriculum. Procedural criteria for selecting purposes include representation, clarity, defensibility, consistency, and feasibility. As with substantive criteria, a balanced approach that uses all the criteria is needed, not a choice of one and exclusion of the others.

Representation

This criterion involves two quite different dimensions. The first is representation of persons who generate substantive criteria; the second refers to balance of substantive criteria themselves.

Since substantive criteria deal with needs, we must ask: Who is to be involved in needs assessment deliberation? One school of thought holds that professional educators should study learners, knowledge, and society and rationally determine the emphasis on and interpretation of each that should be represented in a given educational setting. To use a political analogy, one school of thought holds that professional educators are viewed as selected representatives who have expertise and time to determine what is best for the public. Another school of thought supports more direct representation of community members from a broad base of interest groups, socioeconomic levels, racial and ethnic backgrounds, as well as different levels of professional educators and students. Such groups are often referred to as "citizens' commissions" or "advisory councils." In some cases, it is held that these groups, predominantly governed by noneducators, should determine purposes; and it is the job of professional educators to develop the means to achieve or deliver those ends.

The deliberation that takes place by either professional educators or by advisory councils, whether the participants realize it or not, acts to allocate educational resources that create some form of balance among the interests of learners, society, and disciplines of knowledge. Thus, the second representation issue asks: What should be the balance among these three sources of purposes? Should they be of equal weight? In what order should they be ranked?

One technique used to deal with this issue is to have all participants in the decision-making body list the purposes that they think their schools should serve. Usually such lists are quite extensive. Debate ensues. Questions of feasibility and relevance are entertained in view of the fact that all school systems have limited resources and unique needs. Questions of priority arise due to the fact that schools cannot respond to every need lest their response be watered down to the point of being ineffective across the board. Thus, community and professional representatives should deliberate in an effort to arrive at a list of high-priority needs that they are convinced must be met by the school system for their children and youth. They must also demonstrate that such needs are able to be met by the time and resources of the school system. Moreover, the needs should be translated into purposes that are concrete enough to be understood by professional personnel and experienced by students. Finally every successive level (school districts, buildings, classrooms) that helps to provide purposes to meet identified needs must be represented in deliberations about what the purposes mean and how they should be interpreted in their situations.

Clarity

The second criterion for purposes is that they be stated clearly. Statements of purpose written by school districts are too often saturated with vagueness and ambiguity.

If ten educators were asked to set forth ten purposes each that they deemed worth-while, chances are great that some of the same terms would be used, for example, *basic skills, critical thinking, responsibility, creative expression*, and the like. In fact, I begin an activity that I use with classes and workshops by using just such a listing activity. Students discuss the terms they listed. At first, the perception that a term or phrase is shared causes participants to believe that they are in agreement. However, after I encourage them to explain their use of a given term or phrase and to question those used by others, they sometimes find that they had quite different ideas in mind for the same terms.

Different means are proposed for resolving this difficulty. Some curricularists hold that they will be on the right track if they operationalize definitions (i.e., state clearly and precisely what is meant by each). This position often moves us into the direction of behavioral objectives, performance objectives, learning competencies, and so on. Some go so far as to propose a common language for curriculum discourse, but as we noted earlier, they are opposed by those who see variety of terminology and meaning as a sign of richness of dialogue. Nevertheless, even these advocates of more flexible uses of language promote clarity. They insist that meanings of key terms in articles or policy statements must at least be characterized for those particular documents, even though they might well be used differently elsewhere. Finally, some advocate that enough clarity is needed only to enable those who work together to have a common sense of direction. They hold that this is better than being locked into an operational definition because a sense of direction allows for adaptation and evolution that a fixed definition prohibits.

Defensibility

Purposes should not only be clear and representative; they must also be defensible. Here we return to the level of philosophical assumptions discussed in Chapter Five. Assertions of purpose must hold up logically. If they are based on faulty deduction, unverified induction, or inappropriate dialectic, they need to be revised. There exists, for example, a great deal of confusion of *is* and *ought*. The naturalistic fallacy of deriving conclusions of *ought* from *is* premises is very much alive, though it clearly is not well!

Epistemologically, purposes must be based on openly acknowledged ways of knowing. Depending on the purposes, this might mean an appeal to such sources as empirical evidence, intuition, authoritative sources, religious revelation embodied in scriptures, and experience. The important matter is that the source of credibility be admitted and that it not be confused with or used to mask another. There is a tendency in our day to revere science; therefore, those who want to convince others to buy their product or idea try to put science on their side. Authority, intuition, personal experience, and revelation all have their place in defending certain kinds of assertions, but one must beware of finding them clothed in scientific garb, such as the well-known ads that claim three out of four physicians recommend a certain pain reliever.

Similarly, it is advantageous to keep in mind the axiological distinction between the desired and the desirable. In some cases, we will concede that what is desired is also desirable, but again we should guard against being duped into accepting the desired as desirable without consciously weighing the difference. High scores on standardized achievement tests, for example, are widely desired, but many push for high scores without reflecting on whether they provide evidence for educationally valuable aspects of learning.

There are many ways to defend or justify curriculum. Surely one could turn to the array of philosophical literature on the process of justification. Smith, Stanley, and Shores (1957) devote a chapter to explication of judgmental, experimental, analytic, and consensual procedures for defending curricular content selection (pp. 152–167). Such procedures are easily adaptable to the defense of purposes or other aspects of curriculum.

Perhaps the most practical, general method of dealing with the defensibility of purposes is to assert a purpose and follow it up by asking openly and honestly, "Why is that worthwhile?" When you have an answer that satisfies you on that question, ask again: "Why is that worthwhile?" Continue this process two or three more times, and you should arrive close to the level of basic assumptions.

Consistency

It is possible that statements of purpose could be clear, representative, and defensible, but suffer procedurally because they are inconsistent with one another or with other aspects of the curriculum. Curriculum developers need to be careful to maintain an overall picture of the entire program. Oftentimes, purposes for different subject areas and levels of schooling are developed by groups that seldom communicate with one another. Purposes in the science curriculum could contradict those in mathematics, social science, or the humanities. Similarly, purposes within the same area frequently conflict with one another. Even more prevalent is the likelihood of contradiction (or blatant ignorance) from primary to intermediate to junior high to senior high school, simply due to the lack of articulation among personnel from each of these levels. So often one hears lamentations that students are ill prepared once they arrive at a new level. The fault may be more attributable to differences in purpose than to poor preparation.

Another crucial area in which inconsistencies are frequently found is within the curriculum design process itself. Here I refer to the topics treated in Chapters Eight through Eleven: purposes, learning experiences, organization (including environment and methodology of instruction), and evaluation. Do the plans at these four levels mesh or fit together well? Sometimes we find that they do not. For example, we may find a purpose of fostering self-directed learning, coupled with highly prescribed, didactic content or learning experiences. This, in turn, may be mediated by a restricted organizational environment of desks bolted to the floor, an atmosphere of autocracy, and teaching methods based on prepackaged lessons on responsibility. All of this may be evaluated by a standardized achievement test that relates neither to the ends nor the means.

Feasibility

All of the foregoing criteria may be well accounted for, but fail because of the lack of one central quality: feasibility. In the final analysis, this is obviously a necessity. One must ask whether purposes are feasible. Do finances, resources, attitudes, personnel, the community, and the institution support the purpose? Doubt on this is not sufficient reason to drop the purpose as a "pie in the sky" ideal; however, it does require one to analyze circumstances carefully. Based on work of Kurt Lewin (1948), one can do a force-field analysis. Essentially, this is an accounting of supportive and resistive forces, and a careful analysis of what it would take (including the costs and benefits thereof) to convert enough resistive forces into supportive (or at least neutral) forces to carry out the plan in question successfully. This helps to reveal whether there is a real possibility of actualizing purposes proposed.

SUBSTANTIVE PURPOSES

We have considered orientations to purpose and both substantive and procedural criteria for purposes. Now we will enter the realm of purposes themselves (i.e., the kinds of messages they carry). The significance of curricular purposes is, of course, to advocate or assert that something (a skill, area or aspect of knowledge, value, or appreciation) should be taught. Implicit in such advocacy or assertion is the message that the purpose is worthwhile. Here, the term *purpose* may be treated as synonymous with such terms as *goals, objectives, aims,* or *ends.* Or, as many choose to do, these terms may be arranged in a hierarchy from general to specific. These are matters of form. Regardless of the form, all statements of purpose have a substantive orientation.

In the sections that follow I present four general categories of substantive advocacy into which many purposes fall. It is not intended that all purposes be classified into these four groups. There are exceptions; in addition, some purposes may overlap two or more of the four areas. The intent of the analysis that follows is to provide four guideposts that curriculum developers might look at in order to classify any one purpose; they might also check the range and variety of purposes that they advocate in an effort to determine if their overall program is balanced in the way that they had intended. The four categories of substantive thrust found in purposes are (1) socialization, (2) achievement, (3) personal growth, and (4) social change.

Socialization

Socialization refers to the intent to use curriculum to induct the young into the ways of living in a society or culture. This includes initiation into the folkways, mores, attitudes, information, skills, customs, values, and ideals of the social group. The *social group,* as used here, is a generic reference to a range of societal dimensions: family, community, ethnic or racial background, socioeconomic class, nation, and so on.

Examples.   The young are socialized through both the intended and hidden curricula. School rules and routines socialize students to the rules and routines of other institutions. Since school teachers and administrators are largely from middle-class backgrounds, the values and behaviors that they model exert a strong, unidirectional impact. The disciplines and areas of study are intentionally designed to socialize. The social studies of most nations is strongly oriented to conveying interpretations of history, geography, economics, government, and social issues through the lenses of that country's outlook. The sciences, arts, and humanities socialize by providing a vision of what human culture (often with particular emphasis on the national) has accumulated and envisioned.

Intent.   As a socializing agency, the school designs curriculum to provide that essential knowledge of the ways of life in society that would be unlikely or inefficiently acquired by ordinary experience in the culture.

Criticisms.   Socialization is seen as a form of indoctrination, especially if viewpoints from outside the social group are unfairly presented or not presented at all. It is also argued that socialization through education, especially in capitalist countries, perpetuates a myth that social mobility is possible; meanwhile, the education system actually cultivates the same social hierarchies and inequities that exist in the larger society (see Apple, 1979; Anyon, 1981). Less radical critics of socialization argue that merely perpetuating the social order is not enough; education should be designed to improve it, to make it stronger and more worthwhile. Still others claim that to socialize focuses attention too thoroughly on the everyday, because occupational preparation becomes a primary goal. The truer purpose of education should be to keep alive the imagination and wisdom of the ages.

Achievement

This purpose is heavily emphasized in industrial and postindustrial nations where achievement is usually defined relative to scores on examinations.

Examples.   In the United States, for instance, elementary school and junior high students are periodically given achievement tests such as the Iowa Test of Basic Skills. Students and schools themselves are judged based on their scores on such tests. Comparisons with other schools and national norms are often published in local newspapers as an indicator of educational or curricular productivity and quality. In many nations, examinations are given to determine vocational, professional, or scholarly tracks, and the future of student lives is sealed in a few hours of testing. At the secondary and university levels, testing of achievement is even more severe. Such private organizations in the United States as the Educational Testing Service (ETS) are powerful gatekeepers for entrance into undergraduate and graduate school. So widespread is the emphasis on measurable achievement that individual nations have devised special programs to assess the overall level of achievement. The most prominent example in the United States is the National Assessment of Educational Progress (NAEP), which provides achievement data in ten areas (art, career education, citizenship, literature, mathematics, music, reading, science, social studies, and writing) using criterion-referenced instruments at four- to five-year age intervals. At the international level, the International Association for the Evaluation of Educational Achievement (IEA), a large-scale, comparative assessment that began in the 1960s, is still operating in more than twenty nations and treats the areas of mathematics, science, literature, reading comprehension, foreign languages, and civics.

Intent.   The emphasis on achievement addresses, from the start, the need for accountability. By identifying concrete measures, one is able to make claims of progress more defensible. Areas such as socialization and personal growth are too nebulous to be used as purposes, whereas achievement is manageable and efficient.

Criticism. The widespread use of achievement is often a subsitute for thinking seriously about purposes. The test publishers define achievement for us. Thus, it is not a construct that we create, but one that we receive or buy. Sometimes achievement tests actually direct purposes of a school system. When no purposes are clearly articulated and implemented, achievement tests are purchased and administered, and the categories of performance on the test printout simply become the curricular purposes. This preempts consideration of other possible ends of curricular endeavors, such as Herbert Thelen's (1981) advocacy of quality of classroom life, Elliot Eisner's (1982) argument that a literacy of the senses is a more reasonable purpose, and A. W. Foshay's (1984) call for attention to the spriritual character of education.

Personal Growth

As a central purpose, personal growth of the learner in this century stems back to the Progressive Education movement, which lasted from the early years of the twentieth century to the 1950s and was a cause championed by John Dewey. The position has arisen under different labels (open education of the 1960s and early 1970s, humanistic education of the 1950s and 1980s, life-adjustment education of the 1940s and 1950s) with somewhat differing interpretations. Nevertheless, the fostering of self-realization is central, requires careful study of the learners' needs and interests, and requires a personally tailored curriculum to meet them.

Examples. The method of education that Dewey developed at the University of Chicago Laboratory School became a paragon of curriculum and method. It is well interpreted in his *School and Society* (1900) and *The Child and the Curriculum* (1902). Some (e.g., Cremin, 1961; Fraley, 1981) argue, however, that Dewey owed a great deal to Francis W. Parker, who administered a teacher education school in Chicago during the late nineteenth and early twentieth-centuries (see Parker's *Talks on Pedagogics*, 1894, for example). Dewey also acknowledged a debt to Parker. Along with his daughter Evelyn, Dewey searched for schools that exemplified his ideal, and together they reported on the exemplary schools they found in *Schools of Tomorrow* (1915). In 1928, Harold Rugg and Ann Shumaker interpreted the idea of the child-centered school that facilitated personal growth. The writings of L. Thomas Hopkins (1937, 1954) represent major statements on the integrated and emerging self as the purpose of curriculum. A. S. Neill's (1960) *Summerhill* is one of the most widely cited examples of giving great freedom to learners with the faith that it would yield personal growth. Not only radicals advanced concern for personal growth as a curricular purpose; the 1962 Yearbook of the ASCD (*Perceiving, Behaving, and Becoming*) remains a best selling yearbook of this mainstream professional organization. Books by John Holt (1964), George Dennison (1969), Herb Kohl (1968), and Jonathan Kozol (1967) provide many examples. So did the open education literature (e.g., Roland Barth, 1972; Charles Silberman, 1973). That personal growth is alive today as a curricular purpose is represented by demand for a 1983 update of Carl Rogers's *Freedom to Learn*.

Intent. The intent of all this literature, although differences certainly abound among the representatives, is that education begins with the interests of learners. This does not refer to their superficial whims, though the educator might begin with these. Instead, the teacher or facilitator of learning probes more deeply into fundamental life concerns. Sometimes this takes place through a problem-solving process and sometimes by means of self-study similar to autobiographical methods used by reconceptualists, as discussed earlier. The major aim is not achievement of tasks imposed from without and not a molding of conformity with the social order. It is a continous pursuit of increased maturity.

Criticism.   Maturity cannot be measured. It is too fleeting, too intangible. The same is true of self-realization. Both are too subjective, dependent upon the idiosyncratic decisions of teachers and students themselves. Educators have studied such matters far more than the students; thus, they have the responsibility to tell them what is best for their needs, not merely to cater to their interests. Moreover, if everyone is treated differently, there is a lack of equity that could result from a core of similar learning experiences for all. To focus on personal growth may be inimical to society. If everyone goes his or her own way, there is no assurance that the institutions that hold the nation and world together will be preserved. Thus, the benefits of socialization and/or achievement may be destroyed by heavy attention to personal growth.

Social Change

This purpose is sometimes referred to as the reconstructionist orientation. Reconstructionists hold that schools can and should lead the way to social improvement. This goes beyond both socialization and social mobility, which accept the system as it is, to advocate the need for a better society.

Examples.   There are many different levels of this approach. One more closely tied to those who see themselves as change agents and advocate planned change is Bennis et al. (1976). A more recent correlate of the latter includes the vast array of organizational development specialists, who refer to themselves as O. D. researchers and consultants. Schmuck et al. (1977) have summarized this work. Others see schools as centers of democratic involvement and express great faith in democratic institutions (e.g., Dewey, 1916; Hopkins, 1941; Brameld, 1956). They clearly see change as evolution. Still others see revolutionary change as an important goal of curriculum (e.g., Counts, 1932b; Freire, 1970; Apple, 1979, 1982; Giroux, 1983). Futurists (Shane, 1977; Shane and Tabler, 1981) and advocates of global education such as some members of the World Council for Curriculum and Instruction, would fall in this general classification.

Intent.   The schools and other forms of education have the responsibility to reconstruct the social order. Students should be taught critical skills of reflecting on the justice and equity of the prevailing socioeconomic system. They should be enabled by the curriculum to think of constructive alternatives, ponder their probable consequences, and exercise political power to attain desirable consequences.

Criticism.   This approach politicizes education. The curriculum must function as an agent of the social system that it serves. Otherwise, the schools become subversive and disloyal. Children and youth should find out about their society and culture, not turn against their heritage. Furthermore, there is little to worry about since schools reflect the social order. They are, and will be, docile preservers, not powerful activists.

COMMENTARIES

Each guest will now comment on his or her perception of the treatment of purpose in this chapter. Each has been asked to note positions with which he or she agrees and disagrees.

Intellectual Traditionalist

My orientation to the style of writing educational purposes is a combination of global and expressive with a minor touch of the evolving. I believe in global purposes for schooling insofar as they relate to the disciplines of knowledge, but not the broad and vague Cardinal Principles type that replaces academic needs with general societal needs. The global purpose should be to acquaint learners with the disciplines of organized knowledge. This is the embodiment of our culture. What more is there? I add to this expressive purposes because surely increased acquaintance with the disciplines brings novel expressions. Whenever a great work is studied, it interacts with the personality of the student, creating a new expression that cannot be fully anticipated in advance. Further, as Phenix (1962) cogently argues, disciplines contain a dynamism or power of renewal that leads those who study them toward further analysis and synthesis. Thus, we see the evolving function. I dismiss behavioral objectives out of hand. They are the pseudoscientific attempt of pompous sophists to appear educated, organized, intellectual, and professional.

On the matter of substantive criteria for purposes, the disciplines of knowledge should be foremost. This criterion incorporates social needs without wedding itself to a particular nationalistic force, social system, or ideology. It includes basic human needs of individuals by virtue of the fact that the classics offer the best that culture has to offer the individual in granting freedom (liberation as in liberal arts) without license. Procedural criteria such as clarity, defensibility, and consistency should obviously be expected. One must be careful not to confuse feasibility with the mundanely pragmatic. The great works are feasible for everyone to experience, and they are their own representatives.

Finally, achievement is my substantive purpose, but not the behavioristic, measurable kind presented earlier. Instead, I refer to an achievement of knowledge and love of the great works in all disciplines. This provides the best kind of socialization, socialization to the highest achievements of human culture, and in turn, yields personal growth and social change. People improve as they become more sophisticated in the disciplines, and as a broader spectrum of people change in this direction, society also improves.

Social Behaviorist

Behavioral objectives are panned by experientialists and intellectual traditionalists who fail to realize that schools, like all other institutions in society, are business enterprises. Schools are special, along with other public institutions, in that their stockholders are taxpayers. Thus, they must represent the tacit "vote" or will of the public. What the public wants, the knowledge and skills that it desires for its young, should be what schools are mandated to disseminate. Professional educators should help the public to clarify what it wants and then design or engineer the means to achieve it. While it may be useful to begin this engineering process with global objectives or even a general sense of direction, it is necessary to refine it into highly explicit goal statements. This procedure usually moves from general aims to general purposes, to global goals, to behavioral objectives.

The technology of specification has advanced considerably since the early days of Bobbitt and Charters, and it has made great strides since the work in the 1960s and 1970s of Robert Mager and James Popham. In fact, Mager is called upon, time and again, to consult with business and industry. The training of both labor and management has taught us a great deal about the analysis of tasks into instructional components. What task analysis does for performance specification, concept analysis does for cognitive knowledge. The greatest breakthrough exists in the design of computer programs where the work requires one to be specific and exact; we can learn much from this process whether we are dealing with instruction that can be directly translated to computerized instructional software or not. This refinement in behavioral objectives gives us a technology that far surpasses global, expressive, and evolving objectives. It is analogous to the quantum jump from armchair philosophizing about the human mind to current brain research, or from the shoemaker and his apprentice to mass production, from phrenology to modern psychiatry, or from bloodletting to modern medicine.

The criterion of greatest importance is social needs. One must find the greatest good for the greatest number, as John Stuart Mill admonished us to do as "father of utilitarianism." This position, of course, relies on knowledge from the disciplines, and it helps to fulfill basic human needs. Needs of the society must come first, however. Here I do not refer to the revolutionary arm of social needs advocacy that says that society should be changed.

One of the most thorough needs analysis approaches has been developed by the Educational Products Information Exchange (EPIE). EPIE, a consumer service dedicated to objective assessment for selection of educational materials, has developed a system that includes the following: establishment of priorities, community needs analysis, learner needs analysis, and analysis of teacher beliefs and needs (EPIE, 1979). All these factors must be considered in a comprehensive analysis of educational needs.

It is through careful, comprehensive needs assessment that professional educators establish procedural criteria in a representative fashion. The professionals assess the needs of all parties involved. They do this with scientific survey instruments, not by inefficiently sitting around a table and conversing with representatives from all major interest groups. Clarity is a criterion that comes naturally when objectives are specified in terms of specific observable behaviors. The specifications, of course, must be consistent and feasible. If they meet societal needs, then the purposes are defensible as well.

The substance of purposes must remain the product of the needs assessment. Purposes are merely a pragmatic interpretation of needs that demonstrate a plan for their satisfaction. In a democracy, this might mean needs of socialization, achievement, personal growth, social improvement, any combination thereof, or even something not included among these categories. The central point here is that the professional educator should be the instrument that can deliver the services that the relevant publics need, and delivery is indefensible without specific purposes that are its source, its starting point.

Experientialist

Once again the social behaviorist, great believer in parsimony, is longer-winded than the intellectual traditionalist. But this is minor among the contradictions of that commentator. The major confusion is the equating of needs with desires in some of the commentary and at other times giving full reign to "professional educators" as if they are the best judges. A related confusion is the "we know best" syndrome: we know the components of knowledge, the needs of communities, students, and teachers. How pompous!

Each individual is the best judge of what he or she needs. Even tiny babies know when they need to eat, change position, have their diapers changed, and so on. We all know our needs at some level, and we can know them better if the educative environment positively encourages us to study them with greater breadth and depth. As we do this, we begin to realize that our needs are similar to those of others and that others can assist us in meeting our needs more fully. Thus, thorough study of one's own needs leads to a desire to engage in democratic action. This points to the inextricable connectedness of the social with the individual. Further, as the social individual strives to learn more about his or her needs in the broad context, the disciplines of knowledge become perceived as indispensable. Thus, knowledge, society, and the individual are thoroughly interdependent; it becomes silly to refer to one as separate from the others. However, the center is the human being striving to become more fully human.

Possibility (which I prefer to feasibility) becomes the key procedural criterion, but not in the sense of feasibility as the social behaviorist and intellectual traditionalist view it. Possibility, to see in new ways, to look beyond the manacles that bind us to the taken-for-granted, to imagine new paths of action and thought for ourselves— these are purposive criteria. Sometimes this means that old icons of reality must be broken or reshaped. These might include our very conceptions of what it means to be clear, defensible, and consistent. And representation need not be the dreary consideration of who serves on committees. It should begin with a deeper experiencing of what it means to represent oneself, below the surface of proprieties, habit, and unexamined custom. The best representation of purpose is to probe deeply toward the purpose that lies within our own depths, that enables us to be purposefully creative together.

This leads directly to the issue of substantive purposes. Personal growth is the center of true education. It is an immeasurable achievement that far transcends tests that masquerade as significant accomplishment. If persons grow individually, the substantive purpose must be more than socialization, because growing individuals are the seedbed of a growing society. Social change that does not have personal growth as a prerequisite is the story of revolutions in which new power is as corrupt as the old. But social change that is the flowering of personal growth moves toward the ideal of a democracy that is ever educating itself.

SUGGESTED READING

If you would like to read one seminal source on each of the orientations to purposes, you would do well to choose the following: *Cardinal Principles of Secondary Education* (Commission on the Reorganization of Secondary Education, 1918) for global purposes, *Preparing Instructional Objectives* (Mager, 1962) for behavioral objectives, *Democracy and Education* (Dewey, 1916) for evolving purposes, and *The Educational Imagination* (Eisner, 1985) for expressive objectives.

The Emerging Self in School and Home (Hopkins, 1954) is an excellent source for the criterion of individual human needs and for personal growth as a substantive purpose. The several national commission reports that appeared in the United States in the early 1980s exemplify the socal needs criterion, especially *A Nation at Risk* (National Commission on Excellence in Education, 1983). Such commission reports place heavy emphasis on achievement as defined by test results; so too do studies of effective schooling that swept the United States in the early 1980s. Often-cited reports such as Coleman (1961, 1981), Coleman et al. (1966) and Jencks et al. (1972) have the effect of equating achievement test scores with realization of purpose. King and Brownell (1966) provide a good example of curriculum rooted in the disciplines, as do Broudy, Smith, and Burnett (1964) who join excellence in the disciplines with the fostering of democracy. The social renewal dimension of social needs purposes is well exemplified by Counts (1932b), Brameld (1956), Apple (1979), Giroux (1983), and Pinar (1975).

John Goodlad's *A Place Called School* (1984) provides empirical evidence and compelling argument that relates to the need for consistency of purposes. Smith, Stanley, and Shores (1957) treat procedural criteria skillfully.

Two sources are noted for book-length discussion of purposes: Nisbet's (1968) *Purpose in the Curriculum* and Morris's (1972) *Objectives and Perspectives in Education*. Also, the reader would do well to scan major synoptic texts of the curricular past and present for sections on purposes (objectives, aims, etc.): Harap (1928), Hopkins (1929), Caswell and Campbell (1935), Gwynn (1943), Tyler (1949), Taba (1962), Zais (1976), Johnson (1977a), Tanner and Tanner (1980), and McNeil (1985). Summaries of what these and other authors said are contained in such texts and in turn lead to other writings.

RECOMMENDATIONS FOR REFLECTION

1. Return to your response to activities 2, 3, and 4 of the "Recommendations for Reflection" section in Chapter One. There you were asked to reveal some of your ideals. In activity 4 you focused on one ideal and translated it into curriculum. Recall

that ideal or another one and describe it in the form of the following orientations to purpose: (a) global, (b) behavioral, (c) evolving, (d) expressive.

2. Which one of the forms best fits the ideal that you selected? Which fits least? If a form fit well, do you think that it did so because it had a natural affinity with the particular ideal that you selected? Or do you think the form that seemed most compatible reflects your own philosophy more fully? Try to express other ideals. Do the same consistency patterns emerge?

3. Philosophically, which form of purpose do you hold in highest regard? What are some reasons for your selection? With which do you differ most?

4. Reflect on your own situation as an educator. Identify two or three activities in which you are currently engaged, for example, lessons, units, or other curricular thrusts. Which form(s) of purpose guide(s) them: global, behavioral, evolving, or expressive?

5. Are your answers to activities 3 and 4 largely the same or different? If they are the same, does this mean that the institution for which you work is essentially in harmony with your own curricular philosophy? If they are different, what explanations can be given?

6. If you had to rate the substantive criteria for selecting purposes in order of importance, where would you place each of the three (individual human needs, social needs, disciplines of knowledge)? How are these three criteria interrelated or interdependent?

7. Obtain a statement of purpose for any curriculum area from a school system, state department of education, educational agency, or publisher of instructional materials. Analyze the statement in terms of the procedural criteria of clarity, defensibility, consistency, and feasibility. Are any clues given about representation?

8. Is your own work as an educator geared more toward the substantive purpose of socialization, achievement, personal growth, or social change? Is your response to this question largely your own decision or is it primarily a function of institutional policy? If the latter is the case, what is your own position? Is there any way to move your position and that of your institution closer together?

9. With which of the three commentators do you most agree on the issue of purpose? Least? Reasons? Identify three aspects that you can support and three points on which you disagree with each commentator: intellectual traditionalist, social behaviorist, and experientialist.

10. Obtain a statement of purpose from your school district (or simply reflect on your experience with purposes there if a statement is unavailable). Which orientations to purpose are most prevalent? Which are most neglected? Which substantive and procedural criteria are most prevalent? Which are most neglected? What explanations can you provide for your answers? In other words, what contributes to the character of curricular purpose in your school or institution?

11. Categorize the purposes, goals, or objectives in a document (teachers' manual, curriculum guide, etc.) relative to the four categories of substantive purpose:

socialization, achievement, personal growth, social change. Which are dominant? Which are neglected? What are some possible reasons for the neglect or dominance?

12. Reflect on the consistency between purpose and practice in your educational setting. Discuss your reflections with others in similar and different settings.

13. Think of purposes that guide your own personal life. Do they most closely resemble the global. behavioral, evolving, or expressive form? What criteria (substantive and procedural) guide their selection and development? Are they more concerned with the end of socialization, achievement, personal growth, or social change? What kinds of purposes in your life can be categorized in each of these topics?

14. What implications can you draw from purposes in your personal life for the way that purposes are treated in professional education?

9

✦ Paradigm of Perennial Analytic Categories: Content or Learning Experiences ✦

One thorn of experience is worth a whole wilderness of warning.
> JAMES RUSSELL LOWELL "Shakespeare Once More" *Among My Books* (1870)

. . . Purposes, interests, and meanings constitute the underlying facts of human experience.
> LEWIS MUMFORD "Orientation to Life" *The Conduct of Life* (1951)

Life is a succession of events which must be lived to be understood.
> RALPH WALDO EMERSON "Illusions" *The Conduct of Life* (1860)

SETTING THE STAGE

In Chapter Eight we considered purposes, the first category presented in Tyler's (1949) paradigm. His second category deals with the perennial question of content, which he labels *learning experiences* to distinguish it from what he considers less desirable notions of content. Over the years three widely divergent interpretations of content have played central roles in curriculum thought and practice: (1) a subject matter emphasis, (2) a learning activities emphasis, and (3) a learning experiences emphasis. Each of these is characterized in this chapter relative to example, advocacy, and criticism.

Whether content leans in the direction of subject matter, activities, or experiences, it is important to analyze the sources or criteria from which it derives. Eight such criteria are analyzed in a second major section of this chapter: (1) social needs, (2) survival, (3) disciplinary structure, (4) utility, (5) publisher decision, (6) politics, (7) learner interest, and (8) democratic action.

A final section of the chapter deals with images of content or interpretations given to the disciplines. Entire books are devoted to curriculum and instruction in subject areas such as reading, social studies, music, or science. This book, since it deals with many dimensions of curriculum and not content alone, cannot provide a great deal of depth on content. It is important, however, to point out that the way in which content is viewed differs substantially depending on one's curricular philosophy or orientation. Thus, the three curricular orientations represented by our guest commentators (intellectual traditionalist, social behaviorist, and experientialist) are used as alternative lenses through which five overarching content areas might be interpreted. Mediated by each commentator, these areas (social studies, language arts, science and mathematics, the arts, and specialized studies) can be seen to be quite different indeed.

ORIENTATIONS TO CONTENT

Content has long been considered a central curriculum concern; many would go so far as to consider it the major topic for curricularists to determine. Some see it as the second question in sequence, following and fulfilling the question of purpose. Nevertheless, content does directly address the question: What shall be taught? In the practice of curriculum development, this *what* question is often addressed without much attention to purposes or the *why* question. When content is determined, some argue, purposes are implied. Unfortunate as this may be, it is often the case that some educators are satisfied with this unreflective derivation of purposes. The relation of purposes to content varies as content is conceived as subject matter, learning activities, or learning experiences. Each is more fully characterized in the paragraphs that follow.

Content as Subject Matter

Traditionally, content has been treated as knowledge to be acquired. Such knowledge takes the form of information, concepts, principles, ideas, and so on. Even these terms may take on quite different meaning depending upon the author writing about them or the curricularist leading the curriculum development process. But regardless of definition, the emphasis is on knowledge to be disseminated from educators to learners.

Examples. The most traditional example of content as subject matter is found in the lecture. That which is lectured about is the subject matter to be remembered. The advent of printing, and later textbooks, brought a new form for subject matter delivery. Content became equated with material covered in the text, and curriculum syllabi or curriculum guides often list pages that are to be covered or mastered by different dates on the calendar.

Although lectures and textbooks remain dominant purveyors of content as subject matter, new modes of subject matter presentation have emerged in the past twenty-five years. Workbooks and ditto sheets are a mainstay of classroom life, especially at the elementary, middle school, and junior high levels of schooling. This is so much the case that a major market has emerged for publishers of textbooks, who now design instructional packages of ditto masters and other consumable materials to accompany their texts.

Some companies have produced elaborate sequences of ditto masters. For example, a plan known as IPI (Individually Prescribed Instruction) was developed at the Learning Research and Development Center at the University of Pittsburgh in the 1960s and was disseminated and tested by Research for Better Schools. IPI included behavioral objectives, diagnostic instruments, and ditto materials, all organized in a massive management system designed to coordinate the curriculum of an entire school in the use of this plan. Other publishers have developed integrated systems of worksheets and individual study, programmed materials for self-instructional use, a variety of audiovisual or multimedia materials, and computer software, all focusing in different ways on the same topics.

Advocacy.   Although major strides have been made from the days of subject matter conveyed exclusively by text and lecture to the individualized learning materials, multimedia systems, and computer software programs of today, the intent is much the same. It is to deliver knowledge, skills, concepts, principles, and ideas to learners. Curricular content is, in fact, that which is to be learned, namely, the subject matter derived from the disciplines of knowledge and rendered appropriate for different age and ability levels.

Criticism.   The subject matter emphasis takes for granted that curriculum is a matter of prespecification. This implies experts who assume that they know what is best for teachers to teach and learners to learn. Thus, it is elitist in exerting control over the education of others without allowing them to have active participation in their own learning. Furthermore, the subject matter emphasis relegates content to disciplines of knowledge alone. The position presupposes that personal experiences and activities of learners both in and out of school have little bearing upon what they learn in school. Thus, the content of learning is a product to be received, not a process to be experienced.

Content as Learning Activities

The history of curriculum practice prior to the twentieth century was almost exclusively dominated by a subject matter approach to content. A few notable exceptions (e.g., Rousseau, Pestalozzi, Herbart, and Froebel) can be identified, of course. It was the advent of scientific and technological progress, however, that caught the eye of some early twentieth-century curricularists. Most prominent among them was Franklin Bobbitt (1918), who argued that curriculum should respond to needs of contemporary society. He sought to identify needs by studying what effective adults do, by translating their salient activities into objectives with a behavioral flavor, and by converting the objectives into learning activities for students (Bobbitt, 1918, 1924). This, coupled with the practical emphasis sponsored by the Cardinal Principles of Secondary Education (discussed in Chapter Eight), promoted an activity-oriented mode of content. Bobbitt's activity analysis purported to be scientific, and it was designed to yield an efficient technology of curriculum construction. From this point onward, the reference to learning activities rivaled subject matter as legitimate content for curriculum. More emphasis is placed on what students do than on what subject matter is bestowed upon them.

Examples.   Today we hear the term *learning activities* used with great frequency. The use refers to what we have students do as contrasted to that with which they are presented and expected to learn or know. Instead of reading about how a bill becomes a law in the legislature or instead of hearing a lecture on the functioning of the United Nations General Assembly as subject matter, students are engaged in the activity of simulating such processes. Instead of listening to the teacher say that it was exceedingly difficult for ancient homo sapiens to fashion stone implements with only other stones as tools, students might be given stones and a pair of protective goggles to facilitate becoming engaged in the activity of fashioning implements as prehistoric humans might have done. Dewey (1902) often involved students in reenactment of the past by having them spin thread or churn butter. Today, students take part in the activity of working out their own classroom management problems through classroom meetings (Glasser, 1975). They learn about democracy by helping each other learn through cooperative learning activities (Johnson and Johnson, 1975). Instead of merely telling students about scientific discoveries or the process of scientific discovery, projects such as "Science—A Process Approach" sponsored by the Commission on Science Education of the American Association for the Advancement of Science (AAAS) seek to involve students directly in activities that use the scientific method.

Advocacy.   The activity approach to content emphasizes the observable. One can see an activity, but one cannot see subject matter become assimilated or an experience take place. Activities, thus, serve a similar purpose as do behavioral objectives; they make what is to be done explicit; it is there to be seen; one can know if it exists or not. A second advantage is that to involve students in activities recognizes the active, social nature of learners. The subject matter emphasis assumes that learners are passive recipients, which negates much that developmental and cognitive psychologists have made known to us.

Criticism.   To focus on the behavioral is to attend to the superficial rather than the deep structure of learning. Students who have different life experiences (and they all do) prior to encountering a learning activity will invariably have different learning outcomes. The meaning, interpretation, and sense of direction derived from the activity will be markedly different for each. The same activity may help one student and harm another. Further, to focus on activity detracts from the fundamental substance of learning. It becomes a way of involving students in something that grasps their attention but does not attend to their basic needs. In practice, the activity actually becomes an end in itself. Merely doing the activity emerges as the purpose, rather than using the activity to fulfill a purpose. One often hears students say: "I'm finished with school," or "I had that subject." Education that could be a stimulus to learning in life often becomes a quagmire to be gotten through. Moreover, content that emphasizes activities also falls prey to the criticism of subject matter that views prespecification by experts as elitist control.

Content as Learning Experience

Tyler (1949) intentionally used a term that was quite Deweyan—*learning experience*. He used it to differentiate his own position from those before him who emphasized subject matter and activity as content. In Tyler's words (1949),

> The term learning experience *is not the same as the content with which a course deals nor the activities performed by the teachers. The term* learning experience *refers to the interaction between the learner and the external conditions in the environment to which he can react. [p. 63]*

This interpretation has been viewed in many different ways, both behaviorally and phenomenologically. If learning is seen as outward behavior and if *external conditions* refers to prespecified controllers of learning environments, the behavioral interpretation is in order. If, on the contrary, learning is thought to be centered in consciousness, it is more appropriate to use phenomenological or progressive interpretations that see *experience* as an interaction within the learner's mind between a dynamic repertoire of experience and new environments with which he or she interacts. Some of both positions can be found in Tyler's writing. The more progressive or phenomenological interpretation, however, is the one that differentiates the *learning activities* and *learning experiences* positions on content.

Examples.   Learners and teachers engage in dialogue. Teachers usually have broader experience relative to the general purposes of curriculum; however, learners have greater expertise about their own life experience. Together they work out what is in the best interest of the learner to experience, that is, what will enhance his or her growth. The skillful teacher begins with current, often superficial, interests of students and, through discussion, helps to develop a mutual realization of deeper interests that these surface interests represent. Again, the excellent teacher will be able to draw upon an eclectic awareness of the disciplines of knowledge and will be able to relate existing knowledge to fundamental needs and interests of the learner. The pursuit of knowledge, skills, values, and appreciations that fulfill these deeper needs and interests leads to new needs and interests. The process, once in motion, can continue throughout a lifetime. Good teachers are good facilitators of this process (Rogers, 1983).

Advocacy.   The conception of content must move beyond that which is externally imposed on the learner to that which is internally realized as valuable for growth. The content is a psychological construct (Kelly, 1963), as contrasted to a good (subject matter) or service (activity) to be delivered. When content is conceived as learning experience, it is a part of the learner's being, real to his or her life, a springboard to self-realization, and governed by self-control as opposed to elitist control.

Criticism.   To conceive of content as experience in the minds of others, or as what they realize as the result of experience, is much too intangible. Educators cannot get inside the minds of other persons to monitor how every environmental episode that they encounter affects their outlook. If we could, it might be useful, or it might turn into "big brother." If educators cannot know how the environment (be it readings, activities, social interactions) influences student outlook, then they have no basis for input. This position leaves too much of the learning process in the control of students who are too immature to know what is best for them to learn.

CRITERIA FOR SELECTING CONTENT

Decisions about what content should be offered rest on many influences. Some are laudable and genuinely flow from the questions: What knowledge is most worth-while? What kind of life is good to live? Other influences reside in the demiworlds of expediency, personal gain, and desire to control others. Let us consider eight areas, noting that each may contain dimensions of both the admirable and the base, that there is overlap among the criteria in practice, and that curriculum developers need to prioritize and balance extant criteria rather than merely select one over the others.

Societal Needs

Part of the reason for the existence of schools is that they fulfill social needs. Societies ostensibly establish schools to help further their goals and promote their values in successive generations.

Examples.   Schools in most societies promote loyalty to the society and its political leadership. Schools develop curricula that enable the young to enter the labor market. Thus, curriculum perpetuates the socioeconomic values and structures that exist in the society.

Advocacy.   Curricular content is selected because it is deemed worthwhile to the maintenance and renewal of the values, institutions, and relationships for which the society stands. This pertains to both long-term cultural needs and to those that arise because of changing conditions exemplified by change of climate, imposition of other societies, desire to move in new directions, and depletion of economic material resources.

Criticism.   A great deal rests on the nature of the needs that a society sees for itself. Schools, for instance, have perpetuated the rise of Nazi Germany. Thus, there must be a higher order of judgment than that which exists within the social structure. For example, pragmatists might say that a society's perception of needs should be judged relative to consequences, while advocates of democracy often argue that a democratic society has a built-in process of criticism, renewal, and growth. Others assert that schools can do nothing other than perpetuate the social order and act as an arm of the government, religious group, or private agency that supports them.

Test of Survival

The duration of time is thought to be the best indicator of what should be taught. If content has endured the changes of decades and centuries, it must be worthwhile.

Examples.   The classics are taught, the great books are considered great, because they have persisted. For this reason, Mortimer Adler (1982, 1983, 1984) advocates the study of great works of the Western world and the study of enduring ideas such as truth, beauty, goodness, liberty, equality, and justice (Adler, 1981). These, and the value of sound reason, have been advocated as valuable curricular content since the days of Plato and Artistotle. Even in recent times one can see that curricular areas that have been in effect for only a few years are difficult to discard. Once such patterns of three years of Latin or the sequence of Algebra I, Geometry, Algebra II were established for secondary schools (or long vowel sounds followed by short vowel sounds at the primary school), it is difficult to see how they can be replaced. In the modern world of education, the test of survival can be a mere ten years, or even less.

Advocacy.   If something persists, and is selected for use again and again, it must be worthwhile. It would be a sad commentary on human nature to say that humans tend to choose what they do not need.

Criticism.   That which persists is often not a result of conscious choice; rather, it obtains from mindless habit. Thus, as Alfred North Whitehead (1929) perceptively observed, we are beset with a load of "inert ideas" in education. It is easier to perpetuate the old than to arrive imaginatively at more relevant and defensible content.

Structure of the Disciplines

This criterion suggests that each discipline has a deep, inherent structure and that curricular content should be presented in a form that enables students to comprehend this structure (Bruner, 1960; Elam, 1964; Ford and Pugno, 1964). This was a major position that emerged during the post-*Sputnik* curriculum reform of the 1960s.

Examples.   In chemistry or physics class, we all remember the two or three students in laboratory exercises to whom all of the others flocked for answers. Somehow these students had grasped the structure of the discipline. The structure seemed magnetic in that seemingly diverse fragments of information or data from experiments fastened themselves in meaningful ways somewhere on the conceptualized pattern of the discipline. Mathematics is another obvious example. A central purpose of so-called "modern mathematics" and interdisciplinary programs in the sciences such as the Biological Sciences Curriculum Study (BSCS) and the Physical Science Study Committee (PSSC) was to help students see interrelationships more fully. Those who, for example, could see practical interconnections among mathematical, chemical, and physical properties represented in the periodic chart of the elements had a handle on both disciplinary and interdisciplinary understanding.

Advocacy.   To comprehend the structural framework on which a discipline is built provides efficient access to the wide range of knowledge within that discipline. Bits and pieces of information fit together and make sense when they are viewed through the lenses of, and in relation to, the structure of the discipline. Thus, the intent is to select content that brings the structure into full view and reinforces it.

Criticism.   Although those who advocate the structure of the disciplines as a basis for content selection imply that all disciplines and areas of study have inherent structures, there is little evidence that French literature, English poetry, American history, psychology, sociology, modern painting, business management, and education (to name a few areas) have an inherent structure. Moreover, apart from a few obvious basics, it is even difficult for experts in mathematics and the hard sciences to agree on dimensions of the structure of their discipline. While some learners may develop an intuitive grasp of a field of inquiry, this is much more elusive than something that can be taught as a matter of fact. The failure of the 1960s curriculum reform projects supports this criticism.

Utility

Curricular content is selected because it is useful to the learner, to the school, or to the society as a whole. In the latter case, this criterion closely resembles the social needs criterion discussed first. In a discussion as brief as this one, it is not possible to treat all the possible realms of usefulness; therefore, only three are touched upon in the examples that follow.

Examples.   Some argue strongly for a criterion of utility that is designed for students. In a rapidly changing world, it is necessary to develop coping strategies or life skills. These might include critical thinking, problem solving, and the kind of resourcefulness that allows one to find one's way around in novel or difficult circumstances.

Some views of utility are given to the student with a kind of false benevolence that actually benefits the school more than the child. When students score high on standardized achievement tests, the school is praised for its productivity. Thus, content is selected that contributes to earning high achievement test scores, to making high scores on the college boards, or to winning highly touted contests in music, science, athletics, and the like. A more cynical view may even see the school as a kind of duper that convinces the public to want whatever commodity (knowledge) the school has to offer (e.g., a student should know phonics rules, how to multiply and divide fractions, name the muscles and bones of the body, recite the monarchs of England, and match the capital cities of the world with their countries). These, the public becomes convinced, are marks of the educated person. Their utility may be dubious to either the individual or society, but it helps to perpetuate schooling and is even reinforced by popular game shows on television.

A third example, perhaps the most frequently acknowledged sign of utility of schooling, is that it provides jobs for graduates. This is especially the case with jobs that raise the social station of the student. Content is selected because, in either the short or long run, it provides jobs. Vocational education or work-study programs are usually reserved for members of lower socioeconomic classes and those who are less academically inclined. Math and science courses are justified for the more able students on the grounds that they support jobs in medicine, engineering, business, and related domains of high technology.

Advocacy.   If something is useful, instrumental to desired ends, it should be provided. To learn for the sake of learning is not enough; it should be for the purpose of acquiring an end that enables greater achievement and success. This might include qualifying for higher education as a means to better jobs.

Criticism.   The instrumental criterion is opposed on the grounds that the utility is for someone else's benefit. School teachers' jobs are perpetuated, barons of industry get their workers, and government officials receive strokes of praise because students do what is "useful." The job market of today provides little indication as to kinds of work that will be needed in the future. Even the life skills of today soon become outmoded. Content that enables people to learn how to learn and to appreciate learning is more truly useful. True usefulness derives from genuine interest in the world, not in seeking utility directly. To be preoccupied with the latter is to fall prey to the dictates of trendish social forces rather than to personal growth and the good life.

Publisher Decision

Although it may not appear as altruistic as some of the other criteria for content selection, some argue that curriculum developers at the school level exert little impact on the content taught. They merely select which textbook series or instructional system to adopt. Cynics might add that there is little difference among the extant choices. It is, in the final analysis, the publishers who make the curriculum. According to the Educational Products Information Exchange (EPIE), more than 90 percent of classroom time is spent using published materials (EPIE, 1979). Thus, published materials *are* the curriculum content.

Examples.   One has only to spend time in classrooms and observe that the daily regimen is governed by published materials (texts, teachers' editions, worksheets, and other instructional systems), to realize that publishers' decisions govern the classroom and the content taught and learned there.

Advocacy.   Publishers have greater expertise at their disposal than schools have. Publishers can hire noted scholars from the disciplines to develop content for their texts, they can consult with top educators and psychologists on the best way to sequence and present material for grade levels in question, and they can hire excellent writers and editors to put the material in a form that appeals to students' interests and motivates them. Moreover, the free marketplace at its best guides publisher decisions. Through marketing strategies, they find out what educators in schools want to buy and what appeals to and works well with students. Then they provide it. This is an effective way of tapping the needs and interests of those concerned. Furthermore, if the school people did not think the materials were good, they wouldn't buy them. Clearly, they wouldn't buy them if students didn't like them.

Criticism.   This is a blatant example of capitalism overextending itself. The desired is confused with the desirable. School people are wedded to the habit of thinking that they need published materials for effective teaching. So they buy them. The range of selection available is meager. It is akin to engaging in deep deliberation over what view of the news is best by focusing on comparisons of televised news on ABC, NBC, and CBS, or of products they advertise. Decisions about what is best for the growth of children should not be relegated to the same level as deodorants, toilet cleaners, and trash bags. The claim that students, teachers, and administrators have a creative role in the materials published is unfounded. The materials are purchased and then mandated for student use. Their use is the result of authoritarian control, not free decision.

Political Pressure

Like it or not, those who serve in leadership positions in schools are forced to cater to the demands and whims of partisan politics. Such demands surface at many levels: from school to community, from state to nation, from interest group to international conflict. Pressures are brought to bear and schools respond, using the demands as a basis for selecting curricular content.

Examples.   Fundamentalist Christian groups object to language in certain novels on the English reading list, and the books are removed or made optional. A group from the Hispanic population in the community requests more representation of its cultural origins in history classes. Regional pressures cause the school to give equal time to "creation science" in biology classes. Publishing companies, as curriculum creators, are far from immune to such pressures. It is well known that different versions of reading, literature, and social studies texts are written for different populations; it is not uncommon for them to delete examples and issues that are objectionable and to include ones that are more palatable on racial, ethnic, and moral topics.

Perhaps the most profound examples of political pressure at work as a criterion for content selection exist at the national level. Government officials in advanced, industrialized nations look at their ranking as compared with those of other countries in international comparison studies and call for a major emphasis on aspects of achievement to improve their relative ranking. They know that achievement measures emphasize verbal and quantitative skills; thus, they advocate and fund development of these skills. A Third World nation may, for example, see its handle on independence obtainable from a strong nationalistic thrust that overcomes a colonial past or tribal differences. Thus, it saturates its social studies curriculum with patriotic messages. Also very prevalent is fear of sturdy competition by corporate powers from other nations, as with the recent international concern for high-tech industries. Barons of business influence government leaders who establish blue ribbon commissions that assess schools and find a need for skills that prepare students for positions that, in turn, benefit those barons of business. The government has then created justification to filter money into research and curriculum development that improves the capacity for high-tech industry.

Advocacy.   Political interests should continuously emerge in order that the public will is aired. Schools need to be responsive to the public will, which curriculum content should reflect and promote.

Criticism.   The will reflected is usually that of power wielders who can muster the economic clout to be heard. This is seldom a highly representative sample of what the public wants. Furthermore, what the public wants is not always what it needs. Just as the public turns to the medical profession for advice on the content of medical diagnoses, so too should it turn to professional educators who are in a better position to identify the needed curricular content. Curriculum developers should listen to and investigate the claims of all parties and interest groups involved, but they should decide what best fulfills the overall needs rather than be bounced about like political Ping Pong balls.

Learner Interest

It is possible to base curriculum content on the interests of the learners. A. S. Neill did this as vividly revealed in *Summerhill* (1960). Dewey (1916, 1938a) advocated that we begin with the psychological (learner interest) and proceed to the logical (disciplinary knowledge). The point is that learners be allowed to study what they are interested in studying.

Examples. The range of examples is exceedingly great. Content based on momentary whim is at one extreme. In such cases, students are told simply to do as they please, and teachers stand aside as in some of the free schools of the 1960s. Far removed from this position is one that asserts that learners have indispensable and subtle insight into what they need to know. Through dialogue, sensitive teachers can help students to discover the more fundamental interests that undergird their momentary whims. Some go so far as to argue that these fundamental human concerns are dealt with in the great literature of the disciplines. Thus, they see student interests as a central means to the acquisition of extant knowledge.

Advocacy. Content should be selected according to the interests of the learners. Either these interests are seen as a motivating device by which to lead students to knowledge deemed relevant to them, or it is believed that students actually know what is best for them. Of course, many positions lie between these extremes.

Criticism. Adults are in a better position to determine content for students. They have greater experience and knowledge. This counters the position that students know best what they need. They do not; they are immature, and would not be students if they knew what they needed to learn. The other position, to use student interest as a means to a predetermined end, is deception. It makes a sham of their interests and degrades the students as human beings while claiming to uplift them to a level of self-determination.

Democratic Action

Does the curriculum content foster democratic action? The assumption is that if educators want to build a society that can live better together and make decisions more effectively through cooperative deliberation, they must ask whether the curricular content leads students in this direction.

Examples. If we want students who verbalize appreciation for democracy, we might obtain this by presenting them with teachers who can deliver inspirational, patriotic lectures. However, this is not democratic action. The ability to engage in democratic action does not automatically result from listening to twelve years of lecture. It must be born in the opportunity to live democratically. For those who attend school, this means the opportunity to experience life in democratic classrooms. In such classrooms, teachers and students would work out together the rules to live by and the meaning of an education. Both rules and conceptions of education would continuously change and evolve. In fact, the process of discussion and study that brings such change and evolution is education. It is learning how to live and learn together.

Advocacy. The curriculum content that best prepares one to live in a democracy is actual experience in democratic life. It is not mere voting, which taken alone is a mere facade of democracy. Democracy involves inquiry, as individuals and as groups, into the meaning of life and the direction one's action should take. It is a continuous imagining of possibilities and the consequences of acting upon them.

Criticism. Students are not mature enough to consider accurately what they need, how to live together, and what the consequences of all this are. To involve the young and immature in democratic action is an inefficient, time-consuming, and wasteful way to determine curricular content. Students need to be told to learn that which will help them live democratically when they are adults.

IMAGES OF CONTENT

Book-length treatments of curricular content are not uncommon in areas of social studies, language arts, science, mathematics, the arts, and specialized areas of education. In fact, subareas of each of these are also given extensive treatment, to wit, books on reading, drama, or bilingual education within the language arts category; books on music, art, or literature within the arts curriculum; and so on.

Since this book is not intended to cover the curriculum in the content areas—a task that is unlikely to be possible, although some have done a good job of sampling (e.g., Shepherd and Ragan, 1982; Steeves, 1968; Ulich, 1964)—a different tack is taken here. We examine five general categories of content from the perspective of each of our guest commentators. The first four content areas are rather traditional ones in schooling: social studies, language arts, science and mathematics, and the arts. You will notice that commentators' orientations even question those general categories. The fifth category relates to a variety of specialized curricular areas, too numerous to discuss separately, for example, vocational education, physical education, and special education. Each commentator will provide an image of the content area in question and some examples.

Social Studies

Intellectual Traditionalist. Social studies is unfortunately a sorry amalgamation of the social sciences. The social sciences (such as sociology, political science, anthropology, economics, and psychology) have come into their own as somewhat credible disciplines in the twentieth century. Personally, I think school curriculum was better off when it had history and geography rather than "social studies." History is established in the humanities and geography is a natural science. While I do not deny that some writers in each of the so-called "social science" areas have provided some worthwhile knowledge and ideas, the realm of social science is still in its infancy. Before the outcomes of its study are disseminated to schools as defensible curricular content, it should reach a higher level of maturity. One could probably summarize in a few pages what social scientists have found to date. My own opinion is that the whole realm is an attempt by social theorists to generate credibility by usurping the methods of natural sciences. The best of social science, I predict, will move back into the humanities as social theory when the pseudo–love affair with science is over.

Thus, my recommendation is to continue to offer history and geography as the prime areas of social studies content and to intersperse relevant perspectives from the "social sciences" as the need arises. I also support a chronological sequence of such material. One final caveat—knowledge from social sciences should not be presented as truth but as interpretation, which is what history is after all.

Social Behaviorist.   In recent years, a positive trend has occurred, namely, the move from the vagueness of history to social science as a basis for the social studies. Some historical work is, quite admittedly, based upon sound, scientific research but much remains shrouded in a veil of speculation and imagination of the authors. The advent of social science, with psychology and economics leading the way, has fashioned new forms of inquiry from which several viable disciplines emerged. Thus, social studies content should be drawn from the findings of psychologists, economists, sociologists, geographers, political scientists, archeologists, anthropologists, and linguists. History, formally among the softer disciplines in the humanities, has profited from competition with new social sciences, and historiography itself has become more scientifically sound.

Content for social studies should be selected from the social sciences and should be determined by asking: What content or learning activities fit the purposes? Purposes should, of course, be based on needs analysis, before content is discussed. To discuss content before purposes is to put the cart before the horse. When purposes finally reach the stage of behavioral objectives, there is less decision making needed than might be expected in the realm of content. The task of integrating the most up-to-date social science findings with overall purposes actually produces content and prespecified learning activities in the form of behavioral objectives. The magnitude of this task cannot be adequately accomplished at the school level or even at the school system level. It requires more expertise than is available in all but the very largest school districts, if even these. It is the job of curriculum researchers in universities, private and governmental agencies, and publishing companies to pull together teams with the needed competence. Thus, the best content for social studies is found in materials carefully designed by publishers who use teams of curriculum designers and subject matter specialists as consultants.

Experientialist.   Social studies is the study of people. The best way to understand people is to interact with them. Classrooms are too often places where 25 to 35 students sit in isolation from one another. They need to engage in a variety of group process activities through which they can share experiences, values, and interests. They need to participate in the governance of their classroom and school.

Students must realize that there is a connection between their social life in and out of school and the subject called social studies. If there is no connection, the topic should be dropped from the curriculum. Social studies, the study of social life, should focus on the vast interest students have in developing relationships with their peers. Students should actively connect school and community life by moving back and forth between the two in a process of active investigation of social problems. Such problems will frequently be actual problems that they face, that their experience has made known to them. Since experience can be vicarious, they may also study problems that they have read about or have discovered through the media. Thus, books and related materials can be useful resources, but they should not be the organizing center of curricular content. The latter should be experience itself.

Language Arts

Intellectual Traditionalist.   The term language arts is a curious one indeed. It has come to mean reading, writing, spelling, and grammar, which are essentially skills, not arts. They are, for the most part, prerequisites to arts, however. The art of language, presumably what the term *language arts* should mean if it means anything at all, is found in poetry, plays, novels, short stories, and films. This includes many languages, not merely the dominant one in the country where the curriculum is offered. Students should study these if they are to learn the art of language. They should emulate the great authors as they learn to speak and write with greater artistry. At all costs, they should eschew textbooks that purport to teach language arts. They, ironically, are among the poorest examples of the art of language.

Social Behaviorist.   The language arts are an integration of reading, writing, spelling, grammar, study skills, literature, speech, drama, mass media, and any other studies that enhance the ability to communicate. Reading, speaking, and writing are perhaps the most fundamental of skills in language arts. We should add to this computer literacy, the key to tomorrow. These are basic to other content areas as well. Skills that contribute to language facility should, therefore, be carefully delineated and based on the best scientific findings that educational research has to offer. If the skills are developed well in the early years of schooling, then students will be able to choose whatever they might like to learn when they are older. To acquire these skills makes future choice wide-angled. Adults will not choose what they cannot do. Thus, the prime job of language arts education is skill development; the enjoyment of literature, theater, poetry, and everyday reading materials (magazines, newspapers, how-to manuals) is contingent upon acquisition of language arts skills.

Experientialist.   Language arts content involves the skill and enjoyment of communication. Too many, notably the social behaviorists, forget about the importance of enjoyment. We rarely become sufficiently involved in learning something if we do not enjoy it and foresee the acquisition of increased skill as a means to greater enjoyment. No, I am not a blatant hedonist, for when I say "enjoyment," I refer to the pragmatic concern for consequences. Thus, it is to enjoyment for self *and others* that I refer. I am assuming here that enjoyment comes from genuine growth. Just as I argued that social interaction yields social growth when I discussed social studies content, experience with language fosters growth in communicative arts. Social interaction allows students to see the integration of the search for meaning and direction with social intercourse, body language, values clarification, resourcefulness, problem solving, and other contributors to personal and social growth. This is not to deny the importance of skills of reading, writing, grammar, usage, spelling, and even the use of computers. Nevertheless, it recognizes that such skills are tools, not ends in themselves. And of great import, these tools can only be acquired meaningfully as they are needed in the process of social life. They cannot be learned effectively prior to the realization of their need by the learner, as social behaviorists and intellectual traditionalists advocate. The content for language arts is found by students in their natural pursuit of communication in social endeavors. This is how they learned to talk when they weren't privy to language at all; and most students learn to speak rather well. If they had to learn to speak prior to application, as social behaviorists and intellectual traditionalists want students to learn to read, write, and so on, we would likely wind up with a huge population of nonspeakers equivalent to the nonreaders of today.

Science and Mathematics

Intellectual Traditionalist. Mathematics is a kind of universal language, particularly the language of the natural sciences. It has a beauty, elegance, and conceptual utility that students must be taught to appreciate. There is so much of logic and aesthetic form presented to learners through the study of mathematics that it should be taught separately from the sciences. The natural sciences (physics, chemistry, astronomy, geology, biology, etc.) should also be taught as separate disciplines. The conceptual utility of mathematics will become clear to students who study any of these sciences in depth. Knowledge of the sciences provides insight into the natural world and, thus, opens the door to metaphysics, the greatest of speculative realms. Students should, of course, become familiar with both basic knowledge within the disciplines and the methods of scientific inquiry and expression. At the same time, as they learn that science is necessary to a liberal education, they should realize that it is not sufficient for such an education. There are other realms of meaning and other avenues to truth.

Social Behaviorist. The method of scientific research is the greatest invention of the modern age. Science content should be designed to enable students to learn to inquire as scientists do. A variety of published materials do an excellent job of teaching this process. Such materials also integrate mathematics into the scientific research process. The content of topics learned should, of course, be drawn from the disciplines: physics, chemistry, biology, astronomy, geology, the behavioral sciences, and the like. It should be selected to give students a working knowledge of the everyday world in which they live, a world that is becoming increasingly sophisticated technologically. Even with this guideline, it is impossible to design curricula with all the content that should be covered. Due to the knowledge explosion in science, we must be content to sample subject areas and hope that students will study more science on their own. The sorry state of scientific knowledge in our world is indeed a problem. We need to teach the basics of mathematics to all and help them understand the process by which scientific research is conducted. If these purposes are incorporated into behavioral objectives and, thus, converted into content, the remainder of the science and mathematics content should be the result of deliberations on particular needs analyses conducted cooperatively by local educators and community representatives.

Experientialist.   Science is not primarily something that credentialed experts do in laboratories, even though the social behaviorist thinks it is. As John Dewey (1910, 1929b, 1938b) ably taught us, science is the process of intelligent problem solving. It does not primarily involve the disciplines of physics, chemistry, biology, and so on, although it certainly may pertain to them. Accordingly, the content of science curricula should be the concerns and dilemmas in social lives of students. Students should learn to clarify dilemmas, thus converting them into clearly stated problems. They should learn to search out precedent from others who have faced similar problems. This often involves a good deal of library work informed by personal and social encounters with relevant others. It involves the formulation of informal hypotheses or possible courses of action and the anticipation of probable consequences of acting on these alternatives. Students learn to formulate logically and carry out proposed courses of action; and they learn to become aware of the continuous, often subtle, flow of consequences that streams from any action. They learn to judge and assess what they do relative to the contribution that it makes to themselves, others, and the environment. This interpretation sometimes involves more formal knowledge and skill drawn from science, mathematics, and technology, but the central focus is life, not academic content. As students pursue many life problems in this manner, they do in fact learn a considerable amount of science and mathematics, but such knowledge is instrumental, not an end in itself. Since it is instrumental, personally useful, it is more fully comprehended and sticks with learners more than academic content delivered in isolation from personal meaning and self-direction.

The Arts

Intellectual Traditionalist.   It baffles me as to the reason why language arts and arts are separated. We do commonly refer to "the arts and sciences" as the basic curriculum of a liberal education. Witness the title, "Arts and Sciences," given to most colleges in universities that grant liberal arts degrees. Languages and the arts are part of the great humanistic tradition that should be the mainstay of any education. Yes, I say *the* mainstay. This means that the arts are more important than the sciences, which are surely not unimportant. But it is the arts as humanities that include philosophy, history, fine arts, languages and literatures, and theoretical studies of many kinds. Even mathematics is more at home among the humanities or arts than the sciences.

Children should be exposed to the arts from their early years. Discretion, of course, should be used in selecting arts that are commensurate with the knowledge of learners. My point is simply that at all ages of schooling, there are more than enough arts to go around. I am often asked about youngsters in primary grades. Even before this, children can deal with philosophical problems (Matthews, 1980). Anyone who has been around children knows how well they like stories of history, folk stories, myths, fairy tales, and so on. See Bruno Bettelheim (1976) on the value of fairy tales. And the love of children for painting, music, dance, and theater is unquestioned, especially those who are fortunate enough to be exposed to it from the very earliest years. Therefore, I recommend that children be exposed on a continuous basis to examples of the best art available. More exposure, I submit, will point students toward a more pure and virtuous life.

Social Behaviorist.   The arts are nice but not necessities, as contrasted to science, mathematics, language arts, and social sciences. It is very nice indeed to know about painting throughout history, play a musical instrument, and dance well. Many enjoy the opera, ballet, the symphony, and the theater. But these are not essentials, as is witnessed by the fact that many good citizens in every country lead productive lives without much acquaintance with the arts. In fact, most ordinary folks fall in this category.

As curriculum content, the arts should receive secondary emphasis to subject areas discussed earlier. Only to the extent that schools can demonstrate adequate progress in the more essential areas, some exposure to the arts should be provided. Music and art classes on a once-a-week basis, as is usually the case in elementary schools, is about right. Some school systems have magnet schools, or at least elective courses, for those who have the inclination to go on in the arts. Yet it is obviously the case that jobs in the arts areas are few and far between. If parents seek training for their children in the arts, there are plenty of skilled artists hoping to offer private lessons. To the extent that the arts are taught in school, however, they should be carefully delineated. The rather frivolous character of arts education has given the field a nonrigorous image. Carefully specified behavioral objectives for skills in the various arts would be a good start. Useful content would be implicit in such objectives.

Experientialist.   The aesthetic imagination and sensitive perception are central to every realm of life. Eisner (1982) argues this position well. To teach the arts does not imply curricular content about singing and construction paper art alone. These, by contrast, are a very small part of what the arts curriculum should be. It should, of course, be exposure to high-quality live performances in the several realms of the arts. But it should also, and with at least equal importance, include experience in the arts. The purpose of this is not that jobs might be available but that human growth of all kinds has its roots in the aesthetic perception of form and grace. We understand our world better and see our relationship to it more clearly as we aesthetically perceive the overlapping patterns that situate ourselves. Art enables us to fashion possibilities for our experience that go beyond the taken-for-granted. The best of science, language, and social interaction is sparked by artistic vision. Curriculum content needs to be revitalized with an artistic spirit that beckons students to create a life for themselves and an environment to live it in. We must move beyond separate subject conceptions of curriculum to see students who are engaged with meaning and direction in the creation of their lives. This form of education has art at its very center.

Other Specializations

A host of curricular content areas come and go with social and economic pressures. They reappear under different labels; yet a few are quite permanently with us: physical education, special education, vocational education, and bilingual education. Each deserves elaborate consideration, but such is beyond the scope of this book.

Nevertheless, the perspective of each of our commentators on these specializations, though brief, is revealing.

Intellectual Traditionalist.   Schools are already beset with too much to teach and not enough time in which to teach it. One can scarcely deny the importance of health, the handicapped, language, and the world of work. These areas are, however, either treated by other areas of the curriculum or they are the job of other agencies in our society. In truth, I believe both to be the case. Health is the province of natural sciences, especially biology, while sports should be handled outside the school. Languages should receive more emphasis, and all students should be bi- and trilingual. Then the problem of students whose first language is another becomes moot. Vocational education is not appropriate for public schools; it can destroy their efforts to provide general education. Besides, the rapid changes in occupations make it better for technical schools and employers themselves to provide vocational education. Students should, however, learn about the world of work when they study economics and history. The best preparation for jobs, however, is the development of a sound mind, the product of general education.

The most difficult problem is that of education for the handicapped. Provisions should be made for the physically handicapped to participate in regular classrooms whenever possible. We have gone much too far in our labeling jargon with the other areas of special education. Many of those with behavioral, learning, and emotional disabilities would likely do well if they had better teachers. Poor teachers and parents undoubtedly cause some of these problems, as well. Separate facilities need to be provided for the profoundly handicapped, both mentally and physically. The remainder should be provided for by the regular schools and can be with good teachers.

Social Behaviorist.   Great strides have been made over the past twenty to thirty years in education for the handicapped. Special education research has identified a carefully delineated set of categories for special learner needs. This, coupled with Public Law 94-142, which requires that all such students be provided for, is a major stride, especially with the emphasis on writing an IEP or individualized educational plan for each student. All areas of the curriculum could profit from the example of special education. Language disadvantage is another form of handicap as I see it. Researchers in the area of bilingual education, with the help of federal funding, have identified different kinds of needs that are served by alternative types of specialized programs.

Vocational education is an absolute necessity. Look at the vast unemployment of the unskilled and semiskilled. Our society and economic system need schools to provide a much elaborated program of vocational education. It is, after all, the school's main task to provide students for their future, and their future is jobs.

Physical education is with us and should remain so. It does need more rigorous standards, for the physical health of our citizenry is at stake. The relatively new lifetime sports emphasis makes a good deal more sense than does the old "throw out the ball" technique.

Experientialist.   If the curriculum is integrated around experiences of students, and if students share together to develop curricular content, then the classroom becomes akin to the cooperative family that works together to solve special problems and meet special needs. In such an environment, one would have the essence of the main-streaming ideal. All but the most severely handicapped would be accommodated, and I would not be surprised if the behavioristic labels and categorical distinctions would no longer be needed. Students who did not know the dominant language would be a positive influence on an experiential class, not a liability, for other students could teach and learn with them. This could result in more students learning a second or third language than merely those being assimilated. Health is essential to sound learning; thus, physical education would be treated as a necessity to other forms of growth. Vocations should be taught for better understanding of one's present. This would involve visits and interactions with participants in many work situations. While this might enhance one's sense of direction for future work, specific preparation for the long-term future would be avoided unless students especially requested it. Work with the hands would, however, be encouraged, as it enables qualities of development not available through nonmanual means.

COMMENTARIES

Rather elaborate commentaries have already been provided on each presenter's image of curriculum content. Therefore, each will now respond quite briefly by identifying his or her position on the first two categories: orientations to content and criteria for selecting content. Each will then add any further comments he or she might wish to make.

Intellectual Traditionalist

My position on content is a subject matter orientation; therefore, I turn to the disciplines that have stood the test of time as a criterion for selecting content. This provides content that meets social and individual needs, although it is often more desirable than desired.

I caution readers to be wary of the social behaviorist who, in the final analysis, is afraid to seek wisdom and turns curriculum into technique that follows social pressure. I also caution readers to guard against the false idealism of the experientialist, who believes that the common man is as capable of intelligent decision as the educated and wise; if this were the case, what would be the point in becoming educated? The social behaviorist skirts responsibility to decide what is worthwhile content, while the experientialist thinks all are equal to the responsibility.

Social Behaviorist

Learning activities combine with subject matter to form my orientation to content, and my criteria for selecting content derive from the analysis of social needs, utility, and the structure of the disciplines. I do believe that some excellent curriculum materials are available as a result of publishers and scholars working as partners.

I warn the reader, as did Harold Benjamin (1939) in his *Saber-tooth Curriculum*, to watch out for intellectual traditionalists who perpetuate inert subject matter long after it has lost its utility. Benjamin, as Professor Peddiwell, told us that prehistoric tribes of the north country taught fish-grabbing-with-the bare-hands and saber-tooth-tiger-chasing-with-fire long after the glaciers froze the streams of fish and pushed the saber-tooth tigers hundreds of miles to the south. Continuing the analogies to prehistory, the experientialists are just as dangerous because they want everyone to rediscover the wheel. Of greatest importance, however, is to realize that the purpose of content is consistently to facilitate purposes and objectives. It is the second step in the process of curriculum design.

Experientialist

We must focus as best we can on the ever-fleeting learning experiences of students; we must try our best to understand how students' outlooks are influenced by what we do. Better yet, we need to enable students themselves to be more aware of the ways in which learning takes place within them. Criteria for selecting experiences must, therefore, include learner interest. Since learners are social, it must also include democratic action.

The division of the content of human experience into separate subjects is the major error of the intellectual traditionalist, who believes that life comes in organized categories. The social behaviorist also derives false security from chopping up reality and putting it in little bundles that are to be parceled out mindlessly to fit demands of social expedience. The intellectual traditionalist lives in the past while the social behaviorist preplans for a future that never arrives. Meanwhile, both miss the best opportunity there is—to experience the present. Few authors speak as well as Louise Berman and Jessie Roderick to a personal and interdisciplinary approach that integrates the curriculum around processes most meaningful to the experience of human living (Berman, 1968; Berman and Roderick, 1977). By interpreting the practical spirit of Deweyan educational philosophy, Berman (1968) calls for curricular focus on perceiving, communicating, loving, knowing, decision making, patterning, creating, and valuing; Berman and Roderick (1977) move to the true basics of creating a worthwhile life by advocating that teachers and students learn to pursue the "what, how, and why of living."

SUGGESTED READING

Apart from sources already listed in the text of this chapter, I suggest that you survey some of the synoptic curriculum texts in an effort to identify how issues of content are treated. I especially suggest Smith, Stanley, and Shores (1957). For a treatment of elementary school curriculum content areas, I recommend Shepherd and Ragan (1982). For a fine collection of articles on curricular content areas, I recommend Steves (1968). Perhaps Phillip Phenix, in *Realms of Meaning* (1964), most creatively investigates the epistemological and personal value of alternative content areas.

I also encourage you to survey texts on curriculum and methods in the subject areas. One might look at Moffett and Wagner (1976) in language arts, Jarolimek and Walsh (1974) in social studies, Copeland (1982) in mathematics, Victor (1985) in science, Eisner (1972) in the arts, and Heitmann and Kneer (1976) in physical education. One might also be advised to search out journals in each of the content areas, survey teachers' editions of textbooks used widely in schools, and skim curriculum guides. This exercise would help the curriculum generalist to become more fully aware of current developments in specialized content areas. It would also help him or her to acquire a method for making periodic surveys to become updated in content areas.

Although it is difficult to find pure-form examples of each of the commentators, and in spite of the fact that each includes considerable variance, one could turn to the following examples for each position: for the social behaviorist, one might consult Gagné (1977), Johnson (1977a), Pratt (1980), Mager (1962), and Popham and Baker (1970); for the intellectual traditionalist, see King and Brownell (1976), Broudy, Smith, and Burnett (1978), Adler (1982, 1983, 1984), and Ulich (1964); and for the experientialist, Dewey (1916, 1931), Hopkins (1937), Kilpatrick (1936), Freire (1970), Rogers (1983), Berman (1968), and Berman and Roderick (1977).

RECOMMENDATIONS FOR REFLECTION

1. Reflect on the purpose(s) that you identified in reflections for Chapter Eight. What orientation to content would best fit the ideal purposes that you want to strive for as an educator? Is it subject matter, activities, or experiences? Which of these characterize the orientation to content in the educational institution for which you work?

2. Think of some content that you believe is worthwhile to teach. What criteria did you use (implicitly or explicitly) to select this content? Why?

3. Return to each criterion for content selection and develop a counterargument to the criticism section.

4. In the "Images of Content" section, with which of the characterizations of content do you most agree relative to (a) social studies, (b) language arts, (c) science and mathematics, (d) the arts, and (e) other specializations? Does one commentator best fit a particular content area?

5. What is your own image of content in each of the five areas? Write a fourth opinion and compare it with the other three.

6. At this juncture in the book, which position most appeals to you: intellectual traditionalist, social behaviorist, or experientialist?

7. Which orientation to content, criteria for selection of content, and image of content is most prevalent in schools that you know?

8. In the "Commentary" section, each of the commentators offered criticism of the other two. Where do you stand on their criticism?

9. If you were required to develop worthwhile curricular content that focused on an insignificant object—say, a paper wad—what could you have students do? Make a list of five to ten worthwhile aspects of content that could stem from a paper wad. Simply brainstorm some possibilities. What do the items on your list reveal about the way that you think about content? Your orientation? Criteria? Images? Other?

10

✦ Paradigm of Perennial Analytic Categories: Organization ✦

Good order is the foundation of all things.
> EDMUND BURKE *Reflections on the Revolution in France* (1790)

Peace is present when man can see the face that is composed of things that have meaning and are in their place. Peace is present when things form part of a whole greater than their sum, as the diverse minerals in the ground collect to become the tree.
> ANTOINE DE SAINT-EXUPÉRY *Flight to Arras* (1942)

Watch out for the fellow who talks about putting things in order! Putting things in order always means getting other people under your control.
> DENIS DIDEROT *Supplement to Bougainville's "Voyage"* (1796)

Order is the shape upon which beauty depends.
> PEARL S. BUCK "The Homemaker" *To My Daughters, With Love* (1967)

SETTING THE STAGE

Among the perennial categories of curriculum analysis, organization is the most multifaceted. It includes the problems of scope or range and depth of curriculum offerings and issues about sequence or how to order the content. Whether content is considered subject matter, activities, or experiences, scope and sequence are crucial organizational decisions. Therefore, the initial section of this chapter deals with alternative responses to the problem of scope, and a second section investigates criteria used in determining sequence. Learning environment is another complex area of study that has arisen in recent years; while it can be viewed as a separate domain of inquiry from curriculum, it surely must be considered within the purview of curriculum organization. Therefore, a third major section of this chapter discusses dimensions by which learning environments may be analyzed and presents examples of several different kinds of learning environments.

One of the most controversial issues that has plagued perennial curriculum debate is instruction. Should instruction be considered separate from or part of curriculum? Operating on the assumptions that curriculum is affected by and sometimes transformed by instructional practices, and that instruction gives further pattern to curriculum, I conclude that the topic must be considered as a major feature of organization. Therefore, orientations to instruction, models of teaching, arrangements for instruction, and types of instruction are addressed.

Due to the extensiveness of this chapter's topics, it is necessary to use almost a shorthand method of presentation in which alternatives are set forth, along with brief explanations or examples, advocacy statements or assertions of intent, and criticisms.

SCOPE

The continuous expansion of knowledge yields new fields of inquiry each year. A knowledge explosion was felt in the late 1800s with the emergence of professional societies in many fields of study. This proliferation has continued and expanded throughout the twentieth century, a point convincingly made by Shane (1977) and a cast of 132 world-class scholars whose views he assembled for a look toward education in the next millennium. Considering the magnitude of knowledge, it was only natural for the question to arise: How much of what knowledge should be provided by school curriculum? Clearly there is not enough time to offer all existing knowledge to students, nor is it possible even to sample a small portion from each area of study. Thus, before midcentury, at least five approaches to scope had emerged: separate subjects, broad fields, projects, the core, and integration. Each of these responses is prevalent today, although labels have changed with authors and circumstances.

Separate Subjects

Educators carefully select the subjects most worthwhile and offer those, while rejecting other areas of knowledge as less basic.

Examples.   Reports by the Carnegie Commission (Boyer, 1983) and the National Commission on Excellence in Education (1983) both advocate increased emphasis on English, science, and mathematics. This deals with the problem of scope in the traditional manner of selecting certain disciplines and discarding others deemed less essential. Most secondary schools, and many elementary schools, have used this approach for years.

Advocacy.   Scope should be based on the assumption that disciplines represent discrete bodies of knowledge that should be studied separately and that some disciplines are more essential than others.

Criticism.   Problems in life do not come packaged in disciplines, and it is a sign of miseducation to hold that one discipline, such as science, is highly useful and another, such as music or art, is a frill.

Broad Fields

Responding to criticism just presented, some curricularists correlated subject areas and fused them together in practice.

Examples. Mathematics and science or language arts and social studies seemed to be natural pairs. In a unit on World War II, students might read appropriate literature and write essays or journal-like episodes as well as study the historical, geographical, and socioeconomic background. Sometimes the arts might be added to make the field of inquiry even broader.

Advocacy. Curricular scope should demonstrate to students the linkages between and among disciplines, and in this spirit some schools have established permanently fused broad fields of study such as LASS (Language Arts Social Studies).

Criticism. The frequency of the use by schools that already use broad fields approaches and mini courses, to whet intellectual appetites and present new subjects, is evidence that broad fields are not broad enough. This tacking on of additional subjects demonstrates the artificial, nonlifelike character of this approach to scope.

Projects

The project method, developed by W. H. Kilpatrick (1918), involved students in an overarching project and related many subject areas to it.

Examples. As intended by Kilpatrick, the topics would be derived from student interests, but in practice topics were often established by teachers: the native American, holidays in foreign lands, or the zoo. A project or *unit* (as the method became reinterpreted) on the zoo might involve measuring animal cages or the size of animals in arithmetic, studying biological characteristics in science, the economics of and social need for zoos in social studies, drawing pictures of animals in art, writing and reading animal stories in language arts, singing about animals in music, and moving like animals in physical education. According to Karl Frey (1985), modern interpretations of the project method are becoming increasingly widespread in European educational settings.

Advocacy. The project method demonstrates to students that it requires many different disciplinary perspectives to understand any single facet or problem of our culture, society, personal lives, or intellectual interest.

Criticism. Projects or units are planned without sufficient background on the interests or needs of students. This continued the criticism that projects are artificial rather than genuine outgrowths of student interest.

Core

The core curriculum (Alberty, 1947; Faunce and Bossing, 1951) brought the disciplines together under the organizing center of social problems.

Examples. A social problem such as war and peace, ecological destruction, world hunger, overpopulation, or prejudice might be studied by engaging students in research that enables them to draw insights from many different disciplines as well as from practical experience.

Advocacy. The core demonstrates the use of knowledge by applying it as it is learned. It motivates students by engaging them in study of problems that are of broad, general interest. By focusing in greater depth on a few areas, students can see more interconnection than they perceive in broad survey courses. Core curricula are usually offered for junior high and secondary students, while projects are reserved for elementary grades.

Criticism. Social problems are too abstract for most students; they don't see a connection to their own lives. The subjects are not systematically presented; since students learn only what is required for a particular problem, much within each discipline is missed. Also, *core* has a totally different meaning today; it now refers to a basic set of required courses in a program after which students may select electives.

Integration

The individual student (or group of students) is the organizing center that defines scope. Together and/or as individuals, students pursue their own sense of direction in a process guided by the overall purpose of personal and social growth.

Examples. Students are engaged in dialogue with responsive, facilitating teachers. They develop and articulate a sense of direction that they believe enhances student growth. They pursue this direction, drawing upon a wide range of personal and academic resources, until another direction emerges, and the process continues through a continuous series of interests.

Advocacy. Integration enables students to realize that they are authors of their own life and learning and gives them experience in taking responsibility for their education.

Criticism. Students are not mature enough to take such responsibility. They do not have the background to provide a balanced curriculum for themselves, and schools could not guarantee to the public what students would learn at different levels. Balance is necessary if the problem of scope is to be resolved adequately.

SEQUENCE

The problem of sequence addresses the order in which content is taught. Sequence and scope go hand in hand as two coordinates on a graph of curricular content. If curriculum developers are to be able to reflect consciously on what they offer, they must be able to articulate the bases by which they sequence content. Six widely used criteria for determining sequence are presented next along with statements of advocacy and criticism for each: textual presentation, educator preference, structure of disciplines, learner interest, learning hierarchies, and developmental appropriateness.

Textual Presentation

The most common ordering of content used in schools today is the sequence of the textbook. Teachers usually follow the text, be it a book, prepackaged learning system, or locally developed instructional unit. In fact, teachers often feel that trouble would await them if they questioned the text.

Advocacy. Experts who wrote the text thoroughly studied the problem of sequence and utilized the most defensible criteria in their design.

Criticism. Curriculum design cannot be made defensibly *en masse*; it must be tailored to the needs and interests of individuals in learning situations. Moreover, those who design texts are more often entrepreneurs than curriculum developers; thus, they provide what is desired, not necessarily what is desirable.

Educator Preference

Teachers vary the curriculum at will, according to their mood or judgment. Research indicates that teachers are not passive implementors; they are active decision makers (Hunter, 1977). They often decide to alter the prescribed sequence. This allows them to base sequence more squarely on their assessment of student need.

Advocacy. Teachers should be allowed to exercise their role as curriculum developers who determine sequence. Publishers and even curriculum designers at the school system level can only operate on generalizations about populations to be served by texts, packages, units, and other documents that they create. It is mandatory that they offer their products and documents as guides, not lawlike, teacherproof orders. Teachers must be treated as professionals who decide the extent to which these guides work in their situations. They need to accept, reject, adapt, and supplement what is given to them.

Criticism. Experience shows that many teachers cannot be trusted to make wise judgments, or even informed ones. They alter the prescribed sequence on a whim or change of mood. It is well known that many elementary school teachers simply do not find the time to teach science because they do not like or understand it well. If they do something this blatant, changes in sequence appear as minor infractions.

Structure of the Disciplines

That existing bodies of knowledge are assumed by some to have an inherent structure (e.g., Bruner, 1960; Elam, 1964; Ford and Pugno, 1964) was established in Chapters Eight and Nine. This structure also implies sequence. For example, principles of economics are built upon concepts, which are built on data; and in mathematics, subtraction and multiplication are sequentially prerequisite algorithms for long division.

Advocacy.   Curriculum developers should rely on the expert interpretation of subject matter specialists who reveal the logical patterns that give shape to their discipline and imply the order in which its elements should be learned.

Criticism.   Most areas of study do not have an inherent structure, especially when we move beyond mathematics and hard sciences such as physics and chemistry. Even in these areas, specialists admit that the structure changes shape as new discoveries are made. If we do accept the existence of structure, sequence still depends on other factors such as prior knowledge, learner intents, and perceived relevance. Recent investigations in cognitive psychology reveal that a large number of variables should be considered when making decisions about sequence (Posner, 1982), not merely structure of the disciplines.

Learner Interest

When learners are interested in problems, they should study them. Pursuit of one problem opens doors to new problems that then should be pursued.

Advocacy.   Sequence should be based on the supposition that knowledge is most relevant when it fulfills learner interests. When knowledge is relevant, it is more readily learned than when it is presented according to an outsider's conception of need or logical order. This is what Dewey (1916) meant when he advocated moving from the *psychological*, or interests of the learner, to the *logical*, or knowledge contained in the formal disciplines. He did not mean that teachers should merely cater to student whims, but through dialogue they should look for deeper interests and needs that momentary interests represent. It is these deeper interests or perennial human concerns that lead students to disciplines of knowledge.

Criticism.   Student interests are too transitory to use as a basis for sequence. They flit from one whim to the next with little reflection. To cater to such momentary caprice would do learners great disservice in the long run. They need the controlling hand of adult guidance. Professional educators can carefully study students as a basis for developing sequence according to their needs and development, not mere interest.

Learning Hierarchies

Learning should proceed from simple to complex (Gagné, 1977; Gagné and Briggs, 1979). Sequence should be commensurate with what we know about learning theory. It should gradually build constructs and principles from data and concepts; thereby it fashions understanding of wholes from a systematic, analytic presentation of parts.

Advocacy.   Sequential order should be based on results of empirical research and resultant theory about validated conditions that foster learning.

Criticism.   Neither learning theory nor research, which serves as its basis, points to conclusive evidence that supports the overall effectiveness of hierarchical modes of sequence. Some researchers suggest that we should move from the particular to the general, while others favor beginning with the general, or image of the whole, and moving to the particulars. Similar arguments persist on the relation between concrete and abstract dimensions of content. There are those who say that sequence should begin with that which is near to children's lives (such as the family and neighborhood treatment in many basal readers and social studies texts) and move toward the state, nation, and world in later years. Yet others (Egan, 1983) claim that childhood preoccupation with fantasy implies that we should sequence from the far-off and imaginary and work back to reality. There may be some truth in all these positions; one may work well for some students and another for others. One thing is certain; the verdict is not yet in on this matter, and the hope for definitive hierarchical recipes may be a hope for a will-o'-the-wisp.

Developmental Appropriateness

Piaget's theory of developmental psychology (1970) holds that learners move from sensorimotor, to preoperational, to concrete operational, to formal operational stages of cognitive development. While curricular implications of Piaget's theory of development offer much potential, they are exceedingly complex to determine relative to specific situations (see Doll, 1983). Similarly, L. Kohlberg (1976) has formulated six stages of moral development: obedience and punishment, reciprocity, conformity, law and order, social contract or constitutional orientation, and universal principles or personal philosophy of right conduct. The point here is that curricular content should be correlated with or designed appropriately to the stage of development, cognitive or moral, at which students function. Examples of such work are presented by Reimer et al. (1983).

Advocacy. Curricular sequence should correlate content with the sequence of human development by making curriculum consonant with the stage of development on which learners are functioning.

Criticism. Not enough is known about how to translate stages of Piaget or Kohlberg into curriculum sequence. Work by Nucci (1982) reveals that this whole process is much more complex than it appears at first glance and that the interactions among cognitive functioning, moral reasoning, and social conventions need much further study. Furthermore, Gilligan (1982) poses a feminist alternative to what she criticizes as a masculine orientation in Kohlberg's conception of moral development. Given the ambiguity of instructional implications of developmental theory, perhaps the best that can be done at present is to act in Deweyan good faith by encouraging teachers to continuously pose the sequence problem to themselves and ask: What is developmentally appropriate for this student in this or that situation? This may be the best guide for the future as well in order to avoid the curricular recipe trap.

LEARNING ENVIRONMENTS

In the 1970s, international attention of a number of educational researchers was directed to learning environments. Barry J. Fraser reviewed that literature as it applies to curriculum evaluation (Fraser, 1981). Pioneering work in the measurement and evaluation of learning environments was done by R. H. Moos (1979), and a variety of perspectives on educational environments is available in a volume edited by Herbert Walberg (1979).

Other more practitioner-oriented books appeared in addition to those just mentioned. Edgar Dale's *Building a Learning Environment* (1972) provides a progressive education perspective on the matter, while Therese Herman exemplifies the behavioral approach in *Creating Learning Environments* (1977), and Mario Fantini (1976) and Allan Glatthorn (1977) both present an array of alternative educational programs that emphasize the profound differences made by alterations in learning environments. Practical suggestions for the design of educational environments are suggested by Taylor and Vlastos (1975), and a collection of perspectives on learning environments is provided by a number of different authors in *Learning Environments* (David and Wright, 1975). Further research reveals the need for teachers to conduct a form of research by reflecting on and monitoring their own teaching situations (Stenhouse, 1975; Elliot, 1976–77; Schubert, 1980b; Fraser, 1982).

Dimensions of Learning Environments

To analyze different types of learning environments, it should be realized that each possesses a range of attributes: physical, material, interpersonal, institutional, and psychosocial. When considering the value of any existing or proposed learning environment, one should not neglect any of these five dimensions. Together, they serve as criteria by which learning environments can be assessed. Each is characterized in more detail in the paragraphs that follow. Here we are only focusing on environmental features internal to specific teaching-learning situations, not wider contexts such as community and socioeconomic surroundings, which are treated in Chapter Four.

Physical Dimensions.   The range of physical environment characteristics within a school is rather great, extending from classroom to schoolwide attributes. At the classroom level, one must view the arrangement of desks, chairs, and tables. Are they movable? Are there learning centers or interest centers, and what is their function with relation to desks and chairs? How are lighting, ventilation, storage areas, and the teacher's desks and files situated with regard to functioning of the class as a whole? At the building level: Is the school arranged in traditional egg-carton fashion with rooms lined up on either side of a hall, or is the environment organized in other ways to differentiate and maximize space? How are different floors, staircases, restroom facilities, food services, libraries, safety provisions, travel paths from area to area, counseling facilities, auditoriums, teacher's areas, special learning facilities, gymnasiums, and administrative offices situated with relation to each other and to the overall learning environment?

Material Dimensions.   Here I refer to curricular or instructional materials. How are they organized? Are they readily accessible to students? To teachers? This pertains to books, consumable worksheets, laboratory equipment, instructional systems packages, art and music materials, audiovisual materials (machines, films, tapes, etc.), computer hardware and software, athletic equipment, home economics appliances, and industrial arts tools and materials. What rules and regulations govern the uses of consumable and nonconsumable materials in these and related domains? To what extent do such rules and regulations inhibit or facilitate learning? How do the sets of materials relate to the overall curriculum design of purposes, learning experiences or content, organization, and evaluation?

Well-designed materials should have characteristics that are consistent with and parallel to the overall curriculum and program design. For example, the organization of social studies texts, related worksheets, and audiovisual supplements should be a microcosm of the curriculum design for the entire school. Similarly, the design characteristics of computer software should be consistent not only with the hardware, but with curriculum design for the whole school program. This is why curriculum design itself must be the basis for judging and selecting all types of curricular and instructional materials. Materials themselves embody implicit (if not explicit) positions on purposes, learning experiences, organization, and evaluation.

Interpersonal Dimensions.   This category of analysis refers to ways of organizing human beings. On what basis are students placed into certain learning groups? Are they grouped homogeneously or heterogeneously? If homogeneously, what criteria govern the placement of students into groups? This pertains as much to groups within classes such as reading groups as it does to different sections of the same grade level. There are those who argue that although tracking is prohibited in some states, it is still carried out by virtue of sections in high school for college preparatory, general education, commercial or technical preparation, honors classes, and advanced placement classes. The positioning of teachers with students relates to the grouping issue. For example, various forms of team teaching make a marked difference in the personal character of learning environments.

Institutional Dimensions.   The governance style of an institution affects the overall learning environment. It makes a great deal of difference if the central administration of a school is essentially autocratic, democratic, or *laissez-faire*. This tendency filters into the local school and the principal is expected, as an arm of the central office, to carry out policy in a similar manner. Teachers, in turn, as the next level of policy implementors, are counted upon to follow suit, which serves as a model for students. Although many principals and teachers hold personal philosophies of organization that differ from those of the central office, and although some make valiant attempts to alter the central office thrust, they face resistance all along the way. Moreover, some would argue that the depersonalization that accompanies institutionalization in any large organization has an adverse effect on learning environments. The converse, of course, may also be the case; institutional governance styles may have positive educative value as a model for teachers and principals.

Psychosocial Dimension.   Clearly the most intangible aspect of learning environment, ambience or atmosphere, is not concrete and easily observable, but is changing constantly. Thus, what one knows about it may change momentarily. Some teachers refer to this dimension of learning environment as the "chemistry of situations." Although not particularly amenable to empirical investigation, good teachers intuitively grasp insights about psychosocial dimensions of learning environments. Such insights have been key ingredients in the arts of teaching and curriculum development since schooling began.

	Physical	Material	Interpersonal	Institutional	Psychosocial
Self-Contained Classroom					
Departmentalization					
Non-graded					
Open-Space					
Open Education					
Tutorial					
Community-based					
Alternative Schooling					
Non-School Education					

FIGURE 10-1.   *Analyzing Dimensions of Learning Environments*

Examples of Learning Environments: Old and New

Although there is not space to analyze each of the examples that follows, an open-ended matrix (Figure 10-1) is provided as a stimulus to consider how the foregoing dimensions of learning environments relate to each of the examples. A brief characterization, a statement of advocacy, and a sample of criticisms are provided for each example. This portrayal is intended to be illustrative but certainly not inclusive. Other types of learning environments and more specific dimensions might be added to the matrix.

Self-contained Classroom.   Still the most prevalent form of environmental organization at the elementary school level, self-contained classrooms consist of one teacher and a group of twenty to forty students who remain together throughout the day. The teacher is responsible for all subject areas, although modified versions involve specialists for such areas as music and physical education.

Advocacy.   Teachers can be autonomous and flexible, having the entire day with the same group of students; they can combine or integrate subject areas, get to know students better, and relate content to their needs and interests more fully.

Criticism.   Few teachers can have a high degree of expertise in all subject areas, and teachers and students who do not have good rapport must remain together for an entire year.

Departmentalization.   The characteristic organizational environment in the secondary school finds teachers placed in departments based on subject matter credentials.

Teachers teach two to five courses within their credentialed area of expertise, and students move according to schedules among teachers and classrooms. Modular scheduling is an effort to provide flexibility. Begun by Lloyd J. Trump (Trump and Miller, 1968), the school day is cut into "mods" of fifteen or twenty minutes each. By combining the modular plan with computerized scheduling, it is easy to vary the length of periods and the composition of groups to provide for large groups, small groups, and independent study within the same week for any individual student.

Advocacy. Students are provided with teachers who are subject matter specialists rather than generalists; thus, the variety and depth of course offerings are increased in both required courses and electives.

Criticism. Discrete, disconnected subject areas remove subject matter from lifelike problems; subject matter is the central focus because a teacher cannot get to know hundreds of students who visit his or her classroom for a few minutes each day; both the subject matter emphasis and the lack of interpersonal contact between teacher and student contribute to the separation of education from life through a process of depersonalization.

Nongradedness. Goodlad and Anderson (1959) advocated a nongraded elementary school, and Brown (1963) promoted the nongraded high school. The essential characteristic of both is that grade-level designations should be eliminated to enable students to progress through prescribed studies at their own pace. Later, John Goodlad (1977) and others developed a form of individualized education known as IDEA (the Institute for Development of Educational Activities) that developed within a league of schools in Southern California and spread to other centers throughout the United States. An ecological perspective on curriculum improvement was used in which the local school was treated as the optimal unit of change and in which innovation required a holistic rather than piecemeal outlook. A related program was initiated by the Wisconsin Research and Development Center under the label "IGE (individually guided education) Wisconsin Design" (see Klausmeier, 1977).

Advocacy. IDEA and Wisconsin Design were consistent efforts to further the spirit of nongradedness by establishing flexible mechanisms for students to engage in advisory dialogue with teachers, to become aware of their own sense of direction, to learn individually and in groups, and to make use of a variety of personal and material resources for learning. About forty IGE (IDEA) schools were developed in the 1970s by the Board of Education of the Archdiocese of Chicago.

Criticism. Schools and the public are so thoroughly conditioned to the graded system that they are highly resistant to this change. Most schools are not willing to put forth the time, effort, and finances needed to reeducate teachers, most of whom are not prepared to implement this type of curricular environment. Popkewitz, Tabachnick, and Wehlage (1982) provide critical ethnographies of IGE schools (Wisconsin Design) and deduce that the value systems adhered to by different schools greatly constrain the ways in which students can "become conscious of the world and act in it" (Popkewitz, 1983, p. 68). Thus, the effort to tailor curriculum to individuals is sorely hampered by curriculum leaders who neglect to investigate and reflect on the ideological and ethical values that guide their work.

Open Space. During the late 1960s, American educators became intrigued with a form of education practiced in some British primary schools. During World War II, to avoid bombing raids over England, teachers were known to take their charges into nonschool settings, often in outdoor areas. There, faced with an openness of space, they were forced to invent new modes of curriculum and instruction, which they took back to the classroom when the war was over. They pushed aside desks and created enriched centers for active, social, informal learning. The Plowden Report in Britain and books by Dearden (1968), Walton (1972), Nyquist and Hawes (1972), and Silberman (1973) characterize the movement. American architects caught the winds of sentiment for this idea and sold a multitude of school systems on the idea that if they built schools that consisted of large open spaces instead of walled rooms, they could save money used to build walls and spend it on carpet, air-conditioning, and instructional materials.

Advocacy.   Just as these schools were open, architects and other advocates argued, so would be the interaction and learning among human beings who worked and studied in them. Thus, flexibility and exploration would reign supreme.

Criticism.   Neither teachers nor curriculum leaders were prepared for open-space environments. While rare cases of successful adaptation exist, the usual story was one of teachers who could not work well together, students who felt alienated and confused, and groups of students who bothered other groups. Walls were built out of book cases; expandable doors were bought, installed, closed, and seldom reopened; and traditional education was reestablished. Some new buildings were built in a podlike construction to provide more manageable and smaller open spaces, but most of these were also discontinued in the final analysis. Educators were caught up in the perpetual bandwagon of pseudosolutions when they bought open-space structures without knowing what curricular philosophy was required for them to work.

Open Education.   Implemented on a much smaller scale was the philosophy of open education, which holds that students are active, social learners who learn best when they pursue their own life problems. While this line of thought is well represented by Dearden (1968), Walton (1972), and Nyquist and Hawes (1972) as well as other collections (e.g., Rathbone, 1970; Silberman, 1973; Spodek and Walberg, 1975), its historical roots trace back to Dewey and the progressive educators who followed his philosophy of education (Schubert, 1980c). In this light, open education is a curricular ideology rather than a particular arrangement of materials, physical layout, interpersonal grouping pattern, or institutional arrangement.

Advocacy.   Open education is a psychosocial atmosphere in which teachers and students engage in dialogue in order to develop a meaningful sense of direction for their learning.

Criticism.   Teachers are not prepared to teach in this way. Moreover, a teacher cannot feasibly engage in this kind of dialogue with thirty students at once. Even if it were possible to reduce class size, the idea that students have enough background to guide their own learning is suspect.

Tutorials.   This ancient university tradition of learning through a process of one-to-one exchange is still maintained at Oxford and Cambridge and certain prep schools. The image of a teacher engaging in discussion with a student on an issue or idea, or that of the teacher offering a critique of a student's paper, can be a setting of profound learning. Recent research by Bloom (1984) and his students indicates that the tutorial may be the best setting for the achievement of mastery.

Advocacy. To provide an environment in which maximum interaction and input directly related to learner needs and interests can take place, one should establish a tutorial relationship.

Criticism. Unless funding for education does a complete reversal, we can never expect the tutorial to be a realistic proposal for any but the wealthiest schools. Even if this were to occur, students would miss valuable socialization experiences if all learning took place in one-to-one settings between a teacher and a student.

Community-Based Curricula. A large number of schools have adopted work-study programs that engage students in academic study for half a day and then schedule them to work with a business or industry for the other half. The purpose of such programs is to acquaint high school students with the world of work and at the same time ease their eventual transition into the job market. A considerably different image of community-based curricula was developed under the title "school without walls," sometimes referred to as the Parkway Plan (Bremer and Van Moschzisher, 1971). Here, the idea had nothing to do with the wall-less schools of the open-space variety; instead, Bremer and others proposed that the community itself is a better learning environment than the classrooms and school. Thus, students were involved in expeditions to all parts of the community to learn from the richness of experience it embodies.

Advocacy. Students learn best by becoming more thoroughly immersed in the community rather than from being isolated from it in schools.

Criticism. Work-study programs indoctrinate young people in certain occupations without giving them opportunity to make choices. It is a subtle means of tracking those from lower socioeconomic classes into low-level jobs and thus preventing social mobility. The school without walls could never become a widespread policy because the community would soon be overrun by students. After all, one of the economic purposes of students is their custodial function. If schools without walls, or community schools, as they are sometimes called, persist at all, it will be to accommodate only those who are difficult to manage in school environments.

Alternative Schooling. In the 1960s and 1970s, a host of alternative schools emerged to offer private alternatives to public schools. The alternatives included but went beyond those offered by religious and college preparatory private schools. Many were called free schools or freedom schools and represented the values espoused by counterculture radicals of the day (Reich, 1970). Sometimes patterned after A. S. Neill's Summerhill (1960), the ideology is represented in sources including Kohl (1968), Kozol (1967), Dennison (1969), Holt (1976), Illich (1972), and Freire (1970). Excellent overviews of alternative schools of different kinds were developed by Glatthorn (1977) and Fantini (1976). These sources reveal that, although established public and private schools looked with disdain on the counterculture movement and its schools, the idea of alternatives began to creep into the established schools as well.

By the mid-1970s many public and private school systems offered choices among a number of alternative schools, and other alternative schools emerged as a response to a variety of ideological interests. For example, in Minneapolis, parents and students could choose from among four types of schools that offered different balances of authority between teachers and students: (1) open or developmental schools strongly emphasized both teacher and student input into the curriculum, (2) traditional schools saw teachers as having strong input and students following their direction, (3) free schools had students provide input as to what they wanted to do while teachers acted as facilitators, and (4) materials-based schools placed authority in the hands of publishers rather than teachers or students. The late 1970s and early 1980s brought a strong emergence of Fundamentalist Christian schools as carefully investigated by Peshkin (1983) and other Fundamentalist schools that fostered authoritarian values and an emphasis on basics (Meyers, 1977). On the other end of the ideological continuum, this period also brought a movement to educate one's own children (Holt, 1981) and the development of alternatives to fulfill desires of diverse racial and ethnic communities.

Advocacy. John Stuart Mill (1859) argued that the only purpose for a public system of education in a free society is to offer a competitive or model alternative to the host of private alternatives that should evolve. The variety of private schools should be maintained because it serves different needs and interests.

Criticism. The public schools offer a low-quality alternative that is not a worthy standard of competition. If by the issuance of vouchers or tax credits parents were allowed to select from a range of alternatives, all sorts of charlatans and quacks would enter the advertisement campaign for schooling with the same kind of seductive appeal that they do when selling cigarettes, soap, toothpaste, used cars, and deodorants. Even if these alternative schools had high-quality programs, they would be likely to cost a great deal more than vouchers would cover. Thus, the hiatus between rich and poor classes would be accentuated.

Nonschool Education. This category is distinguished from alternative schooling by the fact that it does not act as a schooling institution. It does not teach lessons based on a formalized curriculum. I refer here to the implicit curricula and learning environments that saturate our culture through television, radio, popular music, church, scouting, movies, Little League sports, street gangs, homes, families, peer groups, jobs, and the like. Each of these is a learning environment.

Advocacy. The impact of nonschool educative organizations and relationships often goes unrealized or even unintended. More focus needs to be granted to this expanded view of curriculum (Schubert, 1982c) and to the anthropological study of curriculum advocated by David Moore (1981),who initiated a Special Interest Group on Education in Field Settings in the American Educational Research Association. A 1985 Yearbook of the National Society for the Study of Education is devoted to studies of nonschool learning (Fantini and Sinclair, 1985).

Criticism. This expansion makes the study of education and curriculum roughly equivalent to the study of human beings. This is unwieldy as a scholarly domain, to say the least. It is much better to concentrate on school learning and see if that can be improved.

INSTRUCTION

The final topic within organization is instruction. First we grapple the perennial issue of whether instruction is an art or a science; we then consider an array of models of teaching, arrangements for instruction, and types of instruction, along with statements of advocacy and criticisms about them.

Instruction as a Science

The turn of the twentieth century fired the interest of American educators with the spirit of experimentation and measurement exemplified by the psychological laboratory of Wilhelm Wundt in Germany. G. Stanley Hall of Johns Hopkins University, Charles H. Judd of the University of Chicago, Edward Titchener of Cornell, and James McKeen Cattell and Edward L. Thorndike of Columbia University represent different styles of Wundt's protégés. Thorndike claimed that if something exists, it exists in a certain amount and, therefore, can be measured. From such personages as these grew the science of instruction. Yet it awaited the late 1950s and early 1960s for instruction to become a technological outgrowth of scientific research. Beginning with the first *Handbook of Research on Teaching* (Gage, 1963), major breakthroughs were summarized and discussed in each decade that followed; see also handbooks by Travers (1973) and Wittrock (1985) and a related volume by Peterson and Walberg (1979). These renditions are primarily directed toward other scholars; however, Dunkin and Biddle (1974) developed a summarization of findings about research on teaching for practitioners. Recent years have seen a strong research emphasis on conditions that contribute to effective teaching and effective schools. Purkey and Smith (1982) provide a helpful synthesis of research on effective schools, and in an AERA Symposium in Montreal, David Berliner, Thomas Good, and Lee Shulman (Good, 1983) discussed the progress of teacher effectiveness research during the previous decade. The burgeoning research on instruction and teaching has led noted educational researchers such as Gage (1978) to claim that we now have a scientific basis for teaching.

Intent.   To develop a massive body of empirical data on instructional context and process would build a theory of instruction as called for by Bruner (1966) and Hosford (1973). Such a theory could be refined constantly and would be used to explain, predict, and control instruction and teaching. The research on teaching field is making great strides in this direction.

Criticism.   Instructional decision is situationally specific. There are few, if any, guidelines or recipes that fit the technological model that most instructional scientists envision. The effective schools' research is criticized by Ralph and Fennessey (1983) on the grounds that it actually uses scientific jargon to mask its mission to reform schooling by directing educational policy, and Cuban (1983) raises further questions about the research and issues a warning to policymakers who seek to convert findings into practice. This is merely one example of the propensity of educators to desire quick answers or recipes for complex problems. For the most part, educational problems have idiosyncratic answers. This requires an artistic mode of inquiry that continuously alters its shape to meet the ebb and flow of situations. Even setting this criticism aside, research on teaching has simplistically selected achievement as the indicator of effectiveness, but little attention is given to defining this construct. Instead, advocates naively accept achievement tests as the definition of achievement. This is not scientific efficiency or parsimony; it is muddled simple mindedness. In his forthcoming book, *The Practice of Teaching*, Philip Jackson exemplifies a view of teaching that requires continuous philosophic and practical reflection. He illustrates the need for a study of teaching that draws upon artistic, scientific, and everyday modes of inquiry.

Teaching as an Art

Some prefer to refer to *teaching* rather than instruction. *Teaching* is a more comprehensive term that relates to the artistry of everyday intuition and decision making in the educational milieu by those who have the experience to be connoisseurs of their craft (Rubin, 1984). In both his *The Art of Teaching* (1950) and *The Immortal Profession* (1976), Gilbert Highet emphasizes the artistry of teaching as built upon knowledge and love of subject, knowledge of and concern for learners, the skill of communication, the value of continuous growth and self-renewal on the part of the teacher, and the benefits of studying and emulating great teachers such as Socrates, Aristotle, Jesus, and Schweitzer, among others. Broudy and Palmer (1965) similarly suggest that great teachers are the best exemplars of teaching method. Herb Kohl (1976) wrote of teaching as a craft or kind of skilled know-how that might be acquired more through apprenticelike involvement than by following technological rules derived from scientific research.

Elliot Eisner (1979, pp. 153–155) identifies four senses in which teaching is an art: (1) it can be performed with such skill and grace that it can be regarded as aesthetic; (2) it, like performance in painting or music, involves the making of judgments based on the perception of qualities that unfold in the course of action; (3) it is best carried on without the domination of rigid prescriptions or routines because it must respond to the unpredictable; and (4) it involves the creation of ends in the process rather than prior to it through minute prespecification. In treating teaching as an art, Eisner (1982) reminds us of Herbert Read's classic argument, in *Education Through Art* (1943), that art is necessary to education, not merely a nicety that might spice up the process. The January 1983 issue of *Educational Leadership*, entitled "Teaching as Art and Craft," was guest edited by Eisner and contains a variety of visions of aesthetic teaching by Carolyn Mamchur, Thomas Barone, Madeleine Grumet, Robert Donmoyer, and Louis Rubin as well as Eisner, who said, "Teachers are more like orchestra conductors than technicians. They need rules of thumb and educational imagination, not scientific prescription" (Eisner, 1983, p. 5).

Intent.   To admit that teaching at its best is a continuously fashioned art form, as Eisner (1983) describes it:

> When one finds a school climate that makes it possible to take pride in one's craft, when one has the permission to pursue what one's educational imagination adumbrates, when one receives from students the kind of glow that says you have touched my life, satisfactions flow. . . . The aesthetic in teaching is the experience secured from being able to put your own signature on your own work—to look at it and say it was good. It comes from the contagion of excited students discovering the power of a new idea, the satisfaction of a new skill. . . . It means being swept up in the task of making something beautiful. [p. 12]

Criticism.   Artistry in teaching can't be mass produced, and we have educational needs that require mass production. The art of teaching makes good rhetoric, and those who write about it are often talented writers, but what they say needs to be verified empirically. It needs to be operationalized in order that it can be tested and implemented. Otherwise, we cannot know its utility. If we cannot predict its usefulness, we cannot defensibly advocate it as policy.

MODELS OF TEACHING

The term *models* has come to be used more loosely than when it was first introduced. Applied to teaching, it refers to a coherent method, approach, or strategy. A model should be able to be discussed in terms of assumptions, propositions, essential characteristics or attributes, supportive theory, research, and practical precedent. Over twenty years ago, Herbert Thelen set forth four models for education or teaching: (1) personal inquiry, (2) group investigation, (3) reflective action, and (4) skill development (Thelen, 1960, pp. 89–187). In 1972 and again in 1980, Bruce Joyce and Marsha Weil provided a comprehensive overview of more than twenty models of teaching that have been quite thoroughly researched and practiced. Joyce and Weil group their models into four families: (1) information processing, (2) social interaction, (3) personal, and (4) behavioral. These families "represent distinct orientations toward people and how they learn" (Joyce and Weil, 1980, p. 9). The point is not for educators to select one model or even family and use it dogmatically; rather, it is to develop a repertoire to draw upon to meet situational needs. In this way the models and their uses point to a melding of the science of instruction and art of teaching. Models are warranted by scientific inquiry and their use is artistically applied.

Information Processing Models

These models deal with "ways people handle stimuli from the environment, organize data, sense problems, generate concepts and solutions to problems, and employ verbal and nonverbal symbols" (Joyce and Weil, 1980, p. 9).

Examples.   The inductive thinking model (Taba, 1966); the inquiry training model (Suchman, 1962); the scientific inquiry model (Schwab, 1965); the concept attainment model (Bruner et al., 1967); the cognitive growth model (Piaget, 1970; Kohlberg, 1976); the advance organizer model (Ausubel, 1963); and the memory model (Lorayne and Lucas, 1974).

Intents.   The inductive and inquiry training models are designed to foster academic reasoning and theory building. The scientific inquiry model focuses on student learning of research methodology and problem-solving used in the scientific or social science disciplines. Concept attainment enables students to formulate and acquire concepts by inductively investigating examples and counterexamples. Cognitive growth models intend to move students from concrete to more abstract levels of cognitive and moral functioning. The advance organizer model seeks to increase efficiency of knowledge acquisition by providing systematic overviews of material at the onset of study. The memory model uses techniques of association to enhance recall.

Criticism.   To train cognitive functioning alone provides distorted learning and development by neglecting the social, personal, and behavioral.

Social Interaction Models

This family of models is designed to help students relate to others more effectively with the goal enabling them to function better as members of democratic society.

Such models "focus on the processes by which reality is socially negotiated" (Joyce and Weil, 1980, p. 11).

Examples.   Group investigation (Dewey, 1916; Thelen, 1960); social inquiry (Massialas and Cox, 1966); the laboratory methods of the National Training Laboratory (NTL) of Bethel, Maine (Bradford, Gibb, and Benne, 1964); the jurisprudential model (Oliver and Shaver, 1966); role playing (Shaftel and Shaftel, 1967); and social simulation (Boocock and Schild, 1968; Guetzkow et al., 1963).

Intents.   Group investigation is designed to show students that interpersonal and academic skills have a reciprocal, positive impact on each other. Social inquiry proposes to develop logical reasoning through group problem solving, while the laboratory method of NTL provides personal awareness and adaptability through interpersonal skills. The jurisprudential model seeks to develop the kind of group problem solving that one finds in the legal profession. Role playing builds social and personal insights through reflection on students' own active behavior and values, while social simulation engages students in the kind of social experience they are studying in an effort to acquire concepts and reflect on their own response to such situations.

Criticism.   Group work is a more time consuming and less efficient way to cover subject matter and reach goals. As such, it often sacrifices knowledge and allows educators to be aware only vaguely of changes in behavior that result from teaching.

Personal Models

This family focuses on affective development of the self or individual. It emphasizes the growth of persons who create meaning and personal direction through interaction with and reflection on their environments.

Examples.   Nondirective teaching (Rogers, 1971, 1983), awareness training (Perls, 1968; Schutz, 1967), synectics (Gordon, 1961), and the classroom meeting model (Glasser, 1965, 1975).

Intents.   Nondirective teaching assumes that individuals are naturally capable of self-understanding, independence, and enhancement of self-concept and builds on these tendencies. Awareness training emphasizes the capacity to experience more fully through the senses and to explore connections among body, mind, emotions, sensory, and interpersonal experience. Synectics involves students in creative growth and problem solving through the use of imaginative metaphor and analogy. The classroom meeting model engages learners in the process of taking responsibility for both themselves and their social group.

Criticism.   Preoccupation with feelings and self-development neglects acquisition of knowledge and information that is necessary to function in the world. If done with those who are immature, at any age, it could lead to deep psychological problems. Most teachers are not capable of dealing with such matters.

Behavioral Models

This family shares a basis in behavioristic theory, and the goal of implementing these models is to change or modify overt behavior. More empirical research has been generated as a basis for these models than for those of most other families. For the past twenty-five years, behavioral models have been widely used in special education.

Examples. Contingency management and self-control (Skinner, 1953); relaxation, stress reduction, and desensitization (Rimm and Masters, 1974; Wolpe, 1969); assertiveness training (Wolpe and Lazarus, 1966), and direct training (Gagné, 1962; Smith and Smith, 1966).

Intents. Contingency management seeks to teach facts, concepts, and skills based on stimulus control and reinforcement. Most of the behavioral models use variations upon these principles toward the end of self-control. Relaxation develops personal goals through reduction of stress and anxiety, and stress reduction and desensitization are processes of substituting relaxation for anxiety in social or individual situations. Direct training involves the hierarchical building of patterns of skills and behavior based on psychological and/or cybernetic principles of learning.

Criticism. Behavioristic models deal only with outward, observable behavior and pay no heed to alterations in consciousness. Proponents often claim that the methods they adhere to do not reveal insight into consciousness. Consciousness relates to inner dimensions of learning provided by personal, information processing, and social interaction models.

Using the Models

Joyce and Weil (1980) devote extensive treatment to methods for reflecting on and using the models that they so ably present. They discuss the following: (1) matching learning environments to individuals based on the work of Hunt (1970); (2) incorporating the models into approaches to mastery learning developed by Bloom and Carroll (Block, 1971); and (3) organizing instructional models to take into account conditions of learning that relate to six varieties of performance (specific responding, chaining, multiple discrimination, classifying, rule using, and problem solving) devised by Gagné (1977). Joyce and Weil (1980) also discuss the need to analyze the kind of learning each model promotes, strategies for combining models, ways to learn a repertoire of models, and the value of inventing new models. As Joyce and Weil reiterate throughout the book, those who rely on the pure form of each family or model usually operate on limited perspective. Most authors of models favor the development of cognitive, personal, social, and behavioral dimensions of learners. They add, "It is the rare educator who is not concerned with more than one aspect of the learner's development, or who does not use more than one aspect of the environment to influence the learner's development" (p. 11).

ARRANGEMENTS FOR INSTRUCTION

Arrangements for instruction are closely related to learning environments, but they are more specific with respect to the setting in which teaching occurs. Some arrangements have been practiced for a very long time; others are relatively new; examples of each are characterized briefly in the paragraphs that follow in terms of intents and shortcomings or criticisms. It is, of course, noted that in the following discussion, only the main arrangements are presented; a comprehensive treatment would probably be impossible because new forms are devised frequently in schools. Most of the latter are, however, variations on those noted here.

Large Groups

Large-group instruction is the mainstay of traditional education. Conventionally, it ranges from large lecture hall to whole class presentations, which may include speeches, recitation sessions, dramatic or inspirational presentations, demonstrations, and other types of teacher-centered performances. The *intent* is to convey or deliver efficiently a fairly large quantity of information, ideas, or affective input in a relatively short period of time. The success of large group instruction depends upon the quality of performance of the teacher and willingness to pay attention on behalf of learners. Some of the most successful forms of large-group instruction in real life are not derived from lecture hall or single-person presentations, but from films, television, concerts, plays and other staged performances, and sporting events. While the instructional character of some of these is great and of others minimal, those who instruct large groups in schools might learn from some of the techniques employed. Disadvantages or *criticisms* include lack of personalization, ineffective performances, lack of teachers who are able to interest large groups, and the unlikelihood that all learners in a large group would want or need to know the same things. Some argue that the advent of the printed page, or recently, electronic forms of communication, preempt the need for traditional, large-group lectures.

Small Groups

Small-group instruction ranges from discussion groups, seminars, and inquiry sessions to laboratory investigation and workshops. The basis for grouping learners is a perennial issue, which raises the debate between homogeneous and heterogeneous grouping. Most small groups are established on some basis of homogeneity: interest in a topic, readiness for a particular level of study, or ability to perform. Minicourses, electives, and even workshop sessions for the inservice training of teachers are examples of homogeneity on the basis of interests or perceived needs of learners. The widespread use of reading groups in the elementary school classroom bears witness to their perceived usefulness. Thus, it is the *intent* of small groups to provide for differences in need and/or interest that cannot be provided by large-group instruction.

Many grouping patterns are flexible and change frequently as new needs and interests emerge; however, when groups become rather permanently established, *criticism* espousing the need for heterogeneity surfaces quite strongly. It is argued that grouping patterns often separate students on the basis of racial, ethnic, and socioeconomic status, even if the intent was to place students of like ability or achievement together. Students grouped homogeneously do not learn from experience what it means to live in a pluralistic culture. In addition, they experience academic disadvantages from association with only those who are most like themselves. For example, those in the lower half of the highest groups may have leadership potential thwarted, and those in the lowest groups may have fewer models. Moreover, strong evidence exists for the power of self-fulfilling prophecy (Merton, 1948) or "Pygmalian effect" (Rosenthal and Jacobson, 1968) in influencing those who work with and/or are members of prelabeled groups to accept characteristics implied by the label (Shulman et al., 1982). Small groups that do change frequently are certainly not immune to allegations that they promote the self-fulfilling prophecy and carry other disadvantages of homogeneous groups. Nevertheless, advocates of large and/or heterogeneous group instruction are chided for not providing for differences in need, interest, ability, and achievement. There are logistical criticisms as well; when one teacher attempts to orchestrate learning activities for several groups simultaneously, some are necessarily neglected because it is possible to focus directly on only one group at a time.

Individualized Instruction

A number of types of instruction fall under this topic, some of which are quite different from others. To individualize generally means that the *intent* is to provide for individual differences, a sentiment that stems back through history to all who were wealthy enough to hire tutors for their children. Dewey recommended attention to individual interests and needs in most of his educational writings, and the first volume of the 1983 NSSE Yearbook is devoted to the complex relation between individual differences and the common curriculum (Fenstermacher and Goodlad, 1983). The plethora of literature on the topic that spans the distance between Dewey and the present is too great to summarize here.

Central distinctions do need to be made, however, to reveal the variety of intents that fall under the *individualization* umbrella. Advocates of independent study see students working on separate projects tailor-made to their needs and interests. This tailor-making, however, may occur at the level of publisher, or it may be done by the classroom teacher. Publishers have developed complex diagnostic devices and materials that supply ready-made prognosis for any one of several categories of diagnosis. These elaborate sets of pretests and instructional materials (with built-in options) are sometimes referred to as "skills management systems" or "instructional packages." Some of these systems or packages include textbooks, consumable materials, tests, record-keeping devices, multimedia equipment, computer software, and teacher's guides that deal with alternative uses for the materials.

Another version of individualized study is created and conducted by teachers at the school or classroom level. Teachers informally diagnose pupil needs and interests and design projects for and with students. Sometimes teachers draw up contracts for students to sign, indicating what work is to be done, when it is due, and the quality and quantity of performance expected.

Both published and teacher-made approaches to individualization may vary on a continuum that ranges from great to little teacher involvement once the students begin work on projects. Teachers may carefully monitor progress and understanding that accrues, or self-monitoring may be built into the system through programmed learning or computer-assisted instruction accompanied by answers. Some teachers individualize by means of conferences. They budget time to talk on a one-to-one basis with students about their studies. Such conversations often reveal personal dimensions of student lives that allow teachers to be in a better position to make learning meaningful. Thus, some educators, such as Margaret Carroll from Northern Illinois University, have led teachers to translate individualization into "personalization." Still others, such as Mel Hetland and Charles Elmlinger, who exerted instructional leadership in the Downers Grove, Illinois, schools for many years, interpret individualization as doing what will most benefit students. This may mean a unique combination of large-group, small-group, and independent study for each learner. A variety of interpretations of individualized instruction is illustrated by Howes (1970) and Talmage (1975).

Criticism of individualization centers on the point that it is overly ideal. An elementary teacher who is in charge of a class of 25, 30, or more cannot provide this kind of attention, and a high school teacher who sees 175 to 200 students daily for only forty-five minutes each certainly cannot individualize in the sense of creating and monitoring a program for each. The next best approach is to utilize a packaged system from a publisher or the school district that incorporates different options. This usually involves students in independent work that prevents socialization, causing them to spend most of their school day in drudgelike labor with materials, only to be rewarded upon completion with another set of materials. Teachers cannot adequately monitor such activity, and no machine can replace the empathic teacher as he or she engages with students to assess their level of understanding. Students sometimes work for days and months harboring vast misconceptions about content studied because teachers are unable to monitor their independent study.

Team Teaching

Team teaching refers to a wide variety of arrangements in which more than one teacher works with a group of students. Due to financial constraints, this tends to be a larger group of students. For example, a group of 150 may be taught by 6 teachers, the equivalent of 1 per 25 in self-contained or departmentalized environments. The *intent* is to allow teachers to capitalize on their strengths, realizing that most teachers do not do all aspects of teaching equally well. In team teaching, different teachers can specialize in large-group, small-group, or individualized learning; or teachers can specialize in subject matter areas, or styles of instruction, such as loud or quiet activities; or different learning styles; or affective, social, cognitive, and psychomotor domains.

Teams of teachers may be expanded through the use of *differentiated staffing*, which refers to the hiring of teacher aides, interns, or other adults instead of one of the teacher slots. This allows for a higher ratio of adults to students. A greater number of student teachers might also be acquired, and certain teachers could specialize in supervising them. The greater number of adults would provide for more curricular offerings. With more adults, a wide range of minicourses can be offered on different topics, and alternative instructional styles can be offered within one teaching-learning team.

If the team is inclusive enough, it can become a self-contained unit, and thereby have the advantages of both departmentalization and the self-contained classroom without the disadvantages of either, while offering all subjects and a community spirit so often absent in the large, impersonal schools of today. In this spirit of community, learning might be of a continuous progress variety envisioned by advocates of non-graded schools. Students of different age groups might be included in the same team, providing for the advantages of cross-age, multigrade, or family grouping (Ridgway and Lawton, 1969). There is a clear similarity between this image of team teaching and that of individually guided education discussed earlier under the topic of "Learning Environments."

Criticism of team teaching centers on the institution of school and its personnel. As an institution, most schools are not physically styled for team teaching; either vast remodeling needs to take place to accommodate the functioning of large teams, or new schools need to be built. Today's financial situation does not allow for either. The ideology usually found in schools would need to be revamped. Emphasis on cooperation, alternative conceptions of learning, options, and teacher creativity would all have to be supported and rewarded. The implications for team teaching would be quite alien to most schools, and the reeducation of personnel requires institutional support. Teachers who are placed in team teaching situations often lose their strengths in the larger group, and the result is a watered-down version of all involved or unceasing conflict among them.

COMMENTARIES

The guest commentators have been asked to speak on their general assessment of topics presented in this chapter. At the same time, they were invited to present additional approaches to curriculum organization that they believe should be mentioned.

Social Behaviorist

I will hurry over the first topics, all of which are important, and add a number of well-researched modes of instruction.

I have no quarrel with a separate-subjects approach to curricular scope. We need to analyze carefully the needs of society and determine which subjects are most useful, especially in projections about job market needs. The various commission reports aired in the United States in the 1982–1984 period all agree that schooling in America is in dire need of reform. The relevant point is that general agreement exists on weaknesses in subject areas: science, mathematics, English, the basics of reading and writing, basic knowledge of literature and social science, and foreign language. There are other weaknesses, of course, but these reports and the response revealed by scientific opinion polls indicate that the public agrees with the needs criterion for sequence. This gives more specific definition to scope, which should already be defined generally by prior decision on content and purpose. Sometimes broad fields approaches are useful, but project, core, and integrated responses to scope are much too vague and ill researched to rely on.

If a publisher's text or instructional package is well researched, it is probably the most reliable source of sequence. It will incorporate a format commensurate with the structure of the disciplines and learning hierarchies. Although some of my colleagues turn to Piaget for sequential guidance, I do not believe that his work readily translates as a basis for curriculum development. Those who design computer software are probably in the best position to develop sequence, because their work focuses on such detail directly.

Learning environments are being researched. I am glad to see sound empirical work done in this area by people like Moos (1979), Fraser (1981), and Walberg (1979). What must be selected is the particular environment that is demonstrated by research to fit needs revealed by the unique combination of students, teachers, backgrounds, objectives, and content or learning activities. Often, well-designed instructional materials will specify learning environments needed for implementation. Sometimes the connection is obvious; computerized instructional software requires compatible hardware, but sometimes schools buy one of these without considering its relationship to the other.

This leads directly to instruction. The behavioral models of Joyce and Weil (1980) are much better researched than the others, although several information processing models are reasonably well researched, as are a few of the social interaction models. Some of the others, however, like the so-called personal models, are the product of indefensible rhetoric, fantasy, and first-person testimonial. Arrangements for instruction all have their usefulness and must be linked with content, environment, and instruction necessitated by a given treatment prespecification or purpose.

One of the best ways of making such linkages is through ATI (aptitude treatment interaction) and TTI (trait treatment interaction) studies. Such studies enable educators to see how background characteristics of learners interact with certain prespecified treatments, and thereby allow for more exact explanation, prediction, and control. This research provides a basis for specific, rather than general, claims about probable results of certain modes of instruction. This, in turn, leads to ability to adapt instruction to specific configurations of learner characteristics (Glaser, 1977).

Considerable research is available on inquiry and games or simulations as methods of instruction (see Orlich et al., 1979). Inquiry provides structured approaches in the utilization of Socratic-style questioning, and games and simulations allow the students to be entertained while they learn. Instructional games can be patterned after entertainment games that students enjoy. One of the best examples is computer games, since increased sophistication allows computer-assisted instruction to relate to similar characteristics that young people find so intriguing in recreational computer games. The increased time on task relevant to inquiry or discovery learning provided by games, simulations, and computer-assisted instruction allows for more individualized attention by teachers.

Technology frees teachers to engage in more productive interaction with students, during which they may match teaching styles to learning styles. Research on learning styles by Dunn and Dunn (1979), Gregorec (1979), and others has produced diagnostic instruments, instructional materials, and strategies that match teaching to the styles by which students learn best. While difficult to facilitate by one teacher with thirty students, the task can be made quite feasible with the help of the computer.

Computers also utilize direct teaching as teachers should be encouraged to do. As we all know, there are times when learners need to be taught directly, for example, in some aspects of reading instruction. Here, through the work of Rosenshine and others (1978) on Follow Through, it was revealed that students learn skills and concepts when taught in a straightforward, fast-paced fashion, providing ample opportunity for student response and monitoring, cues, and positive reinforcement. This method of direct instruction is incorporated in a widely used reading package called Distar. This, then, is the essence of a mastery-learning situation; the students are, through advantages of educational research and technology, able to reach more of their potential through acquisition of more carefully prescribed material designed especially for them. This is certainly a major component of my vision of the future.

Experientialist

The computer won't save the world; people will, if it is to be saved. Any intelligent teacher tries to get students to master what they are trying to learn and does not use one method or approach exclusively. It is only common sense to look for learning styles of students, but I submit that there are many, many more styles than represented in the flaccid categories of those who make a mint from selling diagnostic instruments and instructional materials that pigeonhole students more than they liberate them. Inquiry teaching is worthwhile, but only if it is spontaneous interaction between teacher and student, as it was with Socrates and his charges. There is nothing so incongruous as a kit of prespecified questions that are billed as Socratic!

Games, too, are best if not purchased. Simply let teachers look at the games and activities their students enjoy and then encourage them to build related games for whatever teachers and students together decide is worth learning. Most of the time, however, learning is fun if it is genuinely interesting to learners. It need not be sugar-coated. It is both humorous and depressing that the ATI and TTI, so highly touted by social behaviorists, are the crux of their downfall. If these researchers would suddenly become able to explain, predict, and control, which is the goal of their efforts, they would be dealing with the level of individual situations. That is where we experientialists have always been. As a matter of fact, Snow (1976), a major researcher on ATI, concluded a review of this body of research by saying, "While some ATI findings are plausible and some are replicable, few are well-understood and none are yet applicable to instructional practice" (1976, p. 50).

There are, of course, approaches to teaching that I consider highly palatable, namely, the personal models of teaching (Joyce and Weil, 1980) and less structured interpretations of social interaction models, such as group investigation, social inquiry, role playing, and the laboratory method. Even such ostensibly behaviorist strategies as Bloom's mastery learning and his taxonomies of educational objectives can be useful conceptually. As a teacher, I keep these in the back of my mind, certainly not to use as recipes, but to use to question my own efforts. For example, I might ask myself, "Am I thinking of enough avenues to reach this student who is not grasping an idea or skill? Do my questions and assignments probe all of the taxonomical levels of thought and affect identified by Bloom (1956) and Krathwohl (1964)?"

Beyond this, I believe that there is far too much competition in school. Students are taught *about* sharing and democracy, but they experience punishment if they share work on assignments or tests, and they live under autocracy. Cooperative learning, developed by Johnson and Johnson (1976), is a move in a positive direction away from this contradictory state of affairs. Students in classrooms that apply principles of cooperation are engaged in helping and sharing; thus, they learn values more consonant with democracy.

We need, too, to turn to new dimensions of mind-body awareness as well as interpersonal awareness. That the mind can respond in powerful new ways is revealed in *Superlearning* (Ostrander et al., 1979) and in *Powers of Mind* (Smith, 1976). Gay Hendricks has led the way for teachers to understand a great many roads to awareness through widely selling books on centering and transpersonal education (Hendricks and Fadiman, 1975; Hendricks and Wills, 1976; Hendricks and Roberts, 1977). In these books, Hendricks reveals the importance of centering the mind and body and derives awareness activities for teaching through fantasy, meditation, intuition, relaxation, communication, and parapsychology. Regarding the latter, noted psychologist H. J. Eysenck recently reviewed ESP research and concluded that it rests on solid evidence carefully substantiated (Eysenck and Sargent, 1982). Hendricks and Roberts (1977) provide lengthy bibliographies for further reading. Those who want further legitimization for these areas of human functioning should consult such noted scholars as Sigmund Freud, Carl Jung, and Arthur Koestler (1972), and Robert Ornstein (1976), who developed numerous implications of splitbrain research from insights of the Eastern mystic, Idries Shah.

The fact that Shah and others of Eastern orientation find insight for education through stories reminds me of a quite different, but useful, suggestion that young children learn best through stories, and therefore, we should build curriculum around the story form (Egan, 1983, 1979). Others rightly suggest that the most worthwhile story to study is that of one's own life, one's growing autobiography. (See Hopkins, 1954, 1983; Grumet, 1980; Pinar and Grumet, 1976; Pinar, 1980; van Manen, 1979.) The ability to look deeply into one's own being, to assess, reconceptualize, and reconstruct the story therein does not come automatically. Years of being educationally oppressed by teaching that autocratically demands and controls us are difficult to discard. When this is compounded with similar, but more overt, domination by political and economic power, it becomes even more embedded in our beings. Thus, as Paulo Freire (1970) writes, we must move from a banking mode of teaching to a problem-posing mode in which teachers and learners are both willing to grow through dialogue that breaks down the ideological walls between them and emancipates both to experience higher levels of consciousness.

I could go back through the chapter and note why I believe that scope should be handled by integration, why sequence by genuine student interest is developmentally appropriate, and why the psychosocial atmosphere of learning environments is the most important dimension. I could recount my allegiance to progressive or open education, community-based learning, nonschool learning environments, personal models of teaching, and the ideal individualization of instruction within an arrangement of a democratic learning community. But the reasons seem too obvious in view of what I have said already.

Intellectual Traditionalist

For once I can be very brief. This long chapter and the lengthy comments of the first two speakers are rather tedious to me. If we know the content that we want to teach, and if we have a great teacher—which is the only kind worth having—then the content will be conveyed. We don't need scores of labels for different learning environments, sequences, instructional strategies, and scopes. An excellent teacher who knows the subject will inspire others to learn it, too. He or she will keep in mind that lecture, recitation, discussion, and tutorial methods exist and will use them according to needs that he or she perceives. Usually, the subject matter itself directs the choice of method.

The problem is that most teachers don't know their subjects. If this is the case, it is impossible for them to do what Adler (1982) productively labels as a teaching method, namely, *coach* the students to an understanding of a skill, concept, or basic idea within a discipline of knowledge. I must say that I find it amusing that so-called scientific research praises itself for discovering such things as direct teaching, the inquiry method, mastery, individualization, and even behaviorism. Excellent, even good, teachers have known about all of these for thousands of years. I cringe when I think of the money spent to reveal that wondrous insight that we are more likely to learn something if we are exposed to it—time on task. I surmise that this is why we call the work *re*search! This labeling of genus, species, and minute variety of teaching method is pseudoscience. I am more than ready to move on to another topic.

SUGGESTED READING

This chapter is replete with parenthetical notes on the topics discussed. Therefore, my suggestions are very brief.

For discussions of scope, one might consult Smith, Stanley, and Shores (1957, pp. 229–421) and Taba (1962, pp. 290–309), and for sequence see Smith, Stanley, and Shores (1957, pp. 169–195).

Learning environments are discussed in light of curriculum evaluation by Fraser (1981), and Dale (1972) presents considerations to address when building a learning environment.

A plethora of sources exist on teaching and instruction. Those interested in further pursuits in this area should become acquainted with Joyce and Weil (1980), Orlich et al. (1979), Thelen (1960), Highet (1950), the January 1983 issue of *Educational Leadership*, Broudy and Palmer (1965), Gage (1963), Travers (1973), Wittrock (1985), and any issues in the new journal, *Phenomenology and Pedagogy*. For the newer literature on effective instruction and effective schools, I recommend Levin and Long (1981) and the October 1984 issue of *Phi Delta Kappan*. The related topic of teaching and learning styles is treated well in a full issue of *Theory into Practice* edited by Henson (1984).

For more elaborate treatments of many organizational patterns, including instructional strategies, see Rubin's two-volume *Curriculum Handbook* (1977a,b). The classic presentation of the organization dimension of the perennial paradigm is, of course, found in Tyler's *Basic Principles of Curriculum and Instruction* (1949). Beyond this, those interested in more elaborate theory, research, reports of practice, and critical assessment of any features of organization should conduct a computer search of the literature.

RECOMMENDATIONS FOR REFLECTION

1. Reflect again on the conception of curriculum that you have been building in Chapters Eight and Nine. You will recall that you derived a response to purposes and content that related to a characteristic that you believe worthwhile to develop in others. Now, you are asked to refine this idea further by considering how it could be organized relative to the following: (a) scope, (b) sequence, (c) learning environments, (d) models of teaching, and (e) arrangements for and types of instruction.

2. Reflect on your own situation as a professional educator. Which organizational patterns do you use most frequently for (a) scope, (b) sequence, (c) learning environments, (d) models of teaching, and (e) arrangements for instruction?

3. Does your practice agree most with the orientation of a social behaviorist, experientialist, or intellectual traditionalist?

4. Does your theory, or ideal position, seem most similar to that of a social behaviorist, experientialist, or intellectual traditionalist?

5. Does your practice match your ideal when you compare your responses 1 with 2 and also 3 and 4 above? If there is inconsistency, can you think of impediments and constraints that prevent you from realizing your organizational ideals? Discuss these inhibitors with other educators (e.g., classmates). Can you determine strategies for altering the situation so that you can actualize your ideals more fully? Or do reasons exist that make you have second thoughts about your ideals? Are there any features inherent in the very idea of schooling that contradict your ideals? If so, what are the implications of these factors?

6. Reflect on the organizational categories that are necessary for curriculum developers to consider as presented in this chapter: (a) scope, (b) sequence, (c) learning environments, (d) models of teaching, and (e) instructional arrangements. Which options presented for each do you accept? Why? Which do you reject? Why?

7. Weigh the advocacy statements or intents and criticisms presented for the options in each category of organization. Which is most compelling for each: the statement of intent or the criticism?

8. Select statements of criticism for each category and (a) rate each as likely to be offered by a social behaviorist, intellectual traditionalist, or experientialist and (b) continue the argument by imagining how the author of the intent statement might deal with the criticisms set forth.

9. Which options presented on each of the categories of organization would you like to learn more about? Why? How and where can you find out about them?

10. Identify five of the most important things that you have learned in your life. Describe the conditions, learning environment, mode of instruction, and other organizational factors that contributed to these learnings. Did they occur in or out of school? How do these factors compare with those that characterize the organization of your professional situation? Your ideal for curriculum organization? What implications might be derived from your own valuable learning experiences that could be applied to your work as a professional educator?

11. Do you consider teaching primarily an art or a science? Instruction? Defend your view with literature and experience.

11

◆ Paradigm of Perennial Analytic Categories: Evaluation ◆

He that judges without informing himself to the utmost that he is capable cannot acquit himself of judging amiss.
> JOHN LOCKE *An Essay Concerning Human Understanding* (1690)

We are mistaken in believing the mind and the judgment two separate things; judgment is only the extent of the mind's illumination.
> FRANCOIS DE LA ROCHEFOUCAULD *Maxims* (1665)

SETTING THE STAGE

If one category of the perennial curriculum paradigm has emerged into a field of its own in the twentieth century, it is evaluation. In fact the evolution of public policy analysis as an interdisciplinary area of inquiry has contributed to an emphasis on evaluation in such disciplines as sociology, political science, and economics, and professional areas such as business, industry, medicine, law and criminal justice, health and physical education, as well as education. Much of the history of evaluation, however, can be located in education and, particularly, the curriculum field. This chapter, therefore, begins by tracing the history of curriculum evaluation. Contemporary orientations to evaluation are presented and are followed with a discussion of issues and controversies that pervade evaluation literature today.

THE EMERGENCE OF CURRICULUM EVALUATION

The theory and practice of curriculum evaluation has moved through several stages in this century. It began with an emphasis on grading, marking, and judging and proceeded to develop a specialized connection with systematic measurement. The

Eight Year Study (1933–1941) greatly expanded the notion of evaluation beyond that of mere measurement. As a result, evaluation began to focus on the improvement of programs rather than the assessment of students alone. More recently, a number of evaluators have sought to discover large-scale perspectives and trends, while a good deal of evaluation at the level of local schools and government agencies has been spurred along by accountability pressures. There is also an emphasis on evaluation that guides specific decision and action, as well as varieties of qualitative evaluation that paint curriculum within a complex context.

Each of these is characterized more fully in the paragraphs that follow, along with statements of advocacy and criticisms for each.

Grading, Marking, and Judging

Anyone who has taught in schools, or even anyone who has attended them, learned that a prime symbol of student progress is the grade or mark. Examinations, class participation, daily assignments, special projects, and papers are appraised by the teacher, who rates them according to a hierarchy of grades. Grades might be based on norms, criteria established in advance, or impressionistic judgment. The latter is usually a major factor in any formula for grading, even though it is less often acknowledged. When criteria are established, for example, or when test items are chosen, we should not forget that a good deal of judgment went into the equation. This is the approach to evaluation that guided educators throughout history, and it is still widespread today despite the emergence of many alternative conceptions that now exist.

Advocacy.   Teachers, with their broader range of knowledge and experience, have the right and responsibility to judge students and mark them accordingly. The purpose of judgment as a basis for grading and marking students implies a faith in wisdom that comes with experience. Teachers who experience student life in classrooms provide the best kind of grade when they give an overall impression. Grades and marks may be given to different aspects of classroom performance and then averaged according to weightings attributed to these aspects, but these are only part of the teacher's composite picture of students. The final grade symbolizes the teacher's best estimate of student work.

Criticism.   To rely so heavily on judgment is to overemphasize the subjective. Both research and experience reveal that it is human nature to let nonessential factors intervene. Personal prejudice plays too large a role in grading. We know that different teachers judge the same student's performance quite differently. The process needs to be conducted more systematically and measured relative to established criteria or norms.

The Measurement Movement

Early in the twentieth century, many educators became interested in measurement of student performance, being influenced by Wilhelm Wundt in Germany, by French psychologists Alfred Binet and Theodore Simon, and by Frances Galton in England. Wundt established the first experimental psychological laboratory at Leipzig in 1879. Galton experimented with intelligence tests in the 1870s, and Binet and

Simon developed an intelligence scale in 1905 that consisted of a series of questions of graded difficulty that corresponded to norms (see Cremin, 1961, pp. 185–192). From the United States, G. Stanley Hall, Charles H. Judd, and J. McKeen Cattell visited Europe and Britain to study with the giants of scientific experimentation and measurement during the late nineteenth and early twentieth centuries. They brought back scientific methods and a steadfast hope that a science of education could be created. When Hall's student H. H. Goddard translated Binet's work, intelligence tests were available in the United States, and achievement tests soon followed. Foremost among the advocates of measurement was E. L. Thorndike, student of Cattell. His early research began to build a critique of the taken-for-granted benefits of subjects in the classical curriculum as the builders of mental discipline. Because of Thorndike's work, there was evidence to support a reduction in classical subjects such as Latin and Greek in the curriculum.

From the 1920s through the 1940s, faith in measurement grew steadily, and its techniques were applied to many other areas of education. During the post-*Sputnik* curriculum reform movement and the Great Society programs that followed it, behavioral scientists designed research to evaluate the level of project success for accountability purposes. This brought a great deal of technical sophistication into evaluation during the 1960s and 1970s.

Advocacy.   Measurement is a means to overcome the subjectivity of fallible human judgment. To have uniform standards and systematic procedures, to be objective, and to produce valid, reliable, and replicable results were valued as superior to the usual subjective assessment of student work that accompanies grading. These values predominate among evaluators today.

Criticism.   Many aspects of learning cannot be measured, but they can be realized by the insightful, experienced intuition and perception of teachers. The measurement movement overdid the classification of students into groups, and some of its proponents were heatedly criticized for practicing a pseudoscience of deterministic assignment of students of certain racial, ethnic, or socioeconomic groups to educational classifications that prejudged their potential as low. Even the majority who did not engage in such practices were guilty of overemphasizing those aspects of education that could be measured and thereby drawing attention away from the intangibles that could be artistically and intuitively apprehended, but not scientifically measured.

The Eight Year Study

The Eight Year Study is often regarded as the most important educational research project in the first half of the twentieth century. Despite its infrequent mention today, it is surely the most extensive curriculum research project that occurred between 1900 and 1950.

As we learned in Chapter Three, the study revealed that on a range of outcome measures students who attended progressive, experimental secondary schools were superior or equal to those who attended traditional schools (Aikin, 1942). Superiority was determined on the basis of how a student from one of the experimental schools compared in college with a comparable student from a traditional high school. Students from experimental and traditional schools were placed in 1475 matched pairs. The matching was done by placing students of similar background and other salient characteristics together. Comparisons were not only made in academic areas, but relative to honors, intellectual curiosity, systematic thinking, drive, formulation of ideas, resourcefulness in meeting new situations, planning of time, adjustment, aesthetic experiences, participation in religious and service activities, attitude or judgment about schooling, vocational decision making, and interest in world affairs. The performance of the two groups of students in college is detailed in Volume IV of the five-volume set (Chamberlin et al., 1942).

Never before had the effects of curriculum on a large group of students been studied so thoroughly and systematically over a number of years. Not only were long-term effects studied, longitudinal studies being rare in education, but a great range of different dimensions of the student was investigated for the first time. This was in large part due to the efforts of Ralph W. Tyler, research director of evaluation staff. Brought in as a young researcher in his early thirties who had done notable work on achievement testing, Tyler and his staff developed an array of new kinds of evaluation instruments. Instruments were developed and used to evaluate aspects of thinking, social sensitivity, appreciation, interests, personal and social adjustment, as well as standard areas of achievement (Smith and Tyler, 1942). Students were evaluated on these and other aspects of growth throughout the study, not just after they went to college. Students who did not attend college were studied for success in occupations as well (Tyler, 1980a).

A less formal but equally important contribution of the Eight Year Study was the continuous effort of the evaluation staff to help teachers. They visited the thirty school systems involved in the experimental group, entered into dialogue with personnel, and designed workshops in which they could reflect and prepare curricula for their students. This, too, was a breakthrough because it led to continuous curriculum renewal.

Thus, the Eight Year Study was a seedbed of curricular evaluation: (1) it exemplified a longitudinal, experimental study; (2) it showed that progressive or experientialist education could be formally evaluated; (3) it developed a host of evaluation instruments and procedures that would set a much broader tone for the conceptualization of evaluation in decades ahead; and (4) it recognized the informal, reflective dialogue between practicing educators and scholars (and often students) as a meaningful form of evaluation. The Eight Year Study made one further massive contribution through the people who helped develop and implement the study. In addition to Tyler were Oscar Buros (who was later responsible for the Mental Measurements Yearbooks), Louis Raths (who later founded the idea of values clarification), Bruno Bettelheim (whose work in psychoanalysis, child development, and fairy tales is well known), Hilda Taba (who went on to become a notable in the curriculum area), Harold Alberty (who did much pioneering work on the core curriculum in the high school), Lee J. Cronbach (who became one of the most highly regarded researchers in measurement and evaluation), and Robert Havighurst (one of the foremost educational sociologists). These and many more noted scholars and excellent practitioners of education were associated with the study; even James Michener was involved in the Eight Year Study before he became a renowned novelist.

Advocacy. The ultimate goal of the Eight Year Study evaluation was to develop and implement a plan of investigation to determine the effectiveness of the thirty schools that engaged in curricular experimentation and self-determination. "Evaluation was conceived as an integral part of the educational process" (Smith and Tyler, 1942, p. 29). Thus, evaluation was conducted to indicate points for overall improvement, not merely final judgments. It was designed to validate hypotheses on which the schools operated, to provide information for student guidance, to provide a sense of security for those involved in the schools (students, staff, and parents), and to provide a defensible basis for public relations (Smith and Tyler, 1942, pp. 7–11). Implicit in the evaluation exemplified by the Eight Year Study is the need for evaluators to know thoroughly the situation evaluated by becoming professionally involved in it.

Criticism. Historically, the study was a milestone in its day, but several of its design features would not hold up against today's more rigorous standards. Matched pairs is not as effective as random assignment because one can never match students on all nonexperimental characteristics. This leads to the question of what the experimental characteristics were; no operational definition of the specified treatment exists that fits all of the schools involved. Thus, it is impossible to know which characteristics contributed to student and curricular success. The Hawthorne effect must have been operating (i.e., they performed more enthusiastically and with greater interest because they were in an experiment). Besides, the schools applied to be experimental; thus, their accomplishment could not be generalized to other schools that might not choose the treatment. The dialogue among teachers and evaluators could not be considered evaluation because it was mere informal interaction. In addition, it often led to changes that altered the prespecified intent.

Curriculum and Program Improvement

Building upon the tenor of work in the Eight Year Study, Lee J. Cronbach (1963) called for course improvement as the most important outcome of evaluation. Evaluation, to Cronbach, was designed not merely to judge outcomes of what students learned, but it was to serve as a basis for assessing the entire process. That this broadened emphasis was influential among school people as well as researchers and theorists is supported by the 1967 Yearbook of ASCD entitled *Evaluation as Feedback and Guide* (Wilhelms, 1967). Meanwhile, many evaluators sought course improvement by adhering to a rigid, behavioristic treatment-specification model that tied evaluation directly to precisely stated goals, often behavioral objectives.

Three major articles appeared in the later 1960s that increased the purview of evaluators who sought course improvement: Scriven (1967), Stake (1967), and Stufflebeam (1969). Scriven (1967) introduced the terms *formative* and *summative* evaluation, which became major guideposts in the language of evaluation (see Bloom et al., 1971). *Summative evaluation* refers to a final appraisal of a program; *formative evaluation* provides information to guide the program while it is still progressing.

Stake (1967) augmented the complex countenance of evaluation and its context. He suggested that it "consists of *antecedents* (e.g., goals, materials, student aptitudes), *transactions* (e.g., classroom processes, interactions between student and teacher), and *outcomes* experienced by students or other program participants" (Fraser and Houghton, 1982, p. 140). These three features should be examined relative to four tasks that evaluators should be aware of and distinguish among; these are *intents* of the program; *observations*, which often include unintended effects; *standards* that might be considered valuable by different reference groups; and *judgments* about the worth of different standards. Stake admonished evaluators to distinguish between judgmental and empirical or descriptive acts of evaluation. Further, he suggested that evaluation findings can be handled in two major ways: (1) by focusing on empirical congruences between intents of a program and what is actually observed and (2) by identifying *logical contingencies* that characterize the ways in which antecedents, transactions, and outcomes relate to each other.

Stufflebeam's (1969, 1971) contribution is often referred to as the CIPP model, emphasizing the need for attention to context, input, process, and product. The first three of these terms help to characterize formative evaluation, while product refers to summative evaluation. All four elements of the CIPP model are necessary background for "the process of delineating, obtaining, and providing useful information for judging decision alternatives" (Stufflebeam, 1971, p. 19). "The four basic questions answered by the CIPP model involve what objectives should be accomplished, what procedures should be followed, whether procedures are working properly, and whether objectives are being achieved" (Fraser and Houghton, 1982, p. 151).

Advocacy.   Evaluators must move beyond mere focus on student outcomes and evaluate the whole curriculum or program under investigation, rather than laying ineffectiveness at the doorstep of students. Students may not be acquiring curricular objectives, because the program itself is ineffective. To evaluate for course, curriculum, and program improvement is a complicated job, but to do less is to comprehend inadequately the educative process.

Criticism.   To focus on the whole process is too time consuming and too costly. It may even be a ruse conjured up by evaluators to see that they are hired for a longer period of time and paid more; it also opens the door for complex jargon and educational double-talk instead of straight answers to well-stipulated questions. Moreover, if we really want to portray the full complexity of situations, we would need an impossible amount of data and interpretation. Think of the novel *Finnegan's Wake* by James Joyce (1939). It is a long book indeed and deals with the images of only one character during a summer Saturday night's sleep. Now that is complexity. Consequently, if we want to give complexity its due when we evaluate the interaction of curriculum with the lives of teachers and students, we need something comparable to a *Finnegan's Wake* for every day and night that the curriculum is experienced and continues to have an effect for each person. This is, of course, impossible; besides, it would be impractical if it could be produced. We would soon be overrun with books. This is why we should adhere to behavioral evaluations that get to the point directly.

Large-Scale Perspectives and Trends

Just as the longitudinal nature of the Eight Year Study was noted as a laudable attribute that contributed to the study's renown, other large-scale studies have been conducted during the second half of this century. One of the most extensive studies, still in progress, is known as the IEA Study.

Funded by the Ford Foundation and the United States Office of Education, the

International Association for the Evaluation of Educational Achievement (International Association, 1976, nine volumes) is a cross-cultural, comparative assessment of achievement in science, mathematics, reading comprehension, foreign languages, literature, and civic education. It involves some 250,000 students and 50,000 teachers in twenty-two nations. Started in 1959, data thus far accumulated reveal, among other things, that home background is a good predictor of achievement; achievement in reading is central to achievement in other subjects; many school variables associated with instruction do not correlate highly with achievement; low-level cognitive processes (e.g., remembering information) dominate requirements in school practice; achievement is associated with amount of exposure or time on task, especially in science, which is more school dependent than other subjects; and the top 5 percent of students in all nations studied achieve on an essentially equal basis despite differences in the remainder.

Several studies of national significance have been conducted in the United States in recent years. Perhaps the most overarching is the National Assessment of Educational Progress (NAEP), which began in 1969 with federal funding from the United States Office of Education and private funding from the Carnegie and Ford foundations. It was originally governed by the Education Commission of the States. Through this study census-type data are available from large samples of four age groups: 9, 13, 17, and young adults (26–35). Data are gathered in five-year cycles in relation to ten academic areas: reading, writing, social studies, citizenship, science, mathematics, art, music, literature, and occupational development. The tests are criterion referenced rather than norm referenced, and findings are reported by geographic area, type of community, parental education, age, sex, and racial and ethnic group. By repeating the tests in cycles, comparisons can be made at the four age intervals. Many curriculum developers and other educational policymakers use results of NAEP studies to reveal strengths and deficiencies as a basis for curriculum revision. Up-to-date assessment results can be received by writing: National Assessment of Educational Progress, Educational Testing Service, Princeton, New Jersey 08541. A number of scholars have obtained tapes of the NAEP data to use in conducting secondary analyses (i.e., reanalyses of the data in differing configurations).

Just as Conant's (1959) *American High School Today* called for a revision of schooling in response to the post-*Sputnik* perception of economic and political crisis, the economic ills of the 1980s were met with a host of reports that are evaluations of educational practice in the broad sense. The Carnegie Foundation for the Advancement of Teaching, under the leadership of Ernest Boyer and Paul L. Houte, prepared a report on the status of secondary education in America published under the title *High School* (Boyer, 1983), and perhaps the most widely publicized report was that of the National Commission on Excellence in Education funded by the United States Department of Education and chaired by David Gardner, entitled *A Nation at Risk* (1983). Both reports decry the deplorable state of schooling and call for a core curriculum of traditional subjects with heavier doses of science, mathematics, language, and technological literacy, coupled with more rigorous requirements that prepare students to score higher on tests and perform more productively in college, personal and social life, and in occupations. Similar pronouncements were made by the National Science Board (1983), the policy-setting arm of the National Science Foundation Commission on Pre-college Education in Mathematics, Science, and

Technology; the study of high schools by the National Association of Secondary School Principals and the National Association of Independent Schools under the leadership of Theodore Sizer (1984a); the Twentieth Century Fund's Task Force on Federal Elementary and Secondary Education Policy; the Education Commission of the States' Task Force on Education for Economic Growth, which prepared a report entitled *Action for Excellence* under the leadership of Governor James G. Hunt; the Educational Equality Project of the College Board, which concluded a ten-year study called *Academic Preparation for College* under the leadership of Adrianne Bailey; and John I. Goodlad's "Study of Schooling" published under the title, *A Place Called School* (Goodlad, 1984). (These reports and others are summarized in Chapter Six, Figure 6-1.)

In the study of schooling, Goodlad and his associates base interpretations on detailed observations of 129 elementary, 362 junior high, and 525 senior high classrooms in an effort to understand more fully what these three levels of schooling do and how they connect with each other. In addition to observations, the evaluation methods Goodlad used include interviews, questionnaires, and collections of documents. Praising Goodlad's use of a multidisciplinary advisory committee to deliberate about its design and to help interpret the data, Ralph Tyler (1983, p. 34) called the study, "a more comprehensive basis for understanding United States schools than any previously published." Goodlad sees the study as a basis for improvement of schools, which he describes as fraught with discrepancies, observing that "The gap between the rhetoric of individual flexibility, originality, and creativity in our statements of goals and the cultivation of these in our schools reveals a monstrous hypocrisy" (Goodlad, 1983, p. 17). He concludes that the dire state of schooling need not be the norm and admonishes educators to realize that "the time has come for us to look more carefully into what we have wrought and the alternative we might seriously endeavor to create," but he warns that "either we must come to terms with unrealistic expectations and settle for schools just a little better than what we now have or put our money where our mouths are. So far we have designed and supported schools capable of doing only the simplest parts of the whole" (Goodlad, 1983, p. 19).

Advocacy.   Large-scale studies provide generalized data that inform educators and the public about the overall picture of schooling and the educative process. They are offered as a basis for both understanding and policy decision.

Criticism.   Large-scale studies reveal such broad generalizations that they neglect emphasis on specific situations. For example, the results of the Coleman Report (Coleman et al., 1966) suggest that greater expenditures on school programs do not make a difference in measures of schooling outcomes associated with a given socio-economic group. However, Good, Biddle, and Brophy (1975) point out that when one looks more closely at situations, it can be concluded that teachers do make important differences. The problems that large-scale studies inform are drawn not from the world of educative practice, but from the highly generalized conceptualizations of evaluation researchers. By remaining detached onlookers, evaluators who guide large-scale studies do not derive the insight that accrues to an insider who interacts with situations on a daily basis. (Recall the discussion of Schwab's critique of *theoretic* research in Chapter Seven.) Large-scale studies usually seek laws that explain and predict educational phenomena, although they rarely reach the level of being able to do this. Thus, their findings often wind up in the archives of educational research literature and only benefit researchers whose promotions depend on publications. They seldom inform practice.

Some argue, too, that we must watch carefully the sources of funding and consider the hidden agendas of funding agencies. While one might expect federal and state funding sources to support their own political and economic interests, Berman (1983) argues that it is often overlooked that such ostensibly altruistic foundations such as Ford, Carnegie, and Rockefeller perpetuate American corporate and political interests in Third World nations. Similarly, Fruchter (1983, p. 17) argues that the numerous commission reports falsely assume that economic productivity is "dependent on the quality of educated labor produced by our schools" and that "investment in education is . . . beneficial for everyone, rich and poor, majority and minority." He continues by observing that the reports suffer from a reversal of causality; the economy influences schooling far more than schooling influences the economy. To assume that the answer lies in strict standards and longer hours smacks of "traditional bootstrap solutions that treat a diverse student body, segmented by race, class, and gender, as a unified elite sector" (Fruchter, 1983, p. 17) that knows about bootstraps, how to pull them, and what strings pull them.

Evaluation for Accountability

The pressures for schools to become more accountable emerged during the widespread public critiques of most established institutions in the late 1960s and early 1970s. Schools, once held in high public esteem, experienced a great loss of public confidence over the past two decades. They were called upon to prove their worth, usually by using quantifiable data. Schools in Florida responded by establishing the Florida Educational Accountability Act of 1976 to provide systematic basic skills tests in grades 3, 5, 8 and a minimum competency test for high school graduation. Many states and local districts developed plans that often required careful prespecification of behavioral objectives and verification of their acquisition as criteria of productivity. Others relied heavily on improved performance on standardized achievement tests as indicators of success. Those who could afford it brought in professional evaluators to tailor-make evaluations to their particular needs and goals.

Advocacy. Despite the system selected, accountability is "reporting the congruence between agreed-upon goals and their realization" (DeNovellis and Lewis, 1974, p. x). According to Shepherd and Ragan (1982, p. 475), strategies geared to provide accountability include systems management programs, behavioral objectives, and performance-based contracting. Schools must demonstrate to their publics that they are performing well, and these are the kind of indicators the public demands and values.

Criticism. Who is accountable? Who is responsible for good schooling? How can it be recognized if it exists? Can legislative edicts really do the job of providing accountability? Moffett (1971) suggests that teachers, as lowest members of the schooling hierarchy, have the bulk of accountability pressure pushed along to them. As the least powerful decision makers in most school systems, teachers are also in the poorest position to initiate change. Thus, the usual buck-passing down the hierarchy puts teachers in the ironic position of being responsible without power to make changes. Recent criticism and plans for securing competency pushes the blame to the one level weaker than teachers—students; thus, the victim is blamed once again. Such a state of affairs leads Saylor, Alexander, and Lewis (1981) to ask: "Are we moving to the time when students, schools, teachers, homes, and communities will share in accountability?" (p. 363).

The accountability movement is also criticized for its behavioristic methodology. Arthur Combs (1972) chides behavioristic solutions as simplistic and unresponsive to the complexity of human education. He asserts that most individuals are capable of being responsible for themselves. When systems of control are imposed upon them, they lose this essential human characteristic through loss of morale. Goodlad (1978) suggests an ecological model of accountability that engages the many who contribute to curriculum together in mutual responsibility rather than in a process of stealthily checking up on one another. He adds that those who issue atomized, behavioral objectives as a basis for accountability have no epistemological or logical ground to stand on. Such objectives are vagaries cloaked in exactness that allow administrators to appear to justify any course of action that seems expedient.

Evaluation for Decision and Action

The work of Schwab (1970, 1971, 1973) on practical inquiry provides a basis for giving attention to local-level problems and needs. To focus on decision and action by school administrators, curriculum decision makers, and teachers is another form of evaluative research. Practical studies by Leithwood (1982) and Reid and Walker (1975) analyze decision making and innovation at the local level, thus providing examples of how evaluation might provide precedent for practitioner decision through carefully developed case studies.

Advocacy. Evaluators who zero in on the complexities of local curriculum decision making provide a basis for understanding situational problems. Such evaluation can be used as feedback to decision makers, including teachers, who can revise their situation. Those who work in situations can become collaborators in the process and, thus, play a meaningful role in evaluating their own situation. This idea has its roots in the action research movement spurred by Corey (1953) in the late 1950s and early 1960s and is recently developed by collaborative research efforts of Donmoyer (1983), Lieberman (1983), Griffin and Barnes (1984), Jacullo-Noto (1985) and others.

Criticism. To focus on the local level is to be preoccupied with the idiosyncratic. If many researchers were content to deal with particular circumstances, we would soon be overrun with data that have little or no generalizability. Moreover, those at the local level are neither technically advanced nor politically independent enough to conduct their own evaluations. The field is sophisticated, and objective specialists are needed to do the job.

CONTEMPORARY ORIENTATIONS TO EVALUATION

Some of the examples in the previous section are quite contemporary, and are thus related to this section as well. This especially applies to aspects of evaluation for course improvement, large-scale studies, and decision and action. I encourage you to notice roots of contemporary approaches in developments that occurred as the field of curriculum evaluation emerged. In this section, we highlight the following approaches to curriculum evaluation: goal-based, goal-free, naturalistic, criticism, teacher-as-researcher, theorizing, and responsive evaluation, as well as evaluation models drawn from other professions. Each is briefly characterized, noting advocacy and criticisms.

Goal-Based Evaluation

Evaluation today remains dominated by a goal-oriented model. Purposes are identified and clearly stated; they serve as criteria for evaluation. Tyler (1949, pp. 195–196) defines evaluation thusly:

> *The process of evaluation is essentially the process of determining to what extent the educational objectives are actually being realized by the program of curriculum and instruction. However, since educational objectives are actually changes in human beings, that is, the objectives aimed at are to produce certain desirable changes in the behavior patterns of the student, then evaluation is the process for determining the degree to which these changes in behavior are actually taking place.*

When Tyler uses the term *behavior* we should recall that he means thinking, feeling, and acting (1980b). Regardless of the kind of goal, behavioral or global, the interest is in discovering the extent to which its implementation realized it.

Most goal-based evaluators prefer to be brought into a curriculum project at the onset because then they can help to specify and clarify goals. During implementation, they can use formative evaluation procedures to discover the extent to which practice adheres to plans. Thus, goals are used as criteria to evaluate process and to make readjustments if practice is not in line with purposes. If investigation of practice does not verify that goals are implemented, then one can hardly conclude that implementation will bring goal realization as a product. Attention to the process-product relationship is, thus, linked to goal-based evaluation. Process-product studies are seen as refinements on the goal-based model because they verify the extent to which the prespecified treatment or goal is implemented.

Advocacy. Goal-based evaluation overcomes the frequent tendency to evaluate without regard to purpose. Many schools, for example, write curricular purposes and essentially forget about them when they purchase tests and other evaluation devices. Thus, their evaluation does not fit their purposes and does not reveal whether purposes are achieved or not. Evaluation that is goal based connects evaluation to the goals. Similarly, selection of content and decisions about organizational patterns are processes that must be consistent with purposes and evaluation. Evaluators should see themselves as consultants who help schools to maintain consistency among purposes, processes of delivery, and product delivered.

Criticism. If goals are the evolving outcomes of experience, as Dewey and other experientialists assert, then evaluation cannot rely on predetermined goals. If goals are designed to provide a learning environment or atmosphere conducive to expressiveness, as Eisner (1985) advocates, then a goods and services delivery system is an inadequate image of curriculum. This delivery system conception of curriculum does not fit the spontaneous and creative style by which learning takes place. Instead, it seeks to control human beings by fitting them to a mold. Evaluation should move beyond the mold; that is, if evaluators find that implementation takes on new purpose, they should reconstruct their purposes. The new purposes may be a result of greater insight, through involvement, than was available when prespecifications were made. Evaluators should not adhere too closely to rigidly prespecified goals.

Goal-Free Evaluation

Scriven (1973 and 1977) coined the term *goal-free evaluation* that set goal-based evaluators on their ears. Whereas goal-based evaluators desire to know the purposes of a curriculum so they can develop evaluation instruments that relate to those purposes, goal-free evaluators do not want to know the purposes prior to their site visits to conduct evaluations. Goal-free evaluators look carefully, gather a wide array of information, and prepare an interpretation and assessment of what they find.

Advocacy. Goal-free evaluation seeks actual effects, unencumbered by knowledge of goal statements. It assumes that intended effects should be fully evident and that goals are able to be inferred from them. The goal-free evaluator is more likely than the goal-based evaluator to discover unintended effects because he or she is unprejudiced by knowledge of goals. Being less prejudiced implies greater objectivity on the part of the goal-free evaluator, a point met with rage by goal-based evaluators, who pride themselves in being objective.

Criticism. In theory the position may sound reasonable, but it is impractical. It takes a great deal of time to get to know a situation to be evaluated, even when one is informed about it directly. Without advance knowledge of purposes, goal-free evaluators either flounder in ignorance or they resort to their own notions of what is worthwhile to teach and learn. In either case, they are farther from the mark than if they based their inquiry on goals. Both ignorance and personal preferences are usually more subjective than the goals of the institution to be evaluated.

Evaluation Models from Other Professional Areas

Evaluators have used different disciplines and professional areas as analogues from which to fashion new styles of evaluation. The evaluator might act as an investigative reporter (Guba, 1979) or skilled, sensitive interviewer, as Studs Terkel does in his insightful character protrayals (e.g., *Working*, 1975). Robert Wolf (1979, 1975) uses a mode of evaluation patterned after the judicial process, complete with investigative teams, case analysts, case presenters, forum moderator, clarification panel, and panel facilitator. Malcolm Provus (1971) draws upon management theory and provides an evaluation that serves as a continuous inquiry into discrepancies at program design, installation, and product stages; cost-benefit analyses of the entire program are developed by discrepancy evaluators. Art and literary criticism (Eisner, 1985; Willis, 1978; Mann, 1968–69) are also used as metaphors for educational or curriculum criticism; this is discussed as a separate topic.

Advocacy. Each of these evaluation modes is modeled after a creditable type of investigation used successfully in another field and can be used to illuminate and clarify educational practice. The specific intent of each differs, of course, with the form of investigation employed as a metaphor.

Criticism. In addition to being highly time consuming and costly, these forms of evaluation deprive education and curriculum from becoming viable areas of study in their own right. When researchers rely on methods from other disciplines or professional areas, they remain in adolescence, unable to reach maturity. What is needed, instead, is the development of forms of inquiry that respond to the unique needs of educational phenomena (Reid, 1978).

Naturalistic Evaluation

By drawing its methodologies from anthropology, ethology, and ethnography, naturalistic research is patterned after the likes of Jane Goodall's treatises on apes and the writings of Margaret Mead and Ruth Benedict on different cultures. Utilizing careful observation and description, the approach is exemplified in education by Smith and Keith (1971), Smith and Geoffrey (1968), Wolcott (1973), and many others. Essentially, naturalistic evaluation is a generic category with numerous subvarieties. Sometimes referred to as qualitative research, it may involve numeric representation as well. Common to most of the varieties is an attempt to characterize situations or phenomena as thoroughly as possible. This provides a rendition of what occurred that might not be available to those who focus only on that which can be quantified.

According to Guba and Lincoln (1981, pp. 56–63), naturalistic assumptions hold that reality is multiple, divergent, and interrelated, as opposed to the singular, convergent, and fragmentable characteristics focused on in traditional evaluation. While the researcher and subject are kept separate in the traditional scientific mode, they are interrelated in the naturalistic. Traditional evaluation holds that truth is found in generalizations or nomothetic statements that focus on similarities among situations, whereas naturalistic evaluation sees working hypotheses as truth statements that focus on the idiographic or situationally specific knowledge that reveals differences among situations (Allport, 1951; Getzels and Guba, 1957). By looking at the subtle uniqueness and complex context of school situations it is possible to come to different conclusions about the quality of educational practice than is revealed in broad surveys of practice based on achievement test scores and other discrete indicators of school effectiveness. In vivid portrayals, for instance, Lightfoot (1983) points to the existence of excellent schools, in *The Good High School*, thus, providing a refreshing alternative to the spate of negative assessments of high schools in the early 1980s.

Advocacy. To portray the reality of situations and to reveal their merit and worth by using the human being as the primary instrument of evaluation, naturalistic methodology includes detailed observation, record keeping, and interviews.

Evaluators might act as participants, fellow teachers, or administrators and conduct their research at the same time. Different standards of rigor are applied to naturalistic approaches; in other words, the traditional canons of science (validity, reliability, and objectivity) are replaced by new criteria. Instead of internal validity as an indicator of truth, one asks if the evaluation has credibility; instead of external validity or generalizability as an indicator of applicability, one seeks fittingness; instead of reliability as a measure of consistency, one seeks an audit by a qualified judge; and instead of objectivity as an indicator of unbiasedness, one seeks confirmability (Guba and Lincoln, 1981, pp. 103–127).

Criticism. Despite the alternative tests of rigor just noted, naturalistic research indefensibly lets go of the canons of science. Parsimony or economical treatment of subject matter is certainly not provided by the lengthy protocols or portrayals. Another researcher cannot replicate the findings because the evaluator is the instrument of inquiry; thus, every evaluation of the same phenomenon is different. Since no precise procedures exist to determine credibility, fittingness, and auditability, they must be discarded as less adequate avenues to truth than validity, reliability, and objectivity. While some traditional scientists regard naturalistic research as adequate for hypothesis generation or as a means for filling in the gaps between generalizable data, they clearly relegate it to a subsidiary role.

Educational Criticism and Connoisseurship

A form of evaluation developed by Elliot Eisner, educational criticism and connoisseurship, draws its image from the arts (Eisner, 1977). To be an illuminating critic of painting, opera, theater, film, wine, and the like, one must first be a connoisseur. That is, one must have a great deal of knowledge and experience with the type of phenomenon one criticizes if the criticism is to be warranted. A good critic has an awareness and appreciation of subtle qualities and through writing about them can help others to become more aware. The critic uses language to provide a "vivid rendering" (Eisner, 1977, p. 352) that enables those who lack experience or perception to see more fully.

While educational connoisseurship is "the art of appreciating the educationally significant," criticism makes it public through description, interpretation, and assessment (Eisner, 1985). Instead of scientific validity, Eisner uses *referential adequacy* and *structural corroboration* (Eisner, 1985, pp. 241–245). Referential adequacy involves checking to see if critical observations and interpretations are empirically grounded, allowing readers to experience the evaluated phenomenon in a new and better way. Structural corroboration refers to a continuous inquiry about whether the various parts of the criticism fit together as a consistent whole. Just as one might understand more of the significance of lives of poor Londoners from reading a Dickens novel than reading a statistical encyclopedic account of the same time period, educators who read educational criticism will be moved to different insights than will those who read scientific educational research papers. The following excerpt of criticism written by Thomas Barone (1979, pp. 240–245) makes it obvious that many insights could not be provided through quantitative data alone.

"Of Scott and Lisa and Other Friends," by Thomas Barone

Setting: *a classroom, 43 first and second graders, two teachers, two aides, in an apparently affluent part of California.*

Critic's Intent: *the disclosure of life in the classroom.*

The splendid houses perched majestically upon the hills peek out from between the lush growth of trees and well-tended foliage that dress them. Many seem to snicker at the laws of gravity as they balance themselves so casually upon the slanted land. They stare straight ahead, haughtily ignoring the bright green carpet at their feet. The houses maintain a distance from each other; they wrap their fences around their land as if to insist that it is theirs alone.

As I drive past, I wonder about the people in these lavish houses with their redwood paneling and their thoroughbred stallions in the adjacent fields. What are they like? How do they live? Do they balance their lives as effortlessly as they have balanced their houses on these hills? Do they ever stroll through their woods and sniff the honey-colored air and listen to the California mist as it steals softly over the hills? Or do they gaze straight ahead, like their houses? . . . And most of all, because I am a teacher, I wonder what kinds of lives they desire for their children.

(In the classroom.) The room invites me in. It is a large, extended room drawn together at the waist: It was once two single rooms that have come together to talk. Surely, I could spend a whole childhood here. A wealth of learning materials engulfs me, each piece beckoning me to pick it up.

Soon I am not alone. The other children are pouring through the door, infusing the room with life, brimming with energy, hankering for release. . . . Each seems to be drawn to his own corner of the room, his energy pulling him toward a special task. One moves to the bookshelf and snatches up a book. Several take themselves to the math table. Three crawl in the Honeycomb. One tickles the dinosaur with a paint brush. Others string pull-tabs or watch a film.

Several are my special friends. We had become friends on my previous visits to the school. One day I decided that I would become one of them. So I shrank a little in my mind and revisited a world I had left so long ago.

We help each other a lot; the teachers like us to. They don't teach us to compete; so we don't put our arms about our work and guard it with ourselves. . . . The air is perfumed with collaboration. You see no petty bickering.

But now I guess it's time to tell you of a sheet of paper that each of us keeps faithfully by his side as we move about the day. It's called a contract, and it is implanted in our lives by the teachers when the day is still an infant. It's our constant companion to the very end. This is how it works: When finished with an activity, we give the contract to a teacher or an aide, who scratches her initials onto the paper. We have to finish six "core" activities that Mrs. Abramson once called "obligatory," and some other things that don't seem to be as important. "Fun things," Mrs. Abramson has called them. Sometimes we can swap three or four of the "fun" activities for a certain "core" activity.

What do we do all day? Well, lots of things, but mainly reading and math. They're very important, sitting at the tip-tip of our contracts. Why else would the smiles of our teachers become so broad when we have finished them?

We read every day from programmed texts that a Mr. Sullivan named after himself. We read a line and guess the answer. Then we check to see what (not whether the) answer's right. I think that knowing that we got it right is supposed to replace Mrs. Abramson's friendly pat on top of your head. My friends and I agree that Mr. Sullivan does not deserve a pat on top his head. He doesn't have the answers that he thinks he has. And yet we faithfully read his books.

Scott asked me to listen to him read. As we sank into the wordy sofa, I noticed that he had already begun. He was skimming across the surface of each word, licking the sentences but not tasting. Soon he had strip-mined the paragraphs of their superficial meaning so rapidly that I wondered how much he really understood. I asked a question about the content of the story, and his answer was so pointed that it struck me. He had devoured half a book (even if it was a very short one with lots of pictures) and digested it with amazing speed and never once paused to savor it.

(Even though, Scott's contract gets signed.)

Already he had darted to the teacher's side to announce his victory, "Miss Rogers, I've done fourteen things today."

"You did, Scott. Well, that's really great!"

Now I think it is truly great that Scott has learned to read and write (and maybe charm his older friends with one disarming smile). But at least one of those fourteen things wasn't great, as I'm sure you will agree. Thirteen would have been greater. Even one thing—don't you think?—if it really sparkles, can be greater than fourteen that have no luster.

As I whiz on my way (back home, passing by splendid houses), I notice that many of the apricot blossoms have fallen now, lying shriveled on the road. Just before they are pressed beneath the insistent wheels of my automobile machine, in a flash I wonder if my good pals Scott and (other students in the class) will forever gaze past them—straight ahead. Or will they learn to see their colors?

That would be really great.

Advocacy.   Criticism renders to educators a different and insightful perspective on educational situations. It refers directly to their own situations and enables teachers to see their classroom in a new light. Hamilton et al. (1977) refer to this as an illumination function of evaluation, and Willis (1978) provides further conceptualization of the idea of criticism as well as numerous cases that demonstrate how qualitative renditions portray insights that traditional behavioristic evaluation is unable to provide.

Criticism.   Education is a social science area of inquiry, not an art. Therefore, criticism and connoisseurship should conform to the canons of science or leave the area. A critic of film, novels, or symphonies provides an opinion in the final analysis, and critics often disagree on matters of taste. But educational evaluation should be more defensible than merely deferring to taste. Educational policies and decisions should be based on empirically verifiable knowledge. Even if we believe that the idea is useful, we haven't enough Shakespeares, Dantes, Tolstoys, and Twains to go around, or the time and money to pay them. What we would have at best is shoddy stories about practice that do little, if any, good.

Teacher-as-Researcher

Lawrence Stenhouse (1975) called for teachers to be the primary researchers in educational situations. He argued that teachers might begin in collaborative dialogue with educational researchers who spend time in and devote reflection to the teachers' situations. This reflection, dialogue, and any serious form that it might take is deemed worthy of the label *research*. In this sense, careful reflection on one's situation that reconstructs meaning and direction in the course of action is also worthy to be called evaluation. Stenhouse conducted numerous curriculum research projects in

England and developed case studies that record his unique synthesis of action research and the education of teachers (see May, 1982; Skilbeck, 1983).

Advocacy.   Stenhouse held that research is "systematic, self critical inquiry made public" (May, 1982, p. 24). This is a process of evaluation whereby teachers and other educators are able continuously to renew their perspectives and practices. Without collaborative dialogue and research by scholars and practitioners, the efforts of both are weakened greatly.

Criticism.   While the foregoing may be useful for the inservice education of teachers, it is not professional or scholarly research and evaluation. It is subjective, not objective, and is merely what good teachers have done throughout history.

Theorizing

Theorizing as treated by reconceptualist curricularists can be conceived as a form of evaluation. Personal theorizing, with its emphasis on autobiographical analysis, is a continuous evaluation of the interconnections between one's past and one's anticipation of the future as they converge to create the present (see Pinar and Grumet, 1976; Pinar, 1980). Ideological theorizing focuses inquiry on the socioeconomic conditions of labor, social class, domination, and control that one bears and bestows (e.g., Freire, 1970; Apple, 1979; Apple and Weis, 1983; Giroux, 1983).

Advocacy.   Theorizing enables the theorizer (educator or student) to see through new lenses, to question taken-for-granted forces in his or her life, and to reconceptualize his or her own outlook on and interaction with the world. The purpose is to enhance personal and social growth through emancipatory pedagogy. This often involves the study of existentialism, radical psychoanalysis, phenomenology, and neo-Marxist criticism as a means to broaden one's perspective in an effort to evaluate one's life and situation.

Criticism.   Theorizing is a highly personal and subjective form of evaluation and should not fall under the label of *evaluation* at all because of its lack of scientific rigor. It is an extension of the radical leftist thought of the 1960s, and its emancipation, as Tanner and Tanner (1979) assert, is not so much from the bonds of ideology and oppression as from difficult and rigorous tasks of research. Thus, theorizing is seen by some as a twisting of reality and a selective use of sources not only to counter the dominant ideology and its epistemology but to dangerously promote another.

Responsive Evaluation

Robert Stake, author of the countenance model of evaluation (1967), which did much to raise the image of complexity associated with curriculum evaluation, gradually developed an orientation that tailors evaluation to the concerns of those whom the evaluation will affect. This does not mean that it should relate to only those who pay for the evaluation, but to all "stakeholding audiences." Described by Stake in a book that portrays responsive evaluation applied to arts education, "It is an approach that trades off some measurement precision in order to increase the usefulness of the findings to persons in and around the program. . . . An educational evaluation is responsive evaluation if it orients more to program activities than to program intents, responds to audience requirements for information, and if the different value perspectives present are referred to in reporting the success and failure of the program" (Stake, 1975, p. 14). This requires extensive observations, conversations, and interactions with relevant audiences in and around the situation to be evaluated. According to Guba and Lincoln (1981), responsive evaluation is a further refinement of naturalistic evaluation. Methods of the latter are used to come to a better understanding of what the human instruments should do, how to gather data, and how findings and interpretations should be reported to relevant audiences. Reports may resemble traditional written evaluations, or they may include "discussion sessions, round table discussions, newspaper articles, films, exhibits, or whatever may be deemed appropriate" (Guba and Lincoln, 1981, p. 16).

Advocacy.   Responsive evaluation is designed directly to fit issues and concerns of its specific audiences or stakeholders. Contrasted to traditional *preordinate evaluation*, which is formal, assumes the values of traditional science and uses program intents, goals, and hypotheses that are preordained by program developers, responsive evaluation is informal, accepts a pluralistic value perspective, and uses audience concerns, problems, and issues as bases for a continually evolving design. Responsive evaluation is designed to help those who are evaluated provide better curricular experiences for students in contrast to preordinate evaluation that primarily benefits only those who direct the evaluation.

Criticism.   Like other ideal modes, responsive evaluation is fine for schools that have unlimited time and finances. But there are none of these. Even if there were some, the process requires the idealized version of a Solomon, Socrates, Abraham Lincoln, or other infallible judge to represent fairly all parties who might be affected. Clearly, there are not enough such figures to go around. As long as we are functioning in the realm of the ideal, why not just posit that every human being should be a responsive evaluator? Alas, then we would have no need for the job of outside evaluator. Evaluation would overcome the need for itself.

CONTEMPORARY ISSUES AND STANDOFFS

Numerous issues face evaluators today and are subject of much debate: (1) the relative value of quantitative and qualitative methods and the possibility of integrating the two; (2) the worth of theoretic and practical epistemologies, which invokes the issue of outside expertise versus locally developed evaluation; (3) the relative value of different disciplinary metaphors that should undergird evaluation, which principally refers to scientific technology or artistic criticism but may pertain to legal, journalistic, anthropological, and literary images of evaluation; and (4) conflicts over personal and political aspects of evaluation and the kinds of critical discourse that can help to unravel them.

COMMENTARIES

Each of the guest commentators is invited to respond to the issues and standoffs noted in the preceding discussion. They are each also asked to comment on the historical and contemporary conceptions of evaluation that they deem worthwhile and/or worth criticizing.

Intellectual Traditionalist

Let me begin by noting points of agreement and disagreement with orientations advanced during the short history of evaluation. Perhaps that in itself is a formidable problem; evaluation does not seem to have much of a history. Many evaluators have the pseudoscientific outlook that knowledge is somehow cumulative, and the best insights remain while the less useful ones are weeded out. There is, for example, a massive unstudied legacy of grading, marking, and especially judging, that traces back to antiquity. How, for example, did Socrates, Jesus, Buddha, Quintillian, Abelard, Pestalozzi, Froebel, and other great teachers judge their pupils' progress? How did they communicate progress to their students and relevant others? To develop a history of this kind of educational evaluation would indeed be a most beneficial intellectual task. But, alas, most educational researchers of today are too enamored with science to think such a history of thought in prescientific times would be useful. This is evidenced by the fact that all such contributions are lumped together and looked upon as "those silly times prior to serious thinking about evaluation." I submit that there was probably more serious thought on the topic before the beginning of this century than after. Great literature is saturated with insightful commentary and portrayal about how humans judge their fellow beings.

Beside this rich and virtually untapped history, the academic literature of evaluation pales. The so-called measurement movement is mostly mismeasurement, as revealed by Gould (1981), who was rather ironically given an award for his book by the AERA (many members of which adhere to measurement principles that Gould criticizes). It takes a massive reverence for *techne* and an equally great lack of *aréte* to put as much faith in measurement as many educational researchers exhibit. The tendency to parrot physical science research methodology was anticipated by Dewey (1929b, p. 26), who said:

> *Educational science cannot be constructed simply by borrowing the techniques of experiment and measurement found in physical sciences. This could happen only if some way had been found by which mental or psychological phenomena are capable of statement in terms of units of space, time, motion, and mass. It is unnecessary to state that this condition has not been fulfilled.*

Fortunately, a number of evaluators have heeded Dewey's warning and have moved in directions that develop the capacity of human judgment. This spirit of inquiry can be seen, for example, in the Eight Year Study, but it must be remembered that traditional education in the 1930s was at least as abysmal as it is today. It was not difficult to compete with it. Today, the move to demonstrate the complexity of evaluation is a step in the right direction, but a very small step, because so much of it is merely adding more boxes and arrows to silly systems charts. This is such a minuscule move compared with the complexity of judgment and value found in great literature.

One must not forget, as have most evaluators preoccupied with techniques and recipes, that *value* is embedded in the term *evaluation*. It is, therefore, a disgusting joke that they want to make their work value free, as if anything could be value free! Data on both large-scale trends and data used to prove one's accountability are both so superficial that I wonder how so many people are duped into believing in their importance. Finally, the recent emphasis on evaluation for decision and action seems promising, but it is curiously devoid of historical and literary perspective. Without such ballast to prevent floating with the winds of expedience, evaluators will surely sink into a sea of trial and error.

As for the contemporary orientations I find that goal-based evaluation fits the critique I have already offered. Goal free is mildly interesting because it is imaginative and must rely on a wise person. This is the case with teacher-as-researcher, the naturalistic observer, and the responsive evaluator. All these will bring excellent results only if the evaluator is well educated, imaginative, and highly perceptive, and that is exactly what is needed. Models from other disciplines have potential if they stick to the disciplines. Law is questionable, while journalism and business are clearly suspect. Anthropology is more of a discipline; although it has been around rather briefly, I find its use in ethnographic and naturalistic evaluation of interest.

Most intriguing is the arts metaphor of Eisner. We need a broad artistic and literary perspective in order to evaluate well. Evaluation is aesthetic because of the interdependence between the aesthetic and the ethical. We need the most subtle of imaginative perceptions to detect the ethical implications of what we decide as we develop curriculum. Curriculum decision making is clearly an ethical act because it deals with what ought to be done. The Willis (1978) collection demonstrates this value, especially in a 1968–69 article by John S. Mann, who relates curriculum evaluation to literary criticism. That "theorizers" move in this direction, too, is demonstrated by their examples of criticism, also in the Willis book.

I would, however, be a bit happier if the image were one of artist and not critic. Critics are usually plodding cynics by comparison to artists. This clearly puts me on the side of evaluation as an art rather than a science, unless, of course, we invoke the best scientists. At that point we have a similarity between poet and scientist as aptly demonstrated by Jacob Bronowski (1956) in his play, "The Abacus and the Rose," and captured by Northrop Frye (1981) in his phrase, "Where metaphors and equations meet." This puts me on the qualitative side, but my interest in the power of mathematics as one of the humanities persists, causing me to argue that mathematics reveals qualities as well as quantities. In short, we need both, but we do not need all the ardent followers of formulas who make statistics, not problems, the end of their inquiry (as is implied by Pagano and Dolan, 1980).

As for the other three issues, I think that we need both theoretic and practical knowledge, but the theoretic should not come from puerile results of studies but from intuitive insight into life's great mysteries and events. Second, we need to draw upon the disciplines to find metaphors that guide curriculum evaluation. Metaphor is the highest level of intellectual thought as far as I am concerned. Third, evaluation is both personal and political. Sadly, evaluators who take pride in their work are often rubber-stamping agents for school boards, government agencies, and administrators. This is why I prefer to trust the judgment of good teachers rather than rely on self-credentialed experts called professional evaluators. In the final analysis, one must judge oneself educationally, relative to the standards of the disciplines.

Experientialist

Let me begin with the four issues posed at the end of the chapter and then move to the history and orientations.

We have far too great an emphasis on quantitative research today. The following of statistical formulas and the adherence to the Campbell and Stanley (1966) bible of research design is a substitute for thinking. We need more emphasis on problems; procedures should assist the study of problems, not guide their formulation. In short, we must move to discover that which illuminates educative situations by going "beyond the numbers game," as Hamilton et al. (1977) put it. This leads almost automatically to practical research that must begin with a search for goodness, or "the human quest," as Thelen (1960) puts it. This is a journey that must be taken by everyone; thus, it is more situationally specific than the school district, building, or even classroom levels. It must be pursued by each person as he or she engages in self-evaluation, decides the quality and kind of life worth leading, and considers the consequences of such living. Broad insights about human nature may come from such inquiry, and they may seem theoretic, but they act to emancipate rather than control. Conclusions that humans need to guide their own destiny, for example, are much different from attempts to specify invariant cause-effect relations or a discrete number of factors that predict human behavior and can be used to control it.

As each person grows in the capacity to lead a life of meaning and worth, he or she can become enriched with metaphors from many areas of study: the arts, sciences, professions, and many nondisciplinary aspects of ordinary life experience. The latter is probably most important, for we learn by making analogies between past and present experience, by making connections between old and new aspects of what Herbart called our "apperceptive mass." It is we, not some outside experts, who are the real evaluators of our lives. As creators of knowledge we must free ourselves from the hold of controlling epistemologies and ideologies. This necessitates political action. It also calls for *interaction* with others in the creative spirit of democracy (Hopkins, 1941), which is political activity, but of a quite different kind from that which frees one from overt control. It is the Deweyan ideal of conjoint living that builds ideas through democratic community. Thus, we need both political action that frees us from imposition, and we need to join our experiences with those of others in order to grow educationally. Both are evaluative experiences that pertain to life, not a formalized and brittle evaluation that is tacked on to life. This kind of political activity continuously reconstructs a personal outlook; thus, evaluation in the course of human experience (the only kind that is worthwhile) is a synthesis of the personal and political.

Let us now reflect on the history of evaluation and orientations to its study in light of the foregoing tenets of my philosophy. Grading and marking students relegates them to the status of products on the assembly line and has no place in education. (See Kirschenbaum et al., 1971; Simon and Bellanca, 1976). Judgment, at the other extreme, is one of the most important traits that we can cultivate; it is the essence of evaluation. It is the very trait that too many measurement advocates seek to overcome in the interest of objectivity.

The Eight Year Study was a great advancement over the measurement ethos that surrounded it, not so much because of its design, but due to the role that reflection and judgment played in it. The most important outcome of the Eight Year Study was not its design or even that it revealed the prowess of progressive schools; rather, it was in its example as an evaluation performed by all involved, especially teachers and students who learned that an education is the continuous evaluation of one's life, the acquisition of new sources of meaning, and the shaping of a sense of direction. There is no human endeavor more complex than this process; thus, the evaluative models that evolved later were scarcely more than footnotes on the Eight Year Study.

Evaluation for accountability, large-scale studies of trends, and goal-based evaluation are massive steps backward; they are a return to the measurement era and a search for theoretic generalizations that only benefit researchers who want longer lists of publications. The practical emphasis by Schwab and others (Reid, 1978) on decision and action reminds me of discourse that took place during the Eight Year Study, although the connection is seldom mentioned. How quickly we lose sight of our past. Nevertheless, we need their reminders of what we should have learned from Dewey.

Goal-free evaluation is partially a tongue-in-cheek way of pointing to the pseudo-science of goal-based evaluation, but it still sees the client as guided by outside expertise. I applaud the pluralism of models based on other disciplines, including the naturalistic, which draws the researcher's embeddedness in situations from anthropology, and connoisseurship and criticism, which build upon the arts. The only problem that I see in these approaches is an imbalance between outside expertise and client, in which the former is giver of insight and the latter is receiver. The purpose of criticism, as elaborated in various sources by Lawrence Stenhouse, Gail McCutcheon, Elizabeth Vallance, George Willis, Thomas Barone, Robert Donmoyer, Robert Bullough and others, moves in the direction of more teacher involvement in criticism. The involvement of all who have a relationship with a curricular situation in the evaluative process is recognized by proponents of teacher-as-researcher, theorizing, and responsive evaluation. This kind of critical democratic orientation accepts all participants as having valuable insight and knowledge at their disposal (see Willis, 1981; Kemmis, 1982; Hamilton, 1982).

Social Behaviorist

I am certain that I can be more parsimonious than the previous commentators. Let me respond to the four issues first.

1. Quantitative research is much more rigorously developed than qualitative; quantitative research techniques fit the needs of evaluation. Evaluation must be cost-effective, precise, and able to provide concrete evidence; it must be valid, reliable, replicable, and objective. Quantitative evaluation provides all, while qualitative methods succeed in meeting none of these standards. By being creative, however, qualitative types can sometimes help to generate hypotheses that can be systematically explored by quantitative methods.

2. Both qualitative and practical orientations suffer from being, ironically, highly impractical. They both take immense amounts of time, provide reports that are too voluminous to read, and are usually vague and imprecise. Libraries would overflow with these reports if practical researchers achieved the dominance they seek. What is more, no one would read them because they are situationally specific (i.e., nongeneralizable). What we need is to maintain theoretic and quantitative evaluation research. Large-scale studies of trends, sound measurement, and goal-based evaluations contribute best to decision and action, and they satisfy the reasonable request for accountability. Those who need accountability studies (school boards, government officials, and school administrators) are busy people. They don't want to be engaged in months of discussion, getting-to-know-you activities, and incomprehensibly complex reports. Of course, evaluation is complex; the world is complex. Thus, the purpose of evaluation is to simplify without making simplistic, to point out the issues, generate data, explain results, and make policy recommendations. You can't do this with theorizing, goal-free, jurisprudential, journalistic, naturalistic, artistic, teacher-as-researcher, and responsive forms of evaluation. When you call in experts, you don't want them to ask you to do the evaluation. Similarly, students want and need grades and marking systems; they don't want you to ask them what they deserve.

3. The third issue is easy given what I have already said. The discipline on which to base evaluation is, purely and simply, science.

4. The fourth issue is almost a nonissue. The personal and political have no place in evaluation. Science is objective and value free, not a purveyor of ideology or personal sentiment and prejudice. Granted, evaluators have to deal with political and personal problems in their work, but this is not part of the evaluation or its design.

In the past thirty years, evaluation has come into its own as a discipline. It is precisely because of the characteristics I have enumerated that it has reached this level, and this is the orientation that should be maintained and refined. I venture to add that evaluation has now become the central category in curriculum inquiry and development. Any act of curriculum development should begin with evaluation in diagnosis or needs assessment, continue with formative evaluation during implementation to keep personnel on the track of prespecified treatment, and conclude with summative evaluation tied to the goals and standards laid down at the outset of planning.

SUGGESTED READING

The most comprehensive overview of the curriculum evaluation literature is an annotated bibliography prepared by Fraser and Houghton (1982). It provides amazingly accurate and balanced summaries of main points covered in nearly all the major books and articles up to 1982. An international perspective, something that we have too little of, is provided on curriculum evaluation in a UNESCO publication edited by Arieh Lewy (1977).

Two topics only hinted at in this chapter, but which have important relationships to curriculum evaluation, are (1) measurement and its applications to teaching at the classroom level and (2) the whole arena of psychological testing. Gronlund (1985) and Hopkins and Antes (1978) provide the former with sizable treatment of the topic of testing. For a more research-oriented treatment of testing and measurement, see Cronbach (1970) and Thorndike and Hagen (1977). More recent editions of each of these texts may be available upon publication of this book. Anyone considering the purchase of a test should consult reviews provided in the latest editions of Buros's *Mental Measurements Yearbooks*. See Tyler and Wolf (1974) for a discussion of issues in testing.

Those interested in the Eight Year Study should read Aikin (1942). Subsequent volumes, also published by Harper and Brothers in 1942, elaborate on curriculum, evaluation, and success in college and offer stories of each school involved. The third volume, Smith, Tyler, et al. (1942), focuses most directly on evaluation in the Eight Year Study.

Since many important statements on evaluation appear as articles rather than book-length treatments, I suggest the following anthologies of evaluation literature: Taylor and Cowley (1972), Weiss (1972), Worthen and Sanders (1973), and Payne (1974).

Classifications of evaluation models differ with author, but a survey of extant schemes can be helpful. Popham (1975) provides an overview with a distinct goal-based flavor, while House (1978, 1980) presents models that focus on assumptions and validity. Stufflebeam and Webster (1980) offer an analysis of evaluation studies based on political questions and values.

The most comprehensive explication of naturalistic and responsive evaluation is provided by Guba and Lincoln (1981), while a more traditionally scientific orientation to qualitative evaluation is detailed by Patton (1980). Good and Brophy (1973) provide an early example of how naturalistic researchers might observe life in classrooms. The traditional, systematic, goal-based program evaluation is specified by Rossi, Freeman, and Wright (1979).

Theorizing as evaluation is represented in the reconceptualist articles in the evaluation section of Giroux, Penna, and Pinar (1981) and is exemplified as autobiographical study in Pinar and Grumet (1976), Pinar (1980), and Grumet (1980). Ideological critiques of school practice may be found in an edited volume by Apple and Weiss (1983).

Origins of evaluation that draw from artistic modes are collected in a reader by Hamilton et al. (1977). Eisner's book entitled *The Educational Imagination* (1985) is his most comprehensive statement on connoisseurship and criticism (Chapters 10 through 13). Eisner (1981) argues for realization of the differences between artistic and scientific forms of qualitative evaluation. Willis (1978) provides a set of articles that blend theorizing and artistic criticism as a basis for evaluation. He provides an insightfully argued introduction that develops the need for this type of evaluation and elaborates on it with concepts and case studies by a variety of authors. As this book goes to press, I have learned that Elliot Eisner and Thomas Barone are preparing a book on criticism and connoisseurship.

The teacher-as-researcher position, explicated by Stenhouse (1975) and May (1982), reveals salient features of the history of the cooperative inquiry into curriculum by teachers and university researchers spearheaded by Stenhouse in Britain.

I suggest that readers look at evaluation sections of synoptic curriculum texts and collections of articles, for example, Doll (1982), Pratt (1980), Saylor, Alexander, and Lewis (1981), Oliva (1982), Zais (1976), McNeil (1982), Tanner and Tanner (1980), Gress and Purpel (1978), Bellack and Kliebard (1977), and Orlosky and Smith (1978). These treatments might be compared with that of Tyler (1949).

In the final analysis, evaluation is an axiological problem, not merely a technical one; therefore, the student of evaluation should be a student of values. In this regard, Philip L. Smith's book, *The Problem of Values in Educational Thought* (1982), illustrates the kind of thinking that curriculum evaluators should be prepared to do.

RECOMMENDATIONS FOR REFLECTION

1. Despite the turn taken by evaluation literature at midcentury in the direction of curriculum and program evaluation, student evaluation is of considerable importance and takes place in some form daily in schools. Discuss the relationship between program and student evaluation. Do some of the same issues apply to student evaluation as this chapter depicts for curriculum evaluation? Draw from your experience in evaluating students as a teacher and respond to the following questions: Is student evaluation more complex than it is usually billed to be? Should student evaluation be used as a basis for classroom improvement? To what extent can averages of class performance be used as a guide for decision making about individuals? To what extent should outside expertise be called upon for student evaluation (e.g., teacher-made versus published tests)? How much of the evaluation that guides your grading is goal based, statistical, and formal? How much is informal, interactive, and responsive? How much of your daily interaction with students is guided by formal, systematic evaluation? How much is a function of informal, personal theorizing?

2. Based on your responses to the questions in activity 1, an analysis of your own evaluation beliefs as a teacher, are there analogies that you can offer to the conduct of curriculum evaluation on a larger scale?

3. Reflect again on the ideal characteristics for which you have developed responses to purposes, learning experiences, and organization for the reflection sections concluding Chapters Eight, Nine, and Ten. How would you evaluate the curriculum sketched by your responses?

4. Carefully review your responses to items at the conclusions of Chapters Eight through Ten that led to activity 3. Is anything missing that should be considered if a whole picture of curriculum is to be presented? Are the aspects that relate to purposes, learning experiences, organization, and evaluation consistent with one another?

5. If you were going to design an Eight Year Study today, what would it be like?

6. Focus on the criticism at the end of each topic within the section of this chapter that deals with the emergence of curriculum evaluation. To what extent do you agree with the criticism? Imaginatively project a response that an advocate of the position criticized might provide.

7. Provide the kind of imaginative projection requested in activity 6 for criticism of each of the contemporary orientations to curriculum evaluation.

8. Which of the conceptions of curriculum evaluation seem most beneficial to you, ideally? Is it realistic to assume that they would be used? Why or why not? Do you think it is possible to overcome inhibitors to their use? How?

9. Have you ever been involved in an institutional self-study evaluation (e.g., an accrediting evaluation)? If so, use it as a basis for your response to this item. If not, reflect on how you think your school would respond to a self-study evaluation. Which one(s) of the types of evaluation discussed in this chapter would be most likely to be selected for use? How does this selection compare with your own ideal represented in activity 8? If there is a difference between the actual and ideal in your own experience, how can you adjust to it as a professional? If the two are compatible, what accounts for their compatibility?

10. Which orientations to curriculum evaluation would you like to learn more about? Develop a plan to do so and report what you find to your classmates.

11. Where do you stand on the four issues raised just prior to the guest commentaries: qualitative and quantitative evaluation, theoretic versus practical or expert versus local evaluation, the disciplinary basis of evaluation, and the role of personal and political aspects of evaluation?

12. Now, how does your position relate to that of the experientialist, social behaviorist, and intellectual traditionalist?

13. Where do you stand on the issue of self-evaluation as contrasted to formal, systematic evaluations conducted by experts?

14. This marks the conclusion of the four topics, represented by Chapters Eight through Eleven, of the perennial analytic curriculum paradigm built upon Ralph Tyler's *Basic Principles of Curriculum and Instruction* (1949). Review Tyler's book and note the ways in which curricular concerns and issues have been elaborated during the time that has elapsed since its publication. Which positions on the perennial curriculum topics are consistent with Tyler? Which are not? What is the basis of your classification?

15. Can you identify any topics that might be added to the perennial ones drawn from Tyler (1949)? How all encompassing are they?

12

✦ Paradigm of Practical Inquiry ✦

To foresee future objective alternatives and to be able by
deliberation to choose one of them and thereby weigh its chances
in the struggle for future existence measures our freedom.
JOHN DEWEY *Human Nature and Conduct* (1922)

The world is sown with good; but unless I turn my glad thoughts
into practical living and till my field, I cannot reap a kernel of the
good.
HELEN KELLER *Optimism* (1903)

The grand result of schooling is a mind with just vision to discern,
with free force to do: the grand schoolmaster is Practice.
THOMAS CARLYLE "Corn-Law Rhymes" (1832)

SETTING THE STAGE

We now enter a new realm of curriculum inquiry, a different way of thinking about
curriculum problems than that presented in Chapters Eight through Eleven. The
perennial, analytic paradigm, drawn from the Tyler Rationale (Tyler, 1949) and other
authors' elaborations of it was presented, advocated, and criticized in the foregoing
chapters. Greater space is devoted to the perennial paradigm than to alternatives to it
because of the substantial impact that categories of purposes, content or learning
experiences, organization, and evaluation have had on curriculum thought and practice in this century. This chapter and the next, however, deal with alternative
paradigms for curriculum theory and practice. In this chapter, we consider the
practical paradigm, and in the next, we sketch alternatives drawn from reconstructionist and reconceptualized political criticism that often falls under the label of
praxis. Both the practical and the critical have roots in the progressive education
movement, although both have developed in different ways in recent years.

In this chapter, we examine categories of practical inquiry as they apply to curriculum. First, four assumptions of practical inquiry are examined in light of four commonplaces of curricular situations: teachers, learners, subject matter, and milieu. These were briefly identified in Chapter Seven. Second, the commonplaces are developed relative to their contributions to arts of eclectic inquiry. Third, influences that each of the commonplaces have on each other are discussed in light of ways in which they create the unique character of practical situations. These discussions are followed with guest commentaries, recommendations for reflection, and suggestions for further reading.

The character of practical inquiry is that of everyday problem solving and meaning seeking done well; thus, it directly affects the style in which this chapter is written. Since practical inquiry is based on the assumption that situations are essentially unique, it would be out of character to provide specific guidelines without knowledge of particular states of affairs in which they would be employed. Therefore, the writing focuses more on the kinds of questions to be asked than on substantive categories to be considered as presented in dealing with the perennial paradigm in Chapters Eight through Eleven.

Practical inquiry centers on deliberation, the human search for meaning and understanding that enriches groups and institutions as they continuously refine their sense of value and direction and the means to move toward it. In deliberation, human beings are creators of knowledge who inform action in situations they encounter. Their search for meaning probes beyond the surface features of daily existence into the realm of intersubjective (created among persons) meaning shared by those who experience a similar historical, political, and social context. Central to deliberation within such a milieu is an ethical commitment to contribute good and worthwhile decisions that enable those involved and those affected by action that emanates from these decisions to grow in increasingly human ways. The vagueness of this statement is intentional. It reveals a commitment to not answer problems generally; rather, they can only be dealt with effectively in specific situations.

The roots of such conceptions of practical inquiry stem from the practical interests and interactive or democratic social organization of pragmatic philosophers such as Charles Sanders Peirce, William James, George Herbert Mead, and John Dewey. Dewey, of course, was the exemplar for progressive curricularists such as Harold Rugg, William H. Kilpatrick, and L. Thomas Hopkins in the United States and many others throughout the world. Joseph Schwab has written recently in the same vein in the United States while William Reid's work in England moves in similar directions. One has only to look at recent program books of the AERA Annual Meetings to see the increased attention devoted to the nature of curriculum deliberation. Roots also trace to phenomenological and existential writings of Martin Heidegger, Jean-Paul Sartre, Albert Camus, Maurice Merleau-Ponty, Alfred Schutz, and Hans-Georg Gadamer. In curriculum and pedagogical studies Ton Beekman, Madeleine Grumet, Janet Miller, Valerie Polakow-Suransky, Ted Aoki, William Pinar, James B. Macdonald, Maxine Greene, George Willis, Max van Manen and others associated with the *Journal of Curriculum Theorizing* and *Phenomenology and Pedagogy* contribute to practical inquiry through hermeneutic human sciences.

Despite the multitude of names one could conjure up in association with practical inquiry, tracing back to both Aristotle's work and a long succession of hermeneutic entries in ancient Judeo-Christian texts, this form of inquiry has a strong populist tone. It is to be carried out not so much by credentialed experts as by those in everyday situations. In curriculum this refers to life in classrooms, other educative institutions, and more informal educational relationships such as families and friendships. Therefore, the questions raised in the discussions that follow are offered with a minimum of citations, recognizing full well the debt owed to pragmatic philosophers and progressive educators as well as philosophers and pedagogues of phenomenologist and existentialist origins.

One final point in setting the stage: this chapter separates the practical from the perennial quite abruptly. This is a fault of analysis that by its nature draws distinctions and separations. There is, in actuality, a blending of the pragmatic and phenomenological within many of the subtopics presented under perennial categories (purposes, content and learning experiences, organization, and evaluation) in Chapters Eight through Eleven. It is important for curriculum workers to ask seriously whether they see the perennial and practical categories as primarily complementing or contradicting one another.

ASSUMPTIONS OF PRACTICAL CURRICULUM INQUIRY

Practical curriculum inquiry carries four predominant assumptions:

1. The source of problems is found in a *state of affairs*, not in the abstract conjuring of researchers who tend to imagine similarities among situations that cannot be grouped together defensibly.
2. The method of practical curriculum inquiry is *interaction* with the state of affairs to be studied, rather than detached induction upon it and deduction about it.
3. The subject matter sought in the process of practical curriculum inquiry is *situational insight and understanding*, instead of lawlike generalizations that extend across a wide range of situations.
4. The end of practical curriculum inquiry is *increased capacity to act morally and effectively* in pedagogical situations, not primarily the generation of generalized, publishable knowledge.

If these assumptions are carefully adhered to, it follows from them that the most important curriculum deliberation occurs at the local educational site. Pronouncements made in more distant realms such as state departments, federal offices, legislative chambers, research and development laboratories, university seminar rooms, publishing companies, suites of prestigious blue ribbon commissions, and the like are bound to be too far removed to engage in the most meaningful level of curriculum inquiry and development. The inquiry that can attend to actual states of affairs can best develop curriculum that meets needs of those affairs. Inquiry that proceeds by interaction with a state of affairs cannot be served best by token visits of outsiders who enter a problematic situation for a few hours, days, or even weeks to emerge, leave, and write about their conclusions or to issue policy changes based on their limited exposure. Practical curriculum inquiry must engage primarily those who live in the educational setting in question, and outside authorities only secondarily. Inquiry that seeks situational insights and meanings that lie behind the observable is best conducted by those whose personal orientations, sets of beliefs, or everyday philosophies, and lives are acted out according to continuously redefined, intersubjective meanings. Finally, inquiry that increases capacity for moral action, contributes to personal growth, enhances personal and public meaning, and renews sense of direction can best be generated by those with the greatest vested interest—those in the situation.

If it is the case, as has been argued, that deliberation is best for curriculum if carried out by those at the local site, then the central question becomes: What exactly is the local site? Is it the state as opposed to the federal government as provided in the United States Constitution? Is it the local school board and central office administration? Is this also too far removed from the state of affairs in large urban school districts? Or is the central office too far removed even in small cities and towns if they are serviced by more than one school building? One hears accolades of principals and even central office administrators who devote several days each year to actual teaching in classrooms. The public relations value of such strategy is unquestioned among faculty, parents, and students alike; however, questions can surely be raised about the extent to which such activity is a sound basis for curriculum deliberation. Does the visiting administrator, because of a mysterious superior wisdom, somehow gain greater insight in brief visits than those who live in the classroom day in and day out?

Does this mean that the individual school building is the proper setting for practical curriculum inquiry to take place? If this is the case, then what happens to the vast array of curriculum decision-making bodies that lie beyond the individual school? Surely they have a role to play, but a much reduced one when compared with the usual top-down curriculum decision-making structure found in systems that utilize perennial curriculum categories as recipes.

Although not inherent in the rationale developed by Tyler (1949), and quite the antithesis of Tyler's work with schools in the Eight Year Study, top-down curriculum development has predominated uses of the perennial categories. Typically, committees put together by central office administrators devise responses to matters of purpose, content, organization, and evaluation. Resultant guidelines are usually quite specific in terms of goals and objectives, content to be covered, standards to be met, and textbooks and other materials to be used, and testing and other modes of evaluation are usually specified quite explicitly. The route used to arrive at such a curriculum design is almost always more political and circuitous than rational and direct. Teachers, building principals, parents, and even students are asked occasionally to sit in on such committees along with central office administrators and supervisors. While such committees can undoubtedly serve a useful function in setting the tone and general direction of curriculum development at the building level, the approach violates principles of practical inquiry when a larger proportion of curriculum development is done away from the local site than within it. As soon as the teachers, parents, students, and principals leave their local site to make decisions that affect other sites, their interactive expertise is lost. They begin to project their own needs, problems, and interests on others. When the consent of the governed is ignored, curriculum deliberation ceases to be practical. Here we clearly see that the Deweyan union of democracy and education is at the heart of practical inquiry.

Schwab (1983) proposes that the school itself be the center of practical inquiry. He suggests a "curriculum group" composed of the principal, representatives from the community, teachers, and students and a chairperson who leads in deliberations about the ongoing status of the commonplaces. The chairperson should be skilled in the process of deliberation, should lead investigative reporting to discover imbalances of emphasis upon the commonplaces of teachers, learners, subject matter, and milieu. Schwab addresses other skills needed by the chair and means for maintaining his or her "refreshment" or education. He notes how the chair should be an habitual reader of the literature, a staunch pursuer of a liberal education, a well-versed student of behavioral and social sciences who can relate them to educational problems, and one who is well acquainted with the array of past and present curriculum practices. All this the chair should inspire in others as well.

An important issue emerges in this proposal, however: Does Schwab intend this chairperson and committee to be an actual entity, requiring extra expenditures and time from already beleaguered school systems? Maybe; after all, Schwab subtitled this fourth major paper on practical inquiry, "Something for Curriculum Professors to Do," because he is saying that curriculum professors would find more worthwhile work if they left academe and entered school buildings to serve as chairs of curriculum groups. Perhaps he is admonishing curriculum professors to educate others who could lead these curriculum groups. In either case, however, two questions must be asked: (1) How is an impoverished educational budget expected to provide resources for such a committee in every school? (2) Would it be possible for such a committee to adhere to assumptions of practical curriculum inquiry? The second question must be seen in light of the large comprehensive schools that we now have. Could a committee actually get to know all of the settings in such schools, or would it be necessary to have several curriculum groups per school? This would compound the first question still further.

In the likely event that resources of finance, time, and personnel would not permit such curriculum groups to come into being, is there any alternative means of fostering practical inquiry? Furthermore, if a miracle funded them, it is not at all certain that their inquiry would be consonant with practical assumptions. They might turn out merely to pursue another form of theoretic inquiry that remains closer to home. What then? Is there any place for practical inquiry to occur and flourish?

Once again to the rescue come ideas of John Dewey. The democratic classroom might well provide an answer that prevents further cost and simultaneously is the precise state of affairs required by the principles of practical curriculum inquiry. Classrooms already exist; thus, there would be no need for extra resources. Moreover, the classroom itself could be considered a curriculum group. The commonplaces could be conceived metaphorically as being in a state of deliberation because they combine and recombine continuously to reshape curriculum. Surely, students and teachers could enter into actual dialogue about what is worthwhile for them to do. The teacher, with broader experience, would be analogous to Schwab's chair of the curriculum group, and together learners and teachers could engage in practical deliberation about the curriculum or course of classroom events that affects their outlook and lives. Whether or not Schwab's curriculum group is intended to be metaphoric of the classroom, the tack taken in the remainder of this chapter is that the most appropriate place for the conduct of practical curriculum inquiry is the classroom.

This does not imply that practical curriculum inquiry exists only in the classroom setting. It can exist anywhere that the consequences of problems studied redound upon decision makers who determine policy and guide action. Thus, legislatures,

	Teachers	Learners	Subject Matter	Milieu
State of Affairs				
Interaction				
Situational Insight and Understanding				
Increased Capacity for Moral Action				

FIGURE 12-1. *Relating Assumptions of Practical Inquiry to Curricular Commonplaces*

publishing companies, national commisssions, and school boards are bodies that can engage in practical curricular inquiry. But all of these must play a supportive role in relation to the classroom. It is in this very specific learning situation that the bulk of practical curriculum development must occur. It has been said on many occasions that the teacher is the curriculum. This, however, is only part of the picture of curriculum, defined by practical inquiry, which includes a unique and ever-changing configuration of teachers, learners, subject matter, and milieu. Figure 12-1 is offered to facilitate reflection upon the way in which these curricular commonplaces can achieve practical inquiry. Each cell of the matrix can be read as the interaction of one of the commonplaces with one of the assumptions of practical curriculum inquiry. It should be added that excellent teachers from time immemorial have orchestrated practical curriculum inquiry in their learning situations. They were imaginatively perceptive of the kinds of interactions represented.

Practical Assumption and Teachers

Teachers are deeply embedded in the state of affairs known as the classroom. It is the hub their professional lives. Their daily decision, meaning, and action are the central governing forces in the culture of classroom life. As Thelen (1981) indicates, the classroom is a society. Societies develop cultures, and those cultures can be growth supporting or growth inhibiting. Thelen calls for the emergence of the "classroom society" in which teachers lead the classroom group in the construction of educational experience. He argues that quality of classroom life is more important than measurable products of knowledge acquired.

The teacher's work is carried out by interaction. Although many teachers may think they independently arrive at the daily design of classroom learning, this design is a product of interaction with students, subject matter (policies and materials), and milieu (environmental form and function). Each of these commonplaces continuously reshapes and mediates the teacher's decisions. No one is in a position to be as intimately aware of the power of classroom interaction as the teacher. Connelly and

Clandinin (1985) report extensive research into the personal practical knowledge that informs the lives of teachers.

The teacher, likewise, is interested more in specific insights that guide daily activity than in the construction of general knowledge about teaching, learning, and curriculum that can be applied to other schools and situations. Driving to and from school, lying in bed at night, during a break between classes, and even in the course of classroom activity, good teachers reflect on the meaning of what they do with students and what they ought to do next. Rarely would teachers be likely to label these reflections as phenomenological or practical inquiry. Nevertheless, this is a continuous part of being a teacher who strives for greater meaning, understanding, and sense of direction.

The end of teachers' activities and deliberations is constantly renewing. It results in decision, action, and/or increased personal and professional meaning. This, in turn, brings into clearer sight other problems to be pursued, other needs to be met, and further meanings to be recovered.

Practical Assumptions and Learners

Students are usually engaged in the overt process of receiving curriculum. But this only partially states the case. They mediate, interpret, and relate the content presented in light of their own experiences and consciousness. Sometimes they ignore content presented, but most frequently they bring it into their own repertoire of experience, and it alters the student's image of the world and how it works. Sometimes it contradicts what they already know or believe; sometimes it bolsters and refines. All of this simply points to the fact that students are involved in curriculum development, whether invited to participate or not. By virtue of their active social nature and past experience, learners profoundly influence the consequences of any curriculum.

The practical paradigm, however, offers a more active role to learners in curriculum development. Students of any level are deemed capable of legitimately addressing the questions: What is worthwhile for me to learn about and experience? How can I move in that direction? How can I know when I am growing in that direction?

Practical curriculum is infused with these questions. Thus, students become creators of curriculum along with teachers. Together they engage in dialogue on these questions. What they are able to do with the possibilities entertained in their dialogue depends on constraints and directions carried by policy statements, adopted texts, and other curriculum materials that teachers are required to follow. Choice also depends on the presence, absence, support, and resistance of environmental and financial resources.

Despite possible limitations to engagement of students in practical deliberation, it is a policy that fosters personal responsibility rather than adherence to generalized, expert authority. Thus, learners are granted a preeminent role in practical inquiry, balanced with that of teachers, in the development of curriculum for their own lives. Student involvement in curriculum development is rarely treated in the literature and seldom found in practice. One sometimes finds reference to students who sit on curriculum committees or student councils that are given the right to determine school colors and slogans. Such participation is condescending as compared with active involvement in the creation of purposes, learning experiences, organization, and evaluation.

Students who engage in these important curriculum considerations operate on assumptions of practical curriculum inquiry. They are saturated with the state of affairs that gives rise to their own interests and needs. If school needs are to be representative of needs generally in student lives, then it follows that more must be known about the nonschool lives of students. No one is in a better position than students to tell educators about those life situations, concerns, and needs. Rarely, however, do children and youths express their needs directly as adults might do. They express interests, rather superficial ones at first. Such interests require translation into needs through dialogue with perceptive teachers. This dialogue is interaction or deliberation of the practical paradigm, a method by which students become better able to articulate their needs as they more consciously experience their surroundings.

Thus, the process of more perceptively engaging with one's environment in light of one's past and in view of one's future is the practical curriculum. This is the organizing center around which students seek insight and understanding. Motivation to learn is always present when learning means becoming engaged in choosing a curriculum or journey that grows a more fully developed self and community in which to live. Students are not engaged in some process separated from their lives called curricular design; instead, practical curriculum deliberation implies that learning and growing are the continuous processes of reconstructing curriculum personally and with others with whom one lives. Hence, creating and receiving curriculum are part of the same process that results in increased capacity to act, grow, and mature.

Practical Assumptions and Subject Matter

It is difficult to view subject matter as a participant in curriculum deliberation. After all, curriculum policy documents, textbooks, and other instructional materials are inanimate. However, one must realize that they are created by human beings. Moreover, they are animated by interaction with teachers and students. A book, a worksheet, or media presentation becomes something different for each person and group who interacts with it. Even if not selected to match the needs and interests of students and teachers, materials used and the subjects or topics taught alter the character of teachers and learners who use them. A particular story in a reading book or literature class may be humorous to some students and deadly serious to others; still others may see no connection with it.

The point here is that subject matter itself, normally considered quite static, is dynamic relative to the other commonplaces when viewed through the lenses of the practical paradigm. The effect of interaction enlivens and adapts subject matter even if it was not tailored to the situation in the first place. Tailoring goes on naturally as subject matter is exposed to the unique character of teachers, learners, and milieu. But in the practical paradigm, curriculum involves still more. Subject matter should actually be built within the public space in which the commonplaces interact. This does not mean that books are not chosen from the array made available by educational publishers and libraries, but it does mean that the problems, needs, and interests of the learning situation are given priority. The latter determine what to look for among the disciplines of knowledge. Many projects grow out of life in the situation while others are inspired by something read or observed in subject matter that lies outside the classroom.

With subject matter, as with teachers and learners, we see the assumptions of practical curriculum inquiry and development. Subject matter is selected because of needs and interests in a particular state of affairs. It becomes filled with the life of the situation as it is studied and, thus, becomes something different from what it might be in other educational settings. It is the interaction among the commonplaces that gives meaning to a subject studied. Anyone, for example, who has written a story and shared it with a group, read a great novel, or engaged in a political discussion knows well that the experience would have been quite different in other circumstances. If the people were different, or if the events of one's personal life were altered, or if the immediate environment were changed, the learning experience would be different. The difference may be minute, or it may be profound; always it is important.

Having noted the significance of state of affairs and interaction to subject matter, let us turn to situational insight and capacity to act. Subject matter derived from practical inquiry is selected to meet situational needs and interests. It may serve as a novel journey through which learners become exposed to a broader and richer realm of experience, it may serve more instrumental interests of a particular problem in a student's life, or it may serve as stimulation to probe beneath the surface features of one's outlook and action.

When it does these things, subject matter increases capacity for moral action. Thus, subject matter achieves value when it contributes to moral action. But one asks: What is moral action? Within the practical paradigm, the answer is not a product, rule, or operational definition; to make it such would be to accept tacitly the theoretic paradigm. Instead, the answer is a continuous asking of the question: What is moral action? Such asking in every situation, as Dewey would say, is itself whole-hearted striving toward defensible moral action. Drawing upon Dewey's *Human Nature and Conduct* (1922), Rucker (1970, pp. 123–125) identifies three criteria for enhancing and justifying moral action: harmony, variety, and expansion. Applying this to the impact of subject matter, it follows that when subject matter moves teachers and learners from discord toward harmony, from monotony to variety, and from constraint to expansion, it has moved them in the direction of moral action.

Practical Assumptions and Milieu

The curriculum milieu comprises the physical, social, cultural, and psychological aspects of the learning situation not included in the categories of teacher, learner, and subject matter. For example, a certain *esprit de corps* develops within a group of teachers and learners. The *gestalt* of personalities is greater than the sum of each individual personality. The ways in which students emulate teachers or other students has a marked impact on the kind of learning that transpires. Whether a classroom or the school around it is essentially autocratic, democratic, or *laissez-faire* can profoundly affect learning. These examples pertain primarily to psychological, social, and cultural dimensions of milieu.

Consequences of physical features are equally important. Small classrooms, crowded conditions, damaged facilities, desks bolted to floors, and the positioning of desks and tables can profoundly influence learning. Still another dimension of milieu consists of the rules, expectations, and other aspects of hidden curriculum that govern the classroom life. Thus, it is obvious that if curriculum is the learning that takes place in schools, the milieu plays a major role in it. It clearly affects teachers, learners, and subject matter and, in turn is affected by them.

While curriculum is a function of milieu in any kind of school situation, the kind of milieu that fosters practical curriculum inquiry has a distinctive character. It allows all participants to consider an array of possible courses of action and project possible consequences of choosing from among them. It encourages teachers and students to choose courses of action that will enhance their educational growth and to evaluate the consequences of their action.

Relative to the four assumptions of practical inquiry, the milieu is itself a major feature that defines the state of affairs. It is by nature an interaction of many physical, social, cultural, and psychological factors, both within and outside of school. Insights and meanings about curriculum in a given situation should take into account the impact of milieu. It follows that curriculum decision and action must be firmly grounded in study of moral as well as technical consequences. It is not enough, from the practical standpoint, to solve a problem in a mere technical sense. The goodness and justice that flow from the act of problem solving must be assessed in terms of both direct and indirect effects. To upset the milieu of an educational situation is analogous to intervening in a natural environment and upsetting the balance of nature. To devote too much or too little attention to teachers, learners, subject matter, or milieu is to disturb the ecological balance of the classroom or other educative situation.

THE CURRICULAR COMMONPLACES AND ECLECTIC ARTS

Just as John Dewey's proposals for practical inquiry were faced with unwarranted criticism asserting that he advocated a curriculum based on student interest and neglected the disciplines of knowledge, Joseph Schwab's notion of practical inquiry was criticized on the basis that it was a mere trial and error approach devoid of theoretical sophistication. Neither objection could be more incorrect, and understanding the error of each is essential to comprehending the nature of practical inquiry and its relevance to curriculum.

Dewey's emphasis on interests of learners is integrally dependent upon his high regard for the disciplines of knowledge. To him, the teacher's job is first to get to know the students and their expressions of interest. The perceptive teacher realizes that these often superficial interests symbolize a quest within the human being to understand life's great problems. These problems such as death, love, poverty, greed, power, suffering, and alienation are dealt with in great literature and other disciplines that also treat conceptions of positive virtues such as beauty, truth, goodness, wisdom, equality, justice, and happiness. Dewey referred to the pedagogic movement of learners from interest to the disciplines as a continuous transition from the psychological to the logical (Dewey, 1916).

Similarly, Schwab's emphasis on practical inquiry condemns what he called the *theoretic*; however, his condemnation is not of theory or philosophy in general. Recall that by *theoretic* he refers to research that purports to be useful to educational situations but takes its problems from abstract bits and pieces of many situations rather than from an actual state of affairs with all of its contextual variables. The *theoretic* keeps the researcher detached from situations investigated and searches for lawlike generalizations that can be published. This is more a misapplication of research technology than a condemnation of theory. Schwab (1971) responded to unwitting critics by explaining the centrality of three "arts of eclectic" to practical inquiry.

Like Dewey, Schwab argues that the disciplines that are built upon a foundation of theory are essential to practical inquiry. Three eclectic arts are

1. The capacity to *match* theoretical or disciplinary knowledge and perspectives to situational needs and interests.
2. The capacity to *tailor and adapt* theoretical or disciplinary knowledge and perspectives to situational needs and interests. (This is necessary because extant theories only account for a small proportion of phenomena in the world, thus, making matching a limited strategy.)
3. The capacity to *generate alternative courses of action* and to anticipate the consequences of such action for moral good. (This is necessary because extant theories are irrelevant to much of the world's phenomena even if they are tailored, adapted, combined, stretched, and modified in all conceivable ways.)

To carry out practical curriculum inquiry using these three eclectic arts, one must be steeped in both literature and direct experience. Direct experience is needed for sensitivity to and understanding of situations. Literature is broadly conceived to embrace great works of fiction and artistic creations as well as philosophy, psychological and social theory, and the results of research in natural, social, and behavioral sciences. It also includes knowledge in the professions, such as medicine, law, engineering, architecture, education, and vocational and technical training.

Indeed, to understand practical curriculum problems requires acquaintance with the broad range of human culture; it is the essence of what Elliot Eisner (1985) calls connoisseurship. This is the case because curriculum workers must look at the accumulated knowledge of humankind and ask: What is worth preserving? What of all that exists should this child or group experience? What knowledge, skills, values, and appreciations will help them grow personally and contribute to a better world? To engage in such questions is an awesome responsibility and an honor. The practical curriculum inquirer realizes that these questions cannot be answered for someone else without their participation in the process. Thus, practical curriculum developers become teachers and students cooperatively asking these and related questions.

There is another reason for practical curriculum developers, especially teachers, to be steeped in the literature of a liberal education. Their work requires the subtlest of insight into human nature in order to engage students in dialogue that helps them embark on a lifelong adventure in learning.

How then do practical curriculum developers seek to enable this kind of educative growth? One could argue that each subject in the traditional school curriculum could be taught using arts of eclectic. This, however, would be a compromise position since it accepts the disciplines rather than the learner as the initial organizing center.

A position more in harmony with practical inquiry would have the learner and learning groups become the center of study. Subject areas would be relegated to a subsidiary role as disciplines that could facilitate the study of problems and needs growing out of student interest and teacher-student dialogue. For example, college

	Teachers	Learners	Subject Matter	· Milieu
Matching knowledge and theory to situations				
Adapting knowledge and theory to situations				
Anticipatory generation of alternatives and invention to meet unique situational needs				

FIGURE 12-2.   Uses of Eclectic Arts by Curricular Commonplaces

students in teacher education would pose problems related to their interest in becoming a teacher. Preparatory to observing teaching practice, they might be exposed to a succession of theorists and be asked to interpret and assess what they observe through the lenses of, say, Dewey, then Freud, then Plato, then Froebel, and so on. As theory upon theory accumulates, they would be asked to sort through the layers in an effort to match theories to situations, adapt and combine theories to give situations greater meaning, and finally to invent interpretations of events that theoretical literature seems not to address.

"Yes," some may admit, "eclectic arts could be an organizing center for college curriculum, but what about the elementary and secondary levels?" The same form could be used, but with different subject matter. Obviously, theories of Plato, Dewey, and Freud would be inappropriate for most elementary school students. For the term *theory,* one can merely substitute *disciplinary knowledge.* As students attempt to meet needs or solve problems, knowledge can light the way to action carried out with greater facility. This is how we teach an infant who tries, for example, to set a lid on a jar, or fit a block into a hole, or relate a word to an object. We do not teach an instructional unit on blocks, then one on lids, then one on words. Instead, common sense moves us to focus on the problem at hand and to bring new concepts or perspectives to the child so that he or she perceives more clearly. From this we should learn that curriculum is most successful when it evolves to bring disciplinary perspectives to bear in meeting actual interests, needs, and problems.

Let us consider in more detail what a curriculum might be like that is rooted in practical inquiry. How could the three eclectic arts transform the curricular commonplaces of teachers, learners, subject matter, and milieu? Consider Figure 12-2.

Eclectic Arts and Teachers

Teachers have a repertoire of sources in the back of their minds: Bloom's taxonomies, Skinner's behavior modification theory, Gagné's hierarchies of learning and instruction, Dewey's notion starting with interests of the whole child, and other oft-cited literature in education. Situations arise and teachers may actually think to themselves, "I will try to reinforce positively this child who usually speaks out of turn by praising her when she asks permission to talk." Or "I have beset the students with too much that I think they need rather than listening to their expressions of interest as Dewey suggested that we do." Or "Look here, I am teaching and testing at Bloom's lowest cognitive level, memorization; I need to integrate higher-level thinking into this set of lessons." Without the literature, such observations would probably not be made. Teachers do find solutions in the literature that they recall; however, they need to be aware of more literature. More exposure raises the potential for matching of theories to situations.

Similarly, exposure to theories and practice in using them to interpret situations enhances teachers' capacity to adapt, tailor, and combine theories. In the same classroom, for example, it is not unusual to find some students who work best with a highly structured form of behavior modification and others who function better in loose, self-scheduled situations with a free flow of dialogue. In fact, there may be needed as many or more pedagogic perspectives than there are students in a class, because the same student differs in pedagogic needs from circumstance to circumstance. Indeed, there is much tailoring to be done, especially since each individual student profits from different orientations to teaching, depending on the situation in which he or she is, the mix of students nearby, and the expectations set forth.

This multiplies the need for theories by factors large enough to conclude that there aren't enough theories to fit practical needs. Even if there were enough, it would be impossible for the teachers to learn and make use of them. Therefore, teachers develop their own responses to situations. By combining their storehouse of experience with ideas gleaned from a host of different sources, teachers begin to create a practical theory of classroom life; every new student with whom they interact and every situation that they encounter feeds their evolving theory of teaching. Eventually, they operate on a body of precedent of past experience that helps them to respond to practical problems, derive meaning, generate imaginative alternative possibilities for action, and judge the moral and educative value of consequences of the curriculum that they create with students.

Eclectic Arts and Students

Under a practical curriculum, students would pursue problems and meet needs derived from their deepest interests. The process of doing this would emerge as students engage in dialogue with teachers and other students. Students' own interests, not the usual subject matter, would be the center of the curriculum.

Students would become exposed to disciplines of knowledge as they pertain to the pursuit of interests or the solution of problems. Interests, needs, and problems would vary greatly from student to student. Some students might have carefully defined problems that could be attacked scientifically; other students might simply want to interact with one another and learn more about the interests of their teachers and classmates. In any case, the perceptive teacher will point out areas of knowledge that can enliven and enrich an emergent interest, help to gratify a need expressed, or solve a problem posed.

As students become immersed in the process of tapping relevant literatures for knowledge that provides practical benefit to their lives, they begin to appreciate the roles that the disciplines can have for them. In this process of moving from the psychological to the logical, students realize that they must play an active role in interpreting, tailoring, adapting, and combining knowledge to relate it to their needs, interests, and problems.

Finally, students see themselves as knowledge creators. Knowledge does not just come from outside experts; teachers and students, too, are experts, especially when it comes to their own situation. No one lives it but them. Thus, they are in the best position to generate alternatives, interpret meanings, and judge consequences. In the final analysis, they discover that they must take responsibility to ask fundamental curriculum questions for their own lives.

Eclectic Arts and Subject Matter

Balance must be maintained among the commonplaces. It is inappropriate to say that students take priority over subject matter because the two are so inseparably entwined. Teachers who are committed to practical inquiry enter the pedagogic scene with a repertoire of knowledge derived from the disciplines. The disciplines in the form of the teacher are one access route to subject matter. Good teaching provides the introduction of knowledge at developmentally appropriate times for students. This is an art as well as a science that, when done well, gives rise to the phrase, "The art of teaching."

How does the practical paradigm relate to the usual texts, instructional materials, curriculum guides, and related policy documents associated with subject matter? An enriched environment of texts, worksheets, learning packages, audiovisual materials, computer software, and the like could facilitate practical inquiry if these materials were not laid out in rigidly required doses as prespecified by outside experts. Similarly, curriculum guides and policy statements should be no stronger than the most general sense of direction; they should be no more than possibilities for teachers and students to entertain.

Sometimes good materials and well-developed curriculum guides can lead as well as facilitate. When students and/or teachers look at such subject matter, it may elicit needs, interests, or problems that heretofore remained unrealized or at least unarticulated. Perceiving their efficacy, teachers and students may choose to be guided by well-designed materials, but the choice should be theirs to make.

Thus, subject matter that comes from good teachers, from packaged products, or from students may lead or follow sound learning. The point is that subject matter should be available, even given a good sales pitch, but it should not be forced. Nevertheless, it should be there to be matched with, adapted to, and generative of needs, interests, and problems of learners and teachers.

Of greatest import to practical curriculum inquiry is the development of subject matter that is appropriate to those engaged in situations. This does not mean that teachers must spend forever writing units for each student and situation. It means that the teacher becomes an orchestrator of students who design subject matter in the form of experiences that they pursue. This does not mean that students write it all out; very little is written, but it is carefully *thought out*. Students imagine what will help them grow, they estimate its consequences, try alternatives, reflect on the consequences of what they do, and begin again to develop other subject matter for their own curriculum.

Eclectic Arts and Milieu

Like the subject matter, the milieu in which practical curriculum thrives must be malleable enough to be altered easily to facilitate the pursuit of interests, the satisfaction of needs, and the resolution of problems. Like subject matter, a well-designed learning environment can creatively evoke interests, needs, and problems, as well as discover and respond to them.

It should be possible to alter both the psychosocial atmosphere and the physical surroundings of a learning situation if they are judged to inhibit growth of teachers or students or the improvement of subject matter. The milieu must be continuously monitored. If it is complex, its detail needs to be examined to determine which aspects, when matched with students, teachers, and subject matter, result in better learning. Likewise, those who live within the milieu need to ask how it can be tailored better to facilitate student growth, meaning, and sense of direction, and when these are better served by reconstructing the physical or psychosocial dimensions of the educational situation.

INTERACTIONS AMONG COMMONPLACES

In the practical paradigm, curriculum is defined as the continuous interaction among the four commonplaces: teachers, learners, subject matter, and milieu. This is a much broader conception of curriculum than one finds used in the perennial paradigm, where it is variously characterized by different curricularists as intended learning outcomes, subject matter to be delivered, statements in curriculum documents, or behavioral objectives. The practical definition admits as curriculum the entire culture of the classroom. Everything that happens there, everything that could influence a student, is assumed to fall within the four commonplaces. Curriculum is, thus, anything that influences or shapes the thought, feeling, outlook, and behavior of learners in schools or other educative institutions.

How then does one study curriculum and what does it mean to do curriculum work from a practical frame of reference? Let us look at the second part of this question first. Practical curriculum work entails the conscious orchestration of the commonplaces to have a desirable influence on the thought, feeling, outlook, and behavior of learners. To conduct such an orchestration, one must thoroughly be involved in the educational situation in question. No persons are in a better position to develop curriculum of this sort than teachers and learners. It is further assumed that teachers and students are in the best position to determine that which is desirable for themselves, not merely that which they desire. They should use myriad resources, but ultimately the best decisions about what is desirable for meeting one's needs reside with oneself in light of carefully assessed consequences for others.

The first of the questions (How does one study and assess curriculum?) requires a continuous attentiveness to interaction, interdependence, and influence among the commonplaces. Again, it is teachers and learners who are in a position to put forth that degree of attentiveness. It is their situation, and they must take responsibility for understanding and improving it. If they don't, no one is likely to do so, with compassion and defensible facility.

Teachers and learners, or administrators, researchers, and the public who want to

	Teachers	Learners	Subject Matter	Milieu
Teachers	1	5	9	13
Learners	2	6	10	14
Subject Matter	3	7	11	15
Milieu	4	8	12	16

FIGURE 12-3. *Discovering the Interdependent Influences Among Curricular Commonplaces*

comprehend better the curriculum that affects thought, feeling, outlook, and behavior would do well to consider the interaction among commonplaces in the educational setting with which they are concerned. This can be facilitated by the use of a matrix or table of invention (to credit the work of Francis Bacon). Each cell in the matrix in Figure 12-3 represents a possible point of influence between two of the commonplaces. (Clearly three or more could also intersect; similarly, each cell might be broken into component parts and analyzed in great detail. Both of these are beyond the scope of examples presented here.) Presented here are the sixteen two-cell interactions possible among the four commonplaces. The discussion simply illustrates questions invoked by the pairing of each two-cell combination. Posing questions (rather than asserting answers) is consistent with the practical paradigm because the latter gives precedence to situationally specific as opposed to highly generalized substantive knowledge. Questions presented are designed as springboards for reflection on curriculum in any educational situation. The purpose of these questions is to encourage those who work in particular settings to think of more situationally relevant questions.

Cell One: Teachers and Teachers

How do teachers view other teachers in this situation? What effects does this have in terms of compromises that some teachers need to make in an effort not to step on the toes of other teachers' prejudices, pet ideas, and general modes of operation? How do teachers positively encourage and assist one another? How do teachers respond to teachers who try innovative ideas and approaches?

Cell Two: Teachers and Learners

What aspects of learners' personalities does the teacher bring out? What aspects does he or she suppress? How does the teacher view different students? Does the self-fulfilling prophecy seem to be operating? In what ways does the teacher model attitudes and behavior? What image of an educated person does the teacher give students? How does the teacher convey messages about what he or she considers important and valuable? What does he or she convey is worthwhile to students?

Cell Three: Teachers and Subject Matter

How does the teacher's attitude about a subject affect the subject matter? For example, if an elementary teacher dislikes science, how will his or her interpretation of it compare with that of an enthusiastic teacher who uses the same materials? What image of science will each be likely to give students? How does a teacher's broader knowledge of a subject affect his or her teaching of it? For example, how might the impact of a teacher who has read a great deal about the American Revolutionary War differ from one whose primary source of knowledge is derived from the adopted textbook?

Cell Four: Teachers and Milieu

How does a teacher's behavior, attitude, and general personality influence the classroom atmosphere or ambiance? In *A Place Called School*, John Goodlad (1984) writes of the important difference that ambiance makes in quality of an educational situation. How might the same set of classroom rules be different depending on the teacher? How does the teacher's orientation to teaching influence the physical environment? The psychosocial environment? How much variation in the design and decor of physical classroom settings is dependent on the teacher's outlook?

Cell Five: Learners and Teachers

Teachers sometimes use the term *chemistry* as a metaphor for the atmosphere created by a particular group of learners. How does the chemistry of a group of learners influence the teacher? The same teacher who is quite effective with one group of students might be quite ineffective with another. The teacher's teaching style may not fit well with one group of students but may mesh perfectly with the learning style of another group. How might one disruptive student or a clique of students affect the teacher's interaction with the whole class? What group process techniques could improve the interactions among persons in a particular group of teachers and learners?

Cell Six: Learners and Learners

How might one dynamic student leader among a group of learners affect other learners? What if this leader is not interested in the subject matter or does not like the teacher? How can a small coterie of learners affect the attitudes of other learners? How powerfully do attitudes forged by peer pressure influence learning? Can such attitudes be used to inspire further learning? How?

Cell Seven: Learners and Subject Matter

How does prior experience with a subject area affect current and future response to that subject? If, for example, a learner had very positive experiences in mathematics in the previous year, how might it affect his response to the subject this year? To what extent does prior knowledge of a subject influence learning? If a learner's home or community or religious group fosters an intolerance toward evolution, or attributes great value to creative writing, how might this influence learning?

Cell Eight: Learners and Milieu

To what extent do learner attitudes, behavior, and general outlook influence class-room rules and expectations? How do these same characteristics affect the flexibility of physical use of space and materials in the classroom? In what ways do learners influence the overall ambiance or psychosocial atmosphere?

Cell Nine: Subject Matter and Teachers

What constraints are placed on teachers when they are asked to be subject matter specialists and teach algebra, physics, or home economics rather than the genuine interest areas of learners? What freedoms come with specialization? How do materi-als purchased for the classroom control the type of teaching that can be done there? What kind of view of the teacher is implicit in the materials purchased, the district-wide curriculum guides, and overall policy statements about curriculum? Do they show regard for the teacher's professional judgment, or do they strive to "teacher-proof" the curriculum?

Cell Ten: Subject Matter and Learners

What if the subject matter required to be taught is developmentally inappropriate for students? For example, what if the content has little or no bearing on the experience of the learners? Or what if the content is conceptually relevant but is too difficult for the students to read and comprehend? What image of knowledge is given to learners about the nature of knowledge by the way it is presented in the subject matter materials? Is knowledge set forth as neutral information, nonproblematic, certain, and proven by experts; or is it presented as value-laden, created by all who inquire, and always open to question and subject to improvement? What image of learners is implicit in the subject matter? Are learners primarily deemed active, social creators of knowledge or passive recipients of it?

Cell Eleven: Subject Matter and Subject Matter

Are curriculum policy statements consistent with curriculum guides? Do purchased texts and materials harmoniously further the curriculum philosophy represented in these documents? Do purchased tests and other evaluation strategies? Do purposes and goal statements fit learning experiences selected, and do the learning experi-ences or content and organizational patterns facilitate those purposes? Is a consistent philosophy of teaching and learning represented by different purchased curriculum materials? Across subject areas? Are these consistent with teacher-made materials? With daily lesson plans? With the subject matter that evolves spontaneously through the daily interaction among teachers and learners?

Cell Twelve: Subject Matter and Milieu

How does the physical environment signify the nature of the subject matter taught in that environment? What kinds of rules or general modes of operation are demanded by the subject matter? What ambiance or psychosocial atmosphere does the subject matter permit? How flexible are the possibilities? How constraining? Where are the purchased materials located and how are they organized for classroom use? Does more freedom to learn exist because of them, or less? Does higher or lower quality of learning prevail because of the location, organization, and substance of purchased materials?

Cell Thirteen: Milieu and Teachers

How do the physical characteristics of the school and classroom support and/or hinder what teachers want to do for students? In other words, how does the configuration of desks, chairs, tables, audiovisual equipment, stairs, floors, heat, water, restroom facilities, light, and so on affect the quality of teaching? In discussing the Carnegie Commission Report, *High School*, Ernest Boyer (1984) said that all that is wrong with education in America is symbolized by the public address speakers affixed to the walls of so many classrooms; though humorously overstated, his point was that the P.A. system symbolizes the physical intrusion, lack of sensitivity, and blatant interruption that are too common in public education today. How do the multitude of social service tasks of schools, school building regulations, and extracurricular functions create an atmosphere that affects the work and personality of teachers?

Cell Fourteen: Milieu and Learners

How do the general regulations of school buildings, the peer culture, the extracurricular activities, the learning to defer gratification, the rules and regulations, the crowded conditions, the daily life with agemates, and the grade reports create an ambiance that affects learners' conceptions of themselves? How does this affect their images of what the world is like and what one must do to get along in it? How does classroom life form student images of what an education is and what it can provide? How does the tenor of authority (i.e., administration and teachers who are democratic, autocratic, or *laissez-faire*) affect learner performance, attitude, behavior, and outlook?

Cell Fifteen: Milieu and Subject Matter

Are there ways in which the rules and regulations of the classroom, the general ambiance, and the physical environment resist or constrain the subject matter that is intended to be taught? Do they support and nourish the subject matter in other ways? How? What kinds of alterations in the milieu might be made to improve the acquisition of subject matter? Do particular areas of the curriculum fare better because of the milieu?

Cell Sixteen: Milieu and Milieu

How do rules and regulations, physical features, and ambiance of the school and individual classrooms affect each other? How do they facilitate one another and how do they clash? Within either the classroom or the school as a whole, are the rules, physical features, and ambiance congruent in intent and philosophy, or are they sometimes at odds? If at odds, how might they be brought more into harmony?

COMMENTARIES

Each of our guests will now present his or her perspective on the practical paradigm and its curricular implications.

Social Behaviorist

I see very little value in the so-called "practical" position; in fact, it seems a step backward to me. Almost everything that we do in life or education is based on abstraction and generalization. If we had to resort to the concrete for every decision and action, we would be rendered immobile. Inquiry is done by persons; it must begin with a state of mind (or abstract conceptualization) rather than a state of affairs as suggested by practical researchers. Practical researchers say that they search only for situational specifics, but what good does finding them do if the next situation is substantially different? We must search for generalizable findings with a faith that we will arrive at explanations and predictions for curricular phenomena more generally. If researchers gain knowledge of phenomena by interaction, as practical researchers advocate, rather than by detached induction, they contaminate the situations and data gathered there. Furthermore, we need basic or pure research as well as applied or practical research. Science has always profited from basic research that has no utilitarian value when produced. Witness the numerous unanticipated outcomes that have flowed from the space program to provide benefits to many areas of human endeavor from recreation to medicine.

I agree that teachers, learners, subject matter, and milieu all affect learning of students; however, there is a big problem in making *everything* the curriculum. It becomes too unwieldy to conceptualize or research. If all influences are the curriculum, then curriculum is life itself. That approaches the ludicrous.

Another thing that I cannot tolerate about the practical position is its naive conception of democracy. Here, I particularly refer to student roles in curriculum design. Students' lack of knowledge, after all, is the reason to have schools. They need to be introduced to the world. They cannot be expected to tell you what they need. For goodness sake, that is what professional educators have studied so long to be able to do!

Already, we have a great deal of empirically verifiable research on such topics as teachers, learners, subject matter, and environment (a term that I greatly prefer to *milieu*). We need to utilize that knowledge rather than the indefensible ponderings of teachers who know little about what they are looking for. Researchers are sorely needed to chart the course of curriculum policy.

Intellectual Traditionalist

It was Aristotle who invented the distinction between practical and theoretic inquiry, and he asserted that there is room for both. Some kinds of problems should be pursued with practical inquiry and some with theoretic. Writers such as Dewey and Schwab, as insightful as they are, go too far on the side of practical inquiry without sufficiently acknowledging the need for balance with the theoretic. Undoubtedly, part of their emphasis stems from the seemingly dominant position of theoretic research in education today. I say *seemingly* because the problem is a deceiving one.

My contention is that much of educational research (and this includes curriculum research) is simply poor research. This, I believe, is what Schwab condemns rather than the Aristotelian *theoretic*.

When I think of the brilliant theoretic research done by Robert Merton, for example, on the self-fulfilling prophecy (1948), his emphasis on the value of unintended outcomes (1936), and the chain of educational studies that are built upon Merton's work (e.g., Rosenthal and Jacobson, 1968), I know that theoretic research has its strengths. It can produce great ideas quite similar to those found in the great books. Both theoretic and practical research have the potential to focus in on life's great events and mysteries. When research is at its best, it reveals the profound that lies dormant within the mundane, just as a great novel or play does. However, the problem is to find scholars and practitioners in education who have the insight, imagination, and humanistic understanding to conduct such research. The ability to do this does not flow from recipes or formulas, nor does it stem from merely muddling through isolated situations. Instead, it comes from a broadly based humanistic education, a truly liberal education that actually liberates the mind.

To find such an education requires scholars and practitioners who try to actualize the potential that William Reid sees in uniting the practical with the humanities to develop "a humanistic discipline of curriculum" (Reid, 1978):

> *The function of a humane study is to explain, interpret, and evaluate a specific type of human activity and achievement in terms of the principles by which it is given meaning, significance, and value. [p. 106]*

Reid continues to argue for a humane discipline of curriculum studies that (1) determines how curriculum problems are unique and should be studied by methodologies that are uniquely curricular, (2) determines the levels of data and procedures to be used in illuminating and resolving such problems, (3) determines how other disciplines can contribute to the study and resolution of curriculum problems, (4) determines how judgments are made about the worth of solutions proposed and attempted, and (5) determines the extensiveness of the context of curriculum problems whereby consequences and interdependencies may be attended to and judged. In brief, Reid calls for a critical tradition in curriculum studies that is embedded in the long tradition of the humanities. This would provide much greater perspective than the historically limited rationalism (or what Schwab calls *theoretic*) that has dominated educational research in the twentieth century. This is why the eclectic arts are so sorely needed.

One of the values of practical inquiry as presented in this chapter is its use of tables of invention deemed so important to inquiry by Francis Bacon. Despite the criticisms leveled at practical inquiry by critics of limited vision, I contend that the most sensitive scholars and practitioners (like the great playwrights, poets, and novelists) do provide theoretic insight that is highly generalizable. These insights, however, are not of the mundane variety of pointing to mere commonalities, which is what too many empiricists do. Rather, I speak of a theoretic beyond the theoretic that Schwab castigates, one that intuitively unlocks mysteries of human nature that apply to all time and all places.

This raises the major inhibitor that I see in moving toward the ideal of universal education, namely, the lack of highly insightful persons to populate the teaching force. This leads me to one further bone to pick with the practical image of the curriculum as an interaction among teachers, learners, subject matter, and milieu. I would not by any means advocate balance among these commonplaces. Subject matter, as presented in most curriculum guides, published texts, and materials, constitutes one of the lowest forms of literature I know. This is because it is usually written by pseudoscholars and downright entrepreneurs. Too great a proportion of teachers are incapable of telling the difference between the usual swill found in textbooks and knowledge truly within the disciplines. Excellent teachers, those with liberal education backgrounds, can tell the difference. It is their responsibility to help students learn to appreciate the arts, sciences, and humanities. Students are not yet capable of determining their curriculum; otherwise, they would not be students. Milieu is something to overcome, not to allow to dictate policy. Teachers, great teachers that is, are the curriculum along with the classics whose authors are the greatest teachers throughout history.

Experientialist

I heartily agree with the thrust of this chapter. It represents a direction in which educational inquiry should move. It is more scholarly, by far, than the prevailing theoretic tendencies. This is primarily because it requires inquirers who are steeped in the liberal arts, but more as well. It requires those who can bring the insights of the ages to bear on the essential question of how to develop and improve the human race. After all, that is the mission for which curriculum scholarship and practice strives.

Who is capable of moving us toward that mission? One first asks: What kind of experts? But that is the wrong question; in a sense it begs the question. It implies a curriculum determined by expert authority rather than by personal responsibility. The latter is what is needed in great abundance. This implies a radically different image of who conducts curriculum inquiry than either the social behaviorists or intellectual traditionalists advocate. The former want credentialed experts to decide, and the latter want great teachers to do the job. To be sure, more reflective practitioners (Schön, 1983) are needed to begin the process, but it is necessary to ask who falls in this group.

Neither the social behaviorist nor intellectual traditionalist adequately prepares human beings for life in a democracy. Neither recognizes the vast potential that each individual has for determining his or her own meaning and direction in life. We need to have faith that learners of any age have the capacity to contribute meaningfully to dialogue on what they should learn and how they should grow. My own experience with babies as well as adults convinces me that this is indeed a warranted assumption.

The most neglected dimension of practical inquiry, however, lies in its directionality. It must be realized that it is not merely the process of technical problem solving. Neither Dewey nor Schwab saw the process as being devoid of ideals. In fact, the most central feature of practical inquiry is its relation to the humanities as Reid (1978) rightly points out. Implicit in the humanities is the quest to realize and achieve greater human goodness. Thus, all practical inquiry is a search posed in this direction. Van Manen (1982) speaks directly to the point when he writes of curriculum theory that is edifying, that serves the good.

Similarly, the curriculum itself in every educational setting must also be infused with the quest for greater human goodness. Thus, as interests and needs of learners are identified, their satisfaction is directed by the quest for greater human goodness. Here learners not only strive to realize greater goodness in the meanings that guide their lives, but in the justice meted out as consequences of their striving to grow. I think, however, that many advocates of practical inquiry do not probe such consequences fully enough. They need to push their inquiry further into the culture and more deeply into the deeper recesses of the human psyche. They need to develop a clearer vision of the inequities in a society and culture and the impact of control and suppression on human inquiry and growth. Some researchers in both the progressive and present eras have addressed these questions. These are taken up in the next chapter.

What is important here is the need to realize that what human beings become in any culture is a result of a broad array of social, economic, and psychological forces. Similarly, we must admit that the impact of any educational situation (such as a classroom) on a learner's outlook and growth is holistic. If the term *curriculum* is to have meaning, it must be the interaction among teachers, learners, subject matter, and milieu.

Finally, the kind of questions set forth as examples derived from each of the cells in Figure 12-3 could lead to a new type of resource provided by educational research. To study the types of questions raised requires anthropological or case study research as well as the best literary or artistic portrayals. One-shot quantitative studies will not do. A large-scale effort to interpret curriculum situations and the results of curriculum deliberation could result in a body of precedent similar to that used in the legal profession as a basis for judgment.

As important as this could be, still more important and too subtle to record are the daily interactions of teachers and learners in educational situations. In the final analysis, the essence of practical inquiry is the art-science of deriving increasingly greater insight, and acting on the goodness and justice embodied within it.

SUGGESTED READING

The best sources to read on practical inquiry in education are written by John Dewey and Joseph Schwab. Dewey's work in both philosophy and education consistently supports as ideal the everyday character of excellent problem solving. *Democracy and Education* (Dewey, 1916) is the best thorough statement of Dewey's position on education and its relation to democratic inquiry. In *How We Think*, Dewey (1910) elaborates the problem-solving process. In Dewey's most philosophical rendition of his position on practical inquiry, *Logic, The Theory of Inquiry* (1938b), he sets forth a notion of logic as the theory of ways in which people solve problems and meet their needs. In this book as well as in *How We Think*, Dewey delineated the steps that are now commonly referred to as "the scientific method." Probably his best brief treatment on the nature of educational research is found in Dewey's *The Sources of a Science of Education* (1929b).

Other progressive educators developed and perpetuated the notion of practical inquiry, although neither they nor Dewey often used the label. Standing out among the later progressives in this regard was L. Thomas Hopkins, who characterized a form of inquiry into the improvement of self and social groups in *The Emerging Self in School and Home* (1954) that draws assumptions from biological research as well as psychology and educational practice.

The major rekindling of interest in the practical paradigm and the use of the Aristotelian label are the result of three essays in *School Review* by Joseph Schwab (1969, 1971, 1973). These are now available in a collection of Schwab's essays edited by Westbury and Wilkolf (1978). In that book, one should see as well Schwab's essays on the nature of scientific inquiry and *eros* as the driving force of a liberal education. Most recently, Schwab developed a fourth statement on practical inquiry in *Curriculum Inquiry*, Summer, 1983.

One should also see the work of William Reid (1978) on developing a practical-humanistic discipline of curriculum studies, that of Lawrence Stenhouse (1975) on teachers as researchers through reflection and study of their own work and experience, early work on action research by S. M. Corey (1953), and D. Schön's (1983) treatment of how practitioners think in action. Reviews of literature on practical inquiry include van Manen (1977), Schubert (1980b, 1982c), Westbury and Steimer (1971), and Westbury (1972); and Pereira (1984), and Roby (1985) on the nature of practical deliberation.

The emergent literature of a phenomenological vein should be consulted because it provides a perspective on ways to describe and portray lived experience and deeper meanings that lie behind it. Foremost among North American authors in this area is Max van Manen of the University of Alberta, editor of *Phenomenology and Pedagogy*, a journal that characterizes phenomenology as "all those forms of thinking or inquiry which in some way maintain a perspective on the lived human experience. In the phenomenological attitude we creatively seek approaches which may yield a deeper understanding of the nature of pedagogy: the way we are to live with children or those, young and old, with whom we stand in a pedagogic relationship" (from the statement of purpose in the front of each issue of *Phenomenology and Pedagogy*). Among authors who contribute to this form of literature are those listed in back issues as authors and editors.

Along with those whose writing is phenomenological, alternative sources within the qualitative evaluation domain, especially Willis (1978), should be consulted for portrayals of practical educational situations. Work by Robert Stake, Alan Peshkin, Elliot Eisner, Egon Guba, John S. Mann, Robert Donmoyer, Elizabeth Vallance, Gail McCutcheon, Thomas Barone, and others does much to recognize the character of curriculum viewed practically and phenomenologically. In their vivid, sensitive, artistic interpretations, they serve as critics who can help readers (especially those engaged in practical situations) become better connoisseurs of their own educational situations; thus, such writing can add meaning and direction to lived experience.

RECOMMENDATIONS FOR REFLECTION

1. Reflect on your own work as a teacher. How well is this work characterized by practical inquiry as portrayed in this chapter? To what extent and under what circumstances does your teaching fit the practical paradigm? The theoretic paradigm? What accounts for tendencies toward the practical or theoretic in lives of teachers?

2. Reflect on your experience as a student. To what extent and under what circumstances does your experience as a student fit the practical paradigm of inquiry?

The theoretic paradigm? What accounts for tendencies toward the practical or theoretic in the lives of students?

3. Reflect on your everyday learning outside of school. How is it practical? How is it theoretic? Which predominates in what kind of situations? If it is one's tendency to learn practically in everyday affairs, should it also be one's tendency to learn practically in schooling? Or should schooling be more formal and theoretic?

4. As a teacher did (do) you think more about the categories of teachers, learners, subject matter, and milieu or about the perennial categories of purposes, content or learning experiences, organization, and evaluation? Why? While the first set of commonplaces represents the practical paradigm, does the second or perennial set represent the theoretic? Or can they both enhance and be enhanced by practical inquiry? Should these two sets of categories for conceptualizing curriculum be seen as opposites? Do they primarily contradict or complement each other?

5. What theories or bodies of literature make up the mainstay of knowledge that you draw upon eclectically to solve educational problems and meet needs in situations that you encounter? Give some examples of how you have (a) matched theories to situations, (b) adapted such knowledge to situational needs, and (c) developed new alternatives for situations that seemed to have no precedent in the literature.

6. Do you think it would be possible to develop a massive body of precedent for education that is similar to precedent in the legal profession? This might include detailed descriptions and interpretations of problems encountered by teachers and the methods developed for dealing with them. Such precedent might even be made available through a giant computer bank. Would this be commensurate with the practical paradigm? Would it be practical in the ordinary sense? Why or why not?

7. What could teachers do to gain greater knowledge of the "ecology" of learning from the culture that shapes the outlooks of their students? How necessary is such knowledge for teachers and for curriculum development? How could school systems provide support facilities that enable teachers to acquire such knowledge? How might students help to generate such knowledge?

8. Focus on your own school or educational situation in view of Figure 12-1. Interpret each cell of the matrix in light of the ways in which teachers, learners, subject matter, and milieu relate to or act on the assumptions of practical inquiry.

9. Focus on your own school or educational situation in view of Figure 12-2. Interpret each cell of the matrix in terms of the ways in which teachers, learners, subject matter, and milieu engage in the three eclectic arts.

10. Focus on your own school or educational situation in view of Figure 12-3. Interpret each cell (or selected cells) of the matrix relative to the influence of each of the commonplaces upon one another. How well does the resultant depiction characterize the curriculum that influences learners in your situation? Is anything important omitted? Are any additional categories needed?

11. Look again at the sample questions listed in the discussion of cells one through sixteen of the matrix in Figure 12-3. What kinds of questions would you add to each cell or selected cells? Think of questions that might help you gain more insight into your own educational circumstances.

12. What is your assessment of each guest commentator's response to the practical paradigm? With whom do you agree most? Least? Why?

13. Identify the best teachers whom you have known: elementary? secondary? college? nonschool? List three to five salient characteristics of each. What made them good teachers? Were they more practical or theoretic? Compare your list of characteristics with any published report of the research on teaching literature.

14. What would need to be done for educational practice and scholarship to move more fully into the practical domain? Could this be done?

15. What do you see as the main strengths and weaknesses of the theoretic paradigm? Practical paradigm? Perennial curriculum categories? Practical curriculum categories?

16. What kind of inquiry, practical or theoretic, helps you derive meaning and goodness from daily experience? List some of the most meaningful nonschool learning experiences that you have encountered. Were they more practical or theoretic in character? Were they a blend of the two or were they different from either? Please explain. What implications does this analysis have for curriculum theory and practice?

13

✦ Paradigm of Critical Praxis ✦

Why should there not be a patient confidence in the ultimate justice of the people? Is there any better or equal hope in the world?

ABRAHAM LINCOLN *First Inaugural Address* (March 4, 1861)

I am the people—the mob—the crowd—the mass. Do you know that all the great work of the world is done through me?

CARL SANDBURG "I Am the People, the Mob" *Complete Poems* (1950)

Justice is the great interest of man on earth.

DANIEL WEBSTER "On Mr. Justice Story" (September 12, 1845)

Rebellion, in man, is the refusal to be treated as an object and to be reduced to simple historical terms. It is the affirmation of a nature common to all men, which eludes the world of power.

ALBERT CAMUS *The Rebel* (1954)

No pedagogy that is truly liberating can remain distant from the oppressed by treating them as unfortunates and by presenting for their emulation models from among the oppressors.

PAULO FREIRE *Pedagogy of the Oppressed* (1970)

SETTING THE STAGE

Thus far, I have presented curriculum through the lenses of two paradigms: the empirical-analytic or technical and the hermeneutic or practical. The curriculum field has adopted, for the most part, an empirical-analytic orientation to knowledge. Because of the dominant influence and contributions of this orientation to the curriculum field, Chapters Eight through Eleven treated each of the four analytic categories of the Tyler Rationale: purposes, content and learning experiences, organization, and evaluation.

In Chapter Twelve, a practical paradigm was presented as another conceptual orientation to curriculum studies. Many interpretations of the technical, empirical-analytic interests are designed to "work on" others, namely, students, to ensure that a curriculum design molds them in certain prespecified ways. In contrast, the practical paradigm derived from Dewey, and more recently Schwab, serves interests of establishing meaning and direction amid a continuous flow of problems encountered in educational situations. The practical orientation sees curriculum as evolving from the educational situation rather than being predesigned and subsequently delivered to those situations. Thus, the practical is characterized by an interactive mode of social organization that engages teachers, learners, and curriculum developers in ongoing deliberation about their influence on subject matter, milieu, and one another. In contrast, the technical interests of the empirical-analytic paradigm, or what Schwab labeled *theoretic inquiry*, use a mode of social organization that is hierarchical, as illustrated by work situations. The work to be delivered is predesigned curriculum. Delivery is ensured by administrators and supervisors, who monitor progress, and by evaluators, who assess results of products that students become.

In this chapter, a third paradigm of curriculum inquiry is presented. It is labeled *critical praxis*, a term that can be used to refer to a unity of inquiry and action. This action-inquiry is political in nature; it offers a broad perspective on the meaning of educational endeavors within the context of economic and ideological life. It includes an effort to look critically at impingements of ideology and economics on human growth and development. Moreover, it seeks vigorously to point out inequities of educational access, opportunity, and quality, experienced on the bases of race, gender, socioeconomic class, and other differences. Not only does inquiry in this paradigm point out constraints and inequities, it strives to overcome them. In other words, praxis is a form of study that integrates political action with intellectual inquiry in search of understanding and justice.

At this point it is very important to emphasize again that the three paradigms sketched throughout Part II are not diametrically opposed to one another. In fact, it is possible to provide examples of overlap for all three. For example, although Tyler is credited with the rationale for an empirical-analytic mode of study that serves technical interests, it is quite clear that much of Tyler's own consultation on curriculum and evaluation (during the Eight Year Study and thereafter) was practical in character. He was concerned with the process of enabling teachers, learners, and curriculum developers to articulate sources of meaning and direction in their lives. The influence of Dewey on Tyler is evident to those who know him best (Strickland, 1984). Those less acquainted with Tyler's ideas and interests did much to translate them into a purely technical formula. This is not to deny that Tyler offered the perennial categories of his rationale as empirical-analytic topics; yet, it is to admit that Tyler also worked toward practical interests in the spirit of Dewey's philosophy of inquiry.

Just as Tyler is not a pure form representative of curriculum studies of an empirical-analytic mode that represents technical interests, it will be seen that inquiry advocated by Dewey does not serve practical interests alone. First of all, Dewey was not a phenomenologist; he did not draw heavily upon the work of Husserl, Heidegger, and others who strove to interpret meanings that lie behind and give impetus to the thought process and lived experience. If he engaged in the hermeneutic sciences, it was in an everyday sense. This is the sense in which hermeneutics (the interpretation of texts) is interpreted metaphorically as a continuous "rewriting" of one's own sense of direction while one "reads" the consequences of action and assesses the contributions one makes.

Due to its emphasis on assessment of consequences, this version of hermeneutics is imbued with a desire to achieve social justice. For this reason, it blends with the paradigm of inquiry to which this chapter is devoted—critical inquiry or praxis. The search for meaning and direction cannot be adequately conducted while focusing on a classroom or school alone. The lives of teachers and students, the sociocultural conditions of classroom life, and the subject matter to be taught are much greater than classroom life.

To understand the culture of classroom or school life, one must probe deeply and broadly into the culture in which those classrooms and schools have come into being. Critical praxis asks about origins of inequities in classrooms and schools and what can be done about them. Educators cannot be content to tinker with within-school problems in hopes of making a difference if the roots of those problems lie deep within the culture itself.

Today, critical theorists who are concerned with education ask such questions as

1. How is knowledge reproduced by schools?
2. What are the sources of knowledge that students acquire in schools?
3. How do students and teachers resist or contest that which is conveyed through lived experience in schools?
4. What do students and teachers realize from their school experiences? In other words, what impact does school have on their outlooks?
5. Whose interests are served by outlooks and skills fostered by schooling?
6. When served, do these interests move more in the direction of emancipation, equity, and social justice, or do they move in the opposite direction?
7. How can students be empowered to attain greater liberation, equity, and social justice through schooling?

A number of curriculum scholars in the 1970s and 1980s have been raising questions of this kind. Foremost among them are Michael Apple (1979, 1982a,b, and 1983 with Weis), William Pinar (1974, 1975, and 1976 with Grumet), and Henry Giroux (1980, 1983, and 1981 with Penna and Pinar). Sometimes these and other writers are referred to as *reconceptualists*, a loosely defined term used to designate curricularists whose theorizing stems from a number of nonmainstream sources and falls to the left of center on the political spectrum. Similar questions were raised in more popular education literature of the 1960s by such authors as Jonathan Kozol, John Holt, George Dennison, and Herb Kohl. The questioning of education that runs through the topic of schools back into the nature of society and culture itself, however, is not without precedent in the curriculum field. Many of those who followed John Dewey's ideas in the progressive education movement from the 1920s and 1930s took the stand that education should critique and reconstruct society.

In this chapter, ways are considered in which proponents of reconstruction and reconceptualization have developed curriculum orientations that build upon assumptions of praxis in the critical paradigm of inquiry. After such assumptions are sketched, their relevance to the foregoing questions is discussed.

CRITICAL THEORISTS, RECONSTRUCTIONISTS, AND RECONCEPTUALISTS

The first important clarification to be made is that there is great diversity of viewpoint among both reconstructionists and reconceptualists. Some would argue that so great is the diversity, the labels should be dropped from usage. The fact, however, that certain similar assumptions about curriculum can be found within each of these groups is reason to continue their use. Moreover, I argue that between these two general groups can be found a number of common perspectives. This is not to say that they are the same but that they have enough in common to provide a strong alternative position on the problem of how to study and develop curriculum.

Reconsidering Curriculum Paradigms

Let us first review and elaborate the character of praxis or critical theory as a paradigm for curriculum inquiry that was sketched in Chapter Seven. How does it compare and contrast with the perennial categories of the empirical-analytic paradigm and the categories of the practical paradigm? As set forth in Figure 7-3 in Chapter Seven, the empirical-analytic, hermeneutic, and critical paradigms of inquiry or science (as typically referred to in continental European circles) can be contrasted in several ways.

Each of these paradigms should be viewed relative to its curriculum applications to both ways in which scholars conduct inquiry on curriculum matters and to ways in which all educators reflect when they ask: What knowledge and experience do and should people acquire through the educative process? The way we think about or conceptualize curricular phenomena has considerable impact on what those phenomena become. Therefore, it makes a great deal of difference whether the paradigm within which we operate tends to be more of the empirical-analytic, hermeneutic, or critical variety. If we translate these three positions into the language used in chapter titles for Part II of this book, we result in the relationship portrayed in Figure 13-1.

Any diagram or chart is, of course, overly simplistic. Figure 13-1 does not indicate complexities and divisions within each orientation identified, and it does not exhibit the great deal of overlap that exists among curriculum scholars and practitioners as they engage in curriculum study and development. However, the intended value of the chart lies in its clarification of the relationship between general paradigms of inquiry and those that have emerged in the curriculum field. The match between them is not perfect, but then what is on earth (except my wife)? I will now attempt to sketch some of the connections as well as displace some of the misconnections among categories that have been used in preceding chapters. Thus, this chapter is partially a summarization of Part II as well as a presentation of the critical paradigm.

I labeled Chapters Eight through Eleven *Perennial Analytic Categories* because purposes, learning experiences or content, organization, and evaluation are the main topical ingredients in the dominant way in which curriculum has been treated since the origins of this field of study in the early twentieth century. Topics studied as

Chapter	Title (Curriculum Inquiry Orientation)	General Paradigm of Inquiry	Interest Served	Social Organization
8, 9, 10, 11	Perennial Categories 8 Purposes 9 Content or Learning Experiences 10 Organization 11 Evaluation	Empirical/ Analytic	Technical	Work
12	Practical Categories	Hermeneutic	Practical	Interaction
13	Praxis Categories	Critical	Emancipatory	Power

FIGURE 13-1. *A Comparison of Paradigms of Curriculum Inquiry*

analytic categories cogently summarized and clarified by Tyler (1949) reveal the dominance of an empirical-analytic form of inquiry. Such inquiry serves technical interests; it provides a framework and mechanism through which curriculum can be designed as well as studied. A technical enterprise that develops and delivers service to a broad range of recipients is usually structured socially or institutionally according to the hierarchy of the workplace.

Chapter Twelve presents an alternative paradigm, one that has come to be known through the work of Schwab (1969, 1970, 1971, 1973, 1983) as practical inquiry. This paradigm provides a critique of theoretic inquiry, which is a mode of rationality depicted as empirical-analytic by Hultgren (1982), Giroux (1980), Bernstein (1976), and Habermas (1971) (see Figure 7-3). The label *hermeneutic* is a bit misleading here, because it is only by some stretching that Schwab's work can be considered phenomenological, which is the interpretive philosophy usually associated with hermeneutics. Originally defined as the reinterpretation of religious texts, contemporary *hermeneutics* has taken on a metaphoric use that refers to the ongoing process of reflectively interpreting the meaning of lived experience. If we refer back to the questions posed in Chapter Twelve on the interaction among Schwab's (1973) commonplaces of teacher, learner, subject matter, and milieu, it is easy to see that a broad notion of the hermeneutic is at work. Practical inquiry according to Schwab does involve the continous interpretation of lived experience, but it has more of an instrumentalist, problem-solving flavor than many contemporary educational phenomenologists accept. For example, Max van Manen, Loren Barritt, Ton Beekman, and Valerie Polakow Suransky hold greater allegiance to the kind of questioning or "thoughtfulness" that derives from Martin Heidegger, Maurice Merleau-Ponty, and Hans-Georg Gadamer than to that of the pragmatic philosophical tradition such as William James, Charles S. Peirce, and John Dewey.

The search for virtue and goodness, implicit in the Greek *aréte*, points the hermeneutic phenomenologists more toward praxis or the critical paradigm in curriculum literature. Such a search is implicit in Schwab's writing, especially in "Eros and Education" (1954), but it is much more explicit in the work of contemporary educational writers who work from phenomenological or critical perspectives. In other words, the hermeneutic inquiry of the practical paradigm in curriculum today is the act of creating and recovering meaning that enables the individual to grow in his or her own niche.

A major difference between the practical or hermeneutic position and that of critical praxis is that the latter assumes a state of more severe oppression of individuals in their niche that emanates from ideological and socioeconomic forces in the broader world. These oppressive forces inhibit educational growth. To the critical theorist, it is necessary, therefore, to expose these impeding forces and to take action to overcome them. Hence, the term *critical praxis* refers to an integration of theoretical critique of society and action or practice that seeks to improve society and the individual through education. While phenomenologists engage in a personal search for meaning and understanding, some of them are more committed to political critique and revision, and are often referred to as critical phenomenologists.

Critical Theory*

Central assumptions of praxis in the critical paradigm can be discussed by comparing them with the empirical-analytic and the practical paradigms. The interests served by empirical-analytic conceptualizations of curriculum are primarily technical, and the mode of social organization is that of the workplace (i.e., the business and industrial hierarchy). In contrast, the practical or hermeneutic paradigm serves the end of insight and understanding in situationally specific settings. In doing so, it uses the social organization of interaction in which participants engage in deliberation about the meaning of dilemmas faced and generate a sense of meaning and direction cooperatively. This sense of direction is then acted upon. Thus, practical inquiry is, of course, a form of praxis in its own right, but it differs from critical praxis, which focuses on large-scale social and ideological critique and revision.

Critical theory is directed in the interest of emancipation. Here, emancipation refers to a freeing of one's self to enable growth and development from the taken-for-granted ideology of social conventions, beliefs, and modes of operation. It strives to renew the ideology so that it serves as a basis for reflection and action. This requires modes of social organization that emphasize power. It is perceived necessary to empower people, whatever their station in institutionalized education, to question the value of such forces as the governance structures that direct their political life, the systems by which goods and services are generated and delivered that govern their economic life, the rules and conventions that define their social life, and the beliefs and ideals that contribute to their psychological life. All these forces both symbolize and combine to create the overriding ideology that critical theorists argue should be brought into greater consciousness and criticized. It is assumed that inquiry that results in criticism must be fueled by a value system. Such a value system can only be whole if it holds a conception of social justice. It is further assumed that the conception of justice and the values upon which inquiry is based must be ex-

---

*While *critical theory* specifically refers to the Frankfurt school, I also use it in a broader sense as characterized here and in Chapter 7.

plicated by all engaged in curriculum inquiry and development (Macdonald, 1977a).

This offers a stark contrast to the empirical-analytic paradigm that assumes that knowledge is value free and accepts social reality as it is, instead of asking what it might be, as would be foremost on the mind of one inquiring in the interest of emancipation. On the latter point, the practical inquirer, who has strong ties to hermeneutic phenomenology, would want to know what lies behind the surface structure of that which reality seems to be. What, for example, lies at the heart of the human psyche that impels one to be pedagogic? Could it be a parenting impulse that lies deep within the essence of humanity and symbolizes the desire to perpetuate humankind? Many critical theorists are compelled to ask such questions. Thus, the critique of ideology runs much deeper than mere aversion to one form of governance, say, and the implantation of another.

The critical inquirer also draws heavily from the practical assumption that knowledge of reality is intersubjectively constructed meanings created within an historical, political, and social context. If the ideology that propels a society is itself created rather than received, it follows that it can be re-created. The assumption that humans are creators of knowledge, culture, and thus ideology is sharply contradictory to the empirical-analytic assumption that knowledge is received by the masses from credentialed experts who have used value-free methods of inquiry. Proponents of critical theory argue that this assumption itself belies the value-laden nature of the empirical-analytic paradigm. It accepts principles of credentialed certainty and thereby asserts control over those who receive (i.e., those who are placed in the role of learner).

Accepting the status of learner is something that is not a mere matter of free choice within one's niche. Rather, it is forced upon all but the economically elite in a competitively oriented society where one must be credentialed with diplomas and certificates to survive. To take this example of critical argument a bit further, people become enslaved by participation in a highly capitalist system. They soon value their certificates to the point that the symbols of intelligence become reified or take on a life of their own. The person begins to turn not to his or her own resources and those with whom he or she is intimately involved, but to credentialed experts, and eventually prefers existence as a passive recipient—he or she becomes a patient, a client, a student (as folk educator Terry Doran puts it). It is the false consciousness of this form of existence that the critical theorist seeks to expose, and from it that emancipation is sought. The need, then, is to foster a spirit of what Maxine Greene (1978) calls "wide awakeness." This is a major aim of curriculum from the perspective of the critical paradigm.

Today's tendency of some curriculum writers to expose the distorted conceptions and unjust values in any society that surrounds and gives birth to an educational system is not without precedent. While the recent (1970s and 1980s) impetus is often identified as *reconceptualist* (Pinar, 1975), a position labeled *reconstructionist* emerged in the 1930s and continued into the 1950s. I am not suggesting that reconceptualists are merely revived reconstructionists but, rather, that it is important to characterize both orientations briefly and note some of the well-known figures associated with each label. Labels, however, have an unfortunate way of pigeonholing people and ideas, and considerable variation exists within each of these loosely connected groups. Nevertheless, it is important to sketch the development of reconstructionists, because they offer much precedent for critical praxis.

Reconstructionists

A reconstructionist orientation clearly lies in the work of John Dewey. One might consider his *Reconstruction in Philosophy* (1920), which, like all of his works of philosophy, sees education as a crucial ingredient in the development of social and moral life. In *Democracy and Education* (1916), however, one finds Dewey's most thorough statement on the matter. He defines education itself as

> that reconstruction or reorganization of experience which adds to the meaning of experience, and which increases ability to direct the course of subsequent experience. [p. 76]

Herein we see an idea that, when coupled with democracy, points not only to the ideal of individuals reconstructing their own outlook, knowledge, and capacity to act intelligently, but to that of a reconstructed social system as well.

It awaited the Great Depression of the 1930s for the reconstructionist movement to have full-blown curricular implications. In addressing progressive educators—supporters of Dewey's educational philosophy—George S. Counts (1932a) set the context for reconstruction:

> No longer are there any grounds for the contention that the finer fruits of human culture must be nurtured upon the exploitation of the masses. The limits set by nature have been so extended that for all practical purposes we may say that we are bound merely by our own ideals, by our power of self-discipline, and by our ability to devise social arrangements. . . . We hold within our hands the power to usher in an age of plenty, to make secure the lives of all and to banish poverty forever from the land. [pp. 260–261]

Counts and others within the Progressive Education Association saw education as the only means to rectify the crumbling social order of the day. In his classic book, *Dare the Schools Build a New Social Order?* (1932b), Counts wrote of a different curriculum, one that would not neglect the basics and the disciplines, one that might look much the same to a superficial glance, but also one that would be infused and enlivened with a new spirit, a new social foundation. Later he characterized it as follows (Counts, 1934):

> Motivation would follow unwonted channels. The appeal to egoistic and possessive tendencies would be strictly subordinated; the emphasis everywhere would be placed on the social and cooperative. . . . No individual would be rewarded for merely overcoming or surpassing another. . . . The curriculum would be given a social meaning. [pp. 544–546]

In discussing the social reconstruction position, Michael Schiro (1978, p. 249) identifies three central assumptions: (1) that society is unhealthy and threatening to individual survival, (2) that something can be done to prevent the self-destruction of society, and (3) that education is the means to that end. By the 1938 meeting of the Progressive Education Association, a schism developed between advocates of child study (a kind of practical, problem-solving position holding the child as the organizing center of curriculum development) and proponents of social reconstruction who sought to heal social ills through education.

Probably the best rendition of the social reconstructionist position is provided by Theodore Brameld (1956) in *Toward a Reconstructed Philosophy of Education.*

Brameld identifies a wealth of characteristics of the reconstructionist position, beginning with a statement of precedent to be found in Utopianists from Plato and Augustine to "recent heralds" such as Karl Marx, Karl Mannheim, Bernard Shaw, Lewis Mumford, and of course John Dewey among others, including an array of poets, novelists, and artists. Brameld then discusses central beliefs or assumptions about reality, knowledge, and value. He situates human expression as a creation of cultural and historical factors and calls for an organismic epistemology (one that recognizes the vastness of the principle of interdependence). He offers self-realization as "the supreme value, encompassing all others" and identifies "this as the criterion by which we appraise and advocate the specific goals proposed for a reconstructed, and eventually earth-wide, democracy" (Brameld, 1956, p. 145). As educators seek to rebuild society toward this end, they must realize that their goal is to develop citizens who "possess maximum sensitivity, yet are capable of penetrating criticism" in order that they may be "constantly engaged in seeking and achieving agreement about the details and relations of the ends they desire" as they "continue their critique of past and present cultures and as they unify their actions in behalf of future goals" (Brameld, 1956, p. 167). The learning that transpires from such critique is "social-self-realization," the social emphasis being ballast that gives the individual stability through the culture of a group (Brameld, 1956, pp. 168–210). An educative process that is based upon a continuous quest for a better society is, according to Brameld, the best contributor to democracy. In the full exercise of democracy toward these ends resides the continuous growth of self-realization. Few authors did as much to communicate this position to teachers and curriculum leaders as did L. Thomas Hopkins (1954), who wrote of an IS curriculum organized around the needs that students experience:

> The IS curriculum celebrates the experiential. . . . [p. 211] The IS curriculum is biological and holistic; it deals with the whole pupil who develops through internal control of the learnings that he or she self-selects to recreate into the self for personal growth. . . . In other words, it is what each pupil can take from the teacher-pupil relationship to help him or her better understand and develop the self, for growth toward the highest possible maturity is the direction of all living organisms. [Hopkins, 1976, p. 213]

The advent of *Sputnik* and the curriculum reform movement that followed brought the termination of social reconstruction, firmly establishing the empirical-analytical paradigm. During the years that followed (the late 1950s, 1960s, and early 1970s), a few writers emerged who dared to question the mainstream that was then clearly of the empirical-analytic variety. Scholars who most compellingly took issue with this dominant paradigm were brought together and identified as curriculum reconceptualists (Pinar, 1975).

Reconceptualists

William F. Pinar, a young curriculum scholar in the early 1970s, sensed emergent discontent with the empirical-analytic paradigm that dominated conceptualizations of curriculum. He brought together both established and beginning scholars who shared criticism of this form of inquiry. Among the former were James B. Macdonald, John Steven Mann, Ross L. Mooney, Dwayne Huebner, Maxine Greene, Philip Phenix, and Herbert Kliebard (Pinar, 1975).

Philip Phenix, whose background is in physics and mathematics as well as theology and philosophy, argued that curriculum should be related to images of the common good (1961b), that curriculum theory and practice should be sensitive to a variety of realms of meaning (1964), and that transcendence of the mundane and taken-for-granted should be the *raison d'être* of curriculum (1971).

As early as 1957, Ross Mooney raised important questions about the attitude and orientation of the researcher, the ways in which curriculum research reflects assumptions about consumption and production inherent in capitalism and its impact on the human personality. Mooney also expressed realization that curriculum insight can be presented defensibly in different forms such as poetry (see Mooney in Pinar, 1975, pp. 173–174).

Maxine Greene has contributed greatly to the expansion of literature studied by educational philosophers, researchers, and curriculum theorists. Her early work (1965) explored contradictions and commonalities between the private vision and the public school. The literature she brings to bear on curriculum issues includes fiction and poetry as well as philosophy, all of which is a blending of existentialist, phenomenological, and pragmatic sources. Of particular interest is Greene's relating of the existentialist predicament of alienation to teachers (1973) and her call for a critical wide-awakeness that empowers educators to create curriculum or "landscapes of learning" that inspire praxis (1978).

James B. Macdonald did much to encourage a serious humanistic school curriculum by focusing on the meanings embedded in product-oriented language of curricular discourse from the empirical-analytic paradigm (Macdonald and Leeper, 1966). Later, along with Bernice Wolfson and Esther Zaret, Macdonald (1973) drew up a conceptual image of how schooling could be based on an ethical, humanistic dedication. Two years later, Macdonald and Zaret (1975) edited a volume that attempted to raise the consciousness of educational leaders and arouse their realization of the widespread (but often unconscious) use of schools to control the lives and thoughts of those who live in them. Contributors argued for the need to depoliticize schools and make them places where meaning is explored in the interest of liberation. It is significant that all three of the above works were written for members of ASCD, which is heavily populated by educational leaders in schools, because so much scholarly effort in curriculum results in books and papers that remain in the hands of scholars alone.

Macdonald's notion of *liberation* was not merely a catchword; instead, it represented the result of long-term attention to critical theory by the Frankfurt School of social philosophy, especially the work of Jürgen Habermas (1971). Macdonald (1975) pointed to the importance of emancipation through dialogue between teachers and students, with the latter being recognized as essential participants in the curriculum development process. Such dialogical processes were inspired in Macdonald's thought by Paulo Freire's (1970) work in educating Brazilian peasants by use of interactive discussions about cultural experience and artifacts. Such dialogue enabled the identification of needs and interests of students that existed at deep levels of consciousness behind the superficiality of overt behavior. In the 1980s, Macdonald attributed even greater import to this process of curriculum theorizing, which he claimed was akin to religious inquiry in its worth to educators and students who seriously engaged in it (Macdonald, 1980):

The act of theorizing is an act of faith, a religious act. . . . Curriculum theorizing is a prayerful act. It is an expression of the humanistic vision in life. [p. 13]

This religiousness of curriculum inquiry is sometimes explored directly through study of theological writing that provides insight for human transcendence and thereby empowers praxis (Macagnoni, 1984).

One can look at the work of Dwayne Huebner in a similar fashion. In fact, his critical and phenomenological work on curriculum issues eventually led to his early retirement from the Teachers College of Columbia University and his acceptance of a post in the Yale Divinity School. This is not to impute direct cause and effect, nor does it suggest that curriculum actually deals with religious doctrine. The connection to religiousness lies in the depth of devotion necessary to address questions about the kind and quality of life that one wants to develop in ways that bespeak of religious metaphors in educational language (Huebner, 1984). Huebner's earlier curriculum work dealt with such considerations as the incongruous dimensions of poetry and power politics in the curricular enterprise (Huebner, 1975b); the quality of human relationships (1963); the implications of technical, political, and scientific language modes for curricular thought and practice, and the need for ethical and aesthetic language (1975a); implications of the issue of human temporality for curriculum (1967); and the impact of political economy on human development and curriculum (1977).

Herbert Kliebard has contributed to a reconceptualization of curriculum studies through subtle and complex historical studies (1970), analyses of the impact of bureaucracy on curriculum theory (1971), a critique of the Tyler Rationale (1975), and studies of metaphoric language on curriculum thought and practice (1972, 1982b).

John Steven Mann's (1968–69) use of literary criticism as a basis for assessing educational situations and writings anticipated the emphasis of others a decade later, as did his call for a unique discipline of curriculum studies (1968). Both must be based on an education of curriculum workers for the political spheres in which they work and for the liberation that is their responsibility to empower (1970). This requires that curricularists become more widely acquainted with literature and praxeological experience that serves as a basis for criticism and reform.

These sources illustrate the diversity of perspectives that Pinar (1975) brought together under the rubric of *reconceptualists*. So great is this diversity that it is somewhat unfair to look upon any of these writers as part of a movement. From discussions with Pinar, I feel sure that he did not intend that homogeneity exists among those included in his book, those who serve on the Board of Advising Editors, contributors to *The Journal of Curriculum Theorizing* (which Pinar edits), or participants in the annual curriculum theory conferences sponsored in part by the journal. In fact, if there are commonalities among such persons, they lie in their unwillingness to be labeled, in their willingness to criticize seriously the taken-for-granted in curriculum scholarship and practice, and their intense determination to create curriculum perspectives that point to a better life experience for all members of our world.

As delineated in Chapter Seven, Paul Klohr (1980), mentor of William Pinar and a number of others who participate in activities that bear a *reconceptualist* label, identified nine points that help to characterize this new and pluralistic orientation to curriculum inquiry. It is interesting to reflect on similarities and differences between these points and principles inherent in the reconstructionist position of several decades before. It should be added that there was probably as much diversity between reconstructionists such as John Dewey, W. H. Kilpatrick, George S. Counts, Harold O. Rugg, L. Thomas Hopkins, and Theodore Brameld, as among those labeled *reconceptualist* today. Both reconceptualists and reconstructionists have an overall interest in *theorizing* (the process of continuous reflection) in contrast to the making of extant theories of the traditional descriptive and prescriptive variety. Most of Klohr's (1980) nine characteristics of reconceptualist theorizing describe principles of reconstructionist thought as well (Schubert, Willis, and Short, 1984):

1. *Both hold organic and holistic views of people and their interdependence with nature.*
2. *Both conceive of individuals as agents in the construction of knowledge.*
3. *Both draw heavily upon a basis in experience and value personal knowledge as well as public knowledge.*
4. *Both recognize the important resource that resides in preconscious knowledge.*
5. *Both draw upon a broader array of literature from the humanities than do most who work in the empirical-analytic paradigm.*
6. *Both value personal liberty and higher levels of consciousness.*
7. *Both value diversity and pluralism as means and ends.*
8. *Both advocate the necessity of reconceptualizing (or reconstructing) social and political operations or processes.*
9. *Both set forth new language forms to account for new ideas that could not be expressed in the conventional language of the day.*

One might come away from these assertions of commonality with the observation that reconceptualists might as well be called neoreconstructionists. However, this is not the case. Although there is similarity in the general adherence to *theorizing*, there is not sameness. Reconceptualist curricularists are situated in a different historical and cultural milieu than are reconstructionists. Because of this vantage point, they are able to realize different insights, and they are faced with different dilemmas. Seven of these differences illustrate special contributions of reconceptualists.

1. Current reconceptualists are conscious of the profound differences among paradigms of inquiry. To be able to articulate differences of intellectual orientations to inquiry is a big step forward from merely implying them, as was the case in reconstructionist literature. For example, Schwab's distinction between theoretic and practical inquiry, and distinctions between empiricism, analysis, hermeneutics, and critical theory (Habermas, 1971; Bernstein, 1971; Bernstein, 1976; Hultgren, 1982; Bredo and Feinberg, 1982) do a great deal to explicate epistemological bases of different forms of curriculum inquiry.
2. Critical theorists in curriculum, such as Michael Apple, Henry Giroux, Jean Anyon, Nancy King, William Pinar, Madeleine Grumet, George Wood, and Janet Miller, among others, have raised consciousness about the influence of differences of gender, race, and socioeconomic class on the reproduction of knowledge and quality of experience in schools. Given the lack of general social consciousness of unequal treatment based on race, gender, and class in

decades past, it is understandable that reconstructionists did not attend as carefully to these matters despite their genuine striving for social justice.

3. Reconstructionists, and the progressive movement that spawned them, shared with much of society prior to the 1950s a great faith in the power of science and technology to solve problems, or at least to set a stage of less drudgery on which problems could be more readily pursued. Moreover, many viewed science as a model for inquiry and scientific theory as a model for curriculum theory (see Herrick and Tyler, 1950). Today, the faults of empirical-analytic or theoretic inquiry that takes these models as the basis for developing curriculum technologies are well exposed. Limits and inadequacies as well as the strengths of empirical-analytic inquiry have been more carefully examined. The view of theory, not as a product but as a process of reflecting or theorizing, attends to the reconceptualist emphasis on *currere* (the verb, the act of experiencing) rather than *curriculum* (the product to be distributed). These differences in orientation are better understood by modes of inquiry such as artistic and literary case studies set forth by George Willis and others (1978) and by autobiographic interpretations illustrated by Pinar and Grumet (1976).

4. Reconceptualist emphasis on preconscious processes is given less attention by reconstructionists. Although something is said by Brameld (1956) about Freud, Fromm, and others of psychoanalytic perspective, Dewey, Counts, and other reconstructionists rarely tapped these sources. The introduction of psychoanalytic literature into curriculum discourse gives it a new character indeed, when contrasted to the previously dominant behaviorist psychology.

5. Many reconceptualist writers advocate alternatives to science that they assume are part of an overarching search for meaning that lies deep within human nature. They assert that the need for meaning-seeking is often obfuscated by the overly direct instrumentalist problem solving. Uncompromising attention to immediate problem solving, which occupies considerable time in the curriculum field, obscures the larger human context of curriculum. While Dewey recognized experience as the foundation for the context of beliefs that guide curriculum (see Willis, 1975), he did not fully anticipate the debilitating effects of institutional bureaucracy on the search for meaning and direction. Attention to this problem is foremost among many whose studies are critical and/or phenomenological.

6. While both reconstructionist and reconceptualist curricularists express praise for diversity, pluralism, and democracy, it seems to some that reconstructionists have a value agenda of cooperation and world government that leans toward indoctrination. Most reconceptualists would not support curriculum that hinted at indoctrination. In fact, many who espouse critical theory see as their primary mission the exposure of imposition of values and myths from one socioeconomic class to another, one race to another, or one gender to another.

7. Finally, reconceptualist writers carefully and rigorously draw upon a wider array of literature than do reconstructionists who are linked heavily to pragmatic philosophers and a much greater range of literature than that represented by mainstream curriculum literature that is dominated by behavioristic psychology. By drawing upon literary and artistic sources as well as

phenomenological, existential, and critical traditions from Europe, a rich, new diversity of perspectives has been brought to curriculum discourse by a range of reconceptualist authors.

PRAXIS AND CRITICAL QUESTIONS

In setting the stage for this chapter, seven questions were raised as examples of concerns of critical theorists in curriculum. Now that exemplars of praxis have been portrayed from both reconstructionist and reconceptualist positions, it seems appropriate to demonstrate the kind of perspectives they would be likely to offer teachers and curriculum leaders. One way to illustrate this is to reflect on each of the seven questions in an effort to reveal what critical praxis offers to those who develop and live curriculum in schools on a daily basis. What follows is written from an advocacy standpoint.

1. How Is Knowledge Reproduced in Schools?

Many educators take for granted that knowledge is knowledge and that it looks the same to everyone. Explorations by critical theorists indicate that this is an unwarranted assumption. Anyon's (1980) study of the relation of social class to curriculum experience points out that schools reproduce social class hierarchies and divisions by the different ways in which they teach students from different social classes. Moreover, there is a tendency to present differentiated expectations to students from different socioeconomic classes. Working-class students are prepared for passive, routine, and mechanical jobs in which their work is managed by others; in contrast, there is preparation for activities that require creativity, assertiveness, and self-management in proportion to increased socioeconomic status. Such messages come as much from the hidden as from the intended curriculum. Lower-, working-, and middle-class students, according to many critical theorists, are taught that if they study hard and behave well, they will be socially mobile. Yet few actually experience substantial mobility. As Willis (1977), Apple (1982b), and Giroux (1983) point out, this is not purely a deterministic process. It is one in which the personalities of those in each class are uniquely affected by modes of governance, beliefs, and economic forces. As a result, they mediate, contest, resist, and are ultimately affected greatly by ways in which knowledge and experiences are brought to them through schools. This is revealed in cogently argued interpretations of five kinds of school programs by Bullough, Goldstein, and Holt (1984), who observe that the dominant technocratic orientation to education limits the capacity to think and act; thus, it prevents cognitive, moral, and aesthetic growth that could evolve from critical praxis.

2. What Are the Sources of Knowledge That Students Acquire in Schools?

From the work of Counts (1932b) to that of contemporary critical theorists, the values implicit in the capitalistic system are held responsible in the long run for the kind and quality of knowledge students receive in schools. In the shorter run, textbooks deliver packaged, homogenized knowledge to students. Perhaps better than any other source, due to their widespread use as *the curriculum*, textbooks symbolize the capitalistic system in action. Publishers too often look to the desired rather than the desirable. Thus, they respond to superficial interests of potential purchasers in such matters as bindings, color photos, attractive covers, plenty of activities to keep students occupied, traditional content with which teachers are familiar, and noncontroversial content that prevents public protest. Thus, the marketing of textbooks, like that of mouthwash and toothpaste, often lacks critical dialogue that should accompany educational decision and action. Michael Apple (1984) has explored the political economy of textbook production at some length, and is currently completing a book under the title, *Teachers and Texts.*

Teachers are certainly another major source of knowledge for students. Most teachers are from middle- or working-class backgrounds; thus, the values that they exemplify and promote are of those backgrounds and constitute a one-sided orientation to knowledge. Knowledge is implicitly viewed as a commodity to be received by teachers and passed along to students. Little credit is granted to students' abilities to be knowledge creators or agents of their own learning and moral agents of their own behavior and directionality. Students who tend to operate in such modes are soon "set right," and they are taught to conform to rules and to accept knowledge kindly offered by those who know better. The students are taught deference to information prefaced by "*They* say this is so" or "*They* say that is so." The identity of the mysterious *they* is rarely divulged, though a kind of reverence for it is frequently promoted.

Students, too, are sources of knowledge transmitted in schools. They come to school with repertoires of experience. As individuals, students use these repertoires to mediate what they see, hear, read, and otherwise experience. Moreover, students form groups that develop a kind of subculture within the school (Sarason, 1982) or classroom society (Thelen, 1981). The norms, values, and conventions of these groups interact with the covert and overt messages of teachers to convey the actual curriculum that enters students' repertoires of knowledge, and this is often quite different from the prespecified curriculum.

3. How Do Students and Teachers Resist or Contest That Which Is Conveyed Through Lived Experience in Schools?

Resistance and contestation are not always consciously designed processes, although they sometimes are. Just as people from tropical environs who see snow for the first time cannot distinguish between different types of snow, curriculum developers who bestow curriculum materials on inner-city students accustomed to poverty, street gangs, and lives of unpredictability cannot adequately anticipate their responses. Middle-class teachers, who strive by "the rules" for a house and yard in the suburbs, have difficulty responding to lower-class students who must steal, fight, lie, and cheat in order to obtain both the material and psychological goods and services necessary to survive. Similarly, such teachers may not be fully awake to the fact that students from upper-class backgrounds have ancestors who have "written" societal rules that allow them to steal, fight, lie, and cheat with grace and receive positive feedback to boot.

Students and teachers also resist school knowledge and experience quite consciously and overtly as well. They have ideas of their own, and when they feel threatened or contradicted, they speak out as individuals or in groups. Students may band together to report a teacher they feel to be unjust, or with parental assistance, they may utilize the courts to challenge alleged inequities. Teachers send forth grievances through their unions or professional associations or, more informally, they may resist unfair administrative practices. Experience in any of these situations and others like them produces knowledge, by affecting the belief system of teachers and students. Case studies such as those provided by Apple and Weis (1983), Bullough, Goldstein, and Holt (1984), and Wood (1983) help to illuminate the process of resistance and contestation.

4. What Do Students and Teachers Realize from Their School Experiences? In Other Words, What Impact Does School Have on Their Outlook?

Despite the fact that it may be easier for curriculum researchers to look at observable behaviors as signs of success or productivity, the real outcome of curriculum lies in the mysterious realm of human consciousness. Curricularists have little indication about the impact they have on student outlooks; they operate in ignorance of the value of their efforts. How can knowledge about educators' impacts on student outlooks be obtained? Surely, the vast array of standardized tests available can tell us more than we know, if we would begin systematically to design a network of cognitive, affective, social, and psychomotor tests to give a broader picture of student educational health. However, vast holes exist in what tests can do.

More holistic and situationally specific knowledge can come from qualitative evaluation approaches such as literary and artistic criticism (Willis, 1978; Eisner, 1985), naturalistic and responsive evaluation (Stake, 1975; Guba and Lincoln, 1981) and phenomenological theorizing (van Manen, 1984a; Pinar and Grumet, 1976). Moreover, teachers who work closely with students need to develop greater ability to communicate with students, to see how they respond to the schooling experience. This needs to become as great a part of the work of teachers as teaching and classroom management, because it is impossible to teach students effectively when teachers and curriculum developers know little about them. A great need, then, is to put teachers in a work situation that gives them the time to get to know their students well. This in itself may require a radical restructuring of schooling as it is known today.

5. Whose Interests Are Served by Outlooks and Skills Fostered by Schooling?

Linda McNeil (1983) argues that teachers uncritically perpetuate schooling that values external credentialing more than personal growth or the acquisition of knowledge, meaning, and purposeful direction. She claims that this is done by a process that she labels "defensive teaching." Defensive teaching is the prevalent habit of teachers apologizing for making assignments to students. Teachers often note that they realize how busy students are, and therefore give them a summary of required reading or other abridged assignments. Inadvertently, they are saying that the appearance of completed work, grades, and diplomas are more important than genuine learning and growth. Thus, compliance takes precedence over critical self-development, and external control dominates.

When schooling is designed, developed, and conducted by uncritical educators, the interests of the dominant social classes are almost invariably served by the curriculum. If rules that legislators make are tailored to fit the interests of the wealthy classes, if public administrators promote and execute those rules, and if cases in dispute are adjudicated and interpreted by courts who owe allegiance to the wealthy classes, then, the very fabric of society itself is sewn by classes in power. Thus, those who by gender, race, ethnicity, and class do not fit with the ruling minority are granted less of the societal pie than are those who do fit. According to Bourdieu (1971), those who do not fit into power positions and strive to do so, must make their way through at least two of three avenues: (1) knowing powerful people, (2) acquiring money and property, and (3) obtaining official credentials such as diplomas, and so on. Powerful interests, of course, are rarely in the hands of those who occupy official positions in the public sphere. They are usually granted access to office by gatekeepers, who possess major shares of personal and corporate wealth.

It is better, according to most critical theorists, to stimulate a sense of justice through schooling than to perpetuate the myth of progress up the class hierarchy through hard work alone. A sense of justice would have the effect of equalizing all members at a comfortable level, thus eliminating class bias. Only then, when more equal footing is achieved for all members of a society, can there be hope of democratic functioning.

6. When Served, Do These Interests Move More in the Direction of Emancipation, Equity, and Social Justice, or Do They Move in the Opposite Direction?

When the interests of a greedy, self-serving, nonempathic upper class are served, it is clear that liberation, equity, and social justice are replaced by constraint, control, inequality, and injustice. Yet it is rare to find leaders who see themselves as operating upon the latter set of principles. Rarely is there a conscious conspiracy; at the same time, rules have a way of accumulating to favor those who make them. What appears to be in the interest of justice, equity, and emancipation is often its opposite. This misunderstanding in a class society derives from lack of interaction among widely separated classes. They live in the same society but seldom meet; they are part of vastly different cultures and institutions.

7. How Can Students Be Moved Toward Greater Liberation, Equity, and Social Justice?

Most critical theorists who work in curriculum see this as a primary goal of schooling, although they realize quite fully that it requires the support of the surrounding society to do this. There is a rather powerful faith, however, among reconstructionists and some reconceptualists that schools can initiate movement toward greater social justice.

If this process is to evolve, it must do so by modeling the principles of equity, justice, and liberation in the school. This means creating schools based on these principles, not merely schools that talk about them. Such schools would need to enable students to see the rules that govern their lives as problematic. They would need to be places where students could genuinely search for meaning and direction; not just as individuals but together, offering cooperative inspiration and assistance to both those who started with less resources, and to those who have more and believe it is due to the fact that they are more deserving. According to Sharp and Green

(1975), such curricular experiences must transcend liberalism or the usual image of progressive education to make problematic for students the penetrating impact of a complex, stratified society on their lives and personalities. It must be an education in which dialogue among all members of society continuously illuminates the practice of freedom and social justice, as Freire (1973) contends in *Education for Critical Consciousness*. Giroux (1983), in similar light, calls for "a radical pedagogy . . . informed by a passionate faith in the necessity of struggling to create a better world" (p. 242). This involves the kind of interest and effort that does not take place in the strident, control-oriented workplace, but through a continuity of experience and reflection (*praxis*) that Arthur Wirth (1984) calls *productive work*—the business of humans striving together, in harmony with nature, to "become persons again" who can create a society that perpetually renews itself through education.

COMMENTARIES

Social Behaviorist

I assume that since this is the last chapter on the so-called topic of paradigms, it is reasonable for me to clarify my own paradigmatic preference. This seems fitting for another reason as well: the critical theorists keep saying that we should clarify our value base. That is fine for someone whose writing is armchair speculation, political cajolery, or impromptu problem solving. But when I write, I write research papers; therefore, I value objective description, based upon empirically verifiable and replicable data, which I use as a basis to explain, predict, and control phenomena logically. In other words, my value base is to be value free. Of course, people who have value and policy agendas may use my services. I explain what is, and they decide what they ought to do. My work is technical scientific analysis, and it is empirical; therefore, I must have allegiance with the empirical-analytic paradigm.

As for the other paradigms—the practical or hermeneutic and the critical or emancipatory—I have little use. We have come a long distance intellectually since monks and rabbis added interpretation upon interpretation to religious texts. That image has little use as far as I am concerned, even when applied metaphorically to problem solving in specific situations. Why muddle through when you can systematically utilize the results of scientific inquiry?

The critical praxis alternative is just as bad, if not worse. It sounds as if the emancipation is to free oneself from having to do rigorous empirical investigation and conceptual analysis. What's more, the *critical* part is even more naive. All societies have classes, especially those that claim to be classless. There have always been the rich and the poor. In the United States and a few other industrialized nations, we have successfully—for the first time in history—created a working and middle class that is rather well off economically and culturally. This is in no small measure due to the fruits of science, technology, rugged individualism, and capitalism.

Schools are institutions within society, at best well-oiled parts of the societal machine. Educators cannot, and should not if they could, change society at will in their own image. If they could do this, they would be exercising the most hideous form of indoctrination in an exercise of power over the minds of children that far exceeds prejudices on the basis of social class, gender, race, ethnicity, and the like.

In fact, we may be bending over backward in some of these areas (but that is a personal comment, not one that represents other social behaviorists). Finally, and of utmost importance, these critical theorists write their stories, compose their poetry, and paint their portrayals, but out of it all comes no concrete plans that are operational and replicable. It is mere criticism for its own sake as far as I can see. The idea of praxis is a nice-sounding ideal, but in making theory and practice the same process, theory loses its most important function—that of explaining, predicting, guiding, and controlling practice. In an ideal world, practitioners would be experts in philosophy, research, history, and so on, and could qualify as the scholar-practitioners that advocates of praxis want. But I have news for such advocates—we don't live in such a world; practitioners need to be led.

Experientialist

I had hoped to have the last word because I feel so close to the idea of critical praxis, but the luck of the draw was not with me. In following the social behaviorist, however, I can try to refute some of the gross misinterpretations of that orientation. First, I should say that the social behaviorist simply does not comprehend what praxis is, or what critical theorists try to do.

I agree quite fully with the critical position and believe it to be both a logical and ethical extension of the paradigm of practical inquiry. Sometimes critical theorists are criticized for not having a complex enough philosophy (Bowers, 1984a). This critique may be correct for many who write in that mode, but their philosophy is developing. Let them evolve.

Meanwhile, I prefer to turn to Dewey, whom I believe to be the original critical theorist in the curriculum field. It is inappropriate to separate practical inquiry from liberation and critique when it comes to Dewey. He was a paragon of a philosopher, a sensitive practitioner, a social critic, and a radical activist rolled into one. As persuasive as Counts and Brameld were in their reconstructionist writings, Dewey was more comprehensive. The bookshelves of his works constitute an educational position that builds upon all realms of philosophy.

What is more, his philosophy of education is a thorough basis for praxis. A Deweyan philosophy of education is never complete except as developed and refined in the continuous flow of experience. The pity is that it has never been tried on a large scale. I am both a reconceptualist and a reconstructionist. I agree with Klohr's (1980) nine characteristics of reconceptualist thought and believe that Dewey would as well. As Haggerson and Garman (1981) indicate, theorizing is at once a metaphor, a method, and an act.

As for the paradigms of curriculum thought, I eschew regimented classification systems and would rather talk and think about what individual writers say than place them in categories. In fact, the same authors may differ because of the situation about which they are writing. If I must classify myself, I am both of the paradigm of practical inquiry and that of critical praxis. I am rarely in the empirical-analytic tradition because of the great rigidity that it has taken on in recent years. For example, the social behaviorist identifies values such as objectivity, parsimony, replication, and so on, and proceeds to claim to be value free. He or she lacks historical and epistemological perspective in a myopic tendency to allow only one vision of inquiry. Worse than all this, the social behaviorist fails to try to learn from researchers with differing views.

I want to add that the chapter was a bit brief on the role of the teacher and student in emancipatory pedagogy. The student as well as the teacher must together develop curricula (journeys of learning experiences). This very process of critically questioning oneself and the world in which one lives *is* the best curriculum. Students and teachers who do this do not follow operational definitions. They follow their intuitive insight into questions about the meaning and goodness that they can create. This kind of questioning and growing together is what makes a better society, not some predesigned formula to follow, which would be indoctrination. True reconstruction of this kind is within the Deweyan ideal, and it is the antithesis of indoctrination. It is indeed the harbinger of equity, liberation, and social justice, because of the continuous experience it provides in becoming responsible for the consequences of one's influence.

Intellectual Traditionalist

I am beginning to think that the social behaviorist is the real traditionalist here. Remember, I am an *intellectual*, not a political traditionalist. The social behaviorist is quite a political conservative, it appears. Enough of that!

As for paradigms, the notion is only mildly intriguing. I prefer the term *philosophy*; it is more comprehensive, whereas those who deal with paradigms seem only to treat epistemology (with a dose of axiology here and there). I am an idealist with some overtones of realism and scholasticism. I would rather not align myself with one of the paradigms.

The so-called critical paradigm of praxis has quite a tradition (and the ahistorical social behaviorist thinks it is new!). It stems at least from Hegel and Kant and remains the dominant orientation to inquiry in many prestigious European centers of learning. I recognize the importance of the critical position in intellectual history and ask those in the curriculum field who espouse it to become as thoroughly aware of that history as they can. Furthermore, I put one additional question to advocates of critical theory: What is the basis for your critique? In other words, what image of social justice do you have and how do you defend it?

One further point from the history of ideas: While there is overlap among critical theory, phenomenology, and existentialism in certain authors, they represent quite different intellectual traditions. This should be recognized, and the tendency to say all three in the same breath should be avoided, unless one is sure of overlap in a particular work or scholar. We can see important differences, due to intellectual ancestors selected, among van Manen, Apple, and Pinar, for example, despite their similarities along certain lines.

A very bright spot in all this literature is the intense concern for justice, one of the most problematic of the virtues; another hopeful sign is the willingness of a new breed of curriculum scholar (whatever the label) to probe new intellectual turf, especially that of nonanalytic and nonpositivistic philosophy, fiction, poetry, psychoanalytic writings, and the arts. I must add, however, that one need not be a Marxist to support a liberation ideology. Thomas Jefferson, Benjamin Franklin, John Jay, Alexander Hamilton, and others involved in the American Revolution strongly advocated a liberating or emancipatory praxis. In his 1983 presidential address to the

Association for Supervision and Curriculum Development, O. L. Davis (1983) eloquently brought this sentiment to educational practice by calling for curriculum that liberates students to participate in the deepest spirit of democracy and excellence. Thus, one can see a critical praxis both implicitly and explicitly present in the best of democratic theory, such as that provided by John Dewey in *Democracy and Education* (1916).

SUGGESTED READING

The work of Paulo Freire is one of the best, fully developed renditions of praxis that offers a blend of ideas and experience that appeals to scholars, teachers, and curriculum leaders. In an incisive critique entitled "The Problem of Individualism and Community in Neo-Marxist Educational Thought," C. A. Bowers (1984a) criticized many critical theorists in education for having incomplete philosophies, but notes that Freire is a prominent exception. Freire's *Pedagogy of the Oppressed* (1970) is probably the best example, but his more recent books, *Education for Critical Consciousness* (1973), *Pedagogy in Process* (1978), and *The Politics of Education* (1985) further develop his ideas. One of the few general texts on curriculum planning that deals with praxis for teachers and curriculum developers is Dale Brubacker's *Curriculum Planning* (1982).

Freire, in the foreword to a recent book by Henry Giroux (1983), *Theory and Resistance in Education: A Pedagogy for the Opposition*, called it "a book of great importance . . . [and] should be read by anyone interested in education, social theory, and critical practices" (p. x). Recent writings of Michael Apple go considerably beyond mechanistic and deterministic positions on knowledge reproduction. Too often, it is assumed that schools are rather efficient conveyors of the ideology that dominant social classes want conveyed. This inadequately accounts for the resistance and contestation that teachers, students, curriculum leaders, and communities offer. *Education and Power* (1982a) by Apple, and *Cultural and Economic Reproduction in Education* (1982b) edited by Apple, point far in this direction. Moreover, Giroux (1983) and Apple and Weis (1983) move further in the interest of practicing educators by discussing both how they do and might oppose this hegemony that faces them. Of particular interest to teachers is the Apple and Weis volume, *Ideology and Practice in Schooling*, a collection of cases of practice that indicates ways in which curriculum leaders, teachers, and students respond to and are imposed upon by ideology that penetrates their lives through textbooks, children's literature, aesthetic curriculum, classroom management, school structure, business education, and play. Overriding this analysis is a sensitive attention to the impact of gender, race, and class on classroom life and its relevance to economic, cultural, and political production of knowledge. Authors of contributions to the Apple and Weis (1983) book are also acknowledged for their other curriculum writings on these and similar topics: Jean Anyon, Nancy King, Landon Beyer, Linda McNeil, Linda Valli, Lois Weis, Joel Taxel, and Robert Everhart. Similarly, *Human Interests in the Curriculum* (Bullough, Goldstein, and Holt, 1984) provides critical interpretations of curricular practices that work against human emancipation and growth. Earlier work by Apple (1979) and Giroux (1981) should not be neglected as a basis for the above.

Publications of British and European authors have contributed markedly to thought of this genre, for example, M. F. D. Young's *Knowledge and Control* (1971), P. Bourdieu and J. C. Passeron's *Reproduction in Education, Society and Culture* (1977), and especially *Learning to Labor* by Paul Willis (1977), which gives a vivid account of the hidden curriculum taught to working-class students.

Two journals need to be given special recognition here because the articles they publish often are critical and/or phenomenological in character: *The Journal of Curriculum Theorizing*, edited by William Pinar, and *Phenomenology and Pedagogy*, edited by Max van Manen. To appreciate such writing, it is important to acquire background in these areas. Reconceptualized curriculum theorizing is introduced well by a range of articles in Pinar's *Curriculum Theorizing: The Reconceptualists* (1975) and by Giroux, Penna, and Pinar (1981) in *Curriculum and Instruction: Alternatives in Education.* (Both selections provide a range of articles by such authors as James B. Macdonald, Herbert Kliebard, Michael Apple, John Steven Mann, Ross L. Mooney, Dwayne Huebner, Maxine Greene, Philip Phenix, George Willis, Francine Shuchat Shaw, Henry Giroux, Alex Molnar, Madeleine Grumet, Anthony Penna, Ulf Lundgren, Thomas Popkewitz, Jean Anyon, Robert Donmoyer, and Stanley Aronowitz.) Further, Karen Mazza (1982) presents a useful historical criticism of reconceptualist inquiry in curriculum.

Writings by van Manen such as "Edifying Theory: Serving the Good" (1982) portray the character of continental phenomenological writing on curriculum, and "Creating Curriculum Knowledge from Students' Phenomenologies" by George Willis (1982) illustrates phenomenological writing that stems more from a Deweyan practical stance. Theme articles in *Phenomenology and Pedagogy* (Vol. 2, no. 1) interpret and explicate phenomenological writing and research for those who might wish to conduct it and/or understand it more thoroughly.

It is difficult to deal with reconceptualist writers of today, however, without background in the literature of progressive education, particularly the writings of John Dewey and Boyd Bode. Dewey's *Democracy and Education* (1916) and *Experience and Education* (1938a) are musts, and Bode's *Modern Educational Theories* (1927) is as contemporary as it was when written in its insightful, often witty, criticisms of fads and movements in curriculum and educational psychology. Dewey's work is the foundation for understanding both progressive education and its reconstructive offshoots by Counts, Hopkins, and Rugg. *Dare the School Build a New Social Order?* by George S. Counts (1932b) is acknowledged as something of a manifesto of the reconstructionist movement. In *Interaction: The Democratic Process* (1941), Hopkins argued that if schools are to engage students in democratic processes in preparation for democratic society, they must admit their role in continuously revising society. Again in 1954, Hopkins vividly showed that if the individual is to move toward self-realization, it is necessary that he or she function within an organic, growing group, the logical extension of which is the democratic society. While many of Harold Rugg's writings are reconstructionist, it is perhaps his controversial social studies textbooks that make his major contribution to praxis (as revealed in a dissertation by Schipper, 1979, and a paper by Donald Robinson, 1983). Finally, Brameld's (1956) treatment of reconstruction is the most comprehensive.

Those interested in more philosophical problems associated with critical praxis might turn to Jürgen Habermas's *Knowledge and Human Interests* (1971), *Theory and Practice* (1973), and *Communication and the Evolution of Society* (1979). This work is complex, especially for those without strong philosophical background; therefore, I recommend secondary sources. *Praxis and Action* by Richard J. Bernstein (1971) provides an excellent comparative study of *praxis* in the work of existentialists (Kierkegaard and Sartre), pragmatists (Peirce and Dewey), and analytic philosophy through critical theory derived from Hegel, Marx, and major figures of the Frankfurt School. The Frankfurt School is the major developer of post-Marxist political theory, including the work of critical theorists such as Marcuse, Adorno, Horkheimer, and Habermas; a concise interpretation of critical theory is provided by Raymond Geuss (1981) as it evolved within the Frankfurt School. Thomas McCarthy, translator of Habermas into English, presents a careful rendition of Habermas's critical theory (McCarthy, 1978). Finally, those concerned with the paradigm problem in curriculum inquiry should consult sources listed at the conclusion of Chapter Seven.

RECOMMENDATIONS FOR REFLECTION

1. Do you believe that you live in a society that has different social classes? If so, in what socioeconomic class do you classify yourself? What is the basis for your decision? What is the socioeconomic class of your students, currently, and in other schools in which you have worked?

2. Can you think of instances in which students whom you know or have known from different socioeconomic levels were treated differently in school? If so, what explanations can you give for this? Are the differing treatments inequities?

3. How do students whom you have known to be from different socioeconomic backgrounds respond differently to school? What are some of the prominent consequences of this response?

4. Have you noticed that students of different race, gender, religion, or ethnicity are treated differently in schools that you have known? Do the different treatments represent inequities? Injustices?

5. Do you ever find yourself in situations as an educator when you become part of differential treatment of students on the basis of class, race, ethnicity, gender, or religion? If so, what accounts for this? If not, why do you think some foster differential treatment? Is differential treatment categorically wrong, or only if it produces inequities?

6. Did you enter teaching because you wanted to exert a renewing influence on society? Do you know others who have done so? Is this a laudable goal or is it self-serving?

7. How do you relate to the notion of teacher as curriculum theorizer? Should teachers critique the society in which they live, or should they support it and teach what they are told to teach? Is it possible for people to criticize a social system of which they are a part?

8. If teachers are critical theorizers, how might it help their students? Hinder them?

9. What do you think about the assertion that reconstructionism perpetuates indoctrination? Read Brameld's (1956) account and construct a case for and against this assertion.

10. Which of Klohr's (1980) nine principles of reconceptualist inquiry do you consider part of your own curricular philosophy? Why do you accept some of his points and reject others? Which do you accept, by your actions as an educator, as well as by your philosophy?

11. Do you agree or disagree with some critical theorists who think that capitalism is detrimental to personal and social growth? Explain your reasons.

12. Would you want your own children to be taught by an emancipatory educator from the critical paradigm?

13. Identify the best teachers whom you have experienced as a student: Elementary? Secondary? College? Nonschool? List three to five salient characteristics of them.

14. Would you classify teachers identified in activity 13 as practical inquirers? Emancipatory theorizers? What are the implications of this exercise?

15. As a teacher, are you a practical inquirer? Are you a theorizer? Where do you stand on the claim that schooling should be emancipatory or reconstructionist?

16. How do you now align with each of the commentators: intellectual traditionalist, social behaviorist, experientialist?

17. What would teacher education need to include if teachers were to become more practical and/or emancipatory?

18. Or do you think that good teachers have always operated in the practical and emancipatory paradigms? If so, what contributed to these perspectives? What are the major inhibitors?

19. On a class list of students whom you know well, give each student a rating for each of the following traits using a 5-point scale with 5 being highest: *achievement* (How well does this student accomplish what he or she is asked to do?); *happiness* (How well adjusted does he or she seem in the classroom?); and *justice* (How fair is the classroom experience for the student?). Notice discrepancies among the three ratings for each student. What accounts for them? Notice discrepancies among students and patterns for the class. What accounts for them? Can you think of plausible, alternative explanations? How might you describe the response as a critical theorist? How might a critical theorist explain low ratings on social justice in particular?

20. Socrates condemned sophists because they requested and accepted payment in exchange for providing education. Today, all professional educators accept payment. A critical theorist might argue that such acceptance sets in motion a chain of events that makes the curriculum a commodity. Argue in favor of this position. Now argue against it. Which argument do you believe most?

21. Where do you stand on each of the seven sample questions that might be asked by critical curriculum theorists? To what extent do you agree or disagree with the responses provided to these questions in the last section of the chapter, just prior to the commentary section? How would you respond to the questions in the concreteness of your own educational situation?

22. To what extent should students engage in critical theorizing about the meaning and direction of their own education? To what extent should they theorize about the kind of society that is best and be encouraged to criticize the one in which they live?

23. Do you find your own thinking about curriculum matters to be more in harmony with (a) the perennial curriculum categories (purposes, content or learning experiences, organization, evaluation) of the empirical-analytic paradigm, (b) the paradigm of practical inquiry, or (c) the paradigm of critical praxis? If your own theory and practice is a combination, or if it differs from any of the above, characterize it.

24. How do the three guest commentators (intellectual traditionalist, social behaviorist, and experientialist) relate to the three paradigms (empirical-analytic, practical inquiry, and critical praxis) presented in Part II? Is there a direct match, primarily bypassing, or extensive criss-crossing and overlapping? Explain your assessment.

25. What is your own approach to curriculum inquiry as a professional educator? Do you feel that you have had essentially the same approach throughout your career? If so, is it due to consistency or stagnation or something else?

26. What plans do you have for growing in your capacity to inquire about curriculum in an effort to improve the praxis in which you engage?

PART III

✦ Possibility ✦

14

✦ Problems Facing Curriculum ✦

If way to the Better there be, it exacts a full look at the Worst.
> THOMAS HARDY "In Tenebris II" *Poems of the Past and Present* (1901)

Our problems are man-made, therefore, they may be solved by man. And man can be as big as he wants. No problem of human destiny is beyond human beings.
> JOHN F. KENNEDY Address, the American University, Washington, D.C. (June 10, 1963)

Whoever fights monsters should see to it that in the process he does not become a monster.
> FRIEDRICH NIETZSCHE *Beyond Good and Evil* (1886)

SETTING THE STAGE

Part III deals with three intersecting and interdependent domains that give possibility to the future of curriculum theory and practice. The first of these, the subject of this chapter, deals with curriculum problems and proposals. The second, considered in Chapter Fifteen, is the relationship between curriculum improvement and teacher education at the inservice and preservice levels. Finally, in Chapter Sixteen, promising directions are treated in a discussion of ideals and practices that give meaning and direction to curriculum, and aid in the resolution of problems facing the curriculum field. In short, if the possibility of improved curriculum in schools is to be realized, it is necessary that current problems and proposals be addressed. Furthermore, if the impetus for improvement is to grow, become more defensible, and remain sustained, there is no substitute for improved and continuous teacher education. Only with serious attention devoted to these prerequisites can the hope of fundamental change become a realistic possibility.

Throughout its history, the curriculum field has been beset by a constant barrage of problems that has inhibited the pursuit of ideal possibilities. Proposals for innovation from partisan interest groups also fall under the general category of problems. Problems might be classified relative to their emphasis on the three sources of curricular balance that, as noted earlier, can be traced to the work of Tyler, Rugg, Dewey, and others: students, subject matter, and society. For example, attention to student apathy and disciplinary problems focuses more heavily upon students than on subject matter and society. Nevertheless, at a deeper level, what we ask students to do may be derived from unquestioned societal conventions; thus, society may be more important to consider in these realms. Or, perhaps, the subject matter is irrelevant to student needs and therefore critical in dealing with matters of discipline and apathy.

Sometimes social needs are tacked on to the curriculum without taking anything away. Perceived social needs, such as the need for more jobs, fewer teenage pregnancies, greater prevention of drug abuse, and a higher level of competitiveness in the world market have resulted in vocational training programs, family life curricula, drug abuse counseling, higher academic performance standards, and consumer education. These become part of the curriculum along with more traditional subjects, making overcrowding yet another problem.

There is an historical trend from the early twentieth century when curriculum dealt with the presentation of subject matter to recent decades when schools are expected to handle major social problems as well as disseminate knowledge and cultivate the thinking process. When students, knowledge, and society change markedly, schools are expected to adjust curriculum to meet those changes. The "knowledge explosion" in the twentieth century, especially pronounced in the post-*Sputnik* perceptions of scientific and technological needs and in the current computer revolution, has brought a multitude of calls for change in the school curriculum.

Similarly, in the societal realm, increased perception of needs of the poor, the handicapped, those who do not speak the dominant language or come from a minority cultural background have brought great pressures on schools. Schools responded by altering the experiences or curricula that they provide.

Emphasis on social needs is often juxtaposed with attention to needs of learners. Responses have ranged from carefully listening to student perceptions of needs to providing more technical diagnosis of student abilities in areas that adults deem necessary. The results of attention to students have brought child-centered schools and open education on one side, and programmed instruction, life skills curricula, and continuous progress learning packages on the other. Thus, curriculum problems can be analyzed relative to their origins in an emphasis on society, subject matter, and students.

Sometimes problems are not so much a matter of conscious reckoning as they are blatant impacts. The openness of discourse and expression of feelings that characterized the 1960s can be seen in consequences that spilled over into schooling, for example emphasis on affective or emotional development, sensitivity sessions which promoted the open expression of feelings and personal values, and death education which symbolized the need to air our most fundamental beliefs. In the more austere period of the 1980s, we find spillover in the form of tougher standards, testing to ensure accountability, and an emphasis on more homework to provide more time on task.

This current push for basics, for example, is reminiscent of the post-World War II conservative "back to basics" movement, which in turn is similar to a basics movement that followed World War I. The increased attendance in high schools by out-of-work youth during the Great Depression required curricula that met the needs of the new student population. Today, the greater school attendance of poor, minority populations brings problems to schools that were essentially absent from schools a half-century ago, although these problems were always part of society as a whole. A vivid example is provided in a list published in the March, 1985 issue of *Harper's*; it compared discipline problems in schools between 1940 and 1982. The top five discipline problems in 1940 were talking, chewing gum, making noise, running in halls, and getting out of turn in line; in 1982 the top discipline problems were rape, robbery, assault, burglary, and arson. Surely, this is not only symptomatic of an influence of poor and minority populations, but of substantial shifts in attitudes, actions, and perceptions of American society as a whole.

The foregoing examples are designed to illustrate that one productive way to analyze curricular problems is to focus on the ebb and flow of emphasis placed on students, subject matter, and society. As you read discussions of problems throughout the remainder of this chapter you might attempt to mentally classify them as having origins and/or consequences primarily centered on students, subject matter, or society. To identify one as the center of attention cannot be the point of closure on reflection, however. It is necessary to ask whether the emphasis is accurate or misplaced. Moreover, it is important to defend your assessment on this issue. Should, for instance, a kind of equal balance always be maintained among students, subject matter, and society as the sources and effects of well-designed curriculum? Or, do certain circumstances merit a priority ranking among them? Or, should an absolute rank ordering govern all situations holding, for example, that students should always come first, then the needs of society, followed by subject matter?

As you read the examples that follow, you may wish to use this categorization to interpret and assess the significance of curricular problems. You may, however, wish to select an alternative or additional schema for analysis. Drawing upon the empirical-analytic paradigm, you might ask about the implications of a given problem for purposes, learning experiences, organization, and evaluation. Using the practical paradigm, you might assess the significance of a problem for its impact upon the teacher, learner, subject matter, and milieu, and upon the interactions among these curricular commonplaces. Focusing upon the paradigm of critical praxis, you might ask how a given problem or proposal affects and reflects socioeconomic class, race, gender, ethnicity, and age. Similarly, you might find it helpful to question the impact of a problem or proposal on the economic, cultural, and political ideology of the society in which it exists. A sound analysis using any one of these conceptual structures may begin with obvious relevance to one dimension of the scheme, but almost always reverberates subtly throughout the other dimensions. In addition to the conceptual schemes presented here you may be interested in developing your own basis for criticizing the problems presented for discussion throughout the remainder of the chapter in an effort to better understand their implications for curriculum and the entire schooling process.

Beyond this, one further point should be added, drawn from a powerful question raised by Seymour Sarason. Noting that schooling in America has been viewed as both a means to salvation and a scapegoat for the problems of the day, Sarason calls for serious questioning of the axiom that: "education best takes place in classrooms and school buildings" (Sarason, 1983, p. 5). He challenges educators to ask whether the axiom is defensible, and to be willing to address the possibility that this time honored value may no longer be true (or may never have been true). What if it is not true? He continues:

> *If education can better take place outside the traditional classroom in the traditional school, what do we do? How do we do it? Isn't this notion widely impractical? These are productive and fair questions only if you have concluded that schools cannot be interesting, intellectually stimulating places and that alternative educational settings must be seriously considered. The millennia-old view has such a hold on our minds that when it is challenged we retreat to what is familiar to us. The fact is that there are many ways to answer these questions. [p. 6]*

I encourage you to ask Sarason's questions in many ways as you read the commentaries on problems discussed. What problems take traditional schooling for granted? What ways of responding to the problems move beyond the axiom articulated by Sarason? And most of all, how do you respond to the problems and the alternative commentaries presented?

Using the Goodlad and Richter (1966) categories, I have identified two sets of problem areas for curriculum. The first set pertains to the instructional and institutional levels, and the second set relates to the societal and ideological levels. Instructional and institutional problems are presented first. While they often have their origins in society at large, the particular form they take is unique to schools. Such problems include apathy, discipline, standards, individual differences, basics, high-tech education, skills management systems, vocational preparation, brain-based teaching, mastery, teacher effectiveness, life skills, death education, drug abuse education, sex and family life education, consumer education, testing, accountability, bilingual or multicultural education, global education, mind-body education, and the school's responsibility for social ills. All of these instructional and institutional problems have curricular implications that depend upon the orientation of those drawing them. To illustrate these differences, comments are presented on each problem or proposal from an experientialist, social behaviorist, and intellectual traditionalist perspective.

Societal and ideological problems facing curriculum are broader cultural and philosophical dilemmas that have general relevance to humanity as a whole and indirect but powerful relevance to curriculum. Examples include the following: autocracy, poverty, inequity, indoctrination, ill-health, supression of inquiry and expression, nationalism, dissolution of the family, ecological imbalance, prejudice and provincialism, alienation, threat and fear, control and coercion, war, and greed. As with the instructional and institutional problems, these societal and ideological problems are responded to through lenses of the intellectual traditionalist, social behaviorist, and experientialist.

It should be remembered that both the commentaries and problems selected for commentary are samples. They are illustrative, not all-inclusive. Each problem topic is briefly sketched and followed by three commentaries for the institutional and instructional problems, and the societal and ideological problems are treated in an integrated discussion from each perspective. Clearly, discussion of each problem could be immense, each a book in its own right. The point is to stimulate reflection on the problems and to encourage attempts to interpret, analyze, synthesize, and assess them by bringing different conceptual schemes (such as those noted in the foregoing paragraphs) to bear on their illumination.

INSTRUCTIONAL AND INSTITUTIONAL PROBLEMS

School problems and proposals emerge and recede with social conditions, and they have a way of returning again for those who wait ten years or so in the profession. The labels may change, but many of the problems and proposals are perennial. In this section we look at a sample of these recurring problems and proposals in an effort to examine their curriculum implications from three different perspectives.

Apathy

Social Behaviorist. Apathy produces absenteeism, and that, of course, markedly reduces time on task. We need a structured system of incentives that will bring students to school. This is especially needed in our poor rural areas and in the impoverished ghettos and barrios of our inner cities. Once students are enticed to school, another system of rewards can be used to engage them in productive learning based on the best research on instructional design, delivery systems, and technology. Such instruction can be informed by research on motivation to reduce apathy in school.

Intellectual Traditionalist. Apathy is a perennial human condition that often stems from alienation. Poor teachers alienate students because they have little grasp of their subject area. They treat their discipline as information rather than as doorways to understanding and fulfillment. To reduce alienation, and thus apathy, students need to be exposed to teachers who know their discipline. Such teachers derive meaning and direction from their own study because they realize that within their discipline lies insight into the great events and mysteries of life. Teachers who realize this, and who enjoy working with students, convey this realization and joy to students almost automatically. This does much to prevent apathy.

Experientialist. Apathy simply comes from students honestly realizing that what is taught has little or nothing to do with their lives. The curriculum must be radically reconstructed so that it grows out of cooperative dialogue about how the resources of school can be used to help students overcome the problems they experience. People are not apathetic when it comes to creating more worthwhile lives for themselves. If schools show students that they can achieve more meaning and direction in their lives by participation in the curriculum, there will be no apathy or attendance problem.

Discipline

Intellectual Traditionalist. Students first must be made to pay attention; only then will genuine interest be possible. Fine music will never be appreciated unless it is listened to; moreover, it must be listened to with increasingly sophisticated perception. Intricacy of perception is basic to all realms of scholarly knowledge. Thus, attendance must be required for students to come to know the best that culture has to offer. If students are then exposed to teachers who know and love their subject, they should soon realize the great personal enrichment that a liberal education offers. At that point discipline will switch from required to self-initiated.

Experientialist.   Discipline is inherent in human nature. When students know that inquiry, problem solving, exercise of imagination, reading, and other kinds of study help them to meet needs and become better persons, they will engage in the most difficult work. The teacher's central job is to get to know students well enough to enable them to discover knowledge that helps to meet their needs. It is only when knowledge that is irrelevant to student experience is forced on students that discipline problems occur. Unfortunately, this is much of the time.

Social Behaviorist.   People are *not* born self-disciplined. One of the school's major functions is to mold the rather primitive child into a disciplined individual who fits into society. A variety of systems of reward and punishment can be orchestrated to accomplish this. At best, some form of behaviorist technology derived from the range of operant conditioning strategies available should be devised for each child. Realistically, resources and time do not permit this; therefore, schools must design behavior modification strategies that fit classes of students and subcategories within these classes. Teaching that is well prepared, direct, rather fast paced, and task oriented keeps students on their toes and interested.

Individual Differences

Experientialist.   How to deal with individual differences has long been a problem in schooling. To treat everyone the same is certainly not to provide equality. If we treat all students alike, their differences become exaggerated. What is needed is careful attention to the needs and interests of each individual and to each group of students. The latter is needed because every group develops a spirit or character of its own. Provisions for differences, however, should not be done *for* students. They need to participate in the process, not just for affective value, but because their insight contributes to better curriculum. Curriculum in a democracy cannot merely be designed *for* students; rather, it must be designed *of* and *by* students as well as *for* them.

Social Behaviorist.   The vast literature on learning styles that has emerged in recent years illustrates well one of the best ways to provide for individual differences. Students are given diagnostic tests, categorized according to their style or orientation to learning, and matched with appropriate instructional materials. The more sophisticated learning styles materials include comprehensive curriculum systems that integrate teaching styles, environmental organization, and evaluation methods within a programmatic thrust. This is only one example of the kind of systematic approaches available to deal with individual differences of many kinds. Essentially, they all begin with rigorous diagnosis, provide a program consistent with diagnosed needs, and conclude with evaluation that fits the program goals.

Intellectual Traditionalist. Individual differences are much exaggerated today in education. We are all human because we are more similar than different. All persons are concerned with birth, death, love, ambition, threats, hope, and other great ideas and forces. At the root of all individual problems and needs, we can find common ideas and problems. These are treated in great literature, and this is the reason the classics and the disciplines are of perennial value. They speak equally well to different cultures, historical eras, and socioeconomic classes. Hence, I dispute the emphasis on differences and argue that our attention should focus on similarities of a deep, profound, and enduring kind.

Science and High Technology

Social Behaviorist. Science and technology give modern society the greatness it has today. Yet it could be so much greater if children and youth were better trained in science and technology. This pertains to students of both sexes and particularly to females who have been told implicitly and explicitly that science and technology is not for them. Science and technology infuse all aspects of our life in some way or another. It is imperative that these areas be given highest priority in elementary and secondary education. Further, it is necessary that teachers have both an appreciation for and knowledge of science that excels the current level in the teaching force by far. They must teach students what it is like to think as scientists, and they must develop in students greater appreciation for the formative role of science and technology in everyday life. Such an introduction to science will push students toward jobs in high-tech industries. This is much needed for any nation that seeks to hold its own in the world of commerce and international relations. It is a good sign that the National Science Foundation in the United States is pouring more money into science and technology education again.

Intellectual Traditionalist. Sciences are clearly recognized disciplines. Physics, chemistry, biology, astronomy, and earth sciences are surely among the most respected domains of inquiry today. Unfortunately, we have a state of affairs that is considerably unbalanced. The humanities and arts have diminished because their market value is less in the business world (except insofar as television, popular music, and movies count as arts). The point is that technology runs rampant without imaginative and ethical direction. This can come from serious inquiry in the humanities. Perspectives of history, philosophy, literature, and the arts are desperately needed to give a sense of virtue, wisdom, beauty, and justice to technology and thus to human life.

Experientialist. Science and technology are important for the good that they can offer the general public. The sad fact, however, is that they too seldom serve the general public (especially the poor) because they are used to make the rich wealthier. This is the bottom line of the so-called emphasis on more "high-tech" jobs. High-tech jobs serve the interests of corporations primarily. Science should be reconceived as the method of inquiry that gives greater meaning and direction to human experience. It is this everyday notion of science that truly responds to the needs of *public* education, not the science of laboratories and high-tech corporations that cater to the interests of an elitist few.

Handicapped Learners

Intellectual Traditionalist.   Throughout history, the handicapped (mentally, physically, emotionally, socially) have borne the brunt of criticism, rebuke, physical punishment, and scorn. This is a terrible blot on human history. Great literature often helps us see our lack of compassion with regard to the handicapped. We do too much classifying and separation. We need more treating of the handicapped in ways that resemble the empathic relation of Nicholas Nickelby to Smike. As in the case of Smike, most handicapped persons can learn about the virtues of life along with others. All are handicapped in some ways. Only the most severely handicapped need to be set aside and given special treatment. Most can profit from the classics well taught.

Experientialist.   We can all learn from the experiences of others. Only when we meet and interact with others can we learn of their situation and needs. The subject matter of public education should be mainly the public itself. To separate people in homogeneous units is a disservice to what education can be. We can learn from the handicapped and they from us. Too many people are afraid to be associated with handicapped populations. We must learn from experience that they are not pariahs; handicapped persons can be as fully functioning in their own ways as those not labeled "handicapped" are in theirs.

Social Behaviorist.   No area of the curriculum, or education in general, has progressed as much as that of special education in recent years. In fact I contend that the twentieth century, especially 1950 to present, will be seen one day as the most revolutionary period in educational history. We have learned to diagnose and categorize a host of physical, mental, emotional, social, and behavioral handicaps. We have developed sciences for studying them and technologies for preventing and remediating such handicaps. The theory of behaviorism and bioengineering and pharmacological technologies have given sound lives to many who would not have survived or would not have wanted the miserable survival they would have suffered in years past.

Basics

Experientialist.   We have heard a lot of "back-to-basics" rhetoric in the 1980s, but we have heard little serious debate on what *basics* means. If we simply think for a few moments about what is basic or fundamental to important aspects of our daily lives (family, friendship, work, marriage, raising children, enjoying oneself), it rarely turns out to be phonics rules, math facts, spelling, and handwriting. This is not to say that these areas are unimportant; instead, it is to say that they are not key pillars in the grand scheme of things. Human relations, the ability to inquire deeply into problems, to identify needs and respond imaginatively to them, to attend to the consequences of action in view of personal and social good, and to express oneself articulately and artistically are much more basic than are the mundane, discrete skills that are mindlessly referred to as "basics." The schools would have a hard time "going back" to these real basics, because they have never been there before, except in certain rare instances.

Social Behaviorist. The basics are the building blocks of communication and cognitive performance; they are the modern correlates of reading, writing, and arithmetic. Yet educational and psychological research reveals that these and related skills can be taught more directly and efficiently than ever before. Cognitive psychology, behavior modification, research in the content areas, evaluation research, and research on delivery systems and organization development are prominent among the thrusts that enable children and youths to acquire the skills needed to participate in the society in which they live.

Intellectual Traditionalist. Basics in reading, mathematics, grammar, and composition can be taught by drill. Many so-called traditionalists have used this method, and to an extent it works. However, there is a better way, namely, the way that an appreciation for the value of liberal arts has been taught best since the time of Plato and Aristotle. This involves the student in a pedagogic relationship with a great teacher. Such a teacher tells the student about the wonders of culture, shows the student the beauty of the arts, presents science as a key to mysteries, and provides humanities as a door to the human mind and spirit. These are basics of a meaningful life on earth. If students are truly inspired to learn these areas, they will acquire the skills to do so without repetitive tutelage.

Standards

Social Behaviorist. One of the most important developments in recent years is the widespread acknowledgment of the value of educational standards. This does not mean that every attempt to provide standards is laudable. Nevertheless, the fact is that local school boards, state departments of education, teachers' unions, professional associations, and national agencies are taking an active role in developing standards and in judging performance relative to standards. There was a day when standards were used by accrediting agencies and that was about the only place. Today, more of those who are closely involved with situations to be assessed play a part in setting standards of performance. Human beings need the challenge of well-substantiated high standards to motivate them. Thus, experts who derive their expertise from sound research play a central role in educating policymakers at the local level.

Intellectual Traditionalist. Standards are implicit in the disciplines themselves. So long as curriculum is discipline centered, as it should be, the disciplines provide the rules of inquiry and expression. The quest for standards on the part of commissions located outside the disciplines (be it in the community or the political and economic arena) is a pseudoquest. To say that standards reside in the disciplines is not to say that they are static because every legitimate discipline has its own built-in capacity for renewal.

Experientialist. To require a certain number of minutes of each subject per week, a specified amount of homework time, "x" number of courses in a subject, and so on is to confuse standards and standardization. Standards are best when they are derived from personal responsibility of those who guide and assess their own lives. This means that the classroom itself is the best place for standards to be created. Students and teachers must see their work as the continuous refinement of standards that reconstruct and reconceptualize their lives together and individually.

Jobs

Intellectual Traditionalist.   The purpose of curriculum is to enrich the person intellectually. It is to help the individual become increasingly aware of the true, the beautiful, and the good. It provides a greater sense of equity, liberty, and justice and presumably informs action and creates better personal and social interaction. This would have the side effect of better job preparation regardless of the job. All jobs can improve when held by those who have a liberal education. The business world is beginning to realize this and is hiring more liberal arts graduates than those who are trained in specialties. A liberal arts education enables people to learn to meet new situations. But only in this way would I advocate vocational training. Vocational training should never be a direct part of general education. In addition, the job market should never dictate course offerings.

Experientialist.   It is good for students at the elementary and secondary levels to have exposure to a variety of ways of life. Jobs are part of our ways of living, so students should be exposed to jobs. This might take the form of classroom visits from persons in different lines of work, or it might involve on-site visits to various jobs. It might involve work-study relationships with businesses at the secondary school level. At the elementary school level, it might involve a playful, Deweyan reenactment of jobs in the classroom setting, such as the setting up of a community in which students take on occupational roles of different community members. All this, however, is never laid on the student authoritatively; if it emerges at all, it is from dialogue about the students' interests. Schools should not be job marketing centers. As a matter of fact, jobs (which are so emphasized by social behaviorists) may be largely outmoded. People need meaningful activity and a supply of goods and services to meet basic needs. Jobs soon may be an archaic way to get goods and services. Schools need to help learners question the value of mundane jobs and jobs that serve evil purposes. Likewise, students need to be encouraged to ask how they can contribute through worthwhile activities. The issue of jobs should be secondary to this issue.

Sociologist Christopher Lasch (1984a) argues that the current society in the United States, in fact, depends on low-caliber schools because business and industry actually need janitors, clerks, cashiers, and other service jobs that require few sophisticated skills; thus, the economic system benefits from poor schools, in contrast to "high-tech" needs pushed by curriculum reform reports of the 1980s. Lasch further points out that if education is to be truly reformed, it requires a reconstitution of society that gives primacy to all citizens, not merely credentialed experts, to make the most important decisions. This, in turn, necessitates a new conceptualization of self, fashioned on the interdependence among human beings and nature (Lasch, 1984b).

Social Behaviorist.   Schools exist to serve society. Society is run by the economic system, which means by the labor force. Therefore, occupational needs of the society must play a pivotal role in curricular offerings of schools. Students don't live in the idiosyncratic vacuums of their own lives. They live in a society; thus, their behavior must be responsive to the needs of that society. Often, students are not broadly aware enough to see these needs. Occupational demographers must help generate this awareness. Students need to know the job market. In our era to have schools that ignore occupational preparation is indefensible. Too many students have no idea of the range of possible jobs available, how to locate them, and the training they require. This should be a much larger part of our curriculum than it is currently.

Instructional Packages

Social Behaviorist. One of the most important innovations in educational practice is the instructional or curricular package or skills management system. Actually, I prefer the label *instructional system*. This is a cohesive, coherent set of materials that may include textbooks, consumable worksheets or workbooks, audiovisual materials, self-instructional tools such as programmed learning games and booklets, and computer software. All of this is organized around carefully delineated objectives, systematically described procedures for implementation, and evaluation materials that assess acquisition of the objectives. The best packages have been designed by expert curriculum developers, and they have been carefully field tested so that they arrive in a highly refined state.

Intellectual Traditionalist. Books make the best learning packages that I have ever seen; they are far more attractive and easier to carry than computers or audiovisual machines. Moreover, the great books are filled with far more wisdom than computer and multimedia packages. From my standpoint, packaged learning materials do far more to inhibit genuine learning than to stimulate it. Their acceptance and use assumes that an invariable sequence exists and that curriculum organization can be fashioned around it. Intellectual development, however, proceeds by all kinds of imaginative and intuitive leaps as well as by the logic of deduction, induction, and dialectic. Prepackages cannot possibly anticipate these and other modes of learning. Learning depends on the great teacher who can mold method and curriculum to intellectual needs of learners.

Experientialist. The real instructional packages are not skills management systems. They are people. Each person embodies purposes, learning experiences, orientations to scope and sequence, modes of instruction through commmunication, experience with learning environments, and perspectives on evaluation. These, however, are alive in continuously changing interaction with each other. They are an integral part of the teacher and learner. They are not discrete entities that one finds in the teachers' manual for skills management packages. Thus, the only meaningful notion of *instructional packages* is a metaphorical one; it refers to persons who share meanings, ideas, hopes, knowledge, and dreams.

Mastery

Intellectual Traditionalist. Mastery is always a kind of unreachable goal to strive toward in intellectual endeavors. In practical and productive work during the emergence of cities following the Middle Ages, systems of preparation for craft occupations consisted of apprentice, journeyman, and master. The master was the highest and most skilled member of the craft. The analogy to intellectual endeavors is good to a point; the pedagogue or master teacher should be an exemplar of teaching method. The problem, however, in educational practice is one of substituting credentials for genuine quality. Hence, we see master teacher plans, master's degrees, and so on. Too many parents and students unfortunately see salable skills as the most important outcome of education. True mastery, however, for teachers and students alike, is never fully achieved. It is always able to be improved through further acquaintance with great literature.

Experientialist. The intellectual traditionalist emphasizes great literature as the sole means to mastery, and also sets the intellectual apart from other aspects of human growth and development. The term *intellectual* itself is unfortunate because it rules out the emotional, social, spiritual, physical, and other dimensions of humanness. In reality, these are all integrated in the continuous process of reflective inquiry. Personally, I don't care much for the label *mastery*; however, if it is used, it should refer to ongoing self-development that should be the center of all educative experience.

Social Behaviorist. The point is seriously missed by both the experientialist and intellectual traditionalist. The term *mastery learning* has a specific, technical meaning. Mastery learning is a concept and practice developed through the brilliant research of James Block, John Carroll, and especially Benjamin Bloom. As with all great conceptions, much has been lost in some practical interpretations that use the *mastery learning* label in schools. Nevertheless, the central idea is that students should not merely be moved through curriculum without regard to the extent to which they acquire the knowledge and skills set forth in objectives. In contrast to traditional educational practice, students should be worked with in such a way that their individual progress is continuously monitored and furthered. Although some argue that this requires the ultraexpensive ideal of one-to-one tutoring, the pioneering work of Bloom and others (Bloom, 1981, 1984) points to methods of group instruction that approximate the effectiveness of tutoring in terms of achievement outcomes.

Teacher Effectiveness

Experientialist. What I am about to say does not fit the rhetoric of teacher effectiveness or effective schools literature in vogue today. But, then, what I say rarely is in vogue. Teachers are effective if they are able to get to know their students well enough to look deeply behind and broadly beyond their superficially expressed interests to perceive their genuine interests. Such teachers are able to enter into dialogue with students about sources of meaning and experience that will enable them to pursue those genuine interests, by helping them see the relevance of the disciplines of knowledge to their own growth and development. In essence, the effective teacher is one who is able to transfer the spirit of inquiry to students who take charge of their own learning and use many resources to create a better life for themselves.

Social Behaviorist. Again, teacher effectiveness is not an abstract concept treated only by the polemics of armchair philosophizing or by aimless experiencing. Teacher effectiveness and school effectiveness are sizable bodies of research. Major centers of research at Michigan State, Stanford, and elsewhere have studied teaching effectiveness and have identified characteristics of teachers and schools that are associated with (and sometimes argued to be causal of) higher student achievement. Syntheses of such research are readily available in the literature. What is more, good packages of instructional materials are beginning to be made available with characteristics of effective teaching built into them. Since today's instructional systems, if used as intended, are entire learning environments, I am not speaking of a mere book or package of dittos. Instead, I refer to an entire instructional environment, complete with print and nonprint materials such as learning games, computer software, and audiovisual materials.

Intellectual Traditionalist. The effective teacher is first a person who is in the process of becoming more liberally educated. He or she is driven by the image of excellence. Moreover, this person is a natural pedagogue; by this I mean one who enjoys helping others learn and has an intuitive grasp of how to connect knowledge with the intellectual needs and interests of learners. This is the art of teaching. Often, this involves putting the right literature in a student's hands at the right time. An effective teacher is one who introduces students to the great conversation of literary and philosophic giants, of great scientists and artists, whose insight has ascended to rare heights throughout history.

Life Skills

Social Behaviorist. The public should be very much concerned with life skills. What should curriculum provide if not skills to deal with life? We need more carefully designed research to determine what skills contribute to successful living in any society. If we would identify the skills that most successful persons in society possess, then we could isolate and reprocess them for children and youth of different ages and abilities. I suspect that we would find that basic skills of communication (the three R's), study skills (how to locate and process information), occupational preparation skills, skills that deal with the technology of ordinary living, and personal economic skills are most needed. People who are preparing to live in a society should acquire skills that contribute to successful life in that society.

Intellectual Traditionalist. The skill of successful living is basically the same in every society. Superficially, it is different, but one must probe beneath the surface to discover that human meaning derives from the skill in the arts, humanities, and sciences. Insight, knowledge, and imagination in these areas of inquiry enhances performance, decision, and action in the ordinary experiences of any society. It is a great mistake merely to train students in the conventions of a society. When this is done, as the social behaviorist wishes, educators take for granted the goodness of the society as it is. The alternative is to delve into the literature from other cultures and periods of history. This develops a basis for criticizing one's own culture. An educational system that merely imitates the culture in which it exists suffers from provincialism. A liberal education liberates one from the chains of provincialism. A liberal education is not a skill, but it educates the mind to be able to learn skills in yet unknown domains.

Experientialist. Life skills should not be viewed primarily as capabilities for the future. Any reasonable conception of life skills should deal with the present. Skillful dealing with present problems, needs, and interests is the best way to prepare for yet unknown futures. Students should look to their own lives now. Empathic and well-educated teachers should offer guidance in this process. The best skills are those of seeking meaning and defensible direction amid the flow of events and attending to the goodness wrought by consequences of one's decision, action, and being. The skill of growing a better life as an individual and in consort with a group is the overriding life skill.

Drug Abuse Education

Intellectual Traditionalist. While I agree that drug abuse is one of the major social problems among youth today, I do not believe it should be a part of the curriculum. Drug abuse is not a discipline of knowledge, and children and teenagers should rarely, if ever, be expected to study pharmacology. If the primary disciplines among the arts, sciences, and humanities are taught well, I submit that society's young will have their sight turned toward virtue. This will do much to counteract a plethora of social problems. It is precisely the number and expansiveness of social problems such as drug abuse that can lead to a terribly watered-down curriculum. If schools try to provide courses to combat every serious social problem, the curriculum becomes unmanageable and lacks purpose. To a large extent, this is what is happening today. Schools cannot be the creators of solutions to social problems by confronting them face to face. Schools must try to create wise and virtuous human beings; in the long run, this will address a multitude of social problems.

Experientialist. Drug abuse is clearly a growing problem among children and youth. It once was relegated mainly to larger cities, but it is quite widespread. Thus, if students are involved with drugs, have questions about them, or just want to talk about the peer pressure associated with them, schools should provide opportunity to pursue this interest. Doing so is commensurate with the principle of beginning where the learner is. Drug education could be an excellent center from which to organize the curriculum. It is easy to see that all disciplines can be applied to drugs. The social studies implications are great; the scientific aspects are an obvious necessity; music, art, and literature abound on the topic. It is indeed a rich area for study, and it has the added advantage of involving teacher and student in a guidance-oriented form of dialogue.

Social Behaviorist. The market of instructional materials already has a number of well-designed instructional packages on drug education. More research needs to be done on their effectiveness in reducing drug problems among children and youth; however, the testimony of teachers and principals (though this is subjective) attests to changes in attitude and behavior brought by such materials. This, of course, needs greater empirical verification, but it indicates that some schools are learning how to meet their obligation to help solve one of society's most destructive behavior problems.

Death Education

Experientialist.   Death is an existential reality that plagues all of us. Most people repress it deeply into the recess of their subconscious, only allowing it to emerge when serious illness is experienced on the part of self or loved ones or when a member of one's close circle of family and friends dies. Talk of death is generally sparse, even among the closest of family and friends. Little is known by the general public of the growing knowledge of how to help people deal with fears of death. For example, more should become aware of the excellent work of Elisabeth Kübler-Ross. The fear of death is generally relegated to the sanctuary of one's private imaginings, which can become unduly frightening and repressive. For this reason, it is better if a public forum exists in which private anxieties can be shared, probed more deeply, and explored together in a support group atmosphere. Schools should be such a forum where the most vexing human problems can be discussed.

Social Behaviorist.   One can teach about death as one can teach about any subject. First, objectives need to be clarified and the rest (activities, scope, sequence, environment, materials, evaluation) is engineered from that point onward. The only problem that I see, and it is a major one, is whether there is a public mandate to teach on this topic. The rather aberrant counterculture movement of the 1960s was a time when death education emerged as a part of what grew into sensitivity training and related movements. I think that time has passed, and it is clear that the public call is for basics rather than the fads of radical groups. We should respond to public demands if we are truly public schools, and I feel quite certain that if a poll were taken today, the public would overwhelmingly oppose teaching about death in schools.

Intellectual Traditionalist.   Again the myopic provincialism of the social behaviorist is exhibited. The human concern with death is anything but a fad! In fact, if anything is basic, it is death. Great literature and art in every culture clearly reveals that concern about death occupies a prominent place all throughout human history. Perhaps, along with love, it is the most written-about topic in literature. Indeed, the perennial nature of the topic of death is what makes much literature about it classic. This, however, does not mean that I think that there should be required courses on death. That would be unnecessary to anyone who is pursuing a liberal education because of the massive attention to death in the literatures of humanities, arts, and sciences. Readings in such courses at the advanced high school or college level in history might use, for example, Norman O. Brown's (1959) provocative study of the psychoanalytic meaning of history, *Life Against Death*.

Family Life and Sex Education

Social Behaviorist.   Much of what is taught and learned about sex and family life occurs in the home and peer group. It seems as if many communities and cultures want it to remain that way. If so, this desire should be honored. The public seems to want the schools to stay away from indoctrinating their children in the realm of values. Clearly, family life and sex education can be fraught with values. However, it doesn't have to be. Values and facts can be separated easily in this domain. Parents and the public in general seem insecure in teaching the biological aspects of sexual reproduction, growth, and development. Both instructional materials and strategies have been developed and field tested in this area. It is important for schools to provide family life and sex education information either in specific courses devoted to this topic or as units of study in biology, health, and guidance courses at all levels. These courses, however, should stick to the facts and not impose values. Schools should, when possible, utilize services of medical experts in the area and should also disseminate background information to parents.

Intellectual Traditionalist.   It is naive, if not silly and simpleminded, to think that values and facts can be separated in teaching as the social behaviorist indicates. Values, actions, information, and misinformation about all human processes and events are integrated in great literature as they are in life. What is even better, sex is not separated from love and other value-filled emotions. Sex and family life education should definitely not be a separate course. It should be taught as it emerges in the teaching of humanities, arts, and sciences.

Experientialist.   No—I don't advocate sexual experience in laboratory settings in public schools! But I do realize, as do all sane adults, that our students have sexual experiences, and are often confused about them. These, and their family problems (which are indeed plentiful) are on students' minds frequently, if not continuously. Students don't leave their families, friends, and adolescent sexuality behind when they enter classrooms. Classrooms that ignore these important dimensions of children and youths cannot adequately relate to them. If anything is basic to humanity, it is family life and the love of children and adolescents for one another. Moreover, if this topic is ignored by schools, the prevailing disturbances in family and sexuality will be perpetuated through inattention, ignorance, and lack of empathic dialogue.

Consumer Education

Intellectual Traditionalist.   The only kind of consumer I am concerned with is persons who are connoisseurs of literature, the arts, scientific and mathematical elegance—in short, consumers and producers of beauty, truth, wisdom, and justice. Educative institutions should not be in the business of producing consumers who are good clients for advertising agents. Persons steeped in the best of culture become connoisseurs and critics of goods and services. They need no specialized training in it.

Experientialist.   Consumerism is part of daily life. Ralph Nader has done much to show how much the public is deceived and "ripped off" by rampant producers. Great need exists for curricular experience that enables students to be critical and perceptive consumers: not just in the future, but right now in their lives. Daily life is filled with consumer situations, from lunch money, to collectables that students may trade with one another, to the barrage of televised commercials that bombards them daily. Profiteers are everywhere, and schools need to prepare students to meet them. This means far more than comparing one roll of paper towels with another for durability, absorption, number of sheets, and so on. It is important to generate an awareness of the origins and consequences of producing and consuming goods and services. Such awareness does not derive from laying before students a diet of units of predigested, homogenized information. It must grow out of students' lives, needs, interests, and interaction with teachers and others.

Social Behaviorist. All the ideals in the world are for naught if they can't be put in concrete form. Students need particular skills of consumerism. They need experience in comparative shopping, preparing budgets, and setting priorities. They need to become alert to the use of specific propaganda techniques such as appeal to status, the use of technical jargon, and association with authority or prestige. It is quite clear that many high school and college graduates lack the knowledge of basic economics and finance intelligently to acquire housing, invest savings, and plan for their futures and those of their children. Indeed, courses are needed in these areas, and more abstract courses (such as economics, mathematics, and sociology) need to take on a more practical consumer character, especially for students who are not college bound.

Accountability

Social Behaviorist. During the past twenty years, great strides have been made in educational accountability, because evaluation research and educational measurement have advanced significantly. We now know how to operationalize objectives in behavioral terms carefully, verify their implementation in the activities that transmit those objectives, and assess acquisition of learnings implicit in the objectives. The latter is now enhanced by greater expertise of major test production institutions such as the Educational Testing Service. The point is that all major producers in the corporate world must be accountable. For them, it is somewhat easier because making a profit is the bottom line. In education, achievement test scores must be the equivalent standard, and they must be increasingly refined in terms of validity and reliability.

Intellectual Traditionalist. The acquisition of knowledge is the standard for all education. Thus, general knowledge tests are better than typical aptitude tests that focus only on verbal and quantitative skills. Yet tests themselves do not do justice to the breadth and depth of knowledge acquisition. It remains for artistic, intuitive educators to judge the level of knowledge acquired. It is great teachers, then, who must be accountable for the knowledge acquired by their students.

Experientialist. Everyone involved in the educative process must become accountable for the consequences of their action. This means more than technical achievement of whatever ends are set forth. It means a careful analysis of the value of those ends for the individual and society. This requires study by credentialed experts, but, to as great an extent, it necessitates the involvement of each person. Accountability is a matter of personal responsibility. Of particular importance is the engendering of a sense of accountability on the part of students, along with all others who participate in the educative process.

Standardized Test Scores

Intellectual Traditionalist.   Testing has become big business. Purchased tests are a substitute for serious thinking about the knowledge that is and should be acquired. Teachers should have the primary responsibility for assessment of student progress. Standardized aptitude tests can be of some use in determining who has a propensity to study an area. Similarly, achievement tests give insight into comparisons from place to place. But both these functions are overblown when compared with the ongoing testing program that should be developed by excellent teachers. Only they can tailor examinations to the liberal arts traditions that they have chosen to provide. There is, of course, something attractive about the European tradition of national examinations of the essay and oral variety. This, too, should be continued.

Experientialist.   The use of standardized test scores as the prime measure of productivity by school districts and researchers alike is a farce. The public and the educational establishment both have been duped severely by capitalistic entrepreneurs who have a rather shoddy product to sell. The sad fact, however, is that the public and many professionals have reified test scores; they have given them a life of their own. In discussions, planning, and interaction, children and youth are thought of not as whole people, but as embodiments of labels—IQs, achievement test scores, or even as persons of *A, C,* or *F* caliber. What is more, parents and teachers perpetuate that pseudolife onto their children. The children devalue other aspects of their unique identity, and are treated as labels instead of fingerprints.

Social Behaviorist.   We can't measure educational products in terms of dollars as corporations measure their profit in the quarterly report. The best that we can do, in the interest of objectivity, is to use standardized test scores. Granted, the tests are not perfect, but they are better than subjective impressions. Instead of throwing out the tests because they have some faults, we should work together to revise and reform them. We should probably turn to a broader use of standardized tests of various types (personality, aptitude, attitude, achievement, social adjustment, etc.), rather than continue to use a narrow version of testing in which one score provides the whole picture.

Bilingual-Multicultural Education

Experientialist.   Most nations, and a huge percentage of communities, today have within them persons of more than one racial, cultural, and language background. We have moved beyond the narrow ideal of a melting pot. We need to realize that individual and social growth is fostered by a cultural mosaic in which differences are seen as enriching. This is the origin of democracy based on dialogue. Democracy stagnates in an environment of homogeneity. It flourishes because of the ability to bring different backgrounds, ideas, hopes, modes of reasoning and expression, and experiences to bear on the ongoing consideration of how to create a better life for all. This spirit of creativity through pluralism must begin in the home and school at the earliest ages. Only then will it become fully infused in adult living at later stages.

Social Behaviorist.   It is possible, of course, to design instructional materials to fit any cultural or linguistic bias. This can, however, be extremely costly and time consuming. What is better is to identify the core values and ways of life that exist in a culture. Curriculum should provide these basics for all; then aberrations can be dealt with as needed to satisfy the social demands of different racial, ethnic, and language subgroups within a culture, region, or community. It is very important to realize that whatever the cultural or language differences, all should be judged relative to achievement of basic skills and knowledge of subject matter. In the final analysis, the same objective standards of performance must be used for everyone.

Intellectual Traditionalist. The great literary and artistic traditions are by their very nature cosmopolitan. The historical centers of culture at Athens, Alexandria, Constantinople, Rome, Paris, Moscow, London, and New York are examples of the joining of many languages and cultures. The literature, art, and ideas that have sprung from these centers represent great diversity. Thus, when one studies the classics, one becomes immersed in a multiplicity of culture and language. One will, of course, note that classics in the West suffer to some extent from noninclusion of the great traditions of the Far East, Islandic cultures, Latin America, and Africa. Our notion of liberal education would be more pluralistic, would exude greater depth and breadth, if these domains were included. Their inclusion is the major task for liberal educators of the future.

Global Education

Intellectual Traditionalist. It is impossible, in my view, to become more global than the kind of liberal arts education that I characterized earlier. In fact, nothing has so transcended idiosyncratic cultures as a liberal education. Throughout history, great artists, authors, scientists, and religious figures have moved far beyond the confines of their national origins. The liberal arts provide a global education that far surpasses flimsy political attempts to speak of world government. It is through the global character of intellect and the creative mind, not self-serving political and economic systems, that a global human spirit will emerge. Thus, curriculum programs that cater to the superficial interests of certain ethnic groups by providing instruction in their language and extra emphasis on their culture actually do a disservice to individuals who need a broader perspective, and in a practical—even banal—sense, need to exist competitively in a culture that is not of their origins. They need to learn the dominant culture and language as well as others.

Experientialist. Human experience is global. Despite differences in the clothing of language, culture, and convention, the basic moral, spiritual, intellectual, and physical character of human beings forms a unity. Time and again, people are surprised when they finally share a deep feeling, experience, or problem with others and find that they too have had similar experiences. When classrooms become centers of sharing and dialogue, and when schools form a similar hub for communities, globalism will not be far away. Global spirit comes from "walking in another's shoes" and from the empathy this brings. Compassion is the outgrowth of empathy, and compassionate consequences of action build global unity. Exchanges within schools, communities, states, and nations, and exchanges among them as well, are the seeds of one world—a world that remains diverse and pluralistic but one in human embrace.

Social Behaviorist.   There have been movements in history to establish world government. Soundly designed instructional units could be developed to teach about these movements and to enable students to develop critical thinking skills by which they can assess their pros and cons. Teachers and curriculum developers should not take a stance on this issue. If they do, they cease to present it objectively. They should only try to change behavior if they receive a strong societal or governmental mandate to do so. It is unlikely that this is forthcoming. If it were received, however, instructional strategies could easily be developed to convince children and youths of the desirability of a one-world government. The mass media and exchange programs could be particularly effective in this process.

Mind-Body Studies

Experientialist.   The usual linear way of learning is disintegrative of mind and body. Numerous sources are known to contribute to human growth and development by integrating the mind and body. Seldom are these sources used in education that occurs in school. Examples listed by Hendricks and Roberts (1977, pp. xvi–xvii) include the following: ecological awareness, honest communication, quiet and solitude, shared fantasies, meditation, nutrition, yoga, Tai Chi, relaxation techniques, movement expression, intuition, personal responsibility, and centered as opposed to scattered awareness. Realms of psychic phenomena, altered states of consciousness, dream sharing and analysis, and massage techniques are all worth exploring for their educational value as contributors to human growth and development.

Social Behaviorist.   Most of the so-called centering techniques have not been scientifically verified. A few, such as hypnosis and certain aspects of psychic communication, have been studied rather thoroughly over the past twenty years or so. Yet their educational value has not been studied thoroughly enough. Students should not be guinea pigs for radical educational techniques. One way to study new developments in education is not to grab hold of fads but to consult the best international scholars as Shane and Tabler (1981) did in studies of future educational needs in view of predicted societal changes. This is a more realistic approach. So, too, is the computer revolution and the kinds of head-hand development of powerful ideas in children that Seymour Papert (1980) has shown is possible through computer techniques known as LOGO.

Intellectual Traditionalist.   With the social behaviorist's propensity to revere science, I don't see why he or she doesn't advocate the study of neurological research on the function of the human brain as a means to understand the mind-body problem. I would. Beyond this, anyone who knows the history of ideas knows that the use of psychic powers, dream analysis, massage, prediction, and a host of mind-body integrations is not new in the twentieth century. Their origin, and in some sense their full bloom, was in ancient times—especially in China, India, and Egypt. It was well along in the history of philosophy that the dualism of mind and body was created and promoted. Only in recent times was the integration of mind and body rediscovered. It is still a major philosophic problem, one that is more complicated than current fads and expensive training sessions in mind-body centering give credit. As with other philosophic problems, the mind-body problem is in need of much historical and philosophic study, especially when one asks about its implications for education.

Feminist Studies

Social Behaviorist. More and more textbooks and other instructional materials illustrate a sensitivity to women's equity issues. The problem of women's equity is a major one in today's society. We need more and better instructional materials to enable students to deal with the issue objectively. To the extent that a society, state, or community mandates teaching a position on the topic, it is possible to engineer attitude and behavior changes accordingly.

Intellectual Traditionalist. Throughout history, women's views have been left behind. Whether this is due to time spent in child rearing, to physical domination by males, or to a less aggressive orientation to living on behalf of women, I am not certain. Sometimes I think that this whole realm of studies should become a new discipline, and at other times I think that feminist studies should become more fully integrated within each of the disciplines, for it has surely been omitted in most, and I fear that setting it up as a separate entity may not have the long-term significance that disciplinary strength may lend. Women's studies should not fall into the trap of being an add-on; these are too easily subtracted according to fashion or public whim. Finally, there are fine studies and creative contributions in every discipline that are about women and/or conducted by women that have been inappropriately suppressed. This should indeed be rectified and more should be created.

Experientialist. Experiences of women are in many ways fundamentally different from those of men (e.g., women bear and mother children), and as Noddings (1984b) argues, their sense of ethics and morality derives from an experience of longing for goodness, *caring*, in contrast to male-derived moral reasoning that focuses on fairness and equality. Men generally have not responded to the world and to fellow human beings with the compassion that women seem to have. We need to engage men and women in a great deal of more serious sharing of perspectives and experiences. Men and women need to compare experiences based on gender, learn from one another, and try to reconstruct a fragile and divided world. Zumwalt (1984) demonstrates that insights derived from the experience of reflective mothering have implications for reflective teaching. Miller (1982, 1985) drawing upon both a broad view of feminist studies and detailed interviews with women teachers, suggests that a new basis for reconceptualizing curriculum theory can be found in feminist world views.

SOCIETAL AND IDEOLOGICAL PROBLEMS

The attempt of a society to communicate its highest aspirations and deepest meanings to children and youths is a curricular ideal. Sometimes this ideal meets resistance from forces within the school system, and at other times, curricular hopes are dashed by larger societal, cultural, and ideological problems. Such problems include:

1. Poverty
2. Autocracy
3. Indoctrination
4. Ill health
5. Suppression of inquiry and expression
6. Nationalism
7. Dissolution of the family
8. Ecological imbalance
9. Prejudice
10. Alienation
11. Threats
12. Fears
13. Control and coercion
14. Death
15. War and possible extinction

These pervasive social ills are experienced in almost every culture. Curriculum, as both a purveyor of culture and as a phenomenon within culture, is heavily influenced by the broadest of societal problems. There exists a sense, too, in which curriculum influences society in return. Yet profoundly differing positions persist on the relationships between social problems and curriculum. To illustrate some of these differences, the intellectual traditionalist, social behaviorist, and experientialist commentators will discuss the bearing that the curriculum and the sociocultural problems listed have upon one another. Their discussion need not include each of the fifteen problem areas, and it may include others. The list is illustrative, not inclusive. The point is to portray some of the differences that exist on the too often overlooked relationship between curriculum and problems that reside beyond schools in society at large.

Intellectual Traditionalist

True to the Platonic ideal of the virtuous life, the supreme aim of curriculum should be to set students on a path toward virtuous living. This would be achieved primarily through reading and discussion. Through reading, one can develop a compassionate sympathy for those who suffer from poverty. On the opposite side of the coin, one can easily glean from reading insights into the nature of autocracy and its frequent contribution to poverty. This comes from both political autocracy and an autocracy of commerce in which those who have economic advantages control the rules of society and increase the suppression of the poor.

It must be admitted that all education is a form of indoctrination. We are conditioned to recoil in disgust when we hear the term *indoctrinate*. Yet, whenever educators determine what the curriculum should be, they have made a decision about indoctrination. The point is to indoctrinate toward virtue and away from vice. If that is accomplished, the society and individuals within it will both move ahead. Some will ask: What is virtue? They asked Socrates the same question, and his approach was to force the question to deeper levels. That in itself is progress toward virtue. This emphasis on questioning invokes the issue of freedom of inquiry and expression. This, of course, is necessary, but there is a danger of moving from freedom to license. This occurs when immaturity or unbridled aggressiveness causes a student to lack awareness of ways in which his or her exercise of inquiry and expression hampers that of others.

Ill health, ecological imbalance, and the dissolution of family life are problems in the contemporary world to be sure. Ill health has always been a problem, and the other two have too, although not as widely recognized. Ill health and ecological imbalance are partially treated in the disciplines of biology and geography. Other disciplines pertain more indirectly. Dissolution of the family is researched in sociological and psychological literature. These topics should remain in the disciplines; to teach them as separate courses, units, or minicourses leads to a never-ending chain of such topics, all with their special advocates. Controversial issues need the distance of dispassionate analysis.

The world has, unfortunately, a rich history of prejudice, threats, fear, and alienation. The best insights into these areas lie in the literature of every period. Existentialist literature of Kafka, Camus, and Sartre deals especially well with the problem of alienation. Such literature often deals with such problems as adequately as psychology, though it does so more indirectly. Nowhere better than in the great books are problems of control, coercion, war, and death portrayed and discussed. I refer as much or more to poetry and fiction as to philosophic and psychological analysis.

I do have trouble with two of the topical problems presented to us: nationalism and extinction. Nationalism can be as beneficial as it is detrimental. Just as the *bildungsroman* genre of literature, exemplified by Goethe and Schiller, strives for the glorification of the individual through learning, so too can national pride and glorification help humanity to grow. Sadly, unbridled nationalism has spawned wars, but I think the human spirit is too wise, too intelligent, and too good to obliterate itself into extinction through the kind of warfare that is now possible.

The major problem facing the human race, however, was not listed above. This is ignorance. Note that I did not say stupidity. Educators can combat ignorance by inspiring learning. I contend that nearly everyone is capable of pursuing a liberal education unless they are damaged organically. To be sure, they will engage in that pursuit at different levels, but it still liberates. It liberates because it changes one's guiding philosophy and points one toward virtue.

Social Behaviorist

It is too easy to note how curriculum might ideally affect world problems. It is not a useful response to refer to unreachable ideals; neither is it appropriate to bypass the effects of societal problems on educational institutions. Intellectual traditionalists and experientialists are guilty of both. In reality, societal problems in large part determine what can and cannot be done in schools. Research shows that one of the best predictors of student success in school is the socioeconomic level of the home. Poverty yields impoverished learning; so too do ill health and malnourishment, the offsprings of poverty. Poverty and economic problems are a leading contributor to the dissolution of the family. Yet schools cannot eradicate poverty. Schools are not nearly that powerful. What educators can do is provide greater public knowledge about the need for reduced expectations for children in impoverished areas. They cannot be expected to perform as well as children from more advantaged backgrounds. This, of course, does not mean that nothing can be done to help these children perform well later on; it is precisely the purpose of compensatory education programs to help in this matter. We have more data now from national studies such as Head Start, Follow Through, Upward Bound, and similar studies of local scope. We know more about the kind of instructional strategies that work with these populations.

Let me now turn to the other problems and begin by saying that schools cannot cure all of the ills of a society. This burden should not be placed on schools. Schools should deal with the core knowledge, skills, and attitudes that a society deems important. That is enough. The line should be drawn at that point. Many of the great social problems listed above are so value laden, and public responses to them are so varied, that it is impossible to deal with them fairly in schools.

Teachers can and should model appropriate behavior. This means that the school atmosphere should not be prejudicial, threatening, alienating, fearful, coercive, or indoctrinating. Teachers and curriculum developers should not go into detailed explanations of how these problem areas are and are not defined. Nevertheless, they teach by their example.

Some might say that this is a form of indoctrination, but if it is, it is not of a harmful variety. It must be remembered, too, that teachers and curriculum developers in public schools deal with the immature. They must exercise control and sometimes coercion; moreover, sometimes they must suppress inquiry and expression that is misguided or harmful. They exist as educators in place of parents. Thus, they cannot allow the young to run wild. They have to adhere to the societal rules and expectations in which they live.

I do have a bone to pick with the list of societal and ideological problems set forth. They may be problems, to be sure, but several of them also may be positive characteristics as well. Ill health is always a serious problem, but it sometimes brings learning. Similarly, people have their outlooks altered, sometimes toward greater maturity when they see death or when they admit their own mortality. This is not to say that it would not be better to bypass these realities if possible—certainly, it would; but we cannot. Despite the fact that we all wish we (and our loved ones) could live forever in excellent health, this is not reality. We learn from reality. In the same light, nationalism has contributed greatly to human productivity. Look at the accomplishments of Japan during the past thirty years, for example. Even ecological imbalance has its strengths. We would likely suffer more if humans had not transformed many forces of nature into controlled tools for technological advancement. We learn, too, from fear, threat, alienation, prejudice, coercion, and even war. There are necessary wars.

All this is to reiterate my stance that information, skills, and knowledge disseminated through schools should be as value free as possible. Both sides of every controversial issue should be presented, along with an analysis of pros and cons. Objectivity is the keynote here. Schools should, and can, present major problems and issues without the subjective viewpoint of the teacher and curriculum developer influencing the students. Realistically, not all subjectivity can be overcome, but neutrality should be the goal. The job of education is too valuable to allow schools to become a forum for editorials.

Let me return for a moment to research on these matters. We need to know more about the impact of poverty, illness, suppression, and the like. We need more research studies to demonstrate their impact on society in general and schools as institutions in particular. Knowledge of how these topics or forces contribute to society is invaluable background for curriculum designers and other educators. To serve a society through its schools, it is imperative that professional educators have clear knowledge about what a society perceives as its position on major controversial issues and world problems. To serve society, curriculum designers need to know what are the preferred skills, knowledge, and behaviors. This is a necessary basis from which to generate momentum for a sound delivery system.

In the long run, one further problem must be dealt with as a kind of culmination of all the others. That problem, well recognized by all politicians today, is jobs. To put the people to work on a large scale would reduce poverty and ill health and all of the attendant evils of our age. Only with everyone working can people be economically and socially in a position to be learning as well. Public education has the responsibility to provide a much greater degree of vocational preparation and guidance for all students.

Experientialist

The intellectual traditionalist and social behaviorist miss two absolutely essential points: (1) the inescapable need for education to change and improve society and (2) the embeddedness of schools in society.

It is obvious that these two points are head and tail of the same coin. Schools need to lead the society toward improvement; at the same time, they are a product of that society and reflect many of its conservative elements. This is a great paradox of how education should serve a society. Let us look at it relative to the ideological and societal problems listed.

Schools need to embody the highest and best aspirations of humanity. There is no way that educators can decide on what these are while remaining neutral. It takes values to determine oughts, and curriculum developers are in the business of deciding what students *ought* to have. The reasons for the ought must be justified in terms of a better life for all. This, of course, facilitates the values of democracy.

Democratic values make it possible to respond in principle to each of the large scale problems listed. Poverty and ill health are evils; when people are totally preoccupied with satisfying basic physical needs such as nourishment, shelter, clothing, and freedom from preventable illnesses, it is impossible for them to strive toward higher ideals and aspirations. Thus, educators should lobby to overcome poverty and illness; this means increased funding for research and action to diminish both. Autocracy, even when benevolent, is the antithesis of democracy. Schools should promote democratic deliberation in action as well as in word. Children are never too young to be involved in meaningful decisions about what they need. Indoctrination is the heavy arm of autocracy; people, including students, need to discover meaning and direction through study and dialogue. This requires that inquiry and expression be fostered, not suppressed. Expression of ideas is the basis for moving from individual reflection to family, group, and community deliberation. I emphasize family here because we need to propose a more inclusive definition of family that accounts for the variety of primary group life styles that have emerged in society to enhance everyday, practical inquiry and enjoyment. A new definition of *family* would prevent what now appears to be dissolution and would enable the recognition of other life-styles alongside of the traditional family that should be maintained.

Group, community, and family interchange of ideas should evolve to larger spheres—beyond the national—to world exchange. The planet Earth is too small and too worthwhile to be the center of petty nationalistic bickering. With the technological and nuclear power available today, such bickering and prejudice could lead to the extinction of the human race as Jonathan Schell (1982, 1984) so cogently points out. Contributors to such a horrendous possibility are prejudice, alienation, threat, fear, and the desire to control others. These are problems that need to be eradicated. To say that they have positive features is to compromise with the forces of evil and perpetuate a kind of living death on Earth that is worse, in many respects, than death itself.

I want to add, since the other two speakers added a problem, the problem I consider to be greatest. It is greed. Remember the story of Buddha sitting under the tree until the cause of human suffering came to him? That cause was greed, and I firmly believe it. The social behaviorist emphasis on jobs plays unwittingly into the hand of capitalists who seek personal and corporate gain with little regard to the consequences. These consequences are indeed massive. The poverty and ill health that they promote by taking from those who already have too little, and by the indoctrination and suppression that they foist through advertising campaigns, have a way of filtering into the schools. The unbridled control wanted over production and consumption finds its way into the conduct of teachers who, in turn, seek to control their students. I am not suggesting that a conspiracy is at work. Rather, the effects of greed coupled with inattention to consequences begets a social system in which ecological imbalance, prejudice, alienation, fear, threat, and control prevail.

As an institution within such a social system, the school is a microcosm or miniature universe governed by these values. Teachers become autocrats over students who are considered impoverished or possessing ill health in terms of knowledge, power, and values. The school competes with other schools in sports and academic achievement, much as nations compete for Olympic medals and economic supremacy. Students are treated as material in a packaging machine, where gears must be aligned and prespecified products turned out; thus, they are alienated and controlled by threat, fear, and coercion.

Educators can do something. By looking critically at the sphere of their work (classroom, school, or school system), they can see vast discrepancies between the ideal of democracy and the malignant social system that is emerging in its stead. Those who are fortunate to live a democratic experience in schools may take it from the microcosm to the macrocosm. This, I submit, is a possible avenue toward change that deals with ideological and societal problems. Its seeds are in grass-roots experience, and its effects can be global.

SUGGESTED READING

The possible reading list for this chapter is virtually unlimited. Therefore, I have decided to limit myself to one or two suggestions for each of the topics treated under the heading of instructional and institutional problems. Following this, I will relate a few more general sources that deal with societal and ideological problems.

L. Thomas Hopkins dealt well with the issue of apathy before it was labeled as a school problem. In his *The Emerging Self in School and Home* (1954), Hopkins shows how apathy can be overcome by starting with the students' lives and interests. The writings of George Dennison, Herbert Kohl, Sylvia Ashton-Warner, Jonathan Kozol, and John Holt move in a similar direction.

Many books exist on the topic of classroom discipline. Most are how-to manuals for teachers. While these can be quite useful, there is need for broader conceptual analysis of the sort that Laurel Tanner provides in *Classroom Discipline* (1978).

Individual differences is a topic that is treated in many sources. One might turn to Raubinger and Rowe (1968) for a fine collection of perspectives, to Robert Glaser's (1977) work on adaptive education, to the Eighty-third NSSE Yearbook by Fenstermacher and Goodlad (1984), or to appropriate sections in a broad array of synoptic curriculum texts.

Science and high technology again became a major item of discussion in the 1980s as it was in the post-*Sputnik* era. One would do well to consult periodicals from *Daedalus* to *Kappan* and *Educational Leadership* for a variety of writings.

Literature abounds on handicapped learners; for further reference, consult particular types of handicaps in the card catalogue, *Education Index*, or the *Thesaurus of ERIC Descriptors*.

This literature search strategy is the best way to find out about the latest proposals and controversies on such topics as basics, standards, teacher effectiveness, drug abuse education, family life and sex education, consumer education, and most of the other topics treated in this chapter.

However, I want to note a few particular suggestions relative to certain additional topics. On the matter of education for jobs, Robert Theobald (1976) argues that we need to think of a future society with meaningful activity for everyone, but jobs only for a few, or part-time job rotations for all. Everyone, he contends, should have access to goods and services, but they should not be contingent on jobs in a society that has communication and technological levels that enable a few to do the work of many. One need only read Studs Terkel's *Working* (1975) to realize that much work could be replaced quite readily by the search for meaningful activity, if education or human growth rather than money were the criterion for determining how one occupies one's time.

Some of the better evaluative work on instructional packages is done by the EPIE Institute as it continues its consumer service to schools on instructional materials. Marda Woodbury has produced some useful books in this connection. Eugene Cramer and I did a piece in *Curriculum Review* (1979) in an effort to encourage consumers to be judicious in selecting skills management systems. Some instructional systems build mastery learning into their formulas for sound instruction, but the work of Block (1971) and Bloom (1981, 1984) indicates the significant role of teachers who orchestrate learning environments so that group instruction approximates that of the tutorial. Life skills, too, are often packaged, which is ironic since they purport to enable the sensitive dealing with life's problems. In another issue of *Curriculum Review*, I have argued that deciding one's own purposes is a life skill too often replaced by consumer skills, job skills, basic skills, and the like (Schubert, 1982d).

One of the best sources on standardized testing is still Lee J. Cronbach's *Essentials of Psychological Testing* (1970), and *Crucial Issues in Testing* (1974), edited by

Ralph Tyler and Richard Wolf, airs numerous controversies associated with testing. One of the best statements on accountability is a speech by John Goodlad published by the Society for Professors of Education (1978).

I recommend literature on global education published by those involved in the World Council on Curriculum and Instruction (e.g., Berman and Meil, *Educating for World Cooperation*, 1983; and Overly and Kimpston, *Global Studies: Problems and Promises for Elementary Teachers*, 1976).

Bilingual and multicultural education has had wide treatment, but little directed study in the area of curriculum. An ASCD publication entitled *Multicultural Education* (Grant, 1977), a fine collection by Stone and DeNevi (1971) that treats five multicultural areas, and a theme issue of *Theory into Practice* (Richard Pratte, guest editor, Spring 1984) all study carefully this important problem.

Feminist perspectives are readily available in both the popular and professional literature. I suggest Carol Gilligan's insightful treatment of the differences between men and women, *In a Different Voice* (1982). I also note a Symposium on Gender Education published in the Fall 1984 issue of *Educational Theory* with participants including Ann L. Sherman, James C. Walker, Mary Ann O'Loughlin, and Jane Roland Martin and a book edited by Fennema and Ayer (1984) in the NSSE Contemporary Issues Series, entitled *Women and Education: Equity or Equality?*

On the problem of death education, the several books by Elizabeth Kübler-Ross are monumental (e.g., *On Death and Dying*, 1969). Many novels and poems treat death more sensitively than is possible in prose; I think particularly of James Agee's moving rendition in *A Death in the Family* (1938). The related matter of war is given new meaning by Studs Terkel's *The Good War* (1984) and Jonathan Schell's *The Fate of the Earth* (1982) and *The Abolition* (1984).

The mind-body issue and its educational implications are far reaching indeed. Gay Hendricks has done much to further insight into this area with *Transpersonal Education: A Curriculum for Feeling and Being* (Hendricks and Fadiman, 1976), *The Centering Book: Awareness Activities for Children* (Hendricks and Wills, 1975), and *The Second Centering Book* (Hendricks and Roberts, 1977). The latter has an excellent reference section for further reading on many related topics.

Finally, books and articles abound on education and macrolevel problems. I suggest *Educating for a New Millenium*, by Harold G. Shane and M. Bernadine Tabler (1981), which contains perspectives of more than 130 international scholars on an amazingly wide-ranged display of topics. *Horace's Compromise* (Sizer, 1984a), *High School* (Boyer, 1983), and *A Place Called School* (Goodlad, 1984) all contain insightful observations about the roles of schools amid the larger issues of our day.

Among the best recent books on the impact of world problems on personal education is Erich Fromm's (1976) *To Have or to Be*. Saint-Exupery's *The Little Prince* (1943) offers many of the same perspectives in the form of a beautiful children's book. Hundreds more books on world problems could easily be identified, although it might be better to encourage you to locate your own for each of the topics that interests you most. Allow me merely to conclude with a brief list of some that have influenced my wife, Ann, and myself, especially because of their indirect educational significance: on poverty, *Diet for a Small Planet* by Lappé (1982), *The Two Cultures* by C. P. Snow (1969), Alice Walker's novel *The Color Purple* (1982), and many novels by Charles Dickens; on autocracy, a marvelous children's book entitled *The Boy Who Could Sing Pictures* by Seymour Leichman (1973) and Franz Kafka's *The*

Castle (1926) on the cold terror of institutions; on indoctrination, *Forest Ranger: A Study in Administrative Behavior* by Kaufman (1960) and *The Death of Artemio Cruz* by Carlos Fuentes (1964); on ill health, *Life Extension: A Practical Scientific Approach* by Pearson and Shaw (1982), *The Healing Heart* by Norman Cousins (1983), and *The Well Baby Book* by Samuels and Samuels (1979); on suppression of inquiry and expression, Hermann Hesse's *Beneath the Wheel* (1906), *Soul on Ice* by Eldridge Cleaver (1967), and *Sex and Caste in America* by Carol Andreas (1971); on nationalism, *War and Peace in the Global Village* by McLuhan and Fiore (1968); on the dissolution and potential of the family, *Buddenbrooks* by Thomas Mann (1900) and *On Becoming a Family* by T. Berry Brazelton (1981); on ecological imbalance, *The Closing Circle* by Barry Commoner (1974) and *The Web of Life* by John H. Storer (1953); on prejudice, *The Nature of Prejudice* by Gordon W. Allport (1958), *The Invisible Man* by Ralph Ellison (1952), and *The Burden of Race* by Gilbert Osofsky (1967); on alienation, threats, and fear, *Escape from Freedom* by Erich Fromm (1941), *Teacher as Stranger* by Maxine Greene (1973), and numerous existential contributions by Sartre, Camus, Kafka, and others; on corporate greed, Buckminster Fuller's *The GRUNCH of Giants* (1983); on control and coercion, Viktor E. Frankl's *Man's Search for Meaning* (1963) and, of course, Aldous Huxley's *Brave New World* (1932).

RECOMMENDATIONS FOR REFLECTION

1. What is your position on each of the instructional and institutional problems?

2. Which of the problem areas discussed do you think are most important? Select five. Why are they of great importance?

3. Where do you stand in comparison to the three guest speakers? Are you closer to the social behaviorist, intellectual traditionalist, or experientialist position? Does your answer to this question depend upon the topic under discussion? If it does, is that a sign of consistency or inconsistency? Or is it a sign of a productive eclectic stance?

4. Make a list of the ten most important problems facing curriculum today at the instructional or institutional levels. How many of these are similar to the problems discussed in this chapter?

5. Which problems on your list are different from those discussed in this chapter? In other words, what problems would help round out the list presented here and make it more complete?

6. How might a social behaviorist, intellectual traditionalist, and experientialist respond to them? How do you respond to them?

7. Think back on your experience as an educator. Try to recall the major educational issues, trends, or fads that you have lived through. Make a reverse chronological listing of them. Do you see recurring issues responded to in different ways? Do you see the pendulum swinging back and forth?

8. Take a look at a journal such as *American Educator, Today's Education, Kappan,* or *Educational Leadership* over a period of a decade or two. Make a list of the dominant topics. See if you can find what a school district's in-service education sessions were like for the same period. Can you make observations about the connection between the inservice thrusts and those in the literature?

9. Why should societal and ideological problems be of concern to curricularists? Do you feel that they have bearing on your own professional work? Can you cite instances?

10. What is your position on the relevance that each of the fifteen societal and ideological problems has for curriculum?

11. Do you stand closer to the experientialist, social behaviorist, or intellectual traditionalist on these issues? Explain.

12. What ideological and societal problems would you add to the list? What is the school's responsibility in dealing with them?

13. In order to analyze the problems presented what conceptual structures did you choose from among those suggested at the beginning of this chapter? Why?

14. Which conceptual structures did you find most helpful? In what ways were they helpful?

15. What observations can you make about the relative value of the empirical-analytic paradigm, the practical paradigm, and the paradigm of critical praxis for illuminating problems presented here?

16. Did you devise any conceptual structures of your own that helped you analyze the problems at either level? If so, please explain them.

15

✦ Professional Development and Curriculum Improvement ✦

The spirit of improvement is not always a spirit of liberty, for it may aim at forcing improvements on an unwilling people.

JOHN STUART MILL *On Liberty* (1859)

Think of [your contemporaries] as they ought to be when you have to influence them, but think of them as they are when you are tempted to act on their behalf.

JOHANN C. F. VON SCHILLER *On the Aesthetic Education of Man* (1795)

The urge to save humanity is almost always a false-face for the urge to rule it.

H. L. MENCKEN *Minority Report* (1956)

Every abuse ought to be reformed unless the reform is more dangerous than the abuse itself.

FRANCOIS MARIO AROUET DE VOLTAIRE *Philosophy Dictionary* (1764)

SETTING THE STAGE

If problems exist within the curriculum, and if other problems impinge upon the curriculum from the larger social context in which it exists (as Chapter Fourteen amply indicates), how can they be overcome? Perhaps, a question more to the point is: Who is in the best position to deal with these problems? Some might respond that this is a responsibility of the society or even the world as a whole. But wholes rarely get mobilized before parts. The most salient force in the curriculum improvement process is the professional educator, specifically the curriculum leader and the teacher.

I am arguing that the key to curriculum improvement is professional development. Whether one believes that professional personnel are primarily implementors of curriculum, or whether one thinks of them as actually creating and developing curriculum as they carry on their work, the people in the process are key agents in what the curriculum becomes. As professional educators at different levels (curriculum administrators, supervisors, principals, and teachers) go about their daily activities, they produce overt and covert consequences for learners. Nearly every decision and action of these professional educators has consequences—intended or not—that reverberate throughout the institution of schooling and into the sphere of learner influence. Researchers are only beginning to scratch the surface of subtle but profound influences that school life has on students. Perceptive teachers and curriculum leaders have long known that it is the whole experience of school life that influences the outlook of students. Thus, they realize that they must have a wide-angled perception on the effects of their efforts. They must, as Goodlad (1966) and Goodlad and Richter (1966) admonish, think of the societal, ideological, institutional, instructional, and individual all at once when reflecting on curriculum matters. It is not just leaders in "high places" who should have this broad vision, but those who interact with students on a daily basis. This applies especially to teachers.

In a very real sense, professional development is curriculum development. The two are so thoroughly entwined that it is difficult, if not impossible, to conceive of one proceeding without the other. If teachers and curriculum leaders become more acutely aware of the purposes and consequences of daily action, it clearly affects others. The effect of teacher reflection and development always has some impact on students. If school curriculum pertains to the effects of schooling on student lives, then it is obvious that personnel development goes hand in hand with curriculum development.

To view the process from the curriculum development side first, it is impossible for improved curriculum to be proposed without assuming that some kind of antecedent change has occurred in the outlook of those who propose it, namely, curriculum leaders and teachers in schools. Thus, behind every curriculum improvement project is some kind of change in personnel outlook. This is not to say that all such changes in outlook are laudable or desirable. Some may be fashioned by self-serving political forces or the blatant self-interest of a curriculum leader, but even in these cases, there is a refocusing of attitude or there would be no proposal for change. Other proposals for curriculum improvement may be aptly characterized by critical theorists as hegemonic; that is, as discussed in Chapter Thirteen, they unwittingly perpetuate the kinds of knowledge and experience that support the prevailing stratification of money and power in society. One might think at first glance that this would not be change, yet it could be so conceived if it is change that moves more in the direction of hegemony. One could argue, for example, that the development of magnet schools in large cities does not enhance racial or socioeconomic interaction as much as it serves the needs of corporations by preparing students for certain job markets. In a day when computerization and automation could make it possible to have fewer mundane jobs and enable more people to have freedom to self-style their own worthwhile activities, schools perpetuate jobs. Critical theorists might argue that this is simply the school's way of following the politicians who follow the dictates of those who hold the economic wealth. To keep the masses busy in mundane work enables the richest 1 percent of the American public to own 56.5 percent of the corporate stocks, for example (Harrington, 1980, p. 153). Thus, a curriculum change that perpetuates this maldistribution of wealth may be seen as undesirable for the public as a whole; nevertheless, it represents a difference in focus that in turn symbolizes a change in outlook by personnel who propose the change.

The use of the term *change* here is of considerable importance, and it needs to be differentiated from *improvement*, which is used in the chapter title. The central difference is that *change* is an amoral concept. To say that change has taken place is not to make a judgment about desirability; it is merely to observe or propose a state of difference. To say *improvement*, however, invokes a value that indicates that a state of affairs is assumed to be better or more desirable.

The purpose of professional development should not be to create change for its own sake, but instead to foster improvement of curriculum. Change for the sake of change has been a major problem in education. Any experienced teacher can recount the recurrence of topics in the limelight of curriculum popularity: the "new math," inquiry teaching, open-space schools, differentiated staffing, values clarification, and on and on. Despite the fact that sound ideas often initiated such bandwagon trends, it frequently was a rather vacuous and superficial version that teachers met in faculty development programs. Good teachers saw through the gloss and found emptiness behind many of these approaches. They learned to trust themselves more than the charlatans who came bearing novel panaceas. Experience with educational band-wagonism did not bring an altogether negative outcome; however, many teachers began to distrust any kind of idea for curriculum improvement. No idea for curriculum improvement, regardless of its merit, can succeed without the support of teachers. Teachers must be receptive to any change proposal if it is to become a genuine improvement.

The key question in curriculum improvement at the grass-roots level becomes quite obvious: What kind of environments, situations, and learning experiences contribute to professional development that brings curriculum change? In the next section of this chapter, we consider some of the key ingredients in curriculum change and alternative approaches to providing them. We then move directly into the realm of teacher education. Preservice, inservice, and supervisory spheres of teacher education are discussed as the means to personnel development. Alternative strategies are presented and criticized. The three guest commentators address the relation of curriculum improvement to personnel development. A central notion that runs through the entire chapter is that curriculum improvement is not a one-shot venture. Joyce, Hersh, and McKibbin (1983) refer to this as *homeostasis of improvement*, meaning that schools develop innovation as a way of educational life, not as coercive imposition. Curriculum improvement requires a continuous program of professional development.

KEY INGREDIENTS IN CURRICULUM IMPROVEMENT

Two general approaches to curriculum improvement have dominated the literature. The first is formulated from the top of the power structure of school systems and is implemented by employees who may or may not be involved in the formulation. The other evolves in the course of everyday professional interactions among teachers, curriculum leaders, and students. This is sometimes referred to as "grass-roots" improvement, which is distinguished from "top-down" improvement formulations by its emergence during the course of action and its development by those who are most directly affected by the improved situation. In contrast, advocates of top-down improvement see improvements as carefully formulated prior to application rather than emergent from it, and improvements are drawn primarily from sources outside of the sphere of application.

Both approaches hold that planning is important, but each conceives it differently. The top-down orientation sees curriculum improvements as the result of research conducted by experts. It is carefully tested through development in pilot studies, and only then is it offered for more general consumption or use at the school system level. The task at that level is to convince potential adopters of the worth of the proposed improvement. Kurt Lewin's work (1948, 1951) is considered classic in the field. It advocates the need to "unfreeze" old patterns, introduce new ones through the aid of outside experts, and finally "freeze in" improvements so that the new expertise is built into the system and visiting consultants are no longer required for maintenance of the innovation. Other classics that build and elaborate upon this model of pre-planned improvement are Lionberger (1961), whose work on agricultural change radically innovated the process of farming; Lippitt, Watson, and Westley (1958), who generalized knowledge of change processes to many types of organizations; and Bennis, Benne, and Chin (1969), who elaborated the components of planned change. In more recent years, the field of organization development has sprung from this body of literature. Schmuck et al. (1977) summarize developments and point to the need to involve participants more in the formulations of improvements. Organization developers during the past two decades have created a stockpile of techniques for working with organizations that seek improvement. Much of the literature of this movement has been adopted and adapted by writers in education (e.g., Marks and Nystrand, 1981) and in curriculum (e.g., Doll, 1982).

Probably the greatest source of this kind of contemporary expertise on how to enable organizations to function more fully is in literature for business executives. One of the most popular and highly acclaimed accounts is *In Search of Excellence: Lessons from America's Best-Run Companies* by Peters and Waterman (1982). In a presentation to teachers from the Chicago Public Schools, Ernest Boyer (1984) summarized the book's message:

> 1. *If you want excellence in business, first have a clear vision of your product.*
> 2. *Give recognition to the people who are working to make that product every day.*

A problem with this orientation to improvement is related to its origins in agriculture and business. Hamilton et al. (1977) argue that curriculum cannot defensibly be measured in terms of products produced, as is the case in agriculture, botany, and business. When dealing with people in the process of education, the notion of product is too simplistic and too insensitive. The human being is much more complex than the outcome score on an achievement test can reveal, and the experience of schooling is a curriculum too subtle to represent in charts and graphs. What is needed are forms of evaluation that illuminate curricular experience, for example, Hamilton et al. (1977). Eisner (1979) develops related arguments culminating in his call for imaginative connoisseurs and critics of curricular experience.

Emphasis on the diversity, complexity, depth, and subtlety of curricular experience illustrates the need for a democratic orientation to curriculum improvement. This approach not only involves and caters to those most involved at the school and classroom level, it evolves from their work and insight. In other words, instead of experts conceiving of improvements while using minimal input from personnel who are later required to carry out or implement them, improvements themselves are seen to emerge from the experience of persons intimately engaged in situations. Outside or central office experts may be used as consultants, but they are used at the discretion of teachers, building principals, and students who seek their help.

Let us examine more closely how participants at the grass-roots level go about the process of curriculum improvement. Being immersed in the situation, they have experiential access to a multitude of influences on curriculum. They have an involved understanding of curriculum that influences their students. They see these students every day and can sense the impact of schooling on their outlooks. By involving students in the assessment process, professional educators and students can identify needs together.

To claim that improvement is needed requires an evolving philosophy or defensible and articulate sense of direction. As an area for improvement is identified, two processes go to work almost simultaneously, one convergent and the other divergent (see Guilford, 1977). The convergent force clarifies and articulates the problem, and thereby narrows the focus, while the divergent force unleashes imaginative powers to identify an array of possible courses of action and a host of probable consequences of acting upon those possibilities. As decision and action continue in the course of daily events, the imaginative projection of probable consequences is coupled with exploration of the actual consequences of action. Continuous engagement in this process is the art-science of Deweyan problem solving. It has been called *action inquiry* by Thelen (1960), *practical enquiry* by Schwab (1970), and a *humanistic discipline of curriculum studies by* Reid (1978).

Whether one accepts the grass-roots or top-down position, or any of many hybrids of the two, the dilemma of who is the primary force in curriculum improvement is serious and inescapable. As we examine five key ingredients in curriculum improvement, this becomes even more evident.

Personality

If one agrees that curriculum improvement and professional development are inextricably interdependent, as is the case with either the grass-roots or top-down positions, it must then be admitted that personality is a major factor in the process. People give birth to the ideas for improvement and carry out the improvement process. This process itself constitutes the curriculum that actually affects the lives of students. It affects them not as cold platitudes and brittle information, but as living forces in the personalities of teachers. This is the case regardless of the nature of the particular improvement in question. Furthermore, if the new curriculum has consequence, it resides and grows within the personality of students. It becomes part of the way in which they interact with their world and perceive themselves and others.

In the realm of educational practice, there seem to be two opposing schools of thought. One holds that human personality is largely invariant; one's basic character is thought to be given. The other position assumes that personality is alterable. One can see vestiges of this age-old debate in teachers who say that students are of a particular type or potential and can therefore learn or behave only within certain limits. In contrast to this position, we find teachers who see virtually unlimited potential in all students who are given environments conducive to learning and growth.

This is an argument that is sometimes referred to as the eugenicist (advocates of inborn personality) versus euthenicist (advocates of environmental creation of personality) debate. Eugenicists in curriculum early in the twentieth century advocated ability grouping of students based on standardized test scores, and sometimes blotted the history of equality by asserting that certain racial, ethnic, and socioeconomic groups innately had less potential than others (see Selden, 1984).

When teacher educators look at potential teachers and when school administrators consider how to provide faculty development activities, they often address the problem of personality. They ask themselves whether the teachers have a value system that accepts certain kinds of curriculum improvement and if the teachers have the ability to understand and accomplish needed curriculum improvements. When some consider what should be done to improve the quality of education, they propose that a new breed of teacher be attracted into the profession rather than attempting to retrain those who are currently teachers. In the latter instance, the tendency is more toward genetics than environment.

Today, one rarely finds pure advocates of either the invariant personality or the completely alterable personality. With the influence of Dewey, Piaget, and others who advocate interactionist epistemology, one finds that most curriculum leaders and teachers believe that personality falls somewhere between the two extremes. Even a cursory glance at a general text on personality theory such as *Theories of Personality* by Hall and Lindzey (1978) reveals the incredible complexity of human personality. Yet it is not enough for curriculum leaders to say that human personalities are complex. It is necessary for them to realize where they stand on the alterability issue and how their assumptions can be consistently practiced as they educate personnel for curriculum improvement.

Materials

Instructional materials are often seen as a means to curriculum improvement. This topic indelibly presents the issue of grass-roots versus top-down improvement. A tendency toward grass-roots curriculum improvement might inspire teachers to form study groups and develop curriculum improvements as they see fit. Such an approach might even provide released time for them to do this and resources to facilitate study such as reference materials, supplies, opportunity to visit relevant projects, and finances to tap the expertise of outside consultants. These teachers might be given very broad areas to pursue or, more likely, no mandates at all.

At the opposite extreme is the use of materials to "teacherproof" the curriculum. This was the purpose of some of the packaged programs that came out of the post-*Sputnik* curriculum reform movement. The idea was that teachers could not be trusted to determine sound curriculum commensurate with the structure of the disciplines and to use inquiry and other innovative teaching methods of the day adequately. Thus, both content and methodology were packaged and accompanied by elaborate implementation instructions for teachers to follow.

Funders and writers of such curriculum projects, however, became increasingly dismayed that use did not reap the benefits they anticipated in terms of increased student achievement. Goodlad, Klein, and Associates (1970) investigated the implementation phase by conducting elaborate observations in classrooms. They determined that although schools displayed the rhetoric of innovation, when teachers closed the classroom door they reverted to the more traditional teaching to which they were accustomed. Similarly, the Ford Foundation (1972) assessed the failure of some of their funding efforts at curriculum innovation and concluded that more thorough systems of evaluation were needed to monitor the existence of implementation and to determine its consequences as a project ensued.

Advocates of grass-roots change take these studies one step farther and suggest that failure was due to the fact that teachers were expected to implement projects when they had no stake in their development. The need to overcome this problem is becoming more fully recognized. For example, in assessing the promise and practice of curriculum change, as guest editor of a theme issue of *Theory into Practice* on the topic, Nel Noddings (1983, p. 158) observes that one theme is particularly strong: "The role of the teacher is absolutely central in any discussion of the relation between theory and practice." Some would find this as one among many clear indicators of a move in the direction of scholarly support for greater balance in favor of grass-roots, as opposed to top-down, improvements. Whether this is a mandate for teacher-created materials is open to question; however, it is a sharp strike against teacherproofing. Indeed, teachers must be central figures in the improvement process; whether this means creating curricula entirely themselves or not, it also means that if commercially prepared materials are to be used, teachers should play a major role in their selection. The act of laying change proposals on the doorstep of teachers and expecting them to comply as robots may still exist, but *defensibly* doing so is clearly innapropriate.

Physical Environment and Facilities

As in the case of materials, the issue of using physical environment and facilities also illustrates the grass-roots versus top-down dilemma. Cases abound in which the stage for improvement is set from sources outside the sphere in which improvement is to take place. For example, broad federal demands that state or city school systems must comply with a general mandate for improvement are often made without knowledge of the constraints on the site to be improved. Outside influences may pertain to smaller-scale improvement endeavors as well. A school system official may mandate that an innovation be implemented in school X or a principal may do the same for classroom Y and Z. The phenomenon illustrated here is environment structured from sources outside the realm of application.

An example of this phenomenon is the open-space school movement that dotted the United States in the late 1960s and 1970s. Often, new schools were designed with large open spaces, carpeting, conference rooms, and learning centers, and teachers were placed in them with little or no prior knowledge or preparation. Sometimes, old school buildings were remodeled during the summer. When teachers returned to work, they found a large open space instead of walls, and a group of colleagues with whom to team teach rather than the traditional classroom arrangement that they left in the spring. Teachers who are given no time to consider the match between their educational values with facilities and environments in which they work are likely to function less well than when they are involved in the planning.

Involvement in planning also has extreme positions. It can be condescending by requiring participation for the sake of appearance. In this case, teachers are usually asked to be functionaries on committees designed to rubber stamp decisions already made. At the alternative end of the spectrum are teachers who are genuinely invited to design educational environments and facilities that further the kinds of curriculum improvements they deem worthwhile.

Defensible Ideas

Curriculum improvement is mere change for its own sake or for the sake of appearance, if it is not informed by defensible ideas. Education is too often beset by bandwagonism—the tendency to jump on a slogan or proposal merely because it is popular for the moment or because the wealthy and prestigious school districts are doing it. Such behavior produces negative public relations for the profession. Indeed, it is an unprofessional habit.

Curriculum improvement and professional development alike are vacuous facades if not given impetus by defensible ideas. Why use the adjective *defensible* here? The reason is simply to dispel the notion, based on a false image of equality, that one idea is as good as another. Clearly, some ideas are better than others; therefore, curriculum improvement proposals based on more defensible ideas are better conceived, because they have a rationale that can be articulated.

What gives an idea defensibility? This issue could be discussed for a long time, and it should be in each practical situation that entertains curriculum improvement. The point is to claim not only that a proposal is worthwhile, but to justify the ideas on which it is based. Justification may take the form of logical argument, empirical evidence, testimony of experience, intuitive insight, harmony with authoritative literature, assertion of divine revelation, and pragmatic consequences. The type of justification needed depends upon the theory of knowledge or epistemological assumptions held by both those who propose improvements and those who must be convinced of their merits.

The issue of grass-roots and top-down change surfaces again on the issue of ideas. What is their source? Are they primarily created inside or outside the situation where improvement is intended? On this issue, especially, one can see that it is naive to conceive of the grass-roots and top-down positions as either-or, or mutually exclusive. Clearly, one can have ideas that stem from both outside and inside sources. Trouble may emerge if either of these sources is relied on solely. The central point here is that defensible ideas must be the basis for curriculum improvement if it is to be successful.

Support and Resistance

Every hope for curriculum improvement depends for its survival on a positive balance of supportive over resistive forces. This message was made clear in the work of Kurt Lewin, whose *Resolving Social Conflicts* (1948) has been something of a bible for those who want to understand organizational change, innovation, and improvement. In an article that preceded this book, Lewin (1943) wrote of forces behind the change process. He identified a key term, *gatekeepers*, which refers to those who must approve of an improvement proposal before it has a chance to be practiced. In curriculum literature, Smith, Stanley, and Shores (1957) devoted substantial space to the role of human relations in curriculum development. Drawing upon Lewin and others, they emphasize the necessity of identifying gatekeepers in both the school and the community.

Conventional wisdom might hold that identification of gatekeepers is simple enough. All one needs to do is look at the formal power hierarchy of a school and note who must sign project proposals and see if they will sign. However, anyone who has spent time in schools or other organizations knows well that those who fill the position of formal administrator may not be the key power wielders. One teacher with a good idea may have it continually rejected by the principal for reasons that he or she cannot explain, while another in the same school always seems to have ideas avidly accepted even though they may be less well conceived. The difference may be essentially political or may even boil down to public relations. The formal power structure is often in allegiance with, and not infrequently governed by, even more powerful behind-the-scenes persons. The teacher whose proposals are approved, for example, may have cultivated more powerful support groups within or outside of the school.

The analogy of barons of business and industry, lobbyists, and large campaign contributors influencing legislators and other government officials applies on a smaller scale to schools and school systems. Who knows whom, and what is the history of their connectedness? Who gives the subtle nods of approval or disapproval to the administrators in school buildings and school districts? Sometimes these forces stretch far out into the community to corporate board offices; sometimes they involve local community interest group leaders; and at other times, they emerge from the inauspicious teacher in the room next door. At times, respect attributed to such power wielders is merited because of the record of insight that they have achieved over the years; at other times, the power is amassed by a succession of political moves and the collection of favors owed that comes with it.

The central point for those who want to initiate curriculum improvement is that changing attitudes toward acceptance of proposals is not merely a rational process. To be sure, sound rational argument can help a great deal, but it is a political process, too. This does not mean that it is evil, the pejorative connotation of *political*. Instead, it necessitates the subtle arts of public relations, resistance, and contestation. This applies to all publics to be affected by the new proposal, but most especially to the gatekeepers.

In the twentieth century, for good and for ill, methods of public relations and advertising have increased in sophistication manyfold. Edward L. Bernays, widely recognized as the father of large-scale public relations, promoted origins of many of today's advertising and propaganda techniques. Bernays and filmmaker Frank Capra were called upon in times of war to build public opinion in support of major war efforts in the United States. Applications to curriculum problems may be on a much smaller (but at least as important) scale, but some of the principles are similar, and it might be added that advocates of curriculum proposals have been slow to recognize the power of public relations, media presentations, and political confrontation.

Some of the most insightful authors on curriculum improvement have argued for the need to do informal analyses of supportive and resistive forces. This notion, derived from Lewin's work, is sometimes referred to as the *force-field analysis.* Essentially, the process involves the following kinds of questions that might be asked about a proposal for curriculum improvement:

1. What exactly is the curriculum proposal that is hoped to be put into practice?
2. Given the situational context, why would this proposal constitute an improvement?
3. Who would be most likely to accept this proposal?
4. Who would resist it?
5. What are the needs of time, facilities, money, resources, and personnel for the proposal to become a reality? All of these dimensions need to be spelled out in as much detail as possible.
6. Where does the balance of power lie between supportive and resistive forces?
7. How might key resistive forces—gatekeepers—be led to a supportive position by seeing benefits in the proposal?

An emerging position among curriculum leaders and researchers alike is that the foregoing questions can be answered best when universities and schools enter into collaborative relationships to develop school improvement. Griffin and Barnes (1984) explain how such ventures are derived from both the craft knowledge of practitioners and the research on school change, effectiveness, and improvement.

Summary Note

Five broadly conceived, key ingredients in curriculum improvement have been characterized here: personality, materials, physical environment and facilities, defensible ideas, and supportive and resistive forces. Each of these plays an important role in professional development that leads to curriculum improvement. The neglect of personnel involvement (especially that of teachers) in the planning and doing of any curriculum improvement project can spell disaster for that project. Conversely, the genuine and meaningful involvement of personnel most closely associated with any improvement project can greatly strengthen the project.

PRESERVICE TEACHER EDUCATION

The seedbed of professional development that brings curriculum improvement lies in the education of teachers. Concern about the nature of teacher education has long been a concern of teacher educators. Highlights of the history of teacher education (Borrowman, 1965) reveal a conviction that the curriculum of schools can be no better than the quality of persons prepared by teacher education institutions. Early writers assessed meager developments in the United States in the first half of the nineteenth century as promising, but far short of the ideal promoted by German universities.

As new disciplines emerged, noted advocates wrote of the relevance of their field to teacher education. William James's (1899) *Talks to Teachers* and Edward L. Thorndike's (1910) "The Contributions of Psychology to Education" advocated the need for teachers to know two very different interpretations of psychological knowledge. Similarly, Albion W. Small (1896) argued for the worth of sociological knowledge in the preparation of teachers. With the emergence of scientific research methodology and assumptions in social science and even philosophy, we find philosopher Josiah Royce (1891) asking, "Is There a Science of Education?" In a now classic piece on the relation between theory and practice in education, Dewey (1904) warned of dangers in early exposure to practice of would-be teachers because of their tendency to unconditionally accept conventional coping strategies of experienced teachers without critically examining them. He expressed great faith in the possible shift from a two-year normal school preparatory period to a four-year college education for teachers, assuming that by doubling the time, one might help teachers become much more able. Some wrote of the potential for normal schools if they only sharpened their purpose and mission, and still others, such as George S. Counts (1935), called for a breaking of the lockstep approach to teacher education and a concomitant opening of experimental and imaginative alternatives. In *The Teacher of Teachers*, Harold Rugg (1952) discussed the need for teachers to be leaders; he called for new disciplines in the art of expression, the biopsychological science of behavior, and the science of society and culture and advocated a theory and program of creative imagination as the focus for teacher education.

In 1946, a major commission report, chaired by Edward S. Evenden and sponsored by the American Council on Teacher Education, provided recommendations on five major categories treated by all major reports on the topic during the previous forty years: general education; advanced subject matter preparation; professional preparation in child growth and development, social understanding, and creative expression; direct participation and experience in schools; and student teaching. Critics of teacher education such as James Koerner (1963) called attention to the fact that education majors scored among the lowest of all college majors on the Selective Service College Qualification Test and argued that teachers were miseducated. Probably the most elaborate study of teacher education in recent decades was *The Education of American Teachers* by James Bryant Conant (1963). His twenty-seven concluding recommendations altered the countenance of teacher education that followed. These recommendations deal with the following topical areas:

1. Certification requirements
2. Collegiate or university responsibility
3. Cooperating teachers in practice teaching
4. State financial responsibility for practice teaching
5. Programs of practice teaching
6. State information service
7. Assignment of teachers by local boards
8. Composition of National Council for the Accreditation of Teacher Education (NCATE)
9. Function of NCATE
10. Certification reciprocity among states
11. Initial probationary period of employment
12. Loan policy for future teachers
13. The all-university approach to teacher training
14. Requirements for collegiate or university teacher education programs
15. Foreign language preparation
16. The establishment of "clinical professors"

17. Basic preparation of elementary teachers
18. Practice teaching for elementary teachers
19. Adequate staffing of small colleges training elementary teachers
20. Single-field diploma for secondary school teachers
21. Clinical professors in institutions educating secondary teachers
22. Teaching diploma for art, music, and physical education teachers
23. Revision of salary schedule by local boards
24. Financial assistance to teachers for study in summer schools
25. Leaves of absence for further education of teachers
26. Master's degree programs
27. Inservice education of teachers

This list of recommendations illustrates a kind of curriculum of curriculum. Without a defensible curriculum of teacher education, it would be difficult to conceive of teachers developing defensible curricula for their students. This is not to say that Conant's proposals are the model. Many of them have had great influence on teacher education for almost three decades, while some have been dropped and others were not tried. But use does not equal justification. What Conant's work symbolizes is the realization that reform of teacher education is central to the reform of curriculum generally.

Major reform statements of the 1970s, such as Silberman's *Crisis in the Classroom* (1970), devote much attention to the reform of teacher education. The best examples of the spate of reform reports of the early 1980s (*Horace's Compromise* by Sizer, 1984a; *A Place Called School* by Goodlad, 1984; and *High School* by Boyer, 1983) devote ample attention to teacher education as a basis for reform.

While a great proportion of teacher education occurs on the job through inservice, supervision, and self-education experiences, preservice teacher education begins the professional journey. This is a curriculum consisting of three dominant features: (1) general education courses, (2) professional education courses, and (3) student teaching and other clinical experiences. Reform reports almost invariably discuss these topics when building the case for how reform should take place. In the preservice teacher education program, seeds of attitudes that build curriculum improvement are sown. The relative balance among the three features is a matter worth considering in more detail.

General Education

This term usually refers to the initial two years of college in which the student receives a wide-ranging background in the arts, sciences, and humanities.

Advocacy. Students who plan to be teachers need a broad eclectic base from which to draw. The teaching profession, more than most others, requires a deep and broad understanding of human nature, society, and knowledge itself. This is found nowhere more abundantly than in the traditional liberal arts. Teachers at the elementary school level must be generalists when it comes to subject matter, and those in the secondary school must know a great deal more than their subject specialty if they are to relate it to students, the contemporary world, and other subjects. General education perennially has been acknowledged as one of the prime missions of a college of education (Kridel, 1980), and this should be especially the case with teacher education curricula. Without such preparation, teachers cannot be expected to develop programs of general education in schools such as those proposed by Roberts and Cawelti (1984), Broudy, Smith, and Burnett (1964), and others.

Criticism.   Teachers need to know how to teach; they need to learn techniques and strategies for reaching students and the theories that lie behind them. If they don't know their subjects well enough to keep ahead of grade school and high school students, there is little hope for progress anyway. As for a liberal education, of course, it is worthwhile, but the pabulum that passes for general education in the first two years of college hardly provides profound insight into human nature and society. That kind of a liberal education requires a lifelong commitment to learning. If we can get bright people into teaching, they will have that commitment, and they can spend their college days preparing precisely for the job of teaching by taking methods courses.

Professional Education Courses

For those who plan to teach at any level, there are foundational methods courses, and for secondary, elementary, or middle school teachers who take an area of concentration, there are advanced methods courses in specialized areas.

Advocacy.   All teachers, regardless of teaching level, should have an area (or areas) of concentration. They should know what advanced learning is like in at least one field, and they won't get that in the introductory courses that are labeled "general education."

Methods courses, however, are potentially the most important and currently the most maligned at the university level. No one would ridicule a medical student for studying methods of surgery. Indeed, one would desperately hope that one's own surgeon had taken such courses. Criticism is often promoted by those who have not taken methods courses themselves. It is, of course, necessary that those who have completed two years of general education, and are well on their way to completing their major(s) in a subject specialty, should possess knowledge far in advance of all elementary and most secondary students. What they have not yet acquired is the technique of teaching, perspectives on classroom management, and an overall frame of reference for curriculum, instruction, and program development in the institutional context of a school. High-quality methods courses provide this; further, those who teach such courses realize that a teacher learns more methods on the job. But in the beginning, the frame of reference, repertoire of strategies, lists of resources, and the advice of a seasoned scholar-practitioner are all indispensable.

Criticism.   Students usually come to methods courses knowing little or nothing of what teaching is like, except what they assimilated as a student (which is usually quite meager because they did not perceive from a teacher's vantage point and did not have a teacher's needs at that time).

In addition, it is extraordinarily rare to find good methods courses. They usually involve drab lists of strategies to be memorized apart from any teaching-learning context and are interspersed with requirements to write units and lesson plans according to some rigidly prespecified format. If this is not enough, the student spends too many hours listening to outdated lectures delivered by someone who has had little touch with the real world of school for many years. In short, the poor reputation of methods courses is well deserved.

There are, admittedly, a few fine practitioner-scholars who teach methods courses. Many of these are dropped from university faculties because they have not published much research and are, therefore, not granted tenure. Even if a preservice teacher education student is fortunate enough to have an excellent methods instructor, chances are great that his or her message will bypass the student. Students who have little exposure to schools usually are not in a position to benefit from methods courses. This leads to a recommendation that all methods courses be given at the graduate level, and then only after students have had a year or two of experience in the classroom. Critics may argue that these apprentice teachers resort to trial and error methods that hurt students; however, all beginning teachers use trial and error methods.

As for the areas of specialization emphasis, one must remember Whitehead's (1929) brilliant admonition that "you may not divide the seamless coat of learning. What education has to impart is an intimate sense for the power of ideas, for the beauty of ideas, and for the structure of ideas, together with a particular body of knowledge which has peculiar reference to the life of the being possessing it" (p. 23). To such an admonishment, most universities are as guilty as methods courses.

In the name of general and specialized education, bits and pieces of information are trotted out and briefly displayed for students to gaze upon, with little or no emphasis on connecting them to one another or to students' lives. What is needed is a radical redesign of education for teachers (and everyone else) in a concerted effort to show how knowledge relates to the quest for meaning, interests, and direction that plagues all learners. If a redesign of college curriculum can do this, we will have good teachers in great abundance. There will be enough for schools and other educative institutions as well.

Student Teaching and Other Clinical Experiences

Not so many years ago, student teaching was the first and only exposure to schools provided for teacher education candidates. Today, the situation is quite different. In many university programs, the professional education of teachers includes clinical experiences in schools in conjunction with many or all methods courses.

Advocacy.   It used to be said that teachers earn their A.B. degrees in college and then have to learn the rest of the alphabet of teaching on the job. This is no longer the case, though it will always be true that much about becoming a teacher cannot be learned until one has been a teacher for some time.

Today, the best teacher education programs integrate in-school experiences with every methods course. Beginning with the introductory courses and the social and psychological foundations courses, teacher education candidates meet teachers and students and get perspectives on a variety of kinds of schools. They may visit public, private, inner-city, suburban, and rural settings. They may see firsthand the workings of open schools, traditional schools, and a host of other organizational formats.

When available, they are exposed to schools that have differing racial, ethnic, and socioeconomic composition.

These exposures are not without careful design. Students learn to observe particular methods or social and psychological phenomena. They conduct interviews, carry out formal observations, do research projects, tutor, and intensively interact with and learn from the situations visited. As their program of studies progresses, they learn to interpret school problems and daily occurrences through a variety of models or theories. These they compare and contrast. During a year or more of methods courses that precede student teaching, the teacher candidates begin teaching experiences under the guidance of university supervisors and master teachers in classrooms. By the time they enter student teaching, many of today's teacher candidates have classroom experience that far exceeds that of graduates in days gone by. When it comes to variety, they have a repertoire of different kinds of schools that exceeds that of many experienced teachers. Having participated in a variety of schools, these teachers are able to adjust more fully to new and different situations. Compared with teachers in previous generations of teacher education who experienced only one setting, these teachers are much better prepared. They are equipped to have twenty years of experience rather than one year of experience twenty times, as Harold Spears used to say.

Criticism.   This ideal of teacher education is exceedingly rare. Moreover, it usually provides more rhetoric and paperwork for accreditation and state education offices than a qualitatively different experience.

Even the ideal, however, is wanting. As Dewey (1904) warned over eighty years ago, early exposure pressures the inexperienced to accept uncritically rules, regulations, conventional wisdom, and traditions of school operations. Those who do not yet have a basis for criticizing present practice, and those who lack knowledge of viable alternatives to it, are at a great disadvantage. They are socialized—even indoctrinated—into a system of teaching without having a fair chance to see its strengths and weaknesses in perspective. Without perspectives leading to productive and imaginative questioning, curriculum improvement is stifled. When teacher candidates are forced to cope with classroom life before they can start developing their own curriculum philosophy, a great resource is lost. The result is automatons who follow directions well, but lack the kind of imagination and critical insight that create curriculum improvements. In a sense, early exposure is such a formidable inhibitor of reform because it nips professional development in the bud, before it has a chance to flower.

What is needed, instead, is something patterned after the models of more highly respected professions such as medicine and law. A preeducational four-year education in interdisciplinary studies in arts, sciences, social sciences, and humanities could be followed by one and one-half years of educational theory, research, and methodology. A final year and a half of teaching in different settings could then be experienced with a firm basis for criticizing prevailing practices and for formulating defensible and creative alternatives to them. At this point, teachers would be professionals, ready to embark on a program of continuous growth as educators. Clearly, many impediments make such a program seem like a wild fantasy today; nevertheless, a large number of wild ideals have been actualized throughout history due to hard work, imagination, and dedication.

INSERVICE TEACHER EDUCATION

Frequently referred to as *staff development* (Griffin, 1983a; Beegle and Edelfelt, 1977), inservice teacher education is the education of teachers that occurs after they obtain their college degree and begin teaching. Teachers are, of course, educated by the job of teaching itself, by their interaction with students and other teachers, and by the social system that a school is. Beyond this very important informal education, however, curriculum leaders attempt to influence the professional development of teachers (Speiker, 1976) by providing programs of learning experiences for them. Curriculum leaders have developed a wide range of approaches to professional development because they are convinced that this yields greater curriculum improvement. In this section of the chapter, we point out nine general strategies of inservice education and consider strengths and weaknesses of each through statements of advocacy and criticism. While each of the nine strategies can be treated as an alternative to the others, they are often used in combination.

Workshops

The workshop is one of the most widely used kinds of inservice education for teachers. Some school systems refer to workshop and institute days interchangeably. Such days may have some large-group sessions in which teachers listen to featured speakers from universities, private educational agencies, research centers, consulting firms, or other school districts. Larger school systems sometimes have their own inservice education staffs and therefore tap outside sources less often. When not attending the large-group sessions, teachers meet in smaller groups and work on the development of ideas, concrete approaches, and materials or become more aware of recent research findings. Sometimes, workshops are not part of a full-day event. Instead, there may be an after-school, weekend, or half-day released-time workshop setting. Sometimes, college credit is given for attendance, and sometimes districts provide credit toward advancement on their salary schedules. While the range of workshop settings is great, and while the kinds of topics treated is even greater, workshops usually mean that teachers meet with someone who has special expertise to share with them. This sharing is assumed to enhance professional development and thereby improve curriculum.

Advocacy. The workshop idea came into being on a broad scale during the Eight Year Study, when Ralph Tyler and others arranged for teachers to meet during summers and at other times to develop ideas and practical projects designed to enhance learning in their classrooms and schools. Experts on curriculum and evaluation would meet with the teachers over a period of time as resources for curriculum improvement.

Today, we have some examples of workshops that provide long-term assistance to teachers. Some workshops are taught as university courses, but differ from the usual theoretic or research flavor by being highly practical to the classroom setting. For instance, the College of Education of the University of Illinois at Chicago has developed workshops with representatives of both the Chicago Teachers Union and the Illinois Education Association. Teachers from these groups enter into dialogue with university faculty members to discuss how the university might meet their needs. Together, they design workshops and courses that fit situational needs.

Many "one-shot" workshops exist today as well. In this case, a topic is identified by curriculum leaders within a school district, and experts are invited to present the latest ideas and practical proposals to teachers. This has the benefit of whetting the appetite for further study and giving that extra spark of novel ideas to classroom activity. It is a way of keeping teachers informed of new developments in their field. The best curriculum leaders do not merely select workshop topics off the tops of their heads; rather, they involve teachers on committees to help make selections.

Criticism. It is indeed rare to find any long-term, serious effort to develop workshops that meet teachers' needs. Frankly, curriculum leaders in schools usually decide on topics and presenters using the criterion of expediency. Desperate administrators fill workshop days with speakers from travel agencies who sell vacations, theatrical troupes who present a satire on the teachers and the school visited, or investment counselors who explain how teachers might invest the little money that they have acquired to provide for their retirement. While such workshops may address personal interests, they hardly qualify as professional development, and they surely do little for curriculum improvement.

Workshops that do deal with educational topics are usually of the "one-shot" variety, and they are generally replete with trivial activities: how to make a single construction paper art project, how to make a seasonal builletin board, how to make an instructional gimmick. Some teachers take these trivialities (worksheets galore) back to their classrooms with glee. They soon discover that these projects are all glow with no substance. They may interest students briefly, but the interest soon fades. These same teachers shop for instructional devices that keep students busy instead of those that have educative value. Woe to their students. These teachers give a negative reputation to the education profession. Curriculum administrators and workshop leaders who cater to such puerile interests only exacerbate the problem.

There are, to be sure, "one-shot" workshops of a higher quality—a few steps beyond the "make-it, take-it" variety. These workshops introduce ideas, research findings, and teaching strategies. The only problem is that in a one- to four-hour or even all-day session, it is impossible to get to know teachers. How can a defensible professional service be rendered until the workshop leader knows the interests, needs, and situations of participants? All that even the best workshop leaders can provide is highly generalized presentations that relate inadequately to participants. The workshop idea, as presently practiced, is a waste of professional time and effort. While teachers may glean an idea here and there, the primary benefit lies in the teachers' salary increments if tied to accumulated workshop time and in the pocketbooks of those who make a business at leading workshops.

Idea Exchanges

Some school systems provide the opportunity for teachers from similar grade levels, subject area specializations, or professional interests to meet together. The sessions may or may not have an agenda, but in either case, the purpose is to share ideas, problems, strategies, and the like. An entire inservice day or part of a day may be devoted to this kind of exchange.

Advocacy.   Teachers are among the loneliest of professionals. They come to work, say "hello," and close the classroom door. They are expected to act in this fashion, which is not to say that they do not enjoy being with students. But it is not the same as having another professional with whom to share ideas, problems, and interests. Often teachers are surprised when they learn that another teacher has experienced the same problems. How unfortunate it is to learn about this many years later than would be necessary if the mechanisms had been set in place by curriculum leaders who knew the value of idea exchanges for teachers.

Idea exchanges need not always focus on problems; they are excellent forums for sharing teaching strategies, units, and materials that have worked well. A whole compendium of successful teaching approaches and descriptions of the settings in which they worked well could evolve into a great body of practical precedent. Moreover, with the computer technology available today, such a resource from many school systems could be pooled and designed for easy retrieval through a thesaurus of key words such as ERIC uses for journals and research documents.

Finally, idea exchanges can be excellent brainstorming sessions. One teacher might present a dilemma, and the group could make suggestions about alternative courses of action and their likely consequences. Or a dilemma could be posed such as how to deal with a particular kind of discipline problem, or how to motivate students to want to learn an aspect of subject matter for which students seem to lack interest. The possibilities for idea exchanges are virtually limitless.

Criticism.   The misuses and abuses of idea exchanges are virtually unlimited too. First, teachers let them debilitate into "gab sessions." Gossip rather than learning too often prevails.

In principle, the idea is a decent one, but in actuality, teachers get "uptight" about sharing problems. It is similar to the principal telling the new teacher to come to him or her whenever a problem occurs; when the teacher comes, it is considered a sign of weakness or incompetence. Teachers are indeed leery about sharing their problems or even admitting that they have any.

As for sharing ideas, projects, units, and so on, teachers are exceedingly cautious about sharing anything controversial. Thus, sharing sessions tend to be bland and rarely get at the heart of the real life and concerns of teachers. They say what they think curriculum leaders want to hear, when those leaders are within earshot. Teachers' unions and professional associations are helping teachers to be more comfortable about sharing their true concerns, but even these organizations have not probed deeply into curriculum matters. Perhaps that is not their territory, but something more fundamental than school-sponsored sharing sessions is needed to break the bondage of complacency and fearfulness that characterizes teachers when it comes to organizing on curriculum issues. After all, curriculum is the only defensible reason for schools to exist in the first place.

Visitations

Some schools use released time to enable their teachers to visit other schools and educative institutions. Teachers may observe in classrooms where new or unusual projects are being implemented, or they may merely see how other kinds of institutions that have educational missions conduct their efforts.

Advocacy.   It is much better to see a new or different idea in operation than merely to hear about it secondhand. When one visits, one can get the feeling of the whole situation—one sees and feels it, and even has a chance to discuss questions with those who have experienced problems and successes with new ideas. First, just to meet teachers from other places is interesting. Second, to spend a day with them greatly enriches one's repertoire of approaches and ideas. Third, it is useful to develop networks of colleagues in other places.

Another value of the visitation is that teachers who do the visiting often become participants, sometimes for lengthier periods of time than a day. They do so by bringing ideas from their own background of experience, and by actually participating in the learning environment rather than watching only. Such participation sometimes leads to productive exchanges. It is both a breath of fresh air and an educative experience to trade classrooms with another teacher for a few days. One learns new routines and becomes acquainted with new programs by being immersed in them. Of perhaps greater importance, one learns of students whose backgrounds are different.

Some school districts have used inservice days for visiting nonschool educative settings such as scientific laboratories, training centers for business and industry, seminars, university research offices, think tanks, and the like. Teachers are often surprised at how unlike schools these environments are. They notice how free, open, and often playful the exchange of ideas, individual study, and group discussion is. Frequently, they take these ideas back to their classrooms and adapt them to their elementary or secondary school environments.

Criticism.   Visitations are like the ads that entice tourists to "See Europe in six days." They claim that your visit to ten countries in less than a week will familiarize you with ways of life there. Of course, this is ludicrous. The same is true of visitations by teachers to other schools for a day or two, or even a week-long exchange. The benefit may be to have a brief vacation from one's own routine, but to bill the day as "educational" is to stretch the value of the experience out of proportion.

Moreover, teachers who are visited put on a show for the visitors. Schools visited frequently transform assistant principals into tour guides who provide uncritical and sparkling renditions of schools that have no problems.

School systems should save their money. If they are willing to give their teachers a day without students, they should let them work in their classrooms. They need the planning time. They would be more than grateful for that kind of inservice rather than the conjured-up special event.

Graduate Study

Many school districts and some states require a certain number of hours of graduate study every so many years. The vast majority of school systems give advancement on salary schedules for completion of a certain number of hours of graduate study or the earning of graduate degrees. Some school systems provide inservice education funds to supplement tuition, and a few offer sabbatical leaves. When many school districts invite workshop leaders for their inservice or institute days, they try to negotiate university credit for the sessions. Whether school systems provide funding or convenient opportunity for graduate study, most encourage it as a highly relevant feature of their inservice programs.

Advocacy.   Graduate study is the most rigorous form of inservice education. Rather than the usual "dog and pony" or "cut and paste" variety of workshop, with no basis given in research or theory and no assignments, graduate programs at high-caliber colleges and universities offer courses that are demanding in terms of theory and research, and they require assignments that are intellectually challenging and practically rewarding.

Although one way to take graduate work is to pick and choose a few courses here and there, that is clearly not the best way to proceed. It is better to enroll in a degree program (masters, advanced certificate or specialist degrees, or the doctorate). When this is done, inservice education becomes cohesive and integrated. Teachers who complete such programs are more useful to their school system and are often promoted to better positions.

Some teachers want to remain teachers and continually improve at that station in professional life. Programs are evolving in many graduate schools for precisely this purpose. Instead of a thesis, teachers are allowed to pursue a problem-solving venture in their own situation and thus engage in a more practical form of curriculum research. The Chicago Teachers' Union and the University of Illinois at Chicago have, for example, successfully negotiated and implemented a master's degree program to fit the needs and interests of teachers in the Chicago public schools. Furthermore, B. Othanel Smith (1980) argues that graduate degrees for teachers and curriculum researchers should be oriented not to the conduct of research, but to the utilization of research and practical knowledge in the art-science of pedagogy. He proposes a doctor of pedagogy as distinguished from the traditional doctor of philosophy in education.

Criticism.   Colleges and universities have become large-scale credentialing factories. Their programs, for the most part, are unconnected with practice. The brightest and best teachers refuse to go back to college and endure the humiliation and irrelevance that a graduate program often brings. It brings humiliation because professional educators are debriefed of their expertise, told in effect that their experience is merely "war stories," and informed that the only game toward educational understanding is played with the rules of research and theory. Professional educators are thereby re-created into the images of the researchers and theorists at universities, who are rewarded for publication. These practitioners, however, are not rewarded for publication in their daily work and, therefore, endure hours and even years of degradation for irrelevant results.

The experience of graduate study could be worthwhile if professors and practitioners joined together to integrate the practitioner's experience and intuition with the scholar's theory and research in a collaborative venture to understand better the problems plaguing schools today. But that is almost an impossible expectation due to the extraordinarily different reward and incentive structures that govern the work of these two large groups of professional educators.

Specific Instructional Information

Inservice lectures and study groups are often devoted to the dissemination of information and techniques that curriculum leaders decide should be made available to all of the teachers in a school district. For example, if a new content area, purpose, type of instruction, or evaluation procedure is to be adopted, all teachers must be informed about it. This is frequently carried out with an emphasis on securing awareness of new instructional materials and testing instruments.

Advocacy.   Inservice education should not be piecemeal and disjointed from the daily work of teachers. As new instructional materials, environmental arrangements, testing instruments, and textbooks are adopted, curriculum leaders should inform teachers about their value and proper utilization. One best way to accomplish this is to have workshops conducted by personnel from companies that sell those materials. They, better than anyone, know the materials, can answer questions about their possible uses, and can provide recommendations about how they might be tailored to practical circumstances.

The positive upshot of this kind of inservice lies in its cohesiveness. It builds an overall programmatic consistency that is impossible for those school systems that allow teachers to teach whatever subject matter in whatever ways they wish. Programmatic consistency is an essential characteristic of what institutionalized curriculum is all about. To deny this is to deny the central purpose of institutions in society. Publishers have put a great deal of time, effort, and expertise into the development of institutional systems, and usually have a variety of options within any given purpose. To replace this with teacher-made curriculum is a great mistake, because teachers are primarily implementors. They have not the time, energy, or expertise to teach and develop curriculum at the same time.

Criticism.   Making teachers mere implementors denies their professionalism. Their central mission should be to interact carefully with their own students and, together with them and with sources of outside expertise, determine what is in their best interest at a particular moment. Teachers (and students themselves) are in a unique position (along with parents) to diagnose needs and interests continuously, provide experiences that meet them, monitor student response and learning that accrues continuously, and redevelop curricula that better meet the changing character of student needs and the interests that symbolize them.

This complex work requires the utmost of teachers who are willing and able to engage in an intuitive-empirical art-science of inquiry into the lives of students and their relation to the social milieu that surrounds them. It cannot be done by generic materials published by those who have no knowledge of particular circumstances.

Developing Competencies

Many states, school systems, and teacher education colleges have developed a series of skills or performance criteria that they refer to as *competencies*. They usually tap results of research on teacher effectiveness as a basis for selecting competencies. Given this orientation, inservice education consists of attempts to ensure that competencies are understood and subsequently implemented.

Advocacy.   Research on teaching during the past two decades has increased immeasurably in sophistication and relevance to practice. In 1978, Gage argued that we are approaching a scientific basis for the art of teaching. In the years since that time, research on teaching has been augmented to the point that it is now possible to identify competencies that, if adequately employed, have great chance of improving academic achievement. Many of the characteristics stem from those summarized by Rosenshine and Furst (1971): clarity, variability, enthusiasm, task orientation, directness and indirectness, positive rewards, supportive behavior, structuring comments, high-level questioning, and probing questions. Staff development that builds teaching competencies is also adapted from research on training (Joyce and Showers, 1983) that deals with new conceptions of transfer of training, parallels between teaching and coaching, and strategies for increasing learning aptitude. Recent summaries of effective instruction research for practitioners emphasize the need for (1) active learning time, (2) feedback and corrective procedures, (3) instructional cues, (4) continuous programs of instructional evaluation, and (5) direct implications for teaching and learning that support such classroom climate variables as (a) academic orientation, (b) teacher assertiveness, (c) structure, (d) cooperation and affiliation, and (e) support and concern for individuality.

A good inservice program keeps teachers informed about the latest developments. Much of the relevant research stems from the ongoing IEA studies of international educational assessment. In the final analysis, the search is for teaching characteristics that are associated with (and interpreted as causal of) higher student achievement. Competency need not be developed in rigid, behavioristic ways; in contrast, it can be a process of informing teachers of the latest research as provided in general summaries by Dunkin and Biddle (1974) or in more specific translations of research on teaching for teacher education programs and practices by Zumwalt (1982).

Criticism.   There is a massive construct validity problem in this pell-mell promotion of competence. It lies in the unconditional acceptance of *achievement* as the measure of curricular worth. In most of the literature that promotes a competence basis for inservice education, the published achievement test is the definition of achievement. This omnipresent assumption, and others related to it, are criticized through linguistic analysis by Noddings (1984a), normative or value analysis by Pearson (1984), historical analysis by Johnson (1984), critical praxis by Aoki (1984), and rhetorical analysis by Fagan (1984). As early as 1978, John Goodlad argued that there is little justification epistemologically or logically to support the idea that atomistic competencies can be pasted together to demonstrate accountability for achievement. There is immense need, therefore, to move beyond the superficial adherence to achievement tests and ask the larger question of what it means actually to live worthwhile teaching experience and to engage in pedagogic competence (van Manen, 1984b).

Individualized Consulting

A few school districts have successfully tried an approach by which a consultant (usually from a university) is invited to a school district. The consultant thoroughly gets to know a limited set of school buildings and classrooms. He or she observes in classrooms, engages in follow-up discussion with the teachers, and helps them to solve problems and renew practices.

Advocacy.   This process tests whether the consultants are "worth their salt." Since no college credit is typically attached to this brand of inservice, teachers are not put in the awkward position of feeling that they must offer praise for services for the sake of grades. Thus, consultants are only invited to return if teachers and curriculum leaders judge their services to be practically useful.

The advantages over the one-shot workshop and university coursework are obvious. Teachers are engaged in inquiry continuously to improve their teaching in an effort to meet student needs, and the expressed purpose of this mode of inservice is to facilitate and enrich this process. The motivation to participate is intrinsic; it should be chosen, not required. This does not contradict the fact that some school systems may offer increments in salary schedules for participation, if this type of inservice is made available with alternatives such as college courses, workshops, and so on that also couple salary benefits and professional growth. University professors are often willing to spend time in classrooms in the spirit of the following: collaborative supervision (Griffin, 1983a); criticism and connoisseurship (Eisner, 1985; Willis, 1981; McCutcheon, 1981); teacher as researcher approaches (Stenhouse, 1975); participant observation (Bogdan, 1972); ethnographic inquiry (Smith and Geoffrey, 1971; Berlak and Berlak, 1981); grounded theory (Glaser and Straus, 1967; Janesick, 1982); critical ethnography (Apple and Weis, 1983; Bullough, Goldstein, and Holt, 1984; Weiss, 1983); and research using multiple modalities (Goodlad, 1984). Thus, it is clear that the teacher and curriculum leader incentives to discover better ways to deal with daily experiences of schooling and university professor incentives to produce and publish knowledge do not have to be mutually exclusive. In fact, they are complementary, each making the other stronger, more relevant, and more defensible.

Criticism. This does not sound bad as an ideal, but it is wishful thinking, indeed, when it comes to practice. First, teachers fear being observed. They distrust observers and suspect them of being in linkage with administrators who evaluate them for salary ratings. Thus, they put on airs and do not reveal actual problems for fear that it would hurt their reputations. Second, and probably more to the point, it would be impossible to pay that many consultants for the 16,000 school districts in the United States alone. The idea of a consultant in every classroom or school is ludicrous when one looks at today's level of educational funding. Third, university types are usually liberals, if not radicals, and they advocate ideas that upset well-developed routines, after which they leave all the problematic consequences for school system officials to solve. Fourth, if such consultants are helpful, and if there are not enough for all who want and need them (which would surely be the case), equity problems would run rampant. Teachers would demand consultant policies that could not be financed, and parents would rightly realize that their children were being unjustly treated if their teachers did not have access to consultants when others did.

Invention Strategies

Teachers often lament the fact that the information, theory, research results, and related ideas presented in the usual inservice workshops, university courses, and research literature are not relevant to their needs. Thus, some inservice leaders provide teachers with strategies for use in developing curriculum for their own unique situations.

Advocacy.   Teachers rightly decry the fact that much research and theory propagated by universities is too highly generalized to relate to their practical situations. At the other end of the continuum, teachers turn to popular "idea" books that list strategy after strategy. One finds such books in specialized teaching materials stores and in the large popular bookstores on shelves marked "Education." Such recipelike resources are too specific. Although teachers may adapt some of the approaches to their needs, they usually conclude that the techniques may have worked well for the author, but they do not work in their particular circumstances.

Needed is an approach that recognizes the teacher as a creative problem solver and a capable curriculum developer in his or her own niche. This realization requires inservice approaches that stimulate these capacities; instead of bestowing theory, research, or even concrete techniques, the inservice leader provides invention strategies or springboards for creative decision making. For example, the idea of *limiting* is an invention strategy. Teachers are often beset about what to do tomorrow. They feel an absence of ideas.

Limiting might tell them to reach in their purse or pocket and pull out three useless items. What if tomorrow's lesson had to be based on that gum wrapper, toothpick, and void lottery ticket? Teachers will see their English, math, social studies, or science class in a different light. One might have students build a story around the three items, think of alternative uses for them, probe their origins as cultural artifacts, consider the measurements involved in producing them, discover their social and economic origins, speculate psychologically about why we attributed value to them, develop an art object or musical rendition about them, or produce a creative advertisement using them. A speech teacher who cannot think of an idea might limit himself or herself by asking, "What would I teach in speech class if students were not allowed to speak?" He or she might develop a lesson on mime, the origins of language, or body language. Teachers might look in the back of their desk drawers or storage closets and force themselves to use an item that they meant to throw away long ago. The possibilities for limiting are unlimited.

Another invention strategy is *patterning*. Teachers identify what their students like to do. They identify the games, television programs, movies, music, peer activities, family life, dating, sports, and the like. Then they ask: How could my subject matter be taught on a "Family Feud" format? Might I teach more like a coach interacts during a game? Could I emphasize the familial and adolescent problems in any period of history? The idea is to pattern teaching after the structure of games, concerns, and leisure activities that hold the interest of students so substantially. Could the content of familiar television programs be used to convey basic social studies or English content? Could the inner workings or technology of television, records, stereo systems, photography, and so on be used as a point of departure for science and mathematical content? The answer to such questions is an unconditional *yes.*

Interviewing is yet another invention strategy. Students love to be interviewed and to interview one another using all sorts of questions. *Valuing* is another. The success and popularity of values clarification techniques (Raths, Harmin, and Simon, 1966; Simon, Howe, and Kirschenbaum, 1978) clearly attests to this.

In short, inservice education should capitalize on teachers' capabilities to be creative curriculum developers by presenting invention strategies, providing illustrations and examples of their use, and leading teachers to develop possibilities applicable to their own situations.

Criticism.　In reality, teachers are some of the most uncreative people. Perhaps years of being in schools, surrounded by boredom, has done this. Clearly, I do not share the faith that teachers are creative problem solvers. Unfortunately, hope lies mainly in developing soundly constructed curriculum materials for teachers and in providing recipes for their use. One thing learned from long exposure to schooling, as teachers have had, is to follow orders.

Learning Contracts

Teachers are accustomed to the idea of contracts; they spend considerable time negotiating them with administrators and school boards. But this is not the kind of contracts referred to here. *Learning contracts* are professional agreements that teachers make with administrators who are in charge of inservice education. These contracts spell out how teachers will use their inservice time, their rationale for its use, the plan of action to be carried out, and the form of evidence to be provided to substantiate that the work was done.

Advocacy.　Teachers are professionals, or at least they should be considered at that level. This means that they should know best the kinds of experiences that will contribute to their growth. They should be able to explain how their proposed professional growth will contribute to curriculum improvement. Clearly, they are able to do this when given the chance.

Leaders of inservice education, however, can greatly inhibit this approach if they continually question the motives of teachers who submit unusual and imaginative proposals for professional growth. For example, attending a series of plays, films, or concerts can be illuminating about such dimensions of life as human nature, political action, economic transaction, and aesthetic experience. Insights in such realms relate to life in classrooms and schools; they provide ideas about what is worthwhile to know and why. Thus, there could be no greater justification than this for professional growth that yields curriculum improvement.

Some teachers might want to (1) attend university courses; (2) pick and choose workshops offered in the area (whether or not they are geared to schooling specifically); (3) work more intensively with individual students after school; (4) communicate regularly with parents to develop collaborative teaching of students between school and family; (5) visit other schools and educational institutions; (6) learn more about new ideas by reading journals; (7) conduct research projects in their classroom or school; (8) learn more about the uses of educational media; (9) read novels and/or philosophy and draw implications for the improvement of their own teaching; and (10) develop support groups to share educational ideas, problems, and aspirations. The list could go on and on, but the point is that teachers, like other human beings, are not a homogeneous group. They need to have personalized learning opportunities just as their students do. What is more, if teachers have such experiences and realize the benefits to their own growth, they may be more likely to provide similar choice for the learning of their own students.

Criticism. To make a teacher sign a contract defending his or her personal growth proposal is itself an unprofessional act. It is inherent in the human species, probably others too, to seek that which fulfills real needs (Hopkins, 1954). Curriculum leaders should have faith that teachers will try their best to grow and mature as they continually strive to improve curriculum.

To expect or require action plans and rigorous statements of evidence is a slap in the face of teachers' capacity for personal responsibility. Surely, there are some teachers, too many, who view teaching as a technical nine-to-five job. They should be weeded out of the profession. No amount of coercive requirements will make them perform with personal responsibility. They may walk through the paces, but the genuine interest (which is everything) will not be there. The need for professional development is best served by expecting teachers to engage in it and then offering to support their endeavors in any ways that are feasible.

SUPERVISION AND CURRICULUM IMPROVEMENT

Another form of professional development is supervision. While the best forms of inservice education provide frequent programs and continuity, the best forms of supervision are continuous. Just as the "one-shot" inservice activity is usually disconnected from the mainstream of teacher and student needs, problems, and concerns, so too is the kind of pseudosupervision that takes the form of two or three visits to the classroom during which teachers are observed by principals or other curriculum leaders.

Supervision is an ongoing process that provides inspiration, meaning, helpful feedback, and a greater sense of purpose. Supervisors are usually curriculum leaders, administrative staff, consultants, building principals, and assistant principals whose work is not exclusively discipline and mundane arrangement of resources, and in larger school buildings the job may be given to directors of curriculum and instruction, team leaders in the case of team teaching arrangements, and department heads in the case of departmentalized structures.

Writers in the field of supervision tend to agree that effective supervision is an ongoing process. They disagree, however, as to the style, character, and orientation that best facilitates curriculum improvement. Some of the most insightful recent authors in the field delineate a variety of types of supervision (Glatthorn, 1984; Glickman, 1981; Sergiovanni and Starratt, 1983; Sullivan, 1980). In broad strokes, one can paint the picture of supervision orientations in two camps as does Smyth (1983):

> There are two ways of viewing clinical supervision—as a delivery system or a means of controlling teaching, or alternatively, as a form of personal empowerment by which teachers are able to gain meaning and understanding about themselves. [p. 12] . . . The really difficult part is actually making the move from preaching collegiality and exhorting teachers to work collaboratively, to the point of implementing practices that teachers feel are genuine, valuable and worth trying in their professional practice. [p. 13]

While Smyth refers to "clinical" supervision, Glatthorn (1984) differentiates this approach from several other types. As in curriculum literature, in supervision different authors use the same terms differently; therefore, I have decided to discuss five types of supervision, which are somewhat of an amalgamation of several typologies in the literature. I label them *directive, evaluative, consultative, permissive,* and *collaborative.*

Directive Supervision

Directive supervision is probably the most traditional. Its mission is to tell teachers how to teach in order to conform to curricular policies of the central administration and school board.

Advocacy. Schools are institutions, not merely collections of individuals. Just as orchestra musicians need musical scores, faculties in schools need curriculum to coordinate their efforts. Orchestras also need conductors who interpret, direct, and judge the performance of the orchestra as it works together. In schools, curriculum supervisors fulfill the same type of purpose. Neither schools nor orchestras need virtuoso performers to make and implement new plans independently of the others in the institution.

Schools need institutional missions or philosophies that are, in part, fulfilled by curriculum policy. Supervisors have as their job the seeing of the larger view; that is, supervisors coordinate or orchestrate the performance of curriculum policy. They see when a teacher, through virtuosity or incompetence, deviates from that policy. Deviation means inconsistency, and it produces practice that is both inefficient and dissonant.

Criticism. Schools are not orchestras and the analogy does not hold up. Rather than compare schools to the high culture of the orchestra, it is more appropriate to draw analogy to the mundanity and control of the factory and other dehumanizing workplaces. Supervisors of the directive orientation are hard taskmasters. They set the work to be done and, without consulting workers, require them to do it in the spirit of automatons. Moreover, an orchestra plays Mozart, Copland, or Brahms, and people choose to come and listen. Students are forced to come to school and are given little choice in what they are exposed to and learn. The greatest difference lies in the purpose. The orchestra gives enrichment through aesthetic experience, but an education should provide the capacity to direct the course of one's own affairs toward greater meaning, self-fulfillment, and contribution to others. If teachers are directed by others, it is silly to assume that they can teach their students to be more self-directive.

Evaluative Supervision

This form of supervision is an attempt to judge or assess teacher competence. It may not refer to competence based on discrete skills, but it is an administrative attempt to evaluate teacher performance.

Advocacy. It is evident that in the workplace, whatever the job or profession, many employees try to get away with doing the minimum amount possible. The teaching profession is no exception. This is part of human nature. Thus, it is necessary to develop instruments, objective if possible, to assess performance.

During the past thirty years, a rather sophisticated array of instruments has been developed to assess performance of teachers through supervision. In addition, supervisors are experienced teachers who presumably taught at a high degree of proficiency. They have in their grasp the clinical, diagnostic instruments to rate teachers fairly. When teachers know that they will be rated fairly and comprehensively, and when they know that they will be rewarded for their efforts, they work harder. Then, too, they are open to feedback, so that they can revise and improve their teaching. This, of course, is part and parcel of curriculum improvement.

Criticism.   Supervisors, by virtue (or vice) of the fact that schools cannot afford many of them, are generalists. Thus, it is a rarity when they know a teacher's area of expertise as well as the teacher does. Even more important, the limited time that it is possible for a supervisor to spend in any classroom, makes it impossible to know situational needs as well as the teacher who lives her or his professional life there. A few visits per year will yield little but teacher nervousness. Costa and Guditus (1984) point out that districtwide supervisors are dwindling in number due to financial constraints. This compounds the problem of getting to know the teachers and their situations well enough to make a difference.

Another major problem with the evaluative mode of supervision is its connection with annual ratings that serve as a basis for salary increments, and in the earlier career years, tenure. Evaluative supervision treats teachers like products, not professionals, and certainly not persons. The claim that feedback is helpful in this mode is merely a mask to cover the coercive character of one-shot teacher evaluations. Proponents assume that unless pushed by external sources, educators avoid the effort to grow. In reality, however, the only kind of effort humans consistently wish to avoid is that which does not enhance the meaning and direction of their lives. Both evaluative and directive supervisors need to ask if they are willing to have these same assumptions and techniques applied to them. If not, do they somehow consider themselves a higher form of professional than teachers? Does this not smack of elitism and discrimination?

Consultative Supervision

Sometimes, supervisors fulfill the role of consultant to teachers. They are neither directive nor evaluative; instead, they serve as resource persons who have greater exposure to curriculum research, theory, history, design, and teaching methods than have teachers. They inform teachers about available precedent in the areas of their teaching practice in general, and they provide ideas to help with specific projects as well. They also make outside resources and resource persons available to teachers according to their need. Consultative supervisors offer suggestions and recommendations, but they do not mandate. They are supervisory staff, not part of the administrative line that determines salary and oversees policy implementation.

Advocacy.   To have one with whom to consult is a great asset to a teacher. As Maxine Greene (1973) points out, a teacher is a stranger in many ways. He or she is alone in a group of young persons. This is rewarding and challenging, as well as alienating; yet it is important to have someone with whom to talk. Teachers often wonder if their decisions took a wrong turn; if others had similar dilemmas before; if they adequately surveyed the consequences of classroom life for all of the students; if their image of worthwhile knowledge and experience should be questioned; and if their mode of operation and basic beliefs are too culture-bound.

A good supervisor can be a sounding board, a careful listener, a generator of ideas, a facilitator, a fellow brainstormer, a participant observer, a model teacher, and a resource person. Sometimes, consultative supervisors can organize a team of specialists within a school to help a teacher address a special problem, meet a pressing need, or discuss a particular student. Such a group might consist of other teachers, a school social worker, a school psychologist, a guidance counsellor, a subject matter specialist, a school-community relations specialist, a speech therapist, and a school nurse, among others. These approaches, sometimes known as *staffings*, are common to teachers whose students are being evaluated for special education. This service, however, should be extended to teachers of all students through consultative supervision.

Criticism. Very few supervisors are like this. It would be nice to have a Socrates in every classroom, or at least in every school building, to help probe the mysteries of teaching. It sounds as if this supervisor would be a Carl Rogers too, along with an all-star team of other educational luminaries. I agree that it would be nice to have a staffing on each student, but I see neither the time nor the money flowing in to make this a reality. Furthermore, I doubt that teachers would open up; they would not believe that this supervisor really wanted to be a consultant.

Permissive Supervision

The label *permissive* should not be given a pejorative connotation here. It means nondirective interaction between supervisor and teacher that resembles the nondirective or client-centered therapy of Carl Rogers (1951), the nondirective teaching of A. S. Neill (1960), and the so-called indulgent child rearing attributed to Benjamin Spock (1945). The idea is to give considerable (almost unconditional) regard to the individual to know his or her needs, with the belief that the individual will strive to meet and satisfy those needs. It also assumes that such satisfaction brings growth. The therapist, teacher, parent, and, in this case, the supervisor is a facilitator. This differs from the consultative position because the permissive supervisor does not assume a position of greater expertise. Rather, the supervisor attempts to help the teacher accept responsibility for decision, action, meaning making, and consequences.

Advocacy. The capacity to be one's own best supervisor lies deep within all individuals. Teachers are no exception. Supervisors need to be there to facilitate and draw out this potential. This is not to say that teachers should do the whole job by themselves. One must remember that the supervisor is facilitative; thus, he or she provides resources and expertise when possible. But the key point lies in the term *permissive*; this does not mean that teachers are turned loose to run willy-nilly. Teachers, on the contrary, are *permitted* to exercise their own sense of responsibility in determining meaning and purpose in their work.

Criticism.   Teachers who are given this much freedom will, for the most part, take it as a license. They will do as little as possible, and eventually they will use the supervisor to fulfill their own selfish ends. Admittedly, there are a few highly motivated, self-directed teachers quite capable of supervising themselves. Even so, one cannot create supervisory permissiveness based on a tiny minority who can handle it. If most teachers are allowed to determine their own decision and action, "do their own thing" so to speak, curricular chaos results. There is no cohesive coordination, and there simply will not be enough time for each teacher to try to foresee the consequences of his or her work without someone directing the orchestra. The nondirective approach may work in therapy, but that is a one-to-one relationship. It rarely works in teaching, and it is a chaotic disservice to a whole school or school system.

Collaborative Supervision

Collaboration, a staff development concept with several extant variations (Gehrke and Parker, 1983), provides an integrated view of the supervisory process in at least two ways. The first pertains to persons, and the second to supervisory orientations. Regarding the first, all persons who are affected by the supervisory process should be involved in it. With respect to the second, all orientations to supervision have some merit under certain conditions and in certain circumstances. Thus, supervisors should have at their disposal several supervisory orientations so that they might utilize the more appropriate ones as needs arise.

Advocacy.   In the supervisory process, as in any other phase of curriculum development and improvement, an eclectic position is most practical (Schwab, 1971). Glatthorn (1984) labels this *differentiated supervision* and argues that a supervisor needs a repertoire of supervision modes. Selections from among these modes or orientations need to be based on a host of contextual variables that can only be known by the supervisor who knows the situation well. This is collaboration of ideas or approaches, and it allows for a multiplicity of perspectives to be drawn upon at once.

Collaboration among persons is of at least equal importance. Many persons have a stake in supervision, because its consequences influence them. Participatory governance holds that those affected by a policy, decision, or action should be allowed a role in its formulation and/or approval. Persons who help to develop their own destinies are more satisfied and effective.

Criticism.   The orientations to supervision already presented may have some overlap, but they are also contradictory. There is little that is more simplistic than an eclecticism which pastes together a collage of incompatible ideas or practical proposals. They clearly do not fit with one another in many respects.

As for persons involved, all of them do not have expertise. Surely, students, secretaries, school boards, parents, government officials, teachers, university professors, teacher educators, principals, superintendents, custodial staff, and a host of other persons are affected by many aspects of curriculum improvement and professional development. But this does not mean that they should share equally in supervision of these matters. Curriculum leaders have the greater proportion of expertise and should, therefore, be granted more supervisory power than those who know little about curriculum.

A CONCLUDING NOTE

We have considered professional development as a key to curriculum improvement. In doing so, we have traversed much territory: change and renewal, preservice teacher education, inservice teacher education, and supervision. If these are to be tied together one day by a comprehensive formulation of the whole professional development process, Griffin (1983b) indicates that the following elements must be considered: (1) primary dimensions of people, interactions, and context; (2) secondary dimensions of purpose, activities, and evaluation; and (3) data sources from funded knowledge, craft knowledge, perceptions, organizational history, and policies and practices of the particular organization.

COMMENTARIES

Each of our three guest commentators is asked to address his or her conception of the relation between curriculum improvement and professional development. Each is also asked to comment on approaches to preservice, inservice, and supervisory teacher education.

Experientialist

I am convinced that curriculum improvement is integral to and inseparable from the development of the persons who create, develop, and live it. In schools, this means that teachers and students are the curriculum, as much or more than the subject matter, plans, environmental arrangements, and instructional materials. As people grow, their experiences become enriched—and they grow. This may sound a bit like the Eastern mysticism of Ying and Yang, but if it does, so be it. We in the West can learn from Eastern mysticism.

Note that I have been careful not to use the terms *professional* or *personnel*. Both of them denote objects more than human beings. The term *personnel* grinds on my nerves the most. It makes the person a thing. *Professional* is somewhat more palatable, and I know that many teachers and administrators take pride in being professionals and strive for status with professions such as medicine and law that now are granted greater respect than education. Nevertheless, to be "a professional" makes one a special status of person to be set apart from others—perhaps even on a pedestal. People are all unique, but should some be given special status? Relationships lose some of their value when people enter them at different levels. This is the main reason that I prefer *personal development*. Its use has the positive side effect of expressing realization that curriculum is improved when students, as well as teachers and administrators, grow and develop as human beings rather than roles.

I cannot argue with the importance that personality, ideas, support and resistance, environments and facilities, and materials have as key ingredients in curriculum improvement. I have just listed them in what I consider priority order. The total personality of each person in a learning group gives the group a kind of personality of its own. Ideas are created by that personality, although some are introduced from outside sources.

It might be said that the group personality is an ever-changing "curriculum guide" and that the ideas that flow from it are the curriculum that is experienced. They actually result from the interplay of support and resistance. I don't particularly like the idea implied in force-field analysis that resistance is something to be avoided. When I think of *resistance* as Giroux (1983) uses it to denote a pedagogy of opposition to oppression and constraint, I see resistance and support as two positive forces in curriculum improvement and personal development.

Environments are surely important as facilitators of ideas, human interaction, and growth. However, facilities, materials, and the physical aspects of environments are usually given more credit than they deserve. The atmosphere or ambience of a group is more important, and that is a function of personalities, ideas, support, and resistance.

Preservice teacher education is far too rigid and lockstep. Those who want to become teachers should be given the assignment of using the resources of the university, those of surrounding school systems, and those of the city and state to learn to be a teacher. If they will need to develop curricula for others, they should learn to do so by developing their own curriculum with the guidance of faculty members. For example, they might develop card files of teaching strategies, survey methods books, visit classrooms, interview teachers, develop the rudiments of their philosophy of education, attend lectures, audit classes, keep journals of their experiences and interpretations of them, tutor students, survey instructional materials, spend time in the library stacks, get to know educational journals and professional associations, talk extensively with others who are preparing their own curricula to become teachers, and interview professors at their university.

As for personal development of teachers, it should be much the same. One never fully becomes a teacher; one is always becoming. If anyone claims to have learned it all, he or she is far from it. Teachers should most of all learn from their experience. They should determine what they want to pursue for individualized or group personal growth.

I dislike the term *supervision*. It implies that some people are superior to others; namely, administrators (whether they call them *staff* or *line*) are more perceptive than teachers. I don't buy that for a moment. It is unprofessional to have supervisors who oversee and judge the work of professionals. An administrator's job is to arrange things for more efficient and effective use. Thus, teachers should tell administrators how they want to grow and learn, and administrators should help to facilitate that process. R. F. Butts (1980) pointed to the paucity of studying and practicing civic values in classrooms and throughout the educational enterprise; he suggests that curricular experience should address a "decalogue" of democratic values: (1) justice, (2) freedom, (3) equality, (4) diversity, (5) authority, (6) privacy, (7) due process, (8) participation, (9) personal obligation for the public good, and (10) international human rights. These should be the basis for curriculum improvement, not just a knowledge basis but a lived basis.

Social Behaviorist

Curriculum improvement must involve retraining personnel, planned change, and the rigorous use of organization development strategies.

One cannot adequately retrain personnel unless one consciously alters personality. This means changing mind sets, attitudes, and behaviors. The best work in this area is done in the military and in advertising, where both the best academic psychologists and the best self-educated "psychologists" are hired. They are our experts in human motivation and propaganda (in the positive sense) techniques. This involves systematic delineation of supportive and resistive forces and a thoroughly planned approach to neutralize or convert resistive forces into supportive forces.

Obviously, curriculum change requires new mind sets, but it will not come about without the existence of materials, physical environment, and facilities. Sometimes, systematically prepared materials and learning environments *are* the improved curriculum with all its key ingredients. Ideas are, of course, necessary; they are the driving force behind any change. But these should be centralized and perpetuated from the top of the organization, because leaders have a coordinated view of the whole organization, and they are paid to be aware of the best ideas. The best ideas are, of course, those verified by carefully designed research studies. This does not mean that there is no input from representatives of all categories of personnel. It is the effective curriculum leader who gathers this kind of input and who realizes that when employees are listened to, they work as better organization members.

In an overall sense, the basic ingredients in curriculum improvement (personality, materials, environments and facilities, defensible ideas, and change strategies about converting resistance to support) could be considered basic elements to research in constructing a theory of curriculum improvement. Of course, these broad categories would need to be refined into subcategories, and the contribution one makes to the other could be explicated by causal modeling techniques.

The best developed research and theory used in curriculum improvement stems from the planned change literature (Benne and Muntyan, 1951; Bennis, Benne, and Chin, 1976). The contemporary outgrowth of this movement is the field of organization development (see Schmuck et al., 1977). Not only has this literature incorporated systems theory, but it provides concrete leadership techniques for changing and renewing organizations.

The adage that the best product is produced by using the best materials applies directly to curriculum improvement, starting with preservice teacher education. Teacher educators can fashion these materials—their students—into professionals who are open to curriculum revision based on an appreciation for sound research. While such students need some general education, the bulk of their professional education should consist of acquiring competencies or skills of teaching that research reveals correlate positively with increased student achievement. This means not only learning about these skills, but practicing them under carefully monitored conditions such as microteaching, peer teaching, observed tutorials, and eventually in the classroom. But the latter must be systematically planned and supervised.

All of teacher education that takes place after the bachelor's degree should be systematically coordinated with an overall curriculum design or policy. As attractive as some of the free-flowing, "do-your-own-thing" approaches to inservice education and nondirective types of supervision may seem, they have one overriding deficiency—they do not consider the whole system or organization. Supervisors need to direct or orchestrate the implementation of prespecified goals; teachers need to be evaluated to see if they do their part in implementing them. Inservice education must implement the overall thrusts of the organization. The school and school system should be a cohesive whole, not a collection of individuals all going their separate ways. Many of the inservice strategies listed in this chapter can be geared to this objective, but they should only be utilized when they contribute to it. The same can be said for the forms of supervision, except for the permissive form, which has little sense of purpose connected with it. Again, we need more research on which kinds of supervision and inservice education work better under what kinds of circumstances.

Intellectual Traditionalist

We live in an era when values change merely for the sake of novelty. Change is confused with improvement. We need to practice some of the great ideas of the past rather than give them lip service only. We have an ample supply of ideas, from Plato's *Republic* to the democratic ideals of Thomas Jefferson, Alexander Hamilton, and other Founding Fathers of the United States; from the communal compassion of Jesus to the class consciousness of Marx. Yet the ideals have remained largely rhetoric, neglecting practice. It may seem strange for me to advocate practice, but the topic is curriculum improvement; it requires that I address practice.

The education of teachers should instill within them a deep and abiding acquaintance with the great social idealist literature, the utopian writings of great scholars, and their criticisms of the society of their day. It is within this larger context that curriculum improvement can take place. Proposals for curriculum improvement are for naught, if they cannot be justified and defended within the context of the ideal society and individuals they create. Such improvements do not reach into the hearts and minds of human beings who are told about them, unless those who are taught learn from those who are deeply committed. To be deeply committed, one must have internalized a set of ideals into one's personality. Thus, the two most important ingredients in curriculum improvement are defensible ideas and the personality of leaders who promote their ideals.

For teachers to carry on with curriculum improvement, they must be exposed to charismatic leaders who inspire new motives and rekindle old ones in teachers' personalities. If this is done, such mundanities as materials, environments, facilities, resources, and even support will evolve. Inspiration, if great enough and if sufficiently integrated within the human personality, is the mainstay of curriculum improvement. Teachers who are knowlegeable about their purposes and committed to them will find a way to obtain or create materials, support, facilities, and resources. But it takes great leaders to help great teachers develop.

Preservice teacher education should consist primarily of helping potential teachers to know the disciplines well. This means they should know at least one area of knowledge very well and others well enough to sense the interdisciplinary connections with it. One or two good survey courses on educational theory should do the job for professional education. If teachers know their subject and genuinely want to relate it to students, they will be good teachers. A good grasp of other disciplines such as psychology, history, economics, languages, and their literatures will provide insight into the context of teaching; and the arts, especially theater and music, as well as languages, will enhance communication, which is the essence of pedagogy. Beyond this, the best way to help someone become a great teacher is to surround him or her with great teachers, both in the university classrooms and in clinical experiences in schools.

The most important quality in curriculum improvement is the fact that improvement is incorporated within disciplines of knowledge through methods of inquiry and validation. This means that the disciplines are perpetually in a state of renewal. If teachers, while in service, continue to study the disciplines, they will automatically be engaged in professional development and curriculum improvement.

Thus, inservice education should consist of opportunity to study one's discipline in a systematic way. Workshops rarely do the job. Required is the sustained study of graduate school. Summers should be used for this purpose. Idea exchanges throughout the year can be useful, but they usually debilitate into "show and tell." Such sessions should deal with *ideas*; perhaps, great books discussion groups could be developed for teachers, who would look especially for educational implications. Visits to observe great teachers in action are recommended. The contract idea is relevant, especially for those who are highly self-motivated. This, of course, should be the case for all educators.

Supervisors should be inspirers. They should be exemplary teachers themselves and should virtually overflow with ideas that keep their teachers motivated to learn and grow in their disciplinary expertise.

SUGGESTED READING

Several synoptic curriculum texts have useful sections on curriculum change, innovation, renewal, and improvement (terms that are carefully differentiated by some authors and used interchangeably by others). Among these are Smith, Stanley, and Shores (1957), Taba (1962), Tanner and Tanner (1980), and Wiles and Bondi (1984). Three prominent synoptic texts are organized around the issue of curriculum improvement: *Curriculum Improvement: A Guide to Problems, Principles, and Process* (Oliver, 1977); *Curriculum Development: Program Improvement* (Hunkins, 1980); and *Curriculum Improvement: Decision Making and Process* (Doll, 1982). MacDonald and Walker (1976) focus on theory and cases of educational innovation in Britain and America.

A host of writings from many different orientations speak to the problem of curriculum improvement in quite different ways. In 1950, Hollis Caswell and Associates provided an overview of the evaluation of curriculum improvement through the careful analysis of programs in ten school systems in a volume entitled *Curriculum Improvement in Public School Systems*. A decade later McNally et al. (1960) conducted a similar survey of curriculum improvement in seven school systems and drew implications about the kinds of curriculum development that improve the quality of school programs. It is noteworthy that Caswell wrote the preface for this book. Reid and Walker (1975) presented a set of case studies of curriculum change by authors who have a bent toward practical inquiry perspectives.

Two books that utilize anthropological methods of analysis and interpretation are

The Culture of the School and the Problem of Change (Sarason, 1982) and *Dilemmas of Schooling: Teaching and Social Change* (Berlack and Berlack, 1981). The former insightfully deals with a rather large scope of analysis; the latter is drawn from carefully recorded observations in British primary schools that serve as a basis for a theory (with both analytic and critical dimensions) constructed from sixteen overarching dilemmas of school functioning. A third anthropologically oriented book by Kazamias and Massialas (1965) takes a very broad cross-cultural look at tradition and change in education and forces that lie behind them. Charlotte P. Taylor (1976) sets forth a social perspective on the roles of social groups, government, economics, family, and other forces that could serve as agents to transform schools. Not all useful accounts of change processes are about actual events, as evidenced by Skeel and Hagen (1971), who provide an in-depth fictionalized account of change processes in an elementary school. Joyce, Hersh, and McKibben (1983) contribute an elaborate analysis of the structure, nature, and stages of school improvement that set the large context for curriculum improvement. Finally, I recommend the Summer 1983 issue of *Theory into Practice*, a theme issue devoted to perspectives on curriculum change. The context of curriculum improvement cannot be adequately understood without sociological knowledge of the circumstances faced by teachers, as provided by Dan Lortie (1975).

It is also important to have historical perspective on improvement; therefore, I suggest again Lawrence Cremin's *Transformation of the School* (1961) and Angela E. Fraley's *Schooling and Innovation* (1981). In addition, I have recently come across an unpublished manuscript by Harold B. Dunkel, author of *Herbart and Herbartianism* (1970), entitled *Writ in Water: The Epitaph of Educational Innovation*, which deals with life cycles and contributions of educational movements based upon German educational innovators of the nineteenth century such as Hegel, William T. Harris, Rosenkranz, Herbart and his disciples, Froebel, and Wundt. I suspect that it may be published when this book is available.

The topic of the curriculum of teacher education is well documented in the chapter, and Joyce and Clift (1984) provide a comprehensive discussion of reform in teacher education. I draw your attention to the saga of major commission reports and then suggest that you consult card catalogues on the subject. The reform reports of the 1980s spurred a host of journal articles. One might look at *Kappan* and *Educational Leadership* during the period. Also state reform projects were indeed plentiful, some lasting, some not. A good summary is available in *State Reform Initiatives* (Walsh, 1984) available from the Educational Issues Department of the American Federation of Teachers. The *Journal of Teacher Education* is, of course, an essential resource on this topic.

Inservice education, or more generally *staff development*, is given scholarly treatment and related to school and curriculum improvement in a recent NSSE Yearbook, entitled *Staff Development*, edited by Gary Griffin (1983a). Another excellent resource is Louis Rubin's *Improving In-Service Education: Proposals and Procedures for Change* (1971). Publications of the ASCD frequently deal with staff development as illustrated by Joyce and Showers (1983), who relate it to research on training, and by Beegle and Edelfelt (1977), who drew together a number of authors who address the liberating power the staff development can have. Of particular relevance in the latter are perspectives of James B. Macdonald (1977b) on the context of staff development and Paul Klohr (1977) on alternative curriculum theory perspectives and staff development. Edelfelt and Smith (1978) clearly and influentially stated the case that staff development must be multidimensional and that it must be integrated with curriculum development. The 1981 ASCD Yearbook, *Staff Development/Organization Development* (Dillon-Peterson, 1981), relates these two key terms in the literature. The principal's pivotal role in staff development should be considered (see Yauch, 1957; Klopf, 1974). The process of cooperative learning must be acknowledged for its value to administrators, teachers, and students alike (see Miel and Associates, 1952; Johnson et al., 1984; Slavin, 1983). Finally, a phenomenological treatment of meanings in inservice acts is provided by Aoki et al. (1984); this is an orientation rarely seen applied to this topic and is therefore interesting and helpful.

Supervision is a massive topic and I hesitate to go out on a limb and suggest one best general text, but I will anyway: *Supervision: Human Perspectives* (Sergiovanni and Starratt, 1983). At their 1984 Annual Meeting in New York, Professors of Supervision, counterpart of Professors of Curriculum, were so favorably disposed to the book *Education in the 80's: Curricular Challenges* (Edinger, Houts, and Meyer, 1981) that they gave copies to all members present for both organizations. That teachers feel threatened by supervisors is well known; admitting this and developing the wherewithal to deal with it productively is the theme of *Supervisors and Teachers: A Private Cold War* by Arthur Blumberg (1974). More than any other organization, ASCD regularly produces some fine resources on supervision. I recommend *Differentiated Supervision* (Glatthorn, 1984), *Developmental Supervision* (Glickman, 1981), *Professional Supervision for Professional Teachers* (Sergiovanni, 1975), *Clinical Supervision* (Sullivan, 1980), and the 1982 ASCD Yearbook, *Supervision of Teaching*, edited by Thomas Sergiovanni. One might also examine the April 1984 *Educational Leadership*, as the theme is "The Realities of Supervision." Certainly readers should not neglect the highly influential contribution by Edelfelt and Smith (1978) which called for the integration of curriculum development and inservice education.

Finally, I add literature on critical praxis from Chapter Thirteen, according to which curriculum improvement necessitates a great deal more resistance, contestation, reconceptualization, and reconstruction than provided by conventional orientations to teacher education, staff development, and supervision.

Two sources of enduring value on this topic from the past century are *Talks to Teachers* by William James (1899) and *Talks on Pedagogics* by Francis W. Parker (1894).

RECOMMENDATIONS FOR REFLECTION

1. Think of your own curriculum improvement experience. How have projects that you initiated grown out of your personality? In other words how has your own outlook on curriculum (and life in general) contributed to improvements that you provided for your classroom? For example, changes in attitude or viewpoint throughout one's life may account for changes in curriculum philosophy and practice. I encourage you to reflect on this with reference to yourself and others.

2. How have you seen sparse or abundant materials and environmental facilities enhance or diminish curriculum improvement efforts? What curriculum improvement ideas have you seen dashed because of materials and environments inadequate to facilitate them?

3. What curriculum improvement ideas would you advocate in your environment (or in general) if you had the personalities, environmental facilities, and materials to support them?

4. Select an idea that you are convinced would be very helpful to the curriculum situation in which you now work (or a situation you know well). Why is it worthwhile? Determine its chances of being successfully adopted by conducting a rough version of a force-field analysis. For this purpose, draw up a chart with two columns, one labeled *Resistive Forces* and the other *Supportive Forces*. Down the left-hand side list topics discussed: *Personalities, Materials, Environment,* and *Ideas.* Also include *Feasibility,* which is related to the other four but especially emphasizes matters of money, time, and resources. Next, identify supportive and resistive forces in each of the five areas. How could you use sound argument and public relations to shift the balance from resistance to support, especially with regard to gatekeepers?

5. Reflect on the educational situations in which you have participated as a professional or as a student. Who were the *gatekeepers*? How did they attain that status? Do you see any patterns among them and their uses of power? Gatekeepers also have gatekeepers. To whom do the gatekeepers you just identified turn for support? What happens when you leave the environs of the school system to generate support (i.e., when you seek support from the mass media or business community)? Have you ever tried this? What is the response from the school community? Is this a useful way to generate support? What are its strengths and weaknesses?

6. How did your own preservice teacher education program relate to each of the statements of advocacy and criticism presented in this chapter? What was the major source of emphasis in that program: (1) general education; (2) professional education courses; or (3) clinical experiences, including student teaching? Which of the three contributed most to your success as a teacher? Why?

7. What has contributed most, in general, to the professional educator that you have become? List five major influences. What is it about these influences that affected you so profoundly? Were most of them formal attempts to educate you, or were they experiences that would usually be classified outside of formal education? Of the latter, is there any way that such experiences could become incorporated into teacher education programs?

8. What is your idea of an ideal teacher education program at the preservice level? What kinds of arguments might be leveled against it? How would you defend the program against such arguments? (This might be a good project for small-group work.)

9. What kinds of staff development or inservice education activities have you experienced? How do they relate to the alternatives presented in this chapter?

10. If you were in charge of inservice education for a school district, what kind of program would you develop? Why?

11. What kind of inservice education program do you prefer to be involved in yourself? In other words, what professional development activities help you to grow?

12. Is there any discrepancy between the kind of inservice you prefer for yourself and the kind that you deem beneficial for others? If there is, what are the implications? Does this pertain to the experientialist commentator's distinction between professional development and personal growth? Does it relate to the "golden rule" advice found in many religions of the world?

13. What kind of supervision works best for you?

14. Which of the several varieties of supervision treated in this chapter would you incorporate into a program of supervision if you directed one for a school district?

15. How do you respond to the notions of "developmental supervision" (Glickman, 1981) and differentiated supervision (Glatthorn, 1984), which essentially are efforts to tailor supervision to situational needs and interests? What are strengths and weaknesses of such provisions?

16. Is it realistically possible to have several choices from among which participants may select for preservice teacher education? For inservice education? For supervision? Is there any danger in eclecticism?

17. Return to the statements of advocacy and criticism in sections of the chapter on preservice, inservice, and supervision. Select at least one alternative from each of these sections and continue the arguments. In other words, have the advocate respond to the critic and the critic respond again. (This might be done in writing, as a dialogue or miniplay, a panel discussion, or orally while working in pairs.)

18. Where do you stand with respect to the guest commentators on professional development and its relation to curriculum improvement? On their orientation to teacher education at the preservice, inservice, or supervisory levels?

19. Now that you have heard all the guest speaker commentaries, how does their overall position relate to your own? Are you essentially an intellectual traditionalist, social behaviorist, experientialist, or something different from any of these orientations? If you see your position as a blend of the three positions, as many educators do, what is the nature of that blend? What are the sources and origins of its dominant ingredients? In essence, what is your curriculum orientation? How do you defend it?

16

✦ Promising Directions in Curriculum: A Personal Hope ✦

Knowledge of what is possible is the beginning of happiness.
GEORGE SANTAYANA *Little Essays* (1920)

Round about what is, lies a whole mysterious world of might be, a psychological romance of possibilities and things that do not happen.
HENRY WADSWORTH LONGFELLOW "Table-Talk" *Driftwood* (1857)

So many worlds,
So much to do,
So little done,
Such things to be.
ALFRED LORD TENNYSON "In Memorium A.H.H." (1850)

SETTING THE STAGE

What one curriculum writer deems promising, another might consider ill conceived or wrong-headed. Therefore, any treatment of promising directions must acknowledge that the term *promising* is value laden. Hence, I have chosen the subtitle "A Personal Hope" for this chapter. In using the term *promising*, I am not referring to probability, that which is likely to happen, but to that which I personally believe will bring curriculum improvement, or in some cases already is bringing such improvement.

The first section of this chapter refers back to each of the chapters of this book. My point in doing this is not primarily to summarize but to glean a central message from each for those engaged in curriculum work. In the second part of this chapter, I select central threads that run through several of the chapters and identify them as my personal hopes for the future of curriculum.

PROMISING DIRECTIONS

Preface (Motivations)

In the preface I autobiographically presented some of the background that has led me to curriculum work. More curriculum writers are revealing the deeper sense of meaning and direction that brought them into teaching or related educational endeavors and eventually to curriculum work. Such efforts help aspiring curriculum workers to reassess and clarify the values and motivations that lead them toward careers in the curriculum field.

Chapter One (The Value of Curriculum Studies)

In introducing this book my main point was to recognize that anyone who is involved in the process of educating is engaged in curriculum work. Being involved in curriculum work means a great deal more than writing course syllabi, creating instructional units, and selecting textbooks and other curricular materials. It even involves more than having an overall grasp of program design, prespecification, and its evaluation. Doing curriculum is perceived increasingly as the process of asking fundamental questions such as: What is worth knowing and experiencing? What kind of a life does such knowing and experiencing assume is good for both individuals and the society? How can worthwhile knowledge and experience be provided by educators? How can we know if it is provided?

Part I (The Need for Broad Perspectives)

Part I included Chapters Two through Six and was designed to set curriculum questions in larger perspective. The questions posed in Chapter One cannot be seen adequately apart from their relatedness to broader realms of ideas and circumstances. Curriculum writers are growing in their acknowledgment of the relevance of curriculum inquiry and development to historical precedent; social, economic, and cultural contexts; philosophical assumptions and beliefs; and public policy.

Chapter Two (A Field or Community of Inquiry)

Since the beginning of this century, a network of scholars and practitioners has emerged to address curriculum problems. Through their professional associations, journals, and books, they have created a field of study or area of inquiry. The curriculum field has considerable diversity when it comes to definitions, philosophical and ideological orientations, and classification schemes for analysis. Nevertheless, unity can be found in deep and abiding concern for the kind of world that humans create for themselves and for the character of individuals who make up that world. Sometimes this concern lies beneath a rubble of technocratic mechanisms designed to control or mold learners. The spark that ignites good teaching is often quenched when teachers and curriculum leaders in schools are considered auxiliary to the curriculum field. The essence of democratic curriculum studies involves in dialogue all who play a part in the education. This means that curriculum leaders, teachers, nonschool educators, parents, and even students as well as scholars, need to be considered a part of the curriculum field. Of course, their differing areas of expertise must be recognized and respected. Scholars in a professional field are realizing more fully that they cannot defensibly conduct inquiry and generate proposals apart from collaborative efforts of all who are affected by such endeavors. This implies a community of inquiry.

Chapter Three *(The Need for Curriculum History)*

Curriculum work since the early 1970s has given special attention to history in at least two respects: (1) curriculum researchers, leaders, and developers are beginning to look to the past for precedent; and (2) those engaged in curriculum work are beginning to view their efforts as embedded or situated in a set of historical conditions. To look for precedent is promising because it acknowldges that insight and understanding are not simply modern phenomena. Previous situations and dilemmas may be similar to current ones; therefore, it is beneficial to draw upon historical responses to them as one attempts to deal with contemporary problems. To view oneself as part of an historical process is to become more highly cognizant of the plethora of forces with which one deals. Too often history is viewed as something that deals with others but not with oneself. While the composite of historical forces creates the present, humans also have the power to influence the course of events. Events are not merely dictated forces to which humans can only respond. It is promising, indeed, that curriculum scholars and practitioners are looking more fully to the past for precedent and are seeing themselves as important factors in the course of human history. One of the most neglected historical periods is the progressive education era. I am convinced that we need to explore curriculum insights of that era in light of contemporary problems and proposals. Future study should focus particularly on the ability of progressive teachers and students to ask fundamental curriculum questions about their own lives.

Chapter Four *(Awareness of Contextual Impacts)*

During the past two decades curriculum writers have shown greater awareness of contextual forces that influence curriculum thought and practice. Curriculum leaders and teachers have become more politicized than before, and they are beginning to draw attention to curriculum concerns as well as salary, fringe benefits, working conditions, and the like. Prior to the 1970s, most curriculum development and writing seldom addressed political, economic, cultural, and ideological factors. Some of today's most promising studies deal with ways in which such factors subtly work their way into curriculum practice and provide a powerful hidden curriculum. Moreover, other studies explore ways that curriculum leaders, teachers, and students interact with these forces—both altering them and having their own outlook altered by them. Such studies constitute the root of theory that could lead defensible curriculum improvement.

Chapter Five *(The Necessity of Philosophy)*

Just as a bridge is only as strong as its underlying support, curriculum proposals and practices are only as strong as the assumptions upon which they rest. Merely because a practice or proposal seems attractive or is in vogue is not sufficient reason to accept and promote it. A broad range of curricularists now recognize that it is not enough to develop a proposal and systematically state the underlying assumptions once and for all. Instead, curricularists are recognizing that all persons involved in curriculum, not just those labeled experts, must continuously reflect on their basis for doing what they do. Such *philosophizing* is more important to curriculum work than are formal philosophical treatises. Just as Socrates admonished all persons to realize that the unexamined life is not worth living and encouraged his followers to make such examination a continuous endeavor, the same recommendation should be applied to curriculum work. The unexamined curriculum is not worth offering. To take the principle a step farther into the realm of students, one would advocate that learners themselves should engage in philosophizing about the value of what they are asked to learn and about the role they should have in determining it.

Chapter Six (Curriculum as Policy)

One of the most commendable aspects of the new field of public policy studies is its interdisciplinary character. This illustrates that problems are not neatly packaged to fall within the confines of one discipline or another. Instead, it requires the emergence of a unique configuration of knowledge from many disciplines and professional fields to address most problems adequately. Curriculum problems are no exception. Moreover, most curriculum problems are not amenable to merely technical solutions. They involve fundamental issues about what contributes to public growth. In the words of Tyack and Hansot (1984) educational leaders are no less than "managers of virtue." Thus, curriculum scholars are increasingly linking together with public policy analysts to analyze the consequences of proposals and practices relative to such pervasive issues as freedom, equality, morality, and justice. An important implication for curriculum practice at the school system or even classroom level is that governance procedures or ordinary modes of operation greatly influence the character of what is taught and learned. Decisions about what is taught and learned, the ways in which teaching and learning take place, and modes of assessment used are all policy related. They correspond to policy formulation, implementation, and evaluation. Curriculum researchers are beginning to realize the great impact exerted on public policy by those who create curriculum. Students who experience curriculum, after all, become the adults who formulate, implement, and evaluate public policy.

Part II and Chapter Seven (Paradigm)

Chapters Seven through Thirteen presented three different paradigms or conceptual frameworks for curriculum inquiry. Chapter Seven introduced the idea of alternative paradigms and briefly encapsulated (1) the empirical-analytic paradigm, (2) the practical or hermeneutic paradigm, and (3) a paradigm of critical praxis. Chapters Eight through Eleven dealt with the perennial curriculum categories or purposes, learning experiences or content, organization, and evaluation. Together, these constitute the empirical-analytic paradigm that has dominated curriculum inquiry. Chapter Twelve explained a practical paradigm and Chapter Thirteen presented a paradigm of critical praxis, both offered as alternatives to the dominant paradigm. The central message in this part of the book is that there are multiple lenses through which curriculum problems may be viewed. There is no single avenue to curricular truth. While the three paradigms discussed embody quite different assumptions, it is important to note that they are not mutually exclusive. Moreover, there is considerable variation within each. The realization and acknowledgment of the complex character of curriculum inquiry is promising indeed, because it prevents simplistic, mechanistic, solutions to complicated issues. The tendency to offer recipelike answers ("three ways to improve this or that in your curriculum") should be overcome.

Chapter Eight (Purposes)

The central message of this chapter is that curriculum devoid of purpose is molded by outside forces. Purposes need to be clear and defensible. At the same time, there are many different notions of purpose, not all of which involve prespecification at the onset of the teaching-learning process. Quite promising are notions of purpose that have an expressive or evolving sense of direction that is developed by teachers in dialogue with students rather than for teachers and students by external authorities. Although practiced by progressive educators in the 1920s and 1930s, these notions of purpose are certainly worth exploring more fully in practice than they have been.

Chapter Nine (Content or Learning Experiences)

The issue of curriculum as something to be delivered as opposed to something that is developed is central here. Traditionally, curriculum is seen as a commodity created by experts (a product rather than a process, as Ornstein, 1982, put it) and presented or delivered to the masses of students for their edification. A promising direction that reached fruition with Dewey and other progressive educators holds that curriculum should be developed by those who will be affected by it most thoroughly. This makes curriculum primarily a matter of democratic interaction that is carried on by communication of individual and social needs. Thus, curricular content becomes a process of reflecting, theorizing, and experiencing rather than a mere receiving of predetermined content. Of considerable interest and promise are attempts of researchers who use methodologies as diverse as cognitive psychology, autobiographical method, standardized tests, and teacher-learner dialogue to discover how curricular experiences provide changed outlooks on the part of learners.

Chapter Ten (Organization)

An array of issues falls within the purview of organization: scope, sequence, learning environments, and instruction. Within each of these subdivisions exists many options. Too often in the past, curriculum leaders have settled on one strategy within each of these domains without considering (or even acknowledging the existence of) alternatives. It is most promising to see curriculum workers explicate alternative modes of sequence, responses to the problem of scope, instructional approaches, and learning environments. Many have begun to identify strengths and weaknesses and to project consequences of different courses of action. Sometimes curriculum leaders and teachers keep a range of possibilities at their disposal and in practice match them with the unique needs of their situation as they arise. Here we see a blending of perennial and practical paradigms, a healthy sign indeed.

Chapter Eleven (Evaluation)

Traditionally, evaluation has meant assessment of student performance; more recently, it refers to measures of programmatic success. In both cases the emphasis is a rather linear focus on prespecification, implementation, and outcome. Research that takes this focus is usually of the quantitative and experimental or quasi-experimental variety. Within the curriculum field today a number of promising alternative modes are gaining wider acceptance. Sometimes they are all grouped under the general rubric of "qualitative"; yet their differences are considerable: participant observation, criticism and connoisseurship, and responsive evaluation. These are merely illustrative of attempts to view evaluation as a democratic process that attempts to be helpful to all participants in curricular situations by responding to the ecology of consequences of a program or proposal. It is an important development to see many curriculum evaluators begin to accept the veracity of many varieties of inquiry: from personal, intuitive insight and phenomenological interpretation to literary criticism and dialogic communication, as well as traditional test, measurement, and experimental approaches.

Chapter Twelve (Practical Inquiry)

Practical inquiry, of course, has been used by the best teachers throughout history. They take stock of their situation, interpret its meaning, and pursue a sense of direction based on moral commitment. To them teaching is a moral craft, as explicated by Alan Tom (1984). The example of excellent pedagogues is implicit in many progressive educators' images of what curriculum should be like. A thoughtful, sensitive teacher who looks deeply and broadly within his or her own life and encourages students to do the same is a central feature of practical curriculum. Some renditions, however, cast practical inquiry too much as problem solving of merely an expedient type. It is most promising, therefore, to find curricularists today who emphasize the quest for moral goodness at the heart of practical inquiry. This does not refer to an authoritarian or absolutist notion of goodness. Instead, it refers to an ongoing desire to discover the morally good experience created in every situation.

Chapter Thirteen (Critical Praxis)

The practical and hermeneutic emphasis of Chapter Twelve is intimately related to the critical praxis of Chapter Thirteen. It follows a quest to create morally good action that one would want to attend to the broad context of social and economic life and contribute to a more just society. The tendency of some curricularists to examine critically taken-for-granted aspects of any ideology is promising. It is indeed healthy to develop a perspective or vantage point from which one can leave one's embeddedness in situations and view them from a more detached position. This moves curriculum into a state of genuine inquiry, which is a far distance from curriculum conceived as the arm of the state or economic system. Rather than promote mindless patriotism or unquestioned provincialism, curriculum workers ask whether loyalty is merited. In turn, they motivate such criticism in the action of teachers and students. Criticism, however, does not imply negativism; rather, it openly accepts responsibility for contributing to better quality of life. Admittedly, educational institutions cannot accomplish this alone; nevertheless, to turn away from the quest to create improved social and individual lives is to shirk the moral commitment that curricularists should make to social justice.

Part III (Possibility)

Chapters Fourteen through Sixteen deal with problems facing curriculum, curricular improvement, and promising directions. The overall message of this section is that everyone concerned with curriculum should cultivate a vision of what might be, what ought to be, and how it could be achieved.

Chapter Fourteen (Problems)

Some curriculum problems are perennial while others are transitory. Another way of cutting the pie is to consider instructional and institutional problems as one category and ideological and societal problems as another (see Goodlad and Richter, 1966). A most promising direction is that both curriculum scholars and practitioners are beginning to see both sets of problems as highly significant to curriculum work. A kind of ecological perspective is being realized that acknowledges the interdependence between the two. This not only means that societal and ideological problems influence what goes on in educational institutions and, therefore, curriculum and instruction; it also means that curricular influences on the lives of learners contribute to the character, knowledge, and ability of persons who ultimately grow up to create, conceptualize, and deal with societal and ideological problems. It is impossible for the curricularist defensibly to escape from dealing with either category of problems.

Chapter Fifteen (Curriculum Improvement)

The key to curriculum improvement is professional development. Curriculum leaders in schools and scholars alike are beginning to realize that fundamental improvement requires the involvement of all who contribute to curriculum. This includes teachers as well as administrators and others who make curriculum policy. Moreover, it is essential that their involvement be genuine; in other words, teachers must participate in curriculum improvement proposals because they perceive needs for personal and professional growth and for the growth of their students. In either case, growth does not accrue from being told what should be done. Suggestions should be set forth as possibilities, but those who are most involved in their application should contribute most to dialogue on relative merits.

Chapter Sixteen (Promise and Hope)

In this chapter, I present my own conception of promising directions and personal hopes. I hope that the medium is the message: curriculum workers should be well acquainted with the literature of the field. This familiarity should lead to the advocacy of promising ideas. Furthermore, curricularists should have hope that the future will bring curriculum improvements that are in line with the promising directions they advocate. Advocacy does not mean dogmatic propagandizing. It implies commitment that is always willing and striving to learn and grow.

PERSONAL HOPES

As a curriculum theorist, researcher, consultant, and teacher educator for the past ten years I have had ample time to reflect on my hopes for curriculum. As in the fairy tales in which someone is granted three wishes, I have granted myself ten hopes. In setting forth these hopes I attempt to keep solidly in mind my seven years of experience as a public school teacher. Experiences with both the realities of the practical sphere and the ideals of reflective scholarship should provide a balanced commentary. I intentionally try not to duplicate points made in the discussion of promising directions, although I frequently do build upon them. In essence, my hopes reveal what I believe to be necessary but neglected emphases in curriculum rather than initiatives that already have a strong foothold.

1. Democratic Action

Here I use the term *democratic action* because *democracy* is too often left at the point of rhetoric alone. This is clearly not the case with Dewey's (1916) use of the term in *Democracy and Education*, for he was a staunch proponent of democratic action. I share Dewey's hope that all societal institutions, especially those engaged in education, be democratic. Except for rare instances throughout history, schools have been bastions of autocracy. Children and youths have been seen as incapable of knowing their own needs and developing worthwhile directions for meaningful and valuable experience in their lives. As a result, even in democratic societies where the virtues of democracy are extolled for memorization and appreciation, students are seldom allowed to participate in decisions about their own lives. After students have spent more than a decade under autocratic conditions, it is surprisingly ironic that educators lament the fact that graduates do not know how to participate responsibly as democratic citizens.

It is my hope that educators will soon realize this contradiction and will respond to it by creating democratic learning environments in schools. To do this, educators must understand that students have a deep understanding of what they need, even at an early age. Rousseau, Froebel, Tolstoy, Dewey, and Kilpatrick among others realized this quite fully. L. Thomas Hopkins (1954) developed a biological rationale for it and the notion of organic groups to carry it out. Quite simply, my hope is that teachers will recognize students as fellow human beings who are profoundly interested in their own growth. I hope, too, that curriculum leaders will offer the same kind of recognition to teachers. When a stage is set for democratic deliberation and action, teachers and students will realize that together their insight is stronger than it is separately. Together, they can create continuously evolving curricula of experiences that bring meaning and purpose to their lives.

2. Diversity and Unity

Democratic action reveals the complementarity of the apparent opposites of diversity and unity in society. Every classroom, especially those in our heterogeneous urban areas, is filled with diversity. Unfortunately, many curriculum plans, educational programs, and instructional materials treat students as a homogeneous unit. The superficial assumption of unity in which every student is to be treated alike includes a false notion of equality as same treatment. It is my hope that curricularists will realize the educative power of diversity. The station given to schools in most social systems is middle class; thus, it is easy for those who educate to inculcate uncritically and unwittingly middle-class values. Values should not be held purely for the sake of tradition; rather, they should be developed or accepted through conscious reflection.

I would like to see schools and other educative institutions engage teachers and learners in communicative encounters whereby each could learn from the diverse interests, needs, experience, and knowledge of the others. Through the art of such sharing, argues Jürgen Habermas (1984), "communicative action" can evolve in which humans who seem quite diverse in many ways can discover a bond of common human values. These he asserts can provide principles for the guidance of practical living. I hope that families and schools can be a point of origin for communicative action that grows from the interplay of human diversity and unity.

3. *Curricular Ecology*

Just as biologists realize that the presence or absence of a type of organism or a disturbance of physical environment may upset the balance of nature and produce a state of disequilibrium in natural environments, it is necessary for educators to understand better the ecology or interdependence of curricula in the educational environments of students. Human diversity and unity have their roots in many aspects of culture and society, not merely in schools alone. In modern societies today, persons are bombarded with a multitude of perspectives from many different sources. From a very early age children take in overt and covert messages from families, mass media, friends, communities, nonschool organizations, and informal peer gatherings, and eventually schools, vocations, and avocations. This list is not exhaustive, but the point is that schools are one of many message sources that shape the outlooks of students. The overt and covert messages of schools *are* their curriculum. At the same time that students are influenced by school curriculum, they are also faced with the messages or curricula of many other institutions and relationships. In schools the profound impact of such nonschool relationships on students is rarely acknowledged. Children enter schools and become students, persons defined only by the culture within school. Yet the greater part of their outlook is fashioned by interactions that occur outside of school.

Therefore, my hope is that educators begin to grasp more broadly the interdependent network (or ecology) of curricula (planned and unplanned) that forge the outlooks and ideals learned in a culture, society, or world. This is an insurmountable task, but to make headway in that direction is to come closer to an understanding of *paideia* as defined by Werner Jaeger (1945). Paideia, the ways in which historical processes form human character, ideals, and actions, is at the root of all curriculum inquiry problems. After all, the playing of a significant part in the history of individual and small-group lives is what curriculum is developed to do.

Those who develop curriculum in schools can only contribute to student growth adequately if they know more about the ways in which other curricular forces influence students. There is the growing tendency for leaders in nonschool spheres of culture to see themselves as formative educators. Many individuals consider themselves to be primarily self-educated more than educated by institutions, even though they may have credentials from highly prestigious schools and universities. Even renowned scholars often recount major educative milestones in their lives as, "When I read Goethe" or "During my Hegelian period." In the more technical and executive spheres, corporations are showing a distinct preference to train their own personnel. Television producers clearly may be conceived as curriculum designers. Families are more consciously attending to their educative function as evidenced by sales of books by T. Berry Brazelton (1981) and the myriad classes on parenting, childbirth, nursing, fathering, becoming a sibling, and so on. Balbus (1982) has gone so far as to argue cogently that political, technological, and sexual liberation can only be approached through a dedicated, widespread, and continuous process of parenting in which both parents share equally responsibilities of child rearing. Church groups, scouting organizations, and other youth groups that have performed a supplementary educative function in previous years are augmenting their efforts. Meanwhile, street gangs and other groups are taking on educational responsibilities and are even writing grant proposals for public and private funding to support their efforts.

Cremin (1976) writes of the educational function that an array of societal institutions perform, while Bremer (1979) argues that the community itself should be the focal point around which the many educative institutions and relationships within a society coalesce, concluding that

> *Perhaps education would then be community's way of begetting community, and community would be education's way of continuing education. The ultimate justification of any institution, program or relationship would then be found in the extent to which it contributes to the learning of its members.* [p. 52]

By *community* Bremer (1979, p. 52) refers to the interplay of three meanings: (1) "the ideal society in which we aspire to live," (2) the actual "society or the general neighborhood," and (3) "the joining of these two . . . [and] the social and political skills through which they school each other." John Holt (1981) sees similar benefits emerging within and emanating from the family, perhaps as a microcosm of community, that decides to educate its own children instead of send them to school.

It seems clear to me that education in the future will take place in many different settings. While curriculum scholars and practitioners should continue to devote substantial attention to schools, they will stifle their own potential contributions by confining their efforts to schooling. I hope that more curricularists will see new provinces of educative needs for their expertise, and I hope that they will tailor their communicative style to address problems in languages of parents, corporate managers, street gangs, church groups, producers of television programs, designers of computer software, creators of children's games and toys, and a host of others whose work involves the development of curriculum. This may mean that they consult with such groups, learn to give inspirational lectures, interact in highly informal settings, write popular books and articles, and most of all collaborate in an effort to learn from these groups the insights that they already have about their needs.

4. Dialogue

The need for collaboration is not only satisfid by working together but by genuine dialogue in which differences associated with rank in an institution or class in a society are suspended. In dialogue, people listen carefully, reflectively, empathically, and compassionately to the experience of others, as in Freire's (1970) work with oppressed Brazilian peasants. Roles of credentialed expertise are given a secondary place to insight about needs, interests, and purposes that make sense and are defensible in light of the situations in which they exist. The example of Freire's work should not be construed to indicate that dialogue is only relevant to nonschool populations or to those who are not privy to the languages of educational theory and practice.

On the contrary, dialogue between teachers and students is central to the democratic classroom, and it is the key to professional development relationships between teachers and curriculum leaders. Moreover, dialogue is much needed among representatives of different orientations within the curriculum field as illustrated by commentaries from the experientialist, social behaviorist, and intellectual traditionalist at the conclusion of the foregoing chapters of this book. My hope is that more serious effort will be extended to maintain dialogue among professional educators as well as between curricularists and many constituencies within the community.

5. *Theorizing*

Theorizing is a term that generates no small amount of controversy in curriculum discussions. Its meanings are legion: from the process of creating positivist theories to the act of offering radical social and political critique. The great value of the term, however, lies in its verb form. Theorizing (like philosophizing, reflecting, and inquiring that went before it) denotes a continuous process of questioning and interpretation that gives the person who theorizes increased capacity to deal with problems and dilemmas of life. Thus, theorizing (unlike theory construction) is a populist notion. It is to be done by everyone who has an inclination to look deeply within themselves in an effort to gather and create greater meaning and purpose.

Theorizing is a process that gives direction to what C. A. Bowers (1984b) calls *communicative competence*. It enables the kind of cultural literacy that brings the freedom "to take responsibility for one's own situation" (Bowers, 1974, p. 184). Bowers continues:

> *For educators, this means developing their own critical theory of education that enables them to see the leverage points within that part of the educational system where they find themselves. [p. 184]*

As practitioners form and reform their orientation to curriculum and teaching, they develop a set of values and a conception of justice that guides their action. This is embedded in the work of the best practitioners in many professional fields, according to Donald A. Schön (1983) who has studied carefully the "reflection-in-action" of those engaged in improvisational practice. Although those who theorize may be quite different from one another, one commitment that binds them together is a continuous questioning, a continuous striving to understand thoughtfully their lived experience more fully. I hope that all connected with education, especially teachers, engage in a form of theorizing that fits their unique needs and circumstances. Moreover, I hope that this kind and quality of theorizing will move to the center of the educative process itself.

6. A Theory Within Persons

As persons deal with the problems and possibilities of living, they continuously form and revise their outlooks on the world. To grow is the goal of all life. To be human is to strive to maintain and nurture one's own growth. One's outlook on life is an incredibly complex, and always changing, configuration of perceptions, impulses, habits, values, ideas, strategies, and hopes. If educators are to exert a helpful influence, they must somehow come to know more about this mysterious and unique configuration in each individual whom they teach.

The theory within persons—call it personality, personal philosophy, outlook, orientation, *personal constructs* to use Kelly's (1963) label, or *image* to use Boulding's (1956) term—should be the central focus of the curriculum; it is the repertoire from which interests spring. As Dewey (1916) argued with great persuasion, human interests should be the starting point of the educative process. To proceed from interests or *the psychological* is the only true route to *the logical* or the accumulated wisdom of human culture. This principle will be practiced only when curricularists realize that embedded within human interests are needs that no one perceives better than the person possessing those interests. We have too long operated on the unwarranted assumption that knowledge is the special province of experts (researchers and educators) and it must be prespecified and distributed to the ignorant masses (students). Freire (1970, pp. 59ff) labels this the *banking* concept of pedagogy and calls for pedagogy based upon *problem posing* that genuinely flows from the interests and needs of learners.

Yet the problem remains that learners are often so mired in the necessity of survival that they are unable to identify their genuine interests and needs. Thus, the job of the teacher is to engage in dialogue with students in an effort to help them articulate their fundamental needs and interests. To do this is to enter more deeply within the evolving theory that guides students' lives. Together, teachers and students who know each other well can develop a course of experience (curriculum) that helps to meet their needs and enrich their growth. The structure of schooling today does little to facilitate this process of focusing on the personal theories of learners; nevertheless, if the will is expressed forcefully enough, I deeply hope that a way can be found.

7. The Arts and Sciences

By far the best communication of the theories that guide personal lives is found in the arts. Poetry, theater, novels, short stories, the fine arts, essays, and philosophic treatises are filled with insight about the human condition and responses to it. Portrayals of human experience, the deepest of human thought and feeling, should lie at the heart of curriculum inquiry. Yet the arts are considered expendable and at best background areas to be studied prior to the acquisition of professional technique. It is my hope that educators, both scholars and practitioners, will learn to experience the arts (not as escape or Sunday afternoon enrichment at the museum) for the breadth of perception and perspective they offer to the question of how to create lives worth leading.

Educators have turned primarily to the social sciences for insight, problem solving, and research methodology. While numerous problems can be addressed well by social science modes of inquiry, neither the arts nor the natural sciences have been studied sufficiently by those in the curriculum field. For example, the growing body of neurological research has hardly been addressed by curriculum scholars or practitioners. Notable current exceptions include work by Hart (1983), Chall and Mirsky (1978), and Wittrock et al. (1977). Hopkins (1954) and Kelley and Rasey (1952) illustrate ways in which progressive educators also derived salient insights from the natural sciences.

Beyond the substantive findings of scientific research, great significance resides in broad conceptions of science as methodological activity based on a system of principles and procedures. Dewey (1910, 1938b) wrote of this kind of inquiry in the personal and practical sphere, while today many continental theorists include phenomenological, psychoanalytic, and existential investigation and interpretation under the general label of "human sciences." Commenting on the recent philosophical work of Richard Bernstein (1983), Paul Klohr concludes that pragmatism and phenomenology have much in common, particularly that they both value a "kind of moral intelligence as a fundamental of human existence" (Klohr, 1984, p. 3). That curriculum is fundamental to human survival necessitates the hope that the most perceptive insights, methods of inquiry, and modes of expression (including the vast potential of mass media) be pursued by all who engage in the process of helping young human beings to grow and contribute.

8. *Teachers and Students*

Throughout this list of hopes runs a call to give greater attention to the place of teachers and students in curriculum. In the daily life of teaching and learning, the teacher-student relationship is where curriculum is fashioned. Policy pronouncements, textbook content, and administrative edict are transformed by the interplay of ideas, emotions, action, character, and personality as teachers and students interrelate. Curriculum is created and develops in these interrelationships. It becomes something different from even the best of plans because of the teachers, learners, and their environment.

The literature of the curriculum field has too long neglected to give attention to both teachers and students as creators and transformers of curriculum. Several progressive educators are notable exceptions, and today teachers and students are sometimes acknowledged for the pivotal role they play in what is taught and learned in school, but such acknowledgment is a rarity. Those who engage daily in educative encounters need to be most aware of the legacy of curriculum thought and practice that could enrich their work. But it is quite possible for teachers and students to live up to this curricular ideal. Theodore Sizer (1984) concludes his assessment of the American high school by stating the possibility vividly:

> *Give me, a student, a teacher who inspires me to learn on my own, and the bric-a-brac of schoolkeeping—the course labels, the regulations, the regularities, the rituals—will cease to have much importance. And give me, a teacher, hungry pupils, and I'll teach them in a tumbledown warehouse, and they will learn. Inspiration, hunger: these are the qualities that drive good schools. The best we educational planners can do is to create the most likely conditions for them to flourish, and then get out of their way. [pp. 220–221]*

I hope that more teachers and students will realize that they are curriculum makers. As they interact and reflect on the meaning and purpose of their lives together, they are engaged in curriculum inquiry of the most significant kind. Unfortunately, too many teachers have learned to be implementors of the ideas of others who are labeled experts, and too many students have learned to be receivers rather than creators of knowledge. My hope is that teachers and students will move beyond the *erosion* (to use Suransky's, 1982, insightful label) of institutionalized separations and realize that together they must take responsibility for the growth of the lives they share. As teachers and students share their observations, needs, and ideals, they can grow together. To do this teachers must relinquish their authoritarian position and be prepared to realize (with Jack Greenstein, 1983) what the children teach, not just what they must learn. Teachers and students who both teach and learn prepare themselves, not just to fulfill societal roles, but to engage in a unity of work, leisure, and interpersonal relationships that is personally fulfilling because they contribute to its creation.

9. A Moral, Curriculum Imperative

Teachers and students who learn from and with one another take with them an attitude that all life's encounters have a pedagogic or curricular quality. This does not mean that there is an absence of fun and enjoyment. On the contrary, the curricular quality to which I refer is the drive to encounter increased meaning and growth. This is a source of enjoyment that lies beyond mere entertainment.

A child who experiences the satisfaction of helping others grow, and who knows the love that brings growth with others, becomes an adult who enters situations with a different spirit from those who have not had such benefits. He or she approaches life guided by a kind of pedagogic imperative that says

> *Live as if your life were a curriculum for others, and balance that principle by realizing that every life you meet could be a curriculum for you if you perceive with sufficient perspective.*

This is, I believe, the moral responsibility of everyone. Yet the moral obligation of an educator is even more pervasive. An educator is entrusted with the most serious work that confronts humankind: the development of curricula that enable new generations to contribute to the growth of human beings and society. This means that those who have chosen to devote themselves to curriculum must address the most basic questions that exist: What does it mean to live a good life and how can a just society be created? It is my hope that more persons will study curriculum with the seriousness and depth that these questions imply.

10. An Immediate Hope

I hope that I have communicated a sense of the complexity and worth of curriculum studies to you through this book.

SUGGESTED READING

I have suggested a great many readings for you. Therefore, I ask you: What readings would you like to pursue next? Make a bibliography with annotations about the reasons for your selections.

Take time to wander through libraries and bookstores and ask yourself: What books speak to important curriculum problems and issues? What books, journals, and other writings might help you to grow as a professional educator?

Beyond reading in the traditional literature-oriented sense: What kinds of life experiences would you benefit from "reading"? What would facilitate the needs and interests that you perceive for your own professional growth? Your personal growth?

RECOMMENDATIONS FOR REFLECTION

1. How do you respond to my rendition of promising directions derived from the content of each chapter?

2. What is your own agenda of promising directions for curriculum?

3. How do you respond to each of my personal hopes for curriculum? I would appreciate hearing from you about them.

4. What personal hopes for curriculum do you have and how do you defend their worth?

5. What could you do to contribute to the realization of some of these hopes?

6. One purpose that I have for this book is to provide a basis for you to clarify and develop your own curriculum position by becoming exposed to an array of possibilities and their pros and cons. (Broadening and pondering the possibilities for responding to different curriculum problems helps me in the process of continuously clarifying my own curriculum position.) My ultimate purpose in writing this book, therefore, resides in the hope that you develop images about curriculum contributions that you hope to make. What specific contributions to curriculum do you hope to make? Within the next year? Within the next decade? Throughout your professional career?

7. More specifically: Why are you convinced of the worth of these contributions? How will you proceed to make them?

POSTSCRIPT

If you have comments about this book or suggestions for revision, I would appreciate hearing from you.

I extend all good wishes to you in your efforts to contribute to curriculum. Let me know about your contributions. I would like to learn from them.

✦ References ✦

Adler, M. J. (1981). *Six great ideas*. New York: Macmillan.

Adler, M. J. (1982). *The paideia proposal: An educational manifesto*. New York: Macmillan.

Adler, M. J. (1983). *Paideia problems and possibilities*. New York: Macmillan.

Adler, M. J. (1984). *The paideia program: An educational syllabus*. New York: Macmillan.

Adler, M. J., & Van Doren, C. (Eds.). (1977). *Great treasury of Western thought*. New York: R. R. Bowker.

Agee, J. (1938). *A death in the family*. New York: Bantam.

Aikin, W. (1942). *The story of the Eight Year Study*. New York: Harper & Brothers.

Alberty, H. B., & Alberty, E. J. (1962). *Reorganizing the high school curriculum*. New York: Macmillan. (Previous editions: 1947 and 1953, authored by H. Alberty.)

Allport, G. W. (1951). *The use of personal documents in psychological science*. New York: Social Research Council.

Allport, G. W. (1958). *The nature of prejudice*. Garden City, NY: Doubleday.

Andreas, C. (1971). *Sex and caste in America*. Englewood Cliffs, NJ: Prentice-Hall.

Anyon, J. (1980). Social class and the hidden curriculum of work. *Journal of Education, 162*(1), 67–92.

Anyon, J. (1981). Social class and school knowledge. *Curriculum Inquiry, 11*(1), 3–42.

Aoki, T. T. (1984). Competence in teaching as instrumental and practical action: A critical analysis. In E. C. Short (Ed.), *Competence* (pp. 71–82). Lanham, MD: University Press of America.

Aoki, T. T., Carson, T. R., Favaro, B. J., & Berman, L. M. (1984). *Understanding situational meanings of in-service curriculum acts: Implementing, consulting, inservicing*. Monograph No. 9, Department of Secondary Education, Faculty of Education, University of Alberta.

Apple, M. W. (1979). *Ideology and curriculum*. London: Routledge & Kegan Paul.

Apple, M. W. (1982a). *Education and power*. Boston: Routledge & Kegan Paul.

Apple, M. W. (Ed.). (1982b). *Cultural and economic reproduction in education*. London: Routledge & Kegan Paul.

Apple, M. W. (1984). The political economy of text publishing. *Educational Theory, 34*(4), 307–319.

Apple, M. W. (In Press). *Teachers and texts*. London: Routledge and Kegan Paul.

Apple, M. W., & Weis, L. (Eds.). (1983). *Ideology and practice in schooling.* Philadelphia: Temple University Press.

Aristotle. *The politics* and other treatises are available in several editions.

Ashton-Warner, S. (1963). *Teacher.* New York: Simon & Schuster.

ASCD (Association for Supervision & Curriculum Development). (1962). *Perceiving, behaving, becoming: A new focus in education,* 1962 ASCD Yearbook. Washington, DC: The Association.

Atkin, J. M., & House, E. R. (1981). The federal role in curriculum development, 1950–80. *Educational Evaluation and Policy Analysis, 3,* 5–36.

Augustine (Saint). *Confessions.* (Several editions available.)

Ausubel, D. (1963). *The psychology of meaningful verbal learning.* New York: Grune & Stratton.

Ayers, L. P. (1917). *The Cleveland school survey* (summary volume of 25 volumes). Cleveland, OH: Survey Committee of the Cleveland Foundation.

Bagdikian, B. H. (1983). *The media monopoly.* Boston: Beacon Press.

Baker, E. L., & Popham, W. J. (1973). *Expanding dimensions of instructional objectives.* Englewood Cliffs, NJ: Prentice-Hall.

Balbus, I. (1982). *Marxism and domination: A neo-Hegelian, feminist, psychoanalytic theory of sexual, political, and technological liberation.* Princeton, NJ: Princeton University Press.

Ballinger, S. E. (1965). *The nature and function of educational policy* (an occasional paper). Bloomington, IN: Indiana University, College of Education, Department of History and Philosophy of Education.

Barone, T. (1979). Of Scott and Lisa and other friends. In E. W. Eisner, *The educational imagination* (pp. 240–245). New York: Macmillan.

Barone, T. (1983). Education as aesthetic experience: "Art in germ." *Educational Leadership, 40*(4), 21–26.

Barth, R. (1972). *Open education and the American school.* New York: Agathon.

Barzun, J. (1954). *Teacher in America.* Garden City, NY: Doubleday.

Beauchamp, G. A. (1981). *Curriculum theory.* Itasca, IL: F. E. Peacock. (Previous editions: 1975, 1968, 1961 by Kagg Press, Wilmette, IL.)

Beauchamp, G. A. (1982). Curriculum theory: Meaning, development, and use. *Theory into Practice, 21*(1), 23–27.

Beegle, C. W., & Edelfelt, R. A. (Eds.). (1977). *Staff development: Staff liberation.* Washington DC: Association for Supervision & Curriculum Development.

Bellack, A. A. (1969). History of curriculum thought and practice. *Review of Educational Research, 39,* 283–292.

Bellack, A. A., & Kliebard, H. (Eds.). (1977). *Curriculum and evaluation.* Berkeley, CA: McCutchan.

Benjamin, H. (1939). *The saber-tooth curriculum.* New York: McGraw-Hill. (Author pseudonym, J. A. Peddiwell.)

Benne, K. D., & Muntyan, B. (Eds.). (1951). *Human relations in curriculum change.* New York: Dryden Press.

Bennis, W., Benne, K., & Chin, R. (1976). *The planning of change.* New York: Holt, Rinehart and Winston. (Earlier edition: 1969.)

Bergson, H. (1889). *Time and free will* (See Humanities Press edition. 1971.)

Berlak, A., & Berlak, H. (1981). *Dilemmas of schooling: Teaching and social change.* London: Methuen.

Berlin, I. (1980). *Concepts and categories: Philosophical essays.* Oxford: Oxford University Press.

Berman, E. H. (1983). *The idea of philanthropy: The influence of the Carnegie, Ford, and*

Rockefeller foundations on American foreign policy. Albany, NY: State University of New York Press.

Berman, L. (1968). *New priorities in the curriculum.* Columbus, OH: Merrill.

Berman, L. M., & Miel, A. (1983). *Education for world cooperation.* West Lafayette, IN: Kappa Delta Pi.

Berman, L. M., & Roderick, J. A. (1977). *Curriculum: Teaching the what, how, and why of living.* Columbus, OH: Merrill.

Bernstein, R. J. (1971). *Praxis and action.* Philadelphia: University of Pennsylvania Press.

Bernstein, R. J. (1976). *The restructuring of social and political thought.* Philadelphia: University of Pennsylvania Press.

Bernstein, R. J. (1983). *Beyond objectivism and relativism.* Philadelphia: University of Pennsylvania Press.

Bestor, A. (1955). *The restoration of learning.* New York: Knopf.

Bettleheim, B. (1976). *The uses of enchantment.* New York: Knopf.

Block, J. (Ed.). (1971). *Mastery learning.* New York: Holt, Rinehart and Winston.

Bloom, B. S. (Ed.). (1956). *Taxonomy of educational objectives: Cognitive domain.* New York: David McKay.

Bloom, B. S. (1981). *All our children learning: A primer for parents, teachers, and other educators.* New York: McGraw-Hill.

Bloom, B. S. (1984). The 2 sigma problem: The search for methods of group instruction as effective as one-to-one tutoring. *Educational Researcher, 13*(6), 4–16.

Bloom, B. S., et al. (1971). *Handbook on formative and summative evaluation of student learning.* New York: McGraw-Hill.

Blumberg, A. (1974). *Supervisors and teachers: A private cold war.* Berkeley, CA: McCutchan.

Bobbitt, F. (1918). *The curriculum.* Boston: Houghton Mifflin.

Bobbitt, F. (1924). *How to make a curriculum.* Boston: Houghton Mifflin.

Bode, B. H. (1927). *Modern educational theories.* New York: Macmillan.

Bode, B. H. (1938). *Progressive education at the crossroads.* New York: Newson.

Bogdan, R. (1972). *Participant observation in organizational settings.* Syracuse, NY: University Division of Special Education and Rehabilitation, Syracuse University.

Bonser, F. G. (1920). *The elementary school curriculum.* New York: Macmillan.

Boocock, S., & Schild, E. O. (1968). *Simulation games in learning.* Beverly Hills, CA: Sage.

Booth, W. C. (Ed.). (1967). *The knowledge most worth having.* Chicago: University of Chicago Press.

Borman, K. M., & Spring, J. H. (1984). *Schools in central cities.* New York: Longman.

Borrowman, M. L. (Ed.). (1965). *Teacher education in America: A documentary history.* New York: Teachers College Press, Columbia University.

Boulding, K. (1956). *The image: Knowledge in life and society.* Ann Arbor: University of Michigan Press.

Bourdieu, P. (1971). Systems of education and systems of thought. In M. F. D. Young (Ed.), *Knowledge and control: New direction for the sociology of education* (pp. 189–207). London: Collier-Macmillan.

Bourdieu, P., & Passeron, J. C. (1977). *Reproduction in education, society, and culture.* Beverly Hills, CA: Sage.

Bowers, C. A. (1974). *Cultural literacy for freedom: An existential perspective on teaching, curriculum, and school policy.* Eugene, OR: Elan Books.

Bowers, C. A. (1983). Shop talk: Teaching the introductory foundations course. A symposium presented at the Annual Conference of the American Education Studies Association, Milwaukee, WI, November 3, 1983.

Bowers, C. A. (1984a). The problem of individualism and community in neo-Marxist educational thought. *Teachers College Record, 85*(3), 365–390.

Bowers, C. A. (1984b). *The promise of theory: Education and the politics of cultural change.* New York: Longman.

Bowles, S., & Gintis, H. (1976). *Schooling in capitalist America: Educational reform and the contradictions of economic life.* New York: Basic Books.

Boyd, W. (1965). *The history of Western education.* New York: Barnes & Noble.

Boyer, E. L., for the Carnegie Foundation for the Advancement of Teaching. (1983). *High school: A report on secondary education in America.* New York: Harper & Row.

Boyer, E. L. (1984). Address to delegates of the Chicago Teachers' Union. *Chicago Union Teacher, 47*(8), 18–19.

Bradford, L. P., Gibb, J. R., & Benne, K. D. (Eds.). (1964). *T-group theory and laboratory method.* New York: John Wiley.

Brameld, T. (1956). *Toward a reconstructed philosophy of education.* New York: Holt, Rinehart and Winston.

Brandt, R. S. (Ed.) (1980). *Curriculum implementation.* Washington, DC: Association for Supervision & Curriculum Development.

Brazelton, T. B. (1981). *On becoming a family.* New York: Delta.

Bredo, E., & Feinberg, W. (Eds.). (1982). *Knowledge and values in social and educational research.* Philadelphia: Temple University Press.

Bréhier, E. (1963–69). *The history of philosophy* (seven volumes translated by W. Baskin from original French editions, Presses Universitaires de France, 1931–38). Chicago: University of Chicago Press.

Bremer, J. (1979). *Education and community.* Sheparton, Australia: Waterwheel Press.

Bremer, J., & Von Moschzisher, M. (1971). *The school without walls.* New York: Holt, Rinehart and Winston.

Bronowski, J. (1956). *Science and human values.* New York: Messner.

Broudy, H. S. (1961). *Building a philosophy of education.* Englewood Cliffs, NJ: Prentice-Hall. (Previous edition, 1954.)

Broudy, H. S. (1972). *The real world of the public schools.* NY: Harcourt, Brace, and Jovanovich.

Broudy, H. S. (1977). How basic is an aesthetic education? An address presented to the Association for Supervision & Curriculum Development, Houston, TX, March 1977.

Broudy, H. S. (1979). Arts education: Necessary or just nice? *Phi Delta Kappan, 60*(5), 347–350.

Broudy, H. S. (1982a). Challenge to the curriculum worker: Uses of knowledge. In W. H. Schubert & A. L. Schubert (Eds.), *Conceptions of curriculum knowledge: Focus on students and teachers* (pp. 3–8). University Park: College of Education, Pennsylvania State University.

Broudy, H. S. (1982b). *Truth and credibility.* New York: Longman.

Broudy, H. S., & Palmer, J. R. (1965). *Exemplars of teaching method.* Chicago: Rand McNally.

Broudy, H. S., Smith, B. O., & Burnett, J. (1964). *Democracy and excellence in American secondary education: A study in curriculum theory.* Chicago: Rand McNally. (Reprinted by Krieger, 1978.)

Brown, B. F. (1963). *The nongraded high school.* Englewood Cliffs, NJ: Prentice-Hall.

Brown, B. F., and the National Commission on the Reform of Secondary Education. (1973). *The reform of secondary education.* New York: McGraw-Hill.

Brown, N. O. (1959). *Life against death: The psychoanalytic meaning of history.* Middletown, CT: Wesleyan University Press.

Brubaker, D. L. (1982). *Curriculum planning: The dynamics of theory and practice.* Glenview, IL: Scott, Foresman.

Bruner, J. S. (1960). *The process of education.* New York: Vintage.

Bruner, J. S. (1966). *Toward a theory of instruction.* Cambridge, MA: Harvard University Press.

Bruner, J. S., Goodnow, J. J., & Austin, G. A. (1967). *A study of thinking*. New York: Science Editions.

Bullough, R. V., Goldstein, S. L., & Holt, L. (1984). *Human interests in the curriculum: Teaching and learning in a technological society*. New York: Teachers College Press, Columbia University.

Burton, W. H. (1951). *The guidance of learning activities* (2nd ed.). New York: Appleton-Century.

Butts, R. F. (1947). *A cultural history of education*. New York: McGraw-Hill.

Butts, R. F. (1973). *The education of the West*. New York: McGraw-Hill.

Butts, R. F. (1980). *The revival of civic learning: A rationale for citizenship education in American schools*. Bloomington, IN: Phi Delta Kappa.

Butts, R. F., & Cremin, L. (1953). *A history of education in American culture*. New York: Holt, Rinehart and Winston.

Callahan, R. E. (1962). *Education and the cult of efficiency*. Chicago: University of Chicago Press.

Campbell, D. T., & Stanley, J. C. (1966). *Experimental and quasi-experimental designs for research*. Chicago: Rand McNally.

Caswell, H. L., & Associates. (1950). *Curriculum improvement in public school systems*. New York: Teachers College Press, Columbia University.

Caswell, H. L., & Campbell, D. S. (1935). *Curriculum development*. New York: American Book Company. (Reprinted by R. West, 1978.)

Caswell, H. L., & Campbell, D. S. (Eds.). (1937). *Readings in curriculum development*. New York: American Book Company.

Chall, J., & Mirsky, A. F. (Eds.). (1978). *Education and the brain*. Seventy-seventh Yearbook of the National Society for the Study of Education, Part II. Chicago: University of Chicago Press.

Chamberlin, D., Chamberlin, E. S., Drought, N. F., & Scott, W. E. (1942). *Did they succeed in College?* New York: Harper & Brothers.

Charters, W. W. (1923). *Curriculum construction*. New York: Macmillan.

Cleaver, E. (1967). *Soul on ice*. New York: Dell.

Coleman, J. S. (1961). *Adolescent society*. Glencoe, IL: Free Press.

Coleman, J. S. (1981). *Public and private schools*. Washington, DC: National Center for Educational Statistics.

Coleman, J. S., et al. (1966). *Equality of educational opportunity*. Washington, DC: U.S. Government Printing Office.

Combs, A. W. (1972). *Educational accountability: Beyond behavioral objectives*. Washington, DC: Association for Supervision & Curriculum Development.

Comenius, J. A. (1632). *The great didactic*. (Several editions available.)

Comenius, J. A. (1652). *Orbis pictus*. (Several editions available.)

Commission on the Reorganization of Secondary Education of the National Education Association. (1918). *Cardinal principles of secondary education*. Washington, DC: U.S. Government Printing Office.

Commoner, B. (1974). *The closing circle*. New York: Knopf.

Conant, J. B. (1959). *The American high school today*. New York: McGraw-Hill.

Conant, J. B. (1963). *The education of American teachers*. New York: McGraw-Hill.

Connell, R. F., Ashenden, D. J., Kessler, S., & Dowsett, G. W. (1982). *Making the difference*. Sydney, Australia: Allen & Unwin.

Connell, W. F. (1980). *A history of education in the twentieth century world*. New York: Teachers College & the Curriculum Development Centre of Australia.

Connelly, F. M., & Clandinin, D. J. (1985). Narrative history and the study of minded practice. A paper presented at the Meadow Brook Conference on Collaborative Action Research, Oakland University, Rochester, MI, January 20–23, 1985.

Cook, T. D., & Campbell, D. T. (1979). *Quasi-experimentation: Design and analysis issues for field settings.* Chicago: Rand McNally.

Copeland, R. W. (1982). *Mathematics and the elementary teacher.* New York: Saunders.

Corey, S. M. (1953). *Action research to improve school practices.* New York: Bureau of Publications, Teachers College, Columbia University.

Costa, A., & Guditus, C. (1984). Do districtwide supervisors make a difference? *Educational Leadership, 41*(5), 84–85.

Counts, G. S. (1932a). Dare progressive education be progressive? *Progressive Education, 9*(4), 257–263.

Counts, G. S. (1932b). *Dare the school build a new social order?* New York: John Day.

Counts, G. S. (1934). *The social foundations of education.* New York: Scribners.

Counts, G. S. (1935). Break the teacher training lockstep. *The Social Frontier, 1*(June), 6–7.

Cousins, N. (1983). *The healing heart: Antidotes to panic and helplessness.* London: W. W. Norton.

Cramer, E. H., & Schubert, W. H. (1979). Reading skills management systems. *Curriculum Review, 18*(5), 392–395.

Cremin, L. A. (1955). The revolution in American secondary education. *Teachers College Record, 56,* 295–307.

Cremin, L. A. (1961). *The transformation of the school.* New York: Knopf.

Cremin, L. A. (1971). Curriculum-making in the United States. *Teachers College Record, 73* (2), 196–200.

Cremin, L. A. (1976). *Public education.* New York: Basic Books.

Cronbach, L. J. (1963). Course improvement through evaluation. *Teachers College Record, 64,* 672–683.

Cronbach, L. J. (1970). *Essentials of psychological testing.* New York: Harper & Row.

Cuban, L. (1983). Effective schools: A friendly but cautionary note. *Phi Delta Kappan, 64*(10), 695–696.

Cubberley, E. P. (1920). *The history of education.* Boston: Houghton Mifflin.

Cubberley, E. P. (1934). *Public education in the United States.* Boston: Houghton Mifflin.

Curti, M. (1935). *Social ideas of American educators.* New York: Scribners.

Curtis, S. J., & Boultwood, M. E. A. (1965). *A short history of educational ideas.* London: University Tutorial Press. (Previous editions: 1953, 1956, 1961.)

Dahllöf, U. S. (1971). *Ability grouping, content validity, and curricular process analysis.* New York: Teachers College Press.

Dale, E. (1972). *Building a learning environment.* Bloomington, IN: Phi Delta Kappa.

Darwin, C. (1859). *Origin of the species.* (Several editions available.)

David, T. G., & Wright, B. D. (Eds.). (1975). *Learning environments.* Chicago: University of Chicago Press.

Davis, O. L. (Ed.). (1976). *Perspectives on curriculum development, 1776–1976,* 1976 ASCD Yearbook. Washington, DC: Association for Supervision & Curriculum Development.

Davis, O. L. (1983). Liberating, learning, leading. Presidential address at the Annual Conference of the Association for Supervision & Curriculum Development, Houston, TX, March 1983.

Dearden, R. F. (1968). *The philosophy of primary education.* London: Routledge & Kegan Paul.

DeGarmo, C. (1895). *Herbart and the Herbartians.* London: Heinemann.

Del Novellis, R. L., & Lewis, A. J. (1974). *Schools become accountable: A PACT approach.* Washington, DC: Association for Supervision & Curriculum Development.

Dennison, G. (1969). *The lives of children.* New York: Random House.

DePencier, I. B. (1967). *The history of the laboratory schools: The University of Chicago, 1896–1965.* Chicago: Quadrangle Books.

Dewey, J. (1897). My pedogogic creed. *The School Journal, 54*(3), 77–80.

Dewey, J. (1900). *The school and society.* Chicago: University of Chicago Press.

Dewey, J. (1902). *The child and the curriculum.* Chicago: University of Chicago Press.

Dewey, J. (1904). The relation of theory to practice in education. Third Yearbook of the National Society for the Scientific Study of Education, *The relation of theory to practice in the education of teachers* (pp. 9–30). Bloomington, IN: Public School Publishing Company.

Dewey, J. (1910). *How we think.* New York: D. C. Heath.

Dewey, J. (1916). *Democracy and education.* New York: Macmillan.

Dewey, J. (1920). *Reconstruction in philosophy.* New York: Henry Holt. (Enlarged edition, Beacon Press, 1948.)

Dewey, J. (1922). *Human nature and conduct.* New York: Henry Holt.

Dewey, J. (1925). *Experience and nature.* London: Open Court.

Dewey, J. (1927). *The public and its problems.* New York: Henry Holt.

Dewey, J. (1929a). *The quest for certainty.* New York: Minton, Balch.

Dewey, J. (1929b). *The sources of a science of education.* New York: H. Liveright.

Dewey, J. (1930). From absolutism to experimentalism. In G. P. Adams and W. P. Montague (Eds.), *Contemporary American philosophy* (pp. 13–27). New York: Macmillan.

Dewey, J. (1931). *The way out of educational confusion.* Cambridge, MA: Harvard University Press.

Dewey, J. (1938a). *Experience and education.* New York: Macmillan.

Dewey, J. (1938b). *Logic, the theory of inquiry.* New York: Henry Holt.

Dewey, J. (1940). *Education today.* New York: Putnam.

Dewey, J., & Dewey, E. (1915). *Schools of tomorrow.* New York: Dutton.

Dillon-Peterson, B. (Ed.). (1981). *Staff development: Organization development,* 1981 ASCD Yearbook. Washington, DC: Association for Supervision & Curriculum Development.

Doll, R. C. (1982). *Curriculum improvement: Decision making and process.* Boston: Allyn & Bacon. (Previous editions: 1978, 1974, 1970, and 1964.)

Doll, W. E. (1983). Curriculum and change. *The Journal of Curriculum Theorizing, 5*(2), 4–61.

Donmoyer, R. (1981). The evaluator as artist. In H. A. Giroux, A. N. Penna, and W. F. Pinar (Eds.), *Curriculum and instruction* (pp. 342–363). Berkeley, CA: McCutchan.

Donmoyer, R. (1983). Participatory democratic evaluation: A case study of an emerging model. Paper presented in a symposium on "Collaborative Research" at the Annual Meeting of the American Educational Research Association, Montreal, April 14, 1983.

Donmoyer, R. (1984). Cognitive anthropology and research on effective principals: Findings from a study and reflections on its methods. A paper presented at the Annual Meeting of the American Educational Research Association, New Orleans, LA, April 23, 1984.

Dreeben, R. (1968). *On what is learned in school.* Reading, MA: Addison-Wesley.

Drengson, A. R. (1983). *Shifting paradigms: From technocrat to planetary person.* Victoria, British Columbia: Lightstar Press.

Dressel, P. L. (1982). Curriculum and instruction in higher education. In H. E. Mitzel (Ed.), *Encyclopedia of educational research,* Vol. 1 (pp. 400–405). New York: Free Press of Macmillan.

Dunkel, H. B. (1970). *Herbart and Herbartianism: An educational ghost story.* Chicago: University of Chicago Press.

Dunkel, H. B. (1984). *Writ in water: The epitaph of educational innovation.* Unpublished book manuscript at the University of Chicago.

Dunkin, M. J., & Biddle, B. J. (1974). *The study of teaching.* New York: Holt, Rinehart, and Winston.

Dunn, R. S., & Dunn, K. J. (1979). Learning styles/teaching styles: Should they . . . can they . . . be matched? *Educational Leadership, 36*(4), 238–244.

Durant, W. (1961). *The story of philosophy*. New York: Touchstone.

Dykhuizen, G. (1973). *The life and mind of John Dewey*. Carbondale: Southern Illinois University Press.

Edelfelt, R. A., & Smith, E. B. (Eds.). (1978). *Breakaway to multidimensional approaches: Integrating curriculum development and inservice education*. Washington, D. C.: Association of Teacher Educators.

Edinger, L. V., Houts, P. L., & Meyer, D. V. (Eds.). (1981). *Education in the 80's: Curricular challenges*. Washington, DC: National Education Association.

Educational Policies Commission. (1938). *The purposes of education in a democracy*. Washington, DC: National Education Association.

Educational Policies Commission. (1942). *A war policy for American schools*. Washington, DC: National Education Association.

Educational Policies Commission. (1943). *Education and the people's peace*. Washington, DC: National Education Association.

Educational Policies Commission. (1944). *Education for ALL American youth*. Washington, DC: National Education Association.

Educational Policies Commission. (1951). *Education and national security*. Washington, DC: National Education Association.

Edwards, P. (Ed.). (1967). *The encyclopedia of philosophy* (eight volumes). New York: Macmillan.

Egan, K. (1979). *Educational development*. New York: Oxford University Press.

Egan, K. (1983). Children's path to reality from fantasy: Contrary thoughts about curriculum foundations. *Journal of Curriculum Studies, 15*(4), 357–371.

Eisner, E. W. (1969). Instructional and expressive objectives: Their formulation and use in curriculum. In W. J. Popham (Ed.), *AERA monograph on curriculum evaluation: Instructional objectives* (pp. 1–18). Chicago: Rand McNally.

Eisner, E. W. (Ed.). (1971). *Confronting curriculum reform*. Boston: Little, Brown.

Eisner, E. W. (1972). *Educating artistic vision*. New York: Macmillan.

Eisner, E. W. (1977). On the uses of educational connoisseurship and criticism for evaluating classroom life. *Teachers College Record, 78*, 345–358.

Eisner, E. W. (1979). *The educational imagination: On the design and evaluation of school programs*. New York: Macmillan.

Eisner, E. W. (1981). On the differences between scientific and artistic approaches to qualitative research. *Educational Researcher, 10*(4), 5–9.

Eisner, E. W. (1982). *Cognition and curriculum: A basis for deciding what to teach*. New York: Longman.

Eisner, E. W. (1983). The art and craft of teaching. *Educational Leadership, 40*(4), 4–13.

Eisner, E. W. (1985). *The educational imagination*. New York: Macmillan (second edition).

Eisner, E. W., & Vallance, E. (Eds.). (1974). *Conflicting conceptions of curriculum*. Berkeley, CA: McCutchan.

Elam, S. (Ed.). (1964). *Education and the structure of knowledge*. Chicago: Rand McNally.

Elliot, J. (1976–77). Developing hypotheses about classrooms from teachers' practical constructs: An account of the Ford Teaching Project. *Interchange, 7*(1), 2–22.

Ellison, R. (1952). *The invisible man*. New York: Random House.

Elson, R. M. (1964). *Guardians of tradition: American schoolbooks of the nineteenth century*. Lincoln: University of Nebraska Press.

Emerson, R. W. (1966). *Emerson on education: Selections*, H. M. Jones, Ed. New York: Teachers College Press.

English, F. W. (Ed.). (1983). *Fundamental curriculum decisions*, 1983 ASCD Yearbook. Alexandria, VA: Association for Supervision & Curriculum Development.

English, F. W., & Kaufman, R. A. (1975). *Needs assessment: A focus for curriculum development*. Washington, DC: Association for Supervision & Curriculum Development.

EPIE (Educational Products Information Exchange Institute). (1979). *Selecting instructional materials* (Part 1, Module 3). Stony Brook, NY: EPIE.

Evenden, E. S., for the Commission on Teacher Education. (1946). *The improvement of teacher education*. Washington, DC: American Council on Education.

Eysenck, H. J., & Sargent, C. (1982). *Explaining the unexplained: Mysteries of the paranormal*. London: Weidenfild & Nicolson.

Fagan, E. R. (1984). Competence in educational practice: A rhetorical analysis. In E. C. Short (Ed.), *Competence* (pp. 3–16). Lanham, MD: University Press of America.

Fantini, M. (1976). *Alternative education: A source book for parents, teachers, students, and administrators*. Garden City, NY: Doubleday.

Fantini, M., & Sinclair, R. (Eds.). (1985). *Education in school and nonschool settings*. Eighty-fourth Yearbook of the National Society for the Study of Education, Part I. Chicago: University of Chicago Press.

Faunce, R. C., & Bossing, N. L. (1951). *Developing the core curriculum*. New York: Prentice-Hall.

Feinberg, W. (1983). *Understanding education: Toward a reconstruction of educational inquiry*. Cambridge: Cambridge University Press.

Fennema, E., & Ayer, M. J. (Eds.). (1984). *Women and education: Equity or equality?* Berkeley, CA: McCutchan.

Fenstermacher, G. D., & Goodlad, J. I. (Eds.). (1983). *Individual differences and the common curriculum*. Eighty-second Yearbook of the National Society for the Study of Education, Part I. Chicago: University of Chicago Press.

Firth, G. R., & Kimpston, R. D. (1973). *The curricular continuum in perspective*. Itasca, IL: F. E. Peacock.

Ford, G. W., & Pugno, L. (Eds.). (1964). *The structure of knowledge and the curriculum*. Chicago: Rand McNally.

Ford Foundation. (1972). *A foundation goes to school*. New York: The Foundation.

Foshay, A. W. (1984). The peak/spiritual experience as an object of curriculum analysis. A paper presented for a conference in honor of Benjamin S. Bloom, University of Chicago, March 2–3, 1984.

Foshay, W. R., & Foshay, A. W. (1980). Curriculum development and instructional development. *Educational Leadership, 38*(8), 621–626.

Fraley, A. E. (1981). *Schooling and innovation: The rhetoric and the reality*. New York: Tyler Gibson.

Frankfort, H. D., Frankfort, H. A., Wilson, J. A., & Jacobson, T. (1946). *Before philosophy: The intellectual adventure of ancient man*. Baltimore: Penguin.

Frankl, V. E. (1963). *Man's search for meaning*. New York: Washington Square Press.

Franklin, B. *Autobiography*. (Numerous sources.)

Fraser, B. J. (1981). *Learning environment in curriculum evaluation: A review*, Evaluation in Education Series. London: Pergamon.

Fraser, B. J. (1982). Promising directions in curriculum knowledge: An environmental perspective. In W. H. Schubert and A. L. Schubert (Eds.), *Conceptions of curriculum knowledge: Focus on students and teachers* (pp. 31–36). University Park: College of Education, Pennsylvania State University.

Fraser, B. J., & Houghton, K. (1982). *Annotated bibliography of curriculum evaluation literature*. Israel Curriculum Center, Tel-Aviv: Ministry of Education and Culture.

Freire, P. (1970). *Pedagogy of the oppressed*, M. B. Ramos, Trans. New York: Seabury.

Freire, P. (1973). *Education for critical consciousness*. New York: Seabury.

Freire, P. (1978). *Pedagogy in process*. New York: Seabury.

Freire, P. (1985). *The politics of education, culture, power, and liberation*. South Hadley, MA: Bergin and Garvey.

Frey, K. (1985). The modern project method—Its conceptual origins and historical development. A paper presented at the Annual Meeting of The Society for the Study of Curriculum History, Chicago, March 30, 1985.

Froebel, F. W. (1912). *Froebel's chief writings on education*, S. S. F. Fletcher and J. Welton, Trans. New York: Longman, Green.

Fromm, E. (1941). *Escape from freedom*. New York: Holt, Rinehart and Winston.

Fromm, E. (1976). *To have or to be*. New York: Harper & Row.

Fruchter, N. (1983). Quality of education reports attack the wrong problems. *In These Times*, August 9, 1983, p. 17.

Frye, N. (1981). Where metaphors and equations meet. *The Chronicle of Higher Education*, April 13, 1981, p. 64.

Frymier, J. R. (1967). Around and around the curriculum bush, or in quest of curriculum theory. Paper presented at the Annual Meeting of Professors of Curriculum, Dallas, TX. March, 1967.

Fuentes, C. (1964). *The death of Artemio Cruz*. New York: Farrar, Straus, & Giroux.

Fullan, M., & Pomfret, A. (1975). *Review of research on curriculum implementation*. Toronto: Ontario Institute for Studies in Education.

Fuller, R. B. (1983). *GRUNCH of giants*. New York: St. Martin's Press.

Fussell, P. (1983). *Class: A guide through the American status system*. New York: Summit.

Gage, N. L. (Ed.). (1963). *Handbook of research on teaching*. Chicago: Rand McNally.

Gage, N. L. (1978). *The scientific basis of the art of teaching*. New York: Teachers College Press.

Gagné, R. M. (1977). *The conditions of learning*. New York: Holt, Rinehart and Winston. (Earlier edition, 1965.)

Gagné, R. M., et al. (1962). *Psychological principles in systems development*. New York: Holt, Rinehart and Winston.

Gagné, R. M., & Briggs, L. J. (1979). *Principles of instructional design*. New York: Holt, Rinehart and Winston.

Gehrke, N. J., & Parker, W. C. (1983). Collaboration in staff development—variations on the concept. *NASSP Bulletin*, 67(461), 50–54.

Getzels, J. W., & Guba, E. C. (1957). Social behavior and the administrative process. *School Review*, 65, 423–444.

Geuss, R. (1981). *The idea of a critical theory: Habermas and the Frankfurt school*. Cambridge: Cambridge University Press.

Giles, H. H., McCutchen, S. P., & Zechiel. (1942). *Exploring the curriculum*. New York: Harper & Brothers.

Gilligan, C. (1982). *In a different voice*. Cambridge, MA: Harvard University Press.

Giroux, H. A. (1980). Critical theory and rationality in citizenship education. *Curriculum Inquiry*, 10(4), 329–366.

Giroux, H. A. (1981). *Ideology, culture, and the process of schooling*. Philadelphia: Temple University Press.

Giroux, H. A. (1983). *Theory and resistance in education: A pedagogy for the opposition*. South Hadley, MA: Bergin & Garvey.

Giroux, H. A., & Purpel, D. (Eds.). (1982). *The hidden curriculum and moral education*. Berkeley, CA: McCutchan.

Giroux, H. A., Penna, A. N., & Pinar, W. F. (Eds.). (1981). *Curriculum and instruction*. Berkeley, CA: McCutchan.

Gitlin, T. (1983). *Inside prime time*. New York: Pantheon.

Glaser, B. G., & Strauss, A. L. (1967). *The discovery of grounded theory*. Chicago: Aldine Press.

Glaser, R. (1977). *Adaptive education: Individual diversity and learning*. New York: Holt, Rinehart and Winston.

Glass, G. V., & Stanley, J. C. (1970). *Statistical methods in education and psychology*. Englewood Cliffs, NJ: Prentice-Hall.

Glasser, W. (1965). *Reality therapy*. New York: Harper & Row.

Glasser, W. (1975). *Schools without failure*. New York: Harper & Row.

Glatthorn, A. A. (1977). *Alternatives in education: schools and programs*. New York: Harper & Row.

Glatthorn, A. A. (1984). *Differentiated superivsion*. Washington, DC: Association for Supervision & Curriculum Development.

Glickman, C. D. (1981). *Developmental supervision*. Washington, DC: Association for Supervision & Curriculum Development.

Good, H. G. (1969). *History of Western education*. New York: Macmillan.

Good, T. L. (1983). Teacher effectiveness research: A decade of progress. An invited address presented at the Annual Meeting of the American Educational Research Association, Montreal, April 14, 1983. (With commentaries by David Berliner and Lee Shulman).

Good, T. L., Biddle, B. J., & Brophy, J. E. (1975). *Teachers make a difference*. New York: Holt, Rinehart and Winston.

Good, T. L., & Brophy, J. E. (1973). *Looking in classrooms*. New York: Harper and Row.

Goodlad, J. I. (1966). *School, curriculum, and the individual*. Waltham, MA: Blaisdell.

Goodlad, J. I. (1977). An ecological approach to change in elementary school settings. *The Elementary School Journal*, 78(2), 95–105.

Goodlad, J. I. (1978). *Accountability: An alternative perspective*. The DeGarmo Lecture, Society of Professors of Education, February 23, 1978.

Goodlad, J. I. (1979). *What schools are for*. Bloomington, IN: Phi Delta Kappa.

Goodlad, J. I. (1983). What some schools and classrooms teach. *Educational Leadership*, 40(7), 8–19.

Goodlad, J. I. (1984). *A place called school*. Hightstown, NJ: McGraw-Hill.

Goodlad, J. I., & Anderson, R. H. (1959). *The non-graded elementary school*. New York: Harcourt Brace and World.

Goodlad, J. I., & Associates (1979). *Curriculum inquiry: The study of curriculum practice*. New York: McGraw-Hill.

Goodlad, J. I., & Richter, M. N. (1966). *The development of a conceptual system for dealing with problems of curriculum and instruction*. Los Angeles: Institute for Development of Educational Activities, University of California.

Goodlad, J. I., Klein, M. F., & Associates (1970). *Behind the classroom door*. Worthington, OH: Charles A. Jones.

Goodlad, J. I., Von Stoephasius, R., & Klein, M. F. (1966). *The changing school curriculum*. New York: Fund for the Advancement of Education.

Gordon, B. M. (1983). The emancipatory role of Afro-American cultural knowledge in citizenship education: The politicization of the curriculum. Paper presented at the Annual Meeting of the American Educational Studies Association. Milwaukee, WI, November 5, 1983.

Gordon, W. J. J. (1961). *Synectics*. New York: Harper & Row.

Gould, S. J. (1981). *The mismeasurement of man*. New York: W. W. Norton.

Graber, D. (1984). *Processing the news: How people tame the information tide*. New York: Longman.

Grant, C. A. (Ed.). (1977). *Multicultural education*. Washington, DC: Association for Supervision and Curriculum Development.

Green, T. F. (1984). *The formation of conscience in an age of technology*. Syracuse, NY: The John Dewey Society and Syracuse University.

Greene, M. (1965). *The public school and the private vision.* New York: Random House.

Greene, M. (1973). *Teacher as stranger.* New York: Wadsworth.

Greene, M. (1978). *Landscapes of Learning.* New York: Teachers College Press.

Greene, M. (1981). Educational research and the arts: A dialogue with Elliot Eisner and Maxine Greene. A symposium moderated by J. W. Getzels at the 1981 Annual Meeting of the American Educational Research Association. Los Angeles.

Greenstein, J. (1983). *What the children taught me.* Chicago: University of Chicago Press.

Greer, C. (1972). *The great school legend.* New York: Viking.

Gregorec, A. F. (1979). Learning and teaching styles: Potent forces behind them. *Educational Leadership, 36*(4), 234–236.

Gress, J. R., & Purpel, D. E. (Eds.). (1978). *Curriculum: An introduction to the field.* Berkeley, CA: McCutchan.

Griffin, G. A. (Ed.). (1983a). *Staff development.* Eighty-second Yearbook of the National Society for the Study of Education, Part II. Chicago: University of Chicago Press.

Griffin, G. A. (1983b). Toward a conceptual framework for staff development. In G. A. Grifffin (Ed.), *Staff development* (pp. 228–250). Chicago: University of Chicago Press.

Griffin, G. A., & Barnes, S. (1984). School change. *Teachers College Record, 86*(1), 103–123.

Gronlund, N. E. (1985). *Measurement and evaluation in teaching* (4th ed.). New York: Macmillan.

Gross, R., & Osterman, P. (1971). *High school.* New York: Simon & Schuster.

Grumet, M. R. (1980). Autobiography and reconceptualization. *The Journal of Curriculum Theorizing, 2*(2), 155–158.

Grumet, M. (1981). Other people's children. A paper presented at the Annual Meeting of the American Educational Research Association, Los Angeles, CA, April 13, 1981.

Guba, E. G. (1979). Understanding education through qualitative ways of knowing: five methodological constructs. Discussion at this symposium presented at the Annual Meeting of the American Education Research Association, San Francisco, CA, April 11, 1979.

Guba, E. G., & Lincoln, Y. S. (1981). *Effective evaluation: Improving the usefulness of evaluation results through responsive and naturalistic approaches.* San Franscisco: Jossey-Bass.

Guetzkow, H. and others. (1963). *Simulation in international relations.* Englewood Cliffs, NJ: Prentice-Hall.

Guilford, J. P. (1977). *Way beyond the I. Q.* Buffalo, NY: Creative Education Foundation.

Gwynn, J. M., & Chase, J. B. (1969). *Curriculum principles and social trends.* New York: Macmillan. (Previous editions authored by Gwynn: 1960, 1950, 1943.)

Habermas, J. (1971). *Knowledge and human interests.* Boston: Beacon Press.

Habermas, J. (1973). *Theory and practice.* Boston: Beacon Press.

Habermas, J. (1975). *Legitimation crisis.* Boston: Beacon Press.

Habermas, J. (1979). *Communication and the evolution of society.* Boston: Beacon Press.

Habermas, J. (1984). *The theory of communicative action* (two volumes). Boston: Beacon Press.

Haggerson, N., & Garman, N. (1981). Curriculum theorizing: The metaphor, the method, and the act. A paper presented at *The Journal of Curriculum Theorizing* Conference, Airlie, VA, October 2, 1981.

Hall, C. S., & Lindzey, G. (1978). *Theories of personality* (3rd ed.). New York: John Wiley.

Hamilton, D. (1976). *Curriculum evaluation.* London: Open Books.

Hamilton, D. (1982). On pedagogy and the democratization of educational inquiry. A paper presented at the Annual Conference of the Australian Association for Research in Education, Brisbane, Australia, November 1982.

Hamilton, D., MacDonald, B., King, C., Jenkins, D., & Parlett, M. (Eds.). (1977). *Beyond the numbers game: A reader in educational evaluation.* Berkeley, CA: McCutchan.

Hanna, P. (1984). Panel discussion. Society for the Study of Curriculum History, New Orleans, LA, April 22, 1984.

Hannay, L. M., & White, K. W. (1984). The indirect instructional leadership role of a principal. A paper presented at the Annual Meeting of the American Educational Research Association, New Orleans, LA, April 23, 1984.

Harap, H. (1928). *The techniques of curriculum making.* New York: Macmillan.

Harnischfeger, A., & Wiley, D. E. (1976). Teaching-learning processes in the elementary school: A synoptic view. *Curriculum Inquiry, 6*(1), 5–43.

Harper's (1985). Blackboard jungle, 1940–1982. (A list from the *Presidential Biblical Scoreboard,* a magazine published by the Biblical News Service.) 270(1618), 25.

Harrington, M. (1980). *Decade of decision: The crisis of the American system.* New York: Simon & Schuster.

Harrow, A. J. (1972). *A taxonomy of psychomotor domain: A guide for developing behavioral objectives.* New York: David McKay.

Hart, L. A. (1983). *Human brain and human learning.* New York: Longman.

Harty, S. (1979). *Hucksters in the classroom.* Washington, DC: Center for the Study of Responsive Law.

Harvard Committee on Objectives of Education in a Free Society. (1945). *General education in a free society.* Cambridge, MA: Harvard University Press.

Hass, G. (Ed.). (1983). *Curriculum planning: A new approach.* Boston: Allyn & Bacon. (Previous editions: 1980, 1977, 1974; also 1970 and 1965 under *Readings in curriculum.*)

Havighurst, R. (1981). Education and the revitalization of the central city. Daniel Powell Memorial Lecture at the University of Illinois at Chicago, April 23, 1981.

Heitmann, H., & Kneer, M. (1976). *Physical education instructional techniques: An individualized, humanistic approach.* Englewood Cliffs, NJ: Prentice-Hall.

Hendricks, G., & Fadiman, J. (Eds.). (1975). *Transpersonal education: A curriculum for feeling and being.* Englewood Cliffs, NJ: Prentice-Hall.

Hendricks, G., & Roberts, T. (1977). *The second centering book: More awareness activities for children, parents, and teachers.* Englewood Cliffs, NJ: Prentice-Hall.

Hendricks, G., & Wills, R. (1976). *The centering book.* Englewood Cliffs, NJ: Prentice-Hall.

Henry, N. B. (Ed.). (1942). *Philosophies of education.* Forty-first Yearbook of the National Society for the Study of Education, Part I. Chicago: University of Chicago Press.

Henson, K. T. (Guest Editor). (1984). Matching teaching and learning styles. *Theory into Practice, 23*(1).

Herbart, J. F. (1901). *Outlines of educational doctrine.* New York: Macmillan.

Herbart, J. F. (1904). *An introduction to Herbart's science and practice of education,* H. M. Felkin and E. Felkin, Trans. Boston: D. C. Heath.

Herman, T. M. (1977). *Creating learning environments: The behavioral approach to education.* Boston: Allyn and Bacon.

Herrick, V. E., & Tyler, R. W. (Eds.). (1950). *Toward improved curriculum theory.* Chicago: University of Chicago Press.

Hesse, H. (1906). *Beneath the wheel.* New York: Farrar, Straus, & Giroux (1968 edition).

Hesse, H. (1974). *Reflections,* R. Manheim, Trans. (selected from his books and letters by V. Michels). New York: Farrar, Straus, & Giroux.

Highet, G. (1950). *The art of teaching.* New York: Knopf.

Highet, G. (1976). *The immortal profession.* New York: Weybright & Talley.

Hill, B. V. (1973). *Education and the endangered individual: A critique of ten modern thinkers.* New York: Teachers College Press, Columbia University.

Holt, J. (1964). *How children fail.* New York: Delta.

Holt, J. (1976). *Instead of education.* New York: Delta.

Holt, J. (1981). *Teach your own.* New York: Dell.

Hopkins, C. D., & Antes, R. L. (1978). *Classroom measurement and evaluation.* Itasca, IL: F. E. Peacock.

Hopkins, L. T. (1929). *Curriculum principles and practices.* New York: Benjamin H. Sandborn.

Hopkins, L. T. (Ed.). (1937). *Integration, its meaning and application.* New York: Appleton-Century.

Hopkins, L. T. (1941). *Interaction: The democratic process.* Boston: D. C. Heath.

Hopkins, L. T. (1954). *The emerging self in school and home.* New York: Harper & Brothers. (Also, 1970 reprint by Greenwood.)

Hopkins, L. T. (1976). The WAS vs. IS curriculum. *Educational Leadership, 34*(3), 211–216.

Hopkins, L. T. (1983). My first voyage. In M. R. Nelson (Ed.), *Papers of the Society for the Study of Curriculum History, 1980 and 1982* (pp. 2–6). DeKalb: Northern Illinois University.

Hosford, P. L. (1973). *An instructional theory: A beginning.* Englewood Cliffs, NJ: Prentice-Hall.

Hosford, P. L. (Ed.). (1984). *Using what we know about teaching,* 1984 ASCD Yearbook. Washington, DC: Association for Supervision & Curriculum Development.

House, E. R. (1978). Assumptions underlying evaluation models. *Educational Researcher, 7*(3), 4–12.

House, E. R. (1980). *Evaluating with validity.* Beverly Hills, CA: Sage.

Howes, V. M. (Ed.). (1970). *Individualization of instruction: A teaching strategy.* New York: Macmillan.

Huebner, D. (1963). New modes of man's relationship to man. In A. Frazier (Ed.), *New insights and the curriculum,* 1963 ASCD Yearbook (pp. 144–164). Washington, DC: Association for Supervision & Curriculum Development.

Huebner, D. (1967). Curriculum as concern for man's temporality. *Theory into Practice, 6*(4), 172–179.

Huebner, D. (1975a). Curricular language and classroom meanings. In W. F. Pinar (Ed.), *Curriculum theorizing: The reconceptualists* (pp. 217–236). Berkeley, CA: McCutchan. (Originally published in Macdonald and Leeper, 1966, pp. 8–26.)

Huebner, D. (1975b). Poetry and power: The politics of curricular development. In W. Pinar (Ed.), *Curriculum theorizing: The reconceptualists* (pp. 271–280). Berkeley, CA: McCutchan.

Huebner, D. (1977). Toward a political economy of curriculum and human development. In A. Molnar & J. A. Zahorik (Eds.), *Curriculum theory* (pp. 92–107). Washington, DC: Association for Supervision & Curriculum Development.

Huebner, D. (1984). The search for religious metaphors in the language of education. *Phenomenology and pedagogy, 2*(2), 112–123.

Huenecke, D. (1982). What is curriculum theorizing? What are its implications for practice? *Educational Leadership, 40*(5), 290–294.

Hultgren, F. H. (1982). *Reflecting on the meaning of curriculum through a hermeneutic interpretation of student-teaching experiences in home economics.* Unpublished Ph.D. dissertation, Pennsylvania State University, University Park, PA.

Hunkins, F. P. (1980). *Curriculum development: Program improvement.* Columbus, OH: Charles E. Merrill.

Hunt, D. E. (1970). A conceptual level matching model for coordinating learner characteristics with educational approaches. *Interchange, 1*(3), 68–82.

Hunter, M. (1977). Improving the quality of instruction through professional development. Address to the Annual Convention of the Association for Supervision & Curriculum Development, Houston, TX.

Husén, T., & Postlethwaite, T. N. (Eds.). (1985). *The international encyclopedia of education* (ten volumes). London: Pergamon.

Hutchins, R. M. (1936). *The higher learning in America.* New Haven, CT: Yale University Press.

Huxley, A. (1932). *Brave new world.* New York: Harper & Row (1939 edition).

Ignas, E., & Corsini, R. J. (1981). *Comparative educational systems.* Itasca, IL: F. E. Peacock.

Illich, I. (1972). *De-schooling society.* New York: Harper & Row.

International Association for the Evaluation of Educational Achievement. (1976). *International studies in evaluation* (nine volumes). New York: John Wiley.

Jackson, P. W. (1968). *Life in classrooms.* New York: Holt, Rinehart and Winston.

Jackson, P. W. (1980). Curriculum and its discontents. *Curriculum Inquiry, 10*(1), 28–43.

Jackson, P. W. (forthcoming). *The practice of teaching.* New York: Teachers College Press, Columbia University.

Jacullo-Noto, J. (1985). Interactive research and development on schooling: Possibilities for practitioners. A paper presented at the Meadow Brook Conference on Collaborative Action Research in Education, Oakland University, Rochester, MI, January 21–23, 1985.

Jaeger, W. (1945). *Paideia: The ideals of Greek culture.* New York: Oxford University Press.

James, W. (1890). *Principles of psychology* (two volumes). New York: Dover.

James, W. (1899). *Talks to teachers.* (Several editions available.)

Janesick, V. J. (1982). Developing grounded theory: Reflections on a case study of an architectural design curriculum. In W. H. Schubert and A. L. Schubert (Eds.), *Conceptions of curriculum knowledge: Focus on students and teachers* (pp. 15–22). University Park: College of Education, Pennsylvania State University.

Jarolimek, J., & Walsh, H. M. (Eds.). (1974). *Readings for social studies in elementary education.* New York: Macmillan.

Jencks, C., et al. (1972). *Inequality: A reassessment of the effect of family and schooling in America.* New York: Basic Books.

Jenkins, D., & Shipman, M. D. (1976). *Curriculum: An introduction.* London: Open Books.

Johnson, D. W., & Johnson, R. T. (1975). *Learning together and alone: Cooperation, competition, and individualization.* Englewood Cliffs, NJ: Prentice-Hall.

Johnson, D. W., Johnson, R. T., Holubec, E. J., & Roy, P. (1984). *Circles of learning: Cooperation in the classroom.* Washington, DC: Association for Supervision & Curriculum Development.

Johnson, H. C. (1984). Teacher competence: A historical analysis. In E. C. Short (Ed.), *Competence* (pp. 41–70). Lanham, MD: University Press of America.

Johnson, M. (1977a). *Intentionality in education.* Albany, NY: Center for Curriculum Research & Services.

Johnson, M. (1977b). Priorities in curriculum scholarship. A paper presented at the annual meeting of the American Educational Research Association, New York. April 8, 1977.

Jorgenson, G., & Schubert, W. H. (Eds.). (1985). *Papers of The Society for the Study of Curriculum History.* Cleveland, OH: The Society and John Carroll University.

Joyce, B., Hersh, R. H., & McKibbin, M. (1983). *The structure of school improvement.* New York: Longman.

Joyce, B., & Clift, R. (1984). The Phoenix agenda: Essential reform in teacher education. *Educational Researcher, 13*(4), 5–18.

Joyce, B., & Showers, B. (1983). *Power in staff development through research on teaching.* Washington, DC: Association for Supervision & Curriculum Development.

Joyce, B., & Weil, M. (1980). *Models of teaching.* Englewood Cliffs, NJ: Prentice-Hall.

Joyce, J. (1939). *Finnegan's wake.* New York: Viking Press.

Kafka, F. (1926). *The castle.* New York: Knopf (1954 edition).

Kant, I. (1960). *Education*. Ann Arbor: University of Michigan Press.

Katz, M. B. (1971). *Class, bureaucracy, and the schools: The illusion of educational change in America*. New York: Praeger.

Kaufman, H. (1960). *The forest ranger: A study of administrative behavior*. Baltimore: Johns Hopkins University Press.

Kazamias, A. M., & Massialas, B. G. (1965). *Tradition and change in education*. Englewood Cliffs, NJ: Prentice-Hall.

Kelley, E. C., & Rasey, M. I. (1952). *Education and the nature of man*. New York: Harper & Row.

Kelly, G. A. (1963). *The psychology of personal constructs*. New York: W. W. Norton.

Kemmis, S. (1982). Seven principles for programme evaluation in curriculum development and innovation. *Journal of Curriculum Studies, 14*(3), 221–240.

Kerlinger, F. N. (1973). *Foundations of behavioral research* (2nd ed.). New York: Holt, Rinehart and Winston.

Kerlinger, F. N. (1979). *Behavioral research: A conceptual approach*. New York: Holt, Rinehart and Winston.

Kilpatrick, W. H. (1918). The project method. *Teachers College Record, 19*(4). (Also published as a monograph by Teachers College, Columbia University.)

Kilpatrick, W. H. (1926). *Foundations of method*. New York: Macmillan.

Kilpatrick, W. H. (1936). *Remaking the curriculum*. New York: Newson & Company.

Kimbrough, R. B. (1964). *Political power and educational decision-making*. Chicago: Rand McNally.

Kindred, L. W., & Wolotkiewicz, R. J. (1976). *The middle school curriculum: A practitioner's handbook*. Boston: Allyn & Bacon.

King, A. R., & Brownell, J. A. (1966). *The curriculum and the disciplines of knowledge: A theory of curriculum practice*. New York: John Wiley (reprinted 1976).

Kirschenbaum, H., et al. (1971). *Wad-ja-get? The grading game in American education*. New York: Hart.

Kirst, M. W., & Walker, D. F. (1971). An analysis of curriculum policy making. *Review of Educational Research, 41*(5), 479–509.

Klausmeier, H. J. (1977). *Individually guided education in elementary and middle schools: A handbook for implementors and college instructors*. Reading, MA: Addison-Wesley.

Klein, M. F., Lacefield, W. E., Griffin, G. A., & Burkett, D. (1984). The effects of educational preferences upon curriculum decision making. Symposium presented at the Annual Meeting of the American Educational Research Association, New Orleans, LA, April 27, 1984.

Kliebard, H. M. (1970). Persistent curriculum issues in historical perspective. In E. C. Short (Ed.), *A search for valid content for curriculum courses* (pp. 31–42). Toledo, OH: College of Education, University of Toledo.

Kliebard, H. M. (1971). Bureaucracy and curriculum theory. In V. Haubrich (Ed.), *Freedom, bureaucracy, and schooling*, 1971 ASCD Yearbook (pp. 74–93). Washington, DC: Association for Supervision & Curriculum Development.

Kliebard, H. M. (1972). Metaphorical roots of curriculum design. *Teachers College Record, 72*(3), 403–404.

Kliebard, H. M. (1975). Reappraisal: The Tyler rationale. In W. F. Pinar, *Curriculum theorizing: The reconceptualists* (pp. 70–83). Berkeley, CA: McCutchan. (Originally published in *School Review*, 1970, 78, 259–272.)

Kliebard, H. M. (1982a). Education at the turn of the century: A crucible for curriculum change. *Educational Researcher, 11*(1), 16–24.

Kliebard, H. M. (1982b). Curriculum theory as metaphor. *Theory into Practice, 21*(1), 11–17.

Kliebard, H. M. (1986). *The struggle for the American curriculum: 1890–1958*. London and Boston: Routledge and Kegan Paul.

Kliebard, H. M., & Franklin, B. M. (1983). The course of the course of study: History of curriculum. In J. H. Best (Ed.), *Historical inquiry in education: A research agenda* (pp. 138–157). Washington, DC: American Educational Research Association.

Klohr, P. (1977). Staff development—Resource pak for curriculum reform. In C. W. Beegle & R. A. Edelfelt (Eds.), *Staff development: Staff liberation* (pp. 29–35). Washington, DC: Association for Supervision & Curriculum Development.

Klohr, P. (1980). The curriculum field—Gritty and ragged? *Curriculum Perspectives, 1*(1), 1–7.

Klohr, P. (1984). Curriculum development requires basic theory. *IAAE Chronicle* (a publication of the Institute of the Advancement of the Arts in Education, The Ohio State University), *1*(1), 2–3.

Klopf, G. J. (1974). *The principal and staff development in elementary school.* New York: Bank Street College of Education.

Kneller, G. F. (1984). *Movements of thought in modern education.* New York: John Wiley.

Koerner, J. D. (1963). *The miseducation of American teachers.* Baltimore: Penguin.

Koestler, A. (1972). *The roots of coincidence.* London: Pan Books, 1972.

Kohl, H. R. (1968). *36 children.* New York: Signet.

Kohl, H. R. (1976). *On teaching.* New York: Bantam.

Kohlberg, L. (1976). Moral stages and moralization: The cognitive developmental approach. In T. Lickona (Ed.), *Moral development and behavior: Theory, research, and social issues* (pp. 31–53). New York: Holt, Rinehart and Winston.

Kozol, J. (1967). *Death at an early age.* Boston: Houghton Mifflin.

Krathwohl, D. R. (Ed.). (1964). *Taxonomy of educational objectives: Affective domain.* New York: David McKay.

Kridel, C. (1980). General education and the missions of the college curriculum. *Curriculum Inquiry, 10*(2), 207–214.

Kridel, C. (1984). Student participation in general education reform: A retrospective glance at the Harvard Redbook. *The Journal of General Education, 35*(3), 154–164.

Krug, E. A. (1964). *The shaping of the American high school.* New York: Harper.

Krug, E. A. (1966). *Salient dates in American education, 1635–1964.* New York: Harper & Row.

Kübler-Ross, E. (1969). *On death and dying.* New York: Macmillan.

Kuhn, T. S. (1962). *The structure of scientific revolutions.* Chicago: University of Chicago Press (second edition, 1970).

Lakatos, I., & Musgrave, A. E. (Eds.). (1970). *Criticism and the growth of knowledge.* New York: Cambridge University Press.

Langeveld, M. J. (1983). The stillness of the secret place. *Phenomenology and Pedagogy, 1*(1), 11–17.

Lappé, F. M. (1982). *Diet for a small planet.* New York: Ballantine.

Lasch, C. (1984a). The burden of reform: Schools and American Society. Lecture sponsored by the Illinois Humanities Council, Chicago, October, 1984.

Lasch, C. (1984b). *The minimal self: Psychic survival in troubled times.* New York: W. W. Norton.

Lavatelli, C. S., Kaltsounis, T., & Moore, W. J. (1972). *Elementary school curriculum.* New York: Holt, Rinehart and Winston.

Lee, J. M., & Lee, D. W. (1960). *The child and his curriculum.* New York: Appleton-Century. (Previous editions: 1950, 1940.)

Leeper, R. R. (Ed.). (1971). *Curricular concerns in a revolutionary era.* Washington, DC: Association for Supervision & Curriculum Development.

Leichman, S. (1973). *The boy who could sing pictures.* New York: Holt, Rinehart and Winston.

Leichter, H. J. (Ed.). (1974). *The family as educator*. New York: Teachers College Press, Columbia University.

Leichter, H. J. (Ed.). (1979). *Families and communities as educators*. New York: Teachers College Press, Columbia University.

Leithwood, K. A. (Ed.). (1982). *Studies in curriculum decision-making*. Toronto: Ontario Institute for Studies in Education Press.

Lerner, D., & Lasswell, H. (1951). *The policy sciences: Recent developments in scope and method*. Stanford, CA: Stanford University Press.

Levin, T., & Long, R. (1981). *Effective instruction*. Washington, DC: Association for Supervision and Curriculum Development.

Levit, M. (Ed.). (1971). *Curriculum: Readings in philosophy of education*. Urbana: University of Illinois Press.

Lewin, K. (1943). Forces behind food habits and methods of change. *Bulletin of the National Resources Council*, Washington, D. C., *108*, 35–65.

Lewin, K. (1948). *Resolving social conflicts*. New York: Harper & Brothers.

Lewin, K. (1951). *Field theory in social science*. New York: Harper.

Lewy, A. (1977). *Handbook of curriculum evaluation*. New York: Longman.

Lieberman, A., & McLaughlin, M. W. (Eds.). (1982). *Policy making in education*. Eighty-first Yearbook of the National Society for the Study of Education. Chicago: University of Chicago Press.

Leiberman, A. (1983). Interactive research and development on schooling: Case studies of collaborative inquiry in three contexts. Paper presented in a symposium of "Collaborative Research" at the Annual Meeting of the American Education Research Association, Montreal, April 14, 1983.

Lightfoot, S. L. (1983). *The good high school*. New York: Basic Books.

Lindblom, C. E. (1959). The science of muddling through. *Public Administration Review*, *19*(2), 79–88.

Lionberger, H. (1961). *Adoption of new ideas and practices*. Ames: Iowa State University Press.

Lippitt, R., Watson, J., & Westley, B. (1958). *The dynamics of planned change*. New York: Harcourt Brace and World.

Locke, J. (1913). *Educational writings*, J. W. Adamson, Ed. New York: Macmillan.

Lorayne, H., & Lucas, J. (1974). *The memory book*. New York: Ballantine.

Lortie, D. C. (1975). *Schoolteacher: A sociological study*. Chicago: University of Chicago Press.

Loyola, I. (1599). *Ratio studorum*. (Several editions available.)

Lundgren, U. P. (1972). *Frame factors and the teaching process: A contribution to curriculum theory and theory on teaching*. Stockholm: Almqvist & Wiksell.

Macagnoni, V. (1984). Tillich, transcendence, and insight for curriculum praxis. A paper presented at the Bergamo Curriculum Conference. Dayton, OH, November 2, 1984.

MacDonald, B., & Walker, R. (1976). *Changing the curriculum*. London: Open Books.

Macdonald, J. B. (1975). Curriculum and human interests. In W. Pinar (Ed.), *Curriculum theorizing: The reconceptualists* (pp. 283–294). Berkeley, CA: McCutchan.

Macdonald, J. B. (1977a). Value bases and issues for curriculum. In A. Molnar & J. A. Zahorik (Eds.), *Curriculum theory* (pp. 10–21). Washington, DC: Association for Supervision & Curriculum Development.

Macdonald, J. B. (1977b). Scene and context: American society today. In W. Beegle & R. A. Edelfelt (Eds.), *Staff development: Staff liberation* (pp. 7–14). Washington, DC: Association for Supervision & Curriculum Development.

Macdonald, J. B. (1980). Theory-practice and the hermeneutic circle. Paper presented at the *Journal of Curriculum Theorizing* Conference, Airlie, VA, October 13, 1980.

Macdonald, J. B., & Leeper, R. R. (Eds.). (1966). *Language and meaning*. Washington, DC: Association for Supervision & Curriculum Development.

Macdonald, J. B., Wolfson, B., & Zaret, E. (1973). *Reschooling society: A conceptual model*. Washington, DC: Association for Supervision & Curriculum Development.

Macdonald, J. B., & Zaret, E. (Eds.). (1975). *Schools in search of meaning*. Washington, DC: Association for Supervision & Curriculum Development.

Mager, R. F. (1962). *Preparing instructional objectives*. Palo Alto, CA: Fearon.

Mann, J. S. (1968). A discipline of curriculum theory. *School Review, 76*(4), 359–378.

Mann, J. S. (1968–69). Curriculum criticism. *Curriculum Theory Network, 2*(Winter), 2–14.

Mann, J. S. (1970). The curriculum worker: A view of his tasks and his training. In E. C. Short (Ed.), *A search for valid content for curriculum courses* (pp. 42–46). Toledo, College of Education, University of Toledo.

Mann, T. (1924). *Buddenbrooks*. New York: Knopf.

Marks, W. L., & Nystrand, R. O. (Eds.). (1981). *Strategies of educational change*. New York: Macmillan.

Martin, J. H., and the National Panel on High School and Adolescent Education (1976). *The education of adolescents*. Washington, DC: U.S. Government Printing Office.

Martin, J. R. (1984). Bringing women into educational thought. *Educational Theory, 34*(4), 341–353.

Massialas, B., & Cox, B. (1966). *Inquiry in social studies*. New York: McGraw-Hill.

Matthews, G. B. (1980). *Philosophy and the young child*. Cambridge, MA: Harvard University Press.

Maxwell, W. J., Bernstein, R. J., & Bernstein, J. (1963). *The philosophy and history of education*. New York: Monarch.

May, N. (1982). The teacher-as-researcher movement in Britain. In W. H. Schubert & A. L. Schubert (Eds.), *Conceptions of curriculum knowledge: Focus on students and teachers* (pp. 23–30). University Park: College of Education, Pennsylvania State University.

Mayberry, C. (Ed.). (1980). *Urban education: The city as a living curriculum*. Washington, DC: Association for Supervision & Curriculum Development.

Mazza, K. A. (1982). Reconceptual inquiry as an alternative mode of curriculum theory and practice: A critical study. *The Journal of Curriculum Theorizing, 4*(2), 5–89.

McCarthy, T. (1978). *The critical theory of Jürgen Habermas*. Cambridge, MA: The MIT Press.

McClellan, J. E. (1968). *Toward an effective critique of American education*. Philadelphia: J. B. Lippincott.

McCutcheon, G. (1981). On the interpretation of classroom observations. *Educational Researcher, 10*(5), 5–10.

McCutcheon, G. (Ed.). (1982a). Curriculum theory (special theme issue). *Theory into Practice, 21*(1).

McCutcheon, G. (1982b). Qualitative curriculum evaluation. In H. E. Mitzel (Ed.), *Encyclopedia of educational research*, Vol. 3 (pp. 1503–1506). New York: Free Press of Macmillan.

McLuhan, M., & Fiore, Q. (1967). *The medium is the message*. New York: Bantam.

McLuhan, M., & Fiore, Q. (1968). *War and peace in the global village*. New York: Bantam.

McMurry, F. M. (1927). Some recollections of the past forty years of education. *Peabody Journal of Education, 4*, 325–332.

McNally, H. J., Passow, A. H., & Associates. (1960). *Improving the quality of public school programs: Approaches to curriculum development*. New York: Bureau of Publications, Teachers College Press, Columbia University.

McNeil, J. D. (1978). Curriculum: A field shaped by different faces. *Educational Researcher, 7*(8), 19–23.

McNeil, J. D. (1985). *Curriculum: A comprehensive introduction*. Boston: Little, Brown (previous editions, 1981 and 1977).

McNeil, L. M. (1977). Bibliographical essay. In A. A. Bellack & H. M. Kliebard (Eds.), *Curriculum and evaluation* (pp. 627–647). Berkeley, CA: McCutchan.

McNeil, L. M. (1983). Defensive teaching and classroom control. In M. W. Apple and L. Weis (Eds.), *Ideology and practice in schooling* (pp. 114–142). Philadelphia: Temple University Press.

Mead, G. H. (1936). *Movements of thought in the nineteenth century*, Merritt H. Moore, Ed. Chicago: University of Chicago Press.

Medawar, P. B. (1973). *The hope of progress*. Garden City, NY: Doubleday.

Meiklejohn, A. (1981). *The experimental college*. Washington, DC: Seven Locks Press. (Edited and abridged by J. W. Powell from 1932 edition by Harper & Brothers.)

Merton, R. K. (1936). The unanticipated outcomes of positive social action. *American Sociological Review, 1*, 894–904.

Merton, R. K. (1948). Self-fulfilling prophecy. *Antioch Review, 8*(2), 193–210.

Meyers, H. S., Jr. (1977). *Fundamentally speaking*. San Francisco, CA: Strawberry Hill Press.

Miel, A., & Associates. (1952). *Cooperative procedures in learning*. Bureau of Publications, Teachers College Press, Columbia University.

Mill, J. S. (1859). *Essay on liberty*. Everyman: J. M. Dent.

Miller, J. L. (1982). Breaking of attachments: Feminism and curriculum theory. *The Journal of Curriculum Theorizing, 4*(2), 181–186.

Miller, J. L. (1985). Women as teachers: Issues of self-concept. A paper presented at the Annual Meeting of Professors of Curriculum, Chicago, March 22, 1985.

Miller, J. P. (1983). *The educational spectrum: Orientations to curriculum*. New York: Longman.

Mills, C. W. (1956). *The power elite*. London: Oxford University Press.

Mitchell, D. E., & Encarnation, D. J. (1984). Alternative state policy mechanisms for influencing school performance. *Educational Researcher, 13*(5), 4–11.

Mitzel, H. E. (Ed.). (1982). *Encyclopedia of educational research* (four volumes). New York: Free Press of Macmillan.

Moffett, J. (1971). A presentation on accountability to the Annual Conference of the National Council of Teachers of English, Las Vegas, NV, November 1971.

Moffett, J., & Wagner, B. J. (1976). *Student centered language arts and reading, K–13*. Boston: Houghton Mifflin.

Molnar, A. (Ed.). (1985). *Current thought on curriculum*. 1985 ASCD Yearbook. Washington, D.C.: Association for Supervision & Curriculum Development.

Molnar, A., & Zahorik, J. A. (Eds.). (1977). *Curriculum theory*. Washington, DC: Association for Supervision & Curriculum Development.

Monaghan, E. J. (1982). *A common heritage: Noah Webster's blue-back speller*. Hamden, CT: Archon Books.

Montaigne, M. E. (1899). *The education of children*, L. E. Rector, Trans. New York: D. Appleton.

Mooney, R. L. (1957). The researcher himself. In *Research for curriculum improvement*, 1957 ASCD Yearbook. Washington, DC: Association for Supervision & Curriculum Development.

Mooney, R. L. (1975). Prelude. In W. Pinar (Ed.), *Curriculum theorizing: The reconceptualists*. Berkeley, CA: McCutchan.

Moore, D. T. (1981). Discovering the pedagogy of experience. *Harvard Educational Review, 51*(2), 286–300.

Moore, G. E. (1903). *Principia ethica*. Cambridge: Cambridge University Press.

Moos, R. H. (1979). *Evaluating educational environments: Procedures, measures, findings, and policy implications*. San Francisco: Jossey-Bass.

Morris, B. (1972). *Objectives and perspectives in education: Studies in educational theory (1955–1970)*. London: Routledge & Kegan Paul.

Morris, V. C., Crowson, R., Porter-Gehrie, C., & Hurwitz, E. (1984). *Principals in action.* Columbus, OH: Charles E. Merrill.

Mulcahy, D. G. (1981). *Curriculum and policy in Irish post-primary education.* Dublin: Institute of Public Administration.

National Commission on Excellence in Education. (1983). *A nation at risk: The imperative for educational reform.* Washington, DC: U.S. Government Printing Office.

National Education Association Committee of Ten on Secondary School Studies. (1893). *Report* (chaired by C. Eliot). Washington, DC: U.S. Government Printing Office.

National Education Association Committee of Fifteen Report. (1895). *Addresses and proceedings* (chaired by W. T. Harris). Washington, DC: The Association.

National Science Board. (1983). *Educating Americans for the 21st century.* Washington, DC: National Science Foundation.

Neil, R. (1983). Curriculum and teacher education: An historical case-study. Unpublished manuscript. University of Alberta, September 12, 1983.

Neill, A. S. (1960). *Summerhill: A radical approach to child rearing.* New York: Hart.

Nelson, M. R. (Ed.). (1983). *Papers of the Society for the Study of Curriculum History.* Dekalb, IL: The Society.

Nisbet, S. (1968). *Purpose in the curriculum.* London: University of London Press.

Noddings, N. (Guest Editor). (1983). Curriculum change. Promise and practice. *Theory into Practice, 22*(3).

Noddings, N. (1984a). Competence in teaching: A linguistic analysis. In E. C. Short (Ed.), *Competence* (pp. 17–30). Lanham, MD: University Press of America.

Noddings, N. (1984b). *Caring: A feminine approach to ethics and moral education.* Berkeley: University of California Press.

Nucci, L. (1982). Conceptual development in the moral and conventional domains: Implications for values education. *Review of Educational Research, 52*(1), 93–122.

Nyquist, E. B., & Hawes, G. R. (Eds.). (1972). *Open education.* New York: Bantam.

Oliva, P. F. (1982). *Developing the curriculum.* Boston: Little, Brown.

Oliver, A. I. (1977). Curriculum improvement: A guide to problems, principles, and process (2nd ed.). New York: Harper & Row.

Oliver, D., & Shaver, J. P. (1966). *Teaching public issues in high school.* Boston: Houghton Mifflin.

Orlich, D. C., et al. (1979). *Teaching Strategies: A guide to better instruction.* Lexington, MA: D. C. Heath.

Orlosky, D. E., & Smith, B. O. (1978). *Curriculum development: Issues and insights.* Chicago: Rand McNally.

Ornstein, A. C. (1982). Curriculum contrasts: A historical overview. *Phi Delta Kappa, 63*(6), 404–408.

Ornstein, R. (1976). *The mind field.* New York: Grossman.

Ortenzio, P. (1983). The problem of purpose in American education: The rise and fall of the Educational Policies Commission. In M. R. Nelson (Ed.), *Papers of the Society for the Study of Curriculum History* (pp. 31–34). DeKalb, IL: The Society.

Osofsky, G. (1967). *The burden of race.* New York: Harper & Row.

Ostrander, S., Schroeder, L., & Ostrander, N. (1979). *Superlearning.* New York: Delta.

Otto, L. B. (1982). Extracurricular activities. In H. J. Walberg (Ed.), *Improving educational standards and productivity: The research basis for policy* (pp. 181–210). Berkeley, CA: McCutchan.

Overly, N. V. (Ed.). (1970). *The unstudied curriculum: Its impact on children.* Washington, DC: Association for Supervision & Curriculum Development.

Overly, N. V., & Kimpston, R. D. (Eds.). (1976). *Global studies: Problems and promises for elementary teachers*. Washington, DC: Association for Supervision & Curriculum Development.

Pagano, J., & Dolan, J. (1980). Foundations for an unified approach to curriculum evaluation research. *Curriculum Inquiry, 10*(4), 367–381.

Papert, S. (1980). *Mindstorms: Children, computers, and powerful ideas*. New York: Harper.

Parker, F. W. (1894). *Talks on pedagogics*. New York: E. L. Kellogg.

Passow, A. H. (1984). Tackling the reform reports of the 1980's. *Phi Delta Kappa, 65*(10), 674–683.

Patton, M. Q. (1980). *Qualitative evaluation methods*. Beverly Hills, CA: Sage.

Payne, D. A. (Ed.). (1974). *Curriculum evaluation: Commentaries on purposes, process, product*. Lexington, MA: D. C. Heath.

Pearson, A. T. (1984). Competence: A normative analysis. In E. C. Short (Ed.), *Competence* (pp. 31–40). Lanham, MD: University Press of America.

Pearson, D., & Shaw, S. (1982). *Life extension: A practical scientific approach*. New York: Warner Books.

Pereira, P. (1984). Deliberation and the arts of perception. *Journal of Curriculum Studies, 16*(4), 347–366.

Perls, F. (1968). *Gestalt therapy verbatim*. Lafayette, CA: Real People Press.

Peshkin, A. (1983). Fundamentalist Christian schools: Truth and consequences. Invited paper presented at the Annual Meeting of the American Educational Research Association, Montreal, April 13, 1983.

Pestalozzi, J. H. (1912). *Educational writings*. New York: Longmans, Green. (Edited by J. A. Green with F. A. Colie.)

Peters, T. J., & Waterman, R. H. (1982). *In search of excellence: Lessons from America's best-run companies*. New York: Warner Books.

Peterson, P. E. (1983). Did the education commission reports say anything? *Brookings Review, 2*(2), 3–11.

Peterson, P. L., & Walberg, H. J. (Ed.). (1979). *Research on teaching*. Berkeley: McCutchan.

Phenix, P. (1961a). *Philosophies of education*. New York: John Wiley.

Phenix, P. H. (1961b). *Education and the common good: A moral philosophy of the curriculum*. New York: Harper & Brothers.

Phenix, P. H. (1962). The uses of the disciplines of curriculum content. *Educational Forum, 26*(3), 273–280.

Phenix, P. H. (1964). *Realms of meaning: A philosophy of the curriculum for general education*. New York: McGraw-Hill.

Phenix, P. H. (1971). Transcendence and the curriculum. *Teachers College Record, 73*(2), 271–283.

Piaget, J. (1926). *The language and thought of the child*. London: Kegan Paul, Trench, Trubner.

Piaget, J. (1928). *Judgment and reasoning in the child*. New York: Humanities Press (1962 reprint).

Piaget, J. (1929). *The child's conception of the world*. New York: Humanities Press (1960 reprint).

Piaget, J. (1970). Piaget's theory. In P. Mussen (Ed.), *Carmichael's manual of child psychology* (pp. 703–732). New York: John Wiley.

Pinar, W. F. (Ed.). (1974). *Heightened consciousness, cultural revolution, and curriculum theory*. Berkeley, CA: McCutchan.

Pinar, W. F. (Ed.). (1975). *Curriculum theorizing: The reconceptualists*. Berkeley, CA: McCutchan.

Pinar, W. F. (1978). Notes on the curriculum field. *Educational Researcher, 7*(8), 5–12.

Pinar, W. F. (1980). Life history and educational experience. *The Journal of Curriculum Theorizing, 2*(2), 159–212.

Pinar, W. F., & Grumet, M. R. (1976). *Toward a poor curriculum.* Dubuque, IA: Kendall/Hunt.

Plato. *The republic, The symposium,* and other dialogues are available in many editions and collections.

Ponder, G. A. (1974). The curriculum: Field without a past? *Educational Leadership, 31,* 461–464.

Popham, W. J. (1975). *Educational evaluation.* Englewood Cliffs, NJ: Prentice-Hall.

Popham, W. J., & Baker, E. (1970). *Establishing instructional goals.* Englewood Cliffs, NJ: Prentice-Hall.

Popkewitz, T. S. (1983). The sociological bases for individual differences: The relation of solitude to the crowd. In G. D. Fenstermacher & J. I. Goodlad (Eds.), *Individual differences and the common curriculum.* Eighty-second Yearbook of the National Society for the Study of Education, Part I (pp. 44–74). Chicago: University of Chicago Press.

Popkewitz, T. S. (1984). Soviet pedagogical science: Visions and contradictions. *Journal of Curriculum Studies, 16*(2), 111–130.

Popkewitz, T. S., Tabachnick, B. R., & Wehlage, G. (1982). *The myth of educational reform: A study of school responses to a program of change.* Madison: University of Wisconsin Press.

Popper, K. (1972). *Objective knowledge: An evolutionary approach.* New York: Oxford University Press.

Posner, G. J. (1980). New developments in curricular research: It's the thought that counts. Paper presented to the Northeastern Educational Research Association, Ellensville, NY, October 1980.

Posner, G. J. (1982). A cognitive science conception of curriculum and instruction. *Journal of Curriculum Studies, 14*(4), 343–351.

Posner, G. J., & Rudnitsky, A. N. (1982). *Course design: A guide to curriculum development for teachers.* New York: Longman. (Previous edition: 1978.)

Pratt, D. (1980). *Curriculum design and development.* New York: Harcourt Brace Jovanovich.

Pratte, R. (Ed.). (1984). Multicultural education. Guest editor of *Theory into Practice, 23*(2).

Pressman, J. L., & Wildavsky, A. (1979). *Implementation.* Berkeley: University of California.

Pring, R. (1976). *Knowledge and schooling.* London: Open Books.

Pritzkau, P. T. (1959). *Dynamics of curriculum improvement.* Englewood Cliffs, NJ: Prentice-Hall.

Provus, M. (1971). *Discrepancy evaluation.* Berkeley, CA: McCutchan.

Purkey, S. C., & Smith, M. S. (1982). *Effective schools—A review.* Madison: Wisconsin Center for Education Research, University of Wisconsin, June 1982.

Quintillian. *Institutes of oratory.* (Several editions available.)

Ralph, J. H., & Fennessey, J. (1983). Science or reform: Some questions about the effective schools model. *Phi Delta Kappan, 64*(10), 689–694.

Rathbone, C. H. (Ed.). (1970). *Open education: The informal classroom.* New York: Citation Press.

Raths, L., Harmin, M., & Simon, S. (1966). *Values and Teaching.* Columbus, OH: Merrill. (Revised edition: 1978.)

Raubinger, F. M., & Rowe, H. G. (1968). *Individual and education: Some contemporary issues.* New York: Macmillan.

Raywid, M. A., Tesconi, C. A., & Warren, D. A. (1984). *Pride and promise: Schools of excellence for all the people.* Westbury, NY: American Educational Studies Association.

Read, H. (1943). *Education through art*. New York: Pantheon.

Reich, C. A. (1970). *The greening of America*. New York: Bantam.

Reid, W. A. (1978). *Thinking about the curriculum: The nature and treatment of curriculum problems*. London: Routledge & Kegan Paul.

Reid, W. A., & Walker, D. F. (Eds.). (1975). *Case studies in curriculum change*. London: Routledge & Kegan Paul.

Reimer, J., Paolitto, D., & Hersh, R. (1983). *Promoting moral growth: From Piaget to Kohlberg* (2nd ed.). New York: Longman.

Resnick, L. B. (1985). Cognition and the curriculum. A paper presented at the Annual Meeting of The American Educational Research Association, Chicago, April 3, 1985.

Reynolds, J., & Skilbeck, M. (1976). *Culture and the classroom*. London: Open Books.

Rice, J. M. (1893). *The public school system of the United States*. New York: The Century Company.

Rice, J. M. (1913). *Scientific management in education*. New York: Nobel & Eldridge.

Ridgway, L., & Lawton, I. (1969). *Family grouping in the primary school*. New York: Agathon.

Rimm, D. C., & Masters, J. C. (1974). *Behavior therapy: Techniques and empirical findings*. New York: Academic Press.

Roberts, A. D., & Cawelti, G. (1984). *Redefining general education in the American high school*. Alexandria, VA: Association for Supervision & Curriculum Development.

Robinson, D. W. (1983). The myth of patriotism and the preservation of economic control: A theory of censure of Harold Rugg. In M. R. Nelson (Ed.), *Papers of The Society for the Study of Curriculum History* (pp. 40–48). DeKalb: College of Education, Northern Illinois University.

Roby, T. W. (1985). Habits impeding deliberation. *Journal of Curriculum Studies, 17*(1), 17–35.

Rogers, C. R. (1971). *Client centered therapy*. Boston: Houghton Mifflin. (Originally published, 1951.)

Rogers, C. R. (1983). *Freedom to learn for the 80s*. Columbus, OH: Merrill. (Previous edition: 1969 by Bell & Howell.)

Rosales-Dordelly, C. L., & Short, E. C. (1985). *Curriculum professors' specialized knowledge*. State College, PA: Nittany Press.

Rosenshine, B., & Furst, N. (1971). Research on teacher performance criteria. In B. O. Smith (Ed.), *Research on teacher education: A symposium* (pp. 37–72). Englewood Cliffs, NJ: Prentice-Hall.

Rosenshine, B., Engleman, S., Becker, W., Berliner, D. C., Evertson, C. M., Good, T. L., & Stallings, J. (1978). Direct instruction. A symposium presented at the Annual Meeting of the American Educational Research Association, Toronto. March 31, 1978.

Rosenthal, R., & Jacobson, L. (1968). *Pygmalion in the classroom: Teacher expectations and pupils' intellectual development*. New York: Holt, Rinehart and Winston.

Rossi, P. H., Freeman, H. E., & Wright, S. R. (1979). *Evaluation: A systematic approach*. Beverly Hills, CA: Sage.

Rousseau, J. J. *Confessions*. (Several editions available.)

Rousseau, J. J. *Emile*. (Several editions available.)

Rousseau, J. J. *The social contract and discourses*. (Several editions available.)

Royce, J. (1891). Is there a science of education? *Educational Review, 1*(January–February), 15–25, 121–132.

Rubin, L. J. (Ed.). (1971). *Improving in-service education: Proposals and procedures for change*. Boston: Allyn & Bacon.

Rubin, L. J. (Ed.). (1977a). *Curriculum handbook: Administration and theory*. Boston: Allyn & Bacon.

Rubin, L. J. (Ed.). (1977b). *Curriculum handbook: The disciplines, current movements, and instructional methodology*. Boston: Allyn & Bacon.

Rubin, L. J. (1984). *Artistry in teaching*. New York: Random House.

Rucker, D. (1970). Dewey's ethics. In J. A. Boydston (Ed.), *Guide to the works of John Dewey* (pp. 112–130). Carbondale: Southern Illinois University Press.

Rugg, H. O. (Ed.). (1927a). *Curriculum making: Past and present*. Twenty-sixth Yearbook of the National Society for the Study of Education (Part I). Bloomington, IL: Public School Publishing Co.

Rugg, H. O. (Ed.). (1927b). *The foundations of curriculum making*. Twenty-sixth Yearbook of the National Society for the Study of Education (Part II). Bloomington, IL: Public School Publishing Co.

Rugg, H. O., & Shumaker, A. (1928). *The child-centered school*. Yonkers, NY: World Book.

Rugg, H. O. (1947). *Foundations for American education*. New York: World Book.

Rugg, H. (1952). *The education of teachers*. New York: Harper & Brothers.

Russell, B. (1959). *Wisdom of the West*. London: Rathbone Books.

Saint-Exupery, A. (1943). *The little prince*. New York: Harcourt Brace and World.

Samuels, M., & Samuels, N. (1979). *The well baby book*. New York: Summit Books.

Sarason, S. B. (1982). *The culture of the classroom and the problem of change* (2nd ed.). Boston: Allyn & Bacon.

Sarason, S. B. (1983). *Schooling in America: Scapegoat and salvation*. New York: The Free Press of Macmillan.

Saylor, J. G., Alexander, W. M., & Lewis, A. J. (1981). *Curriculum planning for better teaching and learning*. New York: Holt, Rinehart and Winston. (Previous editions by Saylor & Alexander, 1974, 1966, and 1954 under similar titles.)

Schaffarzick, J., & Sykes, G. (Eds.). (1979). *Value conflicts and curriculum issues*. Berkeley, CA: McCutchan.

Schell, J. (1982). *The fate of the earth*. New York: Knopf.

Schell, J. (1984). *The abolition*. New York: Knopf.

Schiller, F. (1965). *On the aesthetic education of man: In a series of letters*. (Translated with and introduction by R. Snell.) New York: Ungar (orig. 1795).

Schipper, M. C. (1979). *The Rugg textbook controversy: A study in the relationship between popular political thinking and educational materials*. Unpublished doctoral dissertation, New York University, NY.

Schiro, M. (1978). *Curriculum for better schools: The great ideological debate*. Englewood Cliffs, NJ: Educational Technology Publications.

Schmuck, R. A., Runkel, P. J., Arends, J. H., & Arends, R. I. (1977). *The second handbook of organization development in schools*. Palo Alto, CA: Mayfield.

Schön, D. (1983). *The reflective practitioner: How professionals think in action*. NY: Basic Books.

Schubert, W. H. (1980a). *Curriculum books: The first eighty years*. Lanham, MD: University Press of America.

Schubert, W. H. (1980b). Educating teachers to evaluate learning environments. *Studies in Educational Evaluation, 6*(3), 297–301.

Schubert, W. H. (1980c). Toward a theory of open education: Defending open education in the midst of accountability pressures. *Resources in Education*. (ERIC Document Reproduction Service, ED 184213, 43 pp.)

Schubert, W. H. (1980d). Recalibrating educational research: Toward a focus on practice. *Educational Researcher, 9*(1), 17–24, 31.

Schubert, W. H. (1981). Knowledge about out-of-school curricula. *Educational Forum, 45*(2), 185–199.

Schubert, W. H. (1982a). Curriculum research. In H. E. Mitzel (Ed.), *Encyclopedia of educational research*, Vol. 1 (pp. 420–431). New York: Free Press of Macmillan.

Schubert, W. H. (1982b). Curriculum research controversy: A special example of a general problem. *The Review Journal of Philosophy and Social Science, 7*(1 & 2), 216–235.

Schubert, W. H. (1982c). The return of curriculum inquiry from schooling to education. *Curriculum Inquiry, 12*(2), 221–232.

Schubert, W. H. (1982d). The multiple meanings of life skills. *Curriculum Review, 21*(4), 360–362.

Schubert, W. H., & Schubert, A. L. (1982). Curriculum as cultural experience in student lives. In W. H. Schubert & A. L. Schubert (Eds.), *Conceptions of curriculum knowledge: Focus on students and teachers* (pp. 49–57). University Park: College of Education, Pennsylvania State University.

Schubert, W. H., & Posner, G. J. (1980). Origins of the curriculum field based on a study of mentor-student relationships. *The Journal of Curriculum Theorizing, 2*(2), 37–67.

Schubert, W. H., Willis, G. H., & Short, E. C. (1984). Curriculum theorizing: An emergent form of curriculum studies in the United States. *Curriculum Perspectives, 4*(1), 69–74.

Schutz, W. (1967). *Expanding human awareness.* New York: Grove Press.

Schwab, J. J. (1954). Eros and education. *Journal of General Education, 8,* 54–71.

Schwab, J. J. (1965). *Biology teachers' handbook.* New York: John Wiley and Sons.

Schwab, J. J. (1969). The practical: A language for curriculum. *School Review, 78,* 1–23.

Schwab, J. J. (1970). *The practical: A language for curriculum.* Washington, DC: National Education Association. (Revised and expanded version of Schwab, 1969.)

Schwab, J. J. (1971). The practical: Arts of eclectic. *School Review, 79,* 493–542.

Schwab, J. J. (1973). The practical 3: Translation into curriculum. *School Review, 81,* 501–522.

Schwab, J. J. (1978). *Science, curriculum, and liberal education: Selected essays,* I. Westbury & N. J. Wilkof, Eds. Chicago: University of Chicago Press.

Schwab, J. J. (1983). The practical 4: Something for curriculum professors to do. *Curriculum Inquiry, 13*(3), 239–265.

Scriven, M. (1967). The methodology of evaluation. In R. W. Tyler, R. Gagné, & M. Scriven (Eds.), *Perspectives on curriculum evaluation* (pp. 39–83). AERA Monograph Series on Curriculum Evaluation, No. 1. Chicago: Rand McNally.

Scriven, M. (1973). Pros and cons about goal free evaluation. *Evaluation Comment, 3*(4), 1–4.

Scriven, M. (1977). Goal-free evaluation. In E. R. House (Ed.), *School evaluation: The politics and the process* (pp. 319–328). Berkeley, CA: McCutchan.

Seguel, M. L. (1966). *The curriculum field: Its formative years.* New York: Teachers College Press, Columbia University.

Selden, S. (1984). The organizing of human betterment, 1903–1932: Hereditarian thought and curriculum—from the American breeders association to the fitter families contests. Paper presented at the Annual Meeting of the American Educational Research Association, New Orleans, LA, April 27, 1984.

Sergiovanni, T. J. (Ed.). (1975). *Professional supervision for professional teachers.* Washington, DC: Association for Supervision & Curriculum Development.

Sergiovanni, T. J. (Ed.). (1982). *Supervising of teaching,* 1982 ASCD Yearbook. Washington, DC: Association for Supervision & Curriculum Development.

Sergiovanni,, T. J., & Starratt, R. J. (1983). *Supervision: Human perspectives.* New York: McGraw-Hill.

Shaftel, F., & Shaftel, G. (1967). *Role playing for social values: Decision making in the social studies.* Englewood Cliffs, NJ: Prentice-Hall.

Shane, H. G. (1977). *Curriculum change toward the twenty-first century.* Washington, DC: National Education Association.

Shane, H. (1980). Significant writings that have influenced the curriculum: 1906–81. *Phi Delta Kappan, 62*(5), 311–314.

Shane, H. G., & Tabler, M. B. (1981). *Educating for a new millennium.* Bloomington, IN: Phi Delta Kappa.

Sharp, G. (1951). *Curriculum development as the re-education of the teacher.* NY: Teachers College Press.

Sharp, R., & Green, A. (1975). *Education and social control: A study in progressive primary education.* London: Routledge & Kegan Paul.

Shepherd, G. D., & Ragan, W. B. (1982). *Modern elementary curriculum.* New York: Holt, Rinehart and Winston. (Previous editions by Ragan & Shepherd, 1977 and 1971; Ragan & Stendler, 1966 and 1960; and Ragan, 1953.)

Sherman, A. L. (1984). Genderism and the reconstitution of philosophy of education. *Educational Theory, 34*(4), 321–325.

Short, E. C. (1982). Curriculum development and organization. In H. E. Mitzel (Ed.), *Encyclopedia of educational research,* Vol. 1 (pp. 405–412). New York: Free Press of Macmillan.

Short, E. C. (1983). Authority and governance in curriculum development: A policy analysis in the United States context. *Educational Evaluation and Policy Analysis, 5*(2), 195–205.

Short, E. C. (Ed.). (1984). *Competence: Inquiries into its meaning and acquisition in educational settings.* Lanham, MD: University Press of America.

Short, E. C., & Marconnit, G. D. (Eds.). (1968). *Contemporary thought in public school curriculum.* Dubuque, IA: William C. Brown.

Shulman, L. S., Green, T., Cooper, J., Brophy, J., & Kerman, S. (1982). The self-fulfilling prophecy: Its origins and consequences in research and practices. Symposium presented at the Annual Meeting of the American Educational Research Association, New York, March 21, 1982.

Shulman, L., & Sykes, G. (Eds.). (1983). *Handbook of teaching and policy.* New York: Longman.

Silberman, C. E. (1970). *Crisis in the classroom: The remaking of American education.* New York: Random House.

Silberman, C. E. (Ed.). (1973). *The open classroom reader.* New York: Random House.

Simon, S. B., Howe, L. W., & Kirschenbaum, H. (1978). *Values clarification: A handbook of practical strategies for teachers and students* (rev. ed.). New York: Hart.

Simon, S. B., & Bellanca, J. A. (Eds.). (1976). *Degrading the grading myths: A primer of alternatives to grades and marks.* Washington, DC: Association for Supervision & Curriculum Development.

Sitton, T., Mehaffy, G. L., & Davis, O. L. (1983). *Oral history: A guide for teachers (and others).* Austin: University of Texas Press.

Sizer, T. R., for the National Association of Secondary School Principals & the National Association of Independent Schools. (1984a). *Horace's compromise: The dilemma of the American high school.* Boston: Houghton Mifflin.

Sizer, T. R. (1984b). Our nation's schools: Four major reports on policy and practice. An invited symposium at the Annual Meeting of the American Educational Research Association, New Orleans, LA, April 25, 1984.

Skeel, D. L., & Hagen, O. A. (1971). *The process of curriculum change.* Pacific Palisades, CA: Goodyear.

Skilbeck, M. (1983). Lawrence Stenhouse: Research methodology. *British Educational Research Journal, 9*(1), 11–20.

Skinner, B. F. (1953). *Science and human behavior.* New York: Macmillan.

Slavin, R. E. (1983). *Cooperative learning.* New York: Longman.

Small, A. W. (1896). Demands of sociology upon pedagogy. In *Addresses and Proceedings* (pp. 174–181, 184). Washington, DC: National Education Association.

Smith, A. (1976). *Powers of mind.* New York: Random House.

Smith, B. O. (1980). Pedagogical education: How about reform? *Phi Delta Kappan, 62*(2), 87–91.

Smith, B. O., Stanley, W. O., & Shores, J. H. (1957). *Fundamentals of curriculum development* (rev. ed.). New York: Harcourt Brace and World. (1950 edition by World Book, Yonkers-on-the-Hudson, New York.)

Smith, E. R., Tyler, R. W., & the Evaluation Staff. (1942). *Appraising and recording student progress.* New York: Harper & Brothers.

Smith, K. U., & Smith, M. F. (1966). *Cybernetic principles of learning and educational design.* New York: Holt, Rinehart and Winston.

Smith, L. M., & Geoffrey, W. (1968). *Complexities of an urban classroom: An analysis toward a general theory of teaching.* New York: Holt, Rinehart and Winston.

Smith, L. M., & Keith, P. M. (1971). *Anatomy of an educational innovation: An organizational analysis of an elementary school.* New York: John Wiley.

Smith, P. L. (1982). *The problem of values in educational thought.* Ames: Iowa State University Press.

Smyth, W. J. (1983). Clinical supervision as teacher controlled professional development. A revised version of a paper presented to the Annual Meeting of the Association for Supervision & Curriculum Development, Houston, TX, March 1983.

Snedden, D. S. (1921). *Sociological determination of objectives in education.* Philadelphia: J. B. Lippincott.

Snow, C. P. (1969). *The two cultures; and, a second look: An expanded volume of the two cultures and the scientific revolution.* London: Cambridge University Press.

Snow, R. E. (1976). Research on aptitude for learning: A progress report. In L. Shulman (Ed.), *Review of Research in Education, 4* (pp. 50–105). Itasca, IL: F.E. Peacock & American Educational Research Association.

Snyder, B. R. (1970). *The hidden curriculum.* New York: Knopf.

Sockett, H. (1976). *Designing the curriculum.* London: Open Books.

Soltis, J. F. (Ed.). (1981a). *Philosophy and education.* Eightieth Yearbook of the National Society for the Study of Education, Part I. Chicago: University of Chicago Press.

Soltis, J. F. (Ed.). (1981b). *Philosophy of education since mid-century.* New York: Teachers College Press, Columbia University.

Soltis, J. F. (1984). On the nature of educational research. *Educational Researcher, 13*(10), 5–10.

Spears, H. (1951). *The teacher and curriculum planning.* Englewood Cliffs, NJ: Prentice-Hall.

Speiker, C. A. (Ed.). (1976). *Curriculum leaders: Improving their influence.* Washington, DC: Association for Supervision & Curriculum Development.

Spencer, H. (1861). *Education: Intellectual, moral, and physical.* New York: D. Appleton.

Spock, B. (1945). *Baby and child care.* New York: Pocket Books. (Revised, updated, and enlarged, 1976.)

Spodek, B., & Walberg, H. J. (Eds.). (1975). *Studies in open education.* New York: Agathon.

Spring, J. H. (1972). *Education and the rise of the corporate state.* Boston: Beacon Press.

Squires, D. A., Huitt, W. G., & Segars, J. K. (1983). *Effective schools and classrooms: A research-based perspective.* Washington, DC: Association for Supervision & Curriculum Development.

Stake, R. E. (1967). The countenance of educational evaluation. *Teachers College Record, 68,* 523–540.

Stake, R. E. (Ed.). (1975). *Evaluating the arts in education: A responsive approach.* Columbus, OH: Charles E. Merrill.

Stanley, W. O. (1953). *Education and social integration.* New York: Bureau of Publications, Teachers College, Columbia University.

Stanley, W. O., Smith, B. O., Benne, K. D., & Anderson, A. W. (1956). *Social foundations of education.* New York: Dryden Press.

Stenhouse, L. (1975). *An introduction to curriculum research and development.* London: Heinemann.

Steeves, F. L. (Ed.). (1968). *The subjects in the curriculum: Selected readings.* New York: Odyssey Press.

Stone, J. C., & DeNevi, D. P. (Eds.). (1971). *Teaching multi-cultural populations.* New York: D. Van Nostrand.

Storer, J. H. (1953). *The web of life*. New York: Signet.

Stratemeyer, F. B., Forkner, H. L., McKim, M. G., & Passow, A. H. (1957). *Developing a curriculum for modern living*. New York: Bureau of Publications, Teachers College, Columbia University. (Previous edition: 1947.)

Strickland, K. (Ed.). (1984). *Ralph W. Tyler in retrospect: Contributions to the curriculum field.* Collection of papers and transcripts devoted to Tyler's work, presented at the 1981 Annual Meeting of The Society for the Study of Curriculum History in Los Angeles (to be published in forthcoming issue of the *Journal of Thought*).

Stufflebeam, D. L. (1969). Evaluation as enlightenment for decision making. In W. H. Beatty (Ed.), *Improving educational assessment and an inventory of measures of affective behavior* (pp. 41–73). Washington, DC: Association for Supervision & Curriculum Development.

Stufflebeam, D. L. (1971). The relevance of the CIPP evaluation model for educational accountability. *Journal of Research and Development in Education, 5,* 19–25.

Stufflebeam, D. L., & Webster, W. J. (1980). An analysis of alternative approaches to evaluation. *Educational Evaluation and Policy Analysis, 2*(3), 5–20.

Suchman, R. (1962). *The elementary school training program in science inquiry.* Report to the U.S. Office of Education, Project Title VII, Project 216. Urbana: University of Illinois.

Sullivan, C. G. (1980). *Clinical supervision: A state of the art review.* Washington, DC: Association for Supervision & Curriculum Development.

Sumner, W. G. (1906). *Folkways*. Boston: Ginn (1940 edition).

Suransky, V. P. (1982). *The erosion of childhood.* Chicago: University of Chicago Press.

Swales, M. (1978). *The German bildungsroman from Wieland to Hesse.* Princeton, NJ: Princeton University Press.

Swartz, R. (1983). Student choices and a standardized curriculum reconsidered. Paper presented at the Annual Meeting of the Midwest Philosophy of Education Society, University of Chicago, November 11, 1983.

Sylvio, Aenea. *On the education of boys.* (Several editions available.)

Taba, H. (1962). *Curriculum development: Theory and practice.* New York: Harcourt Brace and World. (Also British reprint, 1971.)

Taba, H. (1966). *Teaching strategies and cognitive functioning in elementary school children.* Cooperative Research Project 2404. San Francisco State College, San Francisco, CA.

Talmage, H. (Ed.). (1975). *Systems of individualized education.* Berkeley, CA: McCutchan.

Talmage, H., & Rasher, S. P. (1980). Unanticipated outcomes: The perils in curriculum. *Phi Delta Kappan, 61*(1), 30–32, 71.

Tanner, D. (1982). Curriculum history. In H. E. Mitzel (Ed.), *Encyclopedia of educational research,* Vol. 1 (pp. 412–420). New York: Free Press of Macmillan.

Tanner, D., & Tanner, L. N. (1979). Emancipation from research: The reconceptualist prescription. *Educational Researcher, 8*(6), 8–12.

Tanner, D., & Tanner, L. N. (1980). *Curriculum development: Theory into practice.* New York: Macmillan. (Previous edition: 1975.)

Tanner, L. N. (1978). *Classroom discipline for effective teaching and learning.* New York: Holt, Rinehart and Winston.

Tanner, L. N. (Ed.). (1981). *Papers of The Society for the Study of Curriculum History.* University Park, PA: The Society.

Task Force on Academic Standards of the American Educational Studies Association. (1978). Standards for academic and professional instruction in foundations of education, educational studies, and educational policy studies. *Educational Studies, 8*(5), 329–342.

Taylor, A. P., & Vlastos, G. (1975). *School zone: Learning environments for children.* New York: Van Nostrand Reinhold.

Taylor, C. P. (1976). *Transforming schools: A social perspective.* New York: St. Martin's Press.

Taylor, P. A., & Cowley, D. M. (Eds.). (1972). *Readings in curriculum evaluation.* Dubuque, IA: William C, Brown.

Taylor, P. H. (1966). *Purpose and structure in the curriculum* (inaugural address). Birmingham, England: University of Birmingham Press.

Taylor, P. H. (1970). *How teachers plan their courses.* London: The National Foundation for Educational Research in England and Wales.

Taylor, P. H., & Johnson, M. (Eds.). (1974). *Curriculum development: A comparative study.* Windsor: National Foundation of Educational Research.

Terkel, S. (1975). *Working.* New York: Pantheon.

Terkel, S. (1984). *The good war.* New York: Pantheon.

Thelen, H. (1960). *Education and the human quest.* New York: Harper & Row.

Thelen, H. A. (1981). *The classroom society: The construction of educational experience.* New York: John Wiley.

Theobald, R. (1976). *An alternative future for America's third century.* Chicago: Swallow Press.

Thorndike, E. L. (1903). *Educational psychology.* New York: The Science Press.

Thorndike, E. L. (1910). The contributions of psychology to education. *The Journal of Educational Psychology, 1*(January), 5–12.

Thorndike, E. L. (1913). *Educational psychology.* New York: Teachers College, Columbia University. (Revised and enlarged into three volumes, based on 1903 volume.)

Thorndike, R. L., & Hagen, E. P. (1977). *Measurement and evaluation in psychology and education.* New York: John Wiley.

Tibble, J. W. (1966). *The study of education.* London: Routledge & Kegan Paul.

Toben, B., Sarafatti, J., & Wolf, F. (1976). *Space-time and beyond.* New York: E. P. Dutton.

Tolstoy, L. (1967). *Tolstoy on education,* L. Wiener, Trans. Chicago: University of Chicago Press.

Tom, A. R. (1984). *Teaching as a moral craft.* New York: Longman.

Travers, R. M. W. (Ed.). (1973). *Second handbook of research on teaching.* Chicago: Rand McNally.

Travers, R. M. W. (1980). Taxonomies of educational objectives and theories of classification. *Educational Evaluation and Policy Analysis, 2*(2), 5–23.

Travers, R. M. W. (1983). *How research has changed American schools: A history from 1840 to the present.* Kalamazoo, MI: Mythos Press.

Trice, C. (1984). Curriculum, standards, and testing. Comments at American Federation of Teachers Conference: Meeting the Challenge of Education Reform, Chicago, June 9, 1984.

Trump, J. L., & Miller, D. F. (1968). *Secondary school curriculum improvement: Proposals and procedures.* Boston: Allyn & Bacon. (Also, 1979 edition.)

Tyack, D. (1967). *Turning points in American educational history.* New York: John Wiley.

Tyack, D. (1974). *The one best system: A history of American urban education.* Cambridge, MA: Harvard University Press.

Tyack, D., & Hansot, E. (1984). *Managers of virtue: Public school leadership in America, 1820-1980.* New York: Basic Books.

Tyler, R. W. (1949). *Basic principles of curriculum and instruction.* Chicago: University of Chicago Press.

Tyler, R. W. (1977). Desirable content for a curriculum development syllabus today. In A. Molnar & J. A. Zahorik (Eds.), *Curriculum theory* (pp. 36–44). Washington, DC: Association for Supervision & Curriculum Development.

Tyler, R. W. (1980a). Reflecting on the Eight Year Study. Presentation to The Society for the Study of Curriculum History Annual Meeting, Boston. In manuscript, K. Strickland (Ed.), *Ralph W. Tyler in retrospect: Contributions to the Curriculum field,* forthcoming in *Journal of Thought.*

Tyler, R. W. (1980b). Interview by W. H. Schubert, A. L. Schubert, and assisted by J. Wojcik in transcription. In manuscript, K. Strickland (Ed.), *Ralph W. Tyler in retrospect: Contributions to the curriculum field,* forthcoming in *Journal of Thought.*

Tyler, R. W. (1981). Necessary but neglected sources of curriculum knowledge. Symposium presentation at the Annual Meeting of the American Educational Research Association, Los Angeles, CA, April 1981.

Tyler, R. W. (1983). The contribution of "A study of schooling" to educational research. *Educational Leadership, 40*(7), 33–34.

Tyler, R. W., & Wolf, R. M. (Eds.). (1974). *Crucial issues in testing.* Berkeley, CA: McCutchan.

Ulich, R. (1950). *History of educational thought.* New York: American Book Company. (Earlier edition: 1945.)

Ulich, R. (Ed.). (1954). *Three thousand years of educational wisdom.* Cambridge, MA: Harvard University Press.

Ulich, R. (1955). Comments on Ralph Harper's essay. In N. B. Henry (Ed.), *Modern philosophies of education.* Fifty-fourth Yearbook (Part 1) of the National Society for the Study of Education (pp. 254–257). Chicago: University of Chicago Press.

Ulich, R. (Ed.). (1964). *Education and the idea of mankind.* Chicago: University of Chicago Press.

Vallance, E. (1982). Focus on students in curriculum knowledge: A critique of curriculum criticism. In W. H. Schubert & A. L. Schubert (Eds.), *Conceptions of curriculum knowledge: Focus on students and teachers* (pp. 37–44). University Park: College of Education, Pennsylvania State University.

van Manen, M. (1977). Linking ways of knowing with ways of being practical. *Curriculum Inquiry, 6*(3), 205–228.

van Manen, M. (1979). The Utrecht School: A phenomenological experiment in educational theorizing. *Interchange, 10*(1), 48–66.

van Manen, M. (1982). Edifying theory: Serving the good. *Theory into Practice, 21*(1), 44–49.

van Manen, M. (1984a). Practicing phenomenological writing. *Phenomenology and Pedagogy, 2*(1), 36–69.

van Manen, M. (1984b). Reflections on teacher experience and pedagogic competence. In E. C. Short (Ed.), *Competence* (pp. 141–160). Lanham, MD: University Press of America.

Van Til, W. (Ed.). (1974). *Curriculum: Quest for relevance.* Boston: Houghton Mifflin, 1974. (Previous edition: 1972.)

Van Til, W. (1983). *My way of looking at it.* Terrre Haute, IN: Lake Lure Press.

Victor, E. (1985). *Science for the elementary school.* New York: Macmillan.

Walberg, H. J. (Ed.). (1979). *Educational environments and effects: Evaluation, Policy, and productivity.* Berkeley, CA: McCutchan.

Walberg, H. J. (Ed.). (1982). *Improving educational standards and productivity: The research basis for policy.* Berkeley, CA: McCutchan.

Walker, A. (1982). *The color purple.* New York: Pocket Books.

Walker, D. F. (1971). A naturalistic model for curriculum development. *School Review, 80*(1), 51–69.

Walker, D. F. (1974). What are the problems curricularists ought to study? *Curriculum Theory Network, 4*(2–3), 217–218.

Walker, D. F. (1976). Toward comprehension of curricular realities. In L. Shulman (Ed.), *Review of research in education* (pp. 268–308). Itasca, IL: F. E. Peacock.

Walker, D. F. (1977). Priorities in curriculum scholarship: Toward separatism or synergy.

Presentation in a symposium at the Annual Meeting of the American Educational Research Association, New York, April 8, 1977.

Walker, D. F. (1980). A barnstorming tour of writing on curriculum. In A. W. Foshay (Ed.), *Considered action for curriculum improvement* (pp. 71–81). Washington, DC: Association for Supervision & Curriculum Development.

Walker, J. C., & O'Loughlin, M. A. (1984). The ideal of the educated woman: Jane Roland Martin on education and gender. *Educational Theory, 34*(4), 327–340.

Walsh, D. (1984). *State reform initiatives* (pamphlet). Washington, DC: Educational Issues Department, American Federation of Teachers.

Walton, J. (1972). *The integrated day in theory and practice*. London: Ward Lock Educational.

Ward, L. F. (1883). *Dynamic sociology*. New York: D. Appleton.

Ward, L. F. (1893). *Psychic factors of civilization*. Boston: Ginn.

Warren, D. R., DeVitis, J. L., & the Task Force on Academic Standards. (1978). Standards for academic and professional instruction in foundations of education, educational studies, and educational policy studies. *Educational Studies, 8*(4), 329–342.

Watts, A. (1961). *Psychotherapy east and west*. New York: Pantheon.

Weiner, P. P. (Ed.). (1974). *Dictionary of the history of ideas* (five volumes). New York: Scribners.

Weiss, C. H. (Ed.). (1972). *Evaluation research: Methods of assessing program effectiveness*. Englewood Cliffs, NJ: Prentice-Hall.

Weiss, J. (1983). Critical ethnography: The interplay between research and intervention. A symposium presented at the Annual Meeting of the American Educational Research Association, Montreal, April 13, 1983.

Westbury, I. (1972). The character of a curriculum for a practical curriculum. *Curriculum Theory Network, 10*(Fall), 25–36.

Westbury, I., & Steimer, W. (1971). Curriculum: A discipline in search of its problems. *School Review, 79*(2), 243–267.

Wexler, P. (1977). *The sociology of education: Beyond equality*. Indianapolis, IN: Bobbs-Merrill.

Wexler, P. (1983). *Critical social psychology*. London: Routledge & Kegan Paul.

Whitehead, A. N. (1929). *The aims of education and other essays*. New York: Macmillan.

Wildavsky, A. (1979). *Speaking truth to power: The art and craft of policy analysis*. Boston: Little, Brown.

Wiles, J., & Bondi, J. C. (1984). *Curriculum development: A guide to practice*. Columbus, OH: Charles E. Merrill. (First edition, 1979.)

Wilhelms, F. T. (Ed.). (1967). *Evaluation as feedback and guide*, 1967 ASCD Yearbook. Washington, DC: Association for Supervision & Curriculum Development.

Willis, G. (1975). Curriculum theory and the context of curriculum. In W. Pinar, *Curriculum theorizing: The reconceptualists* (pp. 427–442). Berkeley, CA: McCutchan.

Willis, G. (Ed.). (1978). *Qualitative evaluation: Concepts and cases in curriculum criticism*. Berkeley, CA: McCutchan.

Willis, G. (1981). Democratization of curriculum evaluation. *Educational Leadership, 38*(8), 630–632.

Willis, G. (1982). Creating curriculum knowledge from students' phenomenologies. In W. H. Schubert & A. L. Schubert (Eds.), *Conceptions of curriculum knowledge: Focus on students and teachers* (pp. 45–48). University Park: College of Education, Pennsylvania State University.

Willis, M. (1961). *The guinea pigs after twenty years*. Columbus, OH: Ohio State University.

Willis, P. (1977). *Learning to labor*. Lexington, MA: D. C. Heath.

Wirt, F. M., & Kirst, M. W. (1975). *Political and social foundations of education*. Berkeley, CA: McCutchan.

Wirt, F. M., & Kirst, M. W. (1982). *Schools in conflict.* Berkeley, CA: McCutchan.

Wirth, A. G. (1984). *Productive work—In industry and schools: Becoming persons again.* Lanham, MD: University Press of America.

Wittrock, M. C., et al. (1977). *The human brain.* Englewood Cliffs, NJ: Prentice-Hall.

Wittrock, M. (Ed.). (1985). *The third handbook of research on teaching.* Chicago: Rand McNally.

Wolcott, H. F. (1973). *The man in the principal's office: An ethnography.* New York: Holt, Rinehart and Winston.

Wolf, R. L. (1975). Trial by jury: A new evaluation method. *Phi Delta Kappan, 57,* 185–187.

Wolf, R. L. (1979). The use of judicial evaluation methods in the formulation of educational policy. *Educational Evaluation and Policy Analysis, 1*(3), 19–28.

Wolpe, J. (1969). *The practice of behavior therapy.* Oxford: Pergamon.

Wolpe, J., & Lazarus, A. A. (1966). *Behavior therapy techniques: A guide to the treatment of neuroses.* Oxford: Pergamon.

Wood, G. (1983). The strained relationship in education—Public schools and citizenship education. A paper presented at the Annual Meeting of the American Educational Studies Association, Milwaukee, WI, November 6, 1983.

Woodbury, M. (1980). *Selecting materials for instruction* in three volumes: *Issues and policies; Media and the curriculum;* and *Subject matter areas and implementation.* Littleton, CO: Libraries Unlimited, Inc.

Worthen, B. R., & Sanders, J. R. (Eds.). (1973). *Educational evaluation: Theory and practice.* Belmont, CA: Wadsworth.

Wrigley, J. (1982). *Class politics and public schools: Chicago, 1900–1950.* New Brunswick, NJ: Rutgers University Press.

Yauch, W. A. (1957). *Helping teachers understand principals.* New York: Appleton-Century-Crofts.

Young, M. F. D. (Ed.). (1971). *Knowledge and control: New directions for the sociology of education.* London: Collier-Macmillan.

Zais, R. S. (1976). *Curriculum: Principles and foundations.* New York: Thomas Y. Crowell.

Zumwalt, K. (1982). Research on teaching: Policy implications for teacher education. In A. Lieberman & M. W. McLaughlin (Eds.), *Policy-making in education* (pp. 215–248). Chicago: University of Chicago Press.

Zumwalt, K. (1984). Teachers and mothers: Facing new beginnings. *Teachers College Record, 86*(1), 138–155.

✦ Name Index ✦

✦ Subject Index ✦